An Interpretive Guide to
OPERATIC ARIAS

An Interpretive Guide to
OPERATIC ARIAS

*A Handbook for Singers,
Coaches, Teachers, and Students*

Martial Singher

*Translations of the texts of the arias
by Eta and Martial Singher*

The Pennsylvania State University Press
University Park and London

To the memory of my masters,
to my colleagues on stage and in the studio,
to my students past and present,
to all who love opera
and to Eta, my wife.

Fourth printing, 1991

Library of Congress Cataloging in Publication Data

Singher, Martial.
  An interpretive guide to operatic arias.

  Includes index.
  1. Singing—Interpretation (Phrasing, dynamics, etc.)
  2. Operas—Interpretation (Phrasing, dynamics, etc.)
  I. Title.
  MT892.S5   1983   782.1'07'1   82-42772
  ISBN 0-271-00351-0

Contents

Introduction

A certain aria is probably what the public will remember best when leaving the opera house. For many years, arias were the only part of operas put on recordings. The object of the daily effort of the students, the arias are for the teachers the tools with which they patiently fashion voices and taste. For the performer an aria is an opportunity to detach oneself from the ensemble, to display one's personal talent, and to be singled out. It is the touchstone of success. Within the structure of an operatic composition, the arias are strategically placed milestones where one should pause and reflect while the action, which is pushing ahead the rest of the time, takes a break. For the complexities of the plot, for the skillful combination of various voices, the aria substitutes for a while a single line on which ear and mind can concentrate, presumably to experience great enjoyment. The composer has lavished special care and placed special hopes on his arias. Properly and well sung, a beautiful aria can bring an audience to its feet and decide the fate of an entire opera. The most memorable thrills of an opera singer's life may easily derive from the great arias in his or her repertoire.

For this very reason the aria in performance has been exposed to more alterations than any other part of the opera. The temptation is strong for the singer to take possession of the material entrusted to him and to use it to stress his own best features, thereby substituting the performer for the composer, even attempting to outdo other performers of the same piece, if possible. The honest approach, of course, is to follow faithfully and to the smallest detail the words and the music as written and printed. The knowledge imparted by a scrupulous reading of all the notations of the aria—tempo, intonation, rhythm, indications of style such as *stringendo, rallentando, staccato, con amore, espressivo,* and so on—must be foremost in the mind of the singer at all times.

Yet even the most scrupulous study may fail to discover the vital breath of a piece. Mahler contended that the essential part of his music could never be put down in the printed score. Once, when studying "Asie" from *Shéhérazade* in the presence of Maurice Ravel, my excellent accompanist and I were uncertain about the meaning of two bars in a short interlude. Called to the rescue, Ravel looked at the score and said simply: "My dear, *it's* all in there." To this day we are not sure that we detected "it."

This book is an attempt to assemble and draw attention—only in print, alas—not only to precise features of text, notes, and markings but also to psychological motivations and emotional impulses, to laughter and tears, to technical skills, to strokes of genius, and even here and there to variations from the original works that have proved to be fortunate. In other words, the book will continue the work I have done in master classes and lessons for so many years.

The book, then, should be used as a textbook for the study of the words and lines of the texts and of the precise indications of tempo, style, sometimes even of technical wisdom. It should also be consulted and trusted where it tries to help the interpreter to rise above and beyond the letter and to reach the spirit. As a singer I have performed some hundred operatic roles as well as hundreds of songs, which is not really a different art. Prior to my career as a singer I had graduated with honors and received my diploma, "professor of literature," in France. Whatever I have achieved later in my musical career has been due to the constant union of an often pedantic study of words and music and an abandon as complete as possible to the inspiring demands of the composer. It is my hope that this book will motivate its readers to do the same and show them the way. There may be different ways of understanding the selections discussed herein; there is no other way of studying them.

Recommendations

Study one aria at a time. The very brief synopsis at the beginning of each chapter is meant to provide the reader with the strictly essential information about where, when, and by whom the aria is sung. Read it as a stopgap, useful until you become acquainted with the entire opera, which any serious teacher, student, or performer will want to do. Retain from the synopsis any information about the age, social status, and mood of the character in question. You must know who you are and why you sing what you sing.

Study the translation. It has been made as faithful to the original text as possible, often at the price of some awkwardness in English. Imbue yourself with the meaning of each word, then with the meaning of each verse, then the meaning of the entire piece, literally and in its human significance.

Read the original text aloud. It is your goal to make the listeners hear sounds that are the sum of words and music. The human voice is the only instrument that has been given this double assignment, which is its difficulty and its glory and which makes it the most human of instruments.

Study your music until you know very well all values, pitches, rhythms, modulations, and such. Then, score in hand, check with this book, line by line, sometimes measure by measure. If some suggestion seems odd, read on and you will find a psychological motivation for the suggestion. Carefully mark in your score all you find worthwhile. The wrong procedure would be to read a given section once just to get "a general idea." A general idea of text and music is no idea at all.

A habitual mezzo-forte or a habitual moderato is the slow death of interpretation. A constant fortissimo is an even more dangerous weapon in committing the same crime.

Many sharp, forceful words are used in this book. Trust them. A good interpreter cannot dwell in average elements. These extremes must, of course, be justified by the feelings they reveal and touch by the singer's sincere participation.

Metronomical indications are given in order to protect the inexperienced from grievous errors. They constitute a reliable basis for studying the arias, though I am well aware, having sung *Le Nozze di Figaro* in twelve different countries, that a dozen or more conductors do not all use the same tempi. Nevertheless, some solid premises have to be established. Changing tempi, or changing dynamics without a valid motivation is a betrayal.

I found it impossible to convey my concept of some phrases without including some vocal advice. Aware of the danger of using technical terms, I have tried to put in ordinary words the sensations I know to be right and helpful. Pure vowels are an essential part of singing. It is impossible to insist too much on that point.

In the final analysis, all the precise elements of any interpretation build up to one goal: to express. The inspired mind and the sensitive heart of a good interpreter find in the shape of the phrase, the inflection of the words, the right rhythm, the true nuance, the rare color, the changes of pace, the silences, all they need to convey to the audience the changing emotions of a role. An exceptional vocal endowment is not always indispensable for pleasing, moving, and achieving success. The blessed owners of extraordinarily beautiful voices will no doubt go on dazzling the world with the pure gold of their sounds as they have in each generation, whether books are written about operatic arias or not. And, alas, many who study such books of knowledge with deep earnestness will nevertheless not become great singers. But many more, well endowed, serious, intelligent, and sensitive, may find in these pages the help they need to take a decisive step on the road to success and artistic satisfaction.

An Interpretive Guide to
OPERATIC ARIAS

Beethoven, *Fidelio*

"Abscheulicher, wo eilst du hin?"   *soprano*

Abscheulicher, wo eilst du hin?	Abominable man, where are you rushing to?
Was hast du vor in wildem Grimme?	What do you intend in your savage anger?
Des Mitleids Ruf,	Mercy's call,
der Menschheit Stimme,	the voice of humanity,
rührt nicht mehr deinen Tigersinn.	no longer moves your bestial mind.
Doch toben auch wie Meereswogen	But though like ocean waves
dir in der Seele Zorn und Wut,	anger and fury may rage in your soul,
so leuchtet mir ein Farbenbogen	a rainbow is shining for me
der hell auf dunklen Wolken ruht.	which rests bright on dark clouds.
Der blickt so still,	It looks down so calmly,
so friedlich nieder,	so peacefully,
der spiegelt alte Zeiten wieder,	it reflects bygone times,
und neu besänftigt wallt mein Blut.	any my blood flows quietly again.
Komm, Hoffnung, lass den letzten Stern	Come, hope, let not the last star
der Müden nicht erbleichen,	of the weary woman fade away,
o komm, erhell'mein Ziel,	oh, come, throw light on my goal,
sei's noch so fern,	be it ever so far,
die Liebe wird's erreichen.	love will reach it.
Ich folg'dem innern Triebe,	I obey my inner urge,
ich wanke nicht,	I do not falter,
mich stärkt die Pflicht	the duty of true married love
der treuen Gattenliebe.	gives me strength.
O du, für den ich alles trug,	O you, for whom I have borne it all,
könnt'ich zur Stelle dringen,	if only I could force my way to the place
wo Bosheit dich in Fesseln schlug	where maliciousness put you in fetters
und süssen Trost dir bringen!	and bring you sweet solace!

Florestan, a noble Spaniard, has been secretly seized and jailed by his personal enemy, Pizarro, governor of a prison for political prisoners. His faithful wife Leonore has succeeded in tracing her husband to his present location. Disguised as a young man called Fidelio, she has become an assistant to Rocco, chief warden of the prison. In the scene preceding this aria she has overheard Pizarro asking Rocco to assist him in doing away with Florestan. After the two men are gone, she is free to unburden her heavy heart of its tragic anxiety and to reaffirm her undying hope.

This great aria is written for a great soprano voice, noble, generous, human, of long range and broad scope. The aria itself is written along the lines of Mozart's soprano arias in *Così fan tutte,* in *Don Giovanni,* in *Figaro.* An important recitative is followed by a moving adagio, the last part of the aria being a lively allegro.

The strings play four measures of introduction in great agitation. Leonore's outrage and disgust explode in rapid, violent questions, the last one ending bitterly with the words "in wildem Grimme," said with a biting rather than a somber, heavy voice. After two more tense bars, the accompaniment softens to a much slower tempo. Slowly and in a well-supported piano, Leonore becomes the voice of mercy, then the voice of humanity, which she contrasts with a vehement "deinen Tigersinn." In the phrase "Doch toben auch wie Meereswogen" she vigorously denounces, in a powerful image, the odious soul of Pizarro, taking a long time to stress "dir in der Seele Zorn und Wut." Her voice, much brighter now and adagio, floats above wind instruments to reveal the glow in her soul, "so leuchtet mir ein Farbenbogen," but it darkens anew, for her rainbow rests on dark clouds. In the next eight bars Leonore regains her calm completely and in a rich, low, medium line sings slowly, ♩ = 42, of the happy memories the peaceful rainbow revives in her, soothing her blood. The articulation of these lines must be very precise and soft, the voice limpid, the pace serene. The recitative has taken Leonore from outrage to serenity.

The *adagio*, ♪ = 56, is a cantilena of extreme beauty that calls for a voice with a round, velvety quality, revealing the warmth of Leonore's heart and sometimes her unshakable determination. It is impossible to conceive of it without the most beautiful sounds of the words, sounds faithful to the natural vowels, to the natural inflections of speech, the open vowels /ε/ in "den letzten Stern," the long vowel /y/ in "Müden," the pale vowel /a/ in "erbleichen," the sharp vowels /i/ in "Ziel" and in "Liebe" (how important that one is for a true expression!), the bright vowel /a/ in "erreichen." Breaths must be taken to give eloquence to the phrases, or avoided for the same reason: no breath in "den letzten Stern der Müden nicht erbleichen" but a breath before "erhell" and its repeat; a breath after "Ziel" but not between the two "so fern, so fern"; a breath after "ja, ja" in order to prepare the long ascending phrase. Using some wisdom, the florid five bars, 17–21 of the *adagio*, can be made comfortable: In bar 17, start "erreichen" piano. The ascending pitches provide a crescendo all by themselves. Take a fast breath on the F-sharp carried over in bar 18, sing the chromatic pattern very legato, without any consonant *h* between notes. In bar 19, take a deep breath in the middle of the bar; the ascending line again begins piano and is sung legatissimo to the high B forte—not fortissimo. In bar 21, sing the syllable "-chen" of "erreichen" on the D, breathe, and sing "erreichen" on the last notes of the phrase, with a long fermata on the F-sharp. If the whole *adagio* has been sung naturally, without aiming at constant power, the seemingly difficult five bars will just be the continuation of a long, fluid line. The "komm, o, komm" that follows should now be strong and pressing. After one bar of rest the voice becomes more intense, the plea more urgent, each short phrase increasing in intensity over the preceding one. The repeats of "sei's noch so fern," the repeats of "die Liebe," show a growing passion that expresses its power in the very long E-natural "Liebe," in which the vowel /i/ must be brought to the brightest possible ring. The last bar before the *allegro con brio* should be broad and powerful; in the downward interval between the two E's, bring the ring of the voice completely forward in the mouth in order to maintain its full presence.

The *allegro con brio*, ♩ = 160, is a powerful composition that seems driven by Leonore's fierce determination to reach and to free her husband. Its tempo must be kept up without failing but for a few bars for "und süssen Trost dir bringen." While the tempo never relents, many dynamic changes are indicated. Right away there is a first phrase that in six bars grows from piano to fortissimo, then starts piano again in the seventh bar, to return to fortissimo in the eighth. The first "ich wanke nicht" is piano although extremely firm, but the second "ich wanke nicht" and the end of the phrase return to forte.

The dynamic changes follow the sentimental contents of the text. The fervent wish "O du . . . zur Stelle dringen" is a sustained piano, but "Bosheit" and "Fesseln" are an accusing forte. The short *più lento* must resemble a warm feminine caress, piano and free in rhythm, and the tempo I must be full of energy and determination, ending on the word "dringen," with a fermata on both syllables.

A brief interlude of horns and bassoons prepares a decisive, almost military intensity for Leonore's renewed dedication, a mood that prevails to the end of the piece. The fierceness of her will must make her voice strong and ringing but never pushed, chopped, or bitter. It is possible to suggest all her emotions through a constant legato, carrier of many intentions. The range of some vocal lines must not destroy the continuity of the singing. In bars 24 to 31 of this last tempo I, $\downarrow$ = 160 ("der treuen Gattenliebe"), the impetus of the singing must not be weakened by abrupt changes in the nature of the voice due to an obvious shifting of gears, sometimes called registers. The skill of the singer will consist in finding a constant level of origin for the vibration of the voice (for instance, in the frontal part of the bony palate), in all the pitches, each of them moving to its natural resonance, the high ones upward, the low ones down and in the front of the mouth, never changing the focus of the voice from front to back with gaps in the continuity of the sound. The impetus still increases its urgency in that last page of the aria, where the full power of the voice is needed, but still in legato form. In the very last phrase, a breath is taken after " mich stärkt die Pflicht" and on the tied eighth note G preceding the run to the high B, a run that starts piano but expands to a fortissimo on the high B. The notes marked *ad lib* are neither necessary nor good additions. The unrelenting impulse that drives the piece forward must never become violent or harsh. The soprano must be constantly in command of the continuity of the sound of her voice to meet the demands of the fiery writing without losing her nobility, shall we say, her "class." To be able to give a great rendition of this aria is one of the highest goals for a dramatic soprano.

Bellini, *Norma*

"Casta Diva"

soprano

Casta Diva, che inargenti
queste sacre antiche piante,
a noi volgi il bel sembiante
senza nube e senza vel.

Tempra, o Diva, tempra tu
de'cori ardenti,
tempra ancora,

Chaste Goddess, who strews silver
on these hallowed antique trees,
turn toward us your beautiful face
without a cloud and without a veil.

Soothe, o Goddess, soothe still
the daring zeal of the fiery hearts,
soothe it still,

tempra ancora lo zelo audace,	soothe still the daring zeal,
spargi in terra, ah, quella pace	spread on earth, ah, that peace
che regnar tu fai nel ciel.	that you let reign in the sky.

The story of *Norma* takes place in Gaul about 50 b.c. when that country was occupied by the Romans. In the sacred grove of the Druids the high priestess Norma stands at the altar and addresses an assembly of Gaulish priests and warriors, urging them to renounce temporarily their rebellion against Rome and to pray instead for peace. The moon shines in all its splendor as Norma raises a branch of sacred mistletoe toward the sky and sends her people's prayer for peace to the "chaste Goddess." The interpreter of this aria will find it helpful to imagine the scope of the setting, the nocturnal landscape, the crowd, the theme of Norma's inspiration, in order to give this otherwise simple piece of music its true dimension.

Norma's voice must be a great voice, of very long range and beautiful quality in dramatic as well as in lyric moments. Norma is a tragedian who can nevertheless sing florid passages like a coloratura soprano. Detached from the part in its entirety, the aria "Casta Diva" is a superb cantilena suited to lirico-spinto voices, an aria that every dedicated soprano should try to master.

The tempo marked *andante sostenuto assai* (*assai* meaning "very") can be taken at ♩. = 42–44 at the beginning of each verse and subjected to any number of flexible variations in performance. The accompaniment, all in arpeggios for a while, permits that flexibility. When the aria is sung in concert, one bar of introduction suffices. After the voice enters, the first six bars must establish the magic of the piece. Never was a bright vowel /a/ more indispensable than in the words "Casta Diva," "inargenti," "sacre," "antiche piante." This vowel must originate well forward in the mouth with a velvety sound; its vibration then spins upward and slightly inward. As ridiculous as it may sound, these first six bars of singing must suggest radiant moonlight to the ear and the mind of the listener. The long values must be sustained pianissimo to the end; the short and very short values must be very light but always said in precise, forward vowels. Though rhythmical, the singing cannot be metronomical. A feeling of devotion but also of loving intimacy must appear in the way the word "Diva" is stressed and repeated. Details such as a breath before the first "che inargenti," a very slow turn between the A and the D of "che inargenti," a slight tenuto on the D of "queste" in bar 5 are only a few of the many inflections that a musical imagination will feel instinctively as it aims at winning the favor of the Goddess.

The next four bars are simple, well-sustained lyric phrases kept in the same loving mood. With the first "a noi volgi" the prayer begins. A breath before the second "a noi volgi" will help the start of a crescendo. A detail: the syllable "-gi" of that second "volgi" is sung on the C, as written, but the "il" is sung on the two sixteenth notes B-flat–C, and the "bel" on the two sixteenth notes D–E. A deep breath before "il bel sembiante" must allow the soprano to soar easily to the several A's, repeated in a strong crescendo, the syncopation stressed. The phrase comes to a climax on the high B-flat fortissimo (bar 13), which can be held in a short fermata. Strongly accentuated, the phrase then (on the G and the E, bar 13) becomes a diminuendo, staying strictly on time in contrast with the beginning of the aria. A breath has been taken before "il bel sembiante," bar 13; the next one will be before "senza nube" in bar 14. The last three beats of bar 14 are a rallentando and a diminuendo, the sound of the voice still very bright as befits "senza nube e senza vel." Beyond all those practical indications, the essential element of these four measures is the growing intensity of the prayer, which becomes a supplication through the beseeching repetition of the high A's, expanding to their maximum on the top B-flat. There appears suddenly in the polished aria a primordial outcry of no uncertain greatness, to be sung in great dramatic tones.

After a cut of ten bars (when performed as a solo aria without chorus), the second verse is introduced again by one bar of arpeggios. The first verse was one of worship and adoration; despite its intensity it did not ask the goddess for more than that she turn her face toward the worshipers. The mood of the phrases and the sound of the voice were pure and spiritual. The second verse is more specific, asking for the same peace on earth that the moon preserves in the sky. While a polished and precise treatment of the music is still desired, the voice of the soprano is now fuller and more closely connected with reality. The first six bars are no longer wrapped in heavenly magic. They must be sung on time, still softly on "Tempra" but mezzo forte on "cori ardenti." Beginning on the sixth bar, a progressive accelerando stresses the urgency of the prayer, as in "tempra ancora lo zelo audace." The shorter phrases like "spargi in terra" and "ah, quella pace" are at least mezzo forte and sung without dragging. The ascension to the A comes full voice. In bar 12 the score this time has a full note A, forte. It is certainly possible to sing the bar as printed and to expand that note to a powerful B-flat. But it is also possible, and probably preferable, to repeat here the syncopations on A's written for the first verse and to do so with the same intensity recommended earlier. It is only fair to indicate here the several changes customarily made in the performance of the last bars and the coda of the aria.

seventh bar before the end of the aria:

These changes must not detract from either the noble character of the melody or the vocal dignity of the performance. Although there are and have been few Normas, the performance of "Casta Diva" is a challenge that can be attempted by sopranos who want to experiment with a broad style of basic simplicity but of real greatness. There is no danger there when it is done right.

Bizet, *Carmen*

"Habanera" *mezzo-soprano*

L'amour est un oiseau rebelle	Love is a rebellious bird
que nul ne peut apprivoiser	that nobody can tame,
et c'est bien en vain	and it is utterly in vain
qu'on l'appelle,	that one calls it
s'il lui convient de refuser.	if it chooses to refuse.
Rien n'y fait, menace ou prière,	Nothing succeeds, threat or entreaty,
l'un parle bien, l'autre se tait;	the one speaks well, the other keeps quiet;
et c'est l'autre que je préfère,	and it's the other whom I prefer,
il n'a rien dit mais il me plait.	he has said nothing but I like him.
L'amour est enfant de bohème,	Love is a gypsy child,
il n'a jamais connu de loi.	it has never known any law.
Si tu ne m'aimes pas, je t'aime,	If you don't love me, I love you,
et si je t'aime,	and if I love you,
prends garde à toi!	watch out for yourself!
L'oiseau que tu croyais surprendre	The bird you thought to surprise
battit de l'aile et s'envola.	flapped his wing and flew away.
L'amour est loin, tu peux l'attendre,	Love is far away, you can wait for it,
tu ne l'attends plus, il est là.	you don't expect it anymore, there it is!
Tout autour de toi, vite, vite,	All around you, quickly, quickly,
il vient, s'en va, puis il revient.	it comes, goes away, then comes again.
Tu crois le tenir,	You think you are holding it,
il t'évite,	it escapes from you,
tu crois l'éviter,	you think you are escaping from it,
il te tient.	it grips you.

Note: there is no tilde on the *n* of "Habanera," which must be pronounced like an ordinary English *n*.

The rhythm of the "Habenera" is that of a dance and must stay absolutely steady, ♩ = 72.

This piece was not part of the libretto written by Meilhac and Halévy. In the manuscript of the score (*Bibliothèque de l'Opéra de Paris*), inserted just ahead of the "Habanera," one can read a letter from Bizet to his librettists saying that, as he needed more music to present his leading character, he had taken the liberty of composing an aria in imitation of an existing Spanish song.

The "Habanera" introduces Carmen and must immediately reveal certain features of her character: for her, love is a game of hide-and-seek, of offering and taking back, with danger always an integral part of it. No better information, no better warning, could be given to Don José.

During the three bars of the introduction the singer must establish in her mind and body the rhythm of the aria. The first four bars are to be sung piano and *without* breathing. There is a breath after "l'appelle" so that the vocal line can be well sustained until "prière" without breathing. The portamenti must be light and convey an idea of challenge. There is elegance and warmth in the singing, and no trace of vulgarity. The repeat of the word "l'amour" grows from piano to forte and returns to mezzo piano. Be sure to sing a vowel /u/ on "l'amour" with the help of extended lips: *l'amour* means, of course, "love," and the sound of it must not be confused with *la mort*, "death."

Refrain: "L'amour est enfant de bohème" is piano, extremely rhythmical but legato; the dotted notes are long and tied to the brief sixteenths. During the words "prends garde à toi" sung by the chorus, take two or three fast, rhythmical breaths, which will relaunch the next phrase, both times. A short tenuto is permissible on the D of "m'aimes *pas*, je t'aime." Take the lower octave alternate at the end of the refrain but the high octave at the end of the verse.

Second verse: This is the game of giving and withdrawing. "L'amour est loin, tu peux l'attendre," for instance, should be sung piano, then "tu ne l'attends plus, il est là" crescendo to forte. "Vite, vite" is mezzo forte, "il vient" is forte, "s'en va" is piano, "puis il revient" is mezzo forte, and the ending "il te tient" is fortissimo.

The refrain is the same as above, with a large fermata on the last "prends *garde* à toi."

Remember that sinuous flexibility and warm seduction are dominant and that dark heaviness is fatal. Take advantage of the interesting text built around an idea, not an emotion. The music is made of strong rhythms and contrasts. Taking any liberty would weaken its value and its effect.

"Séguédille" *mezzo-soprano*

Près des remparts de Séville,	Near the ramparts of Sevilla,
chez mon ami Lillas Pastia,	at my friend Lillas Pastia's,
j'irai danser la Séguédille	I shall go dance the Séguédilla
et boire du Manzanilla.	and drink Manzanilla.
J'irai chez mon ami Lillas Pastia.	I shall go to my friend Lillas Pastia's.
Oui, mais toute seule on s'ennuie,	Yes, but all alone it is boring,
et les vrais plaisirs sont à deux;	and the true fun comes when you are two;
donc, pour me tenir compagnie	so, to keep me company
j'emmènerai mon amoureux.	I shall take my lover along.
Mon amoureux, il est au diable,	My lover, he's gone to the devil,
je l'ai mis à la porte hier.	I threw him out yesterday.
Mon pauvre coeur, très consolable,	My poor heart, very consolable,
mon coeur est libre comme l'air!	my heart is free as the wind!
J'ai des galants à la douzaine,	I have beaus by the dozen,
mais ils ne sont pas à mon gré.	but they are not to my liking.
Voici la fin de la semaine:	Here it's the end of the week:
qui veut m'aimer, je l'aimerai.	who wants to love me, I'll love him.
Qui veut mon âme? Elle est à prendre.	Who wants my heart? It's his for the asking.
Vous arrivez au bon moment.	You come at the right moment.
Je n'ai guère le temps d'attendre,	I have little time to wait,
car avec mon nouvel amant	for with my new lover
près des remparts de Séville . . .	near the ramparts of Sevilla . . .

Seguidilla: This is the spelling as it appears in the Schirmer score as the title of the song, and it is the correct Spanish spelling. In the text of the aria, however, the word is spelled "Séguédille," which is its French form. Consequently it is "Séguédille" which must be sung.

Waiting to be led off to jail, Carmen sings this aria with her hands tied behind her back. José, afraid to be swayed by her words, has forbidden her to speak. Carmen therefore pretends to be thinking aloud and to sing only to herself, at least at the beginning of the aria. It starts very subdued in volume, sparkling in timbre, and very legato. The metronomic marking is 160 for the eighth. Keep feeling the rhythm as a fast 1-2-3 throughout the aria; it should never be felt in one. Detaching itself from the original legato, one phrase only is strongly accented: "J'irai danser la Séguédille et boire du Manzanilla." These accents should be more like rebounds than punches. From the start the indication of style has been *pianissimo* and *léger* (light). After the seven bars of interlude and after the faked detachment comes the first tempting insinuation, from "Oui, mais toute seule," still pianissimo, to "mon amoureux." By this change of mood Carmen catches José's attention and arouses in him the jealousy of the male: she has a lover. Two bars later she reveals that she has sent her lover packing and needs a replacement. Sing "Mon pauvre coeur, très consolable" and the following phrase very legato, with a slightly exaggerated crescendo-decrescendo, giving a humorous quality to the complaint. All candidates are then eliminated with scorn—"J'ai des galants à la douzaine"— so that the phrase "qui veut m'aimer, je l'aimerai" is meant for Don José only. Respect the rallentando and the fermata on "m'aimer." Then "je l'aimerai" is risoluto. The next three lines must be sung full voice and the portamenti on "mon âme" and "arrivez" made with force and sensuousness but with a lovely voice, both times keeping the same sound on the vowel, from the lower to the higher octave (not "a-ome" and "arrive-ay"). Those portamenti are an open solicitation from a most knowledgeable woman.

Sing the low line "Je n'ai guère le temps d'attendre" with intensity, in an urgent way, almost as if with clenched teeth. Carmen already seems to be calling José "mon nouvel amant" ("my new lover"). The return of "près des remparts" expresses Carmen's certainty of success: note the plural "nous danserons" as opposed to the earlier "je danserai." The "la-la-la" of the last line bounces enthusiastically. The top B-flat should be spun from the F and started as if the singer planned to sustain it, then cut short, as written. Do not just reach it and drop it before it has had time to settle, if only for a second.

Actually, when the whole scene is sung, the first ending must not be so strong as to preclude a still bigger ending after the duet. As a matter of fact, the duet is so thrilling that it is almost a shame to sing the "Séguédille" as a solo, thus chopping off its passionate importance. But even as a solo it should show the wiles of a clever woman skilled in the art of handling men. Carmen has already changed since the "Habanera;" she is now actually weaving the spell she had only described in the first aria.

Couplets of Escamillo (Toreador's Song)   *baritone*

Votre toast, je peux vous le rendre,	Your toast, I can return it,
Señors, car avec les soldats	Gentlemen, for you soldiers
oui, les toréros peuvent s'entendre,	and we toreros can understand each other;
pour plaisirs ils ont les combats!	their pleasures lie in fighting!
Le cirque est plein,	The arena is full,
c'est jour de fête!	it's a holiday!
Le cirque est plein du haut en bas.	The arena is full from top to bottom.

Les spectateurs, perdant la tête,	The spectators, losing their heads,
s'interpellent à grand fracas!	trade jeers in an uproar!
Apostrophes, cris, et tapage	Insults, shouts, and bedlam
poussés jusques à la fureur!	pushed to the point of furor!
Car c'est la fête du courage,	For it is a festival of courage,
c'est la fête des gens de coeur!	it's the day of stouthearted men!
Allons, en garde, allons, ah!	Let's go, on guard, let's go, ah!
Toréador, en garde, toréador,	Toreador, on your guard, toreador,
et songe bien en combattant	and remember while fighting
qu'un oeil noir te regarde	that a dark eye is watching you
et que l'amour t'attend.	and that love is awaiting you.
Tout d'un coup on fait silence,	All of a sudden everybody is silent,
ah, que se passe-t-il?	ah, what is happening?
Plus de cris, c'est l'instant!	No more shouting, this is the moment!
Le taureau s'élance en bondissant	The bull rushes leaping
hors du toril!	out of the toril!
Il s'élance, il entre, il frappe,	He rushes, comes in, he strikes,
un cheval roule	a horse is rolling,
entrainant un picador.	dragging a picador with it.
"Ah bravo, toro!" hurle le foule,	"Ah bravo, toro" yells the crowd,
le taureau va . . . vient . . . il vient	the bull goes . . . he comes . . . he comes
et frappe encor!	and strikes again!
En secouant ses banderilles,	Shaking his banderillas
plein de fureur, il court,	filled with fury, he runs,
le cirque est plein de sang!	the arena is covered with blood!
On se sauve,	People are running away,
on franchit les grilles!	they jump over the railings!
C'est ton tour maintenant!	It's your turn now!
Allons, en garde, allons! . . .	Let's go, on guard, let's go! . . .

The word *toréador* is seldom used in Spain and means any man who takes part in a bullfight. *Matador* or *torero* would be much better suited to Escamillo, a fact that probably escaped Meilhac and Halévy.

This so-called "Toréador Song" is one of the most famous operatic arias and one of the most misunderstood, by the singers as well as the critics who expect it to be loud and violent, from high range to low. The French tradition accepts a lyric baritone in the role, but almost everywhere else the part is given to a dramatic baritone or even, *hélas*, to a bass-baritone.

Here is the situation: A motley crowd of smugglers, rowdies, floozies, and soldiers welcome to their tavern, for a five-minute visit, the idol of the arenas of Spain, the great torero, comparable in our times to a combination rock star and baseball great. Escamillo accepts the drink they offer him and describes for them his feelings of mastery during a bullfight.

First, as a polished gentleman (that is the way he behaves throughout his role: check the mountain scene), he thanks his hosts and returns their toast, simply and warmly. Then—"Le cirque est plein"—he paints a vivid, cheerful, and animated picture of the sold-out arena bursting with anticipation. The clamor reaches a climax in a large phrase fortissimo: "Les spectateurs . . . s'interpellent à grand fracas." Respect the ritardando on "s'interpellent," take a good breath after "s'interpellent," hold the fermata on the F, then allow for a real silence before "Apostrophes."

Now come several shorter phrases, descriptive, well articulated, mezzo forte to forte but not fortissimo. A hearty "Allons, en garde, allons, allons," then a capitally important diminuendo on the long C, and we enter the key of F pianissimo for the orchestra, piano for the baritone: in the center of the storm the torero has appeared, cool, composed, sure of himself. "Toréador, en garde . . ." is legato, with the dotted eighths and sixteenths very rhythmical but blending without jerking. Already Escamillo sees his reward, a beauty with dark eyes (the E on "te regarde" must be sung with as gorgeous a tone as possible, not blatant but radiant with head resonances and not in the choked quality sometimes called covered). A gracious and ornate diminuendo ends the elegant phrase.

In the second stanza of the aria the bullfight is about to take place, the crowd is at the peak of its expectation. Escamillo stresses the mood in short, half-spoken phrases: "Tout d'un coup on fait silence, ah, que se passe-t-il,'" then exclaims, "Plus de cris, c'est l'instant." Now the bull rushes to his work of gore and destruction, and the dynamic is fortissimo on the longer phrase "Le taureau s'élance en bondissant . . ." Again there are several precise, short phrases mimicking the movements of the bull. Respect exactly the rhythm, and say the words precisely on "le taureau va . . . il vient . . . il vient et frappe encor"—as in the first verse, ritardando, then a breath, then a long fermata on the F. Then, for heaven's sake, *no* portamento downward but a short, striking silence— and the description continues mezzo forte in breathless phrases. The "Allons, en garde" and the following diminuendo bring for the second time the masterful serenity of the torero in the arena, proud, conceited, and as cool as his sword. The ending is the same as the first time.

The listeners in the tavern are on their feet, and Escamillo joins in their rousing chorus. He carries with him the shining glory of the popularity he has won not by brutal force but by skill, courage, and elegance. How is it possible that he is so often mistaken for a noisy bully—in whom Carmen would certainly not have been the least interested? It is his elegance and superiority that attract her to him.

"La fleur que tu m'avais jetée"   *tenor*

La fleur que tu m'avais jetée,	The flower that you had thrown at me,
dans ma prison m'était restée.	in my prison was left with me.
Flétrie et sèche, cette fleur	Wilted and dry, that flower
gardait toujours sa douce odeur.	kept still its sweet perfume.
Et pendant des heures entières,	And for hours at a time,
sur mes yeux fermant mes paupières,	on my eyes closing my lids,
de cette odeur je m'enivrais	with that perfume I made myself drunk
et dans la nuit je te voyais.	and in the night I would see you.
Je me prenais à te maudire,	I would catch myself cursing you,
à te détester, à me dire:	detesting you, saying to myself:
Pourquoi faut-il que le destin	Why did fate have to
l'ait mise là sur mon chemin?	put her across my way?

Puis je m'accusais de blasphème,	Then I would accuse myself of blasphemy,
et je ne sentais en moi-même,	and I would feel in myself,
je ne sentais qu'un seul désir,	I would feel one single desire,
un seul désir, un seul espoir:	one single desire, one single hope:
te revoir, O Carmen,	to see you again, oh Carmen,
oui, te revoir.	yes, to see you again.
Car tu n'avais eu qu'à paraître,	For you had only to appear,
qu'à jeter un regard sur moi,	to throw one glance at me,
pour t'emparer de tout mon être.	to take possession of my entire being.
O ma Carmen, et j'étais une chose à toi!	and I turned into a thing belonging to you!
Carmen, je t'aime!	Carmen, I love you.

The role of Don José demands from the tenor the ability to become dramatic in the second half of act 3 and in act 4. Young and lyric-sounding at first, Don José matures through his ordeal and grows increasingly dramatic with the passing of each act.

Corporal José is a villager, good-natured, trustful, but short-tempered and capable of intense passion. In Mérimée's novel we read that he took refuge in the army after killing a man in a brawl back home. This aria follows a violent scene in which, with sarcasm and open scorn, Carmen has driven José to the point of fury, and the tradition that has him throw Carmen to the floor on the two chords preceding "tu m'entendras" is right. At this point, for this short moment, José holds Carmen in his power. But suddenly he curbs his temper, and while the theme of fate is heard ominously in the orchestra he draws from inside his vest the flower Carmen had thrown at him in act 1 and shows it to her. By so doing he seals his fate and hers. He sings an aria of devotion, of torment, of remorse, of passionate love, ending with total capitulation, delivering himself into Carmen's hands: "j'étais une *chose* à toi" ("I was a *thing* belonging to you").

At the start the tempo is marked 69 to the ♩, the dynamic marking is *piano*, the indication of style *con amore* (lovingly), the melodic line simple and warm. The voice must be intense in feeling, subdued in quantity, legatissimo. The first two words, "La fleur," are written musically in an unusual way, the article "La" falling on the downbeat and the noun "fleur" on the weak beat. The singer must be careful to sing the article "La" softly and to let it melt into "fleur," with the first real accent of the first phrase falling on the last syllable of "jet*ée*." There is a slight crescendo-decrescendo on "sur mes yeux," a slightly stronger crescendo on "je m'enivrais," reaching mezzo forte and suggesting no more than sweet drunkenness caused by the perfume of the flower. Spin easily into the A-flat, avoiding a sudden fortissimo. Then, in the solitude of the jail, resentment has set in (three bars *poco animato*, from "Je me prenais"), to be replaced by wonderment (*a tempo*, "Pourquoi faut-il") followed by four bars of dark remorse, with a crescendo. Only then, stringendo and crescendo to forte, comes the explosion of desire and of incurable passion: the only bars forte in the whole aria are on the words "te revoir, o Carmen, oui, te revoir Car tu n'avais eu." Afterward, note that while the voice returns to piano the tempo becomes faster than the tempo primo, ♩ = 76. This faster tempo will make the end of the aria easier for the voice, which now expresses worship, "O ma Carmen," and then submission, "et j'étais une chose à toi," this last phrase ritardando and coming after the orchestra, as if the words of capitulation were hard to summon. The dynamics *must* be pianissimo here. Don José has turned himself into the antihero, and a heroic B-flat at this point is a bit of painful nonsense even if the public demands it. On "Carmen, je t'aime," said with humble fervor, we must understand that José has surrendered body and soul.

"Je dis que rien ne m'épouvante"   *soprano*

C'est des contrebandiers	This is the smugglers'
le refuge ordinaire.	usual hideout.
Il est ici, je le verrai,	He is here, I shall see him,
et le devoir que m'imposa sa mère,	and the task his mother imposed on me,
sans trembler je l'accomplirai.	without trembling I shall carry it out.
Je dis que rien ne m'épouvante,	I say that nothing scares me,
je dis, hélas, que je réponds de moi,	I say, alas, that I am sure of myself,
mais j'ai beau faire la vaillante,	but in vain I pretend to be brave,
au fond du coeur je meurs d'effroi.	deep in my heart I am dying of fright.
Seule en ce lieu sauvage,	Alone in this wild place,
toute seule j'ai peur,	all alone I am afraid,
mais j'ai tort d'avoir peur:	but I am wrong to be afraid:
Vous me donnerez du courage,	You will give me courage,
vous me protégerez, Seigneur.	you will protect me, Lord.
Je vais voir de près cette femme,	I shall see that woman close up
dont les artifices maudits	whose cursed wiles
ont fini par faire un infâme	have succeeded in making a villain
de celui que j'aimais jadis!	of the man I used to love [of old].
Elle est dangereuse, elle est belle,	She is dangerous, she is beautiful,
mais je ne veux pas avoir peur.	but I will not be afraid.
Non, non, je ne veux pas avoir peur.	No, no, I will not be afraid.
Je parlerai haut devant elle.	I shall speak up in front of her.
Ah! Seigneur, vous me protégerez.	Ah! Lord, you will protect me.

In the dark hideout of the smugglers, Micaëla seems to be a beam of moonlight, and her voice must shine brightly throughout her aria. She is José's hometown sweetheart, and her candor must be a foil to Carmen's fatal powers.

There are four fleeting moods in the short opening recitative. (1) "C'est des contrebandiers . . .": first, a statement of fact; second, a cause for fear. The singer should express a mild but well-motivated apprehension. (2) "Il est ici, je le verrai": hope, expectation, combatting fear. (3) "Et le devoir . . .": awareness of the mission entrusted to her, said very earnestly. (4) "Sans trembler . . .": conviction that she will succeed through her willpower—very firm and confident.

The prelude to the aria must be played espressivo—with deep feeling and not like an indifferent ritournelle.

Sing legatissimo, even if there are various indications of style. Note right away that there are no notes written for the final *e*'s in "epouvante" and "vaillante." The last-but-one syllable must be prolonged by the value of the tied eighth, the final *e* barely alluded to.

Too much is generally done with the sforzando on the words "j'ai." I believe that this sforzando is just the peak of a moderate crescendo before starting a diminuendo. Above all, no ritardando on that G as the voice must flow evenly to the last word of the phrase, "vaillante."

Then Micaëla is overcome by fear, expressed by the big crescendo to "j'ai tort d'avoir peur." The very intensity of her fear, however, turns her heart to her absolute faith in the Lord. "Vous me donnerez du courage," forte, expresses a total confidence that restores her poise and her fortitude, (diminuendo and ritardando to "Seigneur").

The middle part of the aria ♩ = 96, much faster than the original very slow ♩ = 44, is a rehearsal of her confrontation with Carmen, which is the reason for her coming. With all its changes of moods it must be conducted with a basic dignity that precludes violence. Micaëla hopes to win by the use of weapons very different from Carmen's. It is an expression of her love spoiled by that woman, of firmness and courage, and of an authority backed by the protection of the Lord.

Style: Respect exactly the details of the rhythm, which expresses perfectly the meaning of each syllable. Note again, and this is very important, that here is no note written for the last syllable of the words "femme" and "infâme" but a tied eighth instead. Therefore, those two final syllables are made only by a sudden closing of the lips without a sound. The phrase "de celui que j'aimais jadis" is full of nostalgia. (The final *s* in "jadis" is pronounced.) The pianissimo ritardando on "Elle est dangereuse, elle est belle" is the perfect start for the crescendo of six bars climaxing on the B-natural. In order to maintain both vocal beauty and personal dignity, this "Ah" on the B-natural must not be a sudden, separate outburst but must be spun into from the preceding G, spinning during the eighth-note rest as if that silence did not interrupt the vibration of the voice. The following bar, *colla voce*, should be sung slowly, with a comma after "Seigneur" and a flexible and warm rise of the voice (in a vowel /e/) to the A, taking advantage of the grace note as if it were a slow springboard to the A. The next bar is strictly on time, the diminuendo on "vous me protégerez" very confident.

The "Ah" on the next G starts forte, then diminishes to piano, with a written portamento into "Je dis que rien ne m'épouvante." Here, two things are advisable: if you can hold the G, sing the portamento and go without interruption to the end of the phrase; that is very good. If you cannot, then sing the G *and* the portamento downward, then breathe *before* "Je dis." To make the portamento and sing "Je dis" and then breathe does not make sense, either musically or as a way of speaking.

The repeat of part A presents no new problems. The several "protégez-moi" at the end of the aria progressively go to pianissimo but without sinking into indifference and losing the sense of fervent prayer. Fortunately, the practice of singing a high B-flat at the end of the prayer, thereby destroying it altogether, was abandoned by the Met circa 1952 and subsequently everywhere else, or so it seems.

"Air des cartes" *mezzo-soprano*

Voyons, que j'essaie à mon tour.	Let's see, let me try my turn.
Carreau! Pique!	Diamonds! Spades!
La mort!	Death!

J'ai bien lu,	I've read it right,
moi d'abord, ensuite lui,	I first, then he,
pour tous les deux, la mort!	for both of us, death!

En vain, pour éviter les réponses amères,	In vain, to avoid the bitter answers,
en vain tu mêleras,	in vain you'll shuffle,
cela ne sert à rien,	it does not help,
les cartes sont sincères,	the cards are truthful
et ne mentiront pas!	and will not lie!
Dans le livre d'en haut,	In the book up high,
si ta page est heureuse,	if your page is a lucky one,
mêle et coupe sans peur:	shuffle and cut without fear;
la carte sous tes doigts	the card under your fingers
se tournera joyeuse,	will turn up cheerful,
t'annonçant le bonheur.	forecasting your happiness.
Mais si tu dois mourir,	But if you must die,
si le mot redoutable	if the word you fear
est écrit par le sort,	is written by Fate,
recommence vingt fois,	start over twenty times,
la carte impitoyable	the merciless card
répétera: la mort!	will repeat: death!
Encor! Encor! Toujours la mort.	Again! Again! Always death!

This page comes after the optimistic and humourous reading of their cards by Frasquita and Mercedes. Carmen is in a somber mood. In a short recitative preceding this scene she has for the first time suggested that José leave her and has understood that he would rather kill her. Carmen believes in the inexorability of fate and will try to read hers in the cards.

When using this page as a separate aria, the singer should start with "Voyons, que j'essaie à mon tour." The modified theme of fate that also personifies Carmen follows while she throws herself into the test: "Carreau" and "Pique" are forte; "La mort" is fortissimo; then there is a diminuendo for "ensuite lui" and again a forte for "la mort." From that moment on Carmen is certain of her fate, and the aria is an earnest commentary on her conviction and must be sung "with simplicity and very evenly."

It is in the first three lines of the aria, from "En vain, pour éviter" until "ne mentiront pas," that the statement of this conviction is made. The next three lines, until "t'annonçant le bonheur," are a vision of the good fortune foretold by the cards. These lines must be sung with a much brighter voice and with warmth and relish. The brighter color of these lines is an essential element of the aria. From there on we are in the color of tragedy: dark voice starting piano, then with a progressive crescendo (beware of peaking too early!). The F on "vingt fois" must be powerful but must convey a sense of helplessness and, above all, must not be choked by an excessively dark vowel: the right vowel is still an /a/. The low notes on "Encor" and "la mort" must be sung as near as possible to the lips and must vibrate so that they have a chance to be heard.

Note that in the words ending in an *e muet* (a silent *e*)—"amères," "sincères," "heureuse," "joyeuse," etc.—the last two eighths are tied so that the effect is "amèrés," "sincèrés," "heureusé," and so on. We find this way of writing to be more and more frequent in French compositions starting with Bizet and his time.

Bizet, *Les Pêcheurs de Perles*

"O Nadir, tendre ami" *baritone*

L'orage s'est calmé	The storm has abated.
Déjà les vents se taisent;	Already the winds are quiet;
comme eux les colères s'apaisent.	like them, wrath does subside.
Moi seul, j'appelle en vain	I alone, I call in vain
le calme et le sommeil.	for calm and sleep.
La fièvre me dévore,	Fever devours me,
et mon âme oppressée	and my oppressed soul
n'a plus qu'une pensée:	has no longer but one thought:
Nadir, Ah! Nadir doit expirer	Nadir, Ah Nadir must die
au lever du soleil.	at sunrise.
O Nadir, tendre ami	O Nadir, beloved friend
de mon jeune âge,	of my young days,
o Nadir, lorsqu'à la mort	o Nadir, when I delivered you
je t'ai livré,	to death,
par quelle aveugle rage,	by what blind fury,
par quelle aveugle et folle rage	by what blind, mad rage
mon coeur était-il déchiré!	was my heart torn!
Non, c'est impossible,	No, it is not possible,
j'ai fait un songe horrible,	I have had a horrible nightmare,
non, tu n'as pu trahir ta foi,	no, you cannot have betrayed your word,
et le coupable, hélas, c'est moi!	and the guilty one, alas, am I!
O remords, o regrets,	Oh remorse, oh regrets,
ah, qu'ai-je fait!	ah, what have I done!
O Nadir, tendre ami	O Nadir, beloved friend
de mon jeune âge,	of my young days,
o Leila, radieuse beauté,	o Leila, radiant beauty,
o Nadir, o Leila,	o Nadir, o Leila,
pardonnez à l'aveugle rage	forgive my blind fury,
de grâce, pardonnez aux transports	for mercy's sake, forgive the passions
d'un coeur irrité.	of an angry heart.
Malgré moi le remords m'oppresse.	Despite myself remorse oppresses me.
Nadir, Leila, hélas,	Nadir, Leila, alas,
j'ai honte de ma cruauté,	I am ashamed of my cruelty,
ah pardonnez aux transports	ah, forgive the passions
d'un coeur irrité,	of an angry heart,
ah pardonnez!	ah, forgive!

Long ago, on the island then called Ceylon, a community of fishermen appointed Zurga their king. A priestess of Brahma, an inaccessible virgin, is their religious leader. As young men, Zurga and his closest friend, Nadir, had become rivals in their love for Leila, the young priestess. Renouncing their senseless hopes, they had made peace and reaffirmed their friendship. It is suddenly discovered, however, that recently Leila has broken her vows and that she and Nadir have been seeing each other. There is only one way to atone for such a sacrilege, and the people violently demand that both Leila and

Nadir be put to death. Zurga accedes reluctantly, distressed in his heart as much as outraged by the betrayal.

The prelude to the third act of the opera describes a violent storm, symbolic of the turmoil in Zurga's soul. Now dawn has come, the storm has abated, and Zurga, standing on the threshold of his tent, takes stock of his contradictory feelings, that is, of the fight between his duty and his affections. The two culprits are the woman he loves and his best friend. Zurga's voice is a firm baritone, more lyric than dramatic, capable of singing a fine melodic line as well as rising to tragic climaxes. He is a man of passion and deep sensitivity.

The aria consists of an intense recitative and a beautiful and loving cantilena, interrupted twice by violent outbursts of guilt and remorse. The indications of style are many and must be followed exactly, as they are the indispensable foundation for a valid performance. But the opportunities for personal expression are many also.

The recitative begins at a very slow tempo and is free for the voice. The marking ♩ = 58 only applies to the voice starting on the sixth bar. Zurga looks around him and, emerging from the torment of a sleepless night, slowly adjusts to the peace of his surroundings. He sings mezzo forte. Deep breaths seem to fill the silence between the first two phrases. "Comme eux" is almost forte, but "les colères s'apaisent" is piano and very sustained. That appeasement is granted to others but not to Zurga. "Moi seul, j'appelle en vain" is depressed, and the word "le calme," freely sustained, is like a weary prayer. The tempo changes to ♩ = 132, at first only for two bars, then for seven more bars. In between, "La fièvre me dévore" is sung slowly and with a suffering voice. Then the next seven bars, which start piano, become a crescendo of power and sorrow, to the E-flat forte on "Ah," on which the tempo returns to the slow andante. Full of despair and helplessness, the next three bars unfold very slowly. The recitative paints the torment of a strong man hurting deep inside, a condition that stuns and bewilders him.

Aria: It seems that the indication of tempo ♩ = 40 is not acceptable anymore, and ♩ = 58 seems to be right. During the long interlude Zurga revives the happy times of his friendship with Nadir, and his first phrase "O Nadir, tendre ami" is warm and loving, piano and light enough in voice to allow the grace notes to ring clearly and expressively. The same devotion appears in the second "o Nadir." Those first two phrases of the aria must be sung in one breath and with great beauty. With the third "o Nadir" the cruel present comes to cancel the past. Zurga sings intensely, starting piano on the first "par quelle aveugle," growing to mezzo forte on the second "par quelle aveugle et folle rage," but not reaching forte or fortissimo. Those phrases are filled with self-accusation and disbelief and end in sorrow, piano and ritardando on "mon coeur était-il déchiré." It is in the following twelve bars that a first climax will be reached. In his despair over having condemned his friend to death Zurga for a moment sees him as an innocent man and himself as a murderer. The *un peu animé* begins piano and almost speaking ("Non, non"), then becomes progressively louder, the tempo faster on "j'ai fait un songe horrible," and an unbalance is felt in the rubato changes in the next bars. "Non, tu n'as pu trahir ta foi" is forte, with a short fermata on the E of "trahir." The words "et le coupable" are fortissimo and broadly sustained, as is the fermata on "hélas." For three bars, then, the tempo accelerates. "O remords, o regrets" are forte and violent; a short fermata is permissible on the E of "o regrets." Then, while Zurga sings "ah, qu'ai-je fait" in a helpless diminuendo, the tempo within two bars returns to the original andante of the cantilena, $\mathbf{\downarrow} = 58$.

The second verse of the cantilena starts like the first. Love for Nadir is the theme; love for Leila is now added to the happy memories. Zurga's voice rings at its brightest on Leila's name, sung with a slight tenuto on the two thirty-second notes D. The anger the king regrets so deeply is again deplored, the regrets this time turning into a fervent prayer for forgiveness, "de grâce, pardonnez." The pattern follows that of the first verse. There follows a moving coda in an animato tempo, $\mathbf{\downarrow} = 132$. The voice, though interrupted by the overflowing of Zurga's emotion, stays forte and intensely pleading, as if his friends could hear him, "Nadir, Leila, hélas." A sudden piano on "j'ai honte" launches a new crescendo. (Do not hold "cruauté" beyond the written value.) The F-sharp on "ah" must be a powerful and vibrating outcry, a vocal achievement as well as a passionate prayer, very much in the Italian style.

The last bars are a free rubato. "Pardonnez aux transports" is fast and urgent, "d'un coeur irrité" a remorseful apology and slower, with sustained B-flat and B-natural. The last "ah pardonnez" is very slow, with a diminuendo on the fermata going to morendo.

The study in this aria of the character of Zurga and the conversion of his psychological aspects into vocal colors and dynamic changes are of great interest and particularly rewarding. Zurga is a man of power and great authority but also a loving human being. In Bizet's music he alternates among sorrow, remorse, affection, negation of reality, and pleas for forgiveness, with the support of lovely vocal writing well within the normal limits of a good baritone voice, and with a touch of Italian lyricism. A sensitive interpreter can feel entirely sincere in this aria and may combine imagination and feeling with an easy enjoyment of vocal beauty.

Charpentier, *Louise*

"Depuis le jour"

soprano

Depuis le jour	Since the day
où je me suis donnée,	when I gave myself [to you],
toute fleurie semble ma destinée.	my future is blossoming, it seems.
Je crois rêver	I seem to be dreaming
sous un ciel de féerie,	under a magical sky,
l'âme encore grisée	my soul still drunk
de ton premier baiser.	from your first kiss.
Quelle belle vie!	What a beautiful life!
Mon rêve n'était pas un rêve.	My dream was no dream.
Ah, je suis heureuse!	Ah, I am happy!
l'amour étend sur moi ses ailes!	Love spreads its wings over me!
Au jardin de mon coeur	In the garden of my heart

chante une joie nouvelle,	there sings a new joy,
tout vibre, tout se réjouit	everything quivers, everything rejoices
de mon triomphe.	in my triumph.
Autour de moi tout est sourire,	Around me all is smiles,
lumière et joie!	light and joy!
Et je tremble délicieusement	And I tremble deliciously
au souvenir charmant	at the enchanting memory
du premier jour d'amour!	of the first day of love!
Quelle belle vie!	What a beautiful life!
Ah, je suis heureuse,	Ah, I am happy,
trop heureuse,	too happy,
et je tremble délicieusement	and I tremble deliciously
au souvenir charmant	at the enchanting memory
du premier jour d'amour!	of the first day of love!

When, in 1900, the curtain rose on the original set of the third act of *Louise* at the Opéra Comique, the spectators could see a small house and its small garden. On the open porch of the house sat a man and a woman, he idly daydreaming, she looking now at him, now down below her at the panorama of Paris, its lights already blinking in the twilight air. They were Louise and her lover Julien. Against her parents' will and against the mores of the time she has come to live here with him, high up in Montmartre. This is the first time in the opera that they are seen settled in their new life together. With great exaltation Louise in this aria tells Julien of the happiness she has found through him.

The aria is a long cantilena with soaring climaxes, with waves of passion alternating with waves of pride. It is also a song of liberation and of gratitude. Going to live with her lover, Louise has sinned against the laws of the family, of society, of decency. At this hour she has triumphed over all of them, and all seems right to her as she sings this aria.

In order to perform "Depuis le jour" well, the soprano must decide to observe all the markings—and there are many—scrupulously and to conceive her voice as a soaring fountain, unhampered by any weight, darkness, or muscular handling. No note of the printed music will ever be altered, yet the voice must sound spontaneous and as if improvising. It is a skillful artist indeed who succeeds in making those two prescriptions work well simultaneously.

The aria begins very quietly, $\textstyle\frac{}{} = 54$, as if Louise was not quite sure that the proper time had come to reveal her soul's delight; or maybe she wants to respect the intimacy of that moment a little longer. But, once started, she must say the first phrase without a breath, culminating in the essential word "donnée." During the following two bars of her silence the orchestra plays the theme, which is tied to the idea of liberation. The next breath comes after "toute fleurie," never, please, after "semble." The voice should be slim and vibrant, growing to a good mezzo-forte on "destinée," where the orchestra makes an accelerando. "Je crois rêver" starts in this animando, but the tempo quiets down when the voice sings piano on the two notes "-ve-er" and regains some momentum on "sous un ciel de féerie"; there is fervor in the voice for "l'âme encore grisée" before it slows down considerably on "de ton premier baiser." It is this constant flexibility in tempo and in dynamics that makes the aria appear unplanned and spontaneous when each change must be planned most precisely. That remark applies, of course, to the entire aria.

It is not too early for another, most important remark: The melodic sound of the whole piece will be hopelessly distorted if the final vowels of each phrase do not sound exactly right. Here again the apparent nonchalance of the writing of the text, which is prose almost suggesting verse, hides a very well-planned alternation of slim and open vowels. "Donnée" calls for /e/, as do "destinée" and "grisée" and "baiser." Ringing in the same slim groove are the /i/s of "fleurie," "féerie," "vie," so that we have reached the end of the sixth line of the score without coming upon an open vowel at the end of a phrase. All those slim vowels must have a shimmering quality such as high notes have on a violin and must not show any concern for power through bulk. This may well be a typically French concept. Another French feature is the presence of the terminal *e*, the so-called *e muet* (mute *e*), at the end of several of the words just quoted above. These are always a diminuendo from the preceding note. They also require a change in shape of the mouth from the shape used for the preceding vowel, and this new shape is always a slight elongation of the lips where the *e* comes to place itself very lightly and forward.

One more prescription: the pattern used for "de ton premier baiser" will be repeated later. In order to perform it easily and with the effusion it implies, the singer should start it piano, already in high resonances, establish the C of "-mier" in medium resonances, refuse absolutely to reach down in resonance for the F-sharp on "bai-," and spin to the G on "-ser" as if it were no more than a half tone above the low F-sharp, thus minimizing the intervals instead of stressing them. To put it another way: Sing as if you were going from "-mier" to "-ser," but insert between those two notes a very light and unstressed "bai-."

Despite their different spelling, the two vowels in "baiser" are the same /e/. At this point I can only repeat that all changes in tempo must be respected and that exact respect for the many metronomic markings, for the orchestra as well as for the singer, is indispensable. They are the very structure of the aria, as explained above.

With "Mon rêve n'était pas un rêve" we enter into a section where open vowels will be more frequent and significant. We now have several /ɛ/—"rêve," "ailes," "nouvelle." The tempo accelerates, at first little by little, then strongly, to ♩ = 112 at two points. Happiness no longer seems only a dream; it is there for all to see, it communicates itself to the world around (feel how ample the phrase is: "Autour de moi . . . lumière et joie"). Here the voice must have the strength of a spinto but remain capable of crescendos and diminuendos on the high notes, which are never heroic for a long time. The first "Ah, je suis heureuse" starts mezzo forte, increases to forte, but ends piano, passion followed by tenderness, on a slim vowel /ø/, vibrant with great intensity. "Et je tremble" starts also quite forte, with a strong allargando on the end of the F-sharp and on the E-sharp, a deep breath, a great A decreasing to piano while the orchestra accelerates. The last "je suis heureuse" starts pianissimo and grows to forte on the whole value of the B, only to diminish at the end of the A and on the G. Such a *messa di voce* seems to be possible only if the tone is inserted into a vibrant and slim vowel /ø/ once more.

The declamation of the several low D's going to the end of the piece should be made on the lips, without any attempt to sing a rich, chesty tone. It is like a murmur as Louise softens at the very precise memory of her first night of love.

When all the work of learning all the markings of style, all the dynamics, all the changes of tempo, all the intentional changes of vowel sounds have been done and practiced, you may feel shackled and mechanical. The intensely rewarding work of liberation will start when you regain the awareness that Louise is singing this aria at the side of Julien, the man who has taught her physical as well as sentimental love, and that it is the memory of the first pleasures of that love which motivates the outpouring lyricism of the aria. All technical studies, all efforts to master the text and the musical demands of this aria must turn into a sincere performance founded at every moment on the intentions of the composer. There is no disorder in Louise's tender exaltation as depicted in these pages. But there is in her, while she sings, a growing desire for more of the same happiness. In the opera she throws herself into the arms of Julien after the aria. That is what the soprano performing "Depuis le jour" must yearn to do if she has imbued herself deeply with the realistic passion burning behind the melodious phrases of the piece.

Debussy, *L'Enfant Prodigue*

"Air de Lia"

soprano

L'année en vain chasse l'année!
A chaque saison ramenée
leurs jeux et leurs ébats
m'attristent malgré moi . . .
ils rouvrent ma blessure
et mon chagrin s'accroît . . .
Je viens chercher la grève solitaire . . .
douleur involontaire!
Efforts superflus!
Lia pleure toujours
l'enfant qu'elle n'a plus.
Azael . . . pourquoi m'as-tu quittée?
En mon coeur maternel
ton image est restée.
Azael . . . pourquoi m'as-tu quittée?
Cependant les soirs étaient doux
dans la plaine d'ormes plantée,
quand sous la charge récoltée
on ramenait les grands boeufs roux.
Lorsque la tâche était finie,
enfants, vieillards et serviteurs,
ouvriers des champs et pasteurs,
louaient de Dieu la main bénie.
Ainsi les jours suivaient les jours,
et dans la pieuse famille
le jeune homme et la jeune fille
échangeaient leurs chastes amours.

A year in vain drives out a year!
At each returning season
their games and their pastimes
sadden me despite myself . . .
they reopen my wound
and my sorrow increases . . .
I come to seek out the solitary shore . . .
involuntary grief!
Vain attempts!
Lia still weeps [for]
the child she no longer has.
Azael . . . why have you left me?
In my motherly heart
your image has remained.
Azael . . . why have you left me?
Yet the evenings were pleasant
in the plain planted with elms,
when under the burden of the harvest
the large red oxen were led home.
When the work was done,
children, old folks and servants,
workers in the fields and shepherds,
praised the Lord's blessed hand.
Thus the days followed the days,
and in the pious family
the young man and the young girl
exchanged their chaste love.

D'autres ne sentent pas	Others don't feel
le poids de la vieillesse.	the weight of old age.
Heureux dans leurs enfants	Happy in their children
ils voient couler les ans	they see the years flow by
sans regret comme sans tristesse.	without regret or sadness.
Aux coeurs inconsolés,	On disconsolate hearts,
que les temps sont pesants!	how heavily weights the time!
Azael . . . pourquoi m'as-tu quittée?	Azael . . . why have you left me?

Although the "Air de Lia" is an excerpt from a cantata it has been rightly accepted in competitions and concerts as an operatic aria. When Debussy was a contestant for the Prix de Rome, a four-year scholarship for study abroad, he deliberately bent his personal style to Massenet's, the reigning composer of the time, and Lia's aria is meant to be a replica of, say, "Il est doux, il est bon." It is an excellent aria, and Debussy's cantata won the Prix de Rome. It has been my privilege to perform *L'Enfant Prodigue* with a Lia who had sung it under the baton of Debussy himself, and I try to remember.

The Bible tells the story of the Prodigal Son who deserted the prosperous farm of his family to lead his own life elsewhere. After years of absence he returns and is welcomed back lavishly. In this excerpt from the cantata his mother, Lia, still mourns for her lost son long after his departure.

Lia's voice is a lirico-spinto capable of warmth, emotion, and beauty. Although she will speak of "old age" toward the end of the aria, her voice sounds well balanced and mature. It is a firm, easy, natural voice, and we may want to decide that Lia is about forty-five years old.

The first phrase of the aria, sad and slow, must unfold wearily and without a breath. It should suggest the slowness of the passing of time for the bereaved mother. The vowel in "année" is /e/. With the *moderato* a rhythm is established—time marches on after all— ♩ = 72. Lia sings passively and with a certain monotony but for the crescendo on "leurs ébats" and the pathetic accents on "et mon chagrin s'accroit." The *un peu plus lent* introduces a melodic line; the marking says, "with a dreamy voice." Lia seeks solace at the solitary shore, and there is a poetic feeling in the phrase, a fine legato, and an effusion in the long note on "grève." The short recitative, "douleur involontaire," is at first slow, then faster with a feeling of painful helplessness. To give the high A of "Lia" its tragic expression the soprano must spin into it from the preceding E, start it piano, and expand its power by the repeat of a very precise vowel /a/. The end of the phrase is a progressive ritardando; "l'enfant qu'elle n'a plus" is very slow, each syllable stressed, the diminuendo reaching pianissimo.

The *andante ma non troppo,* ♩ = 66, is a lyric legato, beginning piano. The name of the son is "A-za-el", not "Azayel" as often heard. The mother says it like a caress; the sixteenth is soft and sweet. When the name comes again it is mezzo forte, then forte, intense, like a call to somebody who could hear it, but it is certainly neither noisy nor irritated. The end of the phrase melts in a sad diminuendo.

Lia now remembers happier times, the return from the harvest, the prayers of thanksgiving, the young lovers. Her voice is warmer with the glow remaining of the former happiness. The memory of the harvest suggests a time of plenty, heavy wagons slowly drawn by the oxen. The tempo is ♩ = 100, with every eighth note clearly heard.

The prayer after work is more vibrant and animated, ♩ = 112. A short fermata is permissible on the high A forte, provided that no breath need be taken after it and that the end of the phrase stays strictly on time. The next five bars are a lovely lyric line, still very rhythmical, light in mood, with a motherly warmth on "le jeune homme et la jeune fille." A breath can be taken after "échangeaient," and a tender ritardando may be made on "leurs chastes amours," but no fermata on any individual note. The movement of the phrase does not stop until the end of the bar following "amours."

"D'autres ne sentent pas le poids" is sung slower, with a rather darkened voice and a gloomy feeling, and although the words "de la vieillesse" are sung wearily and stentato, it would be better to sing the whole phrase without a breath, repeating the effect of time passing slowly, as indicated for the first phrase of the aria.

A great contrast is created by the next phrase, "Heureux dans leurs enfants." The two syllables of "heureux" have the same vowel /ø/ which does not change with the interval of a ninth. The middle G must be sung as a very slender vibration in the first vowel /ø/ aiming at upper resonances, and the second vowel /ø/ is the exact continuation of the first one, as there is practically no distance between the two sounds, which are also at the same dynamic level, piano. The whole phrase is very touching. Below the gentleness of Lia's singing one must feel the intensity of her yearning for the happiness of her family. During the bar following "sans tristesse" the orchestra gains momentum, and "Aux coeurs inconsolés" rings without reserve and almost loud.

Four times Lia calls the name of her son, at first piano, then with more intensity, then faster and louder, finally very loud, before she bursts into a violent fit of despair. "Pourquoi m'as-tu quittée," a question without an answer, is violently accented, then subsides suddenly in a helpless repeat, very piano. There is no ritardando written at the end of the aria. The effect of despair is more natural without that stylistic addition.

It takes skill and taste to convey Lia's deep and sincere feelings, with great intensity but without excessive loudness, with enough freedom of rhythm but without weakening the structure of the piece, especially in the 4/4 rather long section, which can almost be counted by the eighth notes. On the other hand the aria does not make outstanding demands on the voice and should lie within easy reach of any well-prepared performer.

Remark: In French the vowel *e*, when it is found at the end of a word, as in "année," "ramenée," "quittée," "restée," and on the same pitch as the preceding vowel, is not only "mute" but simply ignored and has neither sound nor value. If it comes on a different pitch than the preceding vowel, then, of course, it must be sung like the usual French mute *e*.

Delibes, *Lakmé*

"Où va la jeune Indoue" (The Bell Song) *soprano*

Où va la jeune Indoue,
fille des pariahs,
quand la lune se joue
dans les grands mimosas?
Elle court sur la mousse
et ne se souvient pas
que partout on repousse
l'enfant des pariahs.
Le long des lauriers roses,
rêvant de douces choses
elle passe sans bruit
et riant à la nuit.
Là-bas dans la forêt plus sombre,
quel est ce voyageur perdu?
Autour de lui, des yeux brillent dans l'ombre,
il marche encore au hasard, éperdu.
Les fauves rugissent de joie,
ils vont se jeter sur leur proie.
La jeune fille accourt
et brave leur fureur.
Elle a dans sa main la baguette
où tinte la clochette
des charmeurs.
L'étranger la regarde,
elle reste éblouie.
Il est plus beau que les rajahs,
il rougira s'il sait
qu'il doit sa vie
à la fille des pariahs.
Mais lui, l'emportant dans un rêve,
jusqu'au haut du ciel il l'enlève
en lui disant: "Ta place est là."
C'était Vishnou, fils de Brahma.
Depuis ce jour, au fond des bois,
le voyageur entend parfois
le bruit léger de la baguette
où tinte la clochette
des charmeurs.
Ah . . .

Where does the young Indian go,
the daughter of the pariahs,
when the moonlight plays
in the tall mimosas?
She runs on the moss
and does not remember
that everywhere people repel
the child of the pariahs.
Along the rosy laurel trees,
dreaming of lovely things
she passes noiselessly
and smiling at the night.
Over there in the darker forest,
who is that lost traveler?
Around him, eyes shine in the dark,
he keeps walking aimlessly, bewildered.
The wild beasts roar for joy,
they are about to jump on their prey.
The young girl comes running
and defies their furor.
She holds in her hand the rod
where tinkles the little bell
of the charmers.
The stranger looks at her,
she is dazzled.
He is more beautiful than the rajahs,
he would blush if he knew
that he owes his life
to the daughter of the pariahs.
But he, carrying her off in a dream,
lifts her into the heights of heaven
telling her: "Your place is here."
It was Vishnu, son of Brahma.
Since that day, in the deep forest,
the traveler hears at times
the light sound of the rod
where tinkles the little bell
of the charmers.
Ah . . .

Against all the laws of her religion Lakmé, daughter of the Brahman priest Nilakantha, has fallen in love with the young British officer Gerald, who is serving his time in India. Nilakantha has discovered this sacrilegious love and swears to kill Gerald, whom he has never seen. Disguised as a beggar, he compels Lakmé to impersonate a street singer and to sing a popular legend in the marketplace where, attracted as one of the crowd, Gerald might be detected by Nilakantha.

Although the aria requires an excellent high range and much agility, it is not meant to serve as a mechanical display of these qualities. "The Bell Song" is the narration of a legend complete with decor, characters, a plot, and a miracle. While the soprano must, of course, endeavor to sing the coloratura lines excellently, she must also catch and retain the rapt attention of her listeners by the colorful and sincere telling of the naive, mystical legend. As a matter of fact, apart from "The Bell Song," the role of Lakmé is written for a lyric soprano, not for a pure coloratura.

The first page of the song, all in coloraturas, is meant to attract the people in the marketplace to the singer's side. It must have an "open-air" ring and resound freely, without pinching or restraining. The first motif has an echo piano, which might be colored with a hidden anxiety, for Lakmé knows that her singing sets a trap for the man she loves. A similar effect can be obtained from the next two motifs with their crescendo and decrescendo. Breaths should be taken as shown.

The *lento* proceeds along the same lines, with its mezzo forte, piano, forte, and piano, if the original text is performed. The alternate line provided may be attractive to coloratura sopranos who enjoy a very high range. Only few singers will gain a positive advantage from its use, though, and the sense of an appealing call may be lost in the process for the sake of displaying a physiological rarity. Of course, only a singer sure to sing brilliantly and with ease should attempt such a display.

The legend contains three vignettes, greatly contrasted. The first one, all charm and poetry, tells of a rare moment of happiness for a girl of the lowest class, free for once to run and dream all alone amid moonlight and flowers. The second, more dramatic, shows the girl saving a traveler from death with her magic bell. The third tells of her reward, filled with mystical grandeur. The introduction of a magic bell justifies the coloraturas for the voice and also provides a sparkling ending. Except for them, the whole text is a lyric ballad and must be sung accordingly.

First vignette ("Où va la jeune Indoue"): The very deliberate tempo *andante*, ♩ = 76, is right for the first eight bars. Voice and expression must with great simplicity suggest the youth of the humble girl, the clarity of the moonlight, the perfume of the mimosa trees, but also, through its legato and respect for the values including the silences, a peaceful, almost silent evening. The marked *a tempo* in bar 9 is more of a rubato, the movement of the triplets becoming playfully faster in bar 9 and peacefully slower in bar 10. The staccati in bar 9 are very light, not jerky, and sung on a pure vowel /u/, as in "I do" and "loose."

The following eight bars reproduce the first eight bars, lighthearted at first, a little more earnest in the last four bars because of the allusion to the girl's lowly condition. Bars 20 and 21 also reproduce the pattern of bars 9 and 10, with a playful lightness followed by a quieter warmth. Bars 22 and 23 demand real sweetness, with light legato triplets and a stress on the last words, "roses" and "choses," in which the vowel /o/ is round and long. The following staccati, leading into "elle passe sans bruit," are again playful and graceful. "Et riant à la nuit" should be said slowly and with delight, the word "nuit" on the C-sharp beams with a smile. The light run upward is a progressive rallentando and stays on the vowel /a/, the last two words "la nuit" being eliminated.

The tempo for the second vignette, *allegro moderato*, could be marked at ♩ = 108–112. Here the soprano should be able to use a round, slightly darkened voice, using darker vowels. The first two phrases will find their right color if the singer mentally turns her back to the charming moonlight in order to scan in the distance a dark forest where a human form is vaguely perceived. Then the form becomes more precise, it is that of a frantic man pursued by wild beasts. A crescendo of intensity fills the phrases "Autour de lui" and "il marche encore" with concern. Then a real crescendo and a strong accelerando climax on the word "proie" (one syllable only; do not pronounce the final *e*) and again on "fureur." The piano subito on "Elle a dans sa main la baguette" does not carry with it a ritardando, which will come only on the second "clochette." The girl's intervention is graceful but swift, and it is only when her feat is accomplished that there is a relaxation on "des charmeurs," sung quite slowly.

To give meaning to the following page of coloraturas, let us think of it as a celebration of the girl's victory and the rescue of the man. That celebration rightly takes the form of an imitation of the magic bell that tamed the beasts. A marking of ♩ = 132–138 will allow the vocalization to stay clear, neat, poised, cheerful enough, and not frantic or dry. If possible, the staccati should be so smooth as to appear an interrupted legato. The written cadenza at the end of the page is perfectly good, the variant to be used only by those who can make it as pretty as the original.

With the third vignette we return to the *allegro moderato*, ♩ = 108–112. Lakmé's voice is clear, warm, and full of admiring surprise. It will dim for a few bars only on "il rougira s'il sait qu'il doit sa vie," when she remembers her humble situation. The next page is a long, progressive crescendo, although not written in the score. From a lullaby-like softness for "mais lui, l'emportant dans un rêve" to a glorious "fils de Brahma," each phrase must grow more majestic until the apotheosis on the names of Vishnu and Brahma. That is actually the end of the narration, its emotional contents being exhausted.

A coda is left; the sound of the magic bell outlives the drama. Purely but calmly, the phrase "Depuis ce jour, au fond des bois . . ." brings back the graceful motif of the bell, sung as previously. The tempo then returns to *più animato* as the celebration of victory starts anew. The color and the meaning of the vocalization must be cheerful and very bright. It is agreed that using several colors of the vowel /a/ will avoid monotony in the sound and help the flexibility of the runs. Nevertheless, the general feeling must be that these vowels ring very near the front of the face, changing resonances with the changes of range, finding amplification in all the resonators of the upper face, the upper pharynx, and the head, completely detached from any heavy handling of muscles and membranes.

Personal and sensitive colors must be inserted in some moments of the singing, such as, for example, a rallentando used with sensitivity before the long trill on C-sharp or a slight accelerando over the last page that rekindles the attention of the listeners. There is no objection to ending the piece at the upper octave.

There is a very touching and elegant naiveté in "The Bell Song." If, instead of trying to turn it into an acrobatic triumph, the soprano, while mastering the vocal demands, still keeps the idea of a legend in the foreground, even in the coloratura passages, she will have achieved a high degree of artistic sincerity and given her listeners a special kind of pleasure.

Donizetti, *Don Pasquale*

"Bella siccome un angelo" *baritone*

Bella siccome un angelo	Fair as an angel,
in terra pellegrino,	a pilgrim on earth,
fresca siccome il giglio	fresh as a lily
che s'apre sul mattino;	that opens in the morning,
occhio che parla e ride,	eyes that speak and laugh,
sguardo che i cor conquide . . .	a glance that conquers the hearts . . .
chioma che vince l'ebano,	hair which triumphs over ebony,
sorriso incantator!	an enchanting smile!
Alma innocente, ingenua,	An innocent, artless soul
che sè medesma ignora,	that ignores itself,
modestia impareggiabile,	incomparable modesty,
bontà che v'innamora;	goodness that makes you fall in love;
ai miseri pietosa,	merciful to the poor,
gentil, dolce, amorosa . . .	gentle, sweet, loving . . .
il ciel l'ha fatta nascere	Heaven made her be born
per far beato un cor!	to render a heart blissful!

Don Pasquale, a wealthy bachelor far from being a young man, has decided to get married. His trusted adviser, Dr. Malatesta, assures him that he knows a young woman who would make a perfect wife for Don Pasquale. He describes her in such terms that we have to understand his speech is really a sales pitch that extols the merits of the woman almost beyond credibility.

In the first part of the aria Malatesta describes the physical beauty of his candidate in some detail, and in the second part her moral virtues, to conclude that such a combination cannot fail to bring her husband bliss. A short interlude between the two parts emphasizes the acute attention Don Pasquale is paying to the speech.

The tempo is *larghetto cantabile*: Malatesta takes all the time he needs to display the outstanding qualities of the chosen bride, but he does not drag since he has to keep Don Pasquale on his toes, so to speak. ♩ = 72 seems to satisfy both needs. The animation will come not from speed but from the liveliness of the tone in the singer's voice and from the constant changes of its color according to the feature depicted. A sense of boundless albeit fake admiration pervades the whole piece.

The voice must be round in the mouth for the first half phrase, and especially so for the very first word, "Bella," the sixteenths well sustained in time with the accompaniment. The accent on "angelo" stresses enthusiasm. The second half of the first phrase is more humble. That angel is seen not in heavenly glory but as a transient on earth, the word "pellegrino" legatissimo. The voice becomes slimmer on "fresca," and "giglio," like "angelo," bursts with admiration. The B-flat on "giglio" is carried over to the C of "che," but it is possible to breathe after the portamento and before "che." A break in the pattern of the accompanying orchestra or piano enables the singer to make a slight ritardando on "sul" and to spin a lovely vowel /i/ in "mattino."

There are no more sixteenths in the next four bars, only a smooth legato line, with a smiling sound on "parla e ride," a crescendo of aroused sensitivity on "sguardo . . ." It is acceptable to sing "conquide" with a slight ritardando, the vowel "-de" stopped after the first C and a deep sigh of sensuousness sung on "Ah" on the fermata C, B-flat, and A-flat. A dark, luscious voice will fit the words "chioma . . ."; a light, soft tone sings in "sorriso incantator," still lighter and softer in the repeat of the phrase, as the singer tries to express the inexpressible delight of that smile.

The description creates strong excitement in Don Pasquale, as shown in the short interlude that follows, but Dr. Malatesta must have made some soothing gesture, as the music quiets down and he can resume his report.

The vocal line is for a while the same as in the first part of the aria, but the voice must acquire an almost spiritual quality, all in upper resonances, with a very light staccato on "ingenua." The dot combined with the accent produces a certain suspense between the D-flat and the F and after the F, but without any jerking roughness. To the contrary, the result is gentle and expresses admiration. The second part of the phrase is said more humbly, almost with disbelief in the voice, the feeling persisting for "modestia impareggiabile" (same effect on those last notes as on "ingenua" above). And suddenly Malatesta's enthusiasm cannot be contained any longer: The short cadenza on "v'innamora" is meant to impress upon Don Pasquale the impossibility of resisting that woman's seduction. Sing the vowel /a/ of "bonta" broadly, and after a short tenuto on the G-natural of "v'in-" sing presto the five sixteenths on a vibrant, bright vowel /i/ and hold the fermata forte on the F before landing with satisfaction and mezzo forte on "-namora." During the next four bars Malatesta almost succumbs to the emotion created by so many virtues and sings piano, almost as if on the verge of sobbing. In order to find a lovely tone on the E-flat of "*a*morosa," be sure to sing as written.

gen - til, dol - cea -mo -

That is, sing "do-ol" on the notes F–G, and "-ce-a-" on the E-flat. It is very easy to find a lovely and gentle E-flat starting with the vowel /e/ rather than directly with the vowel /a/.

As above, the C when repeated can be divided in two: one quarter note on the syllable "-sa," then a break, and a sensuous sigh on "Ah" on the fermata and the notes B-flat–A-flat.

The following four bars are given full voice yet no more than mezzo forte, with round vowels all over, especially the vowel /a/. In the next four bars Malatesta's faked excitement grows in an accelerando and a very accented ascension to an F-flat ("un cor"). Note that an F-natural would have given the ascending scale a triumphant meaning. But the F-flat is more moving and should not be given brutally. In fact, it bears no accent.

The voice, alone, repeats piously, "il ciel l'ha fatto nascere per far beato," then amplifies the feeling of bliss contained in the word "beato" through the use of a whole cadenza. The amplification, of course, verges on the ridiculous and should be treated so. The cadenza should be sung without any changes of the notes but very rubato, as follows: The first group of thirty-seconds is sung fast, the E-flat that starts the second group and the following D-natural much slower. A short tenuto is advisable on the F; then the scale downward is sung very fast to the low C, which is sung much slower, as are the remaining thirty-seconds, and more so the four sixteenth notes, the final two eighths on "-to" very slowly. The effect must be that of a rush of fervor reaching a climax on the high notes E-flat–D-natural–F, reviving on the downward scale, but making room for a delectation beyond words at the bottom of the line, from which the singer will emerge on the last two notes.

What? That much should be done with an innocent-looking cadenza? Yes, that many intentions should be prepared so that some of them have a chance to be exteriorized.

The last words can be sung as written, with the fermata as indicated, given the impression that Dr. Malatesta's inspiration had died down. Italian baritones use several variations with the goal of adding more brilliance to the ending. The most moderate, which does not seem to offend the style of the aria in general, goes as shown, to be sung broadly with a ringing, happy tone.

The above aria is often sung early in a young singer's studies. It calls for only a moderate range and moderate power, which makes it easy to handle. But it will fill its purpose only if the student is encouraged to obtain from his mind and his voice an extreme variety of colors and expressions. This variety is, of course, required just as much from the accomplished performer.

"Quel guardo il cavaliere" (Norina's Cavatina)   *soprano*

"Quel guardo il cavaliere
in mezzo al cor trafisse,
piegò il ginocchio e disse:

"That look stabbed the cavalier
in the very center of his heart.
he bent his knee and said:

son vostro cavalier.
E tanto era in quel guardo
sapor di paradiso,
che il cavalier Ricardo,
tutto d'amor conquiso,
giurò che ad altra mai
non volgeria il pensier."
Ah, ah!

So anch'io la virtù magica
d'un guardo a tempo e loco,
so anch'io come si bruciano
i cori a lento foco;
d'un breve sorrisetto
conosco anch'io l'effetto,
di menzognera lagrima,
d'un subito languor.
Conosco i mille modi
dell'amorose frodi,
i vezzi e l'arti facili
per adescar un cor . . .
So anch'io la virtù magica
per inspirare amor.
Ho testa bizzarra,
son pronta e vivace,
brillare mi piace,
mi piace scherzar.
Se monto in furore
di rado sto al segno,
ma in riso lo sdegno
fo presto a cangiar.
Ho testa bizzarra
ma cor eccelente . . .
Ah . . .

I am your cavalier.
And there was in that look
such a taste of paradise,
that the cavalier Ricardo,
totally conquered by love,
swore that never he would turn
his thoughts to another woman."
Ah, ah!

I, too, know the magical power
of a look at the right time and place,
I, too, know how to set hearts aflame
on slow fire;
of a passing smile
I, too, know the effect,
of a faked tear,
of sudden faintness.
I know the thousand ways
of amorous swindles,
the charms and easy tricks
to trap a heart. . .
I, too, know the magical power
of inspiring love.
I have a crazy head,
I am quick and lively,
I love to shine,
I love to have fun.
If I get furious,
I rarely stay that way,
but to laughter I soon
change the anger.
I have a crazy head,
but an excellent heart . . .
Ah . . .

This aria introduces Norina to us. She is a young widow, at this point unattached although in love with young Ernesto. She has not yet entered the plot that is the subject of *Don Pasquale*, and it is not necessary here to know more about her. From the text and the music of this aria we shall gain a pleasant knowledge of her personality.

Lying on a couch or lounging in an armchair, Norina is reading a novel. Obviously one of the characters in the story is a very seductive young woman irresistible to men. Interrupting her reading Norina takes advantage of the opportunity to compare her own abilities with those of the talented woman in the book.

Norina reads aloud, quietly enjoying every word she reads. She is in her element; she could be reading about herself. The tempo *andante* is about $\flat = 112–116$, subject to several ritardandos and to a constant elasticity. Her voice is easy, warm, smiling, and will stay so throughout the aria. She is a light lyric soprano and must sound young, cheerful, and witty. Coloratura cadenzas are a bonus; they are not the essential part of the aria, which should never sound like a technical exercise but like five minutes of fun.

From the first notes of "Quel guardo il cavaliere" there must be a feeling that Norina, while well pleased with her text, is adding a composite touch of sensuousness and irony to it. She sings very legato, the tone flowing from note to note with an almost excessive smoothness. Each of the short runs is an ironical comment on the mesmerizing woman in the book, but the phrases in between are highly lyric, just a little too highly. The first of the runs, on "trafisse," stays on time. But the overly elegant pattern of "cavalier" calls for a slightly fussy ritard, followed by a very romantic "E tanto era in quel guardo," with a tiny tenuto on "guardo" and two very light sixteenths on the way down. The word "paradiso" is sung exquisitely, the run on a very bright vowel /i/, with a short fermata on the E starting the run, a real fermata on the A (syllable "-so"), and a very languid ascent to the A-sharp.

The next three bars are sung with a little more voice, the run on "conquiso" with again a short fermata on the starting G. With "giurò che ad altra mai" the voice becomes vigorous, either because Norina in her mind sees the taking of the solemn oath or because she becomes irritated at the fussy text, and she sings "non volgeria il pensier" forte, without any romantic feeling, the fermata on "pensier" really ironically. The "Ah, ah" are chuckles of amusement, but light, pretty, and well in character.

The *allegretto*, this time ♩ = 112–116, is as natural and spontaneous as the book was artificial and contrived. Norina, sure and proud of her feminine guile, lets herself go with youthful exuberance, her experience in life adding to her natural flair. A warning: the constant rhythm ♪♪. ♪♪. ♪♪. ♪, etcetera, must not be changed into ♪♪ ♪ ♪♪ ♪ ♪♪ ♪ ♪, etcetera; in other words, the dotted eighth note is a long value into which the preceding sixteenth melts and which carries into the next sixteenth. The whole line is a legato, not a jumping party. When a little bite is needed, the grace notes provide it. Besides, all the moods that Norina suggests, "breve sorrisetto," "menzognera lagrima," "subito languor," must be reflected in the changing colors of the voice and the various ways of saying the words. That is not mugging. It must be worked out as if each of the colors appeared in the voice simply because Norina thinks of them. The expression of her face must, of course, correspond to the colors of the voice and help them exist. A rallentando on "i cori a lento foco" suggests a patient work of seduction, an *a tempo* on "d'un breve sorrisetto" helps the cheerful feeling, a darkening on "di menzognera lagrima" brings out the faked sadness with the help of two sobbing grace notes, and the triplets of "d'un subito languor" must indeed become languid, as triplets really can.

The four short half-phrases, "Conosco i mille modi," are more serious since while enjoying the power of her charms Norina feels, too, that they are not without practical value. After the poised and meaninful "per adescar un cor," she returns to her exuberance, this time going farther in her jocular mood: note the chuckle in "d'un breve sorrisetto" and the crescendo on "l'effetto." The two short "conosco" show some conceit. After "d'un subito languor," sung on time now, the phrase "So anch'io la virtù magica" becomes a strong lyric phrase sung without a breath to the high A of "amor." The two runs, the one originating on a high B-flat and the one starting with a high C, are actually a jubilant comment on the word "l'effetto," which precedes them. The concluding words "per inspirare amor" are very suggestive of how far Norina's seduction might go. A sensuous ritardando will be right for the last words of that section.

A pirouette in the orchestra, and Norina turns to self-examination. More slowly, very pleased with herself, smilingly, she sings "Ho testa bizzarra, son pronta vivace." She repeats this second feature with added pleasure. The same pattern returns in the next phrase, "brillare mi piace," and so on. Then, with strength and taking her time, Norina reveals another facet of her personality. If need be, she can be furious—but only for a short time. "Ma in riso" is humorous and mocking. If done with taste, the phrase can be followed by a burst of light laughter.

During the preceding lines the voice had been free to change its pace, but in between phrases the orchestra must maintain a strict tempo. The voice will now follow suit and be strictly on time for the next nine bars, with a good opportunity to blossom on the long F in "cor eccelente."

The seven-bar trill on F must be very brilliant, a crescendo from mezzo piano to forte, the mind of the singer concentrating on the upper notes of the trill for a cheerful sound. After the four measures following the trill it is customary to cut the next sixteen bars. The next fifteen bars after the cut, starting with "d'un breve sorrisetto" are sung as they were the first time. After the run from the high B-flat a cadenza is substituted for the next run and usually ends the aria. Cadenzas have been composed by many sopranos, and some very good ones can be found in the Ricci book (volume 1), and in the Liebling book. My own taste would be for a rather simple cadenza, as it seems to me that the whole aria must convey spontaneity more than technical virtuosity. A tentative suggestion is shown.

Donizetti, *L'Elisir d'Amore*

"Una furtiva lagrima"

tenor

Una furtiva lagrima	A furtive tear
negl'occhi suoi spuntò:	showed in her eyes:
quelle festose giovani	those merry girls
invidiar sembrò:	she seemed to envy:
che più cercando io vo?	what else am I looking for?
M'ama, sì, m'ama,	She loves me, yes, she loves me,
lo vedo.	I see it.

Un solo istante i palpiti	For just one moment to feel
del suo bel cor sentir!	the throbbing of her beautiful heart!
I miei sospir confondere	To mix my sighs
per poco a'suoi sospir!	for a bit with her sighs!
I palpiti, i palpiti sentir!	To feel the throbbing!
Confondere i miei	To mix mine
co'suoi sospir!	with her sighs!
Cielo, sì può morir—	Heavens, one can die—
di più non chiedo,	for more I don't ask,
ah! Cielo, si può, si può morir,	ah! Heavens, one can die, one can die,
di più non chiedo, non chiedo,	for more I don't ask, I don't ask,
si può morir, ah sì morir	one can die, yes die
d'amor.	of love.

Naive and sincere, the young peasant Nemorino has been grieving over being scorned by Adina, the wealthy village belle. As fate would have it, Nemorino unexpectedly falls heir to a large fortune, and all the girls flock to him. Now it is his turn to ignore Adina. Miffed at first, then sincerely affected by his indifference, Adina sadly leaves him to his new admirers. As Nemorino notices her sadness he slowly understands that she cares for him. In the lovely romanza "Una furtiva lagrima," which has always made the success of the opera, he frees his heart of its heaviness and delights in the discovery that he is loved.

This aria is a graceful piece of music written for a smooth and melodious lyric voice. Although many powerful tenors have scored easy triumphs with it, it is at its best when it stays attuned to Nemorino's character, which is not in the least heroic. The only indication of tempo is *Larghetto*. Some powerful voices have taken it as slowly as ♪ = 66. That tempo makes the aria too solemn. A more nimble tempo, ♪ = 80, would fit a lighter voice better, it being understood that there is no rigidity at all in the style of the singing.

It is during the first verse that Nemorino has the revelation of Adina's love for him. That clear awareness comes to him during the long note on "io vo," prolonged into "M'ama" in the twelfth bar of the vocal line. Before this, he had wondered in his tender heart about the cause of Adina's sadness. That is the mood of the first lines of the aria, a sweet concern for Adina who has shed a tear she tried to hide. The dynamic level is, of course, *dolce*, the voice affectionate and very simple. Turn the grace notes on "suoi" into a caress. "Quelle festose giovani" is a warm remembrance of his recent popularity, mezzo forte and ringing. "Invidiar sembrò" is reflective, diminuendo, and a little slower. Then the truth slowly dawns on Nemorino. "Che più cercando io vo" is piano and sung almost in disbelief; the slow grace notes suggest a question mark. The repeat of "che più cercando io vo," however, is animated. After a breath before "io vo," a long, vibrant crescendo expands into "M'ama," sung forte in a large, well-opened vowel /a/. The enthusiasm of the discovery is carried into "sì, m'ama, lo vedo," the vowel on the A-flat being a round /ɑ/. After a breath between the two "lo vedo" the repeat comes as a sigh of happiness. Sing freely as if the second part of the bar was a fermata from piano to pianissimo. Two grace notes, E-flat–F, precede the slow E-flat, the last eighth note of the bar.

In the second verse Nemorino pictures himself holding Adina in his arms, feeling her heart beating against his body, her sighs responding to his own. To have known such joy would make death acceptable to him. His voice becomes more intense, more sustained, but at first his imagination is still timid. "Un solo istante i palpiti" is still piano, "del suo bel cor sentir" is mezzo forte with well-stressed grace notes on "cor." There is exaltation on "I miei sospir confondere," sensuous enjoyment in "per poco a'suoi sospir," which must be sung pianissimo, as written, and with a delighted ritardando. The same enjoyment lasts through the next two phrases. Note the sensuousness of the repeat "i palpiti." A breath should be taken after "confondere i miei" so as to prepare a long tenuto and a large expansion on "sospir" and its tie with a fortissimo "Cielo," the climactic note of the melodic line. (Remember that "cielo" is pronounced "tchelo" and not "tchielo.") A diminuendo on "si può morir" becomes a piano on the ascending line "di più non chiedo" and its repeat. A warm mezzo-forte will give the F on "Ah, cielo" its intensity whereupon the end of the bar, "si può, si può morir" is sung ritardando and diminuendo. At this point the prevalent custom is to make of the end of the aria a vocal showcase.

Even yielding to the practical need of achieving success by singing glorious high notes, it should be possible to keep the above ending in character with Nemorino's tender soul and to sing the added A-naturals with a spin and not a bang, carrying them to their maximum power in a musical crescendo, and returning as soon as possible to a light lyric quality and quantity. In the same vein, the "si può morir" forte should be a lovely, full-bodied phrase, the "ah sì morir" piano a gift of oneself, the last fermata on "d'amor" a triumphant, happy tone which does not hit but delights.

A beautiful, powerful voice is certainly always welcome, but in this aria it is indispensable to combine such a voice with great charm.

Floyd, *Susannah*

"Ain't it a pretty night" *soprano*

Ain't it a pretty night!
The sky's so dark and velvet-like,
and it's all lit up with stars.
It's like a great big mirror
reflectin' fireflies over a pond.
Look at all them stars, Little Bat.
The longer y'look the more y'see.
The sky seems so heavy with stars
that it might fall right down out of heaven
and cover us all up in one big blanket
of velvet all stitched with diamon's.
Ain't it a pretty night!
Just think, those stars can all peep down
an' see way beyond where we can:
they can see way beyond them mountains
to Nashville and Asheville an' Knoxville.
I wonder what it's like out there,
out there beyond them mountains
where the folks talk nice,
an' the folks dress nice
like y'see in the mailorder catalogs.
I aim to leave this valley some day
an' find out fer myself:
to see all the tall buildin's
and all the street lights
an' to be one o' them folks myself.
I wonder if I'd get lonesome fer the valley though,
fer the sound of crickets an' the smell of pine straw,
fer soft little rabbits an' bloomin' things
an' the mountains turnin' gold in the fall.
But I could always come back
if I got homesick fer the valley.
So I'll leave someday an' see fer myself.
Someday I'll leave an' then I'll come back
when I've seen what's beyond them mountains.
Ain't it a pretty night!
The sky's so heavy with stars tonight
that it could fall right down out of heaven
an' cover us up
in one big blanket of velvet and diamon's.

The scene takes place in New Hope Valley, Tennessee—more precisely, in front of the Polk farmhouse with its rickety porch and its tattered curtains at the windows. Susannah Polk is a "girl of uncommon beauty" who lives on the farm with her brother. Neither of them seems to fit in the bigoted milieu of the village, and they keep pretty much to themselves. Tonight, however, Susannah had gone to the square dance where she attracted the attention of the men and caused the women to gossip maliciously. Back home now, she is "still radiant with excitement." With her is her secret worshiper Little Bat, a shifty-eyed youth "not too strong mentally."

In the lines preceding the aria Susannah and Little Bat have laughed together remembering the clumsiness of the new preacher as he tried to join in the dance. Then a silence falls, and Susannah "looks up into the night." The aria begins in a very slow tempo, ♩ = 50, *adagio sostenuto*. Susannah's voice is a brilliant and flexible lyric soprano. In this aria it must not only celebrate in Susannah's naive way the beauty and the marvels of nature but also color itself with more earthy dreams. The voice starts the aria all by itself, and the first interval shows the shape of things to come. The voice must be ready to stay legato and melodious while entering into the musical character the composer has conceived for Susannah's part. She should sing the lower notes already in the high resonances of the high ones, minimizing for the listeners' ears the physical distance between low and high. In this moment Susannah needs an outlet for her happy excitement and finds it in her admiration of the starry sky, which is all she has. While "Ain't it a pretty night" is piano, there must be an effusion in the words, and the dotted quarter note of "pretty" can be prolonged just a little. Then Susannah improvises a hymn to the sky in long, fluid phrases. If it is possible to sing in one breath from "The sky" to "with stars," and from "It's like" to "over a pond," the singer will have suggested the scope of Susannah's vision, keeping the same very slow tempo.

With the *più mosso* we are back to earth for a few seconds. Susannah needs to share so much beauty with somebody, if only Little Bat, who after all deserves it for walking her home. Then she sings with more intensity of a heavier sky. After a breath after "with stars," the voice rises to forte on the naive but scary thought of the sky falling out of heaven. But it soon softens to a velvety roundness for "in one big blanket of velvet" and shines sweetly for "all stitched with diamon's."

This time "Ain't it a pretty night," one third lower, is wistful and less bright than the first time, and Susannah's mind drifts toward a more personal vision. Still legato but piano, the new thought is introduced, "Just think, those stars . . ." During the ensuing crescendo the interval G-sharp–F-sharp must be treated as indicated above, without breaking the line. The enumeration of the southern cities is made with force and a certain awe. Those big centers are exciting and intimidating, and going again to forte Susannah reaches beyond the obstacle presented by the mountains but softens at the lovely vision of the well-dressed people there. The naive ideal of mailorder-catalog aesthetics is stressed by the chatterlike writing of the many notes of the last ⅜ bar.

With the *ancora più mosso*, ♩ = 80, comes the essential statement of the aria. It must be sung firmly, almost loudly, like a challenge to fate. Some high notes seem to stand out but should not when performed. The F-sharp of "myself" is one high note that should be stressed, for obvious reasons. But "tall" should tie in with "buildin's" and "street" with "lights." A deep breath after "lights" prepares the support for the incoming high A-sharp. This broad phrase will find its scope in a very legato singing, in a round, resounding voice, and not in hammering or punching. The triplet on "one o' them" gives the singer a good opportunity to check on the continuity of the vibration, which will spin into the A-sharp.

But Susannah's exaltation is short-lived. With the 6/4 at rehearsal number 21 she reflects wistfully on the possibility of becoming very nostalgic away from the valley, the valley that has so many attractive features after all. Starting with "fer the sound of crickets," a humble but sincere touch of poetry revives a spontaneous ring in her voice, and this ring becomes forte and rich at the thought of "the mountains turnin' gold in the fall." (Do not hurry the triplet of the high A's.) Having weighed the pros and cons of her dream, Susannah makes a brave decision. "Someday" she will go away. The *con moto,* $\downarrow = 72$, is decided and animated. Observe exactly the changes from triplets to eighth notes and vice versa. The vocal line becomes broken by sharp intervals, as in "an' then I'll come back when I've seen." They surely mean to show the intensity of the fight in Susannah's mind between her desires and the reality of life. Vocally, a good way to master those intervals and to reach in good shape the final B-flats of the phrase is to make a choice of the notes that provide a continuity for the voice, almost ignoring the others, as follows:

I'll   LEAVE an' THEN I'll come BACK when I've SEEN
A -   B - - - - - - D - - - - - - - - - F♯ - - - - - - - - - - G♯ - - -

so that the soprano really sings an ascending, easy line, and then:

what's be YOND them mountains.
- - - - - - - F♯ - - - - - - - B♭   B♭

The *molto allargando* before "mountains" will certainly help this arrangement.

But all that is for some ill-defined future. What exists now is the "pretty night," which for all its beauty is a symbol of Susannah's static life. This third time there is a slight feeling of depression in the musical variation. The last two lines of the song are a calculated rubato. The first bar of the 6/4, rather fast, is a repeat of a previous impression; the second bar expands vocally not only with the fermata on "out" but with the hidden wish of disappearance that follows it. That wish is very subtly expressed in the next bar (molto ritardando) with the sliding portamento from high A to low A. Despite the splendor of the blanket that a starry sky could be, Susannah's aria does not end in the serenity this seems to suggest.

The above analysis is, of course, subjective. It may be disputed and rejected. But, like all the commentary in this book, it is meant to provoke the mind of the singer preparing the aria. By rejecting my suggestions the soprano proves that she has made her own effort at comprehension and used her own sensitivity, as all interpreters should do.

Giordano, *Andrea Chénier*

"Nemico della patria"   *baritone*

Nemico della patria?
E vecchia fiaba che beatamente
ancor la beve il popolo.
Nato a Costantinopoli? Straniero!
Studiò a Saint Cyr? . . . Soldato!
Traditore! Di Dumouriez un complice!
E poeta? Sovvertitor
di cuori e di costumi!
Un dì m'era di gioia
passar fra gli odi, le vendette
puro, innocente e forte!
Gigante me credea!
Son sempre un servo . . .
Ho mutato padrone.
Un servo obbediente
di violenta passione!
Ah, peggio! Uccido e tremo,
e mentre uccido io piango! . . .
Io della Redentrice figlio
pel primo ho udito il grido suo
pel mondo, ed ho al suo
il mio grido unito . . .
Or smarrita ho la fede
nel sognato destino?
Com'era irradiato di gloria
il mio cammino! . . .
La coscienza nei cuor ridestar
de le genti,
raccogliere le lagrime
dei vinti e sofferenti,
Fare del mondo un Pantheon!
Gli uomini in dii mutare
e in un sol bacio
e in un sol bacio e abbraccio
tutte le genti amar!

Enemy of his country?
That's an old fable that blissfully
the populace still swallows.
Born in Constantinople? A foreigner!
Studied at Saint Cyr? . . . A soldier!
A traitor! Accomplice of Dumouriez!
He's a poet? A perverter
of hearts and customs!
Once it was a joy for me
to pass through hatred and vengeances
pure, innocent, and strong!
A giant I believed myself!
I am still a servant . . .
I have changed masters.
An obedient servant
of a violent passion!
Ah, worse! I kill and tremble,
and while I kill, I weep! . . .
I, son of the redeeming Revolution,
among the first I heard her call
throughout the world, and to hers
I joined my call . . .
Have I betrayed my faith then
in the dreamed-of destiny?
How my way was bathed
in glory! . . .
To reawaken conscience in the hearts
of the people,
to gather the tears
of the beaten and the suffering,
turn the world into a Pantheon!
To change men into gods,
and in one single kiss
and in one single kiss and embrace
to love all mankind!

The libretto of the opera *Andrea Chénier* deals with historical as well as fictitious characters. The historical characters retain the main features of their true lives. Chénier was indeed a poet, a liberal, and was indeed executed on the guillotine during the French Revolution. Roucher was also a poet and a friend of Chénier. Fouquier-Tinville was the most merciless of public accusers in the government. One of Chénier's last poems was inspired by the lovely woman he met in their common death cell. The plot of the opera, however, is pure fiction and the character of Charles Gérard an invention. The man who sings the aria "Nemico della patria" had been a servant in the home of the wealthy de

Coigny family before he became a revolutionist and eventually an important figure in the Judiciary of the Revolution. Initially a sincere liberal, power has now corrupted him.

When still a servant, Gérard had fallen hopelessly in love with the beautiful Maddalena de Coigny who loves, and is loved by, André Chénier. Now that he wields the power of life and death, Gérard can rid himself of his rival if he so desires. In this aria we hear him working on the act of accusation that could send Chénier to his death, interrupting his work to reflect on the perversion of his own lofty principles.

A strong baritone voice is required here and a clear and sensitive mind. There are no frills in this music, which stresses straightforwardness and sincerity. It depicts the virile drama of a man's love and lust fighting with his weakening principles. At stake is another man's life. The link among the various sections of the aria is not always obvious. A good study of Gérard's successive mooods will help connect them logically.

Pen in hand, Gérard prepares his accusations against Chénier, assembling a number of facts which, harmless in themselves, can be used to point out the defendant as a life-long enemy of the Revolution. During this first part of the aria the singing lines are as free as speech. The metronomical markings apply only to the orchestra. First, Gérard puts down an accusation he will try to substantiate, "Nemico della patria." That is the kind of allegation that will never fail to doom a man. Gérard tries the sound of it and likes it, so much so that it makes him laugh. Sing these first words between piano and mezzo forte, slowly, tentatively, evaluating their worth. After the laughter Gérard sings full voice "E vecchia fiaba . . ." He knows the weaknesses of the people he should be guiding and banks on them. There is scorn as well as enjoyment in his voice. Then, three different times, he will quote a piece of information about Chénier and turn each one into an incrimination. Each time the quotation is sung slowly and in a questioning voice, the imputation faster and forte, with satisfaction, like this: piano and slowly, "Nato a Costantinopoli"—silence—forte, faster, "Straniero"; piano, slowly, "Studiò a Saint Cyr"[1]—silence—forte, faster, "Soldato." The sudden, welcome idea of associating Chénier with a traitor brings a forte on "traditore" and on the next words.[2] The third accusation, equating poetry with perversion, requires less vocal power; rather, especially on the last words, it calls for an almost sadistic sneer. Such an excess of bad faith disgusts Gérard with himself and changes the trend of his thoughts. It leads him to appraising his present condition in comparison with his memories of the past.

The page beginning "Un dì m'era di gioia" starts very slowly, ♩ = 54. The man here recalling his youth used to be proud and courageous. Sing with extreme dignity, mezzo forte, with an earnest, virile sound. There is no irony, only pride in "Gigante me credea," sung with power and suddenly contrasted with the deprecative "Son sempre un servo," sung piano. "Ho mutato padrone" is also piano but bitter besides.

A sudden indignation explodes on "Un servo obbediente," which must be sung faster and vehemently while forte should be maintained until "Uccido." Sing the phrase "e mentre uccido" much slower, with a short silence before "io piango," which comes al-

---

[1]Saint Cyr: French Military Academy.

[2]Dumouriez (Dü-moo-ryā) is a French general who in 1792 as head of the army of the Revolution won decisive victories that kept the Prussians from invading France. One year later he tried to turn his army against the Revolution, failed, and fled into exile. His name is anathema to Gérard and his friends.

most as a sob. During these last two lines do not hesitate to be loud. Gérard reacts savagely to the ascendancy of his guilt feelings, guilt over the passionate love he cannot resist, guilt as well over the murder he prepares of a man whom he knows to be not only innocent but also of exceptional merit.

As if that explosion had delivered him of his torment, Gérard's mind returns to the days of his idealism, of his faith in the Revolution and in freedom: "Io della Redentrice figlio." The tempo is very slow, ♩ = 44. In order to reach effectively the climax of the page on the word "gloria" twelve bars later, sing piano when starting the page, but with great concentration of energy and a legato that even a few indispensable intakes of breath should fail to interrupt (after "figlio," after "mondo," after "unito").

A rallentando on the word "unito" introduces a new feeling, anxiety lest idealism has become impossible for Gérard, "Or smarrita ho la fede." But he cannot forget its beauty. The phrase "Com'era irradiato di gloria" must be sung with as beautiful a tone as you can muster, culminating with "gloria" and becoming regretful on "il mio cammino."

Forgetting his present troubles, Gérard suddenly revives the humanitarian dream that was his natural climate and for a while basks again in the beauty of his ideals. The tempo is much more animated, ♩ = 84, but not so much so that it precludes a growing animation later. The voice is piano at the start but generous in nature. Powerfully supported, well rounded in the mouth and in the resonances, the voice must now flow freely from phrase to phrase but keep the best forte for the F-sharp on "bacio," which during the opera is backed up by a powerful orchestra. The accelerando on the syncopated measure "braccio, tutte le genti" is very effective and should increase enthusiastically until two bars before the end of the aria, where a good rallentando enhances the last words "tutte le genti amar." How beautiful it would be if the baritone did not take a breath before the last "amar"! That page is, of course, glorious material for the performer to enjoy, for the listeners to applaud. Let us remember that its mood is a call for human beings to love each other and that it would be a superb achievement to make the sound of the voice itself mean "tutte le genti amar."

"La mamma morta" *soprano*

La mamma morta m'hanno	My dead mother they left
a la porta della stanza mia;	at the door of my room;
moriva e mi salvava!	she died and saved me!
Poi a notte alta	Then, in darkest night,
io con Bersi errava,	I wandered with Bersi
quando ad un tratto	when all of a sudden
un livido bagliore guizza	a reddish glow flickers
e rischiara innanzi a' passi miei	and sheds light ahead of my steps
la cupa via.	on the dark path.
Guardo! Bruciava il loco	I look! My birthplace
di mia culla.	was burning down.
Così fui sola.	Thus I was alone.
E intorno il nulla!	And around me, the void!
Fame e miseria!	Hunger and misery!
Il bisogno, il periglio!	Need and danger!
Caddi malata.	I fell ill.

E Bersi, buona e pura,	And Bersi, good and pure,
di sua bellezza ha fatto	bartered off her beauty,
un mercato, un contratto per me.	a deal for my sake.
Porto sventura a chi bene mi vuole!	I bring misfortune to who wishes me well!
Fù in quel dolore	It was in that time of grief
che a me venne l'amor,	that Love came to me,
voce piena d'armonia e dice:	a voice full of harmony saying:
"Vivi ancora! Io son la vita!	"Go on living! I am Life!
Ne' miei occhi è il tuo cielo!	In my eyes lies your heaven!
Tu non sei sola!	You are not alone!
Le lagrime tue io le raccolgo,	I gather your tears,
io sto sul tuo cammino	I stand on your way
e ti sorreggo!	and I support you!
Sorridi e spera!	Smile and hope!
Io son l'amore!	I am Love!
Tutto intorno è sangue e fango?	Everything around is blood and mire?
Io son divino!	I am divine!
Io son l'obblio!	I am oblivion!
Io sono il dio	I am the God
che sovra il mondo	who descends on earth
scende da l'empireo,	from the firmament,
fa della terra un ciel! Ah!	[and] turns the earth into heaven. Ah!
Io son l'amore, io son l'amor!"	I am Love, I am Love!"
E l'angelo si accosta,	And the Angel approaches,
bacia, e vi bacia la morte.	kisses me, and it is the kiss of death.
Corpo di moribunda è il corpo mio!	The body of a moribund is what my body is.
Prendilo dunque!	Take it then!
Io son già morta cosa.	I am already a dead thing.

The scene takes place in Paris in the year 1793, in a room taken over by the Revolutionary Tribunal. For the last three years the power of the king and the aristocracy has been progressively destroyed by the Revolution, at the price of much blood and misery. Maddalena de Coigny, young and beautiful, is a member of an aristocratic family ruined by the Revolution. The man she loves, the poet Chénier, is under arrest and in danger of being executed. His fate hangs mainly on the decision of one judge, Gérard, formerly a servant of the Coignys, now a public prosecutor. To save Chénier's life Maddalena comes to Gérard, knowing he desires her, and offers herself to him. Following their dramatic encounter she is moved to draw for him, who knew her family so well, a picture of her life in recent months.

The main interest of the aria resides in the very strong contrast between the first part, a tale of death and misery, and the second part, a hymn to love. Maddalena's voice is a lyric-dramatic soprano. In this aria its range of emotions is very wide indeed, from drama to ecstasy and again to drama, certainly a very worthy challenge.

As a solo aria the entrance of the voice should be preceded by a short prelude of three measures, with a low B-sharp as an upbeat. The first words are said very slowly, $\quarternote = 44$, with a dark, dull voice filled with horror, and broken after "morta." The feeling of horror intensifies, the voice becomes agitated by some accents, and the words come a little faster, "m'hanno a la porta . . ." A silence after "mia," then sad irony piercing through the words "moriva e mi salvava." The next words are difficult to say for Maddalena.

"Poi" is slow to come, the phrase "a notte alta" is spoken more than sung, haltingly, with a break after "alta." Respect the silence before "quando ad un tratto"; it is still possible to take a breath after "tratto." But suddenly the vision of the catastrophe becomes so vivid that the words to describe it rush from Maddalena's lips at great speed, $\sqrt{} = 108$. Sing without a break from "un livido bagliore" to "la cupa via." The next four bars are again almost a spoken declamation. "Guardo" is pianissimo;; "Bruciava il loco di mia culla" is a desperate murmur. "Così fui sola" are words standing isolated between silences, the one between "sola" and "E intorno" is very strong, stressing the frightening void surrounding Maddalena after the fire. Her helplessness pervades the depressing following bars. "Caddi malata" is entirely passive.

The mention of the devotion of Bersi, her loving governess, brings light to some notes on the words "buona e pura," but the memory of her sacrifice destroys the vocal line, which tumbles in hasty and ashamed triplets, whereupon Maddalena raises her voice in self-accusation on "Porto sventura" before it weakens guiltily on "a chi bene mi vuole."

The second part, which starts at this point, requires a voice as soaring and brilliant as it was depressed and suffering in the first part. In four bars the transition is completed. "Fù in quel dolore" is still in the color of the preceding lines. "Che a me venne l'amor" is already brighter, with a sense of surprise bordering on disbelief. The D-sharp of "amor" should brighten progressively; the eighth notes on "voce piena d'armonia" should be of very even value and prepare a mellow sound for the F-sharps of "armonia." After a fermata of moderate length a portamento into "e dice" opens the way to a flow of vitality that will run to the end of the aria.

The original tempo of this second part is *andantino,* $\sqrt{} = 58$. There will be many indications of tempo, dynamics, and style in the coming pages. The first duty of the performer is to follow them faithfully. The interpretation then consists in finding the "why" of all the changes and conveying those motivations. Maddalena quotes what she believes to have heard the voice of Love tell her. That voice was sweet and distant when she heard it first, as in the seven bars following "e dice." Then it suddenly spoke forcefully, "Ne'miei occhi . . . ," forte and *un poco allargando,* in order to open a horizon of hope, and told her with sweet friendliness, "Tu non sei sola." With an intensity that will grow immensely later on, the voice of Love consoles Maddalena, dries her tears, comforts her, and enjoins her to smile and hope. In a still faster tempo the voice reveals its identity, "Io son l'amore." The singer should take advantage of the gimmick of the suggested outside voice speaking to Maddalena and pretend to listen intently, then react with growing elation to the progressive domination of the voice over her mind. Finally, with the *più mosso,* $\sqrt{} = 100$, the pretense is discarded, and Maddalena gives her all to singing with her own voice.

At the *più mosso,* the memory of the ordeals returns pianissimo, only to be canceled by "Io son divino," a piano but warm tone, and to be swept away by the ringing "Io son l'obblio." The tenuto is on the vowel /i/ of "obblio," the /o/ coming at the end of the value. The accelerando pushes ahead; Maddalena's mood has changed from consolation to exaltation. It is now her own beliefs, her own hopes, that she sings with vehement fervor. To convey that fiery impression, the soprano must be careful not to become loud but to think instead of a ringing intensity so that, when she comes to the climactic B she will not carry a weight of tone impossible to hoist that high but will feel that she just spins into it with the same sound she had been using all along. The repeats of "Io son l'amor" are done in extreme rubato, as indicated. But the singer must decide herself whether they are ecstatic or whether there is a sad premonition in the last one.

It is possible to end the aria here, and this is done often. It is more meaningful, however, to sing the remaining four lines. Maddalena's exaltation stemmed from the memory of another treasure lost. Now her voice suddenly turns sullen, dark, and icy. It is not necessary to make it lugubrious in search of pathos or to resort to chest tones. It seems that the vibrato has died, that the body that provides the sound is already "morta cosa." The words should be enunciated with a kind of indifferent precision, very slowly in the last two lines. No postlude should be played, a terrible silence following the words "morta cosa"—a silence that ought not to be shattered by applause.

"Come un bel dì di maggio" *tenor*

Come un bel dì di maggio	Like a beautiful day in May,
che con bacio di vento	which with a kiss from the wind
e carezza di raggio	and a caress from a ray of sunlight
si spegne in firmamento,	dies on the horizon
col bacio io d'una rima,	so I, with a kiss from a rhyme,
carezza di poesia	a caress from the muse
salgo l'estrema cima	rise to the highest summit
dell'esistenza mia.	of my being.
La sfera che cammina	The clock that keeps moving
per ogni umana sorte,	throughout every human destiny,
ecco già mi'avvicina	already brings me close
all'ora della morte,	to the hour of death,
e forse pria	and maybe before
che l'ultima mia strofe	my last strophe
sia finita,	will be finished
m'annuncierà il carnefice	will the executioner
la fine della vita.	announce me the end of my life.
Sia! Strofe, ultima Dea,	So be it! Strophe, ultimate Goddess,
ancor dona al tuo poeta	give your poet still
la sfolgorante idea,	the passionate inspiration,
la fiamma consueta;	the familiar flame.
Io, a te, mentre tu vivida	I, to you, while you gush alive
a me sgorghi dal cuore,	from my heart,
darò per rima	will offer for a rhyme
il gelido spiro	the ice-cold breath
d'un uom che muore.	of a man about to die.

The scene: "The courtyard of the St. Lazare Prison. Andrea Chénier is seated under the lantern which throws light in the prison yard." At dawn he will be taken to the guillotine. His friend Roucher is with him for a last visit. Chénier reads him his last poem, a last "Credo" and an exalted description of his tragic fate.

The aria, composed for an expressive and eventually powerful tenor voice, is made of three parts, very clearly defined. The first part is lyric poetry, the second bitter realism, the third heroic inspiration. The first part lends itself to reading aloud. For the second part Chénier may have spoken the lines without reading anymore, but surely by the third part, the written word has been discarded and the reading turned into an all-out declamation, the outcry of a noble soul facing irreparable tragedy.

Part 1: The tempo is marked andantino, $\flat$ = 108, a very peaceful, almost placid tempo as Chénier remembers the delights of a beautiful morning in May. The voice is easy, soft, the consonants almost nonchalant, the grace notes smooth and light, the vowels in "maggio," "bacio," "vento" full and lasting. If possible, the whole phrase "che con bacio di vento e carezza di raggio" should be sung without breathing, the breath being taken before "si spegne," the dotted values in "firmamento" well sustained to the end. Those delights compare with the joys of poetic inspiration. The words "bacio" and "carezza" now are applied to rhyme and poetry as they were applied to "vento" and "raggio." The voice must keep the same soft but radiant quality. It indulges in a sensuous ritardando on "carezza di poesia," returns *a tempo* on the next bars, at the same time becoming firmer and more solemn, growing to mezzo forte on "cima," staying earnest and quite broad on the last bar of the section. Thus, the life of the poet unfolded in happiness.

Part 2: The change of tempo, $\quarternote$ = 72, and the change of rhythm, to 2/4, substitute a feeling of matter-of-factness to that of inspired poetry. Without becoming trivial, the voice begins a somewhat bitter speech, but earnest and without fear or rebelliousness. The page starts piano, with a natural crescendo on "l'ultima mia strofe" and a ritardando of two bars on "m'annuncierà il carnefice," words hard to say even for a courageous, clear-minded man. The end of the phrase, "la fine della vita," deals with a matter that no man can help but find very serious. The voice must grow in importance, the crescendo also preparing the next section.

Part 3: The broad tempo, $\quarternote$ = 52, the phrases covering at least two bars in 4/4 each, the enormous power suddenly given to the orchestra, invite the voice to grow to its full scope, and a dramatic tenor voice is needed here. The first bar is sung broadly, the word "Strofe" magnified to the limit, the triplets stressed, the word "Dea" grandiose. With tremendous enthusiasm Chénier prays to find for his last verses all the glories of his genius, ending them with his death as the last rhyme.

The tempo accelerates on the third bar of this section, which is sung mezzo forte, as is the next bar. The voice returns to forte on bars 5 and 6, with the A-flat on "sfolgorante" shining brightly. There is a little less power but fine resonance on "la fiamma consueta." The tempo is still faster in bars 9 and 10, but the orchestra has suddenly become pianissimo, allowing the fast-speaking voice to address the "Strofe" almost confidentially as it flows out of the poet's heart and the singer to enjoy a relative rest before the incoming climax. The ritardando on bar 11 helps the voice to sound proud and strong again. A great intake of breath after "rima" will make the next two bars possible. It is necessary to sing the upper alternate in bar 12, the vowel /e/ on the B-flat long, strong, and vibrant, but calculated in such a way that the singer can sing without a breath until after the fermata on "uom." The grandiose impact of this last phrase of the aria will come not only from the outstanding quality of the B-flat but also from the power and the fierce conviction of all the words, crowned by a long fermata fortissimo on "muore."

Chénier's farewell to his art is an imposing vocal piece and, well performed, is very moving. A strong lyric voice may find it tempting and, with piano accompaniment, may perform it successfully. With the original orchestral score, however, only a dramatic voice can cope with it, helped by the determination to attempt an artistic rendering rather than a vocal tour de force.

Gluck, *Alceste*

"Divinités du Styx" *soprano*

Divinités du Styx,	Deities of the Styx,
ministres de la mort,	ministers of death,
je n'invoquerai point	I shall not appeal
votre pitié cruelle.	to your cruel mercy.
J'enlève un tendre époux	I take a tender husband
à son funeste sort,	away from his deadly fate,
mais je vous abandonne	but I surrender to you
une épouse fidèle.	a faithful wife.
Divinités du Styx . .	Deities of the Styx . . .
Mourir pour ce qu'on aime	To die for what one loves
est un trop doux effort,	is too easy an endeavor,
une vertu si naturelle.	so natural a valor.
Mon coeur est animé	My heart is aroused
du plus noble transport,	by the most noble impulse,
je sens une force nouvelle,	I feel a new strength,
je vais où mon amour m'appelle.	I go where my love summons me.
Mon coeur est animé . . . etc.	My heart is aroused . . . .

Inspired by a tragedy by Euripides, the libretto is a glorification of conjugal love that survives the most cruel ordeals. The beloved King Admète has reached the last hours of his life, but the oracle of Apollo predicts that he will regain his health if another mortal consents to die in his stead. One person only, his wife Alceste, unknown to him offers herself in sacrifice. In the scene preceding this famous aria the high priest of Apollo has informed Alceste that Admète is saved and that she will be taken to her death by nightfall.

Alceste is alone in the temple face to face with her fate, which is to descend to Hades and be taken across the River Styx from which place nobody ever returns. Happy to save the man she loves, she will go without asking for mercy.

"Divinités du Styx" is written for a dramatic soprano capable of singing with equal ease a high B-flat and a low C, without giving the impression that she changes voice. The low tones in particular must be sung in the mouth, using full, natural vowels, no attempt to make the sound more masculine, as it is the same sound that has to become a ringing high B-flat and everything in between.

There are three tempi in this aria, an *andante,* ♩ = 104–108, which is a challenge to the cruelty of the Gods of the Underworld (it comes three times); an *un poco andante,* which means slower, ♩ = 72–76 (it comes twice), in a loving, warm mood; and a *presto,* ♩ = 144, an irresistible élan in the face of sacrifice.

The eight bars of introduction must be played; they create the intense mood, the solemnity as well as the simplicity needed for a successful interpretation. "Simplicity, truth and naturalness are the great principles of beauty in all artistic manifestations," wrote Gluck about his *Alceste*. There is in this aria a compelling directness that banishes any display of superfluous effects. The tempo of the first part must be strict except for the last phrase, as we shall see. Alceste speaks to the deities of death on equal terms, calling them twice by name, piano to mezzo forte the first time, mezzo piano to forte the second time, with a well-sustained value on the full notes and a legato on the eighth notes of "Divinités," which should by no means sound like little hammers. The surprising phrase "ministres de la mort" expresses the recognition of their sinister nature but also a kind of heroic scorn. All vowels are to be sustained in the crescendos, the fermatas long and firm to the end of the sound. No effort must be made to blacken the sound. On the contrary, the vowels /i/ in "ministres" must vibrate forward near teeth and lips, the voice must spin in wide vowels /a/ /o/ on "la mort." The same strict tempo as in the beginning of the aria, the same legato without hammers, brings the voice to the first B-flat, sung in a dramatic forte, slim at first, then greatly amplified by the repeat of the vowel /ɛ/. The repeat of "votre pitié cruelle" is slightly ritardando and still forte. The accompaniment, which had stressed the rigorous determination of Alceste, seems now for a short while to reflect her inner turmoil.

In the second part Alceste, rising to a sublime serenity, weighs the results of her sacrifice. "J'enlève un tendre époux à son funeste sort" is sung mezzo forte with a warm, mellow voice still capable of happiness. There is a proud resignation in "je vous abandonne . . ." The second "je vous abandonne" is slower than the first; the three bars on "une épouse fidèle" are very slow. The fermata on "épouse" calls for a crescendo of pride, and the word "fidèle" reveals a great emotion. (In the last-but-one bar, the effect is that of four eighth notes with an E-natural on the third beat.)

When Alceste addresses the infernal deities again, she interpellates them more boldly, forte on the F, forte on the G. By all means, for the first "ministres de la mort" sing the alternate low C's, in the way indicated above.

In the second *un poco andante* Alceste's serenity and resignation have grown to rapt enjoyment of her sacrifice. Her voice is bright and warm, absolutely legato, radiant with tender love. Starting with "une vertu si naturelle," the voice is raised slightly, and suddenly it becomes ardent in the forte of "mon coeur est animé," with a ringing A on the vowel /e/ and great valiancy on "du plus noble transport." In these two *un poco andante* the rigorous tempo of Part 1 is replaced by a lyricism that demands the flexibility of rhythm prompted by the exalted feelings. The strictness returns with the *presto*.

The first statement lies just above piano, growing to mezzo forte, and the second grows to forte on "m'appelle." Each new phrase is a vigorous crescendo as an irresistible drive takes hold of Alceste. It is wise to sing "mon coeur est animé" with a little less intensity but without destroying the drive, in order to prepare the superb climax, "du plus noble transport." The fermata on the B-flat should be long but not so long that it would force the singer to breathe before "transport," which would be unacceptable.

After the two "Divinités du Styx," this time "ministres de la mort" is marked *adagio*, which seems to indicate that the scornful challenge tries to find an even more expansive expression, a challenge that should stay noble in keeping with the character of the whole piece.

The final page adds no new element to what has been studied before. The soprano must be very careful to increase her crescendo gradually from phrase to phrase in order to preserve her best voice and her greatest strength for the high B-flat and the last "votre pitié cruelle."

This is a very noble piece, which calls for a noble voice as well as a noble heart.

Gluck, *Iphigénie en Tauride*

"O toi, qui prolongeas mes jours" *soprano*

Cette nuit j'ai revu
le palais de mon père.
J'allais jouir
de ses embrassements;
j'oubliais en ces doux moments
ses anciennes rigueurs
et quinze ans de misère.
La terre tremble sous mes pas.
Le soleil indigné fuit ces lieux
qu'il abhorre.
Le feu brille dans l'air,
et la foudre en éclats
tombe sur le palais,
l'embrase et le dévore!
Du milieu des débris fumants
sort une voix plaintive et tendre;
jusqu'au fond de mon coeur
elle se fait entendre.
Je vole à ces tristes accents,
à mes yeux aussitôt
se présente mon père:
sanglant, percé de coups
et d'un spectre inhumain
fuyant la rage meurtrière.
Ce spectre affreux,
c'était ma mère!

Last night I saw again
my father's palace.
I was going to enjoy
his embraces;
I forgot in those sweet moments
his former harshness
and fifteen years of misery.
The ground trembles under my steps.
The sun, indignant, flees from this place
which it abhors.
The fire glows in the air,
and crashing lightning
strikes the palace,
sets it afire, and consumes it!
From amidst the smoking ruins
comes a plaintive, tender voice;
to the bottom of my heart
it makes itself heard.
I rush to these mournful sounds,
before my eyes suddenly
appears my father:
bleeding, stabbed through and through,
and fleeing the murderous fury
of an inhuman specter.
This horrible specter
was my mother!

Elle m'arme d'un glaive	She arms me with a sword
et disparait soudain;	and disappears suddenly;
je veux fuir,	I want to flee,
on me crie: arrête!	somebody cries: halt!
C'est Oreste!	It is Orestes!
Je vois un malheureux	I see a wretched man
et je lui tends la main.	and hold out my hand to him.
Je veux le secourir,	I want to help him,
un ascendant funeste	a fatal power
forçait mon bras	forced my arm
à lui percer le sein!	to pierce his breast!
O toi, qui prolongeas mes jours,	O you, who prolonged my days,
reprends un bien que je déteste,	take back a gift that I detest,
Diane!	Diane!
Je t'implore, arrêtes en le cours.	I implore you, halt their course.
Rejoins Iphigénie au malheureux Oreste,	Reunite Iphigenia with the wretched Orestes,
hélas, tout m'en fait une loi;	alas, everything makes it a law for me;
la mort me devient nécessaire.	death becomes necessary.
J'ai vu s'élever contre moi	I have seen rise against me
les dieux, ma patrie, et mon père.	the gods, my country, and my father.
O toi, qui prolongeas mes jours . . .	O you, who prolonged my days . . .

The story of Iphigenia is an episode of the legends connected with the long-drawn-out war between the Greeks and Troy. Iphigenia is the daughter of King Agamemnon who agrees to sacrifice her on the altar of Diana in order to obtain the winds which for so long have been withheld from the Greek fleet. But the goddess substitutes a doe for the young girl and transports her to the distant land of Taurida (Crimea). There Iphigenia becomes a priestess in the temple of Diana. Agamemnon spends ten years at the siege of Troy. His wife Clytemnestra, in revenge for the supposed death of her daughter, meanwhile takes a lover and banishes Agamemnon's other children, Elektra to the servants' quarters, the infant Orestes to a foreign country. When Agamemnon returns, he is murdered in his bath by Clytemnestra and her lover.

The recitative "Cette nuit . . ." and the aria "O toi . . ." take place at the beginning of the opera *Iphigénie en Tauride*. The overture has just described a furious tempest assailing the shores of Taurida. In front of the temple of Diana, Iphigénie and two priestesses have been praying to the gods for protection and mercy. The storm is over now, and Iphigénie, anguished and troubled, tells her two friends of the tragic dream she has had which, jointly with the tempest, seems to bear dark forebodings for her family.

The recitative starts with three sustained F-sharps preceding the words "Cette nuit . . ." The tempo is largo, the mood slow and mysterious. Iphigénie seems reluctant to speak, so painful was her dream. Mark a comma after "Cette nuit," respect the silence after "j'ai revu," and sing "le palais de mon père" with sadness and nostalgia. On the next phrase, "J'allais jouir . . .," the voice becomes clearer and warmer at the thought of her father's embrace. The same mood persists in "j'oubliais en ces doux moments," but "ses anciennes rigueurs" is severe and forte, followed by the accusation "et quinze ans de misère," which cancels out the affectionate feelings: it is her own father who ordered her sacrifice and caused her exile.

In the orchestra a tremolo piano introduces a new element of the dream: a cataclysm, an earthquake, a thunderstorm, a palace burning. Let the tremolo settle before singing; then use a frightened, half-choked voice for "la terre tremble sous mes pas," a more dramatic sound and an accelerando on "le soleil indigné . . ," and a new tempo will start with "abhorre." The next four bars will be counted in 8, ♪ = 120, with a great crescendo to fortissimo on "tombe sur le palais" and to the end of the phrase. It is permissible to sing a half note on the "-bra-" of "l'embrase" and to sing the final "-se" as the first eighth of the next bar. "Et le dévore" is still fortissimo and very broad. From this point on the tempi change constantly. Let us count bars:

Bars 1 and 2 (orchestra) are presto, ♩ = 120. The two terminal chords and the next five bars are lento, ♪ = 120. The last two beats of the fifth bar and the next three bars are presto again. but the last two beats of this third bar and the next five bars are moderato, ♩ = 80.

The phrases *lento* must be sung with great sensitivity, the phrases *presto* with frenzy, the *moderato* coming after the horrified fermata before "mon père," heavily and as with disbelief. The fermata on the silence after "meurtrière" should be long and should create suspense: Iphigénie has seen the ghost of her murdered father. Now she will be shown the murderer: her mother.

After the fermata, let the tremolo settle again before singing, "Ce spectre affreux." Those three bars are lento, the voice tragic and going from a breathy piano to fortissimo. After the fermata the next four bars are presto again, ♩ = 132, breathless and distracted. The fifth and sixth bars are moderato, ♩ = 80: A voice stops Iphigénie in her tracks, shouting the name of Oreste. She sees her young brother begging for help: after the fermata, six measures lento. The first three are sung piano, with great compassion and love. Starting with the fourth, a tragic forte shows the terrible conclusion of the dream: Iphigénie herself becoming the murderess of her brother. The last bar, "à lui percer le sein" is sung fortissimo and allargando, the last two chords of the piece fortissimo and separated by a large silence.

This extraordinary recitative is a perfect example of the directness of Gluck's style, which realistically notes the pathetic accents and subordinates the purely musical element to the dramatic expression. To recapitulate: the dream as narrated in this recitative encompasses, first, the nostalgic return to a home left long ago, then a cataclysm destroying that home, a call for mercy followed by the vision of a dying father, then of a mother turned murderess, finally of the dreamer herself forced to murder. A fluid and flexible pattern is what the many changes of tempi indicated above want to suggest, all changes being associated with as many vocal colors and dramatic intentions or more, indeed a challenge to make the heart of any true artist rejoice.

When performing this excerpt of Gluck's opera in concert it is customary to leave out the chorus and the two pages of recitative following it and to proceed to the aria in A major "O toi, qui prolongeas mes jours," *andante moderato,* ♩ = 56–60.

Aria: During the four bars of introduction Iphigénie recovers her composure and prepares herself to address, in a moving cantilena, a prayer to Diana to let her die in order to end her ordeal. It must be sung with the most beautiful legato, in words purely and simply said, letting the voice flow from the beginning to the end of each phrase, with a well-calculated, moderate emphasis on the sensitively accentuated words like "jours," "déteste," "implore." The appoggiaturas are worth half the value of the note they precede and mean precise feelings: on "reprends," supplication; on "déteste," distaste; on "arrête," prayer. The general dynamics is a fine-sounding mezzo-forte. The high A on "Je t'implore" should come in a gracious spin, with a slight tenuto on top, the meaning of "imploring" always present.

After the interlude, the lines starting with "Rejoins Iphigénie" constitute a Part B and should be sung appreciably faster than Part A. ♩ = 76 is suggested. While the same legato is to be used, a more declamatory diction should fill the phrases with energy. For instance, "la mort me devient nécessaire" must be sung with somber determination. The reason for that despair is given in the next lines, which become rubato as follows: accelerando and going from piano to mezzo forte on "J'ai vu s'élever contre moi," accelerando and forte on "les dieux," fortissimo with despair on "ma patrie," a deep breath, and "et mon père" ritardando molto and decrescendo, with great and loving sadness.

The return of Part A brings few new elements of interpretation. There is an added sense of urgency given to the prayer. Both "Je t'implore" can be strongly stressed. A slight ritardando on "arrêtes en le cours" will create an effect of rebound and give more intensity to the last "je t'implore," sung forte and always with beauty. The forte will be maintained to the end of the piece.

For my own first operatic debut anywhere I sang Oreste under Pierre Monteux and heard this aria sung in such a way that the conductor interrupted the dress rehearsal to inform the soprano, Germaine Lubin, that the orchestra called her Stradivarius! Such an experience could not fail to set a lifetime standard for the young Oreste.

"Unis dès la plus tendre enfance" *tenor*

Quel langage accablant	What an oppressive language
pour un ami qui t'aime.	for a friend who loves you.
Reviens à toi,	Come to your senses,
mourons dignes de nous.	let us die worthy of ourselves.
Cesse, dans ta fureur extrême,	Cease, in your extreme furor,
d'outrager et les Dieux,	to insult the Gods as well
et Pylade et toi-même.	as Pylades and yourself.
Si le trépas nous est inévitable,	If our death is inevitable,
quelle vaine terreur	what vain terror
te fait pâlir pour moi?	makes you fear for me?
Je ne suis pas si misérable	I am not so unfortunate
puisque enfin je meurs près de toi.	since after all I die close to you.
Unis dès la plus tendre enfance,	United since our earliest childhood,
nous n'avions qu'un même désir;	we never had but one wish;
ah! mon coeur applaudit d'avance	ah! my heart applauds beforehand
au coup qui va nous réunir.	the blow that will reunite us.
Le sort nous fait périr ensemble,	Fate makes us perish together,
n'en accuse point la rigueur.	don't accuse its severity.
La mort même est une faveur	Death itself is a favor,
puisque le tombeau nous rassemble.	since the tomb unites us.

The tempest that has assailed Taurida (Crimea) has swept ashore two young Greeks. They are being held captive by the natives and will be offered in sacrifice to appease the gods. It is the duty of Iphigénie as priestess of the temple of Diana to celebrate the sacrifice. One of the captives, Oreste, is tormented by violent remorse. Not only has he murdered his mother, he now feels responsible for the fate of his friend Pylade, the other captive. Raised together since infancy, the young men are united by a deep, brotherly affection. In the aria "Unis dès la plus tendre enfance," Pylade tries to comfort Oreste by telling him that they will also be united in death.

Recitative: An utmost simplicity is its dominant feature. Each phrase reflects a nuance of Pylade's thoughts and feelings, and his words are direct and sincere. The voice of the tenor must be warm and clear, the words said purely, the phrases aimed at persuading and moving. This page is definitely directed at somebody, a notion which in the performer should create a style of singing different from that of an introspective piece. How useful it would be if Pylade could imagine an Oreste prostrate near him and watch his reactions!

Although the page is a recitative it is a good idea to stay very faithful to the rhythm of the printed notes. Some inflections are, of course, desirable, but too many liberties would harm the beautifully conceived pattern. There are no written appoggiaturas. When singing Oreste in this opera, I was never asked to sing any by such conductors as Pierné, Monteux, and the senior Kleiber, for instance. I have no personal authority in this matter and simply want to put down the fact here.

The tempo stays around ♩ = 84. "Quel langage accablant" refers to the last phrases of Oreste's aria just before this recitative. They were "Gods, open the abysses of hell before me, their torments will still be too mild for me." Pylade speaks sadly, reproachfully, discouraged for a while before his affection overcomes his depression. Sing "pour un ami qui t'aime" with great warmth (and an open vowel /ɛ/ on "aime"). "Reviens à toi" is said firmly, "mourons dignes de nous" with pride. Pylade now uses authority—"Cesse, dans ta fureur extrême . . ."—and indignation—"d'outrager et les Dieux"—and, again, pride—"et Pylade et toi-même," with a slight allargando. There is noble resignation in "Si le trépas nous est inévitable," sung piano, while "quelle vaine terreur" is an appeal to reason. A fermata on the silence following "pour moi" is advisable. Pylade's last phrase, a stoic and touching acceptance of their common fate, must be sung very tenderly. There is no trace of swagger anywhere in this recitative, only firm, quiet resolution based on reason and on love.

The aria, started piano in a very intimate mood, is a melodious cantilena sung in a continuous legato, with warmth and affection. But the voice should never be static or passive. A constant spin, an alert support, should give each phrase a life and a shape, avoiding the pitfall of monotony. When a whole phrase is repeated, a new color, a new dynamic, a new contour should be attempted until the singer feels sincere, personal, and in compliance with the musical and dramatic intentions. A physical picture of the two men would certainly help to find the right mood. Could Pylade see himself, for instance, kneeling beside the prostrate Oreste, trying to make him look at him, to make him raise himself on an elbow, to make him come out of his dejection?

After singing the first two phrases piano the voice rises to mezzo forte on "ah! mon coeur applaudit d'avance," still more on the first "au coup qui va nous réunir." These phrases challenge death courageously and should be sung accordingly and again with simplicity. The second "ah! mon coeur" starts piano, the repeats of "au coup qui va nous réunir" grow to forte and finally to an almost stately nobility.

The middle part ("Le sort nous fait périr") returns to the feeling of intimacy and tenderness, becoming firm and reasonable on "n'en accuse point la rigueur." The first time the phrase "La mort même est une faveur" is sung, it should sound very persuasive and very natural, but its implications are tragic, and when repeated in the higher range it must acquire great force. The singing of the vowel /y/ on the pitch A-natural should present no difficulty if it is shaped precisely in extended lips backed by an open space in the upper pharynx and if the phrase is conceived as passing beyond this A-natural to its main accent on "faveur." The pronunciation of the word "tombeau" must be exact in order to make it singable. It is "ton-bo", /tɔ̃bo/, the vowel /o/ of the last syllable being dark and spinning. It is much better to sing the phrase "puisque le tombeau nous rassemble" without a breath in the middle every time it comes, and the last time with a slight ritardando, full of the simple spirit of sacrifice.

The aria is musically very simple, vocally not overexacting. But it will bring satisfaction to the performer and the listeners only if it rises beyond a correct vocal and musical reading to the level of the Greek tragedies. Oreste and Pylade are two intimate and very human friends, but through the centuries they have grown and reached the rank of legendary figures, somewhat bigger than life. How wonderful if that were suggested in the singing of this aria!

Gluck, *Orfeo ed Euridice*

"Che farò senza Euridice" *mezzo-soprano/baritone*

Ah! Mio tesoro! Amata sposa!	Ah! My treasure! Beloved wife!
Ove trascorsi, ohimè,	Where did you vanish, alas,
dove mi spinse un delirio d'amor?	what did my delirious love make me do?
O mia sposa! Euridice, mia diletta!	O my wife! Euridice, my beloved!
Ah! più non m'ode,	Ah! she hears me no more,
ella è morta per me!	she is dead for me!
Ed io, io fui che morte a lei recava!	And I, I am the one who brought her death!
Oh! legge spietata!	Oh! merciless law!
e qual martir al mio somiglia!	and what martyrdom equals mine!
In quest' ora funesta sol di morir con te,	In this fateful hour, only to die with you,
lasso, mi resta.	alas, is left for me.
Che farò senza Euridice?	What will I do without Euridice?
Dove andrò senza il mio ben?	Where will I go without my beloved?
Euridice! Euridice! O Dio! Rispondi!	Euridice! Euridice! O God! Answer me!
Io son pure il tuo fedele!	Yet I still belong to you faithfully!

Che farò . . .	What will I do . . .
Ah! non m'avanza più soccorso,	Ah! no help comes to me anymore,
più speranza,	no hope anymore,
nè dal mondo nè dal ciel!	neither from this world nor from heaven.
Che farò . . .	What will I do . .

The Greek legend is known to everybody: The Gods have allowed Orfeo to lead Euridice out of Hades and back to life, under the condition that he never look at her during their return. If he does, she will die for the second time.

This aria must not be sung without the recitative preceding it. This is true of almost all arias of the seventeenth, eighteenth, and early nineteenth centuries. The score for *Orfeo* was rewritten several times by Gluck himself, and there are several recitatives to choose from. When the aria is sung in the key of C, the one most often used by mezzo-sopranos and baritones, I recommend the Ricordi version as the most dramatic, a quality indispensable to expressing the cruel disappearance of Euridice and the despair of Orfeo. As I had always heard it, I accepted for a long time the tempo of the aria itself as an adagio with practically no change from beginning to end—until the day when I had to stage the whole scene. I failed in repeated attempts to find a psychological connection between the violently outspoken recitative and the placid aria. I then decided to try Part A as written—alla breve, cut time—and the middle Parts B adagio, as written. The result was instantly satisfying and the possibility of staging obvious. The eminent conductor Fritz Busch trusting my idea, we performed the aria for the first time in this fashion with the Chicago Symphony and received one of the greatest ovations I have ever experienced.

The tempo for part A and its repeats should be approximately ♩ = 58–60, for the two *adagios* twice as slow, ♩ = 58–60. In some scores for voice and piano the accompaniment is written entirely in even eighth notes. The Ricordi edition has dotted values, as does the orchestra, on bars 13 and 14, "Che farò senza il mio ben."

Recitative: If the piece is used as a solo aria, the recitative should start with the four chords preceding "Ah! Mio tesoro! Amata sposa." On these words Orfeo, no longer able to resist the bitter entreaties of Euridice, turns around and looks at her. (The words "O Dei, che avenne, io moro" must be omitted, the chords kept as written.) Euridice falls lifeless. Orfeo, stunned, sings the following bars very slowly, almost without timbre. Then, during the *allegro* (♩ = 160), he tries feverishly to revive her. The *allegro* ends on a long funereal chord. On the words "Ah! più non m'ode, ella è morta per me," Orfeo despite himself has to acknowledge that she is dead: Sing very slowly, with disbelief at first, then with despair. The following *allegro* depicts Orfeo's fury when he realizes that he is responsible for the fate that has befallen Euridice. Sing with fury: "Ed io, io fui che morte a lei recava." Orfeo then seems to pant through the disconnected phrase, which should logically be "O legge spietata! e qual martir al mio somiglia." Minimize the two silences, stress the dotted eighths and sixteenths. Broaden the last line, sung with a darkened voice. Allow yourself a fermata on the F, fortissimo on "Lasso," and connect with "mi resta" without breathing. The resolution is stronger and more tragic without an appoggiatura.

During the introduction of the aria Orfeo's furor is replaced by a growing awareness of the worthlessness of his life without Euridice. The first verse should be sung in an anguished, intense piano. Two strong accents on the C's of "farò" and "andrò," then legatissimo, as the dotted values in the piano score stress the inner tension of the phrase. The two "Euridice" and "Rispondi" are a fervent plea; the long "Rispondi" is a crescendo ending in a vehement forte. The *adagio* is a desolate love song, piano and legato with two accents on the second "pure" and the second "fedele." I believe that the return of "Che farò" should be sung forte: Orfeo now has the strength to voice his despair forcefully. With the *adagio* comes the awareness of his solitude, his hopelessness. Start piano, make a great crescendo and a long fermata on "*nè* dal ciel." The last "Che farò" starts piano: Orfeo's strength is spent for a while. Stay piano until the second "Dove andrò, che farò" (note the inversion of the words), then an upsurge of despair creates a great crescendo to forte and then fortissimo on the last three bars of the vocal line. Above all, *no* rallentando.

The postlude must maintain and increase the tension, still stressed by the syncopation in the last bars. A rallentando is probably acceptable in the last two bars.

Gounod, *Faust*

"Avant de quitter ces lieux" (Valentin's aria)   *baritone*

Avant de quitter ces lieux,	Before leaving this place,
sol natal de mes aïeux,	native soil of my forefathers,
à toi, Seigneur et Roi des cieux,	to you, Lord and King of Heaven,
ma soeur je confie.	I entrust my sister.
Daigne de tout danger	Deign from all danger
toujours, toujours la protéger,	always, always to protect her,
cette soeur si chérie,	this sister so dear,
daigne de tout danger la protéger.	deign from all danger to protect her.
Délivré d'une triste pensée,	Delivered from a sad thought,
j'irai chercher la gloire	I shall look for glory
au sein des ennemis.	in the midst of the enemy.
Le premier et le plus brave	First and bravest
au fort de la mélée,	in the center of the fray,
j'irai combattre pour mon pays.	I shall fight for my country.
Et si vers Lui Dieu me rappelle,	And if God calls me back to Him,
je veillerai sur toi fidèle,	I shall watch over you faithfully,
o Marguerite!	O Marguerite!
Avant de quitter ces lieux,	Before leaving this place,
sol natal de mes aïeux,	native soil of my forefathers,
à toi, Seigneur et Roi des cieux,	to you, Lord and King of Heaven,
ma soeur je confie.	I entrust my sister.
O Roi des cieux,	O King of Heaven,

jette les yeux,	turn your glances,
protège Marguerite,	protect Marguerite,
o Roi des cieux, o Roi!	O King of Heaven, O King!

This aria, sung by Valentin, the brother of Marguerite, has become one of the favorites of all baritones and is used constantly in auditions and concerts. I have often sung *Faust* at the Paris Opéra, both in the present version premiered in 1869 and in the original version with spoken text of 1859. Therefore I was sure of myself when I found the role in my repertoire at the Teatro Colón in Buenos Aires in 1937. At the first musical rehearsal, however, I discovered that my smugness was premature: In the country-fair scene Valentin had an aria that was not in my score and of which I had never heard. It was "Avant de quitter ces lieux." I learned it and sang it, of course—but what had happened?

In 1864, when *Faust* was given in English at Her Majesty's Theatre in London, Gounod yielded to the strong entreaties of the baritone Santley who was unhappy with a role that had no aria. He took the melodic phrase from the prelude of the opera and turned it into the aria "Avant de quitter ces lieux." In 1937 it had never yet been used at the Paris Opéra.

The aria was inserted in the score between the entrance of Valentin, "O sainte médaille," and the "Veau d'Or" strophes sung by Mephisto. It consists of three sections: (A) Valentin, joining the army, entrusts his sister Marguerite to the protection of the Lord; (B) he will be a valiant soldier, and if he falls, he will protect Marguerite from on high; (C) repeat of Part A. The interpretation is very easy. Part A is earnest, religious, and keeps a long, melodious line flowing. The tempo should read ♩ = 69. The first phrase is piano with a touch of sadness. "Sol natal de mes aieux" has, with a crescendo, a feeling of proud devotion. Be sure that the syllable "-eux" in "aïeux" sounds like the German umlaut *ö* in *schön* and not like an open vowel. "A toi, Seigneur et Roi des cieux" is sung broadly and with solemnity. The following phrase has always embarrassed me and may be the reason why the French were reluctant to adopt the aria: The spread of the word "ma" (in "ma soeur") over three notes reaching G is terribly clumsy and goes against the grain of the language. (Try to sing "my-y-y sister" and you will understand me.) Anyway, making the best of a bad situation, sing the "ma-a-a" just above mezzo forte, avoid sustaining the G beyond its written value, and also avoid breathing before "je confie." Breathe after "confie," with the next breath coming between "toujours" and its repeat, which gives some emphasis to the second "toujours." Sing "Cette soeur si chérie" with love and intensity. The next breath is after "la protéger," carrying "danger" over into "la protéger." A very slight ritardando can be made on the repeat of "la protéger."

Part B: This is a march, ♩ = 100. Although this section expresses determination and bravery, it is not a description of a battle, and there is serenity behind the soldierly statement. Valentin's mind is made up, his behavior dignified, his faith in the Lord total. The phrase must be sung with pride and controlled vigor, without rushing or pressing. Sing with a ringing sound, not a heavy or loud one.

The vowel /e/ in "pensée" and "mélée" is the sharp slender one, turning into /ə/ without inserting a diphthong. It is /meleə/ and not /meleiə/. Take a quick breath after the first "gloire," suppressing the second note (B-flat) on the syllable "-re." Conversely, add the conjunction "et" on the tied A-flat on the last syllable of "premier": sing "le premier et le plus brave," taking a quick breath again after "premier." In this way you can ascend with full power to the G-flat "le plus brave," singing the vowel *a* on "brave" with a warm shading of /o/. "J'irai combattre pour mon pays" is broad and proud.

The next six bars are slower and are religious in feeling. The shadow of death has fallen upon the mind of Valentin, lightened by his faith in a new life beyond. While in the marching lines of the aria the triplets of eighths were ascending and aggressive, here the two descending triplets are soothing and peaceful. A progressive ritardando on "O Marguerite" brings back the first tempo.

Part C is piano and legatissimo at the start, with a crescendo on "à toi, Seigneur et Roi des cieux." If it is necessary to create a climax near the end of the aria, do not do it on "ma-a-a soeur" but on the G of "O Roi des cieux," sustaining that G and the next two notes, gaining a little momentum on "jette les yeux" turning to piano, with feeling on "protège Marguerite," and using a final cadence such as that shown here.

Mozart added new arias to his scores or made substitutions, and so did Verdi. Success is a necessary ingredient in the life of a composer, and a good singer singing a good aria means success. Sung with conviction and distinction, "Avant de quitter ces lieux" can be a great success, in spite of some clumsiness in the music and some definite nonsense in the words. "Jette les yeux" as used here means nothing. It must be said, too, that the aria, placed as it is in what should be the bustling animation of the country fair, disrupts a pace that should not have relented until the entrance of Marguerite, much later in the act. I always sang this aria reluctantly, especially at the Teatro Colón and at the Met. But, of course, any baritone who likes it should use it in concerts. It is an excellent vocal piece.

"Le Veau d'Or"   *bass*

Le Veau d'Or est toujours debout!	The Golden Calf is still standing!
On encense sa puissance	People worship its power
d'un bout du monde à l'autre bout.	from one end of the world to the other.
Pour fêter l'infâme idole	In honor of the base idol
rois et peuples confondus	kings and common folk together
au bruit sombre des écus	at the dull sounds of coins
dansent une ronde folle	dance an insane roundelay
autour de son piédestal,	around its pedestal,
et Satan conduit le bal!	and Satan leads the ball!
Le Veau d'Or est vainqueur des dieux!	The Golden Calf is winner over the Gods!
Dans sa gloire dérisoire	In its derisory glory
le monstre abject insulte aux cieux.	the vile monster insults the heavens.
Il contemple, o rage étrange,	It contemplates, o strange wrath,

à ses pieds le genre humain	the human race at its feet
se ruant, le fer en main,	throwing itself, sword in hand,
dans le sang et dans la fange	into blood and mire
où brille l'ardent métal,	where the red-hot metal glitters,
et Satan conduit le bal!	And Satan leads the ball!

Using the medieval legend of Dr. Faust as the basic inspiration for his immense dramatic poem, Goethe allowed his imagination to weave many embroideries into the original fabric. The story of the love affair of Faust and Gretchen is one of them. It is that episode that Barbier and Carré, the French librettists, detached from Goethe's *Faust* and that Charles Gounod set to music. Everybody knows that the aging and disillusioned Dr. Faust has made a pact with Mephistopheles, the spirit of evil, by which he recovered his youth and the enjoyment of all material things and in exchange signed away his soul to Mephisto. The latter, who had at first appeared to Faust as a dragon, or a gray monk, or a black poodle, has assumed in the opera the appearance of a most elegant nobleman, all in red, doublet and tights, wearing a short silk cape, a cock's feather in his hat, and a very pointed sword at his side. In the French tradition he adds to this elegance a jaunty disposition, a jocular way of being sarcastic, and only in some dark flashes of authority does he remind us of his frightening powers.

Having promised Faust a taste of the great and the small joys of life, he has taken his charge to a country fair where the crowd is drinking, dancing, and singing. To the revelry he contributes the "strophes" of "Le Veau d'Or," the Golden Calf, the subject of which is very much to his liking.

The Golden Calf was an idol that Aaron, older brother of Moses, built at the request of the Hebrew people after their liberation from captivity in Egypt. It was a sacred idol of the Egyptians. Moses, in retreat on Mount Sinai, was informed of the transgression of the Hebrews by Jehovah himself. He descended from the mountain in a fury, destroyed the idol and had 3,000 men executed. The Golden Calf symbolizes the materialistic thirst for wealth that is part of human nature.

You must visualize Mephisto, stunning in his red outfit, standing on a rustic table, surrounded by drinking men and women, all irresistibly attracted to him, and enjoying his cynical glorification of a debasing pagan cult.

The two verses have the same structure, after a very noisy introduction to the first one. The tempo is *allegro maestoso*, $\rfloor$ = 92. In order to be heard, the voice must come in fortissimo on the words "Le Veau d'Or" in unison with the orchestra. But that fortissimo must not be made by trying for an enormous bulk of sound, which could put the singer in instant trouble, nor by pushing a darkened "Or" high in the back of the pharynx where it loses all resonance. Those three notes must be sung fully in the mouth with a ringing, vibrant tone, the color of the vowel /o/ in "Or" being the key to strength and security. It is not an "open" tone or a "covered" tone. It is a round warm tone, easily carrying into "est toujours debout" by rolling strongly the /r/ of "Or" and staying fortissimo to the end of the phrase. This first phrase must create an impression of triumphant greatness, without which the whole song is in vain.

The second phrase and its repeat—"On encense sa puissance"—are sung starting mezzo forte but round, with a very legato crescendo on "puissa-a-ance" (avoid at all cost "puissahahahance"). Stay legatissimo on "d'un bout du monde à l'autre bout." We are in 6/8, there are no dotted values, the eighth notes are as round and sustained as the quarter notes. By now, there must be a strong feeling of the size and might of the Golden Calf.

The next nine bars describe the behavior of the human race at the feet of the statue: the orchestra turns pianissimo; the voice mezzo forte, still legato, changes colors, becomes bitter and biting, with the desire to be sarcastic. Make a crescendo on "confondus" and on "ronde folle," like two short waves. Then return to a round legato forte on the next eight bars, "autour de son piédestal." Sing cheerfully "et Satan conduit le bal" and its repeats. Again, I stress that the singing should be legato, without violence. The ease and security of the E-flat will come from the color of /a/ in "le bal", an /a/ colored by a slight change toward /o/ without interference from any covering.

The second verse follows the same pattern as the first. The sarcasm may become still more bitter on "rage étrange" and "dans le sang et dans la fange." Roll the /r/ in "brille" and in "l'ardent" strongly. To stress the biting diction, you may also want to flip the terminal /l/ of "metal."

When the aria is sung in performance and with the chorus around, Mephisto generally avoids singing the nine bars of the chorus's fortissimo singing, singing himself only the last two bars fortissimo. In this case Mephisto must be given some stage action during the nine bars that are omitted.

I have insisted strongly on the character of legato and roundness of all phrases forte in this aria, first because this is the right way, and second because, having sung Valentin many times, I have witnessed with concern the misfortunes of many a Mephisto who started the aria with violence and complicated technical approach only to end with obvious hoarseness, very unwelcome so early in the performance. Power and authority do not go hand in hand with harshness and brutality.

"Salut, demeure chaste et pure" *tenor*

Quel trouble inconnu me pénètre?	What unknown emotion invades me?
Je sens l'amour s'emparer de mon être!	I feel love taking hold of my whole being.
O Marguerite, à tes pieds me voici.	O Marguerite! Here I am at your feet.
Salut! demeure chaste et pure,	I greet you, chaste and pure dwelling
où se devine la présence	where one senses the presence
d'une âme innocente et divine.	of an innocent and divine spirit.
Que de richesses en cette pauvreté,	What riches in this poverty,
en ce réduit, que de félicité!	in this [humble] corner, what felicity!
O nature,	O nature,
c'est là que tu la fis si belle!	it is here that you made her so beautiful!
C'est là que cette enfant	This is where this child
a dormi sous ton aile,	slept under your wing,
a grandi sous tes yeux.	grew up under your eyes.
Là que de ton haleine	Here that, surrounding
enveloppant son âme	her soul with your breath,
tu fis avec amour	you lovingly made
épanouir la femme	this angel from heaven blossom
en cet ange des cieux.	into a woman.

Mephisto has led Faust to the garden of Marguerite's house. It was the enchanting vision of Marguerite that had decided Faust to sign his pact with the Spirit of Evil. Since then Faust has seen the young woman only once again, as she was coming out of church, but she had refused his offer to walk her home. Now Mephisto gives him a great opportunity for another attempt to satisfy his desires. In the dramatic poem by Goethe, it is in Gretchen's neat bedroom that Faust waits for her return. Barbier and Carré, Gounod's librettists, preferred the garden as better suited to Gounod's Faust, who is less aggressive in his approach to love than Goethe's. The general spirit of the original monologue as well as several lines of literal translation are nevertheless present in this aria. But the very absence of physical greed makes this beautiful aria difficult to project. An outspoken passion is easily suggested. Here, we hear of the worship of an idealized woman. The humble garden becomes a shrine, which Marguerite has imbued with a divine presence. Faust places the tribute of his heart at her feet. As a love song, this aria might sound placid and tame. As the exalted worship of a divinity, it will vibrate and move. The tenor should not be afraid to prepare a spiritual build-up within himself prior to singing and to treat each phrase like a vibrant prayer. Only too often do we hear a singer who works his way cautiously through the aria, waiting for the second where his high C will ring powerfully and get him an ovation. That was not Gounod's design.

The aria starts slowly and almost hesitantly. It is imperative to stick strictly to the slow rhythm: Faust has the premonition of something great about to happen. And it does: cresdendo and accelerando, again in exact rhythm, on "Je sens l'amour s'emparer de mon être." Carried by the orchestra, the voice bursts out forte on "O Marguerite" and stays forte on "à tes pieds me voici." In that moment Faust is yearning for the purest kind of love and will delight in the ideas of chastity and innocence. This implies that his voice should be as simple, pure, and devoid of technical complications as humanly possible.

The *larghetto* can be felt at ♩ = 66. It is difficult to advise the singer regarding the first lines of this *larghetto*. All he has to do is to sing pure sounds (pure vowels) in a perfect legato and let the curb of each phrase land on the final long value: "*pu*re," "di*vi*ne." (A concrete remark: There are two almost similar words in French: *de*vine, which means "to guess," and *di*vine, which of course means "divine." Don't mix them up.) At the same time, feed the tone with the inner tension of life.

The two phrases "Que de richesses en cette pauvreté" (with the vowel *e* in rich*e*sse being an open /ɛ/ and not an /e/) are not made of loud tones going up and small tones going down. They are sustained to the end by a true enthusiasm. The fermata on "pauvreté" seems to indicate that Faust has to pause an instant to be able to express his feelings. The next indication of tempo is not acceptable nowadays, and ♩ = 76 is the slowest we tolerate today. The phrase from "O nature" to "sous tes yeux" is sung from piano to mezzo forte with a warm feeling of gratitude toward the motherly "nature," Faust marveling at the fact that such a humble place has nurtured such a divine child— "C'est là que cette enfant a dormi." This is a very affectionate phrase, with a crescendo on "dormi sous ton aile" and a sensitive decrescendo on "a grandi sous tes yeux." I cannot stress enough that there is no possibility of passivity in the voice, which, without as yet becoming forte, must stay alive and vital throughout.

A much greater expansion occurs on the next lines, culminating vocally on the A-natural "avec amour," although sentimentally the climax is on "épanouir la femme,' which follows. The words "haleine" and "âme" indicate that Faust still thinks in almost spiritual terms. The voice, getting stronger, must stay without any edge, any roughness, which would bring it down to a more material level. For the same reason the tenor must avoid a blatant G-sharp on "âme" and a blatant A-natural on "avec." The words "épanouir la femme" need a round, warm, loving tone. If possible, sing "tu fis avec amour épanouir la femme" in one breath, then breathe after "femme" and sing diminuendo and bright "en cet ange des cieux."

The repeat of "C'est là" means a sort of disbelief in what nature has achieved in such a place. The second "c'est là" is very slow and *not* carried over into "Salut." By now, the voice should prepare, in light intensity, for the incoming and long-expected climax. The first time, "où se devine la présence d'une âme innocente" is a large curve with a good crescendo to the A-natural on "âme" (not blatant) and a diminuendo. The vowel /y/ in "Salut" and "pure" must be absolutely pure, made with the lips and not distorted toward /i/. Sing "où se devine la présence," which includes the C, quietly; do not breathe before "la présence" but ascend to the C by a spin from the very released sounds of "où se devine." The vowel in "présence" should be at least /ɑ/ and never /a/. In the time of Gounod this famous C was sung in *voix mixte,* a light head voice. Even today the character of the piece rejects a thunderous, muscular tone and calls for a well-supported voice resounding entirely in head resonances. This implies, of course, that the singer has been trained to use head resonances. The two A-flats that follow the C should stay in the same resonances as the C, thus avoiding a harsh change of tone, the /i/ of "innocence" very slim, from the lips and along the face. Make a long pause before singing "et divine" pianissimo but well supported.

Whatever Faust's behavior in the next scenes and his return to sensuous joys, there is no doubt that Gounod has written for him an aria conceived on a high level of pure sensitivity. The problem is to stay vital while singing in that spirit, and to rise to the level of the music.

"Le Roi de Thulé" and "Air des bijoux"   *soprano*

Je voudrais bien savoir
quel était ce jeune homme,
si c'est un grand seigneur
et comment il se nomme.

Il était un roi de Thulé
Qui jusqu'à la tombe fidèle
Eut, en souvenir de sa belle
Une coupe en or ciselé.
Il avait bonne grâce,
à ce qu'il m'a semblé.
Nul trésor n'avait tant de charmes.
Dans les grands jours il s'en servait,
et chaque fois qu'il y buvait,
ses yeux se remplissaient de larmes.
Quand il sentit venir la mort,

I would love to know
who that young man was,
if he is a nobleman
and what his name is.

There once was a king of Thulé
who, faithful until the grave,
kept in memory of his beloved
a goblet of embossed gold.
He had a nice way about him,
or so it seemed to me.
No treasure held so much charm.
On festive days he always used it,
and every time that he drank from it,
his eyes would fill with tears.
When he felt his death approaching,

étendu sur sa froide couche,	lying on his cold bed,
pour la porter jusqu'à sa bouche	in order to lift it to his lips
sa main fit un suprême effort.	his hand made a supreme effort.
Je ne savais que dire,	I did not know what to say,
et j'ai rougi d'abord.	and I blushed at first.
Et puis, en l'honneur de sa dame,	And then, in honor of his lady,
il but une dernière fois.	he drank a last time.
La coupe trembla dans ses doigts,	The goblet trembled in his fingers,
et doucement il rendit l'âme.	and softly he gave up the ghost.
Les grands seigneurs ont seuls	Only noblemen have
des airs si résolus	such resolute ways
avec cette douceur.	with such gentleness.
Allons, n'y pensons plus!	Well, let's not think about it anymore.
Cher Valentin! Si Dieu m'écoute	Dear Valentin! If God listens to me
je te reverrai!	I shall see you again.
Me voilà toute seule!	Now I am all alone!
Un bouquet—c'est de Siebel, sans doute.	A bouquet—it's from Siebel, no doubt.
Pauvre garçon!—Que vois-je là?	Poor boy!—What do I see?
D'où ce riche coffret peut-il venir?	Where can that rich casket come from?
Je n'ose y toucher, et pourtant . . .	I dare not touch it, and yet . . .
voici la clef, je crois. Si je l'ouvrais?	here is the key, I think. What if I opened it?
Ma main tremble. Pourquoi?	My hand shakes. Why?
Je ne fais, en l'ouvrant,	I don't, if I open it,
rien de mal, je suppose!	do any harm, I suppose.
O Dieu! Que de bijoux!	Oh my God! Such jewels!
Est-ce un rêve charmant	Is it an enchanted dream
qui m'éblouit—ou si je veille?	that dazzles me—or am I awake?
Mes yeux n'ont jamais vu de richesse pareille!	My eyes have never seen such riches!
Si j'osais seulement	If I dared only
me parer un moment	to adorn myself for a moment
de ces pendants d'oreille!	with these earrings!
Ah! Voici justement	Ah! Here, just when needed,
au fond de la cassette	at the bottom of the box
un miroir! Comment n'être pas coquette?	a mirror! How not to be vain?
Ah! je ris de me voir	Ah! I laugh to see myself
si belle en ce miroir,	so pretty in this mirror.
Est-ce toi, Marguerite? Est-ce toi?	Is that you, Marguerite? Is that you?
Réponds-moi, réponds, réponds vite!	Answer me, answer, answer quickly!
Non, non, ce n'est plus toi.	No, no, that is no longer you.
Non, non, ce n'est plus ton visage:	No, no, that is no longer your face:
C'est la fille d'un roi	This is the daughter of a king
qu'on salue au passage.	before whom people bow when she passes.
Ah, s'il était ici! S'il me voyait ainsi,	Ah, if he were here! If he saw me like this,
comme une demoiselle,	like a noble damsel,
Il me trouverait belle.	he would find me beautiful.
Achevons la métamorphose.	Let's finish the metamorphosis.
Il me tarde encor d'essayer	I am anxious to try still
le bracelet et le collier.	the bracelet and the necklace.
Dieu! C'est comme une main	God! It's like a hand
qui sur mon bras se pose.	that grasps my arm!
Ah, je ris . . .	Ah, I laugh . . .

A well-paced performance of the third act of *Faust* lasts exactly one hour, and it is an hour filled with a succession of masterful scenes. Scene 9, a solo for the soprano, is one of the most famous. It is made of two capital pieces, the song of "The King of Thule" and "The Jewel Song." The two pieces are introduced and connected by shorter fragments, which are sometimes recitatives and sometimes measured singing. Marguerite in that act appears as a brilliant lyric soprano, sensitive, nimble, capable of going from melancholy to great joy, very feminine, and a virtuoso. In other parts of the opera she becomes a lirico-spinto, and in the last act a dramatic soprano. The ideal Marguerite is indeed a rare bird. Besides the vocal versatility required, Marguerite needs a warm and appealing personality and a dramatic gift that will carry her from innocence to madness by way of love, happiness, rejection, and crime. In the scene studied below we shall see only how nostalgia and loneliness give way to surprise, to coquetry, and to an almost childish joy. The audience will derive great pleasure from watching a simple, sincere, healthy, and attractive girl in her well-enclosed garden singing light, clear, frank music with a brightly shining voice.

Marguerite is the bait that Mephistopheles, the Spirit of Evil, had offered Dr. Faust to induce him to sign his soul over to him. First in a magic vision, later in a brief meeting in the public square, Faust has seen her and fallen in love with her (see the preceding section). But Marguerite is a modest and a very young girl living alone who has not yet had the company of a man. In order to disturb, confuse, and tempt her, Mephisto has left in her garden a casket full of precious jewels, now hidden under a bouquet placed there by Marguerite's neighbor and admirer, Siebel. As Marguerite returns home, having undoubtedly taken the long road and mused about her encounter with that attractive nobleman, her loneliness seems to her sadder than usual—and she thinks aloud.

The prelude to the scene depicts Marguerite entering her garden from the street (on the ninth measure), walking slowly toward the house, stopping, looking around, maybe reaching the door of the house and leaning her back against it. She starts singing, piano, exactly in rhythm, with a very earnest voice, saying the words very clearly but without particular emphasis. It is the exact rhythm that will give the three short phrases their feeling of depth.

"The King of Thule" paraphrases Goethe's text. For the ancient Greeks, Thule was a northern land surrounded by the Arctic ice, maybe Iceland, maybe the Shetlands or some Norwegian island. The ballad is a melancholy one of mourning, old age, and death but also of faithfulness and lasting love. On the operatic stage it will fit perfectly the mood of Marguerite, who has lost her mother and a young, beloved sister and whose brother has just left for the war. She will sing it without sentimentality; it comes to her lips spontaneously, and she does not have to control its nostalgic flow. But twice the flow is interrupted by the recollection of that recent encounter. There is a counterpoint between the fidelity of the dying king to his love and the very new inclination of Marguerite for the unknown young man.

After the five bars of introduction, Marguerite sings, a little slower than $\goodbreak = 72$, with a very even voice, mezzoforte, round in quality, finding a curve for each phrase, avoiding the syllabic stress on successive quarter notes or eighths. Above all, she must sing not like an opera singer who wants to show technical achievement but like a simple girl in her solitude. There is a ritardando on "une coupe en or ciselé," said with a certain solemnity. The following two and a half bars are much slower. The words "Il avait bonne grâce, à ce qu'il m'a semblé" are said in rhythm but slowly, with a half smile at first and a tenuto on "grâce," then with humility on "à ce qu'il m'a semblé." Marguerite does not fancy herself a good judge of men's charms.

The verse "Nul trésor" starts a little faster than the first one, and with more warmth. Stress the word "charmes" both times. Do not carry over "jours il," but make a real ritardando on "il s'en servait." The following four bars are slower. Little by little Marguerite becomes aware of the meaning of the ballad she had started as if by reflex. There is almost a lump in her throat on the word "larmes," the portamento upward being also a diminuendo but well supported.

There is a change in mood as Marguerite sings the next verse. It is concerned with death; the voice darkens a little, and the ritardando on "sa main fit un suprême effort" shows weariness. Stress "suprême," and drag slightly the sixteenth on "effort," delaying the coming of the syllable "fort." But Marguerite returns to the encounter with a smile, shaking her head at her own shyness: Sing very lightly and freely. It is now obvious that there is, in the soul of Marguerite, a fight between the forces of gloom and the newly found and as yet unprecise hope. The gloom will survive in the last verse of the song, the death of the old king. But the words "en l'honneur de sa dame" are sung heartily, weakening a little the second time, more slowly and earnestly on "une dernière fois." The tempo is now almost lento, the sound piano and hesitating—"la coupe trembla dans ses doigts"—ending in a waning murmur on "il rendit l'âme."

Even if the song had not reached its end at that instant, Marguerite would have freed herself from the gloom. A new spirit carries her away and makes her see everything in bright colors. "Les grands seigneurs" is suddenly forte (open vowel on "-eur," vibrant vowel /y/ on the F), with an equally sudden pianissimo on "avec cette douceur." But she restrains herself for a while and becomes again her quiet self. In that way, after a resigned "Allons, n'y pensons plus," she sings with simple lyricism the following four bars. "Me voilà toute seule" is said piano, as if she were shivering. Gloom has won, after all.

Here starts a masterpiece of a recitative: precision, economy, color, variety are combined to perfection. The young Siebel is disposed of in two bars. "Un bouquet"—mild surprise; "c'est de Siebel, sans doute"—matter-of-fact; "pauvre garçon"—a rejection tempered by sympathy.

The discovery of the casket: The first two bars are slow, with a wondering voice. From the third bar on the tempo is *allegro*. Impatient, yet hesitant and feeling some guilt, Marguerite sings faster as her fingers fumble with the lock. On the C chord forte, the casket is open, and for the following six bars she sings forte with great excitement and animation. Watch the vowel /ø/ in "Dieu," the open vowel /ɛ/ in "veille" and "pareille." The tempo is slightly slower on the four orchestral bars given to the feverish search for the jewels inside the casket and stays slower until the aria itself. Be sure to observe all the short silences in the next two phrases, "si j'osais" and "Ah! Voici justement." Marguerite is breathless with anticipation, curiosity, and surprise. (Note again that the open vowel /ɛ/ is heard in "oreille," "cassette," and "coquette." Don't ever believe that French sounds are basically narrow!)

"Air des bijoux": Marguerite has by now discarded all qualms and restraints and lets herself go in the boundless joy of a girl putting on her first jewels ever and fancying that she would now be mistaken for a princess. The tempo marked in the score may seem a little slow for our time. Let us make it *allegretto,* ♩. = 56. The trill on the first note is forte, an outburst of gaiety. Then a diminuendo indicates almost a chuckle, and the run to the G should assume the character of laughter. A slight ritardando is permissible.

From "Je ris" on the cheerful voice must avoid chopping the musical lines. Each phrase is a legato with every long value well sustained, the eighth notes sung without interrupting the vibration of the voice. The A on "Ah!" before the second "Je ris" is not staccato but a short, sustained sound. "Est-ce toi, Marguerite" is by no means sad, as often heard, but on the contrary the mark of a cheerful disbelief. "Non, non, ce n'est plus toi" is warm, round-voiced, the runs on "la fille" very light, started piano with a crescendo upward. Then a progressive crescendo reaches a strong forte on the second "c'est la fille d'un roi," and there is a decrescendo on "qu'on salue au passage," as if "la fille d'un roi" had been walking proudly and subjects were bowing low on "qu'on salue au passage." For a few seconds Marguerite sings wistfully, "Ah, s'il était ici," her mind returning to the earlier encounter. But that mood disappears on the ritardando following "S'il me voyait ainsi," and the next fourteen bars, "Comme une demoiselle . . ., are sung brilliantly, with sweeping enthusiasm and free fluctuations of dynamics. The soprano singing Marguerite must at all cost avoid using a superficial voice, disconnecting syllables for some juvenile characterization, or minimizing the lyricism of the phrases. Marguerite is not loud or rough, but she is a healthy, vigorous girl, straightforward and without guile, singing frankly and generously. The result should be vocal and musical beauty.

Now she returns happily to the casket, but her feverish excitement has changed to a quiet exploration of the remaining marvels. Sing easily as if with a smile. (A detail: Marguerite enumerates "le bracelet et le collier" in that order. However, she should first put on the necklace as during the first four bars of the *poco più lento*, and only then deal with the bracelet, so that the exclamation "Dieu" comes at the moment when she clasps it on her wrist.) A sudden premonition should make the phrase "C'est comme une main . . ." sound frightened, the voice nearer to speech. This includes the first "Ah," but on the second "Ah" there is already reassurance, and the full joy returns on the B-trill and stays throughout the repeat of the first part of the aria.

The tempo of the coda is faster than the general tempo, ♩. = 72, but not so fast that it leaves the voice no time to soar and expand fully. This is a page where a great, brilliant voice should shine without any restriction. After "non," sing "C'est la fille d'un roi" broadly, with a stentato on each of the three notes, F-sharp, G-sharp, and A. Breathe deeply after the sustained "roi," breathe again after "qu'on salue," taking the time necessary. Of course, "au passage" must be sung as written, not divided in two as sometimes suggested in America. Having made sure of a full breath, sing the trill on the F-sharp, keeping your attention on the upper note of the trill, and use the light turn E-sharp—F-sharp for spinning evenly into the B, which you start less than forte and expand on a pure vowel /a/ while it lasts. A very light portamento downward allows a soft landing on the final E.

"The Jewel Song" is youthful, nimble, charming, but should never become an exercise in technique. It should not be made fussy and coquettish. It has a broad scope. Marguerite is still essentially Gretchen and should never become Peggy.

"Mephisto's Serenade"   *bass*

Vous qui faites l'endormie	You who pretend to be asleep,
n'entendez-vous pas,	don't you hear,
O Catherine ma mie,	O Catherine my love,
n'entendez-vous pas	don't you hear
ma voix et mes pas?	my voice and my steps?
Ainsi ton galant t'appelle	Thus does your suitor call you
et ton coeur l'en croit.	and your heart believes him.
Ah, ah, ah—	Ah, ah, ah—
N'ouvre ta porte, ma belle,	Don't open your door, my beautiful one,
que la bague au doigt!	unless the ring is on your finger!
Catherine que j'adore,	Catherine whom I adore,
pourquoi refuser	why refuse
à l'amant qui vous implore	the lover who implores you
un si doux baiser?	so sweet a kiss?
Ainsi ton galant supplie	Thus does your suitor beg you
et ton coeur l'en croit.	and your heart believes him.
Ne donne un baiser, ma mie	Don't grant a kiss, my love,
que la bague au doigt!	unless the ring is on your finger!
Ah, ah, ah—	Ah, ah, ah—

This short, pleasant page paints Mephisto in a most urbane mood. The text is, of course, inspired by Goethe, and the situation is the same in the drama and the opera. Faust has seduced Marguerite and left her. She is with child, a fact he ignores. Months have passed, and Faust feels an urge to see the poor young woman again. Mephisto guides him back to her house, late one evening. A lamp is burning in Marguerite's room. In the dark street the two men pause for a while, and Mephisto offers to sing for her a "moral song," which will confuse still further Marguerite's already disturbed mind. Goethe's text has Gretchen standing before her lover's door and begging to be let in. The text used by Gounod, on the contrary, has the lover singing in front of Marguerite's house, just as Mephisto is doing now. That change shows Gounod's desire not only to attenuate the cruelty of the plot but also, at the same time, to insert a light episode between Valentin's return from the war and his death at the hands of Faust.

Mephisto sings the serenade, playing the part of a lover under the window of some "Catherine," who is, of course, none other than Marguerite. The burden of the serenade is a warning to her not to yield to a lover until he has given her a wedding ring. That is what Mephisto calls "moral." No doubt it is a sarcastic song, but it would be wrong to think of sarcasm as synonymous with ugliness. Mephisto should sing both verses with all the inflections indicated by the meaning of the phrases, using a voice that he makes seductive and irresistible almost to the point of exaggeration. Never should he use a bitter, "diabolic" voice, as I have heard done sometimes in this aria.

The introduction sounds like a bizarre guitar being plucked by bony, hard-nailed fingers that play a mockingly virtuoso scale before settling into a traditional pattern of accompaniment. First verse: Mephisto sings mezzo forte, cautiously, in order to be heard by Catherine but not by the neighbors. The words "Vous qui faites l'endormie" imply that Catherine is actually awake and listening. The repeat of "n'entendez-vous pas" should be piano and insinuating. "O Catherine ma mie" is a crescendo, openly sung with a decrescendo to "ma voix et mes pas." So far, the singing must be legato and with long phrases: no breath between "endormie" and "n'entendez-vous pas"; no breath between "ma mie" and "n'entendez-vous pas."

"Ainsi ton galant t'appelle" is pressing but elegant, and so is the repeat, with a little more sentimentality. The short phrase "et ton coeur l'en croit" is a spoof. The low A on "coeur" must be sung with emphasis on the basso quality of the tone and with a mixture of pathos and irony. By then Mephisto enjoys his parody so much that he bursts into laughter, four times on the upper D forte, then, as if catching himself at making too much noise, six times on the lower D piano. And, with a serious, warning voice, he delivers his message, mezzo forte the first time, more forte the second time, going to full voice on "que la bague au doigt." The third "que la bague au doigt" is a solemn warning immediately derided by the hard-nailed-fingers playing of the interlude.

The voice becomes still more persuasive, still more legato, above the staccato accompaniment. Things go very much as in the first verse, but there is a touching diminuendo on "un si doux baiser," a stress of emotion on "supplie." After the laughter, the intimate advice, "Ne donne un baiser," will go from piano to a good mezzo forte on the D of "*Ne* donne" and a crescendo on the descending chromatic line. A tenuto on the E-natural forte in "que la bague *au* doigt" is generally accepted, as well as a long fermata on the middle A on the last "*au* doigt."

It is to be hoped that the bass singer can laugh on the right pitches in the final laughter. A very deep breath will help start the laughter. The general attitude must be that of preparing to sing a real phrase, open mouth, lifted face, strong support, and then letting out a big sound of laughter on the four high G's, returning to a normal singing tone on the middle G's. There is a choice for the low G's, either to make them sound very deep and sepulchral or to turn them into barely audible chuckles. I do not think that a loud laugh *al piacere* should be added: the sardonic plucking of the guitar is a good enough conclusion for an aria that does not pretend to be too outspoken.

Let me repeat here that in the French tradition Mephistopheles is an elegant character and that anything gross or vulgar betrays the intentions of the composer. A good artist will have real fun in making the audience feel that Mephisto's powers are so great that he does not have to exert himself in order to achieve his goal. The result of the serenade will be to bring out of the house, not Marguerite, but her indignant brother ready to fight, and even he will be dispatched with the greatest of ease.

Gounod, *Roméo et Juliette*

"Ballade de la Reine Mab" *baritone*

Mab, la reine des mensonges,
préside aux songes.
Plus légère que le vent décevant
à travers l'espace,
à travers la nuit,
elle passe, elle fuit!
Son char que l'atôme rapide
entraîne dans l' éther limpide
fut fait d'une noisette vide
par ver de terre le charron!
Les harnais, subtile dentelle,
ont été découpés dans l'aile
de quelque verte sauterelle
par son cocher le moucheron!
Un os de grillon sert de manche
à son fouet dont la mèche blanche
est prise au rayon qui s' épanche
de Phoebé rassemblant sa cour.
Chaque nuit, dans cet équipage,
Mab visite, sur son passage,
l'époux qui rêve de veuvage
et l'amant qui rêve d'amour!
A son approche, la coquette
rêve d'atours et de toilette,
le courtisan fait la courbette,
le poète rime ses vers!
A l'avare en son gite sombre
elle ouvre des trésors sans nombre,
et la liberté rit dans l'ombre
au prisonier chargé de fers.
Le soldat rêve d'embuscades,
de batailles et d'estocades;
elle lui verse les rasades
dont ses lauriers sont arrosés.
Et toi, qu'un soupir effarouche,
quand tu reposes sur ta couche,
O vierge! elle effleure ta bouche
et te fait rêver de baisers!
Mab, la reine des mensonges,
préside aux songes.
A travers l'espace,
à travers la nuit,
elle passe, elle fuit!

Mab, the queen of fairy tales,
presides over dreams.
Lighter than the inconstant wind
through space,
through the night,
she passes, she slips away!
Her chariot which speedy atomies
draw through the limpid ether
was made from an empty hazelnut
by earthworm, the wheelwright!
The harness, dainty lace,
has been cut from the wing
of some green grasshopper
by her wagoner, the gnat!
A cricket's bone serves as handle
for her whip whose white lash
is taken from the beam which flows
from Phoebe gathering her court.
Every night, in this carriage,
Mab visits, on her way,
the husband who dreams of widowhood
and the lover who dreams of love!
At her approach, the coquettish girl
dreams of ornaments and dresses,
the courtier bows and scrapes,
the poet rhymes his verses!
To the miser in his somber quarters
she opens numberless treasures,
and freedom smiles in the darkness
at the prisoner burdened with chains.
The soldier dreams of skirmishes,
of battles and of thrusts;
she pours him glasses brimful with wine
with which his laurels are watered.
And you, whom a [mere] sigh startles,
When you rest on your bed,
O maiden! she barely touches your mouth
and makes you dream of kisses!
Mab, the queen of fairy tales,
Presides over dreams.
Through space,
through the night,
she passes, she slips away!

"A gentleman . . . that loves to hear himself talk, and will speak more in a minute than he will stand to in a month" (Shakespeare, describing Mercutio through the mouth of Romeo). To this Mercutio himself adds: "True, I talk of dreams, which are the children of an idle brain, begot of nothing but vain fantasy which is as thin of substance as the air and more inconstant than the wind." These two quotations are obvious clues to the meaning of "The Song of Queen Mab" and to the spirit in which it must be sung.

In the play, Mercutio spins his yarn in front of the palace of the Capulets prior to crashing their party. In the opera, he sings it during a lull in the dancing, when the young Montaigues find themselves alone in a part of the ballroom. In both cases the reason for the song and its meaning are the same: Roméo should not agonize over threats received in a dream, as dreams have no foundation and no concrete existence.

The tempo as printed, $\downarrow$ = 100, is to be respected. The aria is an *allegro*, not a *prestissimo*. The tempo used in some recordings is insane and robs this lovely piece of its charm, indeed of its very existence, while depriving the singer of every possibility of doing an artistic job.

During the brief prelude Mercutio, often crude, biting, and sarcastic, makes himself light, charming, and nimble, adding one more role to his repertory of imitations. Lightness and nimbleness are two of the characteristic of the aria, a third being the great variety of colors. A consummate comedian, Mercutio will speak rapidly, with extreme precision, and will have great fun. A detailed mastery of the French text is indispensable, and the voice must be ringing right on the lips, the mouth generally opening but little, its movements small for being rapid, except in two climaxes that we shall indicate and stress.

The first "Mab" bounces from the support; although marked staccato, it should not be so brief as to lose the spin of its vowel. Do as if you were about to sing a tenuto; then cut it short. "La reine des mensonges" is sung legato (no *h*'s before repeating the vowels) and with a smile. The singing of the first page must match the chattering of the orchestra until "décevant." "A travers l'espace" is pianissimo, and there is no crescendo in the following phrase as the ascending vocal line will provide a natural crescendo. In order to convey the impression of a fleeting presence, the singer should imagine Mab coming from a point in space to his left, then passing in front of him, then disappearing to his right or, of course, the reverse.

That was Mab in motion. Now it seems that the tiny fairy has settled in front of Mercutio, who can then describe her. Starting with "Son char," sing very light and legato giving equal strength to all notes, avoiding stress on the long ones. The diction is entirely between tongue, teeth, and lips. Remember that in singing, the French r is rolled by the tip of the tongue; otherwise, a phrase like "par ver de terre le charron" is totally indistinct and will slow you down. No liaison on "Les harnais." The diction stays very dental on "dentelle, ont été découpés." The following phrases need the sounds of their written open vowels, "aile," "verte," "sauterelle," "mèche" /ɛ/, and a bit more voice, the E's and F's sung bright and slim, with no trace of covering. A rallentando is often made on "qui s'épanche de Phoebé rassemblant sa cour," and I think this is a good idea, as a first moderate climax. Make an *a tempo*, then, on the two bars with the G's in octaves.

The description of Mab is finished now, and Mercutio lets his imagination run freely, enumerating and painting the various effects of Mab's visit. Starting with "l'époux" et "veuvage," the singer must find the color of voice and the inflection that will suggest the different characters. It is no longer necessary to sing piano and light; instead, change the dynamics constantly.

"Veuvage," yearning for freedom; "amour," longing for love; "toilette," luxury and refinement; "courbette," servility; "vers," strong inspiration; "soldat," "batailles," forte and military in sound. On the rallentando on "elle lui verse les rasades," sing a glorious phrase forte, taking a good amount of time. The mood changes quickly: now Mercutio sees before him a beautiful young girl asleep, he sees her innocent mouth where Mab will put the illusion of a kiss. Sing from piano to pianissimo, with a real rallentando and a real fermata on "*de* baisers." There should be some sensuousness in the last tender vision.

Then Mab is again in motion, and all the effects of the first page can be repeated, with the addition on the last line of a fading decrescendo. The fortissimo on the last two notes is for the orchestra only; the voice fades pianissimo on "elle fuit."

Throughout the piece the orchestra is marked *pianissimo*, but the voice must make important dynamic changes, as indicated above.

The aria of "La Reine Mab" will probably not bring the interpreter any bravos, probably no more than polite applause. It calls for little bravura, has no fermata on a high note, and the virtuosity of the baritone may not impress that part of the public which is easily moved to exteriorize its pleasure. But it is a challenge for all baritones, most especially the non-French ones, as it requires a most precise study of the text, for correction first, for interpretation second. Monotony or a very short range of colors and moods is too often a defect of opera singers. This aria can be made into a glittering jewel by a baritone who knows how to conceive many moods and use many colors and how to convey all those intentions through the versatility of his voice. After the moderate caliber of voice needed for "Mab" has been established, it is by the correct handling of every word that the song will gain its interest. Words and voice are the same here, maybe just a little more so than usually. Having to stay on one's toes every second and succeeding in doing it is a sensation I remember with great pleasure—and what a delight to match the varied colors of the voice with a measured but eloquent mimicry.

"Je veux vivre" (Juliet's Waltz) *soprano*

Ah! Je veux vivre	Ah! I want to live
dans le rêve qui m'enivre	in the dream that transports me
ce jour encor.	this day still.
Douce flamme	Sweet flame,
je te garde dans mon âme	I keep you in my soul
comme un trésor.	like a treasure.
Cette ivresse	This drunkenness
de jeunesse	of youth
ne dure, hélas, qu'un jour.	lasts, alas, but a day.
Puis vient l'heure	Then comes the hour
où l'on pleure,	when one weeps,
le coeur cède à l'amour	the heart yields to love
et le bonheur fuit sans retour.	and happiness escapes without return.
Je veux vivre . . .	I want to live . .

Loin de l'hiver morose	Far from that sullen winter,
laisse-moi sommeiller	let me linger and rest
et respirer la rose	and breathe the rose
avant de l'effeuiller.	before stripping it of its leaves.
Douce flamme,	Sweet flame,
reste dans mon âme	stay in my soul
comme un doux trésor,	like a precious treasure,
longtemps encor.	a long while still.

Shakespeare's Juliet is not introduced pompously to the guests at the Capulets' party, nor is she in any way singled out at that occasion. Her first words that evening are in answer to Romeo's advances, in the lines that have become the Madrigal in Gounod's score, an exchange of precious and delighted taunts between the two youngsters suddenly struck by love. Gounod's librettists have found it necessary to give Juliette importance, prestige, before her encounter with Roméo—thus the waltz, part of the psychological portrait of Juliette, a joyous outburst of vitality coming from a beautiful, fourteen-year-old girl, rich, happy, surrounded by care and luxury. At her side the librettists have wisely kept her Nurse so that Juliette sings to a partner, thus avoiding a conventional solo display of vocal skill without cause. Her line just before the waltz, "laisse mon âme à son printemps" ("let my soul enjoy its spring"), justifies the existence of the waltz.

Through this somewhat lengthy introduction I hope to persuade the singer to approach the waltz with a desire to add much which is personal to the expected vocal achievement. Start by making of the first vocalise an intense sigh of well-being, youth, and health, as if stretching joyously when greeting a fair morning. That is the meaning of the marking *fortissimo* and of the accents on the nine descending notes. A clear distinction, however, must be made between intensity and loudness. In order to sing the B-flat with ease, the first three notes and the turn must be sung in head resonances, so that the B-flat is already baited by them and the interval between the C and the B-flat smoothed out. A short fermata on the B-flat is welcome *if* it enhances the vibrant quality of the tone and helps the voice to stabilize itself before the descending scale. The diminuendo will be obtained easily if the voice is brought more and more forward with each new pitch downward.

The tempo of the waltz should be such as to allow for charm and poise as well as animation. It may, of course, vary from one soprano to another but a marking of 84–88 to the bar seems basically right, although it is never rigid. The first phrase of the waltz starts piano, the grace notes are on the beat, very light, the main notes as forward as the grace notes, the voice ready to soar on the eleventh and twelfth bars sung allargando, with an *a tempo* on "ce jour encor." That pattern is repeated on bars 27–30 ("âme comme un trésor"), that is, a rallentando and a soaring crescendo on the four bars, with no fermata on the A. Note that the most intense sound falls on the C of "trésor." It precedes a diminuendo to piano on "Je veux vivre." Carrying the voice over into "Je" is a matter of individual taste. The whole fragment is repeated, but the crescendo starts earlier than the first time and does not rise beyond mezzo forte on "âme." The vocalise ending the fragment (sing the high alternate, please) is piano and very tender. "Cette ivresse de jeunesse" introduces a surprising premonition: The fifteen bars following "cette ivresse" must be sung with a sudden sadness, very legato and with a darker sound but *a tempo*. Still entranced by the movement of the waltz, Juliette is invaded by a feeling of frailty, sensing that love may kill happiness. The eleven bars following "à l'amour" are imbued with a sense of tragedy, with their crescendo in the upward lines, their diminuendo on the downward ones, and finally with the long chromatic sigh on the vowel /a/. The premonition has turned into knowledge, and Juliette is fearful of the unavoidable coming of love. Vocally it is helpful to start the chromatic scale in head resonances in order to avoid having to displace the voice upward for the higher pitches and to give oneself the impression that all notes are kept on a horizontal level while very distinctly individualized. At the end of that melancholy run, the cheerful waltz returns with greater strength and with a will in a first wave of crescendo, then in a second wave that culminates in a high B-flat, brilliant and warm, not loud, the symbol of that "sweet flame" kept in her soul.

The score now says *un peu moins vite*, slightly slower, and for sixteen bars it would be helpful to count in 3/4, that is, by the quarter note. Embracing the Nurse, Juliette, nestling on her motherly bosom, asks for more of the carefree, lovely time of her adolescence symbolized by the rose, a flower that will wither and fall apart. The lines must be sung with an extreme legato, darkly on the words "l'hiver morose," with deep yearning and great tenderness until "l'effeuiller." The ability to sing such lines properly distinguishes a great artist from a correct vocalist. The following runs are a transition from the nostalgic mood to the enthusiasm of youth, now triumphant in Juliette's soul. The first two bars are still piano, the next two mezzo piano, the next two mezzo forte, the following run growing to forte. Sing without attacking each of the A's with a jerk. On the contrary, keep an even power on all the notes. The dynamic marking *forte* lasts to the end of the piece but a forte at the same time brilliant and velvety, without any edge or blast.

The last vocalise, starting on a dotted half note on E, comes after the chord and runs with a rubato to a delicate rallentando on "comme un trésor." It is sensible to take a breath before these words. It is convenient to sing the trills on the C, the D, and the E and also the note A on the vowel /a/. The trills should be very light, with a stress on the upper note, taking plenty of time to sing them. There must be no shrillness: Remember the sigh of well-being on the opening scale of the song. A high C is expected from the soprano on the next fermata, and there is no objection to it provided it is within easy reach of the singer and provided it conveys the same happy exaltation as the preceding notes. An optional high note is a good choice only when it is of better quality and of greater beauty than the written note.

Although this waltz is an interpolation that could be dispensed with in the unfolding of the tragedy of *Romeó and Juliette*, it is, when sung with all the intentions listed above, a very human piece of music as well as a triumph of brilliant vocalisation.

"Ah! Lève-toi, soleil" (Cavatine)   *tenor*

L'amour! L'amour!   Love! Love!
Oui, son ardeur a troublé tout mon être!   Yes, its fervor has troubled my whole being!

Mais quelle soudaine clarté	But what sudden brightness
resplendit à cette fenêtre?	shines at that window?
C'est là que dans la nuit	That is where in the darkness of night
rayonne sa beauté.	radiates her beauty.
Ah! Lève-toi, soleil!	Ah! Rise, [fair] sun!
Fais pâlir les étoiles	Make the stars turn pale
qui, dans l'azur sans voiles,	which, in the mistless azure,
brillent au firmament.	sparkle in the firmament.
Ah! Lève-toi, parais,	Ah! Rise, appear,
astre pur et charmant.	pure, enchanting star!
Elle rêve! Elle dénoue	She is dreaming! She unwinds
une boucle de cheveux	a lock of her hair
qui vient caresser sa joue.	which comes to caress her cheek.
Amour, amour, porte-lui mes voeux!	Love, love, carry my vows to her!
Elle parle! Qu'elle est belle!	She speaks! How beautiful she is!
Ah! Je n'ai rien entendu!	Ah! I have heard nothing!
Mais ses yeux parlent pour elle,	But her eyes speak for her
et mon coeur a répondu!	and my heart has answered!
Ah! Lève-toi, soleil . . .	Ah! Rise [fair] sum . . .

> Arise, fair sun, and kill the envious moon
> Who is already sick and pale with grief,
> That thou her maid art far more fair then she;
>
> Shakespeare, *Romeo and Juliet*

The libretto written for Gounod takes some liberties with the Shakespearean play. For instance, it makes the coming-out of their daughter Juliette the reason for the parents Capulet to give a great party. The young Roméo, a member of the Montaigue family with whom the Capulets keep up a running feud, crashes the party and, at first sight, falls incurably in love with Juliette. Later that same night Roméo, deserting his friends, "leaps her orchard wall" and now stands under Juliette's window.

Although Roméo finds himself alone on stage, this is an aria addressed to somebody by one with a burning desire to persuade. On the operatic stage the situation is easily felt by the performer. When the aria is sung in concert or in audition, the first task of the singer is to create inside himself the same conditions: Roméo is still obsessed by his new passion: he has come running and has had to climb over a wall. As a result, the first lines of the aria, "L'amour, l'amour. . ." should be sung not placidly but with great intensity, first mezzo forte, then forte, and the words "ardeur" and "troublé" should be stressed very strongly. The silences between them may show an emotional or physical breathlessness.

The first bar of the *adagio* obviously paints a coming of light: Juliette has lit a lamp in her room. Slowly—the *adagio* lasts six bars—Roméo understands how near he is to her. There is suspense in his voice (it is perfectly permissible to breathe after "clarté"; it is indispensable to sing at the most mezzo forte on "fenêtre," with a spinning tone on the open vowel /ɛ/). Again the music of light, and Roméo is sure now that he is at the right place. Sing the phrase "C'est là que dans la nuit" with adoration, first mezzo forte, then with a lovely decrescendo. This first page is not a free recitative and should be sung exactly on time.

The aria is addressed to Juliette (it goes without saying that *she* is the sun). The "Ah" which starts several phrases should be "attacked" neither by an *h* (Ha) nor by a glottal pinch but should be spun from below as if it had already existed before it is heard. The word "soleil" has two open vowels /sɔlɛij/. The two half notes on "étoiles" and "voiles" are sustained to the end of the value and must not collapse into a portamento downward. Nothing is more foreign to the French style than those portamenti favored by some famous tenors. The first eight bars are piano and mezzopiano. With the ninth bar a crescendo starts (the prayer grows more urgent), reaching its climax on the B-flat. A skillful singer will avoid pinching the vowel /ɛ/ on the top "parais" and opening it wide on the second "parais" (on the G). It is possible to maintain a certain opening of the vowel on the B-flat and to refrain from exploding it open on the G. This is a line which, badly handled, makes a poor impression on the listener.

Now the orchestra unfolds a lovely melodic line with which the voice must blend sweetly. Words like "rêve" and "caresser" are clues to the quality and the quantity of tone to be used. There is a crescendo of intensity on the word "amour" (G-flat) and an almost supplicating feeling on "porte-lui mes voeux."

The following two short phrases stay very mellow. In the French way, the total value of the two eighth notes on "parle" is given to the first syllable, "*par*-le"; it is the same with "*bel*-le." The next four bars can stand some animation (watch "*el*-le"). Follow with a good diminuendo on "a répondu," holding the last syllable to the end of its written value. Then start the return of "Ah! Lève-toi, soleil" at the same dynamic level as "répondu," giving yourself plenty of leeway (seven to eight bars) before the next crescendo on "Ah! Lève-toi." The prayer can be intense without being loud. The same remark applies as above on "parais," first on the B-flat, then on the G. The return to the dynamic marking *piano* on the two "astre pur et charmant" is musically imperative but also very useful for relaxing the voice before the final climax, the final crescendo starting only on the last-but-one "viens, parais," if the singer has decided to finish the aria fortissimo. In this case, the F's and the B-flats of the last bars should be sung not just as sounds, technical and without meaning, but as a deeply felt plea. A certain sentimental intensity always helps to coordinate the energy of the middle and lower body with the vibrant resonances of the upper tones. Although I am not a tenor, I have experienced the fact many times through my students.

This being said, the truth is that this last phrase, with the F's and the B-flats, is not marked *forte* at all but seems to float on top of a last chord piano. Psychologically this dynamic marking of *piano* or *pianissimo* is right. The conventions of the operatic stage are strong and deeply anchored in tradition. But, frankly, who can conceive of a Roméo, now standing for five minutes under Juliette's window very late at night, more probably even in the early morning, and ending his plea with the most powerful note in his voice, while one minute later Juliette will confide to the night the secret of her love in a murmur? The first climax of the aria was part of Roméo's passionate rush away from his friends and into the enemy's garden. How beautiful it would be to let him finish his wooing as an almost religious worship, as Gounod had wanted it. And a B-flat sung in a beautiful pianissimo would woo not only Juliette but the listeners in the opera house as well.

"Que fais-tu, blanche tourterelle"   *mezzo-soprano*

Depuis hier	Since yesterday
je cherche en vain mon maître.	I search in vain for my master.
Est-il encor chez vous,	Is he still at your house,
Messeigneurs Capulet?	my lords Capulet?
Voyons un peu si vos dignes valets	Let's see a bit if your worthy servants
à ma voix ce matin oseront reparaître.	this morning dare reappear at my voice.
Que fais-tu, blanche tourterelle,	What are you doing, white turtledove,
dans ce nid de vautours?	in that nest of vultures?
Quelque jour, déployant ton aile,	One day, opening your wings,
tu suivras les amours!	you will follow love!
Aux vautours il faut la bataille.	Vultures need battle.
Pour frapper d'estoc et de taille	For cutting and thrusting
leurs becs sont aiguisés!	their beaks have been sharpened!
Laisse-là ces oiseaux de proie,	Let them be, those birds of prey,
tourterelle, qui fais ta joie	turtledove, who find your joy
des amoureux baisers!	in loving kisses!
Gardez bien la belle,	Guard the young girl well,
qui vivra verra,	time will tell,
votre tourterelle vous échappera!	your turtledove will escape from you!
Un ramier, loin du vert bocage	A male dove, far from the green bower
par l'amour attiré,	attracted by love,
à l'entour de ce nid sauvage	around that wild nest
a, je crois, soupiré.	has been sighing, I believe.
Les vautours sont à la curée,	The vultures are at their spoils,
leurs chansons que fuit Cythérée	their songs that Cytherea avoids
résonnent à grand bruit.	resound with great noise.
Cependant, en leur douce ivresse,	Meanwhile, in their sweet rapture,
nos amants content leur tendresse	our lovers tell the stars of the night
aux astres de la nuit.	their tenderness.
Gardez bien la belle,	Guard the young girl well,
qui vivra, verra,	time will tell,
votre tourterelle vous échappera!	your turtledove will escape from you!

The scene is a public square in front of the Capulet palace in Verona. The Capulets and the Montaigues, as is well known, are deadly enemies. But Roméo, the young hope of the Montaigue family, having seen Juliette Capulet at her debutante ball, falls in love with her, and she with him. His friends lose sight of him as he secretly enters Juliette's garden and climbs on her balcony. His page Stephano, however, guesses the reason for his disappearance and, delighted by it, teases the Capulets in front of their own house the next morning. It is a very risky undertaking.

Nine bars of a pleasantly bantering prelude introduce Stephano. A page in his teens, he will be properly portrayed by a slim and nimble young woman. He sings with a light lyric mezzo-soprano, in France often even with a soprano voice. Like Cherubino, however, Stephano is in truth a mezzo-soprano. His song includes a brief recitative, two verses, and a very short final cadenza. Stephano is in high spirits; he wears an elegant doublet and tights, and the hilt of his sword is never far from his fingers, be it for fighting or for playing on the blade a mock and mocking guitar. The boy is always moving, changing attitudes, addressing the listeners he hopes to reach from different angles, and the mezzo-soprano, while singing, must feel the physical animation surrounding the aria.

The recitative is *moderato*, the first phrase, merely informative for the audience, addressed to no one in particular, simple and frank. There is no concern in the statement. After the fermata the reason for Stephano's coming to this particular place is revealed, together with his deliberate impertinence. "Messeigneurs Capulet," sung on time, is ironic in its excessive formality. The next phrase, "vos dignes valets," comes as a provocative insult, and the sixteenth notes on "dignes" must be properly sarcastic, as must "oseront reparaître," which is not without self-importance.

In the traditional attitude of a serenader under a balcony, Stephano now sings to Juliette, the "white turtledove," in very melodious and loving lines, but alternates these with a rhythmical description of the vultures that surround her. The first mood, "Que fais-tu, blanche tourterelle," is piano and rather slow, counted at $\quarternote = 72$. The second, "Aux vautours il faut la bataille," is mezzo forte to forte and counted at $\quarternote = 100$. "Laisse-là ces oiseaux de proie" returns to $\quarternote = 72$ in a well-sustained legato, expressing a desire to persuade, then turns lovely on the sentimental ritardando on "des amoureux baisers," the C on "bai*sers*" started with sensuousness and held with a delicate diminuendo. The challenge to the Capulets is made with a poise that reveals great confidence. Despite guards and barriers, the dove will escape. The tempo, *andante*, $\quarternote = 66$, is contemptuous in its very slowness. Two details: Schirmer writes wrongly, "Qui vivra vedra"; "qui vivra *verra*" is the correct way. Also, the eighth note on the A (tourter*elle*) needs to be more than a squeak. The appoggiatura E must be a very light springboard from which the sound spins to A and lasts long enough to spin for a fraction of a second before being stopped. It must have had a life of its own. The crescendo on the E of "échappera" stops with the breath marked, and the run of triplets is extremely light, suggesting the flight of the dove attempting to break away but failing.

With the beginning of the second verse Stephano gives up his role of serenader. He may still vaguely address the Capulet household—he certainly does so at the end of the verse—but he enjoys above all reviewing the present sentimental condition of his master. As he had suggested the sweet charm of the "tourterelle," he now makes his voice firmer and even a bit virile for his description of the male half of the pair. Sing from "Un ramier" to "a, je crois, soupiré" in a good, well-sustained mezzo forte. The vultures seem to sense his presence, becoming violent and noisy. A detail: "Cythérée" is another name for Venus, the goddess of beauty and love. The vultures' nest is not a place fit for beauty and love. Then Stephano delights in the vision of the starstruck lovers. The phrase "Cependant, en leur douce ivresse" is sung with a warm romanticism, almost excessively stressed as it aims at enraging any possible Capulet listener. The two triplets on "douce ivresse" and "leur tendresse" can be very tender indeed, the open vowels /ɛ/ on the syllable "-esse" resounding softly. "Aux astres de la nuit" may be slowed down for expression. As in the first verse, the challenge "Gardez bien la belle" is made with poise. The firmer and more serene it sounds, the more flippant it appears to Capulet ears.

The very short coda is made of a still slower warning, almost in a dragging, sneering voice that will make the sudden flight of the dove—the up-and-down run—impossible to stop. The last "vous échappera" is not a ritardando. The trill and the fermata on the E are like the fluttering of wings. The singer should concentrate on the upper note of the trill to make it sound high and then resolve in exact time on the last two F's. The accompaniment confirms that this abrupt ending is right.

Stephano's aria is not a very important piece of music, and there is no Stephano in Shakespeare. It seems that Gounod's librettists wanted to add some charm to the street scene, which in the drama is violent and tragic from the start. If so, Stephano must have charm and give the listeners pleasure, but he should never try to be cute and affected. Within minutes he will fight like a man. It should be possible to make a brave young boy of him, courageous and frank, and to sing his song in this spirit.

Leoncavallo, *I Pagliacci*

"Il Pròlogo"   *baritone*

Si può? Si può?	May I? May I?
Signore! Signori!	Ladies! Gentlemen!
Scusatemi	Excuse me,
se da sol mi presento:	if alone I present myself:
io sono il Pròlogo.	I am the Prologue.
Poichè in iscena ancor	Since once again the author
le antiche maschere	puts on stage
mette l'autore,	the classic masks,
in parte ei vuol riprendere	he partly wants to follow again
le vecchie usanze,	the old usage,
e a voi di nuovo inviami.	and again sends me before you.
Ma non per dirvi come pria:	But not to tell you as before:
"Le lacrime che noi versiam	"The tears we shed
son false!	are faked!
Degli spasimi e de'nostri martir	By our anguish and our torments
non allarmatevi!"	don't be alarmed!"
No! L'autore ha cercato	No! the author has tried
invece pingervi	instead to paint for you
uno squarcio di vita.	a slice of life.
Egli ha per massima sol	He holds as sole maxim
che l'artista è un uom	that the artist is a human being
e che per gli uomini	and that for human beings
scrivere ei deve;	he must write;
ed al vero ispiravasi.	and he drew his inspiration from reality.
Un nido di memorie	A flow of memories
in fondo a l'anima	in his innermost heart
cantava un giorno,	sang one day,
ed ei con vere lacrime scrisse	and he wrote with real tears,

e i singhiozzi il tempo	his sobs
gli battevano.	beating time for him.
Dunque, vedrete amar	So you will see loving
siccome s'amano gli esseri umani;	just as human beings love;
vedrete de l'odio i tristi frutti.	you will see the sad fruits of hatred.
Del dolor gli spasimi,	Of pangs of pain,
urli di rabbia udrete,	of fury you will hear the outcries,
e risa ciniche!	and cynical laughter!
E voi, piutosto	And you, rather than
che le nostre povere gabbane d'istrioni,	at our poor frocks of comedians,
le nostr'anime considerate,	look at our souls,
poichè siam uomini di carne e d'ossa,	because we are men of flesh and bone,
e che di quest'orfano mondo	and because, just like you, we breathe
al pari di voi spiriamo l'aere!	the air of this forsaken world!
Il concetto vi dissi. . .	I have told you the idea . . .
or ascoltate com'egli è svolto.	now listen how it unfolds.
Andiam. Incominciate!	Let's go. Begin!

A company of traveling players has arrived in one of the villages in Italy where they perform from time to time. Before their show gets underway, a member of the company, Tonio the Clown, steps in front of the curtain to remind the audience that, under their makeup and their costumes, the actors are men and women of flesh, blood, and passions. The sufferings onstage may well be for real and the drama performed lived in earnest.

The "Prologue" is a speech addressed to a large group of listeners. Its goal is to persuade. It must be sung with the constant desire of reaching the minds and hearts of the audience. It must be given a great variety of shapes and colors. Sometimes it is almost spoken, sometimes sung in powerful lyric phrases. And it is presented by the most extroverted member of the company, the clown. But that clown is also an Italian baritone: his voice is round, generous, modulated, and his landsman the composer has given him every opportunity to display his vocal gift and mastery.

The first "Si può" pretends to be timid and should make the listeners smile. The second is firmer, already confident. The salute to the ladies is gracious, to the men virile, broad both in time and voice. "Io sono il Pròlogo" is said with pride and vigor but without harshness.

Certain that he now has the attention of his audience, Tonio will patiently explain the reasons for his presence there. The tempo is ♩ = 52, well sustained and without haste.

Although editions may differ, the first line, "Poichè in iscena . . , should be *sung* on the music of the cello part, as singing is at this point more natural than speaking. The words "in parte ei vuol riprendere" should be sung after the orchestra, unhurried, the balance of the phrase on time except for the final ritardando. The voice throughout the entire page should be poised and friendly, informative in intention.

The 3/8 is thought in one, ♩. = 80. Put a sense of warning in "Ma non per dirvi come pria." The next three lines, "Le lacrime che noi versiam . . ., however, require a light, monotonous voice suggesting superficiality but not jest. To distort the voice comically here would be a mistake and would put the public in the wrong frame of mind. It is the following page that will alert the audience to the seriousness of what will be presented. The tempo is slow, still in one, but ♩. = 50, and solemn. Sing with earnestness, stressing the importance of a new concept. Respect the pause after "vita," as if wanting to give the listeners time to assimilate the idea. (Remember that verism was indeed a new idea at the time Leoncavallo wrote *I Pagliacci*.) Sing with decisiveness the phrase "Egli ha per massima sol," breaking it for a comma after "sol," as the second part of the phrase is the one making the essential statement, "che l'artista è un uom," with a tenuto stressing the word "uom." Thus the actor is defined.

The next line concerns the audience itself. More slowly, make them see that they are meant to be human beings, too, and, still slower, introduce the essential word of the new doctrine, "al vero."

The whole page must of course be sung with a fine voice, but it is also a speech of intellectual intent, a fact that should not be entirely overlooked.

The page in 9/8 and 6/8 is a famous cantilena, to be started piano and legatissimo, with a voice that even in the singer himself should create a sensuous feeling of beauty and ease. All the indications of style needed are plainly written in the score and should be respected scrupulously. The *col canto* in the last line could involve a swift accleerando on "il tempo" and a broad ritardando on "gli battevano."

The next page in 9/8–3/4 is a study in crescendo and accelerando as well as in very well-defined alterations of mood. It starts slowly but faster than the preceding tempo, ♩. = 56. The first indication for the orchestra is *misterioso*, the second is *animando poco a poco*; the last one is fortissimo *con forza*. In between these extremes we have to suggest: human love, "siccome s'amano gli esseri umani," the voice matching the English horn; hatred, "de l'odio i tristi frutti," with the woodwinds; cruel sorrow, "Del dolor gli spasimi," with the horns; rage, "urli di rabbia," with winds and strings; and finally cynical laughter, "risa ciniche," with the tutti. It is up to the singer to find all the colors, all the expressions, all the varied intensities that will convey all the moods a stage can present to an audience. Tonio, in that page, gives the listeners a full performance through descriptive samples.

He now has reached the eloquent epilogue of his allocution, ♩ = 60. Once more he starts piano, returns to the legato of "Un nido di memorie," but aims directly at the audience. "E voi" stands alone between two silences, friendly, pleading, followed by another isolated word, "piutosto," the two short segments preparing by contrast the two incoming majestic phrases, to be sung, the first with humility, the second with force, both with the greatest beauty of voice and in one breath. The final E-flat of "considerate" slows the tempo down to allow a portamento upward, interrupted by a breath, followed by a strong accent on the F "poi," diminuendo, and a very sensitive rendering of "uomini." There is a sense of vulnerability in "di carne e d'ossa" sung piano. For two bars there follows a *rianimando*, which facilitates the buildup for the traditional climax that for many years has been as good as compulsory.

Al   pa - ri di   voi spi - ria - mo   l'a - e - re.

The "Prologue" is so representative of Italian vocal glory that it encourages the desire for a crowning vocal ending. But only those who are absolutely sure of the quality and ease of their extreme top voice should attempt it. Nothing is so disastrous as an added high note that fizzles!

Tonio recovers quickly from his exaltation, addresses his patient listeners once more in two short phrases, then calls for the show to begin. Here, too, tradition has prevailed, and woe to the baritone who would sing a D instead of a high G on the fourth syllable of "incomincia-te." This G will be enjoyable if it is sung by spinning from the E without a jerk and if it stays in a still brilliant color of the vowel /ɑ/ without heaviness and without choking the tone for reasons of "technique."

"Ballatella" *soprano*

Qual fiamma avea nel guardo!	What a fire he had in his look!
Gli occhi abbassai per tema	I lowered my eyes for fear
ch'ei leggesse il mio pensier segreto!	that he read my secret thought!
Oh! s'ei mi sorprendesse . . .	Oh! if he should surprise me . . .
brutale come egli è!	brutal as he is!
Ma basti, or via!	But enough! away with it!
Son questi sogni paurosi e folle!	These are fearful and crazy dreams!
O che bel sole di mezz'agosto!	Oh, what a beautiful sun of mid-August!
Io son piena di vita	I am full of life
e, tutta illanguidita	and languishing all over
per arcano desio,	with some mysterious desire,
non so che bramo.	I don't know what I am longing for.
Oh, che volo d'augelli,	Oh, what a flight of birds,
e quante stride!	and what screeching!
Che chiedon? Dove van?	What do they want? Where are they going?
Chissà!	Who knows!
La mamma mia,	My mother,
che la buona fortuna annunziava,	who used to predict the future,
comprendeva il lor canto	understood their song
e a me bambina	and to me, as a child,
così cantava:	she used to sing like this:
Hui! Hui!	Hui! Hui!
Stridano lassù	Up there they are screeching,
liberamente lanciati a vol	launched free on their flight,
come frecce, gli augel.	like arrows, the birds.
Disfidano le nubi	They defy the clouds
e'l sol cocente,	and the burning sun,
e vanno per le vie del ciel.	and travel over the roads in the sky.
Lasciateli vagar	Let them wander
per l'atmosfera,	through the air,
questi assetati d'azzurro	these creatures thirsting for the blue sky
e di splendor:	and radiant light:
seguono anch'essi un sogno,	they, too, follow a dream,
una chimera,	an illusion,
e vanno fra le nubi d'or.	and keep traveling through clouds of gold.
Che incalzi il vento,	Let the wind blow,
e latri la tempesta	and let the storm roar,

con l'ali aperte	with their wings open
san tutto sfidar;	they can brave it all;
la pioggia, i lampi,	the rain, the lightning,
nulla mai li arresta,	nothing ever stops them,
e vanno sugli abissi e i mar.	and they fly over abysses and sea.
Vanno laggiù verso un paese strano	They go yonder to an unknown country
che sognan forse	of which they dream, maybe,
e che cercano in van.	and which they look for in vain.
Ma i boëmi del ciel	But the gypsies of the sky
seguon l'arcano poter	obey the mysterious power
che li sospinge . . . e van!	which urges them on . . . and they go!

A ballatella, derived from the word *ballare* (to dance), is a simple song sung by simple people while dancing or playing some rustic game. Nedda's "Ballatella" is a song of much greater scope. Nedda is the leading lady of an itinerant company of actors and the wife of its leading man, Canio. She has reached a point in her life, however, where she can no longer stand these conditions. Besides, she has started an affair with a well-to-do young villager, Silvio, and yearns, not without fear, for the chance to leave Canio and live with Silvio. In the "Ballatella" she expresses symbolically her desire to break her chains and escape from her present life.

In a preceding scene Canio, seeing his wife surrounded by young men, has given them as well as her a warning that any attempt to approach her would be met with violence on his part. He then went to the tavern with other men from the village. Nedda, left alone, is confused and distressed as she muses upon her husband's outburst.

The scene is vivid in her mind, the words come rather fast, the tempo is *con moto*, ♩ = 88, the tone is surly and resentful. Nedda's greatest fear is that Canio will discover her secret thoughts that are so dear to her. Sing "Gli occhi abbassai" slyly, but let some sensuousness enter into "il mio pensier segreto" (the score says: *con amore*). Physical fear makes her sing rapidly and tensely "Oh, s'ei mi sorprendesse" and fearfully "brutale come egli è." Then she forces herself to discard her worries. The line "Ma basti! or via" is vocally light and quite free in rhythm. During the two bars of chords, Nedda gets up, stretches in the sunshine, and returns to a mood familiar to her: the enjoyment of having a young and healthy body filled with expectations. The A-natural on "O" is a delighted sigh of well-being, and the lines following it are sung mezzo forte, sensuously and with vitality, avoiding any drag (♩ = 88). The last two bars for the voice are much slower and are sung like a secret.

At this point a flight of birds passes overhead and interrupts Nedda's meditation. Note that there is no change in tempo but that the writing becomes more animated, especially for the orchestra. You must stay strictly on time if the playing of the accompaniment is to be clean and expressive. The words must be on the lips, brisk and unhurried. At first, Nedda is plainly surprised, but quickly, being as superstitious as was her mother, she interprets the flight of the birds as an omen of liberation and freedom for herself.

The two bars of trills are difficult to handle. They are meant, I suppose, to be an imitation of birds' voices and should be sung very lightly, all in head resonances, with the vowels as follows:

Sing the trills on "Hui" with a very light ascending line on the "i"s and a short stress on the upper "i"s. It may be inconvenient to sing "Hu-u-u-i," as the sudden narrowing of the voice on the top "i" is clumsy. Nor is there any improvement in singing "Hu-u-u-a" or something similar.

The "Ballatella" is Nedda's vision of the birds' long and hazardous flight to freedom and expresses her envy of them. The whole aria by its momentum suggests the uninterrupted soaring of the birds, sometimes unimpeded, sometimes labored, but always progressing toward their distant goal. It requires a brilliant lyric voice full of drive and vitality, free of tensions, darkness, and weightiness, capable of maintaining a lively rhythm and flexibility. With all those assets the interpretation itself is easy. The first fourteen bars for the voice are sung with warmth, admiration, and a floating feeling as of wings in the wind. The next fourteen need more strength, as the word "Disfidano" will suggest, and a soaring climax on the G-sharp on "vanno."

With "lasciateli vagar" Nedda suddenly injects her comment into the narration: no obstacle should come in the way of the triumphant flight. A slight allargando stresses her sympathetic interest. "Per l'atmosfera" is already on time, and the words "questi assetati" are said with intensity. Nedda feels in herself the "thirst" that urges the birds on. The whole page is a splendid opportunity that any gifted singer will enjoy singing with a soaring full voice. No advice can help those who do not feel this.

The *animando* on "Che incalzi il vento" opens a new mood: Wind, rain and storms in vain try to slow down the travelers who fight victoriously. The phrases interrupted by silences become shorter; sixteenth notes make the rhythm harsher. In order to suggest that struggle the voice should start this page in a darker hue, in darker vowels, less legato, but stay ready to soar again as the words "sfidar" or "nulla mai li arresta" are already winning words, as is "mar" on G-sharp. The tempo animato is still observed to the end of the section. Nedda in her dream of liberation expects to encounter storms and struggles. Here again she identifies with the birds, and this must appear in her voice, which should grow more intense and passionate.

With "Vanno laggiù" the rhythm broadens. The obstacles have been overcome, the whole sky is open, and so is the universe. The triumphant voice must carry a sense of potent serenity. A short ritardando on the word "arcano" seems to stress anew Nedda's identification with the birds. At the end of her meditation earlier in the scene she had been troubled by an "arcano desio"; the birds follow an "arcano poter." But now, after that short ritardando, the voice pours out the several "e van," ending with a climax presto on the last one. The flight of birds has delivered Nedda from her worries and given new life to her yearning. The singer must enjoy stressing the evolution of Nedda from a surly mood to a mood of triumph, albeit a vicarious one. The "Ballatella" offers a non-Italian soprano the opportunity to improve her Italian style, which is basically and in its pure form the use of a free voice in sonorous words with great lyric expression.

"Recitar"

tenor

Recitar!	To go on stage!
Mentro preso dal delirio	When a prey to delirium
non so più quel che dico	I don't know anymore what I am saying
e quel che faccio!	nor what I am doing!
Eppur è d'uopo . . .	And yet it must be . . .
sforzati! Bah!	force yourself! What?
Sei tu forse un uom? Ah!	Could you be a man? Ah!
Tu se' Pagliaccio!	You are Pagliaccio!
Vesti la giubba	Put on the costume
e la faccia infarina.	and powder your face with flour.
La gente paga	People pay
e rider vuole qua.	and come here to laugh.
E se Arlecchin	And if Harlequin
t'invola Colombina,	steals Columbine away from you,
ridi, Pagliaccio . . .	laugh, Clown . . .
e ognun applaudirà.	and everybody will applaud.
Tramuta in lazzi	Change to jokes
lo spasmo ed il pianto;	your torment and your weeping;
in una smorfia	to a funny face
il singhiozzo e'l dolor . . .	your sobs and your grief . . .
Ah! Ridi, Pagliaccio,	Ah! Laugh, Clown,
sul tuo amore infranto!	at your shattered love!
Ridi del duol	Laugh at the pain
che t'avvelena il cor!	that poisons your heart!

Canio, the leading man of a traveling company of comedians, has surprised his wife and principal partner, Nedda, in the company of a young lover who has fled at his coming. Other members of the company have restrained him as he was about to stab Nedda and have with difficulty persuaded him to prepare himself for the evening's scheduled performance.

Canio's famous aria requires a dramatic voice. It includes the strong declamation of a short prelude and the all-out singing of a page bursting with sarcasm and despair. It can lend itself to outrageous exaggerations. But we have proof in our day that great tenors can display their great voices in it without losing their artistic dignity.

The tempo of the first page is *andante*, changing as needed for the expression. The starting dynamic level is mezzo forte. "Recitar" is said bitterly, in disbelief. Canio is certainly not in the mood to go onstage. Stay mezzo forte and legato on "mentre preso dal delirio." There is dismay on "non so più quel che dico" and some irritation on "e quel che faccio" (long "e quel," a strong accent on "faccio"). "Sforzati" is no longer passive, and an angry swiftness marks "Sei tu forse un uom," the A violent and sustained. The traditional laughter heard here is indeed written in the score. In order to be ringing and convincing it must be preceded by a strong intake of air and supported like actual singing. It also must sound bitter and sad. A phrase like "Tu se' Pagliaccio" in its free rhythm calls for a most sincere sensitivity: what is not felt, the humiliation, the helplessness of Canio, cannot be faked.

"Vesti la giubba" starts with a resigned piano. The same feeling but already colored with some sarcasm continues in "e la faccia infarina." There is a realistic cynicism in the next phrase; the portamento upward on "vuole qua" is angry, the voice forte. An allusion to Nedda's lover colors a tense "E se Arlecchin," and a faked lightheartedness the "t'invola Colombina"—a trifle! "Ridi, Pagliaccio" is hurting, "applaudirà" said with rage (on the optional F-sharps).

The great tragic phrases begin with "Tramuta in lazzi," which grows from an almost spoken start to a broad and ringing "spasmo," "il pianto" following more piano, as if ashamed. Then a fever of bitterness accelerates the line "in una smorfia . . ." "E'l dolor" is very sustained so that it fully prepares the "Ah" on the F-sharp, which then ties with a very broad "Ridi, Pagliaccio" with the greatest possible power. The marking *straziante*, meaning "tortured," applies to the entire balance of the aria. After the biting diction of "sul tuo amore," "infranto" is sustained at will. "Ridi del duol" comes with heavy despair; a breath can make "che t'avvelena" more biting, and "il cor" should be heartrending, an effect that can be achieved without a loud sobbing.

That short page deserves its celebrity. The theme is right, as many of us have experienced. The power of sincerity is overwhelming. But the best-intentioned tenor must be warned, first, against starting to sing too loud too soon instead of finding all the colors that make him eloquent without straining his voice or his nerves and, second, against being deceived by the short range of the aria and singing some of the first high notes in white, open vowels. Without going here into controversial technical advice, let me say that the high-range precautions must be started earlier in this aria than in any other I know. The F's of this aria must already be considered high notes so that the A's do not suddenly feel out of reach. If that is well done, a thrill will be shared by singer and listeners.

Mascagni, *Cavalleria Rusticana*

"Voi lo sapete, o mamma"   *soprano*

Voi lo sapete, o mamma,	You know it, Mamma,
prima d'andar soldato	before going away as a soldier
Turiddu aveva a Lola	Turiddu had sworn eternal faith
eterna fè giurato.	to Lola.
Tornò, la seppe sposa;	He came back, and found her married;
e con un nuovo amore	and with a new love
volle spegner la fiamma	he tried to quench the flame
che gli bruciava il core.	that burned his heart.
M'amò, l'amai, ah!	He loved me, I loved him, ah!
Quell'invida d'ogni delizia mia,	She, envious of my every joy,
del suo sposo dimentica,	forgetful of her husband,
arse di gelosia,	burning with jealousy,

me l'ha rapito!	has taken him from me!
Priva dell'onor mio rimango:	Deprived of my honor I am left:
Lola e Turiddu s'amano,	Lola and Turiddu love each other,
io piango.	I am weeping.

It is Easter Sunday in a village in Sicily. After a large, religious chorus the villagers have gone to church. Mamma Lucia is about to join them when Santuzza stops her. Lucia's son Turiddu, returning from military service and finding his former sweetheart Lola married, has made love to Santuzza who has accepted him passionately. But Turiddu has now secretly returned to Lola, and Santuzza is forsaken and dishonored. Burdened by her sin, she stays out of church.

This aria is a gem of the *verismo* school of opera. Written by a twenty-one-year-old composer, the opera *Cavalleria Rusticana* is a spontaneous and inspired work. Involving rustic characters in the grip of elemental passions, it is, of course, violent and outspoken but in a direct, sincere, human way. And it should be sung in the same spirit. *Verismo* does not imply bad taste, loud noises, and acting quackery.

Santuzza is a dramatic soprano, not a mezzo-soprano, as the present fancy for heavy, dark voices has wrongly decided. In this aria she has a beautiful opportunity to touch the heart of the listeners without hurting their ears. The indication of style in the score is "sadly, with simplicity."

The tempo is *largo*, very sustained, ♩ = 50. There are two reasons for that. First, this is the beginning of a conversation, the subject of which is only being indicated; second, Santuzza informs the public of the plot of the opera and must do so slowly and clearly. In spite of saying "Voi lo sapete, o mamma," she will tell the story of her misfortune for our sake, and if passion keeps her narration alive and vibrant, it has to stay absolutely clear and precise nevertheless.

Santuzza speaks to Lucia piano, calling her "mamma," as Turiddu does, with the intention of winning her sympathy and her help. The next six bars are sung with simplicity, with a well-sustained tone; a comma can be placed after "soldato," another one after "Lola." It is in the repeat of "aveva a Lola eterna fè giurato" that a first wave of passion can be felt. The oath was taken and then betrayed by Lola. Both facts are cruel for Santuzza. The brevity of the text that follows is to be admired: it is impossible to say so much in fewer words. One word, "Tornò," and Turiddu is present. But if the words are short, the marking *legatissimo* stresses the importance of each one of them. With "e con un nuovo amore" the love story of Santuzza surges up in front of us. After the very short "Tornò" and "la seppe sposa," a deep breath should enable the soprano to sing the whole next line to "fiamma" without breathing, as the top of the phrase is "volle spegner la fiamma," which must not be separated from the preceding "amore." "Che gli bruciava il core" expresses the burning intensity of Turiddu's desires, and it takes a good ritardando to stress it. The first "M'amò" is pianissimo. The word is painful to say, but the dotted quarter note is to be sung to the end; "l'amai," mezzo forte and then forte, are words that tear the heart of Santuzza. The triplets must be clearly heard; they are like contained sobs preparing the soaring high A, which must be expanded to its extreme possibility but not exploded with brutality. And the soprano must be very sure to avoid sobbing artificially on "l'amai," keeping the sixteenths and the last two eighths power-fully sustained.

Here a double interlude sings passionately of Santuzza's distress and then her ramp-ant jealousy. Above this striking motif Santuzza sings with bitterness, but restraining herself, of Lola's misdeeds. The first "arse di gelosia" is a little less restrained. With the second, sung with rising rage, faster and louder, the poor woman starts releasing the fury that will make a lightning bolt of the word "rapito." (The vowel must stay a pure /i/, fed from below by an intense ascending vibration.)

For three bars the orchestra plays the theme of Santuzza's dishonor, and she sadly refers to it herself, at first piano, then more forte. Then, overcome by jealousy, she cries despairingly, "Lola e Turiddu s'amano," and obsessed by the thought, she repeats the terrible phrase faster and louder. A fast, deep breath must be taken before the high A so that there is still a strong supply of air for the fermata on "piango." (Instead of "io" sopranos often sing "Ah" on the high A.) The second "io piango" is forte and on time. The start of the last one can be delayed a second; a deep breath is needed for singing the last tenuto notes, and a short silence will give the last words a new eloquence. It is wiser to try to find the "io" in the low B in a forward vibration at the lips rather than to find it in the chest. It is wiser, too, to sing the next note, F-sharp, rather lightly and to spin the sound into the final A in a rather slender vowel /a/ and then to expand it greatly in the A rather than to sing two basically bulky notes on that last "piango."

It is in such places as the last eight to nine bars of the aria that the overwhelming desire to express with great intensity may prompt the soprano to oversing, ending up making noises instead of sounds, or to sob repeatedly. Keeping the singing legato and very strongly supported will result in very strong exteriorization if the performer feels Santuzza's distress intensely in her heart and has learned how to color, to say, to vary her singing lines in accordance with her emotions. There can be *verismo* without vulgar-ity. A sincere Santuzza using a beautiful voice with great conviction and a great musical mastery cannot be a loser.

Massenet, *Le Cid*

"Pleurez, mes yeux"   *soprano*

De cet affreux combat	From this frightful struggle
je sors l'âme brisée.	I emerge broken-hearted.
Mais enfin je suis libre	But at last I am free
et je pourrai du moins	and shall at least be able
soupirer sans contrainte	to sigh without restraint
et souffrir sans témoins.	and suffer without witnesses.

Pleurez, pleurez, mes yeux,	Weep, weep, my eyes,
tombez, triste rosée,	fall, sad dew,
qu'un rayon de soleil	which no ray of sunshine
ne doit jamais tarir.	will every dry.
S'il me reste un espoir,	If any hope is left me,
c'est de bientôt mourir.	it is to die soon.
Pleurez, mes yeux, toutes vos larmes,	Weep, my eyes, all your tears,
pleurez, mes yeux.	weep, my eyes.
Mais qui donc a voulu	But who ever wanted
l'éternité des pleurs?	the eternity of tears?
O chers ensevelis,	O beloved buried ones,
trouvez-vous tant de charmes	do you find so much pleasure
à léguer aux vivants	in bequeathing implacable sorrows
d'implacables douleurs?	to the living?
Hélas, je me souviens. . .	Alas, I remember. . .
il me disait:	he said to me:
"Avec ton doux sourire	"With your gentle smile
tu ne saurais jamais conduire	you could lead only
qu'aux chemins glorieux	to glorious roads
ou qu'aux sentiers bénis!"	or to blessed paths!"
Ah, mon père . . . hélas!	Ah, my father . . . alas!

The immortal tragedy by Pierre Corneille from which derives the libretto of *Le Cid* deals most powerfully with the conflict between love and duty. In medieval Spain two noble, ardent lovers, Chimène and Rodrigue, are promised a happy and brilliant life. But suddenly a deadly feud separates their fathers. Obeying the rules of honor of those times, Rodrigue must fight Chimène's father in a duel. He kills him, and honor now compels Chimène to ask the king to condemn Rodrigue to death. Her duty done, Chimène, overcome with grief, decides to take the veil.

She sings the aria "Pleurez, mes yeux" in the solitude of her room, raising her head from her hands, numb with despair, slowly regaining her clear-mindedness. The role is written for a dramatic soprano, but the aria itself can be sung by a lirico-spinto capable of expressing deep emotions with great intensity.

The tempo is ♩ = 54, and the marking of style "slowly and painfully, with sadness." An introduction of eight measures is necessary to create the mood. Chimène sings at first with a somber voice, the words coming slowly, no notes, including the sixteenths, sung short and dry. The "combat" she mentions refers to the fight within herself that made her denounce Rodrigue to the king. The triplets must be almost dragged, the word "sors" elongated, the half note on "brisée" sustained. A trace of vigor appears with "Mais enfin je suis libre," and her pride finds some relief in the thought that she will be free to suffer in secret. The phrase "soupirer sans contrainte," sung without a breath, has a noble ring in its resignation.

After that prelude, which is not a recitative, the aria begins "with great sensitivity," piano and legatissimo, with a velvety quality of tone. The stresses written on notes like "*mes* yeux," "*tri*ste," and sol*eil*" should be used for a very personal expression and to make the phrases touching without breaking the general legato.

Chimène's resignation, however, would be superhuman if it did not abandon her at times. "S'il me reste un espoir . . . mourir" is a longing for death expressed in a sudden forte with a strong stress on each note of "c'est de bientôt mourir." The following "Pleurez, mes yeux" is still forte in an agitated rubato, ending in an exhausted rallentando, piano.

The *un peu plus animé,* ♩ = 69, brings rebelliousnes, curbed before it explodes too violently. Chimène questions the fairness that gives the dead the right to exact such sorrows from the living. Her voice is now vigorous and ringing, loaded with reproach albeit hesitant to accuse. This appears in the contrast between some strong sounds, "chers," "vous," and the sixteenth notes that suggest weakness. Only "d'implacables douleurs" is an unrestrained complaint.

And the memory, so recent, of happy love invades Chimène's heart. The next page is a quotation of Rodrigue's song of love to her. After two bars of dreamy music she says, piano and slightly remote, "Hélas, je me souviens, il me disait." The very words Rodrigue used come to her rapidly. A crescendo starts right away, her voice brightens at once with "Avec ton doux sourire," and a glorious phrase spreads over the next five bars, the exact repeat of Rodrigue's in act 1. A magnificent, full voice must be used for that phrase, with a lavish rallentando on "conduire," broad stresses in "qu'aux chemins glorieux," and a touching diminuendo and ritardando on "qu'aux sentiers bénis." The soprano should be able to sing the B-flat of "conduire" into a vowel /i/. The tenor will have sung his B-flat on that vowel, and it should be a shame if the soprano felt it necessary to distort the sound toward some other, unexpected vowel.

The moment of exaltation is short. Chimène returns abruptly to reality. "Ah, mon père," forte, is full of sorrow and remorse, "hélas," piano, of sorrow and hopelessness. The repeat of "Pleurez, mes yeux" must be quite piano, the lovely line written for the voice kept legato and melodious. The soft lamentation expands suddenly in an outcry of acute suffering. From the high A of "Ah, pleurez" to the end of the piece, while respecting the written musical text, the singer can stress and sustain all the notes as she deems proper for a dramatic expression. Singing the "Ah" (A–G–F-sharp) in a great forte and ascending to the high B of "larmes," piano, is a superb effect that a serious artist must not neglect. The last phrase, ending in the lower octave, slowly and in a somber voice, stays in the proper mood and should be very moving.

The original voice and piano score offers a different ending, more outspoken, but one which, sung from mezzo forte to pianissimo, is not without its merits.

It is fortunate that "Pleurez, mes yeux" has survived from an opera that contains quite a few impressive pages. It would come as no surprise if in the wake of the present trend to a Massenet revival more arias from *Le Cid* came back to life, to be enjoyed by all of us.

Massenet, *Hérodiade*

"Il est doux, il est bon"   *soprano*

Celui dont la parole efface toutes peines,
le Prophète est ici,
c'est vers lui que je vais.

Il est doux, il est bon,
sa parole est sereine.
Il parle . . . tout se tait,
plus léger sur la plaine
l'air attentif passe sans bruit.
Il parle.
Ah! quand reviendra-t-il?
Quand pourrai-je l'entendre?
Je souffrais,
j'étais seule et mon coeur s'est calmé
en écoutant sa voix mélodieuse et tendre.
Mon coeur s'est calmé.
Prophète bien-aimé,
puis-je vivre sans toi?
C'est là, dans ce désert
où la foule étonnée avait suivi ses pas,

qu'il m'accueillit un jour,
enfant abandonnée,
et qu'il m'ouvrit ses bras!

He whose voice erases all pains,
the prophet is here,
it is to him that I go.

He is gentle, he is kind,
his speech is serene.
He speaks . . . everything becomes silent,
more lightly over the plain
passes the attentive air without a sound.
He speaks.
Ah! when will he return?
When will I be able to hear him?
I was suffering,
I was alone, and my heart has calmed down
listening to his tender, melodious voice.
My heart has calmed down.
Beloved prophet,
can I live without you?
It is there, in that desert,
where the spellbound crowd had followed his
steps,
that he welcomed me one day,
forsaken child,
and that he held out his arms to me!

Who can be sure that some day Massenet's *Hérodiade* will not make a triumphant come-back on some great operatic stage? The story, the score, and the staging require on the part of an opera company an effort almost comparable to that of a production of *Aïda,* and few "grand operas" include so many spectacular arias for all the principals in the cast—tenor, soprano, baritone, contralto, and bass—or such large choral scenes and diversified dance interludes. When I sang Hérode in the early 1930s in France, I felt that I had to meet some of the most exacting demands a composer can make on his interpreters. Shortly afterward the opera went into a coma from which it has as yet not recovered. But other works of Massenet have known a similar fate, yet are again fully alive. So, who knows?

Be that as it may, two arias from *Hérodiade,* "Il est doux" and "Vision fugitive," have survived as solo pieces and are often used in auditions.

In Massenet's version of the time-honored story of Salomé and Saint John the Baptist, Hérode's young stepdaughter appears in the first scene as she furtively leaves the royal palace in search of the prophet who reigns over her life. She is alone in the world but for him.

The original tempo is ♩ = 88. The first phrase, mezzo forte, very legato, unfolds itself with a sense of peace and warmth, a crescendo and a decrescendo, and a stress on "ef-

face," with the eighth notes and the triplets staying absolutely in exact rhythm, without a break. "Le prophète est ici" is forte with a slight accelerando and a large sound while "c'est vers lui que je vais" is piano and very simple, conveying the inevitability of Salomé's move. The next twelve bars describe the spell woven by the prophet, a soothing, serene spell (*andante cantabile* ♩ = 63 quiet but not slow), which is why the D in "sereine" and the G on "plaine" must be sung in a light, floating pianissimo. The tenuto on "parle" is an ecstatic diminuendo still vibrant with emotion.

In the following thirteen bars Salomé expresses forcefully, *avec ardeur,* her yearning for the voice, the words, the presence of the prophet. These bars, from "Ah! quand reviendra-t-il" on, must contrast with the preceding twelve through their prevalent energy. The healing virtues of John's voice are celebrated now not by diminuendos on the high notes but by a warm crescendo on the G of "tendre" followed by a diminuendo on "Mon coeur s'est calmé." The score indicates that the phrase "Prophète bien-aimé" demands "élan and love." The last three bars of the fragment are strongly rubato, rallentando on "Prophète bien-aimé," strong animando on "puis-je vivre, vivre," and a rallentando only on "sans toi." A youthful passion dominates the page.

The next eight bars, starting with "C'est là," are the narration of Salomé's first encounter with John. The start is a little faster than the preceding lines, the tone becomes more dramatic on "avait suivi ses pas" and pathetic in the two short phrases, "qu'il m'accueillit un jour" and "enfant abandonnée." It grows into a passionate forte and allargando on "et qu'il m'ouvrit ses bras," easily the most cherished memory of Salomé's young life.

The return of "Il est doux, il est bon" is identical to the first time, possibly started with a more intimate emotion after the vivid recollection of the unforgettable embrace, sentimental as well as physical in meaning. There is no change until the coda although a sensitive singer will always be able to make subtle changes of inflection, stresses, and dynamics in order to avoid the impression of a mechanical repeat.

The coda is marked *a tempo più appassionato. A tempo* means only that the rallentando on "vivre sans toi" has come to an end. *Più appassionato* means with more passion and emotion. The effect of that marking must be a greater amount of tone, but according to the temperament of the performer it may be an accelerando or a broadening of the phrase. Personally, I feel that more voice on a broader phrase provides the most powerful effect. Salomé's passion explodes here without restraint, and obviously Massenet wants a large display of force but not yet as full an impact as on the last G of "sans toi."

This last G is beautifully set up by the rallentando on the B-flat ("Prophète," four bars before the end), the stringendo on the triplets on "-aimé, puis-je," and the breath, marked by Massenet, before "sans toi." The singer must imbue a slim, vibrant B-flat with love and beauty, sing with impetuosity the impatient "puis-je vivre," and reserve the full impact of her power for the G ("sans toi"), sung with a very round tone and the firm, strong support of her body.

A well-analyzed but purely vocal performance of this aria can provide a modicum of satisfaction. But the piece is long enough to allow the singer to enter into the character of the lonely girl who is irresistibly attracted by a man consoling and protecting her and also embracing her—a very powerful feature of his presence, although Salomé has not yet understood the strongly sexual character of her obsession.

"Vision fugitive" *baritone*

Ce breuvage pourrait me donner un tel rêve!	This potion could give me such a dream!
Je pourrais la revoir,	I could see her again,
contempler sa beauté!	gaze at her beauty!
Divine volupté à mes regards promise,	Divine voluptuousness promised to my eyes,
espérance trop brève	hope all too short
qui vient bercer mon coeur	which comes to lull my heart
et troubler ma raison.	and trouble my mind.
Ah! ne t'enfuis pas, douce illusion!	Ah, do not flee, sweet illusion!
Vision fugitive et toujours poursuivie,	Fleeting vision always pursued,
ange mystérieux	mysterious angel
qui prend toute ma vie,	who takes possession of my whole life,
Ah! c'est toi que je veux voir,	Ah! it's you that I want to see,
o mon amour, o mon espoir.	o my love, o my hope.
Vision fugitive, c'est toi	Fleeting vision, it is you
qui prend toute ma vie.	who takes possession of my whole life.
Te presser dans mes bras,	To clasp you in my arms,
sentir battre ton coeur	to feel your heart beat
d'une amoureuse ardeur!	with passionate ardor!
Puis mourir enlacés,	Then to die entwined,
dans une même ivresse—	in one shared delirium—
pour ces transports, pour cette flamme,	for such exaltation, such [burning] flame,
ah! sans remords et sans plainte	ah, without remorse or complaint
je donnerais mon âme	I would trade my soul
pour toi, mon amour, mon espoir.	for you, my love, my hope.

In his palace in Jerusalem, Hérode, reclining on his bed of carved ivory, cannot find rest. A slave offers him a glass of "vin rosé d'Engaddi," a wine of magical powers. She promises Hérode that by drinking it he will see near him the woman he desires ardently— Salomé. Hérode rises and ("disturbed and radiant," it says in the score), glass in hand, sings of the expected delights.

The marking $\quarternote = 152$ applies only to the two and a half bars of orchestral introduction. The voice starts much slower but in exact rhythm, not in a free recitative, and with a glow of sensuous anticipation. There is no room here for a dark, gloomy voice. Respect the different rhythms of the two phrases "Je pourrai la revoir" (active) and "contempler sa beauté" (with love). From the *moderato* marking on, the melodic line is a perfect legato interrupted only by the silences as written and the two breath signs, after "coeur" and "ne t'enfuis pas." The dynamic markings fit exactly the meaning of the words, "bercer mon coeur" piano and mellow, "troubler ma raison" forte and nervous. A great rallentando and a pianissimo sung on the lips will make a sensuous prayer of "douce illusion."

The prelude to the aria, andante, $\dottedquarternote = 48$, must be played rubato, stressing very romantically the climb to the climactic A-flat and almost exaggerating the expression of the last bar.

The aria, whatever it is worth, truly tests the vocal and stylistic mastery of any baritone. It should be studied by any young hopeful who feels ready to enter the professional field. It also challenges the honesty of approach to it since it requires, or almost requires, an overstatement of feelings, yet must never become vulgar or cheap. (When I sang this aria as part of an examination at the Paris Conservatoire, the famous baritone Maurice Renaud, one of the judges, said to me: "You are not enough of a whore." It is a point to ponder.)

The stylistic indication at the start of the aria says, "with greatest charm and very sustained." Charm, a certain sensuous charm, is without doubt what Maurice Renaud, the most famous Don Giovanni of his time, had in mind—charm, a quality so seldom cultivated nowadays by male singers because nobody asks for it. "Very sustained" means *with absolute smoothness and continuity.* And the score says again, *sans retenir,* without dragging, which calls for a constant vitality and energy. All these elements will play their part in the performance.

The first phrase must be sung without breathing, the stress of the phrase being on the D of "poursui*vie*" and certainly not on the E-flat ("pour-"), as marked in some American editions. The way this first phrase is handled will reveal the degree of culture of the singer.

In the following phrases, make sure that all the eighth notes have the same value, thus avoiding the impression of limping. The voice must be mellow through "o mon espoir," the breaths taken as marked, a slight ritardando helping the stress on "o *mon* amour," a clearly indicated decrescendo on "mon espoir," then a breath before the return of "Vision."

"Vision fugitive" is again sung very smoothly, with a slight decrescendo on "-on" and again on "-ive." The next four bars are very rubato. During the sustained high F the pianist must accelerate perceptibly while the voice joins in the animato in a vehement "qui prend toute ma vie." The high F must be started mezzo forte and amplified to forte by the joint action of deep support and the repeat of the vowel /a/ of "toi" growing taller and more resounding in the upper mouth.

The tempo, *appassionato,* is faster yet only a little faster than *moderato.* The dynamic markings and the intentions of interpretation must follow the meaning of the short phrases, alternating ardor ("Te presser dans mes bras") with frenzy ("dans une même ivresse")—hold a long fermata on "dans," E-natural—and ecstasy ("dans une même ivresse" piano). The following *animando* should not induce the baritone into singing forte right away. "Pour ces transports, pour cette flamme" should be only mezzo forte, the F on "ah" can be forte, but it is only the G-flat on "âme" that should reach fortissimo, not in exploding but in expanding from the preceding notes. For vocal comfort and smoothness, still indispensable for the character of the piece, I recommend breathing after "flamme" (not after "transports"), after "plainte" (not after "ah"), and after "pour toi," descending from the G-flat already with a diminuendo. "Mon amour" is slow, "mon espoir" piano and free. Tying "espoir" with "Vision" by a light pianissimo is permissible if by doing so the haunting quality of "Vision" is stressed.

The first three bars of the coda are faster, the last four bars broadly sung, making sure again that the G-flat on "toi" is neither exploded nor darkly covered but expanded from the F in a vibrant, slim, ascending tone. The D on "espoir" must be sustained to the end of the value by repeating the vowel /a/ actively to the end.

The knowledge that this aria is only the beginning of a long scene of hallucination might persuade the baritone who attempts it that it should be sung with a well-calculated control of his power. It seems that all too easily it induces the singer to try for one super-climax after another, a treatment that would prove very dangerous in a full performance of *Hérodiade*. The aria should be conceived as a long, smooth line, unbroken by outbursts, where even the fortissimi are connected with the more restrained moments by a progressive and well-calibered expansion, where the mellow pianissimo moments are still fed with sufficient energy to prevent them from sagging out of line.

Massenet, *Manon*

"Adieu, notre petite table" *soprano*

Allons! Il le faut!	Come on! It has to be!
pour lui-même.	for his own sake.
Mon pauvre chevalier . . .	My poor chevalier . . .
oh oui, c'est lui que j'aime.	oh yes, he is the one I love.
Et pourtant j'hésite aujourd'hui.	And yet I hesitate today.
Non, non! Je ne suis plus digne	No, no! I am no longer worthy
de lui!	of him!
J'entends cette voix qui m'entraîne	I hear this voice that carries me away
contre ma volonté:	against my will:
"Manon, Manon! tu seras reine,	"Manon, Manon! you will be queen,
reine par la beauté!"	queen through your beauty!"
Je ne suis que faiblesse . . .	I am but weakness . . .
et que fragilité.	and frailty.
Ah, malgré moi	Ah, despite myself
je sens couler mes larmes	I feel my tears flowing
devant ces rêves effacés.	before these erased dreams.
L'avenir aura-t-il les charmes	Will the future have the charms
de ces beaux jours	of these beautiful days
déjà passés?	already passed?
Adieu, notre petite table,	Farewell, our little table,
qui nous réunit si souvent.	that united us so often!
Adieu, notre petite table,	Farewell, our little table,
si grande pour nous cependant.	so large for us nevertheless.
On tient, c'est inimaginable,	One takes up, it's unimaginable,
si peu de place en se serrant.	so little room when pressing close.
Adieu, notre petite table!	Farewell, our little table!
Un même verre était le nôtre,	The same glass was ours,
chacun de nous quand il buvait	each one of us, drinking from it,
y cherchait les lèvres de l'autre . . .	looked for the other's lips . . .
Ah, pauvre ami, comme il m'aimait!	Ah, poor dear, how he loved me!
Adieu, notre petite table,	Farewell, our little table,
adieu!	farewell!

The libretto of Manon follows rather closely the famous novel by the Abbé Prévost, a man typical of the eighteenth century. For a time he was an army officer, at another time a monk, then a preacher in vogue, finally a sincere and sensitive writer whose own experiences in love may have been the source of the plot of *Manon Lescaut*. The simplicity and naturalness of the novel suggest this possibility. The interpreters of the opera should remember that the roles of Manon and Des Grieux are written without artificiality or exaggeration. The Chevalier stays passionately in love with Manon despite her betrayals; she follows her irresistible yearning for wealth, dragging him to dishonor and exile, yet loving him, and him alone, all along. Even under the stress of such exceptional passions, both still express themselves with as much simplicity as the operatic setting allows.

The subject of "Adieu, notre petite table" and of the preceding scene, "Allons! Il le faut," is the fight between love and ambition in Manon's soul. Living in a modest Paris apartment with Des Grieux who plans to marry her in spite of his limited financial means, she has started an affair with the wealthy de Bretigny. She sings of her vacillations, but within moments Des Grieux will be abducted and she will be free to pursue her plans.

The indication *allegro agitato* is more an indication of style than of tempo. It is imperative to count four beats to the bar, the short phrases exactly spaced by the silences. This is not a recitative but an animated scene, with changing moods and a steady pace (May I suggest ♩ = 112?), the 12/8 to be sung at ♩. = 66 as printed.

The first bar is made longer by a fermata: Des Grieux has just left, and Manon must be given the time to let him go away and also to attempt to reach a decision within herself. She is disturbed and looks for a justification for her betrayal: She will leave him "for his own sake." She sings firmly and forte. "Mon pauvre chevalier" is sung forte-diminuendo-piano, the G with affection, on the vowel /e/, not /ɛ/. "Oh oui, c'est lui" must be exactly on time as a true confession escapes from her lips, mezzo forte. The word "j'aime" is made of two long syllables, with a vowel /ɛ/ this time. Mark clearly the silence before "Et pourtant" to show Manon's cruel uncertainty. During the bar of silence before "Non, non" she finds another argument in favor of her betrayal: she is "no longer worthy" of Des Grieux. Sing the phrase "Je ne suis plus digne de lui" without too much conviction, thus preparing the contrast with the following phrase 12/8 of capital importance. The orchestra plays the theme of Bretigny, which is the symbol of wealth, power, glory. Here the delicate Manon suddenly becomes almost dramatic, singing with force, breadth, making crescendos to the high notes and culminating with a B-flat fortissimo. Some remarks: Respect the stresses: "j'*entends* . . . ma *volonté* . . . *par la* beau*té*." Contrast the open vowel /ɛ/ on the two "reine" with the slim vowel /e/ in "beauté," creating an effect of majesty on "reine," of brilliance on "beauté." Remember that the sound of the B-flat must be an illustration of the word "beauty" and not a noisy, brutal high note without a meaning. The ability to suggest a meaning by the quality of the tone is one of the goals of all real artists.

After the fermata, "Je ne suis que faiblesse" is still mezzo forte, said quickly and with irritation, the weakening coming on "et que fragilité," piano and slowly. The following lines will be sung piano, legatissimo, with a simple emotion: regrets already, fears for the future. Note that they are supported in the orchestra by the light figure generally associated with the coquetry of Manon. But with the two chords of the first 4/4 bar there is no more frivolity. All of a sudden Manon realizes that she gives up love and happiness, and her emotion grows deeper. The short aria must be sung in a steady tempo without distortion, piano almost until the last line, but with a well-supported, sustained tone, capable of delivering all the inflections printed in the score. The little table is the symbol of the happy, simple, intimate life shared by the two lovers. Manon, tears in her eyes, a sad smile on her lips, sees the two of them sitting at it, squeezed in the small space it provided, drinking from the same glass. A soprano failing to find the proper tones to suggest this would be very insensitive indeed.

But being moved does not excuse the singer from respecting the markings: *animando* on "On tient, c'est inimaginable," then *espressivo* and *rallentando*. This rallentando delays the second "Adieu, notre petite table" as if Manon had difficulty saying the painful words. Then the memory makes the voice more intense, "Un même verre était le nôtre," and the emotion chops the animated phrase into hesitant spurts, "y cherchait . . . les lèvres . . . de l'autre," before expanding in a large, almost tragic "Ah, pauvre ami" and subsiding to piano on "comme il m'aimait." The return of "Adieu, notre petite table" is again delayed and barely murmured when it comes. The last "adieu" is a sob, intense at first, then dying away. The vowel in "adieu" must always be /ø/ and never /œ/, vibrant and colorful in order to suggest the finality of the word. Throughout the aria the exact sound of the vowels, fitting the great simplicity of the music, will help the singer express and convey the beauty of this short masterpiece of sensitive inspiration and psychological accuracy.

"En fermant les yeux" (Le Rêve) *tenor*

Enfin, Manon,
nous voilà seuls ensemble!
Eh quoi? Des larmes?
Si fait, ta main tremble . . .
Pardon! Ma tête est folle . . .
mais le bonheur est passager
et le ciel l'a fait si léger
qu'on a toujours peur
qu'il s'envole.
A table!
Instant charmant
où la crainte fait trève,
où nous sommes deux seulement!
Tiens, Manon, en marchant
je viens de faire un rêve.

At last, Manon,
we are together alone!
What? Tears?
But yes, your hand is trembling . . .
Pardon me! My head is crazy . . .
but happiness is fleeting,
and heaven has made it so light
that one is always afraid
it might fly away.
To table!
Charming moment
when fear makes truce,
when we are just the two of us!
Listen, Manon, while walking
I just had a dream.

En fermant les yeux je vois là-bas
une humble retraite,
une maisonnette toute blanche
au fond des bois!
Sous ses tranquilles ombrages
les clairs et joyeux ruisseaux
où se mirent les feuillages
chantent avec les oiseaux!
C'est le paradis! Oh non!

Closing my eyes, I see yonder
a humble retreat,
a small house, all white,
deep in the woods!
In its tranquil shade
the fresh, cheerful brooklets
where the leaves are mirrored
sing with the birds!
It is paradise! Oh no!

Tout est là triste et morose,	Everything there is sad and morose,
car il y manque une chose . . .	because one thing is missing . . .
il y faut encor . . . Manon!	it still needs . . Manon!
Viens! Là sera notre vie,	Come! There will be our life,
si tu le veux, O Manon!	if you want to, O Manon!

This aria is rightly considered a test of a tenor's ability to sing a sustained piano line with charm and sensitivity. As the same tenor must be able to provide the dramatic power required by other pages of the score, such as "Ah fuyez, douce image," the test is often a trying one. The role of Des Grieux calls for skill, intelligence, and versatility as well as for power. It is one of the most demanding and rewarding roles in the French repertoire.

Performing "The Dream" alone in concert or in audition is not an easy task. Isolated from the context, it may sound too restrained and almost colorless. That is why I strongly advise the performer to start two pages earlier, with the entrance of Des Grieux, "Enfin, Manon." Those two pages are so animated, contrasted and melodic that they forcefully catch the attention of the listeners so that the subdued mood of the following aria will come as a surprise, planned that way. Let us adopt that idea.

After mailing the letter that makes his intention to marry Manon official, the Chevalier bursts cheerfully into the apartment, to the accompaniment of the brilliant 9/8 theme, which since the first act of the opera is associated with the irresistible élan he feels for Manon, "the enchantress." He sings full voice "Enfin, Manon, nous voilà seuls ensemble." But he notices the tears in her eyes and asks softly: "Eh quoi? Des larmes?" We must necessarily leave out a few words here said by Manon, just as some words must be eliminated after "Je viens de faire un rêve" when the scene and aria are given in concert. Manon will not say "Voici notre repas," and Des Grieux will say "Pardon" instead of "C'est vrai." May these changes be forgiven.

The phrase in 4/4 in the key of A, "mais le bonheur . . .," is most felicitous and must be sung sweetly, with great sensitivity, legatissimo, exactly on time but for the last two bars, "peur qu'il s'envole," which are free. The interval D to G-sharp on "qu'il" calls for a lovely diminuendo possibly going to falsetto, followed by a light and elegant landing on "s'envole." The whole phrase, when done with taste and flexibility, is a delight to the ear.

Des Grieux then sings the two "A table," and the aria itself is almost prepared. One more page of introduction is still provided. Over an undulating orchestra line the voice, with extreme simplicity and a feeling of sweet intimacy, recites on one pitch, rises for an instant on the beloved name of Manon, and returns to simple speech prior to singing "En fermant les yeux."

Des Grieux dreams of a little white house shaded by foliage, of birds and a brooklet singing nearby, a paradise if Manon agrees to live in it. The tragic reality is that such a life has no appeal for her. Des Grieux must sing with the conviction of a man who thinks that happiness is within his reach, yet with the urgency of one uncertain that he will be understood.

The tempo is very quiet, $\downarrow$ = 46, the voice soft and sustained. The values of the dotted eighths and sixteenths must be exact but without edges, firm but not angular, the words said lovingly. The voice soars briefly on the word "retraite," then returns to a caressing softness. The sound is obviously very much forward, with teeth and lips feeling it. The six bars following "bois" need special care, the voice staying in upper resonances on all notes. For instance, on "Sous ces tranquilles ombrages," sing as if the line were ABD–F-sharp, without coming down on the C-sharp, which is already sung with the same resonance as the F-sharp and on the same vibrant vowel /i/. Do the same on the next phrase, the C-sharp on "joyeux" being already in the higher resonance of the F-sharp on "*rui*sseaux." Note that the "-ill-" of "tranquilles" is pronounced like a single *l*, that the word "joyeux" is pronounced /ʒwajø/ and not /ʒo-iœ/, that the *ss* of "ruisseaux" is a hard *s*.

On the next phrase, "où se mirent les feuillages," keep singing the stressed E's, barely touch the B's, reach the G almost in falsetto and on time. The rallentando is on the eighth notes of "chantent avec." Note that the word "feuillage" is pronounced /fœiaʒ/ and that the word "chantent" is pronounced "chante-t'avec" without a nasal *n*.

The brevity of "C'est le paradis" seems to deny the statement even as it is made, a fact confirmed by the strong "Oh non," followed by the words "triste et morose," sung sadly with a darkened tone. "Car il y manque une chose" is mezzo forte on top of a forte chord. Take a good breath after "chose" as if to create a feeling of suspense that resolves in "Il y faut encor . . . Manon." Here the first three notes must already be in upper resonances so that the distance between the D and the A of "faut" is greatly minimized and the *messa di voce* on the A possible, enjoyable but only of reasonable length. "Manon" is said pianissimo and with utmost affection. Then Des Grieux makes his plea, with a round, warm voice: "Viens" (substituted for "non"), "Là sera notre vie." "Si tu le veux" is sung with a ring and with vigor (vowel /ø/, please), and the plea ends diminuendo, tenderly and with a smile.

When the aria is presented as proposed above, there are between the impetuous first phrase "Enfin, Manon" and the warm, hearty "Viens! Là sera notre vie" four pages of sustained singing, the general dynamics of which is piano but which are not restrained in their intensity of feeling, in the frankness of the vibration of the voice. These pages were born brilliant and will end in brilliance. There is no reason for them to be timid; the singer has no cause to feel reined in. The sweetness of love should express itself as freely as the fire of passion. This aria is a great opportunity to prove it.

"Cours-la-Reine" and "Gavotte" *soprano*

Suis-je gentille ainsi?	Do I look nice like that?
Est-ce vrai? Grand merci!	Is it true? Many thanks!
Je consens, vue que je suis bonne,	I consent, given that I am good-hearted,
à laisser admirer ma charmante personne.	to let my charming person be admired.
Je marche sur tous les chemins	I walk on all roads
aussi bien qu'une souveraine.	just as well as a sovereign.
On s'incline, on baise ma main,	People bow and kiss my hand,
car par la beauté je suis reine!	for because of my beauty I am queen!
Mes chevaux courent à grands pas	My horses run at a lively trot
devant ma vie aventureuse.	before my adventurous life.
Les grands s'avancent chapeau bas,	Noblemen meet me, hat in hand,
Je suis belle, je suis heureuse!	I am beautiful, I am happy!

Autour de moi tout doit fleurir!	Around me everything must be in bloom!
Je vais à tout ce qui m'attire!	I go to all that attracts me!
Et si Manon devait jamais mourir,	And if Manon were ever to die,
ce serait, mes amis,	it would be, my friends,
dans un éclat de rire! Ah!	in a peal of laughter! Ah!
Obéissons quand leurs voix appellent	When its voice calls,
aux tendres amours toujours,	let us always obey tender love,
tant que vous êtes belle,	as long as you are beautiful,
usez sans les compter vos jours,	use your days without counting them,
tous vos jours.	all your days.
Profitons bien de la jeunesse,	Let us take good advantage of youth,
des jours qu'amène le printemps,	of the days that spring brings along,
aimons, rions, chantons sans cesse,	let us love, laugh, sing constantly,
nous n'avons encor que vingt ans.	we are only twenty years old.
Le coeur, hélas, le plus fidèle	Alas, the most faithful heart
oublie en un jour l'amour,	in one day forgets love,
et la jeunesse ouvrant son aile	and youth, opening its wing,
a disparu sans retour.	has disappeared forever.
Profitons bien de la jeunesse,	Let us take good advantage of youth,
des jours qu'amène le printemps,	of the days that spring brings along,
aimons, chantons, rions sans cesse,	let us love, sing, laugh constantly,
nous n'aurons pas toujours vingt ans!	we will not always be twenty years old!

This scene starts with the *allegro moderato*, ♩ = 112, one bar before Manon's words "Suis-je gentille ainsi?"

The Cours-la-Reine is a spacious avenue on the right bank of the Seine, in the heart of Paris. There, under the shade of beautiful old trees, it was the fashion in the eighteenth-century for people of leisure to take walks, to see and be seen, to buy trinkets and jewels from noisy vendors, to meet and to flirt. Manon, who in the space of a few short months has risen to a visible position in Paris society, must be seen at the Cours-la-Reine. It is the proper thing for her to do. She is still in her teens, and the enjoyment of her success is boundless, naive, and genuine. She should not be represented as a mature and important lady but as a youth bubbling with excitement and vitality.

Ideally she should be carried onstage in her sedan chair and sing her first phrases through the chair's window. She then sings by the open door and soon is standing outside the chair, splendidly dressed, a beribboned, bejeweled cane in her hand. All her ambitions are fulfilled for the time being, and her singing reflects so much delight that everybody smiles at her, with neither resentment nor reticence. She is radiant and wishes all living creatures well.

Her voice starts light, bright, and vivacious on "Suis-je gentille ainsi," with a bit of coyness on the following "Est-ce vrai" and a touch of good-humored impertinence in "Je consens, vue que . . . " Note the abundance of stylistic markings: *dolce*, with a stress on "bonne," then a comma, then a crescendo to forte, then a stress and a fermata on "personne." Massenet, like Puccini, multiplies these markings, suggesting that besides the exact but rigid values of the notes of music there is a need to constantly change intentions and inflections, which the singer must feel and use adroitly.

Manon now puts on a great act, describing her own triumph and the homage she receives to a crowd which has itself generated that triumph and which at this very moment pays her its tribute. Any trace of vulgarity would make Manon's irresistible impertinence brazen. It is her naiveté that saves her, together with her beauty and her indisputable, accomplished elegance in dress and bearing. Make every effort to sing the rhythm—and it is a difficult one—of the following lines with strict exactness with the exception of the proud stresses on "marche" and "bien." Holding the long value at the end of the phrases is indispensable as it keeps the voice from stalling without a spin. "Car par la beauté [vowel /e/] je suis reine [vowel /ɛ/]," the first time, grows from piano to forte in a swell of pride.

After a good breath the second "Je suis reine . . . " must be sung exactly as written: two even eighths on "je suis"; "reine" includes a first note (middle B) sung lightly, already in upper resonances, then six sixteenths sung fortissimo and slowly with a tenuto on the upper B, then with a distinct diminuendo six fast sixteenths followed by a staccato E piano and a fermata on top of a stress on the quarter note D. No soprano should attempt to sing this scene in public before she has mastered all those details, so that she can be perfectly exact, after which her art will consist in making it all sound spontaneous. A detail: It is possible to sneak in a quick breath after the staccato E, thus making the fermata on the D easy to hold and to feed.

The same remarks as above apply to the following lines, which repeat the earlier pattern. Note that in both those pages the first two lines are a description of Manon's prowess while the third one tells of the humility surrounding her. Those third lines, "On s'incline" and "Les grands s'avancent" call, of course, for a more subdued and condescending voice. "Je suis belle" follows the same pattern as "je suis reine" and must be treated the same way.

It would seem that the whole pattern will be heard a third time, but there are changes coming. "Autour de moi tout doit fleurir" is sung generously; it shows that side of Manon that would like everybody around her to be happy. But the next phrase already reveals the fatal flaw in her nature. Sung much slower and with a contained, intense voice, it expresses Manon's inexhaustible greed. This glimpse of her secret soul is immediately covered up, however, by a spectacular outburst of joy. Early editions of *Manon* do not indicate an *animando* on "Et si Manon devait . . .," in which she challenges even death to put an end to her joy. Such an animando will nevertheless help the expression if used together with a legatissimo, making of the sixteenths added to the quarter notes a way of increasing the tension of the statement.

The singing is free, good-humored, slow, and round in "ce serait, mes amis," staccato and swift in "dans un éclat de rire," where the staccato notes leading to the high C must indeed sound like cheerful laughter. The early editions did not have the coloraturas printed here as they are in more recent ones, such as the Schirmer score. This former-Lescaut-turned-author can report that he had never heard them until quite recently when he was disagreeably surprised by them. He believes that Manon is meant at this point to display not vocal virtuosity but elegance and feminine brilliance and that the coloraturas are totally out of place.

It is necessary to open a parenthesis here: there was no "Gavotte" in the early editions, so that the scene ended after the next bar, the high D providing the final, fitting brilliance. For many years the "Gavotte" was nevertheless performed in this country, a fact which may make the high D unwelcome because of its premature finality. For those who feel this way, it is possible to use alternative notes of the final cadenza of the scene.

The "Gavotte" is obviously an insert and, in a way, slightly incongruous. It befits Manon's personality to urge all young people to listen to the call of love before it is too late, as she has certainly done herself, even to warn her listeners of the disappointments of love. It is hard to believe, however, that her audience is not more experienced than she is and that the advice coming from her very young wisdom will be welcomed by already well-informed ears. Nevertheless, it is a pleasure to imagine Manon addressing herself to a sort of intimate circle kneeling or sitting around her and trading her grand airs for a friendly, confidential tone, speaking to women more than to men.

The 6/8 can be felt as ♪ = 112; the voice is simple and melodious, without any attempt at artificial eloquence, all the values respected in complete simplicity. The rallentando on "toujours" and "tous vos jours" must not be excessive; the staccati on "tant que vous êtes belle" have a certain authority.

The moderato in 4/4 is also at ♩ = 112. While respecting all markings, sing with charm and spirit, thinking of no complications whatsoever. The staccati on "Profitons bien . . ." are softly interrupted legati and not abrupt, edgy tones. The same applies to "Ai-aimons." The vowel /i/ on the G of "rions" must be bright and slim. Be sure to observe the rubato in the line starting with that "rions." It means confidence and carefreeness. In the repeat of the same pattern, the staccati on "aimo-ons," particularly the B, must be very light. The end of the phrase, "que vingt ans," is sung broadly, with joy and pride. The final two "Ah, ah" sounds are very bright and are felt almost behind the teeth, really suggesting laughter.

The second verse of the "Gavotte" is definitely sentimental, and maybe introspective. Did Manon's heart not forget love, at least for the present? The voice should be more intimate than in the first verse, not so brilliant, and should linger discreetly on "amour," more so on the third "l'amour" and on "sans retour." The lines starting with "Profitons bien de la jeunesse" have been dealt with above.

There is a very short coda, as printed in the Schirmer score, the last words of the last verse being changed to "Profitons bien de nos vingt ans." As we have reached the end of the scene, the run upward to D seems a legitimate way to conclude and will stay in character if sung, as written, "light and very fast," the last two exclamations "Ah, ah" sounding like brief, triumphant laughter.

Gaiety, youthfulness, self-confidence make the scene a rewarding vocal task for the soprano, but it is also a study, not in great depth perhaps, of Manon's secret heart. During this scene she should not become a mechanical doll gifted with high notes but should try to feel like a seventeen-year-old girl basking in her success, even if a hidden regret lingers in her heart.

"Ah fuyez, douce image"   *tenor*

Je suis seul! Seul enfin!	I am alone! Alone at last!
C'est le moment suprême!	This is the supreme moment!
Il n'est plus rien que j'aime	There is nothing anymore that I love
que le repos sacré	but the sacred calm
que m'apporte la foi!	that faith brings me!
Oui, j'ai voulu mettre Dieu-même	Yes, I wanted to put God himself
entre le monde et moi!	between the world and me!
Ah fuyez, douce image,	Ah flee, sweet image,
à mon âme trop chère!	too dear to my soul!
Respectez un repos cruellement gagné,	Respect a peace cruelly earned,
et songez si j'ai bu	and think, if I have drunk
dans une coupe amère,	from a bitter cup,
que mon coeur l'emplirait	that my heart would fill it
de ce qu'il a saigné.	with the blood it has bled.
Ah fuyez, fuyez loin de moi,	Ah flee, flee far from me,
ah, fuyez!	ah, flee!
Que m'importe la vie	What does life matter for me,
et ce semblant de gloire?	and this semblance of fame?
Je ne veux que chasser	I only want to chase
du fond de ma mémoire	from deep within my memory
un nom maudit . . .	a cursed name . . .
ce nom . . . qui m'obsède . . .	that name . . . that obsesses me. . .
et pourquoi?	and why?
Mon Dieu, de votre flamme	My Lord, with your flame
purifiez mon âme	cleanse my soul
et dissipez à sa lueur	and dispel at its light
l'ombre qui passe encor	that shadow which still passes
dans le fond de mon coeur.	at the bottom of my heart.
Ah fuyez, douce image,	Ah flee, sweet image,
à mon âme trop chére,	too dear to my soul,
ah fuyez, fuyez,	ah flee, flee,
loin de moi, loin de moi.	far from me, far from me.

Manon and Des Grieux had lived together for only a few weeks when she yielded to her yearning for wealth and deserted him. Two years later Des Grieux is still obsessed with his passion for Manon. He has turned to religion and has brilliantly sustained a thesis in theology. Meditating alone now in the parlor of the Seminary of Saint Sulpice he persuades himself that faith will bring him peace and serenity. That, however, will not be his fate; his love for Manon will dominate his whole life.

The tenor preparing himself to sing this aria should imagine the parlor as a very cold, severe, austere place and Des Grieux as a still very young man, dressed in a cassock, tired by his studies, alone and very tense. Now he will have to put the solidity of his vocation to the test.

There is only one bar of introduction before Des Grieux says: "Je suis seul." These simple words may express different feelings—relief, anxiety, fear, impatience. Two bars later, the word "enfin" reveals that an important moment has arrived. It will be a "moment suprême." The voice, at first very contained, goes to mezzo forte and then swells to forte on "suprême."

The following three bars of interlude suggest agitation and uncertainty. Nevertheless, the voice seems serene and tranquil when it enters. "Il n'est plus rien que j'aime" is firm and legato, and the slower tempo on "le repos sacré que m'apporte la foi" is solemn. Willpower and a certain greatness are reflected in "j'ai voulu mettre Dieu-même." "Entre le monde" reveals his distaste for worldly doings; "et moi" is said with pride, on a well-sustained note. However, even while Des Grieux makes these firm statements, the orchestra plays descending chords that speak of love and contradict the young man. He defends himself in vain against the vision of Manon they conjure up before him. This vision is so charming that, at first, Des Grieux addresses it very quietly and gently. The first "Ah fuyez, douce image" is sung sostenuto cantabile and pianissimo. Vocally the line must be warm and legato. The vowels should not be flat and white but lightly colored to a darker hue, especially the /a/'s becoming /ɑ/'s in "Ah" and "image" and "âme." The word "fuyez" is difficult to pronounce for people not fluent in French. Think of it as follows: "fui-iez," the u like the German ü, the y playing the part of two vowels /i/, one for "fui-", the second for "iez." A careless pronounciation would make the word sound like "fouillez, which means "to rummage, to search." While respecting strictly the rhythm of the double dotted quarter note and the sixteenth, avoid any jerky production. On the contrary, each note must help reach the A-flat on "chère" with a crescendo but without a heavy push (the marking is *espressivo*!). The following eight bars are to be treated in the same style. Des Grieux still speaks confidentially to the vision. On the following bar, "que mon coeur," the voice grows much more intense, suggesting deep suffering that has left its victim weak and wan. "De ce qu'il a saigné" is piano and weary. But the B-flat on "saigné" must be started on high resonances, increased in power by the support, so that the octave jump upward is minimized and a spin stays alive between the low and the high B-flats, even during the quarter-note rest. The vowel on the high B-flat will be resonant without being blatant if it is conceived as /ɑ/ and not /a/. While singing "Ah fuyez, fuyez," minimize also the two G's, singing in your mind B-flat–B-flat–A–flat on a horizontal line and giving little importance to the G's. The last "ah, fuyez" is free, becoming piano almost at the start.

At this point the interlude brings back the theme of Manon the "enchantress," an aspect of hers he is trying to forget. After the repeat of the same theme in the orchestra, Des Grieux fights with all his strength against his memories, now cursing the name he avoids even saying out loud, "un nom maudit . . . ce nom. . . qui m'obsède." Note that the "nom" is pronounced like *non*, the *m* being ignored. The words "et pourquoi" must be slow and bewildered.

Now the sound of the organ in the nearby chapel brings help and support to the wavering young man, and he prays (*andante religioso*, ♩ = 60), piano but with fervor, his main wish being for the deliverance of his soul from his obsession. But while he prays with a voice bright with hope, "et dissipez à sa lueur," the obsession returns. Sing more darkly "l'ombre qui passe encor," still darker "dans le fond de mon coeur." A strong crescendo will bring back "Ah fuyez."

It is advisable to sing from "et dissipez" to "qui passe encor" without breathing and to take a breath after "encor," thus being able to tie "Ah fuyez" to "coeur," with the next breath taken after "Ah fuyez." Avoid bracing yourself tensely when starting "Ah fuyez." Instead, go on singing exactly as you did in the preceding lines, which are so easy for the voice. Take note, too, that the first bar in E-flat, "Ah fuyez," is forte but that the second bar is already much softer; that there is only a rinforzando on the A-flat on "chère"; and that the fortissimo in the fifth bar, "ah fuyez, fuyez," turns into a diminuendo in the sixth bar and into a pianissimo in the seventh. In short, this one page, which intimidates many a tenor, has only one bar of fortissimo singing on B-flat and two moderately strong A-flats. It should be possible to establish the voice comfortably at the level of E-flat and F and to reach from there by a flexible, well-supported spin the few climaxes written. While so doing, it will be of great help to sing the vowel in "fuyez" as an /e/, not as an /ɛ/, provided that a high, open resonance is available at all times behind the ringing vowel.

The aria ends with a fading effect, easily achieved on stage when Des Grieux walks away, suggested in concert and audition by a great diminuendo, the vowel /ɑ/ in "moi" becoming very small and quite dark.

In Massenet's *Manon*, as in the original novel by the Abbé Prévost, the passionate love of Des Grieux for the fickle young woman appears as one of the great tragic passions of literature. The singer must endeavor to perform this aria with a sense of greatness that involves much more than pure vocal strength and skill.

Massenet, *Thaïs*

"O mon miroir fidèle"   *soprano*

Ah! Je suis seule, seule enfin!
Tous ces hommes
ne sont qu'indifférence
et que brutalité.
Les femmes sont méchantes . . .
et les heures pesantes . . .
J'ai l'âme vide . . .
Où trouver le repos?
Et comment fixer le bonheur?

Ah! I am alone, alone at last.
All these men
are but indifference
and brutality.
The women are spiteful . . .
and the hours heavy . . .
My soul is empty . . .
Where to find peace?
And how to retain happiness?

O mon miroir fidèle, rassure-moi.
Dis-moi que je suis belle
et que je serai belle
éternellement.
Que rien ne flétrira
les roses de mes lèvres,
que rien ne ternira
l'or pur de mes cheveux.
Dis-le moi, dis-le moi!
Ah! Tais-toi, voix impitoyable,
voix qui me dit:
Thaïs, tu vieilliras!

Oh my faithful mirror, reassure me.
Tell me that I am beautiful
and that I shall be beautiful
eternally.
That nothing will dry up
the roses of my lips,
that nothing will tarnish
the pure gold of my hair.
Say so, say so!
Ah! Keep quiet, merciless voice,
voice that says to me:
Thaïs, you will get old!

Un jour, ainsi, Thaïs	One day, this way, Thaïs
ne serait plus Thaïs!	would no longer be Thaïs!
Non, non, je n'y puis croire.	No, no, I cannot believe it.
Toi, Vénus, réponds-moi de ma beauté,	You, Venus, vouch for my beauty,
Vénus, réponds-moi de son éternité!	Venus, vouch for its eternity!
Vénus, invisible et présente,	Venus, invisible and present,
Vénus, enchantement de l'ombre!	Venus, magic of the night!
Réponds-moi, réponds-moi!	Answer me, answer me!
Dis-moi que je suis belle . . .	Tell me that I am beautiful . . .

This is a self-contained, brilliant, and varied aria. Once we have placed the plot in the late period of the ancient Greek civilization and have identified Thaïs as a famous courtesan, beautiful but unfulfilled and weary of her life style as well as afraid of the passing of the years, we know enough to study the piece. I feel nevertheless that no serious interpreter of this aria should fail to acquaint herself with the full libretto of the opera.

The aria is written for a lyric soprano and should be accessible to any well-trained such voice. It takes place in a luxuriously furnished room in Thaïs's house, with a statue of Venus much in evidence. During the prelude to the aria, Thaïs waves good-bye from the door to the last guests leaving her party. Then she turns around and leans against the doorframe.

The two bars preceding the voice introduce the aria. The first page expresses Thaïs's boredom and the emptiness of her soul. Her voice should sound morose and sullen, with only some caustic and resentful touches. The dullness of this first mood will, of course, set off the later brilliance of the piece.

There is no free recitative and all the singing is on time, $\quartnote = 76$, unfolding slowly over a slowly unfolding orchestral line. "Ah! Je suis seule, seule enfin" is an expression of relief, not a complaint, and the silence between the long "seule" and "seule enfin" indeed allows for a deep sigh of relief. Men are "indifferent"—say it dully—or "brutal"—say it forte and angrily—and Thaïs cannot stand their company anymore, or that of the women who are "spiteful"—say "méchantes" almost forte and bitterly. Besides, she is bored, and "les heures pesantes" is said heavily. A more serious and directly personal grievance is "J'ai l'âme vide"; therefore, put more sensitivity into a lighter quality of voice. The next two phrases are puzzled and dreamy.

For Thaïs, her mirror seems the immediate remedy for her languid mood. On "O mon miroir fidèle" she speaks to a friend, and her voice becomes firmer and more present. With the *andante cantabile*, $\dottedquarter = 48$, she has regained her charm and is fully alive, so that she sings with élan of her main concern, her beauty.

This second section of the aria relies heavily on the imagination, the liveliness, the charm, and also the taste of the performer, as it is made of contrasted elements held together by the personality of Thaïs. It is also very French, requiring a light and precise diction, especially in the rapid chains of sixteenths. It would be ridiculous to keep all the syllables of "Dis-moi que je suis belle et que je serai" exactly even in value and dynamics. A curve has to be found, slow and sweet to the first "belle," louder and almost hurried to the second "belle" (vowel /ɛ/), and with a spacious feeling for the two "éternellement," an impossible dream. Then the voice grows sensuous, caressing, admiring in frank narcissism, from "que rien ne flétrira" to "mes cheveux." "Dis-le moi" and its repeat resemble the begging of a spoiled child, but the next phrase rises with dramatic urgency (*avec emportement*, "with transport") to a B-flat forte, and hastily—the *serrez*, stringendo, is very important—returns to a murmured "éternellement," only to grow again to a wishful and delirious last "éternellement."

At the moment that Thaïs makes her plea for eternal beauty, her reason speaks cruelly to her, and she tries to silence its voice in the third section of the aria. The tempo stays slow, ♩. = 58, in order to give depth to Thaïs's anguish. The first words, "Ah! Tais-toi," are a revolt against a merciless universal fate, but the voice of reason, like a hallucination, speaks darkly and slowly: "Thaïs, tu vieilliras." With disbelief and in her own voice Thaïs considers this inconceivable future. Note the adoring "Thaïs" piano, preceding the disturbed "Thaïs" forte ("ne serait plus Thaïs"). The anguish, however, does not last because Thaïs lives under an all-powerful protection. The page starting with "Non, non, je n'y puis croire" shows a progressive reassurance in Thaïs's voice, a faith in Venus that very soon brings back her desire to be beautiful forever. "De son éternité" is broad and reaches a passionate fortissimo, whereupon Thaïs throws her arms around the statue.

The invocation to Venus is a murmur of devotion, of intimate confidence, the words flowing slowly like perfumed water, without rigidity but without interfering in the rhythm of the instrumental alternation. "Réponds-moi" is slow at first, its repeat very slow, with a long fermata pianissimo on the G. One feels that during this fermata Thaïs has found the reassurance she was yearning for. A lovely portamento now returns her to the élan that was hers before her spell of anxiety, and she dares ask once more for eternal beauty.

The repeat of section 2 presents no new features but for the fact that in the twelfth bar of that section (a 9/8), on "belle," the *serrez* marked the first time is not marked again, allowing the voice to blossom more freely. In that bar, both times, the custom has prevailed to sing the syllable "-le" of "belle" on the G on the third beat and not into the next bar. The last "Ah, je serai belle" is free (*suivez*), the trill on the F can be prolonged within reason, but the four sixteenths of "éternellement" must then be strictly on time, very fast.

As in many similar cases, the soprano has to choose between alternative final notes, and no advice will satisfy all performers. Having sung the part of Athanael with many Thaïses since my debut at the Paris Opéra in that role, and having stood at her door when she finishes singing her aria, I have nevertheless acquired the conviction that the B-flat sounds like a logical and satisfying ending whereas the D, as thrilling as it may be for some ears, has always sounded outlandish to me.

Thaïs's aria is not widely sung nowadays. Whatever its musical value, which I am not qualified to discuss, it is a great showpiece, dangerous for a tasteless performer given to exaggeration but perfect for a skillful, sensitive, and discriminating young woman.

Massenet, *Werther*

"Air des lettres"   *soprano/mezzo-soprano*

Werther! Werther!	Werther! Werther!
Qui m'aurait dit la place	Who would have told me of the place
que dans mon coeur	which in my heart
il occupe aujourd'hui!	he holds today!
Depuis qu'il est parti,	Since he has left,
malgré moi tout me lasse!	despite myself everything wearies me!
Et mon âme est pleine de lui.	And my soul is filled with him.
Ces lettres! ces lettres!	These letters! these letters!
Ah! je les relis sans cesse . . .	Ah! I keep reading them again and again . . .
Avec quel charme . . .	With what charm . . .
mais aussi quelle tristesse . . .	but also what sadness . . .
Je devrais les détruire . . .	I ought to destroy them . . .
je ne puis . . .	I can't . . .
"Je vous écris	"I am writing you
de ma petite chambre.	from my little room.
Un ciel gris et lourd	A heavy, grey
de décembre	December sky
pèse sur moi comme un linceul;	weighs on me like a shroud;
et je suis seul, seul,	and I am alone, alone,
toujours seul!"	always alone!"
Ah! personne auprès de lui,	Ah! nobody by his side,
pas un seul témoignage	not a single show
de tendresse ou même de pitié!	of tenderness or even of pity!
Dieu! comment m'est venu	Lord! where did I find
ce triste courage	this sad courage
d'ordonner cet exil	to order that exile
et cet isolement?	and that isolation?
"Des cris joyeux d'enfants	"Joyous shouts of children
montent sous ma fenêtre.	rise under my window.
Des cris d'enfants!	Children's shouts!
Et je pense à ce temps si doux	And I think of that lovely time
où tous vos chers petits	when all your dear little ones
jouaient autour de nous.	were playing around us.
Ils m'oublieront peut-être?"	Maybe they will forget me?"
Non, Werther, dans leur souvenir	No, Werther, in their memory
votre image reste vivante,	your image stays alive,
et quand vous reviendrez . . .	and when you will return . . .
mais doit-il revenir?	but will he return?
Ah! ce dernier billet	Ah! this last note
me glace et m'épouvante:	chills and frightens me:
"Tu m'as dit: à Noël,	"You said to me: till Christmas,
et j'ai crié: jamais!	and I cried out: never!
On va bientôt connaître	One will soon know
qui de nous disait vrai!	which of us spoke the truth!
Mais si je ne dois reparaître	But if I should not reappear
au jour fixé devant toi . . .	on the appointed day before you . . .
ne m'accuse pas,	don't accuse me,

pleure-moi!	weep for me!
Oui, de ces yeux	Yes, with those eyes
si pleins de charmes,	so full of charm,
ces lignes, tu les reliras,	these lines, you will keep reading them,
tu les mouilleras de tes larmes . . .	you will wet them with your tears . . .
O Charlotte, et tu frémiras!"	O Charlotte, and you are going to shudder!"

Since the death of her mother, Charlotte, the oldest of eight children, has happily devoted her life to raising her brothers and sisters. By now she is married to Albert, a friend of the family. The peace of her soul, however, has been disturbed by the ardent albeit respectful love of the poet Werther. In spite of her attraction to him, Charlotte has stayed faithful to her duty and has ordered Werther to leave the city, at least for a time. Alone at home the day before Christmas, Charlotte once more reads Werther's letters, which imply that, if he does not come back in time for Christmas, she must mourn him. With growing anxiety she reads aloud from three letters, and we understand that her resistance to the young poet's love is weakening in the face of her fear for him.

An introduction, starting with the C upbeat forte, the last note of the tenth bar before the first "Werther," is necessary before the voice comes in. The dramatic changes of tempi in those nine bars must be stressed in order to prepare the mood of the piece. The basic tempo is "rather slow ♩ = 54" and will remain so until the 6/8 before "Je vous écris." It is necessary also to have a picture of the scene in one's mind: Night has fallen, and the room is quite dark. One lamp only is lit. A solitary woman reads and meditates by its glow. Now and again she gets up and takes a few steps toward the door through which the absent one might suddenly enter. Then she returns to her obsessive reading. The comfortable room appears to her full of gloom and sad premonitions. If the singer succeeds in feeling all this, the color of her voice will be right and the silences full of emotion.

The introduction ends with low, somber notes, which the voice should match. The vowels in "Werther" should be watched. These vowels /ɛ/ are not too open in the direction of /a/ or narrow in the direction of /e/. They are round in the mouth, creating a feeling of warmth and affection, the first "Werther" piano, the second mezzo forte. The next phrase should be sung without a breath, with a sustained sound on "place" and very precisely in rhythm. There is a pressing pattern in the descending chromatic line in either orchestra or piano, and it should be heard in the voice. The crescendo to "malgré moi tout me lasse" is not a mark of strength. On the contrary, a slow unfolding of the words should suggest weariness. "Et mon âme est pleine de lui" has fervor in its resignation.

The very low range of the ensuing interlude suggests a heavy, weary move by Charlotte, who fights the attraction of the letters in vain. Note the strong dynamic changes in the next phrases, also the opportunity to change the color of the voice on words as precise and different as "charme" and "tristesse." "Détruire" is almost violent and is suddenly interrupted by a chord forte, the gesture of tearing up the papers. "Je ne puis" is, of course, weak and depressed.

The reading of the letters is a good study subject. The excerpt from the first one should be read with monotony, on one dynamic level only. It describes grayness and solitude. Charlotte's reaction is swift and strong. Sing a long tone on "Ah" (C-natural) and go on with intensity, with a tenuto on the E-flat as written. A breath is certainly permissible after "tendresse." The phrase from "Dieu" (/ø/) to "isolement" is a strong rubato: very animated until "courage," progressively rallentando until "et cet isolement," which is said very slowly. Charlotte faces with trepidation the fact that she is responsible for Werther's exile and for his solitude.

The second letter is introduced with very animated music. It must be read in a much clearer voice than the preceding lines. It tells of pleasant surroundings and, more importantly, of pleasant memories on Werther's part. There is no sadness here, only a premonition in the last line, to be read wistfully, "Ils m'oublieront peut-être." The mood of the letter rouses Charlotte from her gloom, and with great fervor she assures the absent Werther that he is unforgotten and expected. See how much life you can put in the word "vivante"!

Abruptly this hopeful mood is broken, and the new color is tragic. The tempo changes radically, ♩ = 132, to one of agitation and fright. We have reached the heart of the scene. This last letter is the one that has caused all the anguish. Charlotte has read it many times and is obsessed by it. It does not make an outspoken statement, but it implies the worst. Vocally the mezzo-soprano has to deal here with a range that, without reaching the very top, returns to G-flat and F several times. The first precaution is to avoid loading the lower part of the range with heavy, dark tones. The second is to be aware that the tempo is animated and does not tolerate dragging for reason of weight. The third is to be clearly aware of the vowel written on the high note and to find the size of that vowel and the amount of tone that can be inserted into it.

1.) The low-starting phrases "Tu m'as dit" or "Mais si je ne dois" or "ne m'accuse pas" must find their strength in the forward ring of the voice, aiming at soaring as soon as possible, and will not be allowed to sit heavily on each syllable.

2.) If it is helpful, the 4/4 at ♩ = 132 can be felt as ♩ = 66, a tempo that goes ahead without the weight of individual accents on each beat. This also allows a much greater flexibility in the phrases, which are often heard over a highly adjustable background of tremolos.

3.) The G-flat on "ce dernier billet" must be sung much nearer to /e/ than to /ɛ/ in order to keep a slim vibration and avoid spreading (and tiring the singer). The G-flat on "crié" is a pure /e/, slim and vibrant like the /i/ that precedes it.

The ascension from "ne m'accuse pas" should be started in the resonances foreseen for the G-flat, and the a in "pas" should be nearer to /ɑ/ than to /a/, again to avoid the spreading of the voice.

The repeat of "ne m'accuse pas, pleure-moi" is made with a frightened, wondering voice. Charlotte is afraid to understand how tragic the meaning of the phrase is, but her emotion is an almost silent, inner one.

We return now to a more relaxed tempo, obviously to be felt in 4/4 ♩ = 120 and to be sung with a voice still vibrating with emotion but capable again of legato and softness as she reads the tender words Werther has now written. The phrase ends in a diminuendo on "de tes larmes" but will soar with a savage strength on "et tu frémiras." The long G-flat must be started with less than its full possible power, then increase in intensity, in order to dominate the very strong orchestral writing beneath it. The repeat of "tu frémiras" is mezzo forte. The strength of those two last phrases lies in their perfect legato and the crisp articulation of the *r* in "frémiras." Like a whisper, the last "tu frémiras," although written rather low, is not meant to be swollen by a sudden influx of chest voice. On the contrary, it must be an almost repressed shudder of fear and disbelief.

The above aria is, and rightly so, a favorite of many mezzo-sopranos. Like the entire role of Charlotte, it can also be sung by a soprano. It would be a mistake to use it mostly as a demonstration of power in the low parts of its range. While a warm, round, colorful voice will serve it well in all its pages, that voice must be able, too, to deal without strain with the last pages and also with the prayer that follows later. Sensitivity and distinction are the qualities most required for a successful interpretation of this aria.

"Va, laisse couler mes larmes"   *soprano/mezzo-soprano*

Va, laisse couler mes larmes—	Please, let my tears flow—
elles font du bien, ma chérie.	they do [me] good, my darling.
Les larmes qu'on ne pleure pas,	The tears we don't shed
dans notre âme retombent toutes,	all fall back into our soul,
et de leurs patientes gouttes	and with their patient drops
martèlent le coeur triste et las.	hammer on our sad and weary heart.
Sa résistance	Its resistance
enfin s'épuise;	finally wears out;
le coeur se creuse	the heart grows hollow
et s'affaiblit—	and weakens—
il est trop grand,	it is too big,
rien ne l'emplit;	nothing fills it;
et trop fragile	and, overly fragile,
tout le brise.	anything will break it.

Charlotte's meditation on Werther's letters is interrupted by a visit from her younger sister Sophie. The latter tries in vain to cheer Charlotte up, then sweetly confesses that she, too, has been morose since Werther has left town. At the mention of that name, Charlotte bursts into tears and gives free rein to her sorrow.

There is no way to provide an introduction to the aria, and the singer must put herself in the mood by reliving the preceding scene. The very first note, "Va," is of capital importance. With this single word Charlotte refuses the consolation Sophie offers her and frees herself of the sorrow she has kept secret for so long. The consonant /v/ must be heard strongly, and it is that *V* which starts the sound of the *a* near the front of the mouth from where it can be expanded into a round /ɑ/, growing in size and intensity while it lasts. In your mind tie "Va" to the next words, "laisse couler mes larmes," which must stay at the same dynamic level, forte, and are made of the same vibrant and pathetic sound as "Va." That first phrase should be sung precisely as written rhythmically but as slowly as the singer desires. Note that the indication of tempo, ♩ = 54, is written after that first bar, not before. It is the sincerity and the perfection of that short phrase that will define the quality of this brief but beautiful aria. Sing it explosively, sing it weakly, and the aria will have lost its importance and its emotional impact.

The phrase "elles font du bien, ma chérie," with its interruption in the middle, is almost spoken, in a voice choked with tears although full of affection and gratitude for the loving, sensitive sister. After the outcry "Va . . ." and during the playing of the theme (D–F–A, etc.) Charlotte has had time to regain enough calm to say only a few words. Now she has two full bars to regain her poise and, although still very moved, to use more breadth musically and a more philosophical approach to her thoughts. Now you can give the beauty and the evenness of your voice their proper care. "Les larmes qu'on ne pleure pas" calls for a round legato tone, never stalling on any given note but constantly carried into the next one. Conceive the entire phrase as one unit. Beware of the temptation to sing a heavy chest tone on "âme." The note is low, but the word is spiritual and must be said with a clear tone. The vowel on "toute" is pronounced *oo* /u/, felt on the tip of extended lips, even if it feels small when so conceived.

The same concept as above governs the next phrase: legato, tone carried into the next note, vowel /u/ on "gouttes." Do not try to sing the F's on "martèlent le coeur" with a large, spread voice; keep the sound ringing and slim, with rich resonances still in the mouth. Note that several commas are written for breathing; it is wise to take advantage of them.

So far the subject of the aria has been the tears' slow, constant erosion of the human heart. Now it changes to the heart's resistance to them. The tempo is more animated, the phrases are short, the struggle is painful. To show this, respect the stresses: "Sa *ré*sist*a*nce, en*fin* s'ép*ui*se," and all those written in the next words—"le c*oeu*r," etcetera. They give a seemingly labored quality to your breath. The climactic phrase "il est trop grand, rien ne l'emplit" is still more animated, with no stalling on the eighth notes. Think of them as if they were upbeats to the D ("grand") and the F ("emplit"), which can then be expanded fully. Many mezzo-sopranos distrust the vowel /i/ in "emplit" and consequently distort it into a strange and often unrecognizable sound. It is not only possible but also highly beneficial to keep the vowel /i/, as in *sweet*, on this F. The voice will then vibrate strongly along the face and be able to expand in resonances instead of spreading without vibration. The singer must learn to accept a smaller feeling of a vibrant tone instead of looking for a massive but dull and inexpressive spread sound.

It seems that during the fermata following "l'emplit" Charlotte, having spoken of her fight against her sorrow, yields anew to weariness. The tempo will be slow again, the voice darker, as if defeated. A strong consonant is needed on "tout le *b*rise" to suggest the breakdown of the heart.

Sorrow has won, and the aria ends pianissimo. The last effort of the voice will be to sustain the last /i/ in "brise" to the end of its value but in a diminuendo. The expression must be so touching that the listeners, instead of wanting to applaud, feel a surge of sympathy for Charlotte.

"Pourquoi me réveiller"   *tenor*

Traduire!	Translate!
Ah! bien souvent	Ah! oftentimes
mon rêve s'envola	my dream took flight
sur l'aile de ces vers,	on the wings of these verses,
et c'est toi, cher poète,	and it is you, dear poet,

qui bien plutôt	rather,
était mon interprète.	who were my interpreter.
Toute mon âme est là!	My whole soul is there!
"Pourquoi me réveiller,	"Why awaken me,
ô souffle du printemps,	o breath of spring,
pourquoi me réveiller?	why awaken me?
Sur mon front je sens	On my brow I feel
tes caresses,	your caresses,
et pourtant bien proche	and yet so near
est le temps des orages	is the time of storms
et des tristesses.	and of sadness.
Pourquoi me réveiller,	Why awaken me,
ô souffle du printemps?	o breath of spring?
Demain dans le vallon	Tomorrow to the valley
viendra le voyageur	the traveler will come
se souvenant de ma gloire première.	remembering my original glory.
Et ses yeux vainement	And his eyes in vain
chercheront ma splendeur.	will look for my splendor.
Ils ne trouveront plus	They will find nothing
que deuil et que misère! Hélas!	but mourning and misery! Alas!
Pourquoi me réveiller . . .	Why awaken me . . .

Torn by conflicting emotions, Werther has returned from exile. While with intense feeling he looks at the familiar surroundings Charlotte, hoping to keep their conversation on a not too personal plane, hands him a translation he had left behind unfinished and asks him to read it to her.

The original verses are by a mythic bard from Scotland who as early as the third century allegedly had written some fiery poems which an eighteenth-century British poet pretended to have rediscovered and which created an enormous sensation at the time of Goethe's youth. Goethe incorporated several fragments in his novel, and Massenet uses the last of those for Werther's reading. It deals with the despair of a noble father over the tragic death of his children. That is the fall from "splendeur" to "deuil" and "misère" that Werther talks about.

Rather than starting the aria directly at "Pourquoi me réveiller" it is wise to prepare the mood of the two short verses with the melodic introduction that starts with "Traduire," eight bars before the theme of the aria appears in the orchestra. Doing so will allow the voice to settle in the proper way, and the mood to be set.

The tempo is slow, $\quart = 60$. The word "Traduire," which Charlotte has just used, seems to Werther inadequate to express how closely he identifies with the ancient poet. It is sung piano, as a question, and with a voice already fluid and nimble as it will have to be throughout the aria. The "Ah" on the E-natural is sustained and warm; then there is a diminuendo (the flight of a dream) and a very tender expression in "sur l'aile de ces vers." A little more voice on "cher poète," and the phrase ends piano as with humility on "mon interprète." So far those verses have had the smooth continuity typical of the French style. After a sensitive interlude, first passionate, then full of grace, the short phrase "Toute mon âme est là" should be said, according to the score, "with inspired sadness" and freely.

The tempo of the aria is again $\quart = 60$, the dynamics piano at first. The poet with whom

Werther identifies himself had been unconscious of his sorrow for a while. But the breath of spring, soft as it is, reawakens his despair and causes him to cry out in pain and protest. Consequently, the dynamics piano is not a relaxed and happy one but tense, even on the words "ô souffle du printemps." The second "pourquoi me réveiller" is a reproach, and only on the words "tes caresses" does the sound become soft, especially on the portamento C-sharp–D-sharp on "caresses." A crescendo starts immediately afterward, to forte on "orages." This forte, however, must be less strong by quite a margin than the following fortissimo on "réveiller." In "orages" the voice, ringing in a vowel /ɑ/ almost similar to the preceding /o/, must aim more at a strong ring than at a broad and possibly spread bulk. The rallentando on the bar preceding the A-sharp is very important. The orchestra should start it very clearly, the voice coming in on the sixteenths with poise and without hurry. The ascension to the A-sharp should be a spin from the C-sharp below, not a glottal bang, and should stay on the vowel /e/ rather than stray to some uncertain, shapeless sound. A tenor afraid of the A-sharp will find help in practicing this way: Sing C-sharp–D–F-sharp–A-sharp, without the three other C-sharps of the phrase. When you feel secure in that ascending line, sing the phrase as is, keeping the three C-sharps extremely light, especially the last, which is only a sixteenth note anyway. To pounce on that C-sharp in the hope of baiting the A-sharp is an error. Besides, the A-sharp should not be just a sound. It is an outcry of despair and must be thought of in that spirit, the fermata held to the length the performer feels most appropriate for the expression. It is also both wise and musical to start that note a little less than fortissimo and to increase its power by repeating mentally the vowel /e/ with an expansion in size. A definite silence should follow in order to prepare the last phrase "ô souffle du printemps," piano but with the same ring, the same support, and the same sustained feeling as on the high note. Again, the phrase cannot be without expression: it is a restrained reproach aimed at the breeze of spring.

The second verse follows almost exactly the pattern of the first, but the crescendo and the forte come earlier. There must be a contrast of color between "ma splendeur" (a condition of the past), bright and serene, and "deuil" and "misère" (the present condition). The vowel /œ/ in "deuil" is sad and contained; in "misère," the vowel /ɛ/—beware of spreading—is tragic. A breath is recommended before "et que misère."

The silence before "Hélas" seems to make the approach to the high phrase easier than in the first verse. Again, observe the following rallentando.

The last "ô souffle du printemps" becomes forte this time, staying in the mood of despair of the climactic phrase. The vowel on the F-sharp in "printemps" is an /ɑ/ very near to /ɔ/.

This aria should have the same effect on Charlotte as does the reading of the poems in Goethe's novel; that is, it should make her aware of the love for Werther that she had kept hidden even from herself. But this cannot be achieved solely through the power of a ringing A-sharp.

Menotti, *The Consul*

"Papers, papers"

soprano

To this we've come:
That men withhold the world from men.
No ship nor shore for him who drowns at sea.
No home nor grave for him who dies on land.
To this we've come:
that man be born a stranger upon God's earth,
that he be chosen without a chance for choice,
that he be hunted without the hope of refuge.
To this we've come, to this we've come;
and you, you, too, shall weep.
If to men, not to God, we now must pray,
tell me, Secretary, tell me, who are these men?
If to them, not to God, we now must pray,
tell me, Secretary, tell me,
who are these dark archangels?
Will they be conquered? Will they be doomed?
Is there one, anyone, behind those doors
to whom the heart can still be explained?
Is there one, anyone, who still may care?
Tell me, Secretary, tell me.
Have you ever seen the Consul?
Does he speak, does he breathe?
Have you ever spoken to him?

Papers! Papers! Papers!
But don't you understand?
What shall I tell you to make you understand?
My child is dead . . . John's mother is dying . . .
my own life is in danger.
I ask you for help,
and all you give me is . . . papers.
What is your name? Magda Sorel.
Age? Thirty-three.
Color of eyes? Color of hair?
Single or married? Religion and race?
Place of birth, Father's name, Mother's name?
Papers! Papers! Papers! . . .
Look at my eyes, they are afraid to sleep.
Look at my hands, at these old woman's hands.
Why don't you say something?
Aren't you secretaries human beings like us? . . .
What is your name? Magda Sorel.
Age? Thirty-three.
What will your papers do?
They cannot stop the clock.
They are too thin an armor against a bullet.
What is your name? Magda Sorel.

Age? Thirty-three.
What does that matter?
All that matters is that the time is late,
that I'm afraid and I need your help.
What is your name? What is your name?
This is my answer:
my name is . . . woman.
Age: still young.
Color of hair: gray.
Color of eyes: the color of tears.
Occupation: waiting.
Waiting, waiting, waiting . . .
Oh, the day will come, I know,
when our hearts aflame will burn your paper chains.
Warn the consul, Secretary, warn him.
That day neither ink nor seal shall cage our souls.
That day will come, that day will come!

The stage is the waiting room of a consulate somewhere in Europe. There is a desk for the secretary, with several filing cabinets at hand. Desk and secretary defend the door to the consul's office. Magda Sorel is one of several applicants waiting for a visa to the consul's country. Her own country has become a police state, and all the applicants have compelling reasons for wanting to leave. They cannot do so, however, without a visa to another country. That visa may be the difference between life and death for those suspected of political heresy by the secret police. Getting the visa, however, requires an infinite number of documents made out on precise dates in precise places, often inaccessible under the present troubled circumstances, of information available nowhere, of references impossible to obtain. The consulate is a mechanical device ignorant of human uncertainties and human anguish. It demands, rejects, delays, sometimes stamps papers. It represents total indifference to individual despair, to life and death. Millions of people, I myself among them, caught in the turmoil of war and dictatorship, have experienced such places.

Magda is a woman in her early thirties. Pursued by the police, her husband has fled the country; her child is dead, and she herself is haunted by the secret police. She has come to the consulate countless times already, always in vain because of some irregularity in her papers that she has no way of correcting. This time, despair and a feeling of rebellion overcome her, and after shouting at the secretary she unburdens herself of the accumulated frustrations of weeks or months of tragic futility.

Magda's voice is a vibrant soprano with a full-bodied medium range and the capacity to rise to strong personal indignation as well as to speak grandly in the name of all human beings. Her power lies not in her loudness but in her intensity and conviction.

Using as a solo what is actually a scene, the singer should start at rehearsal number 96. After calling the secretary "Liar" in a fit of rage, Magda realizes that, more than the secretary, it is the age and the world that have become merciless. After a crashing chord in the orchestra, the voice comes in piano and subdued, adagio, expressing the dark helplessness of all the losers, the oppressed, the exiled. Slowly she recites, at first in a monotone enumeration, the vast grievances of the sufferers. "To this we've come" is almost bland in its feeling of inevitability. A breath after "from men" will allow a slight increase of tone on "no ship nor shore"; the two phrase endings "drowns at sea" and "dies on land" are said darkly, in a barely indicated rallentando. The second "To this we've come" shows more intensity, and there is rising indignation on "upon God's earth." The *piano* marking for "that he be chosen" stresses the passivity of the chosen victims, while the forte on "he be hunted" and the forte and accelerando that follow convey the brutality of the oppressors, bringing Magda back to the case of her own family, and the two exasperated "to this we've come" are sung fortissimo. In a striking reversal of her thoughts, singing piano and slowly, Magda now places the secretary among the victims: "You, you, too, shall weep" is not a threat but a prophecy.

The next four bars stay in the same adagio tempo but sound more animated because of the rhythmical writing. Magda's speech acquires a growing vehemence. A clever interpreter can make use of the many commas for contrasts, for sarcasm. "If to men, / not to God, / we now must pray, / tell me, / Secretary, tell me, / who are these men? / If to them, / not to God, / we now must pray, / tell me, / Secretary, tell me." The contrast, for instance, between "to men" and "not to God" is easily felt and easy to use. The episode culminates in the "who" fortissimo on number 100 and the whole phrase is then sung freely and forte.

But with "Is there one, anyone," started pianissimo and rising to forte within a few words, Magda's tortured mind veers to a strange idea: Maybe there is no consul there, after all? The notion of a void behind the forbidden door, coupled with her endless attempts to be heard by the man behind that door, makes her sing the following lines fortissimo. "Heart" and "care" must stand out in the uneasy vocal line. And suddenly, with almost a touch of madness in her voice, Magda asks the secretary in a confidential whisper if she has ever seen the consul.

A short trio during which the secretary offers Magda one more form to fill out, will, of course, be cut when the aria is sung as a solo. Even without this provocation another change in Magda's mind is understandable and acceptable. The next pages show many more, which generally translate into changes of tempi. The singer must be very sure to pass without hesitation from a *presto* to an *andante*, from an *allegro* to an *adagio*, never forgetting to differentiate them strongly. The first *presto* lasts two lines. Magda has snatched one form only from the secretary's hand. There is dismay rather than anger in those first "Papers" and a pathetic appeal in "What shall I tell you?" The short *andante mosso* calls for a moving voice. Some beautiful notes, even sad ones, always prove an efficient tool for a clever singer. By the time Magda reaches "and all you give me is . . . papers," she is practically speaking. The *allegro* gives the impression of a mechanical monotony. Magda can recite in her sleep the list of questions she has answered so many times. As if obsessed with them, she quotes them like a robot and then explodes in an uncontrollable rage. Note that the tempo is moderato, not presto! The many "Papers" must be sung exactly on time. Magda this time has gotten hold of a large stack of forms and "hurls them about the room" in handfuls, alternating gestures and words.

Adagio: after the fermata, in a remarkable non sequitur but with the same fortissimo voice, very slowly, Magda describes her physical decline. At number 107 there is a return to the speaking voice followed by a few bars of the obsessing answers to the form. Three bars before number 108 a new element is introduced. The papers cannot protect against danger or deadlines, and the voice acquires a pressing practical quality that alternates with the mechanical voice of the obsession until number 109. Then, starting "with great dignity and simplicity" and keeping these qualities as long as possible, the page turns little by little into an echo of the obsession itself and finally bursts into the frantic "waiting, waiting," repeated crescendo to an almost hysterical tension.

Then, after three precious beats of silence, very much needed for rebuilding a deep support and conceiving a sense of greatness, Magda prophesies the final triumph of men over papers and seals. Decide to take all the time you need to let the voice pour and expand. The three notes of "the day will come" must be broadly stressed; "when our hearts" is free (the vowel in "our" is an /a/ and must stay /a/ for the high B-flat, the diphthong being completed only at the end of the sound). After that there is no ritardando but a steady, confident, vital progression to the end. Singing the first of the last two "that day will come" just above mezzo forte will allow the concluding one to reach and maintain the needed bright power.

This aria clearly shows the singer that versatility is indispensable, that human expression is the goal of all vocal education, and that the deepest emotions, the most realistic, are to be found in stories of our time and of common people as well as in the stories of traditional operatic heroes.

Menotti, *The Medium*

"Monica's Waltz" *soprano*

Bravo! And after the theater,
supper and dance. Music!
Umpapa, umpapa,
up in the sky
someone is playing a trombone and a guitar.
Red is your tie,
and in your velvetine coat you hide a star.
Monica, Monica, dance the waltz.
Follow me, moon and sun,
keep time with me, one two three one:
If you're not shy,
pin up my hair with your star,
and buckle my shoe.
And when you fly,
please hold on tight to my waist,
I'm flying with you. Oh!
Monica, Monica, dance the waltz,
Follow me, moon and sun, follow me.

What is the matter, Toby?
What is it you want to tell me?
Kneel down before me, and now, tell me . . .
Monica, Monica, can't you see
that my heart is bleeding, bleeding for you?
I loved you, Monica, all my life,
with all my breath, with all my blood.
You haunt the mirror of my sleep, you are my night.
You are my light and the jailer of my day.
How dare you, scoundrel, talk to me like that!
Don't you know who I am?
I am the Queen of Aroundel!
I shall have you put in chains!
You are my princess, you are my queen,
and I'm only Toby, one of your slaves,
and still I love you and always loved you
with all my breath, with all my blood.
I love your laughter, I love your hair,
I love your deep and nocturnal eyes.
I love your soft hands, so white and winged,
I love the slender branch of your throat.
Toby, don't speak to me like that!
You make my head swim.
Monica, Monica, fold me in your satin gown.
Monica, Monica, give me your mouth,
Monica, Monica, fall in my arms!
Why, Toby, you're not crying, are you?
Toby, I want you to know
that you have the most beautiful voice in the world!

In a squalid room of a house on the outskirts of town, Monica and Toby are alone, with time on their hands. Monica is the daughter of Baba the medium and is used to impersonating the dead and speaking or singing with their voices during Baba's séances. Toby is a waif taken in by Baba, who terrifies him. He is very handsome but a mute. Both he and Monica are still in their teens, with the boy being the younger of the two.

There is a puppet theater in the room, and Toby has just given Monica a performance. The ensuing scene involves both youngsters, Toby being, of course, silent, and is a very telling one even when given as an aria without benefit of the stage. In that case the soprano must be even more careful to change the character of her voice depending on whether Monica speaks for herself or for the mute Toby, so that the listeners can follow Monica's change of identity by means of the ears alone. The task is much easier, of course, when the scene is acted out on stage, as part of the opera.

There are two parts in the scene. In the first part Monica, wishing to cheer Toby up, sings an enticing waltz for him, not only giving him the rhythm of the dance but after a while involving herself so much in the game physically that she creates great emotional stress in the adolescent. The first line of the scene is very free, as if improvised. Monica invents a game while she speaks: The puppet show was a play, and after a play people go to nightclubs. Sing "Bravo" loud and sustained, make a silence during which the idea comes to Monica's mind, and sing still slowly "And after the theater" while "supper and dance, Music" come spontaneously and fast. Then the "Umpapa, umpapa" establish the rhythm.

Throughout the scene the text, too, seems a poetic improvisation in the starry vein of Gian-Carlo Menotti, full of fairy-tale touches. In her gloomy life Monica dreams of fairy tales and finds in Toby the right person to share them with. At first, while Toby dances, Monica only sings and devotes all her imagination as well as her voice to making the music and the text sparkle and shine. The first four bars in 12/8–9/8, "Up in the sky," are the clue to the mood of the fantasy. The alliance of "a trombone and a guitar" is a clue to its carefreeness. Take a breath after "sky" and after "tie," then go straight to the end of the two phrases. The next four bars are mostly rhythmical. Then, with the four bars in 12/8 the fairy tale returns, but this time the breaths come after "star" and "waist," the phrasing being inversed.

If Monica starts dancing (one bar mezzo forte, one bar piano) after the fermata on "Oh," she must nevertheless pay attention to a few vocal difficulties: The word "Follow" will be easy to sing if pronounced f[ɔ]ll[o]w, like to-m[ɔ]rr[o]w, the first *o* open, the second slimmer and darker. If the second *o* is thought like /ɔ/, the tone will spread and be difficult to sing. The same caution must be observed with the vowel *e* in "me." It must be sung with a ringing /i/. The last "follow me" is still sung with great zest as if Monica expected the dance to continue with the same verve after a short interruption.

The line before number 4 is free, said with surprise in a very friendly voice, and the words "Kneel down . . ." are also very friendly and persuasive. This voice will stay piano and confidential but becomes intense when it pretends to be Toby's voice, allowing for a great contrast with the voice Monica must use as the Queen of Aroundel. The first line can be phrased as follows: "Monica," comma, then no break until after "bleeding," in a lovely legato. In the second line the first breath comes after "my life," the second after "my breath." There is a strong crescendo on the next two bars, "You haunt the mirror," with a climax on the A-flat on "You," a "You" that is full of love and, although mezzo forte, tender and mellow. If the proper expression has been reached it is possible to hold the A-flat a little beyond the written value. Monica is very good at speaking of love to herself. Are those words she would like to hear from someone but never has? This thought may be confirmed later.

Now Monica as Queen of Aroundel makes herself sound loud and authoritarian but never grotesque. No ugliness must be allowed to creep into the scene, which will grow more and more touching.

When Toby's voice returns, it is at first for speaking again of his humble worship and adoration (four bars), with a sentimental summit of the phrase mezzo forte and ritenuto on "always loved you." On the fifth bar of number 5, however, he sings faster and less confidentially as he talks of more physical details and in the next three bars reaches a sensuousness still dressed in purity; "your soft hands," "the slender branch of your throat." Here Monica's voice must find a way to express an ill-defined trouble, in the rallentando before number 6, for example. And this time, when she stops impersonating Toby she becomes herself, pianissimo subito, and fakes—or feels—a disturbing lightheadedness. Almost immediately she returns to Toby's voice impulsively, as if no longer following her own will but obeying an irresistible urge. The tempo is much faster, and the voice, although still starting piano, grows more intense all the time, the repeated

"Monica" more frantic. The desire has gone from the hands to the mouth and the phrase ends *fff* in a powerful call for physical love. The soprano must be sure to prepare the B-flat by a progressive spin of the voice into high resonances, so that the note flourishes rather than explodes.

Monica is surprised that Toby hides his head in his arms and weeps. Why? Although she had been aware of Toby's feelings for her, she had not guessed their depth, no more than she had guessed her own powerful yearnings, all of which now comes as a surprise. And it is in full communion with the helpless boy that she finds in her heart a stunning word of consolation. In number 7 she must say his name, "Toby," with love, and the short phrase "I want you to know" and the sustained G-sharp on "you have" must very slowly prepare the wondrous line, "the most beautiful voice"—unfold the triplets very slowly and breathe before releasing—"in the world," with a light, floating tone still full of tenderness.

When the aria is performed in concert, that is, in the absence of Toby, a very warm heart and a friendly imagination must reveal the subtle and complex emotions of this piece to the listener, making the voice a very sensitive instrument as the whole style of the performance stays very natural and as far removed as possible from any artificial sophistication.

Menotti, *The Old Maid and the Thief*

"Steal me, sweet thief"   *soprano*

What a curse for a woman is a timid man!
A week has gone by;
he had plenty of chances,
but he made no advances.
Miss Todd schemes and labors to get him some money.
She robs friends and neighbors, the club and the church.
He takes all the money with a smile that entrances. . .
but still makes no advances.
The old woman sighs and makes languid eyes.
All the drawers are wide open,
all the doors are unlocked . . .
He neither seems pleased nor shocked.
He eats and drinks and sleeps,
he talks of baseball and boxing . . .
but that is all.
What a curse for a woman is a timid man!

Steal me, oh steal me, sweet thief,
for time's flight is stealing my youth
and the cares of life steal fleeting time.
Steal me, thief, for life is brief
and full of theft and strife.
And then with furtive step death comes
and steals time and life.
O sweet thief, I pray make me die
before dark death steals her prey.
Steal my lips before they crumble to dust.
Steal my heart before dust must.
Steal my cheeks before they're sunk and decayed.
Steal my breath before it will fade.
Steal my lips, steal my heart, steal my cheeks,
steal, oh steal my breath
and make me die before death will steal her prey.
Oh steal me!
For time's flight is stealing my youth.

In her home, usually devoid of any male presence, the mature Miss Todd has offered hospitality to a young drifter, Bob. Laetitia, her maid, eagerly assists her in taking care of the young man who, in spite of his professed ideals of a free and wandering life, tarries gladly in the house he has singularly revitalized. Alone in the kitchen, mending and pressing Bob's pants, Laetitia in this aria surveys the situation and the state of her own heart.

Laetitia's voice is a young-sounding soprano, a soubrette by trade but a lyric singer in this score.

The recitative preceding the aria is factual and meant to inform the listeners of the progress of the action. But it is, of course, informative also of Laetitia's reaction to the behavior of that fascinating young man. It is noted very precisely, and the best way to perform it, except for some inflections of expression causing a slight retardando here or an accelerando there, is to respect the written rhythms exactly.

The two measures of introduction begin forte and end in a diminuendo. Laetitia, although disappointed and slightly irritated, should not sing the first phrase above mezzo forte but should put a slight stress on "curse" with a mixture of mild scorn and tenderness for the man whose pants she holds in her hands. The next two lines are matter-of-fact, a bit discouraged. Then the thought that Miss Todd, a very busy woman, "schemes and labors" makes Laetitia speak faster in even values, without any stresses; although she may be indignant, she restrains her voice, with a diminuendo on "the club and the church." Quite slowly and forte she now vents her indignation with "He takes all the money" but, attenuating circumstance, "with a smile that entrances," piano, then a fermata on the silence, whereupon "but still makes no advances," unrequited love, is said pianissimo and in disbelief. Laetitia indulges in a partly mocking, partly compassionate imitation of Miss Todd who "sighs and makes languid eyes." Her indignation with Bob grows with the awareness of how far the old lady and she herself have gone to please the man. "All the drawers . . . all the doors" is fortissimo, and again his reaction matter-of-fact, "neither . . . pleased nor shocked." Then it is Bob whom she imitates, rather heavily, for Bob's is not a lithe mind; she imitates him "with disgust." After a very final "that is all" her indignation turns into exasperation, and the repeat of "What a curse" is fortissimo, although the "timid man" is still spoken of gently at the end of the phrase.

The *adagio* aria calls on the sincere sensitivity of its performer. The theme of finding love and happiness now because life is so short is as old as the human mind and the human heart. It has been well exploited here. At first Laetitia fears the empty passing of youth, then, in a moment of great earnestness, the coming of death before love. That thought also lends itself to a plea for love-death almost as earnestly. The soprano sings "Steal me" with a soft, warm voice, with a great underlying intensity. The voice grows stronger on the second "oh steal me, sweet thief," changes to a serious mezzo forte on "stealing my youth," becomes somewhat agitated, losing some of its sweetness, on "the cares of life." "Steal me, thief" in the bar before number 98 is firm and urgent. There is sadness in the slight ritardando in the bar of number 98 itself, the sixteenth notes unhurried. The "furtive step" must be suggested in the way the words are said, and the slight rallentando includes the word "death" in order to delay the coming of the dreaded syllable. A darker color of vowels would fit the gloom of the phrase and help create the required *emozione*. A deep breath before "O sweet thief" at the change of key prepares the coming of a much more important voice; a short one after "thief" is then all that is needed for soaring to the high B-flat forte and ringing, singing it in a bright vowel /a/ that fits the kind of dying desired. But "before dark death . . . prey" again needs a darkening of the vowels, as above.

From here on it seems that in her impatience Laetitia becomes a bit morbid as she confronts her yearned-for lover with gruesome alternatives to his yielding to her desires. Or is it only that she exaggerates the speed of the coming of old age in her panic because she has not tempted a young man yet and fears becoming a spinster? At any rate, the first eight bars from number 100 on, marked pianissimo, offer, two at a time, a strong contrast between the sweet prayers, "Steal my lips," "Steal my heart," and so forth and the frightening pictures of decay, the short prayers said swiftly, the ugly pictures more slowly and reluctantly. The last words of these eight bars, "before it will fade," are so frightening that Laetitia barely dares murmur them. As a reaction to the depressing thought she offers herself body and soul, with an increasing intensity in her voice, which culminates broadly and ritardando on "oh steal my breath" already forte and becoming fortissimo on "and make me die," a strong way of putting it. A great dramatic pathos with a ritardando is heard in "before death will steal her prey." It takes a bar in 4/4 adagio for the very spacious "Oh steal me" and its high B-flat, which for all its urgency is a very sentimental note that should soar intensely but with great beauty above the final phrases. Great attention must then be paid to the detailed rubato of the last three measures. An expressive stress should be put on the G of "time's," a sensitive breath taken before "my youth," the vowel /u/, as in "loose," ringing endlessly between extended lips.

In this aria the "soubrette" Laetitia plays the part of a passionate lover. The generally light character of her part changes here into an intensely lyric character. It takes a fine sensitivity and a beautiful quality of voice to do the aria justice. The soprano must make sure that the two high B-flats are not just big and noisy but vibrant with a passion that is one of the most precious jewels of human nature.

Meyerbeer, *L'Africaine*

"O paradis" *tenor*

Pays merveilleux, jardin fortuné,	Wonderful country, blessed garden,
temple radieux, salut!	radiant temple, hail!
O paradis sorti de l'onde,	O paradise emerged from the waves,
ciel si bleu, ciel si pur,	sky so blue, sky so pure,
dont mes yeux sont ravis,	which delights my eyes,
tu m'appartiens!	you belong to me!
O nouveau monde	O new world
dont j'aurai doté mon pays!	which I will have given to my country!
A nous ces campagnes vermeilles,	Ours the fresh plains,
à nous cet éden retrouvé!	ours this rediscovered Eden!
O trésors charmants,	O enchanting treasures,
o merveilles, salut!	o wonders, hail!
Monde nouveau, tu m'appartiens,	New world, you belong to me,
sois donc à moi, o beau pays!	be mine then, o beautiful country!

The libretto of *L'Africaine*, written by Eugene Scribe, the king of the nineteenth-century librettists, is in French. Meyerbeer composed this opera over a span of twenty years in Paris, for that libretto and for the Paris Opéra. The short and famous aria known as "O paradis" must be sung in French just as Lohengrin's farewell must be sung in German. Both are inconceivable in any other language.

In order to place the aria it is not necessary to know much of the plot. The Portuguese explorer Vasco da Gama has finally, after many failures and betrayals, reached the Indian land he has dedicated his life to attaining. Moreover, he has just married Selika, the lovely native girl who had been his faithful companion and protector.

During the six bars of introduction he enters slowly, admiring the great beauty of the surrounding land. Vasco's voice is a radiant tenor, warm and triumphant in this aria. While it would be an error for a light or a light-lyric tenor to attempt it, a lirico-spinto voice would be proper and a dramatic voice would be right if it rang without any trace of muscular strain. The whole role is written for a dramatic tenor with an outstanding top range.

The tempo, *allegretto*, $\eighth = 108\text{--}112$ should allow the voice to flow unrestrained and with great ease and to indulge in many inflections of joy and enthusiasm. Four short phrases precede the soar of the famous lyric phrase. They are said with a crescendo of admiration. "Pays merveilleux" is piano and very well articulated: "jardin fortuné" is a little louder, the admired marvels closer to Vasco. "Temple radieux," in which he has just been married, is a good mezzo forte, "salut" a cheerful greeting underlined by vigorous syncopations rallentando in the accompaniment. The great lyric phrase "O paradis sorti de l'onde" is marked "very soft, but well sustained." Vasco can hardly believe his eyes, can barely find the words to express his admiration. "Sorti de l'onde" has the fluidity of sea waves. With "ciel si bleu, ciel si pur" the short values express the charm of it all in a strong crescendo. The line "dont mes yeux sont ravis" begins piano and grows into an intense crescendo on "ravis," followed by an ecstatic piano and a broadening of the phrase on "tu m'appartiens." Even the B-flat is piano and sung with a soft quality of voice. (Tenor readers, wait until the end before protesting!) A generous breadth marks "O nouveau monde," a new crescendo "dont j'aurai doté," a good allargando with a slight tenuto on the high G-flat in "dont j'aurai doté mon pays." So far this aria has expressed feelings of personal gratification with elegance and warmth, requiring beauty in the voice but no outstanding power.

As in almost every well-made work of art there will be a contrasting phase. From delight, Vasco will change to a heady feeling of possession, at first for his country, then for himself, of those territories unknown so far. It is the voice of a conquistador that sings "A nous ces campagnes vermeilles" forte, the voice of a happy owner that says "à nous cet éden retrouvé." The sweet enjoyment of such treasures makes the following line very pretty. Sung with a light voice, it concludes with a brilliant "salut." During the next three bars it seems that Vasco is seized by feverish ambition. The tempo accelerates, the voice grows louder and suddenly expands forte on the high G-flat "sois donc à moi." The long value of that G-flat is tied to the following "à moi" and mellows so that "sois donc à moi, o beau pays" (fifth bar before the end of the aria) is beautifully round and serene. But "Monde nouveau" (four bars before the end) is forte and intense. The phrases that follow are sung freely, with or without stops between the "à moi." All expectations, of the listeners as well as of the tenor himself, are now concentrated on the last B-flat. This note must be heroic in size, burning in its ringing quality, and held for as long as the singer wishes. Vasco's ambition and the long-restrained power of the tenor explode at the same time.

Here is an aria that calls for a dramatic voice whose size and nature must be felt from the start, but it is a voice that expresses warm and soft feelings for most of the aria, coming into its heroic own only in a short and memorable ending. What an error it would be to believe that the whole aria should be sung with great power. Its character would be lost, its charm dead, and the famous final B-flat would probably be strained or at least without its essential value of contrast.

Mozart, *Così fan Tutte*

"Smanie implacabili"   *mezzo-soprano*

Ah, scostati! Paventa il tristo effetto	Ah, get out of my way! Fear the sad effect
d'un disperato affetto!	of a desperate love!
Chiudi quelle finestre—	Close those windows—
odio la luce,	I hate the light,
odio l'aria che spiro,	I hate the air I breathe,
odio me stessa!	I hate myself!
Chi schernisce il mio duol,	Who makes light of my grief,

chi mi consola?	who will comfort me?
Deh fuggi, per pietà,	Ah, away with you, for pity's sake,
lasciami sola.	leave me alone.
Smanie implacabili	Implacable passions
che m'agitate	that rage
entro quest'anima,	in this heart,
più non cessate	do not cease
finchè l'angoscia	until this anguish
mi fa morir.	kills me.
Esempio misero d'amor funesto	A wretched example of fateful love
darò all'Eumenidi	I shall give the Furies,
se viva resto	if I stay alive,
col suono orribile	with the dreadful sound
de' miei sospir.	of my sighs.

Is any woman capable of fidelity, or are all women fickle? According to the confirmed bachelor Don Alfonso, they all betray their faith. But two young officers, Guglielmo and Ferrando, in love with the two sisters, Fiordiligi and Dorabella, trust their beloved ones. For a wager the three men decide to put the two young women to the test. Ferrando and Guglielmo will pretend to have been called to arms, will come back in disguise, and will court each other's betrothed. Don Alfonso promptly enlists Despina, the girls' worldly chambermaid, to be his accomplice.

Four arias from this masterpiece will be discussed here. In the first one, when Despina finds the sisters in the depth of depression mourning the departure of their lovers and tries to comfort them with a delicious breakfast, Dorabella reacts vehemently to such a material concern. From the point of view of the young women the situation is indeed very sad. Who knows if and when soldiers going to war will return? From the point of view of the audience, aware of the truth, their grief seems slightly out of place, all the more so because Dorabella is an overly romantic girl who sees herself as singled out by fate and the ancient gods for tragic suffering. The point of the aria for the mezzo-soprano is to let herself go with the vehemence implied in the words and the music without any attempt ever at being funny. If one compares Donna Elvira's recitative that precedes "Mi tradì" in *Don Giovanni* with Dorabella's "scostati," one sees that Mozart has done all that is necessary for making the former pathetic and the latter apt to create at the same time sympathy and amusement. In both cases the singer must treat the text with complete sincerity and leave it to the genius of the composer to convey the desired mood.

The recitative is divided into three phases; aimless fury at first, then self-pity, then a return to fury. It is accompanied by the orchestra so that voice and instruments must follow the same emotional pattern.

Dorabella starts by sending the chambermaid away vehemently, on fortissimo chords, then tells her why, in a dejected but still threatening phrase on pianissimo chords. Prompted by the orchestra (*allegro assai*) she follows this by ordering Despina around in a rage of negation—she can stand neither light nor air nor even herself. Each enraged statement is emphasized by the orchestra. After the last one, "odio me stessa" and its orchestral amplification, she is submerged by a wave of self-pity. The two bars preceding "Chi schernisce il mio duol" are played *andante lento*, as well as the next three bars, with a tearful "chi mi consola." But the fury explodes again in the last seven bars of the recitative. The marking *maestoso* indicates that by now Dorabella has found her style; her despair will be tragic in the manner of the Greek dramas of antiquity.

It would be a mistake to sing this recitative in chopped, clipped words. It must reach unexpected greatness through the broad use of long and well-accented vowels, as in "un disper*a*to affe*tt*o," "La l*u*ce," "l'aria che sp*i*ro," and so on. The young women may be a bit unusual, but they have "class."

Aria: The *allegro agitato* may well be measured at ♩ = 116. For fourteen bars the orchestra only makes wavelets under the voice, which makes it possible for the singer to be very intense without being very loud. That is an important point, for it would be dangerous to translate fury into forced singing. Besides, the dynamic pattern of the first eight bars of the vocal line will repeat itself several times during the aria. As if choking on her own breath, Dorabella chops her sounds in the first bar, stresses them in bar 2, and in bars 3 and 4 finds a relative balance. The same is true for bars 5 (chopped), 6 (stressed), and 7 (a relative legato). There follows a lyric expansion of the voice for six bars. At this point the orchestra takes over the feeling of unbalance, alternating short spans of forte and piano, while the voice gains some continuity, "Esempio misero d'amor funesto."

With "darò all'Eumenidi" starts an organized crescendo, which culminates beyond the G-natural on the G-flat. A bright vowel /i/ is indispensable here. Dorabella is near sobs when she cuts the words "de' miei sospir" in short slices. The quarter notes in these bars should be firm, the eighth notes lighter.

The pattern of the beginning of the aria returns with "Smanie implacabili," but a change occurs with "Esempio misero." The tessitura will be higher than in the first verse, making it still more imperative to follow the dynamic suggestions of the score. "Esempio misero" is piano at first, louder on "misero." The phrase "D'amor funesto" and its repeat are sung full voice, well supported and legato. The following phrases are like waves of sorrow, the strong notes being "Eum*e*nidi," "r*e*sto," and after a big crescendo the A-flat on "orribil*e*," which is really heartrending before the diminuendo on "de miei sospir." At this point it seems that Dorabella is capable only of repeating again and again the same words as if obsessed by them, pausing for one bar here and there to regain some strength. It is right, each time the words come, to sing more forte on "darò all'Eumenidi" and more mournfully on "se viva resta." The words "col suono orribile" going to the G-flat should suggest mental and physical suffering, with a very biting note on that G-flat. This outburst appears to have taken a toll of Dorabella's energy, and a pause must be observed before the next G-flat "col," sung piano. Her strength ebbing, she lets herself weaken but for the two unexpected G's on the words "sospir." Those two notes will be easier to sing if, on the one hand, the singer does not allow the lower notes, middle G–middle F, to lose their support and, on the other hand, she is sure to sing a forward and vibrant vowel /i/ on the two high "sospir."

This aria is most effective when sung in performance and with orchestra. When detached as a solo and out of context, while it may show the skill of the singer it does not convey the double intention of the composer, which is to make the listener smile at the very tumultuous and sincere lament. Nevertheless, what mezzo-soprano would not want to be ready for any part of the role of Dorabella?

"In uomini, in soldati"   *soprano*

In uomini, in soldati,	In men, in soldiers,
sperare fedeltà?	expect faithfulness?
Non vi fate sentir per carità!	Don't let people hear you, for goodness' sake!
Di pasta simile son tutti quanti:	of the same dough are they all made:
le fronde mobili, l'aure incostanti	the moving foliage, the fickle breezes
han più degli uomini stabilità.	have more steadiness than men.
Mentite lagrime, fallaci sguardi,	Faked tears, misleading glances,
voci ingannevoli, vezzi bugiardi	deceitful voices, false manners,
son le primarie lor qualità.	are their chief qualities.
In noi non amano che il lor diletto,	In us they love but their own pleasure,
poi ci dispregiano,	then they despise us,
neganci affetto,	deny us affection,
nè val da'barbari chieder pietà.	and it does not do to beg the savages for mercy.
Paghiam, o femine, d'ugual moneta,	Let's pay, o women, with the same currency,
questa malefica razza indiscreta:	this evil, unworthy race:
amiam per comodo, per vanità,	let's love for convenience, for vanity,
la rala, la rala . . .	la rala, la rala . . .

In the long recitative scene that precedes this aria, Despina uses a number of arguments to persuade her mistresses that the departure of their fiancés is not an irreparable catastrophe. They will return covered with laurels, or else they can always be replaced. In the meantime the girls ought to have a good time and not think that their lovers will be faithful. Men's fickleness is perfectly natural and should always be expected.

Despina's voice must be clear, nimble, capable of many colors and of ringing easily throughout an abundance of words. This textbook chambermaid is a typical soubrette, wise beyond her years, fond of mischief, but always forgiven because of her sunny disposition and her unfailing knack of extricating herself from any embarrassing situation.

The aria, an *allegretto* around ♩ = 92, is made of three sections: the first, a kind of foreword; the second, the truth about men; the third, how to behave under those conditions. The foreword, both sincere and crafty, is a display of Despina's amazement at her mistresses naiveté. The very short musical introduction is like a chuckle half repressed, the words "In uomini" and, after another chuckle, "in soldati" sung as if Despina could barely get them out. Then she regains the composure she had pretended to lose and sings the next two phrases more firmly, the meaning of the words bringing with it a crescendo from "uomini" to "soldati." "Fedeltà" is then repeated with increasing disbelief. The fermata on "fedeltà" must, of course, be observed. In the silent fermata that follows, a clear, ringing, pearly laughter is recommended. Despina, twice repeating "Non vi fate sentir per carità," wants the girls to feel ridiculous, whereupon they are ready to be told some truths.

The second part of the aria is a portrait of men as seen by Despina. It must be handled very lightly, as the clever maid is far beyond indignation at their misdeeds. There is a bounce in her singing as each downbeat becomes a tiny springboard for her voice. Starting with "Mentite lagrime" and "fallaci sguardi," the composer has provided several bars

[1]In some editions there is a misprint. The phrase should read, of course, "non amano che il lor diletto" and not "che il cor diletto."

where mimicry complements the changing colors of the voice. Despina, without clowning, must make the listener hear and see the faked tears, the deceitful glances and voices, the false caresses, and then sing with authority "son le primarie lor qualità" mezzo forte to forte. The two phrases beginning with "In noi non amano"[1] are more serious accusations and require a more sustained, earnest voice and a measure of sincerity. Is Despina not very well placed indeed to distrust men? The thought of expecting mercy from them therefore strikes her as very comical, and she emphatically stresses the two phrases "nè val da' barbari chieder pietà," the second time forte. She even singles out the words "chieder pietà," imitating the pleading voice of an innocent young girl, then repeats the two words with false sentimentality, insisting on them in a long A-flat with a fermata started forte and diminishing to a mockingly pleading "pietà."

The third part of the aria is Despina's advice to the two sisters and incidentally to all women to free themselves from demeaning servitude and to repay men in their own money. Despina makes her voice sound imperative, "Paghiam, o femine . . . , "and very soon becomes impertinent and libertine, "amiam per comodo, per vanità," before turning frivolous and jocular, her crystal-clear laughter delightfully stylized in the repeated "la rala, la rala . . . " From here on the aria is much less a speech or a lesson than a lovely vocal piece where the singer can display the quality of her voice as well as her vocal skill to great advantage. The pattern of the "la rala," with their trills and their dotted values, must be worked out very precisely so that Despina's laughter sounds entirely spontaneous and never creates the feeling that joy has become technique. The last phrases culminate in three A-naturals, which must be sung forte but of course a forte fitting the vocal character of a soubrette. The piece ends with great brilliance without losing its charm or its elegance.

It is indeed easy for Despina to preach such a libertine creed, and she does not have to say a word she does not believe herself. The soprano should avoid any mannerism in singing and, onstage, should blend her singing with the agility and grace required for feeding hot chocolate to two desperate, romantic girls in love.

"Come scoglio" *soprano*

Temerari, sortite fuori di questo loco!	Brazen men, get out of here!
E non profani l'alito infausto	And let the deadly breath
degli infami detti	of your disgusting words
nostro cor, nostro orecchio,	not insult our heart, our ear,
e nostri affetti!	and our feelings!
Invan per voi, per gli altri invan	In vain for you, in vain for others
si cerca le nostre alme sedur:	is the attempt to seduce our hearts:
l'intatta fede	the faith
che per noi già si diede	[which] we already have given,
ai cari amanti	for our dear lovers
saprem loro serbar	we shall keep intact
infino a morte,	until death,
a dispetto del mondo e della sorte.	in spite of the world and of fate.
Come scoglio immoto resta	As a rock stands unshaken
contra i venti e la tempesta,	in winds and storm,

cosi ognor quest'alma è forte	thus this soul is forever strong
nella fede e nell'amor.	in faith and love.
Con noi nacque quella face	With us was born that torch
che ci piace e ci consola;	which gives us joy and comforts us,
e potrà la morte sola	and death alone will be able
far che cangi affetto il cor.	to cause our heart to change its feeling.
Rispettate, anime ingrate,	Respect, unsavory minds,
questo esempio di costanza,	this example of steadfastness,
e una barbara speranza	and may a barbarous hope
non vi renda audaci ancor.	not make you insolent again.

Introduced by Despina and sponsored by their pretended friend Don Alfonso, two noble Albanians have invaded the privacy of Fiordiligi and Dorabella. They are, of course, Ferrando and Guglielmo in disguise. At once they declare their love for the young women in the most pressing terms. While Dorabella listens hesitantly, the stronger Fiordiligi rejects their advances in a capital fashion. That is the theme of the aria "Come scoglio," one of the most impressive arias in all of Mozart's repertoire.

It is impossible even to approach a convincing interpretation of this difficult piece if the intended performer is not vocally ready in the first place. The range of "Come scoglio" encompasses two octaves and one third, from low A to high C. Besides, the extreme notes of the range often fall almost within the same phrase. If the technique of the soprano requires laborious adjustments from low to high and in reverse, this aria is out of reach for her voice. The extreme notes must be the simple and logical continuation of a well-balanced middle range. The middle octave of the voice, from G to G for instance, must be sung into bright vowels, with a forward ring and mixed resonances of mouth and head, never forced and always expressing well-defined meanings and feelings. From that middle octave the voice can soar toward the head resonances or descend into forward mouth resonances without any breaks or bridges, the most extreme notes always preserving some of the basic sound of the middle range in their own sound. Alas, what can be shown and practiced in a few moments in the studio would take pages of explanation here where, besides, they would be out of place. Let me say only that the key word here is *continuity*, and the error to be avoided consists in singing unrelated high and low tones, each of them for its own sake.

The recitative is at first an impetuous *allegro*. Fiordiligi is indignant, offended, and upset, she wants those intruders out of the house. She sings forte and rapidly, finding insulting words such as "l'alito infausto" easily. These she contrasts with Dorabella's and her own dignity, "nostro cor, nostro orecchio e nostri affetti." In this she is helped by the strong punctuation in the orchestra. A slight ritardando on "nostri affetti" will add eloquence to this word. In bar 7 the strong orchestral pattern prepares the finality of Fiordiligi's statement, in a slightly slower tempo: "Invan per voi . . ." There is a certain majesty and a more spacious rhythm in the recitative from this point on. Fiordiligi sings with love from "l'intatta fede" to "cari amanti," and with a challenging pride from her "saprem loro serbar" to "e della sorte." Throughout the recitative her voice must never be edgy or clipped. As she passes from one emotion to another, it must stay sustained and coordinated. Now that she has asserted herself in an impressive way, she will develop the aria's two themes, immovable love and fearless challenge.

As regards the tempi, there are three parts in the aria: *andante maetoso*, ♩ = 72, for fourteen bars and again later for eight bars; *allegro*, ♩ = 116–120, for two long pages and also again later; finally, *Più allegro*, ♩ = 160, to the end of the aria.

What Fiordiligi is reacting to, an unexpected attempt by two improbable suitors to woo her and her sister, another girl would have dismissed with a scornful smile. Not she. She is as exaggeratedly romantic as Dorabella, and her aria seems a reaction to some dangerous assault. It is hardly necessary to oppose a "rock unmoved by a tempest" to two "butterflies in the agony of love," as the two Albanians describe themselves. However, Fiordiligi possesses the greatness of faithful love, and the passion that moves her is a noble one. We sympathize with her despite her excessive reaction.

The *andante maestosa* section: Alternating with a majestic orchestra, the first two phrases of her singing are extremely firm and decisive, forte and legato. That is her own portrait. "Contra i venti e la tempesta," then, is her dramatic interpretation of the offense and requires a very powerful voice in all ranges (see my suggestions above) at the same majestic pace.

The *allegro* section: For sixteen bars Fiordiligi sings of her faithful love with enthusiasm, joy, and firmness. These lines make for beautiful singing, fluid, alive, the voice asserting itself on the long values and floating happily on the groups of sixteenths. But on bar 17 the orchestra adopts a new pattern, which prompts Fiordiligi to return to her aggressive posture and to challenge her offenders. In her exaggeration she is nevertheless totally sincere when she states that only death can change her steadfast heart. The voice must return to dramatic emphasis. There is a suggestion of a forward march in the descending pattern in bar 18 and the following ones, a sweeping bravado in the vocal run in bar 22, a fight as if between life and death in the tortured intervals of bars 24–26 and 28–29, ending piano in bar 29. After three bars of transition piano to mezzo forte, the heart triumphs over all evils in "far che cangi affetto," from bar 31 to the end of the section. As an alternative to the printed notation the soprano can sing the syllable "-to" of "affetto" on the eighth note tied to the full note F (bar 36) and then sing the vocalise in bars 36–38 on the vowel "Ah." It must be noticed that, while a staccato is marked on four notes in bar 36, bar 37 is legato, so that the high C is a strong part of that legato and not a graceful staccato.

The *andante* section is now repeated, shortened to eight bars but rendered still more emphatic than the first time by the four added fermatas. They imply that Fiordiligi has become still more inaccessible to seduction and appears even to have grown physically. The fermatas should be long and have a rich, meaty sound.

The *allegro* section is also repeated in an abbreviated form but always firm and melodious, piano for the most part but ending forte, also in a fermata of absolute finality.

The *più allegro* section: As if the brazen Albanians were not already sufficiently discouraged by Fiordiligi's powerful aria she ends it with a crushing rebuke. The two pages of the *più allegro* must be sung with great strictness of rhythm, unrelenting intensity, and absolute authority. And all this can be achieved only by vocal mastery. Two serious problems must be solved in order to succeed. The first is the handling of the very fast run on triplets. While it is possible to sing the rather long values as in the early words "Rispettate" and "questo esempio" as well as the whole phrase "una barbara speranza . . ." forte, the runs have to be taken with a very light amount of voice, keeping in mind a clear vowel /a/ and never attacking any note with an *h* (ha-ha-ha). Think of the notes as weightless marbles rolling around by themselves inside your mouth in back of the upper teeth, take a breath after the first quarter note C and after the second quarter note B-flat. As in the trill, the less mechanical control the better. Let your reflexes take over.

The second problem lies in the very low range of the two lines following the triplets. Here again, as in the other sections of the aria, enough high resonance must be kept in those low notes so that they do not become heavy, dark, and hard to move. Entrust your voice to very precise words said as forward as possible with your lips. You will achieve no great volume here, but the phrase will run as desired. As soon as the longer values reappear, fourteen bars before the end of the aria, more power should be attempted so that the aria will end in greatness. No edginess must mar the high B-flat of the last lines.

When this *più allegro* is well given it is one of the most compelling scoldings ever delivered to any delinquents. At the same time the character of Fiordiligi will have grown immensely in scope, for our ears as well as in our hearts. "Come scoglio" requires long hours of study and more still of practice. Each of the sections must acquire its own proper style and strength. When each has been mastered separately, they must be assembled with the desire to blend their variety into an irresistible work of intense sincerity and winning conviction.

"Donne mie, la fate a tanti" *baritone*

Donne mie, la fate a tanti, a tanti
che, se il ver vi deggio dir,
se si lagnano gli amanti
li commincio a compatir.
Io vo bene al sesso vostro,
lo sapete, ognun lo sà.
Ogni giorno ve lo mostro,
vi do segno d'amistà.
Ma quel farla a tanti e tanti
m'avvilisce in verità.
Mille volte il brando presi
per salvar il vostro onor,
mille volte vi difesi
colla bocca e più col cor.
Ma quel farla a tanti e tanti
è un vizietto seccator.
Siete vaghe, siete amabili,
più tesori il ciel vi diè,
e le grazie vi circondano
dalla testa sino ai piè.
Ma la fate a tanti e tanti
che credibile non è.
Io vo bene al sesso vostro,
ve lo mostro,
mille volte il brando presi,
vi difesi,
gran tesori il ciel vi diè,
sino ai piè.

Dear ladies, you fool so many of us
that, if I am to tell you the truth,
if your lovers complain,
I am beginning to feel with them.
I mean your sex well,
you know it, everybody knows it.
Every day I prove it to you,
and give you signs of my friendship.
But your fooling so many, so many,
truly discourages me.
A thousand times I have taken my sword
to save your honor,
a thousand times I have defended you
with my words and more with my heart.
But your fooling so many, so many,
is an annoying little vice.
You are beautiful, you are lovable,
heaven has bestowed on you treasures aplenty,
and graces surround you
from head to toe.
But you fool so many, so many,
that it is incredible.
I mean your sex well,
I am proving it to you,
a thousand times I have taken my sword,
I have defended you,
great treasures did heaven bestow on you,
to your toes.

Ma la fate a tanti e tanti	But you are fooling so many, so many,
che se gridano gli amanti,	that if your lovers protest,
hanno certo un gran perchè.	they certainly have very good reason.

Guglielmo, courting the fiancée of his friend Ferrando in fulfillment of a wager, has discovered that her defenses have their weak points. Hearing this, Ferrando has fallen into a revolted despair, which in turn worries Guglielmo. Following a custom of the opera buffi of the eighteenth century, Guglielmo in this aria tells the ladies in the audience what he thinks of the ways of women.

Guglielmo is a baritone. He needs not only a sense of humor but a voice that is round as well as precise and nimble. He must understand that heaviness is incompatible with speed. The *allegretto* of this aria is timed at $\downarrow$ = 126, which is fast but not a *presto*. Although in a state of excited indignation, Guglielmo takes the time needed to express a variety of feelings without running the risk of antagonizing his charming albeit irritating listeners.

The first phrase shows immediately that (*a*) Guglielmo still feels sympathetic toward these tormentors of men—"Donne mie" is a friendly, almost tender, expression; (*b*) he is not going to minimize the scope of his accusations—the several repeats of "a tanti" and the fermata on the last one suggest a great many misdeeds.

The two feelings will alternate throughout a good part of the aria and will even become scrambled at some point. The interpreter must find the right proportion of blandishments and reproaches in his speech and never turn it into either a bitter, aggressive sermon or a grotesque exaggeration. His is the surprised reaction of a friendly man to an unsuspected and disturbing flaw in the makeup of the much-worshiped feminine sex. Ferrando's sorrow prompted his friend to speak out against women's fickleness but not to offend them and run the risk of being deprived of the pleasure of their company. The singing, nimble as it is, must be legato, very fluid, very smooth, never jumpy and dry. The first phrase makes its effect through an insisting crescendo, whereupon the next starts mildly with "se il ver vi deggio dir," fills with sympathy on "se si lagnano gli amanti" and "li commincio a compatir"–no accusation yet. The next four lines are given to the repeated affirmation of his devotion to women, a lavish precaution against any suspicion of prejudice. A smiling conceit colors "lo sapete" and "ognun lo sa." "Ogni giorno," coupled with "vi do segno d'amistà," is boasting lightly if by "segno d'amistà" we understand courtship and love. If it were possible to do so, that phrase should be sung tongue in cheek! It is repeated in a vigorous crescendo. Finally the reproach is formulated, the "Ma" well stressed, the several "a tanti" fading into a slightly ashamed low range, the misdeeds having a depressing effect on Guglielmo. "M'avvilisce in verità" is said sadly, mezzo forte the first time, piano the second time. The first grievance against women is then that they betray their constant servants.

A second grievance is that they also betray their defenders. Now Guglielmo presents himself as a valiant knight always ready to fight for women's honor. He sings forte, well legato at first, then with a well-stressed dotted rhythm full of energy. The reproach is formulated again, this time with some irritation but without going too far—their betrayal is a "vizietto seccator," an annoying little vice.

Guglielmo then embarks on a heartfelt praise of feminine charms, sung with warmth, admiration, and more than a trace of lust. The silences between phrases are like sighs or pauses to regain control of himself. The subject is pursued in great detail, "dalla testa sino ai piè." Saying these words for the second time Guglielmo suddenly remembers the reason for his speech. He can very well tie the last "al piè" to "Ma" and sing two more "Ma" with growing intensity before going as far as insisting that such behavior is unbelievable, "che credibile non è." That was the third grievance; women's beauty precludes trust. Having gone that far, Guglielmo rushes back into a review of all he has said before, again tying the second "che credibile non è" to "Io vo bene al sesso vostro" and mixing praises and grievances at random. Even as briefly as the various moods are hinted at, the singer must try to find their different colors, a virtuoso work.

Suddenly Guglielmo seems to come out of his confusion and to remember once again the subject of his speech and the reason for his presence in front of the audience. Now the repeats of "Ma" and the many "la fate a tanti" are very energetic, and when he comes to "che se gridano gli amanti" he sings full voice and reaches forte in two successive crescendos. The words are strongly articulated in his desire to be severe and impressive. He no longer speaks of an "annoying little vice" but of a "gran perchè," a very good reason for complaining about women. The short, isolated "perchè" seem to answer a silent question from the women. Yes, men do have a reason—Guglielmo thinks of the grieving Ferrando. A short and swift figure in the orchestra keeps the whole episode at the level of light comedy. But Guglielmo can no longer be stopped and will conclude almost gruffly, putting sudden forte accents on unexpected spots—twice on "*un gran perchè*"—and finishing loudly before stalking offstage.

The pace and nimbleness of this aria, especially in the accompaniment, speak in favor of a light comedy style, but Guglielmo wanted to be serious. The combination of the two elements, one comic and the other serious, makes this aria interesting but not so easy to handle.

Mozart, *Don Giovanni*

"Madamina" ("Leporello's Catalog Aria")   *bass-baritone*

Madamina,	Dear little lady,
il catalogo è questo	this is the catalog
delle belle che amò il padron mio.	of the beauties my master has loved.
Un catalogo egli è che ho fatto io.	It is a catalog that I have made.
Osservate, leggete con me.	Look here, read it with me.
In Italia sei cento e quaranta,	In Italy, six hundred forty;
in Almagna due cento e trent'una;	in Germany, two hundred and thirty-one;
cento in Francia,	one hundred in France,
in Turchia novant'una.	in Turkey ninety-one.

Ma in Ispagna—	But in Spain—
son già mille e tre!	there are already one thousand three!
V'han fra queste contadine	Among them there are peasant girls,
cameriere, cittadine,	chambermaids, city girls,
v'han contesse, baronesse,	there are countesses, baronesses,
marchesane, principesse,	marchionesses, princesses,
e v'han donne d'ogni grado,	and there are women of any standing,
d'ogni forma, d'ogni età.	of any shape, of any age.
Nella bionda egli ha l'usanza	In a blond [girl] he usually
di lodarla la gentilezza,	appreciates her gentleness,
nella bruna, la costanza,	in a brunette, her constancy,
nella bianca, la dolcezza,	in the white-skinned, her sweetness.
Vuol d'inverno la grassotta,	In winter he likes a fat one,
vuol d'estate la magrotta,	in summer he likes a skinny one,
e la grande maestosa.	and the tall, majestic one.
La piccina, la piccina,	The tiny little one
è ogn'or vezzosa.	is always charming.
Delle vecchie fa conquista	The old ones he conquers
pel piacer	for the pleasure
di porle in lista.	of putting them on [my] list.
Sua passion predominante	His predominant passion
è la giovin principiante.	is the young beginner.
Non si picca, se sia ricca	He doesn't care if she be rich,
se sia brutta, se sia bella:	if she be ugly, if pretty:
purchè porti la gonnella	provided she wears a skirt
voi sapete quel che fa!	you know what he does!

This aria comes early in the score. Nevertheless, Don Giovanni has already had time to assault Donna Anna, kill her father, and cruelly make fun of his forsaken wife, Donna Elvira. Flashes of true wit have sparkled in some recitatives, and some spirited give-and-take between Don Giovanni and Leporello has taken place. But this aria for the first time justifies the title *dramma giocoso* (dramatic comedy) given the opera by its librettist Da Ponte. The situation is actually not comical. Under the eyes of an indignant wife a brazen servant displays the countless proofs of her husband's infidelity. The comic effect comes primarily from the exaggeration of the figures. If Leporello's accounting is correct, the total of Don Giovanni's conquests reaches well over 2,000, yet the original Don Giovanni was only twenty-one years old and looked it onstage! The choice of a basso buffo voice for Leporello adds to the fun; the marvelous variety and agility of the musical patterns do the rest. This aria demands impeccable musicianship from the singer, virtuoso handling of the voice, and great talent for describing and suggesting. Leporello, who serves, envies, and tries to imitate his master, need not be old and clumsy. What Don Giovanni does, however, with an easy and elegant nonchalance Leporello does fighting a natural heaviness and a tendency to cowardice. Here he finds a defenseless victim to torture. I have always felt that behind the brilliance and the buffoonery of the aria there is more than a trace of sadism, particularly toward the end of the piece.

The first part of the aria is an *allegro*. The tempo, $\, = 96$, is animated but still practical and should be maintained exactly to the end of that part, except for the written fermatas.

The aria is addressed to Donna Elvira and must be acted out, even in concert or audition, with the constant awareness of the presence of a strongly reacting partner. Attention must also constantly be paid to the orchestral patterns, which have been written with such invention and wit. Singing, acting, and music here must form a whole. The first bars of the orchestra suggest at the same time an extreme rhythmical steadiness and a chuckling joy in the repeated staccati of the chord of D. (This effect will be repeated later, as we shall see.) The voice enters mezzo piano, friendly and almost fatherly with the word "Madamina" and very natural on "il catalogo è questo" to "mio." Leporello sees nothing unusual in the existence of such a catalog. Then the voice of its author rises with pride on several D's, mezzo forte. "Osservate, leggete con me" is still very friendly. Donna Elvira must have turned away because Leporello insists more firmly on this last phrase. So far he has taken the attitude of a warmhearted, well-intentioned informer. Now the orchestra (flutes and bassoons) opens the catalog to the first page, prompting a first count: "In Italia . . . ," the singing phrase not overly stressed—Don Giovanni's success in Italy was good but not outstanding. The orchestra turns another page: "in Almagna . . . ," again moderately admiring. The orchestra turns a third page: "Francia . . . Turchia," small business. Then comes the real thing: "Ma in Ispagna." Respect the two fermatas; sing with a happy round voice and a great sensuous legato on the repeat of "Ma in Ispagna." The two repeats of "mille e tre" are piano and light like the violins of the orchestra. The original pattern now returns in the orchestra, and the voice must again be pleasantly informative, piano at first, with a crescendo *poco a poco* on each new phrase, getting strong on "d'ogni grado, d'ogni forma" and fortissimo on the last "d'ogni forma, d'ogni età." In order to stay exactly on time and to give the impression of ease, the singer, even a basso buffo, will find it helpful to "speak" the fast words on the lips, avoiding an excess of bulk in the back of the mouth, and to sing the last two E's with a vibrant quality rather than with thundering power. Leporello does not intend to frighten Donna Elvira; he merely wants to show off the scope of the don's virile power. The orchestra, in a new pattern, returns to the catalog and the flipping of the pages. The recapitulation is made in the same spirit as the first reading. This time, however, the stress is on the countries rather than on the numbers, and the absence of fermatas on "Ma, ma, ma" gives more breadth to the word "Ispagna" when it comes. In the following chatter "contadine," cameriere," and so on, observe the dynamic markings in the orchestra (or the piano part): They reduce the danger of becoming mechanical and monotonous and emphasize Leporello's enjoyment. The ending of the page should, of course, be a triumphant forte. Leporello has gone as far as he could in bravura. To hold Donna Elvira's unwilling attention, he must change his style now.

Second part: *Andante con moto*, ♩ = 76. Leporello becomes a painter of women. Each vignette is interrupted by short silences, as if he were improvising and stalling to find the words. His voice must suggest each of the personalities he enumerates: "Nella bionda," in a clear voice, pleasant, tender on "la gentilezza" (the two middle fragments are just fill-ins, with the voice legato and crisp on the tied sixteenths); "nella bruna," in a much darker voice—roll the *r*—and with a vigorous "la costanza" as prompted by the orchestra; "nella bianca," with a purposely white sound and with some irony in "la dolcezza." Leporello warms up to his subject, and the invention improves: "la grassotta," in slightly overblown tones: "la magrotta," in small, pinched tones. "e la grande maestosa" and its repeat are, of course, a great crescendo from piano, and the long D an expansion of the crescendo (mentally repeat the vowel *o* bigger and bigger). With "La piccina" the fun gets the better of Leporello, who loses control. Babble the words with delight, and sing "è og'nor vezzosa" very legato. With "Delle vecchie" Leporello seems about to make a shocking revelation. Although "fa conquista" is strong, he seems to realize that he has gone out on a limb (hesitation on "pel piacer") but quickly finds a way out: "di porle in lista," said with relief. Now he becomes confidential. "Sua passion predominante": a touch of sadism appears in holding the long E on "dominant*e*" creating suspense so that "la giovin principiante" will revolt Donna Elvira. There follows a summary, rhythmical, strong-voiced.

And then Leporello attacks Donna Elvira personally with "purchè porti la gonnella." He suddenly tells the poor woman, "what he does to all these women he did to you" ("voi sapete quel che fa"). This is simply indecent, and Donna Elvira should hide her blushing face while Leporello repeats the same phrase. I believe that Donna Elvira's fortitude has its limits. It is conceivable that on the fourteenth bar before the end of the aria, Leporello stops abruptly after "voi sapete" because Donna Elvira has slapped him or hit him with her fan. This would explain the growing sarcasm of the last phrases, finally the sadism on the broken syncopated chords of D. Leporello has brought his misdeed to an end and runs away—or we can agree that he finds great satisfaction in a laughing conclusion of his virtuoso performance. The tradition to sing the first chord forte, the second piano, and to hum the third is praiseworthy.

This aria dangerously invites the performer to exhibitionism, not to mention the stage director. The material provided by Mozart is so perfect in every detail and at every second that any willful distortion of it for a laugh or for applause is a real sin. Buffo or dramatic, Mozart is to be served with great enthusiasm but with complete submission to his magic perfection.

"Or sai chi l'onore" *soprano*

Era già alquanta avanzata la notte	The night was already somewhat advanced
quando nelle mie stanze,	when in my rooms,
ove soletta mi trovai per sventura,	where by misfortune I found myself alone,
entrar io vidi	I saw enter,
in un mantello avvolto	wrapped in a cloak,
un uom che al primo istante	a man whom at first
avea preso per voi;	I mistook for you;
ma riconobbi poi	but then I realized
che un inganno era il mio!	that I was mistaken!
Tacito a me s'appressa	Silent, he draws near [me]
e mi vuole abbracciar;	and wants to embrace me;
scioglermi cerco	I try to free myself,
ei più mi stringe,	he grips me still tighter,
io grido!	I scream!
Non viene alcun;	Nobody is coming;
con una mano cerca	with one hand he tries
d'impedire la voce,	to stop my voice,
e coll'altra m'afferra	and with the other he grasps me

stretta così
che già mi credo vinta.
Alfine il duol,
l'orrore dell'infame attentato,
accrebbe sì la lena mia
che a forza di svincolarmi,
torcermi e piegarmi,
da lui mi sciolsi.
Allora rinforzo i stridi miei,
chiamo soccorso,
fugge il fellon,
arditamente il seguo fin nella strada,
per fermarlo,
e sono assalitrice d'assalita;
il padre v'accorre,
vuol conoscerlo,
e l'indegno, che del povero vecchio
era più forte,
compie il misfatto suo
col dargli morte!

Or sai chi l'onore
rapire a me volse,
chi fù il traditore
che il padre mi tolse.
Vendetta ti chieggo,
la chiede il tuo cor.
Rammenta la piaga
del misero seno,
rimira di sangue
coperto il terreno,
se l'ira in te langue
d'un giusto furor.

close, in such a way
that I already think myself defeated.
Finally the pain,
the horror of the distasteful attack,
increased my strength so much
that by dint of disengaging myself,
of twisting and bending,
I freed myself from him.
So then I increase my screams,
I call for help,
the scoundrel flees,
heatedly I follow him into the street,
to stop him,
and from assaulted I become assailant;
my father comes running,
wants to know who it is,
and the felon, who was stronger than
the poor old man,
completes his crime
by putting him to death!

Now you know who wanted
to rob me of my honor,
who the traitor was
who deprived me of my father.
Vengeance I demand from you,
your heart demands it.
Remember the wound
in the pitiable chest,
see the ground again
covered with blood,
if the ire languishes in you
of a rightful wrath.

Since the night of her father's murder, Donna Anna has been hunting for the murderer. Her fiancé, Don Ottavio, faithfully stays at her side and tries to comfort and help her. In the scene preceding this aria, Donna Anna has suddenly discovered with horror that the criminal is none other than Don Giovanni, a friend of theirs. Controlling her emotions with difficulty she gives Don Ottavio a detailed account of the events of that fateful night, which are forever engraved in her memory.

This account is an accompanied recitative. The conductor will impose the tempi as written by the composer for the string accompaniment. According to the meaning and the dramatic impact of the text, and of course after scrupulous study of all the possibilities, the singer will be free to change the pace of her phrases but not their rhythm. The study of such a recitative is never really finished as it must have all the inflections a great actor would find yet be kept perfectly accurate in intonation and rhythm.

In the first scene of the opera we had seen Donna Anna pursuing her assailant. We have witnessed her flight at the appearance of her father and shortly thereafter her discovery of her father's body. But nothing told us where the tragic event had had its beginning. It is only now that Donna Anna tells the whole story, a violent story that still upsets her profoundly. Consequently the recitative is loaded with intense emotions, sometimes repressed, sometimes freed from restraint—a great challenge for the artist.

The orchestra starts *andante*, approximately ♩ = 72, and the voice enters in the same tempo, without much color, as if reluctantly, with a silence after "alquanta," mezzo piano, as if swallowing hard. All the sixteenth notes are very light and almost sotto voce until "per sventura." In "entrar io vidi" there is a little more color but no fright yet, maybe more a feeling of expectation. Donna Anna would not have been adverse to seeing Don Ottavio enter, even at night. "Un uom che al primo istante . . . " may be said with a trace of embarrassment, but at the same time the confession creates a new sense of intimacy between the fiancés, which makes the whole narration easier. "Ma riconobbi poi" is sad and bitter.

The few words interjected by Don Ottavio can be ignored; the chords played by the strings connect Donna Anna's phrases. Now she describes and relives the physical drama: the silent approach of the assailant ("Tacito . . ."), then a crescendo and accelerando on each of the short phrases, with a forte on "grido." (it is possible to leave out the "io" and to sing a quarter note on "grido.")

Here, and when the *tempo primo* returns, the tempo is *allegro assai*. There is a kind of fury in these chords. "Non viene alcun" is helpless. The next phrases are feverishly descriptive of the assault and each move of the assailant. Here as throughout the whole recitative a knowledge of Italian accents is indispensable, and words like "m'afferra" must create a very dramatic impact by their mere pronunciation. "Che già mi credo vinta," with the chords here in andante, recalls Donna Anna's despair at being almost defeated. Her strength, however, returned, and words such as "svincolarmi," "torcermi," and "piegarmi" are intensely active ones. "Da lui mi sciolsi" is exhausted but triumphant, sung piano with a panting feeling.

The following phrases come forte and fast, framed by the fierce chords mentioned above. There is justified pride in "e sono assalitrice d'assalita," but it is short-lived. Sing mezzo piano "Il padre v'accorre," a little slower "vuol conoscerlo," still slower "l'indegno," and so on. The intensity subsides with the phrase "che del povero vecchio era più forte," where commiseration takes its place and the humiliating defeat of the father finds a just excuse. The words "compie il misfatto suo" and their repeat, however, are sung with the energy of a capital accusation: If the assault on the daughter was an evil deed, the murder of the father is an unforgiveable crime. The tempo slows down here in order to render the accusation solemn and powerful, until "col dargli morte" is said, syllable by syllable, as in a last gasp of energy.

Donna Anna's strength seems exhausted but immediately finds new life through her determination to see her father avenged. The aria must be sung with unrelenting drive and intensity but not fast, so as to keep its solemnity intact. The tempo could be a free ♩ = 92 maintaining a regular pace while allowing an expansion for soaring tones, for instance on "pa-a-dre" in the eighth bar, or for the whole ninth bar, or still more for "se l'i-i-ra" in bar 26 or the four eighth notes in bar 28. Throughout the aria the eighth-note upbeat followed by a half note

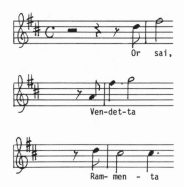

works like a springboard for the voice, creating a sensation of never-weakening vehemence. In order to leave room for growing toward the tremendous ending of the aria, the first six bars are sung no louder than mezzo forte but with an enormous inner force. In the seventh bar the eighth-note upbeat is replaced by a quarter note introducing an exalted legato, the word "padre" used like a term of worship. "Vendetta" is forte with a crescendo to and on the long A on "cor," the power of the voice never becoming harsh but always remaining exalted.

Donna Anna now reminds her fiancé of the horror of the crime with a realistic description of her murdered father. The voice is still vehement and pressing but no more than mezzo forte, singing into darker vowels, putting pathetic accents on words like "piaga" and "seno." It then rises to forte on "rimira di sangue," subsides as if hesitating to say "coperto il terreno," and rises again powerfully to stress the two A's in "se l'i-i-ra." There is a slight ritardando on the first "d'un giusto furor," a stronger one on each note of the second "d'un giusto furor."

The following sixteen bars are a repeat of the first sixteen of the aria. Do not allow that vehement, continuous, legato exhortation to weaken. A change occurs in the seventeenth bar as the words "Rammenta — la piaga" and "rimira — di sangue" are separated by silent sobs or emotional exhaustion. The upper notes are forte, the lower ones piano. The great "Vendetta" phrase is also repeated for six bars followed by the coda, which must be treated almost like an instrumental coda ending a symphonic movement. Start the two ascending arpeggios piano, and end piano after a strong crescendo on the higher notes, bars 7 to 10 of this final piece. In bars 11, 12, and 13 start "la chiede" piano both times, and make a crescendo on the longer values. Bar 14 is mezzo forte, bar 15 forte, and the remaining bars are fortissimo with a progressive allargando, the last "la chiede il tuo cor" very broad. The triplet of sixteenth notes on the last "tuo" is sometimes suppressed, the soprano singing instead a second A on "tuo."

Although this aria does not necessarily require a very dramatic instrument, there are not many voices that should attempt it. An intense ring is needed together with the ability to maintain constantly a surging power unmarred by edges or harshness. Even for such rare voices the aria holds its dangers if the singer forgets to vary the dynamics and the intention of the phrases many times. It is the monotony of the singing, the monotony even of a compelling strength, that creates the danger. A great vocal gift, a clear mind, and thorough training are indispensable for performing this aria and its recitative faithfully and enjoying it deservedly.

"Batti, batti" (Zerlina's Aria)   *soprano*

Batti, batti, o bel Masetto,	Hit [her], hit [her], o charming Masetto,
la tua povera Zerlina.	your poor Zerlina.
Starò qui come agnellina	I'll stay here like a lambkin
le tue botte ad aspettar	waiting for your blows.
Lascierò straziar mi il crine	I'll let [you] pull my hair,
lascierò cavarmi gli occhi,	I'll let [you] gouge out my eyes,
e le care tue manine	and your dear little hands
lieta poi saprò baciar.	I will then kiss cheerfully.
Ah, lo vedo, non hai core!	Ah, I see it, you don't have the heart!
Pace, pace, o vita mia,	Peace, peace, o my life,
in contento ed allegria	contentedly and cheerfully
notte e dì vogliam passar.	we will spend day and night.
Sì, sì, sì—	Yes, yes, yes—

Two young peasants, Zerlina and her bridegroom Masetto, together with a group of their friends were on their way to their wedding when they were intercepted by Don Giovanni. With the help of his servant Leporello Don Giovanni sent everybody off to eat and drink in his castle while keeping Zerlina with himself. Almost yielding to Don Giovanni's charm, Zerlina would have come to grief if Donna Elvira, the discarded wife of Don Giovanni, had not in her turn intercepted her and sent her back to the wedding party. But Masetto does not take the faux pas of his bride quietly. In exasperation he threatens her with physical punishment, calls her names, and finally crumples on a bench, sulking. At this point Zerlina, a clever and resourceful girl, feels that the reconciliation she desires will have to be brought about by some clever move. So she offers herself to Masetto's blows, knowing full well that there is in him more bark than bite. We can imagine the scene: Masetto sitting on his bench, elbows on his knees, head on his knuckles, staring into the distance, trembling with rage. Zerlina, on her knees at one side of the bench, will start singing with her head bowed, arms open, offering herself in sacrifice like a lamb prepared for the knife. She must sound sincere, but many little signs tell us that there is humor in her supposed humility.

The tempo is *Andante grazioso,* ♩ = 52; the indication of style, *sempre legato.* It should be possible to sing from the first "Batti" to "aspettar" with only one breath after "Zerlina," the phrases unfolding with loveliness. Zerlina's goodness must make her irresistible to Masetto. And she knows how to complement humility with flattery. Do not forget to stress "*bel* Masetto" every time it comes. (The blows have not come yet.) "Batti, batti" is repeated, in a higher range and detached, and "la *tua* Zerlina" is stressed. After all, she is his. (No blows.) She comes closer, still on her knees, and partially undoes her hair, offering some strands to Masetto with her hands, resignation in her voice, "Lascierò straziar mi il crine." She feels she has to tempt him further and offers him her wide-open eyes to scratch and gouge. Then, stretching the horror picture beyond any believable limit, she says that when he will have done with her she will kiss his dear little hands. But this is so hard to say that, pretending to be overcome by her own words, she has to take panting breaths in the middle of those words. That is the meaning of the sixteenth rests in "ca-re" and "mani-ne." Do not be afraid to exaggerate that effect; it is obviously wanted. Then sing with a strong voice and with stress on the syllable "-ciar" of "baciar" the concluding phrase of the section. (The G apoggiaturas on "baciar" are eighth notes, as written.)

We guess that Masetto, unable to stand the cruel picture, has gotten up and taken a step aside. Very tenderly now, Zerlina tries another angle. Sing the return of "Batti, batti" piano and with charm. And, as a touch of flattery seems appropriate, Zerlina sings "o *bel* Masetto" with fervor (possibly embracing his legs with both her arms). Sing warmly to the end of the phrase ("aspettar"). The next three lines contain few words ("Ah, lo vedo") and the repeat of a teasing little pattern.

We might decide that Zerlina tickles Masetto lightly in the ribs on that pattern and that he tries to shake her hands off, justifying the words "non hai core," said with a slight chuckle, the phrase ending with a leisurely fermata on both notes of "core."

Let us mark the *allegro* at ♪. = 64. Masetto's resistance is coming to an end, and with it Zerlina's repentance. She will now use the most natural of weapons, the promise to give her man happiness by day and by night. Masetto is seated again and almost relaxed, and Zerlina, standing in the back of him, her hands on his shoulders, will let the rocking movement of the 6/8 invade her little by little and finally pass into the body of Masetto, who will follow it without even noticing it. Sing the first "Pace, pace, o vita mia" mezzo forte, the second piano, "in contento ed allegria" cheerfully. Breathe after "notte e dì," before "vogliam passar," every time the phrase occurs (three times). This way you avoid having to breathe just before the runs "passar," a breath often heard. The runs must be very light and cheerful, a bit frivolous, a bit suggestive of the joys of the nights to come. In order to give meaning to the "si, si, si" Zerlina must imagine Masetto shaking his head stubbornly "no, no, no" on the words "vogliam passar," not so stubbornly the second time. The last lines are sung with gentleness but with the knowledge that Zerlina has regained Masetto's confidence totally and easily. She can now slip smilingly onto his lap.

I have used quite a few suggestions for the staging of this aria in order to stress its meaning. It is essentially a scene. Although staging is not the purpose of this study, it is indispensable for the interpreter, in the case of many arias, to have a clear picture of the physical setup and to act the scenes out mentally even on the concert stage.

"Deh vieni alla finestra" *baritone*

Deh vieni alla finestra
o mio tesoro,
deh vieni a consolar

Ah, come to the window,
o my treasure,
ah, come to bring relief

il pianto mio.	to my tears.
Se neghi a me di dar	If you refuse to give me
qualche ristoro,	some consolation,
davanti agli occhi tuoi	before your eyes
morir vogl'io.	I want to die.
Tu ch'hai la bocca dolce	You whose lips are sweeter
più del miele,	than honey,
tu che il zucchero porti	you who carry sugar
in mezzo al core,	in the depth of your heart,
non esser, gioia mia,	don't be, my delight,
con me crudele!	cruel with me!
Lasciati almen veder,	Let [me] at least see you,
mio bell'amore.	my beautiful love.

With the complicity of Leporello Don Giovanni has enticed Donna Elvira to leave her house. Now, faithful to his custom of seducing without discrimination women of all walks of life, he sings this serenade to Elvira's chambermaid.

The man who sings this graceful tune is the same who fought off a furious crowd in the finale of act 1 and who will later challenge the statue of the Commendatore. But in this moment he plays the traditional part of the Spanish lover singing under the window of his beloved, accompanying himself on the mandolin. His voice must be light and warm. It is totally different from the voice that will reply "Ho fermo il cor in petto, non ho timor, verrò" to the terrifying invitation of the statue.

Above the strumming of the mandolin and the pizzicati of the strings the voice sings a lovely legato, well supported, not too intense, and certainly not in keeping with the text, which speaks of tears and sudden death. Below the vocal line the mandolin nonchalantly gives the lie to the big words and cheerfully goes its playful way. But Don Giovanni is a gentleman when he wishes to be, and his singing must be polished and without flaws.

Remember, Don Giovanni wants to be heard by the chambermaid but not by the neighbors. "Deh vieni alla finestra": Spin the first interval of a fourth with grace and with no rough attack on the D. A quarter-note appoggiatura is generally made on the downbeat on "finestra." Sing long vowels on "*mio*" and "tes*oro*"—same remark as above on the fourth upward on the second "vieni," same possibility of a quarter-note appoggiatura on the downbeat on "consol*ar*." Treat the dotted eighths and the sixteenths on "mio" very smoothly.

During the two-bar interlude, pretend to look slightly to right or left of center and above you, at the window, with some expectation; then resume your singing in a new attempt. The next two lines can be sung mezzo forte with a lyric stress on "ristoro" and a false pathos on "morir vogl'io," darkening the low notes. The expectation becomes more obvious on the next interlude and the voice more caressing on "la bocca dolce" and "più del miele." Note that "più del miele" is more generally sung than "più che il miele." The exaggeration of sweetness must increase on the "zucchero" and "in mezzo al core." During the next interlude, you may show some impatience. The voice becomes pleading and stronger on "con me crudele" and almost heartbreaking on "mio bell'amore." The tiniest ritardando can be made on the word "amore."

The canzonetta sung in this spirit is proof that a strong baritone can also be lyrically light. It also tests the singer's taste. Two great baritones of the early twentieth century have recorded this piece, ending fortissimo on the upper octave. Such a ridiculous error is no longer possible. Today we know that we do not have to demonstrate our vocal powers every minute we are onstage.

"Il mio tesoro"   *tenor*

Il mio tesoro intanto	My treasure, meanwhile,
andate a consolar,	go to comfort,
e del bel ciglio il pianto	and the tears of her beautiful eyes
cercate di asciugar.	try to dry.
Ditele, che i suoi torti	Tell her that her wrongs
a vendicar io vado	I have gone to avenge,
che sol di stragi e morti	that messenger of bloodshed and death
nunzio vogl'io tornar.	I want to return.

This aria, duly performed at the premiere of *Don Giovanni* in Prague, was replaced in the Vienna premiere by another aria at the request of the tenor in that cast. That other aria was "Dalla sua pace." Mozart had had to accept the fact that the tenor, Morella, could not cope with the vocal difficulties of "Il mio tesoro." The final result of that change is that for many years Don Ottavio has sung two arias, one in act 1 and one in act 2.

In the scene preceding "Il mio tesoro" the group of virtuous characters hunting Don Giovanni have acquired the conviction that he is a murderer as well as a would-be rapist. Don Ottavio, one of the group, entrusts his grieving fiancée Donna Anna to the care of his friends and pledges to bring the wrath of justice upon the criminal. "Un ricorso vo far a chi si deve, e in pocchi istanti vendicarvi prometto" ("I will call upon the proper authorities, and within a few moments I promise to avenge you"). And he sings.

Andante grazioso ($\downarrow$ = 84–88): Two moods will dominate the aria, care for Donna Anna and redress of the harm done to her. The first mood calls for warmth, charm, commiseration, the second for firmness, virility, authority. Both show facets of the same man, a refined, aristocratic, sensitive human being, given more to loving than to fighting but bracing himself to fulfill his duty as a man of honor. All these features must be reflected in the quality of the voice of Don Ottavio, in his musical distinction, in the elegance of his vocabulary. The aria can be sung only by a nimble, flexible voice free of inopportune loudness and heavy darkness. The runs as well as the very long sustained notes must sound effortless, the more virile phrases must ring without being noisy. This is a great challenge that every tenor should be ambitious to meet.

After seven bars of introduction by the clarinets, the bassoons, and the violins, the voice enters, singing animatedly and brilliantly. The first words are full of love, the *o*'s in "tesoro" round and warm. The next two fragments establish a pattern that will be used throughout the aria: "andate" is accented on the vowel in "-da-," and the high note is soft and discreet. It is the same with "andate a consolar," where there is a crescendo on the four notes on the vowel [a] and a diminuendo on the following E-natural and the F. "E del bel ciglio il pianto" (supported by the horns) is tender and velvety. The pattern is felt again in "asciugar," the F on the vowel /a/ is sustained mezzo forte, but the following triplets are very light and piano, with a slight ritardando. The word "cercate" now comes three times in succession, the first piano, the second mezzo forte, the third almost forte on the F but again with a real lightness on the G, the E-flat, and the C, with the voice well sustained again on "di asciugar." The final D can be shortened slightly in order to allow a deep respiration before the famous long F on the next "cercate." These are tedious indications when put on paper, and they require time and patience from the reader, but their use can make the difference between a monotonous, insipid performance and warm, musical, and human singing.

It would be ideal if we could hear the long F and the whole phrase sung without taking a breath. If it is possible for the singer to do so without reducing the F to a dull, lifeless sound and without holding the audience in anguished suspense, all will be admirable. It has often been done, but a singer unable to do it may without shame take a breath in the space taken up by the eighth that prolongs the F into the next bar. The resulting silence, however, must be very short and the restart of the tone perfectly smooth and unhurried. Starting the F piano, then repeating the vowel /a/ mentally a number of times, a little bigger each time, and lightening the G and the ensuing run is a good way to avoid the unpopular respiration. At the end of the run the syllable "-te" of "cercate" is generally sung on the last two notes only (E-flat–C) instead of on the last four notes.

We now come to the second mood, revenge. The voice discards its velvet in favor of a vibrant metal. Although the downbeats are strong, do not detach them from the phrase, which must stay strong to the end: "*Di*tele . . . *a* vendicar." The mild Don Ottavio now uses threatening words "stragi," "morte." Pronounce them with great energy. One interval requires vocal wisdom: In "nunzio vogl'io tornar" the second time, from middle G on "tor-" to high A on "-nar," while going down on "vogl'io tornar," keep the voice in the upper resonances, ignore the fact that the interval is a ninth, keep the start of the A in the same resonance and the sound of the vowel /a/ ("-nar") very similar to the sound of the preceding vowel /o/ (tor-), singing as if the two pitches were near each other. The explosion of an open sound on the A must be avoided at all cost.

The following run is the transition from the second mood back to the first. Don Ottavio sings the first four bars of the run inspired by the idea of revenge, then shifts to the tenderness of love in the last two bars. A wise singer, who wants to be safe and to preserve the best quality of his voice, should sing in one breath from "nunzio" to after the half note E-flat, take a breath on the added eighth, sing to the A preceding the chromatic pattern, breathe, and devote his most lovely tones to this pattern, diminuendo and rallentando on the last bar. As I said before, it is true that some singers can go the whole way without breathing. I shall admire them if at the same time they have conveyed with beauty the change of Don Ottavio's mood and reintroduced the sweeter, more touching feeling of "Il mio tesoro." After the long repeat, note the two fermatas on the long F of "vado." The note should be a crescendo to and including a real fermata on the low F. In the run on the next "tornar," the notes starting each section (G, E, C) should be started mezzo piano, the descending lines sung crescendo. Then the F on "nunzio" and the syncopations to the G's on "vogl'io" will be given full voice, the same energy being maintained to the end of the aria.

The long phrases of this aria call for a very skillful handling of the breath. I believe that the concept of "saving" one's breath is wrong. The tenor should work on a very strong buildup of the lower body support and constantly feed the voice in the long phrases by a crescendo of intensity instead of letting the tone stall at one dynamic level in order to "save breath." By the way, all tenors should learn to master "Il mio tesoro" as a challenge they must meet if they want to become masters in singing.

"Mi tradì"   *soprano*

In quali eccessi, o Numi	In what excesses, o Gods,
in quai misfatti orribili, tremendi	in what horrible, tremendous misdeeds
è avvolto il sciagurato.	has the scoundrel entangled himself!
Ah no! non può tardar l'ira del cielo,	Ah no! the wrath of heaven cannot tarry,
la giustizia tardar.	justice cannot wait.
Sentir già parmi la fatale saetta	I seem to foresee already the deadly blow
che gli piomba sul capo.	that will fall on his head.
Aperto veggio il baratro mortal.	I see the deadly abyss gaping.
Misera Elvira!	Miserable Elvira!
Che contrasto d'affetti	what contrasting feelings
in sen ti nasce!	are born in your heart!
Perchè questi sospiri? e quest'ambascie?	Why these sighs? and this anguish?
Mi tradì quell'alma ingrata,	That ungrateful soul betrayed me,
infelice, o Dio, mi fa.	unhappy, o God, he makes me.
Ma tradita, e abbandonata	Yet betrayed and forsaken
provo ancor per lui pietà.	I still feel pity for him.
Mi tradì . . .	That ungrateful soul . .
Quando sento il mio tormento	When I listen to my torment
di vendetta il cor favella.	my heart speaks of vengeance.
Ma se guardo il suo cimento	But when I look at the danger [he is in]
palpitando il cor mi va.	my heart is trembling.
Mi tradì . . .	That ungrateful soul . . .

After the triumph of *Don Giovanni* in Prague, Mozart took the opera to Vienna. For a different house as well as for a different cast he made some changes in the score, adding and substituting, in order to accommodate the singers' vocal personalities and their demands. The aria "Mi tradì" was written to fulfill the wishes of the dramatic soprano cast as Donna Elvira. It followed a duet added for Leporello and Zerlina, number 21*b*, which is never performed anymore. Fortunately, the superb aria has survived, but it comes now immediately after the equally superb tenor aria "Il mio tesoro." There is nothing wrong with hearing two superb arias in succession except for the fact that, opera being theater and *Don Giovanni* being a drama, two static arias coming one right after the other create a long gap in the action. That is why number 21*c*, "Mi tradì," is sometimes performed as number 4*b*, as a reaction by Donna Elvira to Leporello's insulting reading of the catalog. It seems very right in that place, the indignation and the sorrow of a wife betrayed and scoffed at bursting forth in striking contrast with the biting sarcasm of Leporello's aria. Even if the aria is kept as number 21*c*, it is useful for the soprano to feel and act as if Leporello's insults were still in her ear, adding bitterness to her awareness of Don Giovanni's misdeeds. It is in this mood that the recitative starts.

Recitative: The tempo for the orchestra is *allegro*, $\quad$ = 104. The strings play vigorously, with soft inflections at the end of each phrase. Elvira sings forte and more slowly, articulating very strongly the double consonants: "eccessi," "misfatti orribili," and the *tr* in "tremendi." The last two syllables of "sciagurato" are lengthened as if said with shame. What she has heard is almost beyond belief, and she reacts to it with horror. During the next two and a half measures in the orchestra, her thoughts turn toward the inevitable consequences for the criminal. With awe and solemnity, still forte, she senses the punishment will come from above, and it will be a mighty one. Sing slowly, broadening "l'ira del cielo" and, again, "tardar." The vision then becomes more precise and frightens Elvira. Broaden "Sentir già parmi" and speed up "la fatale saetta," which the orchestra then describes unmistakably. Elvira sees it falling on Don Giovanni, "che gli piomba sul capo," once and again. The next phrase is tragic, very slowly declaimed, going almost to a whisper on "il baratro mortal." During the next three bars Elvira frees herself from the tragic vision and turns to reflecting upon herself. The voice becomes warmer and more tender, "Misera Elvira" (stress "contrasto" and "in *sen* ti nasce.") The next two orchestral bars are a wailing, but a noble one, fitting with great beauty the nature of Elvira who asks herself, "Perchè questi sospiri?" After the insistent and sensitive line of the orchestra and a long silence clearly marked, Elvira sighs with anxiety, pianissimo on "e quest'ambascie." She judges Don Giovanni, she suffers from his misdeeds, she clearly foresees his fate, but still she pities him and does not desire any personal revenge. The word *noble* defines her nature and should prompt the color of voice the soprano should use when performing the very difficult aria that follows.

Aria: Once established, the tempo, $\downarrow$ = 126–132, must be kept absolutely steady in 4/4. The aria must be sung with intense feeling and a light, flexible voice constantly able to match the colors of the orchestration. It must continue the even lines of the runs played alternately by the winds and the strings. Voice and instruments together seem to flow endlessly, weaving a shimmering texture of a great many colors, rising and descending around a medium-high level. There is not one sixteenth note in the whole piece, and nothing anywhere should suggest an edge or a jolt; only a gliding continuity is wanted, swelling and diminishing with the shapes and the range of each phrase.

Let me divide the aria into parts and number the measures: part A, bars 1–16; part B, bars 16–40; the return of part A, bars 40–55; part C, bars 56–82; a recall of part A, bars 82–97; and a coda, bars 97–130.

Part A: For the voice, measures 1 and 2, sung piano, are an upbeat to measure 3 where the syllable "-gra-" in "ingrata" accents the phrase. It is the same for bars 4 and 5. The G in bar 6 must come as the exact continuation of the scale played by the bassoon in bars 4 and 5. The next accent is on the E-flat in bar 7, to be followed by an accent on the E-flat in bar 9. We see the pattern: the G's in bars 6 and 8 are not stressed high notes but are light and unstressed. The next phrase goes from the second beat of bar 9 to the first beat of bar 12, without a breath. The ascent to the A-flat in bar 10 is light and fluid, with the accent of the phrase coming on the final E-flat in bar 12. The same pattern holds in the following phrase.

Part B: The effects are the same but repeated with infinite variety. In bar 22 the voice enters the line the flute has played in bars 21 and 22; then, in bar 26, it enters the line of the clarinet in bar 25, and so on, the ascent of the voice to the high notes (A-natural in bar 26, B-flat in bar 33) being always light and evenly matched to all the other notes. In the runs of eighths all notes must be exactly even in value and size, the first of two tied eighths never more accented than the second.

Return of part A: The repeat of "Mi tradì quell'alma ingrata" (bar 40) is treated the same as the first time, possibly sung with more contrasts but without breaking the continuity of the phrases. Elvira yields to the irresistible desire to express her sorrow and does so intensely but with a dignified restraint in both parts A. But she cannot dwell long on her own misery, and in part C her heart goes out to Don Giovanni in spite of herself and the whole world. Her pity nevertheless does not cancel her ever-present sorrow.

Part C sees Elvira behaving like most human beings and thinking of revenge (bars 56–63). Bars 56–59 must be sung with a much darker voice, a voice that speaks of physical as well as sentimental torture. Bars 60–63 are forte, and the G-flat and A-flat show a certain bitterness, for the first time in this aria. But immediately (bars 64–71) Elvira curbs her thoughts of revenge and in a breathless voice reveals the cruelty of her inner fight. Sing the notes in bars 68–71 as a legato interrupted by an overwhelming emotion, not like detached staccato notes. The difficult run (bars 72–77) should be sung if possible without breathing, very lightly, the seemingly erratic intervals creating the impression of a disturbed mind, a woman almost staggering aimlessly. In order to reach the end of the run more comfortably, replace the last "il cor" by lengthening "palpitando" to the last note. To keep the effect of "staggering" alive, it is possible in bars 79–82 to replace "il cor mi va" by "palpitando" again.

In the next repeat of part A, "Mi tradì" is sung pianissimo, almost as an unconscious obsession, something one says again and again almost without knowing it.

The coda (bars 100 and following) is a return to reality. It starts piano but soon grows in intensity. In bars 103–104, "e abbandonata" is mezzo forte. Conductors have allowed a number of modifications in the following run. In bar 105 it is possible to sing "-na-a-ta-a-a-a," to breathe before the B-flat, to sing a vowel *a* to and including B-flat (the first eighth note in bar 107) to omit the notes D–C–A-natural–B (doubled by flutes and clarinets anyway), then to go on with the run on the vowel *a*, to tie it without a breath to "per lui-i" (bar 111), to breathe after the E-flat starting bar 112, and to sing "per lui pie-e-" in that bar. The next breath comes after "lui" in bar 16, the next after the A in bar 118. To the end of the aria, then do whatever keeps the phrase growing in strength and fervor. There is no particular rule restricting you.

Once the prescriptions outlined above have been studied and assimilated and are followed, this remarkable aria becomes highly expressive and consequently highly enjoyable to perform. Patience, and many rehearsals, are recommended, but the result is worth any effort. Feel the aria as the natural, sincere meditation of a sad and noble woman, and it will give you great vocal enjoyment.

Mozart, *Die Entführung aus dem Serail*

"Wer ein Liebchen hat gefunden" *bass*

Wer ein Liebchen hat gefunden,
die es treu und redlich meint,
lohn'es ihr durch tausend Küsse,
mach'ihr all das Leben süsse,
sei ihr Tröster, sei ihr Freund.
Trallalera . . .

He who has found a sweetheart
who means to be true and loyal,
reward her with a thousand kisses,
sweeten all her life,
be her solace, be her friend.
Trallalera . . .

Doch sie treu sich zu erhalten,
schliess'er Liebchen sorglich ein;
denn die losen Dinger haschen
jeden Schmetterling, und naschen
gar zu gern von fremdem Wein.
Trallalera . . .

But to keep her faithful to him,
he must carefully lock Sweetheart up;
for the fickle things try to catch
every butterfly, and taste
all too gladly somebody else's wine.
Trallalera . . .

Sonderlich beim Mondenscheine,
Freunde, nehmt sie wohl in Acht:
oft lauscht da ein junges Herrchen,
kirrt und lockt das kleine Närrchen,
und dann Treue, gute Nacht.
Trallalera . . .

Particularly by moonlight,
friends, watch over her:
often a young lordling is listening then,
cooing and tempting the little fool,
and then, faithfulness, good night!
Trallalera . . .

Osmin is the overseer of Pasha Selim's harem. This scene from the first act of the opera takes place partly outside, partly inside the palace gardens. Inside, Constanze, a Spanish lady, and Blondchen, her English maid, are kept captive. The pasha tries to win Constanze's love, and Osmin, whatever his limitations, the favors of Blondchen. As he sings the following aria from inside the gardens and as we the public are outside, it is customary to have Osmin stand high on a ladder picking cherries from a cherry tree, maybe eating some on the spot, and singing over the garden wall.

The tempo, *andante*, ♩ = 58, should suggest the leisurely ease of a well-fed, middle-aged man dawdling in that cherry tree put there for his enjoyment—or any similar pleasant situation. His voice should be round and meaty although changing in character during the aria.

The first verse is all sweetness and good humor, as if Osmin indeed had a faithful girlfriend and treated her to the best of everything. Delight in such words as "Liebchen" and "treu." The two appoggiaturas on "ihr" and "all" are like two caresses. The vowel /y/ in "Küsse" and "süsse" must be placed well on the tip of the lips. The first "sei ihr Tröster" is mezzo forte, the second almost forte, the repeat of "sei ihr Freund" in the lower octave, comfortable and oozing with goodness. The "Trallaleras" are carefree and light at first, then enthusiastic and forte. The trill on the last A, well done, can add a lot to the suggested fun.

The mood changes sharply in the second verse, in which Osmin reveals his true character. The verse begins piano in a less friendly voice than before, insinuating suspicion.

"Schliess'er Liebchen sorglich ein" is sung firmly and quite naturally, as it expresses Osmin's function in life. Now the two appoggiaturas on "losen" and "Schmetterling" are nasty, and "Dinger" contains some scorn. "Gar zu gern von fremdem Wein" is a reproach, even an accusation the second time, and the lower octave must sound rather disgusted. The "Trallaleras" nevertheless return to carefreeness: Osmin knows how to deal with fickleness of any kind.

With the third verse Osmin reaches the heart of his mission in life. He is the sentinel watching by night for any approaching young man. The voice now sounds a warning, with a certain secrecy in it. The urgent four bars of allegro say it all with irritation and in scornful terms, as the "Liebchen" has become a "Närrchen." The fermata creates suspense: What does Osmin propose to do? Nothing. He returns to the cozy original tempo, for he is not one to worry about such things after all. The low "gute Nacht" could be used to show that he could not care less, and the last "Trallaleras" are just an outpouring of his general well-being, his physical prosperity, and his considerable importance in the palace.

This aria is a delightful fantasy, the love song of the seraglio's overseer, which had to be different. The bass singer should sing it for what it is, not clowning but understanding that with Mozart there is a psychological study even in a trifle and that the cheerful character of the song does not preclude its value as a human document.

"O wie ängstlich"   *tenor*

Constanze, Constanze!	Constance! Constance!
dich wieder zu sehen, dich!	to see you again, you!
O wie ängstlich, o wie feurig	Oh how anxiously, oh how ardently
klopft mein liebevolles Herz!	beats my heart filled with love!
Und des Widersehens Zähre	and the tears of reunion
lohnt der Trennung bangen Schmerz,	reward the anxious pain of separation.
Schon zittr'ich und wanke,	Already I tremble and falter,
schon zag'ich und schwanke,	already I am quivering and shaking,
es hebt sich die schwellende Brust.	my heart is swelling and panting.
Ist das ihr Lispeln?	Is that her whisper?
Es wird mir so bange!	I feel so apprehensive!
War das ihr Seufzen?	Was that her sighing?
Es glüht mir die Wange.	My cheek is burning.
Täuscht mich die Liebe,	Does love deceive me,
War es ein Traum?	was it a dream?
O wie ängstlich . . .	O how anxiously . . .

The plot of the opera is a Turkish story of abduction by pirates, captivity, love, and liberation. Belmonte, a young Spanish nobleman, has been separated from his beloved Constanze, who with her maid Blondchen is held captive in Pasha Selim's house.

But Pedrillo, Belmonte's servant, has managed to enter the service of the pasha and has been able to see the two women. He reports to his young master that Constanze remains faithful in spite of the pasha's entreaties. Furthermore, Pedrillo will attempt to liberate the prisoners. If he succeeds, Belmonte may soon see Constanze again. That hope inspires Belmonte to sing this aria.

Belmonte's voice is a light lyric tenor, capable of romantic lyricism, sweetness, and easy flexibility. In this Mozart opera with its extensive dialogues, the arias are expressions of emotions and do not carry much dramatic impact. It is in the spoken scenes that the plot unfolds and progresses. Belmonte sings songs of love, faith and hope, not songs of action. Within that frame, however, his arias are songs of noble inspiration.

The initial four bars of recitative are very slow. Twice the voice rises pianissimo from the orchestral chord and stops to let the echo by the oboe rise slowly in turn. The sound is just above a sigh for the first "Constanze," stronger but still very tender on the second "Constanze." "Dich wieder zu sehen" is pianissimo and very slow, and if it were possible to express adoration in a single syllable, it would have to be on "dich."

The tempo of the *andante* is basically $\flat$ = 100 with, of course, many small fluctuations in performance. The phrases are alternately very legato and broken into very short spans, as if panting. The first four bars are very legato, the first two piano (with two equal $\flat$ on "wie"), the third and fourth surging to forte on "feurig." Then comes the first panting pattern. From a letter by Mozart to his father we know that the pattern imitates the fluttering impatience of his heart, for he was himself to marry his Constanze very shortly after writing this score, so that he identified himself with the enamored Belmonte. The voice stays piano, warm and alive. A slight stress on the first note of each group of two accentuates the feeling of impatience: "klopft mein l*ie*/bev*ol*/les H*e*rz," and so on. By contrast, until the return of the broken pattern, all the phrases must be sung with the most ideal legato. In bar 9 "klopft mein liebe . . ." begins piano, and the run following, very light in weight, is nevertheless a real crescendo to the final "Herz."

The next two phrases are a lovely and even legato, which lasts through bars 21–24. But in those last four bars there is a lyric stress on the syncopated E of "lohnt" and the F-natural of "T*r*ennung." The two short fragments of the broken pattern have now two stronger tops in "wanke" and "schwanke." "Schon zag'ich" is forte (bar 28) and "und schwanke" (bar 29) piano, the accompaniment also alternating forte and piano. The next six bars, bars 30–35, are a progressive crescendo, each repeat of "es hebt sich die schwellende Brust" being stronger and a little faster than the preceding one, reaching forte—but not a dramatic forte—on the last "die schwellende Brust."

A new pattern, flowing and like whispering, begins with bar 36, suggesting some hidden presence, so that after listening Belmonte says almost hopefully, "Ist das ihr Lispeln?" He should be allowed to say slowly, "Es wird mir so bange," with an emotion that justifies the return of the pattern of the fluttering heart, light at first, very light on "mir die Wange," bar 46. The next five short phrases, bars 47–52, are a progressive crescendo, a mixture of hope and anxiety, with the downbeat notes well stressed ("L*ie*be," "Tr*au*m"). After a forte on the last "Liebe," bar 52, a pianissimo subito and a tenuto on the high A and the next three notes (bars 53–54) and a holding of the E of "Traum" *ppp* for one additional beat create a beautiful effect when done slowly and without losing the intense feeling.

The music of the next fourteen bars repeats what has already been sung and studied earlier. From now on there will be no new elements of interpretation, only some variations of the vocal line based on the same patterns. There is a little more strength than before on the repeats of "es glüht mir die Wange," bars 74–75. The panting pattern stays very light and piano, contrasting with the well-sustained legato in bars 83–84. Bars

86–89, "Schon zittr'ich und wanke," are also legato, with an accent on "wanke" and on "schwanke." Seven bars before the end of the vocal line there is again a well-sustained legato as in bars 83–84. Five bars before the end there is a crescendo to forte going to A ("*mein* liebe-"). The value of the appoggiatura on the A is an eighth note. The repeat of the same figure is piano; the appoggiaturas are equivalent to eighth notes again.

No amount of precise instruction will suffice to insure the beauty of a performance of this aria. The imagination of the tenor and his musicianship must help him to hear each phrase before singing it, to hear his own voice, light and nimble, melting on the legato places, rebounding as if on elfin feet from note to note in the broken lines, singing an interrupted legato and not a staccato, while feeling in his heart the heavenly expectation of a reunion with the beloved one.

How useful and clever it would be for dramatic voices to study and practice such an aria as this, where instrumental precision is united with the most romantic sweetness!

"Durch Zärtlichkeit und Schmeicheln"   *soprano*

Durch Zärtlichkeit und Schmeicheln,	Through tenderness and flattery,
Gefälligkeit und Scherzen,	kindness and joking,
erobert man die Herzen	one conquers easily
der guten Mädchen leicht.	the hearts of nice girls.
Doch mürrisches Befehlen	But grouchy domineering,
und Poltern, Zanken, Plagen	and scolding, quarreling, annoying,
macht, dass in wenig Tagen	cause in a few days
so Lieb als Treu entweicht.	both love and faithfulness to vanish.

This aria introduces Blondchen to the listeners of the opera. The pert chambermaid of Constanze has caught the fancy of Osmin, overseer of the seraglio, a character short of sweetness and refinement. Blondchen, whose heart belongs to young Pedrillo, tries to keep Osmin at a distance and constantly fights a battle of wits with him. In this aria she gives him a lesson in successful courtship as practiced among her English people.

The aria presents a great opportunity for a clear and nimble coloratura voice to show itself to best advantage. On the operatic stage it is accompanied by an all-string orchestra, and there is never a problem for the voice of carrying through. The singer should feel free to use only that amount of voice which fits the music but must never give up sparkle, brilliance, wit, and charm.

The *andante grazioso* is in 2/4, but it is helpful to think it in eighth notes at ♪ = 120. Blondchen will paint in music two approaches to courtship and repeatedly make Osmin hear how love runs away from those who use the wrong approach.

The first approach is made of tenderness, sweetness, and good humor, which means, of course, piano, legato, the voice flowing evenly on all values, a very light and tender appoggiatura on "Schmeicheln" and on "Herzen," a caress in the voice on "Schmeicheln," a smile in it for "Scherzen," a slightly rounder, promising tone on both "der guten Mädchen leicht," a diminuendo on the F-sharp of the first "guten" and on the high A of the second "guten." Blondchen is all milk and honey.

The second approach is characterized by grouchiness, anger, annoyance, and a domineering manner. It is Osmin's approach. In the same way as the musical phrases trade their curves for sharply dotted rhythms, Blondchen's voice turns aggressive, still piano at first but already mezzo forte on "Befehlen," again piano on "Poltern," and again mezzo forte on "Plagen," the crescendos of the two short phrases aimed at Osmin like darts and the repeat of "und Poltern, Zanken, Plagen" reaching a biting forte on the B of "Plagen" in imitation of Osmin's rough ways. Returning to piano on "macht, dass . . ." Blondchen sings her warning very reasonably and softly: In a short time love runs away from such treatment. Again the sweet appoggiaturas make the phrase pleasant and very feminine. The octave jump on "Tagen" sounds like the warning of a dainty finger under Osmin's nose. "So Lieb als Treu entweicht" is serious, with the accent on the double sharp on "entweicht," like a tiny springboard for love to fly away. The same idea is magnified by the run upward after the long E. This long value must be sung piano, in a very clear vowel /a/, the voice spinning lightly while the soprano repeats the /a/ mentally several times and then taking off, if possible without a breath to the top of the run. A breath before "entweicht" will enable a well-trained voice to avoid another breath before the run.

The first low notes of the run must be sung with some of the upper resonances needed for the high B's, the soprano feeling the continuity of the vibration from the start. A short and smooth ritardando can add grace to the three eighth notes, B, G-sharp, and E, before returning *a tempo* for the concluding "so Lieb als Treu entweicht." Osmin must have the impression that he has seen love and faithfulness fly away—and maybe for good.

The repeat of the first approach is not different from the first time. Possibly Blondchen could sing it as sweetly but a little louder, with promising warmth, especially on "der guten Mädchen leicht," to stress the reward one can expect from such an approach. Conversely, the second approach is made more undesirable by strong accents on "Be*feh*len" and twice on "Plagen," the second time maybe reaching forte. The warning has also become more earnest in the broken lines of "dass in wenig Tagen" sung mezzo forte. The pattern of the first verse will repeat itself: a breath before "entweicht," a very clear vowel /a/ in which the voice spins during the long A, the continuation of this spin to the top of the run, a graceful short ritardando on the three A's, the E, and the C-sharp. It will repeat itself again in the next bars, although this time love flies away so high and far that, obviously, it will never return.

If the coloratura singing Blondchen can persuade herself that the high E's at the top of the last run are made of the same vibration as the middle of the run and that this vibration can still be inserted into a slim vowel /a/ at the very top of the line, then she will create the impression of limitless flight needed here. And it goes without saying that the sound of her voice must stay crystal-clear at all times.

Finally Blondchen, with great pedagogical sense, stresses each one of her original prescriptions, pausing after each word said with the proper color and expression, and insisting still more on an almost-laughing "Scherzen." She concludes with a certain vigor, sure to have done her best.

Osmin is not moved to change his ways.

Mozart, *Le Nozze di Figaro*

"Se vuol ballare"   *baritone/bass-baritone*

Bravo, signor padrone!	Bravo, my Lord and Master!
Ora incomincio	Now I begin
a capir il mistero,	to understand the mystery
e a veder schietto	and to see clearly
tutto il vostro progetto;	your entire plan;
a Londra, è vero?	to London, is that so?
Voi ministro,	You the envoy,
io corriero,	I the courier,
e la Susanna. . . .	and Susanna. . . .
secreta ambasciatrice.	secret ambassadress.
Non sarà, non sarà,	It shan't be, it shan't be,
Figaro il dice!	Figaro says so!
Se vuol ballare,	If he wants to dance,
signor Contino,	my dear little Count,
il chitarrino le suonerò, sì.	I'll play the guitar for him, indeed.
Se vuol venire	If he wants to come
nella mia scuola,	to my school,
la capriola le ensegnerò.	I'll teach him the caper.
Saprò, saprò, ma piano;	I'll know, I'll know, but slowly;
meglio ogni arcano	every mystery I shall discover better
dissimulando scoprir potrò.	by dissimulating.
L'arte schermendo,	Through the art of fencing,
l'arte adoprando,	the art of using people,
di quà pungendo,	here stinging,
di là scherzando,	there joking,
tutte le macchine rovescierò.	I shall upset the whole project.
Se vuol ballare . . .	If he wants to dance . . .

Figaro is the manservant of Count Almaviva, Susanna is the chambermaid of the countess; they are very much in love and will be married in the castle this very day. But in the scene preceding this aria, Susanna has revealed to a stunned Figaro that the count plans to revive the ancient right of priority the masters had over the bridegrooms on their wedding nights. Figaro will never allow this to happen, and his fight is the subject of the whole play. Left alone, Figaro in this aria assesses the situation.

Figaro's voice is that of a baritone or a bass-baritone. In Mozart's time all male voices that were not tenors were called bass, and it is impossible to deduce from the original castings which of the singers were higher and which were lower "basses." We know that the original Don Giovanni was a twenty-one-year-old baritone; we do not know whether there was a difference of voice color between the count and Figaro. In our time the custom has prevailed to cast a baritone as the count, a bass as Figaro, although the character and the social standing of the two men should call for more weight and power in the count, more sparkle and sharpness in Figaro. When I sang my first Figaro at the Metropolitan, alternating with the bass Ezio Pinza, Olin Downes of the *New York Times* remarked that "surprisingly, Singher's voice was perfectly suited to the part." At any rate, whatever his usual range, the man singing Figaro should imbue the part with wit, swiftness, and boldness, as opposed to darkness, heaviness, and triviality.

The tempo of the recitative when accompanied by the orchestra at the opera will, of course, depend on the conductor's taste. When given with piano, *moderato* will mean ♩ = 84–88 in the first part, the rhythm exactly as written, and the *andante* in the second part will be around ♩ = 60 and much freer. Figaro is furious, but he tries immediately to gain a clear view of the situation in order to find a way out of it. Susanna's departing words had been: "and you, brains." Brains will help Figaro to temper his anger at times, and both recitative and aria show the alternation of the two moods.

"Bravo, signor patrone" is angry sarcasm, said forte and bitterly, as will be the next two phrases, although Figaro feels a kind of acrid satisfaction in his awareness of the true situation, bad as it is. Stress strongly "mistero," "schietto," "progetto." During the interlude between "progetto" and "a Londra," he seems to reach the peak of his anger (first bar) and then to master it (second bar). He repeats the facts of the project. "A Londra, è vero" is wistful, "voi ministro" stressed pompously, "io corriero" said with false humility. A sudden emotion colors "e la Susanna," and the accompaniment slows down, becoming very sensitive, so that "secreta ambasciatrice" shudders with anguish. At this point Figaro reacts violently and decides on his own behavior. The last two bars are forte to fortissimo, therefore, with a strong stress on "dice."

The tempo of the aria is *allegretto,* ♩ = 144. Having made up his mind to fight, Figaro feels a certain relief, and it is in a subdued way that he formulates his plan of combat using, ironically, pleasant images. "Se vuol ballare" is piano and staccato, without exaggeration, "signor Contino" piano and legato with a stress on "Contino." The twelve bars on the "chitarrino" idea are light and a little bouncy, "chitarrino" itself plucked in imitation. The F on "sì" is either pianissimo or forte but must be slim and ringing.

With extreme urbanity Figaro invites the count to his school of dancing, the irony well dressed in legato. But his resentment explodes suddenly with the repeat of "Se vuol venire," is restrained for one bar, soars again on "la capriola," is dampened again for a while. At this point Figaro cannot go on pretending, not even to himself, and the gnawing desire to know more overcomes him. The several "saprò" are a crescendo on biting tones before the violence is curbed again, "piano, piano . . .," and the admonition to himself to be sly is very legato.

With the *presto* (think it in one, ♩ = 112) Figaro sees himself in action, even sees himself already triumphant. While coloring the voice according to the meaning of the words and pronouncing clearly, the singer must maintain a fluid legato and make a progressive crescendo from "L'arte schermendo" to "rovescierò." Then, after two bars of silence, he must contrast the successive words in forte and piano before allowing himself a good rallentando on the last two "rovescierò."

The return of "Se vuol ballare" is treated as it was the first time, but there must be a subtle change in the mood. Having imagined himself fighting and winning, Figaro has become optimistic so that there is in his singing the smiling satisfaction of the cat digesting the canary, at least for a few bars. From the repeat of "il chitarrino le suonerò" on, the fighting spirit invades him again. This time the F on "sì is very strong, the last "suonerò" fortissimo. Figaro runs off the stage impetuously to start the work that has been cut out for him.

Much has been done in the attempt to apply to "Se vuol ballare" the famous dictum on Beaumarchais's Figaro, "Figaro is revolution in action," and some interpreters have tried to broaden the scope of the aria to include great political strength. Although there is something new in the fact that an eighteenth-century servant plans an attack against his master, it is sensible to feel that at this point Figaro is rebelling against a nasty personal offense, rather than starting a class war and speaking in the name of the people. He is a swift, intense young man deeply in love. That is the key to his behavior.

"Non so più cosa son"   *soprano/mezzo-soprano*

Non so più cosa son,	I don't know anymore what I am,
cosa faccio,	what I'm doing,
or di foco, ora sono di ghiaccio	now I am burning hot, now I am ice cold,
ogni donna cangiar di colore	every woman [makes me] change color,
ogni donna mi fa palpitar.	every woman makes me tremble.
Solo ai nomi d'amor, di diletto,	At the mere words of love, of delight,
mi si turba, mi s'altera il petto,	my heart is troubled, is upset,
e a parlare mi sforza d'amore	and to speak of love
un desio che non posso spiegar	a desire forces me which I cannot explain.
Non so più . . .	I don't know anymore . . .
Parlo d'amor vegliando,	I speak of love [when I am] awake,
parlo d'amor sognando,	I speak of love [when I am] dreaming,
all acqua, all'ombra, ai monti,	to the water, to the shade, to the mountains,
ai fiori, all'erbe, ai fonti,	to the flowers, to the grass, to the springs,
all'eco, all'aria, ai venti,	to the echo, to the air, to the winds
che il suon dei vani accenti	which [carry away with them]
portano via con se	the sound of futile words.
Parlo d'amor vegliando . . .	I speak of love . . .
e se non ho chi m'oda	And when I have nobody who listens to me
parlo d'amor con me!	I speak of love to myself!

"This role can be played by a young and very pretty woman only; we do not have in our theatres a young man sufficiently mature to feel its nuances well enough. Excessively shy in front of the Countess, elsewhere a charming rascal; a restless, vague desire is the essence of his character. He rushes into puberty but without a plan, without knowledge, and throws himself entirely into every occurrence. In short, he is what at the bottom of her heart every mother might want her son to be, even though he would cause her much suffering" (Beaumarchais, "Caractères et habillements de la pièce," addendum to the "Preface" to *Le Marriage de Figaro*, my translation).

This time, then, there is a definite reason for Cherubino to be a "pants role" for a woman, either soprano or light mezzo-soprano. A heavy voice of dark character would not make sense.

In the preceding scene Cherubino has made a pest of himself, trying to kiss Susanna, stealing a ribbon destined for the countess's bonnet, forcing Susanna to accept a love song addressed to all women, prompting her to remark: poor Cherubino, you are crazy. And he agrees, ceasing his mischief for a while in order to reflect upon himself. He is still full of animation, a little out of breath, and the tempo is *allegro vivace*, ♩ = 104. It is not by any means a mad rush: Even Cherubino's quick mind needs time to sort out his feelings and put them into words. Above a very light orchestra (*con sordine*) Cherubino, wondering, sings piano, in rather short spurts and gushes but *not* staccato. The first phrase reaches its natural accent on "faccio" and not before, all the values being sung legato and without gaps—in particular, no gap after the quarter notes, which are long, well-sung values so that the phrase is neither a gallop nor a trot but a curve. The same goes for the second phrase, with the accent on "ghiaccio." In the next phrases, note that the word "donna" is written on two tied notes: sing them with a tender inflection, the B-flat as well sung as the E-flat. On the G the "donna" becomes glorified (bar 10), then tender again on two notes (bar 13). The vowel /o/ in "donna" is bright and never covered.

By now Cherubino has recovered his breath; he will sing two ascending phrases (bars 16–21) with a lyric crescendo on each of them, very legato. Then, leading up to it with a phrase of four rather restrained bars (22–25), he will come to the key word "un desio," repeat it in a soaring phrase, repeat it again alone, finally repeat the soaring phrase ending with a broad crescendo ("spiegar"). The /i/ in "desio" must be vibrant and given its full length every time it comes. Respect the following quarter-note silence: No carrying over to "Non so più" can be permitted, and I am sorry to hear it done sometimes.

Cherubino now recapitulates the symptoms that trouble him. I would advise the performer not to repeat the phrases exactly like the first time. Indicate that by now the boy has reconciled himself to this strange state and can even smile—sheepishly or cheerfully—at his description. After two bars of a kind of lull, Cherubino marvels at the odd things he sometimes does—"Parlo d'amor vegliando" and "parlo d'amor sognando"—asking all nature to witness his obsession. Sing legato with long dotted quarter notes and a progressive crescendo to "ai venti." The length of the fermata belongs to the second syllable "ven-*ti*" but "ven-" is already lengthened and both notes are at the same time forte and light (the wind can be such). Cherubino is thinking of how the wind carries away his "vani accenti," his futile words; start "che il suon" very piano, then make a strong crescendo on "con se," the G and its fermata very sonorous but with a feeling of depression on the tied E-flat, followed by a quiet resignation on the repeated "portano via con se" (vowel /e/ in "se").

Now the repeat of the whole page, starting with "parlo d'amor sognando," is slightly melancholy. The range is lower than the first time, and the soaring line on "all acqua, all'ombra, ai monti . . ." is now divided into short fragments enumerated without enthusiasm. The fermata on the last note of the phrase, "venti," comes on a descending interval, with a diminuendo, but "che il suon dei vani accenti portano via con se" is a strong crescendo, and distress is felt now during the fermata on the G, sadness on the repeated "portano via con se."

The *adagio* will be at least twice as slow as the preceding tempo; "E se non ho chi m'oda" is piano and resigned, the repeat mezzo forte and with a touch of drama: Will we hear some hidden threat? But no (*tempo primo*), it is an adolescent who is singing, sudenly lighthearted and self-centered, who still loves himself (the fermata on "con *me*" is piano and tender), and the last phrase is vigorous, like a challenge to the outside world.

Singing this aria *presto*, it is impossible to indicate all its changes in mood and to reveal Cherubino's mobile, intense heart. A sensitive artist will stress the progressive change from the excited, breathless boy to the adolescent delightfully suffering the pains of approaching manhood.

"Voi, che sapete"   *soprano/mezzo-soprano*

Voi, che sapete	You, who know
che cosa è amor,	what love is,
Donne, vedete,	Ladies, look
s'io l'ho nel cor.	if I have it in my heart.
Quello ch'io provo,	What I feel
vi ridirò,	I shall tell you,
è per me nuovo,	it is new to me,
capir nol so.	I don't understand it.
Sento un affetto	I feel an emotion
pien di desir,	full of desire,
ch'ora è diletto,	which now is a delight,
ch'ora è martir.	and now is a torment.
Gelo, e poi sento	I am freezing, and then I feel
l'alma avvampar,	my soul afire,
e in un momento	and in an instant
torno a gelar.	I return to freezing.
Ricerco un bene	I am looking for something
fuori di me,	outside of me,
non so chi il tiene,	I don't know who holds it,
non so cos'è.	I don't know what it is.
Sospiro e gemo	I sigh and moan
senza voler,	without wanting to,
palpito e tremo	I quiver and tremble
senza saper,	without knowing it,
non trovo pace	I don't find peace
notte nè di,	either night or day,
ma pur mi piace	and yet I enjoy
languir così.	languishing like that.

The page Cherubino is in love with each and every woman. In the first act of the opera he has told Susanna, chambermaid of the countess, of his special attraction to her, which does not preclude his adoration of the countess. He has explained to Susanna the troubles of his heart in the improvised "Non so più cosa son, cosa faccio." But for the countess he has written a song on the same subject, which he is now going to sing for her while Susanna accompanies him on the guitar. The song is the artistic version of the earlier improvisation.

The tempo, *andante con moto*, can be read at either ♩ = 58 or ♪ = 116, with a well-established, elegant, and simple rhythm. Cherubino is standing straight in his white and silver outfit, a blue mantelet on his shoulder, a three-cornered hat with plumes under his arm, shy and delighted, irresistibly attractive. The role is sung by a young and pretty woman, soprano or mezzo-soprano, but never by a heavy, dark voice, which would be in complete contradiction to the spirit of the part.

The first part of the aria, to "capir nol so," is a prelude, frank and open yet courtly, with no passion yet in the singing. Sing to the ladies, paying tribute to their knowledge and entrusting your troubles to their sympathy. Sing the first four bars in one breath, carefully respecting the rhythm of "che cosa è amor" with two notes on the syllable "co-," the same rhythm as in "l'ho nel cor" the second time. Avoid also singing a diphthong in "sapete" and "vedete" (sap*ei*te, ved*ei*te, instead of sap/e/te and ved/e/te). Singing either the shorter two-bar units or the longer four bars, find a lyric line that encompasses all the bars, avoiding a childish syllabic reading. The lines from "Quello ch'io provo" to "capir nol so" show Cherubino very candid, baffled, and mystified and must be sung in a way that arouses the curiosity of Susanna and the countess.

With "Sento un affetto" he starts to describe the phases of his emotions in detail. The words become very important and must have their individual stresses. "Un affetto" is lyric, "desir" is intense, "diletto" is light and smiling, "martir" is earnest and dark. "Gelo" has little time to be colored, but the fact will be strongly quoted a few bars later. "L'alma avvampar" is ardent but will fail to be so if the low notes are swallowed inward instead of being spoken very much forward. The broader phrase, well sustained, from "Ricerco un bene" to "non so cos'è," does not call for details. All the stresses just mentioned are, of course, not violent contrasts of black and white but delicate touches that must be performed with taste and good measure.

The next two confessions are obviously made of an active first half, "Sospiro e gemo" mezzo forte, and a surprised passive second half, "senza voler" piano. The third one, at first seemingly a serious complaint, "non trovo pace notte nè dì," turns out to be a deep enjoyment—"ma pur mi piace languir così." This last phrase must be said with great charm and touching restraint.

Cherubino, having exposed his troubles to the judgment of the ladies, returns to his courtly attitude. The repeat of "Voi, che sapete," possibly more piano than the first time, may also be imbued with a discreet suggestion of more familiarity. The page has shared with his beloved ladies the secret of his trouble, which is their very existence. "Donne, vedete" can be repeated in several different colors and with varied intensity, various degrees of intimacy, before ending in perfectly and gentlemanly formality. Cherubino is a most charming rascal. He will never be a brat. He handles his very normal troubles with grace and distinction.

"Vedrò, mentr'io sospiro" (Count's Aria)   *baritone*

"Hai già vinta la causa?"	"You have already won the case?"
Cosa sento?	What do I hear?
In qual laccio cadea!	In what trap did I fall!
Perfidi! Io voglio di tal modo punirvi:	Scoundrels! I shall punish you in such a way:
A piacer mio la sentenza sarà.	The verdict shall be rendered as I please.
Ma sei pagasse la vecchia pretendente?	But if he should pay the old pretender?
Pagarla!—In qual maniera?	Pay her!—and with what means?
E poi v'è Antonio	And then there's Antonio
che a un incognito Figaro	who to an unknown Figaro
ricusa di dare una nipote in matrimonio.	refuses to give his niece in marriage.
Coltivando l'orgoglio di questo mentecatto	Flattering the vanity of that idiot,
Tutto giova a un raggiro; il colpo è fatto.	everything serves my plot; it's in the bag.
Vedrò, mentr'io sospiro,	I should see my servant happy
felice un servo mio?	while I am sighing?
E un ben, che invan desio,	And a treasure I desire in vain,
Ei posseder dovrà?	should he possess it?
Vedrò per man d'amore unita	Should I see, bound in love

a un vile oggetto,	to a mean creature,
chi in me destò un'affetto,	the one who excited a passion in me
che per me poi non ha!	which she does not feel for me!
Ah no! Lasciarti in pace?	Ah no! Leave you in peace?
Non vo'questo contento.	I don't grant you that satisfaction.
Tu non nacesti, audace,	You were not born, brazen man,
per dare a me tormento,	to torment me,
e forse ancor per ridere	and maybe even to laugh
di mia infelicità.	at my unhappiness.
Già la speranza sola	Already the mere hope
delle vendette mie	of my revenge
quest'anima consola	comforts this heart
e giubilar mi fa.	and fills me with joy.

Beaumarchais says: "Count Almaviva must be played very nobly yet with grace and freedom. The corruption of the heart must take nothing away from his well-bred manners. In accordance with the customs of the times, noblemen treated lightly any undertakings concerning women" (my translation).

Count Almaviva is always humiliated but never debased. When caught red-handed he recovers quickly and regains his confidence in ultimate triumph.

The setting: The count tries to seduce Susanna, chambermaid of the countess and fiancée of Figaro, the count's manservant. He should succeed easily, thanks to the ancient law of *prima nox*, which gives him the right to precéde the bridegroom in the bed of the new bride. But many obstacles have been raised by the members of his household, including, of course, the young couple. In the scene preceding this aria, however, Susanna suddenly not only accepts but offers to meet the count in the garden that evening. He seems to triumph. But, unwisely, Susanna, hurrying out of the room and running into Figaro, whispers "Hai già vinta la causa" (You have already won the case). The count overhears her, and the ensuing aria shows his reaction.

It starts with a recitative, a very important part of any eighteenth-century opera and, in several modified forms, of many later ones. "Hai già vinta la causa": The count repeats with disbelief what he has just heard—that there was collusion between Susanna and Figaro in setting the date with him. Sing that first line slowly, ♩ = 84, almost without timbre, "Cosa sento" more strongly—it is a question, still showing disbelief. "In qual laccio" brings the beginning of awareness (stress laccio, supported by a forte piano chord). The following *presto* should be twice as fast, ♪ = ♩, stressing first indignation, then vindictive anger. But, almost immediately, during the measure given to the orchestra, the count remembers that he is also the judge and recovers confidence and dignity. Sing "A piacer mio" broadly and in exact rhythm. Three pairs of solemn chords punctuate with great authority. Then he reflects upon a possible obstacle, *andante*, ♩ = ♩ (singing piano). But he discards that obstacle as ridiculous: "Pagarla," silent chuckle, "In qual maniera," again a silent chuckle, ♩ = ♩. Now he has overcome surprise, anger, and doubts, and to the end of the recitative he will sing with animation, confidence, and a voice that grows firm and strong above a very energetic orchestra. Broaden considerably "il colpo è fatto."

Aria: *allegro maestoso*, ♩ = 138 at the start. The aria consists of two parts: In the first one, until "Vedrò" repeated four times, the count bemoans his misfortune: Susanna, whom he desires, has denied him, the powerful nobleman, his wishes, giving her love instead to the lowly servant Figaro. His regrets are combined with a righteous indignation because he considers justice to have been distorted. This combination protects him from a vulgar grumbling unworthy of his rank. The singer must respect the dynamic markings, piano to forte in the first two lines (indignation against Figaro), even mezzo forte during the next ten bars (to the second "che per me poi non ha"). Then, on the next eight bars, there is twice a pattern of piano to forte to piano, that is, short revolts of pride followed by scorn for "un servo mio." Ten bars of even mezzo-forte follow, as above, with a growing irritation to forte on the four "Vedrò."

The second part of the aria should be thought in cut time, $\downarrow$ = 108. The count has decided on revenge and, faithful to his character, which allows him to bounce back quickly from his disappointments, savors already his inevitable triumph. Observe the starts piano and the spurts of forte in the first four short lines, stressing "au*dace*" strongly both times it comes. Then, on a dark rumbling of the orchestra—"per dare a me tormento"—sing darkly as the count thinks of what he believes to have been his sufferings. A touch of irritated sarcasm on "ridere" and a touch of lyric self-pity on "mia infelicità" (sing "di mi-a"). With "Già la speranza sola" we feel the onset of a bouncy pattern: The count is again in high spirits, ready to fight and sure to win. Watch again the rapid alternation of piano and forte throughout the repeat of that pattern sung with growing enthusiasm.

We now come to the coda, the last fourteen measures for the voice. Breathe after "e giubilar," before the descending scale of D, and do not breathe again until after the D, which begins the second bar after the triplets. Avoid at all cost singing the triplets as a succession of "ha-ha-ha." They must be conceived as a succession of fast vowels /a/, rolling around the upper mouth like marbles, all at the same level and without concern for the ups and downs of the pitches. (This technical recommendation deserves thought and attention.) The next "e giubilar mi fa" should resound on the upper D and be sung with a real decrescendo to the low D, with a very light trill on the E. It should keep the voice very near the upper resonances so that going to the F-sharp does not change the basic balance of the voice. The F-sharp should have the sound of an /a/ darkened toward /o/ and can be tied to the following D. The phrase is short and can be kept forte to the end without the need to breathe.

Depending on the maturity of the performer the above analysis will seem either tedious or worth studying. Mozart has the gift of suggesting every psychological nuance of the fast-changing mind of his character. It is an endless joy to notice those nuances and to utilize them. As to the acting of such a piece, every gesture, every expression, can be drawn from the text through careful study.

"Dove sono i bei momenti"   *soprano*

E Susanna non vien?	And Susanna does not come?
Sono ansiosa di saper come il Conte	I am anxious to know how the Count
accolse la proposta. Alquanto ardito	received the proposal. Rather bold
il progetto mi par.	the project seems to me.
E ad uno sposo sì vivace	and with such a hot-tempered

e geloso!	and jealous husband!
Ma che mal c'è?	But what harm is there?
Cangiando i miei vestiti con quelli	Changing my clothes with Susanna's
di Susanna, e i suoi co'miei:	and hers with mine:
al favor della notte. Oh, cielo!	under cover of night. Oh, heavens!
A quale umil stato fatale	To what a desolate, humiliating state
io son ridotta da un consorte crudel.	I have been reduced by a cruel husband.
che dopo avermi con un misto	who, with an unheard-of mixture
inaudito d'infedeltà	of infidelity,
di gelosia, di sdegno, prima amata,	of jealousy, of disdain, first loved me,
indi offesa, e alfin tradita,	then offended, and finally betrayed me,
fammi or cercar	now makes me ask for help
da una mia serva aita!	from one of my servants!
Dove sono i bei momenti	Where are the beautiful moments
di dolcezza e di piacer?	of tenderness and pleasure?
Dove andaro i giuramenti	Where did the promises go
di quel labbro menzogner?	of those deceitful lips?
Perchè mai, se in pianti e in pene	Why, since into tears and sorrows
per me tutto si cangiò	everything has changed for me,
la memoria di quel bene	has the memory of that happiness
dal mio sen non trapassò?	not gone from my heart?
Ah, se almen	Ah, if at least
la mia costanza,	my faithfulness,
nel languire amando ognor,	longing and loving as ever,
mi portasse una speranza	would bring me some hope
di cangiar l'ingrato cor!	to change that ungrateful heart!

The countess, the mischievous Rosina from *The Barber of Seville*, has changed greatly after a few years of marriage. She now longs for peace and quiet in her castle and in her married life. "Moved by two contrary feelings she should show a restrained sensitivity only or a very moderate anger; above all nothing which in the eyes of the spectators debases her friendly and virtuous nature" (Beaumarchais, my translation).

It is only to recapture her husband that she lends herself to the deceptions conceived by Figaro; she has not yet given up hope that her own faithfulness will restore peace and harmony to the life of the castle. The plot as it stands at this moment is for Susanna to arrange a date that evening with the count and let the countess, disguised as her chambermaid, keep the date, instead, to confound him. The countess is at the same time amused and rather humiliated at the prospect. It is in that mood that in the opening recitative she reflects on her life these past years.

Recitative: The whole piece is a monologue. Rather than thinking that the countess is talking to herself, let us imagine that we hear her thoughts, of course expressed in her singing lines but as direct and sincere as if they could not be overheard by indiscreet ears. An aria that is a monologue should sound different from an aria that is addressed to one or several persons in order to communicate with them, to influence them, to reveal facts, feelings, or intentions to them. It is not easy to convey from the stage to the audience the sensation that a well-projected voice is the mute speech of the heart.

"E Susanna non vien": The movement, *andante*, suggests a deliberate pace, the silences between short phrases a reluctance to face the situation. Sing very piano (but not muffled) and slowly, with hesitations before "di saper" and "accolse." Allow a good amount of time for the twice-repeated orchestral pattern. Express misgivings on "alquanto ardito," and show an embarrassed fear, with an accelerando on "si vivace e geloso." Then the orchestral *allegretto* dissipates the clouds for a short while, and the countess finds the strength to react—"Ma che mal c'è" (andante)—and to smile at the idea of the deceit—"Cangiando i miei vestiti"—with a short, jocular enjoyment—"al favor della notte." The entire next phrase, from "o, cielo" to "di sdegno" is a crescendo and accelerando expressing at first dismay, then a vigorous denunciation, alternating finally with the chords forte of the orchestra in short, indignant phrases of accusation— "di gelosia," "di sdegno"—before subsiding in an almost tearful "prima amata." The sudden pang of a happy memory should make those two words slow and sustained before returning to the denunciation, forte. Start the last phrase of the recitative with a broadly voiced A on "fammi or cercar" and reach piano on the words "mia serva aita," in which the badly humiliated woman comes as near to bitterness as her noble nature permits.

Aria: The marking is *andantino*, which often means that the unit of time can be the eighth note. The Glyndebourne recording is played at ♪ = 76, which seems at the same time perfect for the mood and negotiable for the voice, a voice that says the words with extreme clarity, sings them piano and legatissimo, and supports them with a concentrated intensity in the middle and lower parts of the body. In order to sustain the line with complete confidence, the singer must feel the tone forward behind her upper teeth where its presence is maintained not by the vague notion of relaxation but, on the contrary, by the feeling that a precisely controlled flow of energy feeds its vibration at all times. The exquisite beauty of the vocal line does not permit the slightest flaw in the quality of the tone, and sopranos who are not in total command of their voices should be discouraged from attempting this aria *in performance*, although any serious spinto student must work on it repeatedly.

The first eight bars of the aria are given to nostalgia for a past full of sweetness and pleasure (be sure to stress the inflection on "dolcezza"). The next ten bars also express a sincere regret but one already colored by an accusation "di quel labbro menzogner," at first restrained (respect the thirty-seconds, but do not stress them), then more intense (the second "di quel labbro," where the voice may become stronger on top of the staff). The very short separation of the two phrases [gner-di quel] can create a problem. The ideal solution is to take such a good breath before the first "di quel labbro" that none is necessary between the two phrases, the shortest comma being indicated between "-gner" and "di quel." It is also possible to sing the first "di quel labbro" very piano with a slight crescendo to the F, take a very short breath, and continue the crescendo to the end of the second phrase; the intention of ending on a strong "menzogner" will carry you to the end without running out of breath.

From "Perchè mai" to "non trapassò" is an easier section because the musical writing creates a feeling of animation that favors the handling of the voice. Be sure to sing the string of syllables on two notes very evenly without introducing *h*'s between notes and without accentuating the first note and weakening the second. The mood is interesting: Although sorrows are part of her life (seven first bars of that section), the countess still enjoys the memories of the happy times. So, no despair in this aria. Beaumarchais said, "she should display a restrained sensitivity only."

The return of "Dove sono" should be pianissimo. It makes greater demands on the breath than it did the first time. Keep the tone present in the back of the front teeth, the energy of the body concentrated, the mind in tender nostalgia. The section is short and halted abruptly: The countess has dwelled long enough on the past and ardently expresses her hopes, her desire to regain her husband through her faithfulness, but also her doubts of success. The first two short phrases are breathless, followed by a spirited *allegro*, ♩ = 138. Sing, still legato, giving to each phrase only one accent on its final syllable "ogn*or*," "sper*a*nza," "c*or*." Do the same on the repeats of the phrase. When "nel languire amando ognor" comes for the second time the tradition is to make a ritardando on "amando ognor" and to go *a tempo* on "mi portasse." When performed with charm and a loving intention, this tradition is certainly correct.

The incoming short "mi portasse" is sung piano; it is a restrained wish. "Una speranza" is mezzo forte, the beginning of exaltation; "di cangiar" on the A starts mezzo forte and may then be amplified on the A-flat and the G as the phrase demands. Then make a diminuendo of sorrow on "l'ingrato cor" so that on the second A you can again sing a mezzo forte amplified until the G as you did the first time. Sing the following "di cangiar l'ingrato cor" no more than mezzo forte and sing the next one going to crescendo to the G, decrescendo to the trilled D, mezzo forte and crescendo for the next, keeping your best for the last A and the end of the phrase.

Those indications may seem much too detailed and restraining. The temptation is almost irresistible to sing forte from the first "cangiar" on the A to the end. I regret to say that I have seen and heard some leading sopranos in difficulty trying to stay forte through all those last lines. Even with voices that can do it easily the effect is no longer as sensitive as it should be. The sensitivity of the countess must be expressed in nuances even in those lines and must keep the musical climax for the last four bars of the vocal text where the notation *forte* comes for the first time after four *forte piano*.

A scrupulous technical performance of this aria would of course mean nothing if the soprano did not feel in herself the lovely, tender, hopeful heart of a sad young woman of distinction.

"Aprite un po' quegl'occhi" *baritone/bass-baritone*

Tutto è disposto;	Everything is ready;
l'ora dovrebbe esser vicina.	the time should be near.
Io sento gente . . . è dessa!	I hear somebody . . . it is she!
Non è alcun. Buia è la notte,	It is nobody; dark is the night,
ed io comincio omai	and as of now
a fare il scimunito mestiere di marito.	I am starting the stupid job of husband.
Ingrata!	Ungrateful girl!
Nel momento della mia cerimonia	At the very moment of my ceremony
ei godeva leggendo;	he was reading with glee;
e nel vederlo, io rideva di me senza saperlo.	and seeing him I laughed at myself without knowing it.
O Susanna, Susanna,	O Susanna, Susanna,
quanta pena mi costi!	how much pain you cost me!
Con quell'ingenua facia,	With such a candid face,
con quegl'occhi innocenti,	with such innocent eyes,

chi creduto l'avria?	who would have believed it?
Ah! che il fidarsi a donna, a donna,	Ah! how the trust in a woman
è ognor follia!	is always a folly!
Aprite un po'quegl'occhi,	Come on, open your eyes,
uomini incauti e schiocchi,	you rash and stupid men,
guardate queste femmine,	look at these women,
guardate cosa son,	see what they are like,
queste chiamate Dee	these so-called goddesses,
da gli ingannati sensi,	by our deceived minds,
a cui tributa incensi	to whom our weak reason
la debole ragion.	offers incense.
Son streghe che incantano	They are witches that weave a spell
per farci penar,	to make us suffer,
sirene che cantano	sirens that sing
per farci affogar,	to make us drown,
civette che allettano	little owls that lure us
per trarci le piume	to pull out our feathers,
comete che brillano	comets that shine
per toglierci il lume.	to take our lights away.
Son rose spinose,	They are thorny roses,
son volpi vezzose,	they are charming foxes,
son orse benigne,	they are good-natured bears,
colombe maligne,	malicious doves,
maestre d'inganni,	masters of deception,
amiche d'affanni,	friends of anxiety,
che fingono, mentono, amore non senton	who pretend, lie, who don't feel love,
non senton pietà, no, no, no.	who have no mercy, no, no, no.
Il resto, il resto nol dico,	I am not saying the rest,
già ognuno lo sa.	Everybody knows it already.

Beaumarchais (Preface to *Le Marriage de Figaro*) describes Figaro as follows: "The sharpest man of his nation who, defending Susanna, his own, makes fun of his master's plans and quite pleasantly becomes indignant because the latter dares challenge his shrewdness, he being past master in that type of fencing." In the aria studied here we shall hear a different Figaro, for Beaumarchais (addendum to the Preface) "knows of nothing more insipid on stage than those stale cameos where all is blue, all is rose, all is the author, whosoever he may be" (my translations).

At the end of the longest and craziest of days Figaro is suddenly convinced that his titanic efforts to protect his fiancée from his master's greed have failed and that his Susanna is yielding to the seducer. The failure is such a shock that this master of subtle intrigue now resorts to melodramatic measures in order to surprise the guilty pair. He places spies in strategic spots in the park. Wrapped in a dark cape, his face half hidden under a black sombrero, he is ready now to lie in wait behind a bush. First, however, he must pause and try to see himself in focus. His dismay at what he sees makes him burst out in a bitter appraisal of women's faithfulness, there for all to see. This is indeed a different Figaro.

Recitative: Figaro enters cautiously, looks around the place, and whispers, "Tutto è disposto." Possibly checking the time against the height of the moon in the sky, he sings "l'ora dovrebbe esser vicina" in quiet eighth notes. He stops, listens, and says rapidly,

"Io sento gente" and, in tempo with the orchestra, anxiously "è dessa," listens again and says more slowly, "Non è alcun." Certain now that he is alone, he complains forte, "Buia è la notte," then explains bitterly the causes of his grief. From "ed io comincio omai" to "marito," sing on time (no change could improve the written values) with violence and self-deprecation. "Ingrata" (forte) is an accusation, but a sad one (long stress on the syllable "-gra-"). Figaro revives the scene at his wedding when Susanna slipped a note into the count's hand. From "Nel momento" to "saperlo" sing rapidly, as with disbelief, and with sarcasm on "io rideva." After the orchestral, strongly accented forte, the words "O Susanna" must be slow, mezzo forte, then piano, and there is almost a sob on "quanta pena mi costi." The sad lover sees her face in front of him and says the next two phrases piano, with a crescendo on "chi creduto l'avria." Suddenly, anger takes hold of him. "Ah! che il fidarsi a donna" to "follia" is a crescendo to fortissimo, with a quasifermata on "è ognor."

Aria: The tempo is *moderato* rather than *andante*, ♩ = 138, and definitely in 4/4. Figaro addresses himself to the audience, warning them in the light of his own experience of the fate that might befall them. Sing forte, strictly in rhythm but not chopped, with great indignation and without ugliness: He speaks from man to man, and he need not distort his voice to do so. Sarcasm will come on "queste chiamate Dee," a feeling of helplessness on "la debole ragion." It is on the next page that Figaro the virtuoso will reappear, coloring each accusation with the proper vocal effect: "incantano" full of charm; "penar" nasty; "cantano" with beauty; "affogar" half-choked; "civette que allettano," the whole line with sharp, cruel sixteenths; "comete che brillano" with grandeur. A new episode in the same spirit begins on "Son rose spinose" but this time starts piano. Here there will be a contrast between the noun and its adjective, one being mild, the other evil, not always in the same order. A conscientious artist must stress all the different intentions without fear of being fussy but must do so very clearly. Figaro then lets loose a torrent of accusations, breathlessly, for no respiration should be taken during the bars in triplets until the silence following "pietà." He sings the "no, no, no" at the top of his voice, easing suddenly on "Il resto" as if realizing the uselessness of his furious advice. It goes without saying that the triplets should be sung exactly on time and that no accelerando is necessary on that line: The composer has provided all the elements of the climax. During that page the baritone should bring his voice very much forward, even more so than usually, to the teeth and the lips, allowing the roundness of sound to return on "non senton pietà."

But Figaro feels that good advice should be repeated in order to be effective. He calls again for the attention of his listeners. "Aprite un po'quegl'occhi" is sung on time but sustained and poised, the phrase "uomini incauti" vigorously, the characterization the same as the first time. The reluctant phrase "il resto nol dico" is said with irony, scorn, disgust, according to the wish of the performer, but with a new color each time it is repeated. The coda, after the surprising D-flat on "ognuno lo sa-a," is handled with a certain detachment and cynicism, well underlined by the horns in the orchestra that make fun of the betrayed husband. (In the European tradition horns are said to be the attributes of a cuckold.)

Figaro, who throughout this aria has suffered badly from what he believes his fate to be, has suddenly decided to share his dreadful experience with all men and has tortured more than relieved himself in doing so. This is a tragic moment in the life of that resourceful and optimistic man. I do not see any reason to turn this aria into a buffo aria, just because it is the generally cheerful Figaro who sings it. The more sincere Figaro's sorrow, the more cruel his furor, the greater will be the impact of the happy discovery that Susanna has remained faithful and devoted to him. The audience, on the other hand, aware of the true situation, may find its enjoyment in knowing that Figaro tortures himself without cause. This slightly comic element is wanted by the librettist and the composer, but Figaro should not create it by singing in a comical way.

"Deh vieni, non tardar" *soprano*

Giunse al fin il momento
che godrò senza affanno
in braccia all'idol mio.
Timide cure, uscite dal mio petto,
a turbar non venite il mio diletto!
Oh come par che all'amoroso foco
l'amenità del loco
la terra, e il ciel risponda.
Come la notte i furti miei seconda!

Deh vieni, non tardar, o gioja bella,
vieni ove amor per goder t'appella
finchè non splende in ciel notturna face
finchè l'aria è ancor bruna
e il mondo tace,
Qui mormora il ruscel,
qui scherza l'aura
che con dolce susurro il cor restaura.
Qui ridono i fioretti
e l'erba è fresca,
ai piaceri d'amor
qui tutto adesca.
Vieni, ben mio, tra queste piante ascose,
vieni, vieni!
Ti vo' la fronte incoronar di rose.

At last comes the moment
that I shall enjoy without fear
in the arms of my idol.
Anxious cares, leave my heart,
do not come to trouble my delight!
Oh, how it seems that to the amorous fire,
the friendliness of the place,
the earth and the sky respond.
How the night favors my secret plans!

Oh come, do not delay, my beautiful joy,
come where love calls you to enjoy yourself
as long as the nocturnal torch does not shine,
as long as the air is still dark
and the world is quiet.
Here the brook murmurs,
here the breeze is playing
which gently whispering soothes the heart.
Here the flowers are smiling
and the grass is cool,
everything here invites [you]
to the pleasures of love.
Come, my dearest, among those hidden bushes,
come, come!
I want to crown your forehead with roses.

"An artful girl, witty and cheerful but not with the almost brazen gaiety of our corrupting soubrettes. She is wise and devoted to her duties. Her guiles aim only at helping her mistress and her own marriage" (Beaumarchais, "Caractères et habillements de la pièce").

The setting: late evening in the park of the castle; darkness. Figaro has learned that Susanna has a date, then and there, with the count. He is furious and depressed. He does not know, however, that Susanna is only a decoy and that at the last moment the countess will take Susanna's place. He is hiding behind a bush when Susanna enters, but she knows he is there.

After four bars of animated and very light orchestra, a ritardando on the last bar, Susanna enters in a rustling of silky petticoats, seemingly going to her date with delight. She sings (on the downbeat) with a crystal-clear young voice, a little slower than the

preceding orchestra. (For this ear, any appoggiatura would only disturb the pure simplicity of the line.) Again there are four bars of orchestra, animated with a slight ritardando on the fourth bar. Susanna on the next phrase should contrast the boldness of
"uscite dal mio petto" with the exquisite "il mio diletto." Only two more bars of animated
music in the orchestra, and Susanna's contrived cheerfulness comes to an end, to be
replaced with a sudden and sincere emotion. She sings more slowly now; her heart in
love feels attuned to the beauty and friendliness of the place. (This is to be her wedding
night.) "La terra," pause, "il ciel" are in understanding with her. Slower still, she sings
"come la notte," a long pause, "i furti miei," "seconda." Delay the coming of the first
chord; delay still more the coming of the resolution.

By stressing the exaggerated joy of the first two lines, by slowing down the tempo
progressively while singing with great emotion, by daring to make real silences before
and between the last two chords, it is possible to create a marvelous mood of tender
expectation. How well Figaro feels it behind his bush I can testify!

Aria: The tempo is slow. The Glyndebourne recording goes to as slow a tempo as
$\flat$ = 88. It is conceivable that a slightly faster tempo, $\flat$ = 96–100, may be preferred. At
any rate the aria should unfold with an exquisite, rocking softness, with no note jutting
out of the line, especially the three F's in bars 8, 12, and 14. The voice must flow with
extreme fluidity, the sixteenths being exact in length and without any edge. This is a
passionate, almost secret call to the lover to appear out of the silent darkness to be
rewarded with joy and pleasure. Do not exert yourself in order to sing two loud notes on
the low B-flat and the A on the word "face." It is enough to have light sounds very much
forward in the mouth. Any loud and darkened sounds are out of place here.

The following lines, from "Qui mormora" to "adesca," are an amplification of the line
of the recitative "l'amenità del loco" (the friendliness of the place). Susanna looks, listens, breathes, feels, and all the delights of this most special night invade her heart
through all her senses. A clear, joyous, flowing voice must ring in these lines, completely free of any artificiality. Then an overwhelming desire to share her happiness with
Figaro turns into a direct appeal to him. "Vieni" is warm, inviting, a crescendo; "tra
queste piante" is more piano, with a knowing smile (Figaro has not deceived her; she
knew all the time that he was there and listening). "Vieni, vieni": While staying on time in
the first bar, lengthen the vowel to the end of the value, breathe, and then sing the
second "vieni" slowly and freely, with great seduction and a melting sound. After a short
pause, start the ascending "ti vo' la fronte" a trifle slower than the preceding tempo,
breathe, sing the tied notes on "in-co-ro-" in absolute legato, and ascend to the A by a
light spin from the F (no covering!). Keep the C very light, another light spin to the F,
and sing "di rose" with a stress on the syllable "ro-." The phrase is repeated in the same
way: The F, $\widehat{\rho\cdot\rho}$ started mezzo forte, will end pianissimo but not weak: Repeat the vowel
/a/ three or four times in your mind to the end of the value. Take a leisurely breath and all
the time you need to give the impression that the last "incoronar" is a delightful message
of love. Respect the fermata on the following silence; then sing the last "di rose" exactly
on time and warmly.

Obviously it is not conceivable in our time that a woman in love should want to crown
her fiancé with roses. We must make an adjustment and try to sense this eighteenth-
century mood of combined sensuousness, elegance, and decorum. An artist will feel

how deeply Susanna is moved. She has tried to conceal her love, but in spite of herself it flows freely to the man she loves. The chambermaid of the countess is in no way inferior to her mistress in this moment of sincerity.

Mozart, *Die Zauberflöte*

"Dies Bildnis" tenor

Dies Bildnis ist bezaubernd schön,
wie noch kein Auge je gesehn!
Ich fühl'es, ich fühl'es,
wie dies Götterbild
mein Herz mit neuer Regung füllt.
Dies Etwas kann ich zwar nicht nennen,
doch fühl'ich's hier wie Feuer brennen.
Soll die Empfindung Liebe sein?
Ja, ja, die Liebe ist's allein.
O wenn ich sie nur finden könnte!
O wenn sie doch schon vor mir stände!
Ich würde—würde—warm und rein,
was würde ich?
Ich würde sie voll Entzücken
an diesen heissen Busen drücken,
und ewig wäre sie dann mein!

This portrait is enchantingly beautiful,
as never an eye has seen yet!
I feel it, I feel it,
how this divine picture
fills my heart with a new emotion.
True, I cannot name this something,
yet I feel it burning here like fire.
Can this feeling be love?
Yes, yes, it is love alone.
Oh, if only I could find her!
Oh, if only she stood already before me!
I would—would—warm and pure,
what would I?
Filled with rapture I would
press her against this burning heart,
and forever she would then be mine!

On his travels through a foreign country Tamino meets with strange adventures. Pursued by a ferocious snake, he is rescued by three mysterious ladies who, a little later, give him a portrait of a young woman of great beauty, for him to keep and to cherish. Left alone, Tamino is absorbed in the contemplation of the portrait, which fills him with wonder and rapture.

The indication of tempo is *larghetto*, a very slow one, and a sensible pace for this piece could be $\decrescendo = 69$, it being understood that this metronomical figure does not mean a metronomical performance. On the contrary, few arias lend themselves to so many inflections, so much elasticity, so much instinctive variety within the general rhythmic frame. The required voice is a lyric tenor, precise and mellow. The singer will not be asked to perform any feats of tessitura. It has been said, as a matter of fact, that *The Magic Flute* was at first received with indifference because the tenor had been given no chance "to prove himself." But there are many ways for a singer to prove himself besides singing stunning high notes.

Tamino must sing with extreme sincerity and conviction. He falls in love with the portrait as soon as he looks at it, and this love will be forever. The mystical emotion he feels imbues the sound of his voice with a noble respect as well as with warmth and purity. Technically, the voice will be as pure as the vowels he sings, as expressive as the shape of the words he says, as melodious as the exact pitches and intervals he chisels. The vowels, for example, are /i/ (there are three identical ones in "Dies Bildnis") as in "Liebe"; /ø/, long and ringing, as in "schön"; /y/ as in "fühl'," "füllt," "würde"; /ε/ as in "Herz," "nennen"; /e/ as in "Regung"; and /a/ as in "Ja, ja," "mein."

Also, the voice should never aim for the same size on all syllables. On the contrary, it should expand or slim down according to each vowel, swell or grow slender during the value of long notes—like a liquid poured into a chain of containers of different shapes and sizes. It almost goes without saying that what is stressed with respect to this marvelous aria applies to singing in general.

Concentrate on all this during the opening chords, then sing mezzo piano and with full delight. The first two phrases are shaped in a similar way: a light upbeat, a lyrical high note flowing into the descending line, and a stress on the last word—"schön," "gesehn"; in other words, a strong high note should not be sung at the expense of neglecting the ending of the phrase.

"Ich fühl'es" and its repeat are centered upon "fühl'," sweetly stressed. The A-flat on "Götterbild" is lyrical, full of admiration, and mellow rather than noisy. The next phrase and its repeat are legatissimo, the word "Herz" well sustained before melting into the following notes, sung caressingly. The appoggiaturas on "neuer" have the value of a sixteenth note; they help to stress the surprising newness of Tamino's emotion.

The line "Dies Etwas . . ." is full of wonder, and the next one, "doch fühl' ich's . . .," is full of passion. The final words, "nennen" and "brennen," are contrasts, the first one subdued, the second full of ardor. Then, piano, so hesitant to believe in his discovery that he has to repeat the question, Tamino guesses that he may have fallen in love. (The first note of that second phrase on "Soll" is a G and not an E-natural as printed in the Schirmer edition.) So he answers firmly "Ja, ja" in a good mezzo-forte and feels the need to say again and again the magic word "Liebe," the first time piano, then with a crescendo to forte the fourth time he says it; finally, quite moved, he sings the last "allein" piano. Note that the vowel /e/ ending the word "Liebe" is not open, almost like an /a/, but is slim and light, more like the French terminal *e* in *mère* or *table*.

During the two bars of interlude Tamino's thoughts of love turn to desires. His first desire is to see the enchanting woman at his side. The two phrases starting with "Oh wenn ich sie" are each one an intense crescendo to the A-flat, ending forte piano. . Tamino barely admits the second wish to himself: "Ich würde—würde—" and in two words describes his pure, ardent feelings, "warm und rein." Amazed at what is happening to him, he must ask himself: What would I do if she suddenly stood at my side? The bar of silence following "was würde ich" must be given its full value. During this silence Tamino, so to speak, commits himself. With rapture he would hold her tight and make her his forever. Sing "Ich würde sie"—a very sensitive "sie"—piano, then more firmly "voll Entzücken"; then, as the wish becomes almost concrete in Tamino's mind, sing "an diesen heissen Busen drücken" crescendo and forte, to return to mezzo piano for "und ewig wäre sie dann mein." In view of the enormity of the wish, the first "und ewig . . ." is sung wistfully. The second one starts in the same vein but follows a crescendo to an assertive "mein." The third repeat is forte in a strong positive statement; the fourth is again piano, expressing sweet enjoyment of the wish fulfilled. The last one, starting with a vibrant "ewig" on A-flat, is gloriously sung, a slight ritardando adding to the scope of the phrase.

In other words, the five repeats reveal changing and contrasting moods. The singer should not only stress each one of them but take advantage of them. The alternation of piano and forte makes the page infinitely easier to sing than would a constant forte. Also, that alternation creates a rocking feeling and a dreamlike atmosphere that allow the tenor to maintain the high poetic level inspired by the music and to suggest the finality of a love that will endure under whatever fluctuations of fate.

"O zittre nicht"   *soprano*

O zittre nicht, mein lieber Sohn!	Oh tremble not, my dear son!
Du bist unschuldig, weise, fromm.	You are innocent, sensible, good.
Ein Jüngling so wie du	A young man such as you
vermag am besten	is best able to comfort
dies tiefgebeugte Mutterherz	this mother's
zu trösten.	deeply depressed heart.
Zum Leiden bin ich auserkoren,	I am destined to grieve,
denn meine Tochter fehlet mir.	for I am longing for my daughter.
Durch sie ging all mein Glück verloren,	With her all my happiness was lost,
ein Bösewicht entfloh mit ihr.	a villain fled with her.
Noch seh'ich ihr Zittern	I still see her trembling
mit bangem Erschüttern,	with apprehensive emotion,
ihr ängstliches Beben,	her anguished quaking,
ihr schüchternes Streben!	her timid resistance!
Ich musste sie mir rauben sehen.	I had to see her be abducted.
Ach helft! war alles, was sie sprach.	Ah help! was all she said.
Allein vergebens war ihr Flehen,	Yet futile was her pleading,
denn meine Hülfe war zu schwach.	for my succor was too weak.
Du, du wirst sie zu befreien gehen,	You, you will go and deliver her,
du wirst der Tochter Retter sein!	you will be my daughter's savior!
Und werd'ich dich als Sieger sehen,	And if I see you victorious,
so sei sie dann auf ewig dein!	then shall she be yours forever!

Tamino is absorbed in the contemplation of a portrait given him by three mysterious ladies when they suddenly reappear. This time they tell him the Queen of the Night, their mistress, has decided that in him she has found the young man worthy and able to free her daughter.

The Queen of the Night usually appears high above the level of the stage, surrounded either by a starry sky or by moonlight playing on some clouds. At first she speaks from this vantage point, sometimes coming to a lower level and nearer to Tamino later, but she always remains in a dominant position. At this point her presence in any case is neither threatening nor in any way frightening.

During the prelude to the aria, *allegro maestoso*, the interpreter must acquire a feeling of great power and majesty. If she is a coloratura more than a lyric, that majesty will come not from the volume of her voice but from the solemn presentation of her text, the rigorous precision of her words, and the studied slowness of her pace.

During the first recitative the orchestra keeps a firm pace, constantly stressing the greatness of the queen. The singing must be much slower. The queen, with all her awesome majesty, wishes to sound benevolent, cordial, and trustworthy. She comes to Tamino for help. In order to bring the character to life, the soprano must immediately find in this short recitative the right combination of these almost contradictory features, stressing the affection in "mein lieber Sohn," the flattering overtones of "ein Jüngling so wie du," the humility of "dies tiefgebeugte Mutterherz."

The *larghetto*, ♩ = 66–69, at first requires great beauty of voice, lyric beauty and a velvety sound in the long phrases, evenly sustained, which will contrast very strongly with the later coloraturas. A deep sadness permeates the first four phrases, the growing intensity of expression going from piano at the start to mezzo forte for the repeat of "Durch sie ging all mein Glück verloren." By now Tamino must be moved. The queen feels the time has come to strike a new chord and says with great resentment, "ein Bösewicht," immediately stressed by the orchestra. She then amplifies it with a long value forte, returning to a grieving piano on "entfloh mit ihr." There follows a dramatic description of the abduction of her daughter, shifting the spotlight from herself to the desperate victim long enough to melt Tamino's heart before alluding again to her own ordeal. Her voice has changed from its velvety texture to a tragic, shuddering tone colored to the meaning of each phrase she sings. "Zittern," "bangem Erschüttern," "ängstliches Beben," all describe the panic-stricken victim. There is a brief return to herself with "Ich musste sie . . .," sung piano. Then the mother recalls her daughter's pathetic cry for help, forte to fortissimo, adding piano a piteous "war alles, was sie sprach." A pleading but hopeless feeling brings a simple lyricism to "Allein vergebens," and depressed slowness invades "denn meine Hülfe war zu schwach." A tragic strength reappears, however, in the first two bars of the repeat of the same words. The last bar of the section is a rallentando; a short fermata is permissible on the last A, "war." In these last lines note the dramatic power of the even quarter notes ("denn meine"); the miraculous use of the grace notes for expression ("allein ver*ge*bens," helplessness; "Hü*l*fe," effort); the descending line of even eighth notes ("meine Hülfe," defeat), two bars before the ending of the section. The soprano ought to study the pages of the *larghetto* with a magnifying glass; they are among the richest and most expressive pages of Mozart's music. Tamino is overcome with emotion, and the resourceful queen will finish winning him over to her side with an extraordinary display of trust in his virtues, a celebration of his victories and of his reward, the possession forever of the as yet unnamed Pamina.

The *allegro moderato*, ♩ = 132: It is very important to find the right tempo for this section, first for the exact character of the music, and second for the speed of the runs. The music must express irresistibly convincing power and overwhelming enthusiasm. The Queen of the Night is sure she has found in Tamino the accomplice she needs in her attempt to get her daughter back, and she uses all of her dazzling brilliance to ensnare him once and for all. It has been said that the ideal voice for the Queen of the Night is seldom found. A voice capable at the same time of the high coloratura written for the part and of the dramatic power of the second half of the score is rare indeed. But in this first aria that dramatic power is tempered by sorrow in the *larghetto* and lightened by enthusiasm in the *allegro*, so that the total demand should not be beyond the range of a very good and well-trained coloratura voice. The only unacceptable feature would be that such a voice would be very small.

In order to stay faithful to the character of the queen the general feeling of the *allegro* must be a sustained legato, a notion absolutely reconcilable with speed. The three syllables "Du-du-du" are sustained in spite of the silences between them. Each of the following phrases is sung in one breath, with a sweeping authority, the repeat of "du wirst der Tochter Retter sein" growing from piano to forte, excluding any doubt from the statement. The same conviction makes the two phrases preceding the runs very firm and even. The runs start with the word "dann," that is, with a clear vowel /a/. It is understandable that this vowel may undergo some changes of color during the long lines of vocalises that follow, but the sound should basically stay as near to /a/ as possible and not drift to some ill-defined /o/ or /œ/ or even /u/. Another basic remark is that no consonant /h/ is to be inserted between notes, so that "hahaha" is never heard instead of "ahahah."

Let us call measure 1, the measure of the first short run on "dann"; the run on bars 2, 3, and 4 ending on a high B-flat is to be sung in one breath, starting piano and staying piano for two bars before a strong crescendo in bar 4. In bar 5 the scale of B-flat starts piano, very light and legato. The same is true for the scale of C in bar 7, so that the staccato notes in bars 6 and 8 come as a cheerful surprise to the ear. That cheerful feeling prevails also in bars 9 and 10—sing with a bouncing animation. The run in bars 11, 12, 13, and 14 is started piano. A breath can be taken after an abbreviated C on the first eighth of bar 13, another before the D (last two sixteenths of bar 13); the singer stays on the vowel /a/ through bar 14 and sings "ewig dein" for the trill and the resolution in bars 15 and 16.

The end of the aria is forte, as spaciously as the voice will allow.

All this advice may seem overdone and tedious. However, the only way to free the mind and the voice for the high notes and to avoid apprehension is to establish in smallest detail all the intentions in the easier places. Variety of dynamics is indispensable for the life of the music as well as to save energy for the singer. The possibility is offered here of playing a highly artistic game. One should try to play it in constant lightness, brilliance, and good humor.

"Ach, ich fühl's" *soprano*

Ach, ich fühl's,
es ist verschwunden,
ewig hin mein ganzes Glück,
ewig hin der Liebe Glück.
Nimmer kommt ihr, Wonnestunden,
meinem Herzen mehr zurück.
Sieh, Tamino, diese Tränen
fliessen, Trauter, dir allein.
Fühlst du nicht der Liebe Sehnen,
so wird Ruhe im Tode sein.

Ah, I feel it,
it is gone,
forever gone all my happiness,
forever gone love's happiness.
Never will you, hours of delight,
return to my heart anymore.
Look, Tamino, these tears
flow, beloved, for you alone.
If you don't feel love's yearning,
then there will be peace in death.

Pamina and Tamino, chosen by the gods to become husband and wife, must pass through severe tests to prove their steadfastness and worthiness. Their recent long separation was only one such test. Pamina is overjoyed to find herself at last reunited with Tamino, but a more cruel test awaits her. She does not know that Tamino has been ordered not to speak and takes his silence for rejection, which, she feels, will be her death.

The aria is an *andante*, but a very slow *andante*. ♪ = 63 is the tempo suggested. The voice of Pamina must flow evenly, encompassing a long range of the vocal line without breaks or discrepancies. Mozart has given her ample time to prepare and perfect the simple beauty of her phrases, the purity of each sound, the coordination of the intervals, and also the depth of her boundless grief.

The dynamic marking *piano* in the orchestra is, of course, valid for the voice also, but in the same way that the orchestral chords are sustained and vibrant, the sound of the voice must be intense, each vowel vibrant to the end of its value, even though the phrase at first stays subdued in deadly hopelessness. That hopelessness will dominate not only the first four but the first sixteen bars. Sing those bars with total conviction, as if you were looking in disbelief at a spot in front of you from where a precious possession has suddenly disappeared. Practically, sing a long "Ach," stress the appoggiaturas on "fühl's" and "hin"; sing the low G of the interval "es ist" very light and already in high resonance so as to match the upper G, which is also a long note. The thirty-seconds on "ewig" are not fast. There is tragic regret in "mein ganzes Glück." The following upper G (vowel /e/) is intense and must clearly convey the meaning "forever." With the words "der Liebe Glück" we face a vocal difficulty that will recur later in the aria, namely, to sing a B-flat on a vowel /i/ and in a word meaning "love," which rules out both shrillness and dullness. The solution is to prepare on the D on "der" a slim vowel /e/, which becomes with almost no change of shape a vowel /i/ on the G of "Liebe" and on the B-flat itself. This vowel /i/ vibrates like a slim blade ascending along the face but resounds into a shell-like space constantly open in the upper back of the mouth. Think of an old, rustic lamp consisting of a candle standing in front of a parabolic mirror and decide to sing the candle while keeping the curve of the parabolic mirror open in the back of it. Moreover, thinking of "Liebe" with worshiping warmth will help you to find the true ring of this all-important note.

Although the mood of hopelessness still prevails, more vocal strength can be used on "Nimmer kommt ihr" until the first "zurück." That phrase as well as the next one, sung legatissimo, must be rich in many slight inflections of piano, very slight crescendos and diminuendos that one must feel instinctively. No doubt in bars 12 and 13 the ascending line on "mei-" and on "Her-" is a crescendo and the two notes on "-nem" and "-zen" are more piano.

In preparation for the run in bar 13, "meinem" is subdued whereas the ascending notes in the run are progressively less piano, aiming at a kind of delayed climax that will take place on the B-flat in bar 15. A breath is tolerated between "meinem" and "Her-zen," that is, between bars 13 and 14, but no breath should be taken after the B-flat at the end of bar 14. If necessary, breathe after the first F in bar 15, but briefly enough to make the breath appear part of the staccato pattern. Sing the run exactly on time with a slight ritardando, if you wish, on the four staccato notes in bar 15, together with a crescendo. There is a decrescendo of depression on the last "mehr zurück."

Pamina now speaks directly to the silent Tamino and with more dramatic force attempts to make him react to her sorrow. She will repeat her plea several times, then, failing to move him, express her yearning for peace in death. Through her strong but never violent insistence her love must still be heard at every moment. The words "Tamino," bars 17 and 18, "dir allein," bars 20 and 21, and the repeat of "dir allein," bars 21 and 22, are overflowing with tenderness. The feeling of hopelessness returns on "Fühlst du nicht," bar 22, the repeat of "der Liebe Sehnen," bars 23 and 24, being full of grief. A darker set of vowels will stress the call for death in bars 25 and 26. The vowel /u/ in "Ruhe" or "Ruh' " is a long *oo* as in *loose*, the /o/ in "Tod" a very dark sound.

In bar 27, "Fühlst du nicht," an outburst of disbelief with a trace of indignation in it, is the phrase most forte of the aria, and its repeat in bars 28 and 29 comes like an echo, sensitive and filled with regret. A tenuto can be made on the top B-flat provided it is sung in a velvety color and piano (see the technical suggestion above).

From here on Pamina gives up her efforts to regain Tamino, only to sink deeper into her yearning for final peace. Even so, her singing must remain extremely even and smooth in order to stay in character. The octave interval G to G, bars 33 and 34, will be smooth if the lower G is already sung in the upper resonance and the upper G in a very slim, forward vowel /u/. Then the low C-sharp is also kept in a high resonance, even if the word "Tode" stays very dark. A progressive, very gradual ritardando seems to come by itself on the two last "im Tode sein." The last one is barely more than a murmur, sung at the tip of the lips, on a very dark vowel /o/, as a sigh of helpless despair.

On the operatic stage the aria is framed by Papageno's materialistic speeches. He is in turn eating, drinking, or trembling with fear. By contrast the aria will easily appear feminine, sensitive, and very sad. Sung in isolation, it demands an even greater amount of charm and grace, coupled with the same easy-sounding mastery of a well-educated voice, to express convincingly and sincerely the hopeless grief which is its essence.

Musorgski, *Boris Godunov*

"I have attained the power"   *baritone/bass-baritone*

I have attained the power.
Six years have pass'd
since first I ruled o'er Russia.
But still no peace returns to my remorseful soul.
In vain the seers and prophets all
foretell long years of life and honour,
glad and peaceful.
Nor life, nor pow'r, nor glory can delight me,
nor plaudits of men—these things give me no joy.
My hopes for those most near and dear are blighted;
I look'd to make a joyful marriage feast for her,

my darling daughter, my pure white dove.
Like lightning death did snatch away her spouse.
The heavy hand of One above doth press
upon my guilty soul, requiring justice!
Around me all is darkness unending,
the future holds nor light nor comfort.
My heart is filled with sorrow; and rack'd with despair
my anguished spirit.
Mysterious terror shakes me, awful visions haunt me . . .
In supplication I kneel to my Saviour,
for respite from pain and sharp remorse.
Enthroned in splendour, ambition's dreams accomplished,
I reign over Russia yet pray to God for tears of consolation.
But God condemns!
My nobles plot against me;
the Poles in secret are conspiring;
famine, pest, and treachery surround me;
while like savage beasts the people roam, plague-stricken.
The country from end to end groans in grief!
These heavy burdens, imposed by Heaven
to punish my crime, still unpardon'd,
my people lay them all at my door.
In the market, in the street, Boris is accursed!
Now sleep has flown from me . . .
In night's darkest hours
the child Demetrius comes in bloodstain'd shroud,
with eyes dilated and hands uprais'd,
imploring for mercy . . .
but mercy was denied him!
I see the gaping wound that gleams so red,
his cry forever haunts me . . .
Great God above, save thou me!

There are many different versions of the opera-drama *Boris Godunov*. The aria studied here is presented as it appears in the Kalmus edition, which is, except for its translation into English, a copy of the Bessel edition, the Musorgski score reviewed by Rimski-Korsakov. The aria covers numbers 103 to 112 of that edition. There are also many different versions of the story of Boris Godunov, his son Feodor, his minister Schuiski, and the false Dimitri who pretended to and won Boris's throne. From the libretto written for the opera by Pushkin and Karamzin it is necessary to retain only some essential features in order to understand the aria.

Boris has been reigning over Russia for six years. He was the brother-in-law and prime minister of the preceding tsar. In order to succeed him, Boris had Dimitri, heir to the throne, murdered and then arranged to have himself called to power by the acclamation of the populace. But his reign is plagued by the misery of his people, the deaths of close relatives, insurrections, and political opposition. Above all, it is marked by growing remorse for his crime. Recently a young man pretending to be Dimitri has begun to raise an army against him from nearby Poland, a heavy blow to Boris's nerves and mental balance. In this aria Boris releases the flow of his sorrows and torments.

The tessitura of the aria, in this particular version, is in the baritone range, but the general weight of the entire role justifies the casting of a bass-baritone or even of a bass. A strong baritone voice with a round and sonorous low range—a rare voice in this day of high notes—should do well with the aria where dramatic power is essential.

There are many changes of mood in the aria, from fatherly love to the hallucination of murder, but gloom pervades all the moods. The man and his power are undermined from all sides. While still invested with the majesty of his rank and the prestige of his own strength, he is fighting a losing battle. The interpreter must be deeply aware of the scope of that battle.

When the aria is sung as a solo, the first two chords must be played very slowly. The voice comes in, slowly also, dark and almost passive, but important. There is no joy for Boris in being the tsar, or in having been the tsar for six years, but still he is the tsar. A forte chord slashes the passive mood. The first suffering words are heard, suddenly mezzo forte, "But still no peace," before the phrase dims and diminishes for "my remorseful soul." In the *più lento* the voice sings above the slowly unfolding theme, which tells of the tsar's anxiety despite notes expressing hopeful thoughts—thus the line from "In vain the seers" to "glad and peaceful," a line hopeful in substance but sung slowly and without hope.

The *più animato* is a strongly voiced rejection of the joys of power, from mezzo forte to forte (a forte that matches the idea of popular acclaim). The first half of the phrase brings with it an accelerando; there can be a stentato on the climactic E, then the second half of the phrase is a rallentando and diminuendo, very slow on "give me no joy." That line calls for the important voice of the tsar.

But the tsar is also a father. With the change of key the sound of the voice, piano to mezzo forte, becomes mellow and, although still full of regrets, reflects his love for his daughter. "My darling daughter, my pure white dove" has a loving sound, slim but warm, more on the lips than before and brighter. Like a blow from fate, "Like lightning" shatters that mood violently, before sadness makes the end of the phrase mournful.

In the *adagio* Boris sings one of the most beautiful melodies in the bass-baritone repertoire, the theme of his punishment at the hand of God. It is a long ascension from E-flat to high G-flat, in a great crescendo. In order to stress its continuity, not much helped by the translation, the singer should go without a breath from "The heavy hand" to "my guilty soul," ignoring the silence after "press." The F-flat on "justice" is all-important and fortissimo. The following four bars, "Around me all is darkness," stay at least mezzo forte, dark and slow in intense hopelessness. In the first six bars of number 107 a progressive accelerando stresses Boris's nervous agitation, while a fearful and restrained sound colors his account of terrors and visions that make him shudder. On the seventh bar of number 107 the tempo returns to *adagio* as in number 106, and the theme of the punishment returns in part, but this time in the form of a prayer for mercy, lasting five bars. The voice here becomes the humble voice of a penitent fallen on his knees.

But (number 108) greatness and glory are not absent from Boris's soul. For four bars the great voice of a sovereign comes back, and the top E-flat must be sung fully, brightly and outstandingly, although the distressed tsar immediately bends his pride to a tearful confession. The end of the phrase must have a sudden touch of human frailty, sung with a slight ritardando.

The moment of self-pity is followed by a feverish review of all the ills of his reign. At number 109 another progressive accelerando begins, this one whipped along by the bells ringing, at first on the third beat of the bar, then frantically twice in each bar. The voice grows harsh and loud until, in the bar before number 110, it falters to a weak piano and a ritardando. (The marking *stringendo poco* in the Kalmus edition makes absolutely no sense.) From number 110 on it is *adagio* all the way. The theme of God's punishment soars anew, pathetically; at the top, "unpardon'd" is an explosion of despair. The repeat of the theme in the abbreviated form (the complete form is in the accompaniment) brings out the public form of Boris's ordeal: His people curse his name. The words "Boris is accursed" can be cried out loud or whispered in a hoarse rasp: the tsar has reached a state of emotion beyond control.

But his private ordeal is even worse than his public one. On the fourth bar after number 111, the theme of the specter of Dimitri sneaks in. Haggard, Boris relives in full daylight the obsession of his nights. Horror enters his voice, which sometimes rumbles in hollow sounds, sometimes soars wildly—"the child," "dilated." Even in the 12/8, however, no change of tempo must occur; the turbulent hallucination is backed by an inflexible fate. Only on the last words of "his cry forever haunts me" does a rallentando of exhaustion take place while the merciless accompaniment vanishes. The last words of prayer are said very slowly, haltingly, no doubt hopelessly, without any rhythm.

That final part of the scene, which starts with the theme of the specter, requires the great, rare ability on the part of the performer to shift from singing tones to declamation and back without breaking the continuity and to keep a strict, even strongly stressed rhythm. In creating a mood of horror for his listeners, he must also avoid any cheap and vulgar sounds. This is tragedy in music, coming from several pages of great, sustained singing. What a joy it is to develop the ability in oneself to feel such emotions as Boris's deeply and yet to be able to master the skill of singing and acting such a scene impeccably.

Nicolai, *Die lustigen Weiber von Windsor*

"Nun eilt herbei"   *soprano*

Nun eilt herbei, Witz, heitre Laune,	Now hurry, come, wit, cheerfulness,
die tollsten Schwänke,	the most fantastic pranks,
List und Übermut!	shrewdness and high spirits!
Nichts sei zu arg,	May nothing be too wicked,
wenn's dazu diene,	if it serves
die Männer ohn Erbarmen zu bestrafen.	to punish menfolk without mercy.

Das ist ein Volk, so schlecht sind sie,	They are folks, so bad are they,
dass man sie gar genug nicht quälen kann.	that one cannot torture them enough.
Vor allen jener dicke Schlemmer,	Above all that fat glutton
der uns verführen will, ha, ha, ha, ha!	who wants to seduce us, ha, ha, ha, ha!
Er soll es büssen.	He shall do penance for it.
Doch wenn er kommt,	But when he comes,
wie werd'ich mich benehmen müssen?	How shall I behave?
Was werd'ich sagen?	What shall I say?
Halt, ich weiss es schon!	Wait, I know it already!
"Verführer! Warum stellt Ihr so	"Seducer! Why do you thus pursue
der tugendsamen Gattin nach?	the virtuous spouse?
Warum? Verführer!	Why? Seducer!
Den Frevel sollt'ich nie verzeihn,	Such misdeed I should never forgive,
nein, nie,	no, never,
mein Zorn müsst'Eure Strafe sein.	my wrath should be your punishment.
Jedoch, des Weibes Herz ist schwach.	However, a woman's heart is weak.
Ihr klagt so rührend Eure Pein,	You complain so touchingly of your pain,
Ihr seufzt, mein Herz wird weich,	you sigh, my heart softens,
nicht länger kann ich grausam sein,	no longer can I be cruel,
und ich gesteh es schamrot Euch ein:	and I confess, blushing with shame,
mein Ritter, ach, ich liebe Euch."	my chevalier, ah, I love you."
Ha, ha! Er wird mir glauben,	Ha, ha! He is going to believe me,
verstellen kann ich mich fürwahr.	I am indeed good at pretending.
Ein kühnes Wagstück ist es zwar,	True, it is a bold venture,
allein den Spass darf man sich	yet that fun
schon erlauben.	one can permit oneself.
Frohsinn und Laune würzen das Leben,	Gaiety and good humor add spice to life,
und zu vergeben ist wohl ein Scherz.	and a joke certainly can be forgiven.
So zum Vergnügen	One may well lie
darf man schon lügen,	just for fun,
bleibt nur voll Liebe,	as long as the heart remains
voll Treue das Herz. Ja!	loving and faithful. Yes!
Drum voll Vertrauen wag ich die Tat,	Therefore confidently I dare the deed,
lustige Frauen, ja, die wissen sich Rat.	cheerful women truly are never at a loss.

Upon the discovery that the impertinent love letter Falstaff has written her was sent in duplicate to her friend Frau Reich (Meg Page) as well, Frau Fluth (Alice Ford) decides to punish the scoundrel and starts planning her revenge. She is in her home, surrounded by her familiar household furnishings, and speaks to herself.

Frau Fluth is still a young woman, steady by nature, active, combative if need be, quick-witted, and at the moment angry. Her voice is a lyric soprano easily covering a long range, nimble and colorful. She must be able to dominate an ensemble with a brilliant legato and to use a light speaking tone in the recitatives.

After a short, very spirited prelude Frau Fluth calls vivaciously for help: She will need wit, good humor, cunning, and recklessness to carry out the prank she has in mind. The spirited music returns and seems to depict the prompt arrival of all those accomplices. The spirit of revenge has also been summoned. "Nichts sei zu arg" is said with severity, and the sudden *andantino*, much slower than the tempo of the recitative, adds solemnity to her plan to be merciless. "Zu bestrafen" is said ominously and a bit melodramatically. With "das ist ein Volk" Frau Fluth releases her scornful anger, the words "so schlecht" are like a whip's lash. Her mind returning to the central object of her anger, she remembers that he is just an old glutton; "dicke Schlemmer" is mugged in a thick, caustic voice, and the idea that he sees himself as a seducer changes her anger into a fit of laughter, light and bright. She is again serious for "Er soll es büssen." Now, slowing down a great deal, she plans her behavior during their date. "Wie werd'ich mich benehmen müssen" is almost in the adagio tempo already, and in the long silence between "Was werd'ich sagen" and the happy "Halt, ich weiss es schon," Frau Fluth has conceived her plan word for word and gives it a try right away.

The run by the violins that starts the *larghetto* launches Frau Fluth on her invective, angry and vehement. As obvious as it is, it must be stressed that the word "Verführer," especially here, is centered on the vowel /y/ and that to sing an /i/ in its place will never do. The soprano must study that vowel to the point where it becomes entirely familiar, even though it does not exist in English. It is customary to sing the second "Verführer" reaching high C on the syllable "-füh-" and going down all the way from there in a double scale of C major, with a fermata on the high C and another one on the low C, this last one with a threatening tone. This tone is right also for the next two lines, the words "Eure Strafe sein" very strongly articulated, the thirty-second notes very brief and sharp. Here appears the cunning part of Frau Fluth's plan: In the two beats preceding "Jedoch," the vengeful mood changes to feigned compassion and the voice becomes friendly and tender. It is compassion that makes the undulating phrase "Ihr klagt so rührend Eure Pein" touching, the next short words so mild. With the change of key the young woman will push her hypocrisy a notch farther. Discarding any resentment—"nicht länger kann ich grausam sein"—she fakes the embarrassment of blushing and is able to speak only two syllables at a time, "schamrot — Euch ein." Even her silences must betray her sudden trouble. But the cat has to be let out of the bag, and "mein Ritter" and "ach, ach" must sound as if Frau Fluth gives up any hope of hiding her sudden passion. The first "ich liebe Euch" is a confidential confession, the second a jocular caricature of passion exploding, the third a capitulation. The performer with her constant vocal and facial mimicry must have a jolly good time during the whole scene. If she does not and clings to some technical preoccupation, the whole fun of the page may be lost.

The laughter marked here must not be perfunctory. The singer must have built up her good humor so well that real, frank laughter, bright and well supported, rings out as singing notes would. A happy Frau Fluth congratulates herself on her acting talent, and for the whole following page she will prolong her enjoyment of the audacious prank. Using her natural voice with gaiety and charm the interpreter must sing the several runs as near the sound of laughter as possible and intersperse them with light staccato notes when indicated. By the time she has repeated "darf man sich schon erlauben" for the last time, she has regained her poise and will, humorously but sincerely, praise the innocent joys of well-intentioned lies and deceits.

While following the indicated changes of tempo throughout the page, it is customary to sing the first two bars of the *poco meno mosso* slowly and the next two fast, then again "und zu vergeben" slowly, with a real fermata, and "ist wohl ein Scherz" not so slowly. The effect is that of a teasing and witty grace, the voice being as brightly feminine as possible. Enjoy saying very clearly the different rhymes ("lügen" and "Vergnügen") and make a sentimental ritardando on "voll Treue das Herz" and "voll Treue and Liebe das

Herz." The cadenza expresses Frau Fluth's—and every woman's—pride in her graceful shrewdness and must be sung with cheerful charm and a touch of irony and daring in the triplets of thirty-seconds. In the third run of that cadenza it is advisable to breathe before the triplet two bars before its end, to sing the chromatic ascending line with a progressive ritardando, and to create with a tenuto on the last B-flat and B-natural a suspense suggesting a kind of "now, wait a second" feeling.

Let us mark the tempo at ♩ = 96 and the following *poco più mosso* at ♩ = 108, just to keep our bearings straight. Frau Fluth proudly celebrates the triumph of daring and cheerful women. Her rhythm has bounce and a feeling of independence, which may have been the 1840 version of women's lib. The mood being established right away, the performance from now on is a vocal affair. A sixteen-bar cut is often made starting at the end of the tenth bar of the *poco più mosso*. That cut does not suppress any new or important element of the piece. A brilliant, vivacious mood should be maintained to the end of the aria, the soprano taking advantage of the notation *piano* on "Ja, lustige Frauen" in order to create much-needed variety. It is traditional to end the piece by singing a high C after the fermata on the G of the last-but-one measure for the voice and to land on the written A-flat.

For all its verve and variety this aria may seem a little lengthy if the soprano singing it does not use a keen imagination in conceiving its several moments, its constant changes of mood, and in participating intensely in Frau Fluth's moods and intentions. There is nothing rare or unusual in these moods. Any young woman can find all the elements of a good interpretation in her own experience.

Offenbach, *Les Contes d'Hoffmann*

"Les oiseaux dans la charmille" *soprano*

Les oiseaux dans la charmille,
dans les cieux l'astre du jour,
tout parle à la jeune fille
d'amour.
Ah! voilà la chanson gentille,
la chanson d'Olympia.

Tout ce qui chante et résonne,
et soupire tour à tour,
émeut son coeur qui frissonne
d'amour. Ah! tout parle d'amour.
Ah! voilà la chanson mignonne,
la chanson d'Olympia.

The birds in the bower,
the sun in the skies,
everything speaks to the young girl
of love.
Ah! that is the nice song,
the song of Olympia.

Everything that sings and resounds,
and in turn sighs,
moves her heart which trembles
with love. Ah! Everything speaks of love.
Ah! that is the cute song,
the song of Olympia.

In Offenbach's colorful score the song of the mechanical doll is one of the most delightful pieces. Born from the joint efforts of the two mad geniuses Spalanzani and Coppelius, Olympia is such a masterpiece that at her presentation at a party she not only seems real to a large group of guests but also wins the love of the poet Hoffmann.

The coloratura singing the aria should use a crystal-clear voice, very simple, very clean, and not purposely devoid of intentions and wit. The mechanical strictness of the doll is still interpreted by a singer of flesh, bones, and brains. The audience must hear the latter under the disguise of the former.

The *moderato* tempo is one without any haste, ♩. = 66–60, the voice poised, happy, even cheerful. It must be noted right away that only a few bars in the whole song are marked *staccato*. Olympia sings an almost constant legato interrupted at will by short silences, as happens for instance at the start of the two first phrases of the song. "Les oiseaux dans la char-" is a legato phrase with short interruptions between syllables but not attacks of jerky support. Birds, sunshine, youth, love, all those elements inspire a delightful song. The suggestion of a mechanical delivery comes on the one hand from the exact repeat of the same phrase, on the other from the musical writing of the runs where we can hear tiny wheels turning and stopping. The first two phrases and their repeats are very monotonous but sung with a cheerful voice. "D'amour" and its vocalise are forte and brilliant, not sentimental. The longer run, however, starting with G is piano and sentimental, its rallentando very enticing (Spalanzani and Coppelius want Olympia to attract Hoffmann), still more so in the ending, "tout parle . . . d'amour." With the fermata and trill on "Ah" (C) starts a demonstration of the technical achievements of Olympia's two inventors. Inside her there is a gear for staccato and a gear for legato, a forte gear and a piano gear. They change abruptly and without transition. That is the way Olympia has been programmed.

"Voilà la chanson gen-" is a bouncy, dainty staccato; the next two bars are an indifferent legato. The last five notes of "gentille" return to the elegant staccato, with a graceful ritardando. The next line returns to the indifferent legato. After the repeat of the single word "d'Olympia" the forte gear is on, precise and well articulated—and changed after two bars to the piano gear, followed by alternating half bars of forte staccato and piano staccato (those gears can be interchanged at will), until an unexpected rallentando reveals that something is amiss in the engine. The staccato staggers for one bar, then the machine stalls on the high B-flats. They come increasingly slower and should create a feeling of anxiety by their seemingly uncontrolled repeats. With the chromatic descent, that feeling is dispelled; the spring only needed rewinding. All B-flats stay forte, each of them a little slower than the one before; the A-natural is still forte, the three following notes diminuendo to pianissimo, to which a portamento downward is generally added, although it characterizes a deflating balloon rather than an exhausted spring. All that bit of comedy should be made with charm, avoiding the trivial and the grotesque. Olympia in her distress is still a very dainty little bit of a doll. Rewound, she returns with new vitality to her previous program, alternating staccato and legato. Two short groups (*re-mi-sol-fa-mi*) forte prepare a dazzling cadenza. The descending part of it is very light and swift, the ascending part, after a breath, could include a small rallentando to suggest that the climb to E-flat is slightly taxing for the mechanism of the doll. The high E-flat is not staccato and can be held that extra fraction of a second which will allow the tone to spin instead of breaking abruptly. The last bars with trills and fermatas are sung full voice with the great satisfaction of a job well done.

The second stanza is musically written exactly like the first. Could one detect one ounce of sentimentality in the words "et soupire . . ." and "qui frissonne," added for the benefit of Hoffmann? Some cadenzas have been added in present-day performances. One of them seems to be at least innocuous and even preserves the feeling of turning wheels mentioned above, but in a slightly different way. It is shown here, in bar 4 and in bar 8:

tour - - - - - - - -

But does this add anything significant? The whole song, as it is, is well balanced, funny, and to the point. It is the debut in society of the pretended daughter of Spalanzani; she does her scheduled number in front of the company and demurely retires to a seat on the side. Later, after getting out of control and forgetting her place, she will indulge in coloratura fireworks exactly fitting the situation. It has proved possible to win great applause by singing Olympia's song as written. Why not work at extracting as much as possible from the original text instead of attempting to gain more personal acclaim from additions not in that original text?

"Scintille diamant" *baritone*

Allez! pour te livrer combat	Go! to do battle with you
les yeux de Giulietta	the eyes of Giulietta
sont une arme certaine.	are a sure weapon.
Il a fallu que Schlémil succombât. . . .	Schlémil had to succumb. . . .
Foi de diable et de capitaine!	On my word as devil and captain!
Tu feras comme lui.	You will do like him.
Je veux que Giulietta t'ensorcelle,	I want Giulietta to bewitch you,
t'ensorcelle aujourd'hui.	to bewitch you today.
Scintille, diamant,	Sparkle, diamond,
miroir où se prend l'alouette,	mirror where the lark is caught,
scintille, diamant,	sparkle, diamond,
fascine, attire-la.	fascinate, attract her.
L'alouette ou la femme,	The lark or the woman,
à cet appas vainqueur	to this triumphant bait
vont de l'aile ou du coeur:	comes on wings or with willing heart:
l'une y laisse la vie,	one gives up its life there,
et l'autre y perd son âme.	the other loses her soul.
Ah! Scintille, diamant,	Ah! Sparkle, diamond,
miroir où se prend l'alouette,	mirror where the lark is caught,
scintille, diamant,	sparkle, diamond,
fascine, attire-la.	fascinate, attract her.
Beau diamant, scintille,	Beautiful diamond, sparkle,
attire-la!	attract her!

Dappertutto is one of the impersonations assumed by the evil power which pursues Hoffmann throughout his life and which, time after time, ruins his love affairs through every means ranging from humiliation to murder. Whatever the concept of the role of Dappertutto—and in the last few years so many have been added to the traditional *Tales of Hoffmann*—his singing must combine elegance, sarcasm, and haughtiness. His goal must at all times be malevolent. A brilliant baritone voice is preferable for the part, and when the singer is cast as Dappertutto only, he should sing the aria in the original key of E-natural. If, as planned by Offenbach and as is now done frequently, the same singer is in charge of all four evil characters, with two of them being more in the bass-baritone range, it is permissible to transpose the aria half a tone down to E-flat, starting the transposition as indicated below. When the aria is used out of context in concert, it may be sung in either key as long as it does not lose its character of haughty brilliance.

The motif that introduces Dappertutto—the "ubiquitous one"—is common to all four evil characters. It starts piano with an insinuating sleekness and grows into a strongly accented, broad ending. While it is being played, Dappertutto watches Hoffmann and his friend Nicklausse as they leave, then directs scornful remarks at their backs. A word of explanation: Giulietta is a courtesan of great beauty whom Dappertutto keeps under a spell and uses according to his whims. Her name is pronounced in the Italian way—we are in Venice—that is, Djoo-liet-ta. Her current lover is Schlémil, whom Dappertutto with her help has robbed of his shadow. Dappertutto speaks of himself as "devil" and "captain." It must be on account of that latter title that he accords himself the right to wear a sword at all times.

The recitative calls for a round voice singing with poise and authority, sustaining all the values, with rather dark-colored vowels, the tempo being ♩ = 76–80. The silences are short and do not disrupt the continuity of the singing. The whole recitative should be felt as one piece. The man who is singing is so strong-willed that when he says "Je veux" ("I want") there is no resisting him.

From the beginning to "que Schlémil succombât," sing mezzo forte with a kind of fateful straightness. The forte on "Foi de diable" for a second allows us a glimpse of Dappertutto's true satanic nature, almost as if the exclamation had escaped his constant control. With the portamento downward we return to more earthly matters. From there on sing with great power, with a strong ritardando on the second "t'ensorcelle," so that the two chords in the accompaniment can be spaced broadly. Note that the two D-sharps on the first "t'ensorcelle" are tied notes so that their total value is three beats, the final syllable "-le" coming on the fourth beat and being stopped immediately.

If you want to sing the aria in E-flat, start the transposition on the last note of bar 12, "Je" on A-natural instead of B-flat. Then sing "veux que Giulietta" in bar 13 on a B-flat and continue a half step lower than the written notes. Finally, sing the aria in E-flat.

Aria: *andante poco mosso.* I have sung this aria on stage in many different tempi, according to the wishes of the conductor. When free to choose I prefer to start at approximately ♩ = 108 with some strong fluctuations later. I also believe in feeling the aria in three and not in one.

The voice should change here. The irresistible power suggested during the recitative might have been that of a destructive force. Now it is a magic power that must be suggested. After the introductory chords and a long silent fermata on bar 8, the voice, as beautiful as possible, enters snakelike in a long line, piano and velvety, the intervals perfectly clean but all sounds tied together without a break. It would be a mistake to use a character voice here. Dappertutto is a magician, not a sorcerer, his strength is seduction, not open cruelty, his bait is a diamond. He will reach his evil goal by ensnaring his victim. The trap he sets is glittering, his prey one more soul, and he profoundly enjoys setting his trap. This enjoyment must show in the subtle inflections, which are very difficult to describe: a way of connecting the B, the F, and the B in "l'alouette"; the cheerfulness of "la femme"; the dynamism of "vont de l'aile ou du coeur."

With the *animato* on "l'une y laisse la vie" the voice becomes suddenly more intense. The cat no longer plays with the mouse. The indication reads *appassionato*. Make the voice more and more vibrant. The words "son âme" must be powerful. The *animato* lasts only nine bars. On the tenth, the *allargando* starts, which will ask for and will favor the full strength of the voice. On the word "vie" you have the option of singing an F-sharp or a G-sharp. Both are fine if they are sung on a bright vowel /i/, ringing and resonant, not muffled or covered.

The next bars are still broader. A breath after "et l'autre" is marked and is useful. The turn on "perd" is triumphant, the fermata long and well sustained. The diminuendo on "âme" reaches mezzo forte, the diminuendo on "Ah" pianissimo. After a breath, "Scintille, diamant" starts in the same pianissimo dynamic.

The magician speaks to his instrument, softly, persuasively, while the glitter of the precious stone is translated in the orchestra. The return of "scintille, diamant," ninth bar of the second part, introduces a new element: Dappertutto orders the stone to attract Giulietta. The first "attire-la" is a crescendo, the second, bars 15 to 17, is both a rallentando and a very strong crescendo, the E on "la" as expanded as possible while the orchestra remains piano. The next "attire-la," bars 20 to 22, is mezzo forte and persuasive. Dappertutto now uses his power to charm. Sing "Beau diamant" piano and caressing, and on the next "attire-la" be sure to stress the crescendo-decrescendo as marked, creating the impression of a force attracting its prey. Cajole "Beau diamant" and "scintille," singing pianissimo, and you will keep your listeners in suspense waiting for the last "attire-la." Start it piano and slowly before letting it grow into a climactic G-sharp held full strength for three bars.

In this aria a skillful singer can show many facets of his talent with a basic simplicity of approach coupled with the desire to make his voice reflect the varied ways of a masterful magician. It is the first aria this writer sang at the Metropolitan. The ovation at the end reassured him that in those short four minutes he had made a niche for himself in that big house.

"O Dieu, de quelle ivresse"   *tenor*

O Dieu, de quelle ivresse	Heavens, with what rapture
embrases-tu mon âme,	do you set my soul afire,
comme un concert divin	like a divine concert
ta voix m'a pénétré!	your voice has penetrated me!
D'un feu doux et brûlant	By a soft and burning fire
mon être est dévoré;	my being is consumed;

tes regards dans les miens	your glances have poured
ont épanché leur flamme	their flame into mine
comme des astres radieux.	like radiant stars.
Et je sens, o ma bien-aimée,	And I feel, o my beloved,
passer ton haleine embaumée	your fragrant breath pass
sur mes lèvres et sur mes yeux!	on my lips and on my eyes!
O Dieu, de quelle ivresse	Heavens, with what rapture
embrases-tu mon âme,	do you set my soul afire,
tes regards dans les miens	your glances have poured
ont épanché leur flamme.	their flame into mine.
Bien aimée, je suis à toi!	My beloved, I am your own!

This beautiful lyric phrase (number 21 in Schirmer's 1959 voice-piano score, number 16 in the 1907 French Choudens score) appears twice in the opera, first in the ardent love scene between Hoffmann and the courtesan Giulietta, the second time at the very end of the epilogue when Hoffmann sings it to his Muse. It has two different endings, a very tender and melodious one the first time, a very brilliant one the second time. If the phrase is to be used out of context for a concert or an audition, it seems possible to use both endings, as will be indicated here, without committing any sin against the music and providing the tenor with an outstanding vehicle for his voice.

Hoffmann's voice is a lirico-spinto tenor of brilliant intensity, displaying great ease in handling a high tessitura, and capable of being nimble and witty as well as tragic.

The tempo, *largo*, runs at ♩ = 50–52 with a sense of great breadth in a superb legato. Ideally the phrase starts piano as Hoffmann speaks of an overwhelming, breathtaking enchantment. The first two notes of the phrase are very light and in upper resonances, so that the slim voice can spin softly to the G on "de" and expand some on the E-flat of "ivresse." The same effect is sought for the second phrase, a very light A, an expanded F ("âme"). In "comme un concert divin" the successive D's are sustained better and better, with again an effect of enchanted lightness on the G's of "ta voix." The same two phrases are repeated with a crescendo of intensity, not of quantity, especially on "mon être est dévoré." Again all notes on the next two bars are very sustained, as above. With the long value on "flamme" the singer can start feeding the voice toward a real crescendo.

So far the voice has squarely sung quarter notes against the three-eighth notes of the 12/8 in the accompaniment. For the next eight bars the voice will sing triplets, that is, the same rhythm as the orchestra. That change helps enormously the feeling of growing passion that invades the piece. The legato is strictly maintained, but the vocal line becomes sinuous and the sensuousness of the text is stressed intensely. The first four bars are a continuous crescendo. The whole line, in high resonances, must nevertheless be said at a level which is still speech and not only sound. The alternation of wide and slim vowels will prevent vocal tensions. The vowels, which normally are /a/ in "astres radieux" and "passer" are now nearer to /ɑ/; the second vowel in "radieux" and the vowel in "yeux" are /ø/ and not /œ/, the vowel in "bien aimée" and "embaumée" is /e/; the vowel in "mes lèvres" is still /ɛ/ but leaning to /e/ in order to avoid a spreading and blatant sound. For the repeat of "passer ton haleine" the tenor needs deep, powerful support and must avoid any feeling of haste. If anything, he should broaden the tempo just a little. With "ton haleine embaumée" begins a diminuendo that continues to the end, "sur mes yeux." This diminuendo conveys a sense of sensuous delight. The word "embaumée" is like a caress; the repeat of "sur mes lèvres" is exquisite. In those short eight bars the tenor must have unleashed a world of passion, in a curve perfectly drawn from piano to fortissimo to piano.

With the return of the quarter notes there is appeasement in the music, and a sensuous satisfaction expresses itself pianissimo in the spinning legato used at the beginning of the aria, but now with greater warmth. The very short coda, with its mellow high A at the start, is all warmth and charm but still very intense. The fermata on the D must not be too long, even less so if we add the following ending: Going now to the epilogue (Choudens, p. 325, 5th bar; Schirmer, p. 316, 5th bar), there is the same B-flat chord on which falls the last syllable of "âme" at the end of the aria. At this point sing the three bars, "Muse aimée, je suis à toi," ending on the high B-flat, the accompaniment being exactly the same as in the aria ending. If this finale is accepted, one word only has to be changed as follows: "*Bien*-aimée, je suis à toi." In the opera the dedication of the aria goes from a woman (first time) to the Muse (second time), from worldly pleasures to poetry. As a solo piece, the aria is a magnificent song of love, any love.

"Elle a fui, la tourterelle" *soprano*

Elle a fui, la tourterelle . . .
Ah, souvenir trop doux!
Image trop cruelle!
Hélas, à mes genoux
je l'entends, je le vois!

Elle a fui, la tourterelle,
elle a fui loin de toi;
mais elle est toujours fidèle
et te garde sa foi!
Mon bien-aimé, ma voix t'appelle,
oui, tout mon coeur est à toi!
Elle a fui, la tourterelle,
elle a fui loin de toi.

Chère fleur, qui viens d'éclore,
par pitié, réponds-moi,
toi qui sais s'il m'aime encore,
s'il me garde sa foi!
Mon bien-aimé, ma voix t'implore,
ah, que ton coeur vienne à moi!
Elle a fui, la tourterelle,
elle a fui loin de toi.

She has fled, the turtledove . . .
Ah, memory too sweet!
Too cruel image!
Alas, at my knees
I hear him, I see him!

She has fled, the turtledove,
she has fled far from you;
but she is still faithful
and keeps you her trust!
My beloved, my voice is calling you,
yes, my heart is all yours!
She has fled, the turtledove,
she has fled far from you.

Dear flower, that has just opened,
for pity's sake, answer me,
you who knows if he still loves me,
if he keeps me his trust!
My beloved, my voice implores you,
ah, that your heart may come to me!
She has fled, the turtledove,
she has fled far from you.

Antonia is a frail and sensitive young woman living in Munich who has inherited her famous mother's vocal talent. But her life is threatened by consumption, and her doctors have advised her to stop singing. Her fiancé, the poet Hoffmann, is absent and not expected in Munich for the time being. Antonia, sitting at her clavichord, yields to her loneliness and longing and sings a song that reminds her of the absent beloved.

Antonia's voice is a lyric soprano that will be taxed to its normal limits in the second part of the act. Here its size is of little importance, but her charm and sadness must find in her voice a clear and sensitive instrument. This is a simple song but an affecting one.

The tempo is *andante,* ♩ = 84–88. Antonia, seated and playing for herself, begins to sing, but her emotion stops her voice. The first short phrase is piano, and it must be noted right away that the phrasing will not stress the F on "la," which is an unimportant word. To the contrary, the voice will be very light on "la," and the stress will be on the downbeat "-relle." This will be true throughout the song. The first words of the recitative are soft, rather slow. "Image trop cruelle" is more intense, with the vowel /ɛ/ opened but not spread on the F. Mark a comma after "Hélas," another one after "je l'entends," the whole phrase tentative, as the memory is still unprecise. The repeat of the same words, however, is allegro, on time and forte. The image of her beloved has suddenly become present in Antonia's mind. With the resulting sadness, "je l'entends" is slow and depressed, and "je le vois" takes quite some time to come. But she regains enough poise to sing the first verse of the song.

"Elle a fui" refers to the fact that, in order to lessen the memory of the dead mother as well as to escape from her physician, Dr. Miracle, Antonia's father had recently moved to Munich with his daughter, thereby also keeping Hoffmann at a distance. The "tourterelle" (turtledove) figures in several French poems as a symbol of a loving girl separated from her love. It is a symbol that fits Antonia's fragile grace very well.

There is no difficulty at all in the singing itself; it is the feeling that counts. "Mais elle est toujours fidèle" calls for just a little more tone, "et te garde sa foi" still a little more. It is on "Mon bien-aimé" that the voice becomes intense: Sing the phrase without breathing. "Oui, tout mon coeur est à toi" becomes passionate but not loud, and the first repeat, with an accelerando, very much more so. The voice must not punch the note A on "toi" but rise to it smoothly, expanding during the value of the half note, a generous half note. The second repeat, piano, is like a confidential murmur to a nearby partner. It is said slowly and with great conviction. There is a sweet sadness in the return of "Elle a fui, la tourterelle."

The short coda: Breathe after "elle a fui," and sing very slowly the last few words. A good fermata on "loin de toi" seems to stress the distance between the lovers.

For a skillful singer, this is an easy song. For others a difficulty may arise in the ascension to "tout mon coeur est à toi." While the pitches are going up, the voice must still originate at the level where words are spoken, its resonances only ascending toward the head. An accelerando on the first "tout mon coeur est à toi" will also prevent the voice from stalling on the repeated F-sharps.

While the first verse was centered on the faithfulness of the singer in the song, Antonia in fact, the second verse will be a passionate call for a response from the distant lover. This call starts with the words "Mon bien-aimé." Until then Antonia sings the words of the printed music, which have no direct relevancy to her, but she should sing them with charm and even with an anxious sincerity when she asks the imaginary flower "s'il m'aime encore, s'il me garde sa foi." From "Mon bien-aimé" on, the words of the song become Antonia's own, very intense this time. "Implore" is a very strong word indeed. It is important for the voice to avoid singing all the F-sharps with exactly the same amount of voice and with exactly the same value. An accelerando should already be made on "Mon bien-aimé," with a diminuendo on "ma voix t'implore." "Ah, que ton coeur vienne à moi" can be quite a bit faster, with a broadening crescendo to the high A.

At the very end of the aria some signs of exhaustion should be discreetly given. "Que ton coeur vienne à moi," very piano and slow, could be carried into "Elle a fui" and a breath be taken before "la tourterelle"—another one after the first "elle a fui," another after the second "elle a fui," delaying the coming of "loin de toi" sung pianissimo, with a long fermata, and ending with a fading on "toi."

Such indications are, of course, artificial. But they can be used to convey a deep sincerity. Once the conviction is present in the heart of the singer, all possible means must be used that fit the music to convey it to the listeners.

Ponchielli, *La Gioconda*

"Voce di donna"

mezzo-soprano

Voce di donna o d'angelo
le mie catene ha sciolto;
mi vietan le mie tenebre
di quella santa il volto.
Pure da me non partasi
senza un pietoso don, no!
A te questo rosario
che le preghiere aduna
io te lo porgo, accettalo,
ti porterà fortuna;
sulla tua testa vigili
la mia benedizion!

The voice of a woman or an angel
has untied my chains;
my darkness keeps from me
the face of that saint.
Yet let her not leave me
without a pious gift, no!
This rosary
that assembles the prayers,
I offer it to you, accept it,
it will bring you good fortune;
over your head shall
my benediction keep watch!

To the superstitious crowd milling in front of the Ducal Palace in Venice, La Cieca (the blind one) has been denounced as a witch. Innocent but helpless, she is seized and physically threatened by the mob. The unexpected arrival of the duke and his wife Laura stops the riot. But not until Laura has interceded in favor of La Cieca is the latter freed from her tormentors. In the aria "Voce di donna" La Cieca thanks Laura and, blessing her, gives her her cherished rosary.

The first act of *La Gioconda* is replete with large and animated scenes written for a numerous and powerful chorus and ranging in mood from festive rejoicing to popular furor. The aria of La Cieca is the first lyrical solo following these scenes. It should create a striking contrast with the turmoil that has dominated the stage heretofore.

The tempo *andante sostenuto* lies around ♩ = 60, very soft and deeply felt right away. When the aria is performed with piano accompaniment, a prelude of four bars should precede the voice. La Cieca has been deeply affected by her ordeal. She has not yet completely recovered her strength or her poise. There is disbelief in her mind and regret over her incapacity to see her deliverer. This complex emotional state must be reflected in the color of the voice, the pace of the words, the placing of the breaths. The first half of the first phrase, to "angelo," which is sung very piano, all notes sustained, including the sixteenths, is kept at such a level that it does not yet cancel out the sound of Laura's voice in the ears of La Cieca. A breath after "angelo" helps avoid the impression that the singer is in command of an unshakable support. The second half of the phrase, to "sciolto," is stronger, as if La Cieca needed to say the words firmly in order to believe the fact. The interval from E-flat to E-flat ("mie") provides a natural crescendo. A comma separates "catene" from "ha sciolto." After the strong accent on the final syllable of "catene," "ha sciolto" is said almost piano, as if in disbelief. The next two bars, to "tenebre," are very sad, in a sustained legato. The following two bars, progressively slower, show a mystical exaltation: The scope of her good deed and the fact that she cannot be seen have made of Laura an object of religious worship in La Cienca's heart. The first "di quella santa" demands a broad sound and the skill to sing all notes of the intervals at about the same level, the differences between low and high being only in resonances. After a breath, the second "di quella santa" is intended to be more piano and morendo, very slow, as if in awe. The eighth-note silence at the end of the bar can be lengthened into a short break, preparing a new section of the music.

Bar 9 of the voice line returns to the original tempo, but bar 10 moves to a tempo faster than the original. La Cieca suddenly is anxious to keep Laura near her a little longer. The singing is more positive and firmer, softening and slowing down on "un pietoso don." The pattern of the accompaniment stresses the change of mood very clearly.

In bars 12 and 13 the two "no" provide the transition to still another mood. The first "no" is still urgent, the second more confident, so that it can be sustained almost at will, provided that the sound expresses the warm affection in La Cieca's soul, now entirely concentrated on her rescuer. Here her soul is inspired to the right gesture. In the original slow tempo, sustaining well a round tone mezzo forte, La Cieca offers Laura her rosary, a humble gift in itself but that of the constant companion and constant solace of the blind woman. With total simplicity she now speaks to her unknown benefactress in the familiar mode, that is, the second person of the singular. No vocal effect is necessary here, all is sincerity; the low B-flat on "aduna," for instance, is not to be stressed, but the words "ti porterà fortuna" have to be said with great conviction, touching as they are coming from the helpless woman. In bar 20 a sense of greatness appears in La Cieca's words. Besides the rosary she gives Laura her blessing, a blessing coming from her whole being, as will be expressed in bars 21 to 26 in a great musical and vocal expansion. A crescendo has started in bar 21. After a breath before "la mia benedizion" in bar 22, a rallentando is added to the crescendo. After a breath before "sulla tua testa" in bar 23 (the breath may take the place of the tied D at the end of the syllable "-zion"), there is a considerable broadening of the tempo, lasting through bar 24, with a very sustained G on "testa" in bar 24. The return to the faster tempo occurs in bar 25 although bar 26 is rather free, as will be explained. A breath should be taken after the high F on the second beat of bar 24, and no other until the low F on the second eighth of the third beat in bar 25. The next breath, however, comes after "la mia" (middle A in bar 26), and the end of bar 26 is sung as shown, with a large rallentando:

mi - a, la mia be - ne - di - zion.

The concluding phrases—"la mia benedizion," the two "vigili"—are generous and lyrical. The fermata on the F, "Ah sulla tua testa," is a bright tone, not held too long, and the following descending pattern is best when kept in the rhythm written. A breath before "la mia" is optional, useful if it helps "la mia" to be slow and very warm. The fermata on the silence that follows allows the nearly exhausted Cieca to rebuild enough emotional strength to sing the last "benedizion" very slowly, very piano, but with an intense fervor.

This aria has beauty. It should be heard for its own sake, not as a vehicle for vocal feats. Its range is just right for a mezzo-soprano. The only error one could make would be to stress deliberately the different colors of the high F's and the several B-flats, to emphasize the distances between high and low notes of several intervals. By singing the low tones very much forward in full mouth resonance, by keeping some of that same resonance in higher tones, by not letting the low tones fall into the low pharynx or pushing the high tones upward, a balance of resonances can be maintained and a continuity of vibration enjoyed. To convey the emotional value of the aria will then be the only goal of the singer.

"Cielo e mar"   *tenor*

Cielo e mar!   Heaven and sea!
L'etereo velo splende   The ethereal veil sparkles
come un santo altar.   like a holy altar.
L'angiol mio verrà dal cielo?   Will my angel come from heaven?
L'angiol mio verrà dal mare?   Will my angel come from the sea?
Qui l'attendo;   Here I am waiting for her;
ardente spira oggi   ardently breathes tóday
il vento dell'amor.   the wind of love.
Ah! quell'uom che vi sospira   Ah! the man who is sighing here,
vi conquide, o sogni d'or!   may he conquer you, o golden dreams!
Per l'aura fonda non appar   In the airy depth appears
nè suol nè monte.   neither land nor mountain.
L'orizzonte bacia l'onda,   The horizon kisses the wave,
l'onda bacia l'orizzonte!   the wave kisses the horizon!
Qui nell'ombra ov'io mi giacio   Hither in the dark where I am staying,
coll'anelito del cor,   with my heart panting,
vieni, o donna, vieni   come, o woman, come
al bacio della vita,   to the kiss of life,
della vita e dell'amor!   of life and of love!
Ah vien! Ah vien!   Ah come! Ah come!

Enzo Grimaldo, a nobleman from Genoa, has returned to Venice, from which he had been banished, in order to see again the woman he loves. Disguised as a Dalmatian sea captain, his boat at anchor away from the harbor along a deserted island, his crew asleep, he waits late at night for the arrival of his beloved whom a mysterious accomplice has promised to bring back to him.

The night is dark but for a few stars, a moon half hidden in a cloud, and a few lanterns on the deck. Alone, Enzo looks at the sea and the sky and directs all his willpower and impatience to bringing to life his golden dreams. From his lonely vigil he calls his beloved with all the strength of his longing. This aria, a solo in the full meaning of the word, is a powerful one, written broadly for a dramatic voice, and should not be attempted by a light or even a lyric voice.

In the full score, five bars provide the prelude to the entrance of the voice. The first two bars of singing, after a sizable silence, are very slow, in keeping with the two elements Enzo refers to, the sky and the sea, and are sung in a dynamic piano, but the piano of a large voice, relaxed in thoughts. With the third bar, a tempo is established, *andante con calma*, possibly ♩ = 63. This figure is a reference only, as it will be in the style of the aria to allow a word or a note to broaden the tempo momentarily without distorting the general pattern. Bars 3 to 6 are a brief, poetic description of the surrounding night. Sing piano, legato for two bars, detached for two bars, aiming at a scintillating effect. The four bars starting with "L'angiol mio" are piano at first, as the question is asked only for the sake of keeping the sky in the picture, but there is already more intensity on "dal mare," a more likely probability. The questions remain unanswered, of course: Respect the fermata on the silence.

From "Qui l'attendo" on, Enzo speaks in the first person. The intensity will soon be growing. After the brief "Qui l'attendo" it would be superb to sing the whole phrase from "ardente" to "dell'amor" without breathing, starting piano, letting the voice make the crescendo, which comes naturally with the higher notes on "vento," and ending mezzo piano on "dell'amor." If that feat proves impossible there is no harm in taking a breath after "spira." The crescendo on "il vento dell'amor" could be coupled with a slight ritardando.

The phrase "Ah! quell'uom" is piano again but the beginning of a crescendo, which will develop throughout the next page. A good breath before "vi conquide" (fifth bar of that section) will enable the tenor to carry the phrase to after the first "o sogni," breathing before the second "o sogni d'or" (seventh bar of that section). A strong animando, which lasts only two bars, begins in bar 8, with a crescendo preparing, by the sudden intensity of the voice, the great climax on "vi conquide" (bar 11). A breath taken after "sospira" in bar 10 will allow full power for the climax as well as a carrying-over until after the first "o sogni" in bar 12. The last bar of the first verse is quite free, with two breaths (after "d'or," after "sogni") preparing and enhancing the beauty and intensity of the few words between them. The last "o sogni d'or" is very slow, with a free fermata on both the G and the F.

Why this insistence on the exact places of the breaths? Because we have here a writing of the vocal phrases that requires a mastery similar to that of a cellist who has to know his bowing exactly in order to obtain the maximum scope from the long melodic lines entrusted to him. The singer performing this aria must, of course, know and feel the meaning of the text, but he is also expected to convey the vocal beauty of the musical lines constantly to its full extent. A bold use of fine vowels—"sosp*i*ra," "conquid*e*," "sogni d'*or*"—will also greatly help his achievement.

The first eight bars of the second verse are given to the description of the vast solitude, the emptiness, surrounding Enzo. They are piano and very legato, but with an important scope in the nature of the voice. The next four bars, starting with "Qui nell'ombra," are much more personal; their intensity comes from a growing anxiety that finds solace only in calling the desired woman, at first softly, then with increasing insistence, which will almost reach frenzy in the last page of the aria. The first "vieni, o donna" sung piano must have a loving softness to it above an impatient urgency that emerges on "vieni al bacio della vita" (a breath after the A-flat of "vita"). Before the change of tempo, "della vita e dell'amor" is declaimed strongly despite the diminuendo.

The *poco più mosso* is usually taken around ♩ = 88–92. The first words are not yet forte but rather a feverish mezzo piano. The mezzo forte, the anxious one, comes on "coll'anelito del cor." On the fifth bar of this section, "vieni, o donna" and the ensuing triplets are forte, the next two "vieni" vehement and speedy. Then the "vieni" preceding the high B-flat must spin, still forte but much more polished than the previous "vieni," preparing the connected spin to the B-flat (vowel /ɑ/), which is expected to be sustained beyond its written value, a breath being taken after "della vita." On the next words, "e dell'amore," the tenor generally omits the syllable "-re" and the G on which it is written. Instead, he sings "dell'amor," breathes, and sings "si, dell' " on the G and the A-flat. The concluding notes on "Ah vien" were meant to be sung piano, with a crescendo-decrescendo like a sigh on the last G. But the custom has prevailed to ask the tenor to end the aria on a resounding B-flat, which is not exactly a sigh. But who will complain, if the B-flat is beautiful?

This aria, written as I said above for a very strong voice, is a powerful invitation to vocal beauty. It can give the listener great joy if this desire for beauty is constantly satisfied by the approach the singer uses in performing the aria.

Puccini, *La Bohème*

"Che gelida manina" *tenor*

Che gelida manina, se la lasci riscaldar.	What an icy little hand, let me warm it.
Cercar che giova?	What is the use of searching?
Al buio non si trova.	In the dark one can't find anything.
Ma per fortuna è una notte di luna . . .	But luckily it is a moonlit night . . .
e qui la luna l'abbiamo vicina.	and here we have the moon close by.
Aspetti, signorina, le diro con due parole	Wait, signorina, I will tell you in two words
chi son, chi son, e che faccio, come vivo.	who I am, and what I'm doing, how I live.
Vuole?	Do you want to?

Chi son? Sono un poeta.	Who am I? I am a poet.
Che cosa faccio? Scrivo.	What do I do? I write.
E come vivo? Vivo!	And how do I live? I live!
In povertà mia lieta	In my cheerful poverty
scialo da gran signore	I squander like a noble lord
rime ed inni d'amore.	rhymes and hymns of love.
Per sogni e per chimere	Through dreams and idle fancies
e per castelli in aria . . .	and castles in the clouds . . .
l'anima ho milionaria.	my soul is a millionaire.
Talor dal mio forziere ruban	Sometimes from my safe
tutti i gioielli	all the jewels are stolen
due ladri gli occhi belli.	by two thieves, two beautiful eyes.
V'entrar con voi pur ora,	They entered with you just now,
ed i miei sogni usati	and my usual dreams,
e i bei sogni miei tosto si dileguar!	my beautiful dreams right away disappeared!
Ma il furto non m'accora	But the theft does not dishearten me
poiché v'ha preso stanza la dolce speranza!	because sweet hope has settled in!
Or che mi conoscete, parlate voi, deh, parlate,	Now that you know me, tell [me],
Chi siete? Vi piaccia dir!	Who are you? Please tell me.

It seems unrealistic on my part to write instructions about this aria, used by so many tenors, glorified by so many great voices, and obviously molded into a traditional pattern that performers follow and that listeners cherish. I believe nonetheless that, for some performers at least, the youthful, sensitive, slightly boastful, cheerful character of the aria should be stressed so that while performing memorable vocal feats they remember to be lovable human beings, as are those in whom love is just awakening.

The first part, until "Chi son? Sono un poeta," starts pianissimo and dolcissimo. In the hand of Rodolfo, Mimi's little hand feels cold. Find an accent of compassion, immediately followed by the offer to help: "se la lasci riscaldar." Rodolfo sees himself as the protector of the humble girl, but he also feels a surge of masculine warmth. Spin easily to the A-flat on "Cercar," then sound wise on "Al buio non si trova." During the lovely four bars of moonlight interlude, Mimi's hand is safely held in Rodolfo's two. Now he can release one and point to the moonlight, to enrich the start of his romance. Stress the romantic rubato, rallentando with individual note stresses, "e qui la luna," speed up "l'abbiamo vicina," starting a rallentando on the last syllable.

Second part: By now Mimi is seated. Rodolfo has an audience and will take advantage of the fact. He feels the time has come to reveal and release his growing warmth for the girl. He introduces himself as a man of great wealth of inspiration and little material means. He does it beautifully. Sing very broadly "Chi son? Sono un poeta. Che cosa faccio?"—then an accelerando on "come vivo." Note also the contrast between "Chi son?" forte and "Sono un poeta" piano. It is an unusual vocation, and Rodolfo is quietly proud of it. Forte on "vivo," as a challenge to the materially hard times. If the artist singing Rodolfo lets himself be invaded by the feelings so masterfully suggested in the music, his vocal task will be easier, his delivery understood.

And now, sincerely yet grandly, Rodolfo basks in the glow of his dreams. The marvelous phrase started piano gaily grows in enthusiasm to the superb "milionaria." Note that from that point to the end of the aria the singer is constantly urged to "sustain broadly," to "broaden again," to "retard": Rodolfo makes the most of his flattering fancy, which compares Mimi's eyes to robbers who have entered his room, looted his safe, and spoiled his dreams—dreams he loves and cherishes (forte and allargando on "bei sogni miei") and might regret (dolcissimo and allargando on "si dileguar").

"Ma il furto non m'accora" must be sung warmly and cozily (make it a marvelous rest for the voice) in a carefree mood, preparing by the release of all vocal tensions the ascension toward the famous high C. The crowning achievement of years of technical work should be started legatissimo from the A-flat and made to vibrate as a slim blade of tone before being amplified in search of beauty and radiance. When it is exploded as a demonstration of muscle and lung power and for its own sake, it does not fulfill the hopes and intentions of the composer.

"Or che mi conoscete" is said with a warm smile. There is a friendly insistence forte on "deh, parlate, Chi siete." "Vi piaccia dir" is a caressing, already affectionate pianissimo.

I believe that it is possible to follow the vocal traditions of the Italian style (portamenti, tenuti, attacca, and so on) and to keep a good touch of flamboyance in the quality of the voice while making the public feel that, together with the coat of Rodolfo, the tenor has inherited his young and vital soul.

"Mi chiamano Mimì"   *soprano*

Sì. Mi chiamano Mimì	Yes. They call me Mimi
ma il mio nome è Lucia.	but my name is Lucia.
La storia mia è breve.	My story is quite short.
A tela o a seta ricamo	On linen or silk I embroider
in casa e fuori. Son tranquilla	at home and outside. I am quiet
e lieta ed è mio svago	and cheerful, and for my pastime
far gigli e rose.	I make lilies and roses.
Mi piaccion quelle cose	I like those things
che han si dolce malìa	that have such sweet charm,
che parlano d'amor,	that speak of love,
di primavere, che parlano	of spring, that speak
di sogni e di chimere,	of dreams and illusions,
quelle cose che han nome poesia.	those things which are called poetry.
Lei m'intende?	Do you understand me?
Mi chiamano Mimì, il perché non so.	They call me Mimi, why, I don't know.
Sola mi fo il pranzo da me stessa.	Alone I cook my own meals,
non vado sempre a messa	I don't always go to mass
ma prego assai il Signor.	but I pray to the Lord very often.
Vivo sola, soletta	I live alone, all alone
là in una bianca cameretta,	there, in a little white room,
guardo sui tetti e in cielo.	I look over the roofs and at the sky.
Ma quando vien lo sgelo	But when comes the thaw
il primo sole è mio, il primo	the first sunshine is mine, the first
baccio dell'aprile è mio,	kiss of April is mine,
il primo sole è mio.	the first sunshine is mine.
Germoglia in un vaso una rosa	In a vase a rose is growing,
foglia a foglia lo spio.	petal by petal I watch it.
Così gentil il profumo d'un fior!	How sweet is the perfume of a flower!
Ma i fior ch'io faccio, ahimè,	But the flowers [that] I make, alas,

i fior ch'io faccio, ahimè, non han odore.	the flowers I make, alas, have no fragrance.
Altro di me non le saprei narrare,	I would not know what else to tell you about me,
sono la sua vicina che la vien fuori d'ora	I am your neighbor who comes at the wrong time
a importunare.	to bother you.

Mimi, who ten minutes earlier had fainted at the door of Rodolfo's garret and had then been revived by a little wine, the modest heat of the stove, and a most friendly reception, has listened wide-eyed and marveling to Rodolfo's flowery speech. Sitting, not daring to look at him, she now overcomes her shyness to answer his question, "Chi siete?" (Who are you?).

Note the tempo, ♩ = 40, which is very slow, and the indication of style: "with simplicity." In the first part of the aria, while describing with simple sincerity her work and her life, she cannot refrain from embellishing its humility in her natural desire to impress her newly found friend. She tells him of the name people have given her, a humble name, Mimi, said with a slight reluctance—that is the meaning of the first portamento: "-no Mimì"—but she stresses that her real name is not so humble: Lucia! Then, pianissimo and modestly, she speaks of her work. After the fermata, on her theme, she grows lyrical for four bars, showing that she is cheerful and contented. Keep this "lieta" (cheerful) in mind; it means a disposition that should be felt beneath the other moods throughout the aria. Mimi and Rodolfo at this point have never seen the fourth act of *La Bohème*.

The tempo quickens a little, *andante calmo*, ♩ = 54, on "mi piaccion quelle cose." There must be a quiet enjoyment in the voice, rising to a mezzo forte on "di primavere," the singer being very careful to sing a true vowel /i/ on the A, allargando, in order to suggest the bright lightness of spring. Now Mimi takes the risk of revealing that she, too, has fancy dreams. But to her anxious question, "Lei m'intende?" (Do you understand me?), Rodolfo replies only with a brief "sì." And Mimi, short of inspiration, quite embarrassed, starts all over again by repeating her name, piano, legato, then very crisply: "non so." At last she finds a subject of conversation again, a subject without pretension: her room and the way that she lives. The words come quickly and easily now, ♩ = 144, an enormous difference from the preceding tempi. "Vivo sola, soletta" can mix a touch of melancholy with a touch of coquetry and catch the smiling attention of Rodolfo.

One more nimble phrase, and after "in cielo," ending on an *eighth* note, there is a silence of the greatest importance. Getting up, looking at Rodolfo frankly for the first time since the beginning of *his* aria, invaded by a feeling of love that had been smoldering in her, Mimi during that silence changes from the shy, hesitant stranger into a vibrant, passionate young woman on the beautiful phrase "Ma quando vien lo sgelo." To ignore the silence and to carry the voice over from "cielo" to "Ma" is to fail to understand that the silence indicates a dramatic turning point psychologically and to transform Mimi into a kind of Rosina who reveals her shrewdness by a similar carrying-over of the voice "mi fo guidar-ma." The *andante molto sostenuto* may well return to ♩ = 54, starting piano and legatissimo and soaring to a great forte. Respect the rhythm of "il primo baccio"; the A is an eighth note but sung with a spin. If possible, take a breath only before "è mio," sustaining the A, which is the climax of the phrase. The repeat of "il primo sole è mio" is piano, with intense emotion: Mimi has seen that first ray of sun all alone, and next spring is so far away. . . With "Germoglia in un vaso" and the next phrases she draws for us a delicate picture of her personal spring, a rose that she takes loving care of. Sing with great charm, making only a very moderate crescendo to the A of "profumo," and sing very clearly the sixteenths of "fior." There is only regret, not despair, on the two "ahimè" (alas) of the next phrase.

The aria ends with a primly suggested good-bye, "Altro di me . . ." Breathe after "narrare." A comma is acceptable after "vicina." Note that there is a longer value on "vien," giving its rhythm to the whole phrase.

When this aria is well sung, that is, with great simplicity and without adornment, showing a great love born in front of the listeners, it is one of the most beautiful arias ever written.

"Quando m'en vo" (Musetta's Waltz) *soprano*

Quando m'en vo soletta per la via	When I walk alone in the street,
la gente sosta e mira,	people stop and look,
e la bellezza mia	and my beauty
tutta ricerca in me,	they search for all of it in me,
da capo al piè.	from head to toe.
Ed assaporo allor la bramosia sottil	And then I savor the subtle desire
che da gl'occhi traspira	which transpires in their eyes
e dai palesi vezzi intender sa	and from my exposed charms knows how to guess
alle occulte beltà.	my hidden beauties.
Così l'effluvio del desio	Thus the flow of desire
tutta m'aggira	envelops me,
felice mi fa.	[and] makes me happy.
E tu che sai	And you who know
che memorie ti struggi	that you consume yourself in memories,
da me tanto rifuggi?	are you avoiding me so strongly?
so ben:	I know very well:
le angoscie tue non le vuoi dir,	you don't want to admit your anguish,
ma ti senti morir!	but you can feel yourself dying!

Let us get acquainted with Musetta through the portrait drawn by the writer who created her, Henri Murger: "Musetta possessed a positive genius for elegance. . . . Intelligent, shrewd, and above all hostile to anything she considered tyranny, she knew but one rule: caprice. In truth, the only man she ever loved was Marcello, perhaps because he alone could make her suffer" (quoted in G. Ricordi & Co.'s *La Bohème, Voice and Piano Score*, p. 177).

In this aria, it is Christmas Eve, and Musetta, tired of the attentions of the aging Alcindoro, attempts to regain the favors of Marcello, from whom she has been separated. In typical fashion she will not hesitate to start a scandal in order to reach her goal. In the pages preceding this aria Musetta has nagged her old beau mercilessly, has broken a plate, humiliated the waiter, behaved like a shrew, all of it in order to catch Marcello's attention. That she has succeeded in doing. Now she suddenly turns on a new personality, all charm and elegance, which she will keep throughout the waltz, the slow waltz, ♩ = 104.

The aria must be felt in 3/4, not in one, and there are many changes of tempi, without which the aria's character of sensuousness and its seductive effect are hopelessly lost. Note with absolute precision the alternations of *allargando* and *a tempo* throughout. It is impossible to indicate all the vocal inflections from phrase to phrase that a talented singer must find, all of them in a mood of warmth, appeal, temptation, without a trace of nastiness—except, maybe, for the last three notes, as will be explained.

Start "Quando m'en vo" strictly on time, with a perfect legato and a velvety voice. Musetta makes herself shrill only when she wants to, and in this aria she does not want to. "La gente sosta" is slower (passersby slow down to look at her), "mira" is *a tempo* (their glances are intense), "e la bellezza mia" legato and round, with pride. Again allargando, take plenty of time on "in me"—then a sudden *a tempo*.

The next page follows exactly the same pattern. An important ritardando, with a fermata on "tutta m'aggira," prepares an *a tempo* forte on "felice mi fa," which is then repeated with a strong rallentando and decrescendo to morendo. By now Marcello must be consumed by jealousy, feeling how much Musetta enjoys other men's greed for her.

On "E tu che sai" Musetta turns brazenly to Marcello as she alludes, in front of the crowd, to their lovemaking in the past, but without losing the enticing beauty of her voice. The alternation of *rallentando* and *a tempo* stops on "tanto rifuggi," and we now have four bars of full-throated singing, followed by an allargando on "So bene . . . ma ti sen-." Take a breath before "ma ti"; the ascending four sixteenths to the B are included in the rallentando and are sung forte, the fermata strong and brilliant, not shrill. Then a sudden piano staccato on the last three notes "-ti morir" can be interpreted as a nagging insinuation or as a sudden breathlessness as Musetta is overcome by the sensual emotion she has created.

I count more than twenty indications of style concerning the voice in those very short four and half pages of music. Puccini asks his interpreter for constant shading, coloring, changing of pace, in order to mirror the many moods of Musetta's mind and heart. She tries to seduce by showing how much she relishes the attempts of seduction on the part of so many men. It takes a very gifted and imaginative soprano to fulfill the demands made by the composer. It would be a capital mistake to use during this aria the shrillness Musetta uses before and after it.

"Donde lieta uscì"   *soprano*

Donde lieta uscì	Where cheerfully she left
al tuo grido d'amore,	at your call of love,
torna sola Mimì	Mimi returns alone
al solitario nido.	to her solitary nest.
Ritorna un'altra volta	She returns once again
a intesser finti fior!	to embroidering false flowers!
Addio, senza rancor.	Farewell without a grudge.
Ascolta, ascolta.	Listen, listen.
Le poche robe aduna	Gather the few trifles
che lasciai sparse.	I left scattered around.
Nel mio cassetto stan chiusi	In my drawer are locked
quel cerchietto d'or	that little gold ring

e il libro di preghiere.	and my prayer book.
Involgi tutto quanto	Wrap all that
in un grembiale e	in an apron, and
manderò il portiere . . .	I will send the janitor . . .
Bada . . .	Please . . .
sotto il guanciale	under the pillowcase
c'è la cuffietta rosa.	there is the pink bonnet.
Se vuoi serbarla	If you want to keep it
a ricordo d'amor!	as a souvenir of love!
Addio, addio senza rancor.	Farewell, without a grudge.

In the preceding scene Rodolfo has told his friend Marcello of the true reason why he made Mimi leave him: he could no longer stand to keep her in his freezing garret, knowing how desperately sick she was, while there was nothing he could do to take care of her. The poor girl has overheard the conversation and now decides to say farewell forever rather than attempt a reconciliation as she had planned before.

This very touching page should not be sung out of context, yet it often is, even if it thereby loses a good part of its impact. It should at least be sung well.

The tempo at the beginning is very slow, *lento molto*, $\flat$ = 66 (that is, to the eighth note, not to the quarter note). The voice enters after Mimi's theme is played very softly and slowly, as she had sung it when asked by Rodolfo to introduce herself at their first encounter, only still slower and almost reluctantly.

Mimi had also said then that she was cheerful, "lieta." Now the memory of that moment brings only sadness. Even a slight crescendo on "d'amore" fails to convey any joy. The ritardando on "torna sola Mimì" is desperately sad. There is an upsurge of more intense sorrow with the *agitando un poco* on the first bar of the 3/4 where the accompaniment plays the theme of the coughing spell at her first entrance, a symbol of what awaits her in her lonely room. The A-flat on "Ritorna" is piano with a small crescendo on "un'altra volta," the voice fluctuating with her emotions, turning to weariness on the slow "intesser finti fior." Here the orchestra actually plays the theme connected with her lonely room. And Mimi says, "Addio, senza rancor" very slowly, like a murmur, in a brave effort to be friendly. At this point it may help the expression to imagine that she is already leaving but cannot quite bring herself to do so; instead, she turns again to Rodolfo. During the first slow "Ascolta" she finds a reason to stay a moment longer, and from the second "ascolta" on the tempo becomes the normal tempo of speech, $\quarternote$ = 84. Mimi's voice is steadier now, dealing with practical matters, but is not without emotion. The melodic line is much more sensitive than the words spoken, and the melodic line tells the truth. Mimi must sing every word with a lovely quality of voice. Indicate a staccato on "quel cerchietto d'or," a religious feeling on "e il libro di preghiere."

Puccini's genius shows in the next line: On the most uninspiring text—I mean a strictly practical one—he writes a very moving line, legato, with a ritardando and a portamento on "tutto quanto in un grembiale" and with a kind of finality on "manderò il portiere." Again Mimi turns to go, stops, and returns. "Bada" has a portamento downward, a wistful appeal to Rodolfo to let her linger a little longer. *Molto ritardando* is the indication for "sotto il guanciale," a place of very intimate memories. And quickly, in order not to start crying, Mimi says, "c'è la cuffietta rosa," probably the only gift Rodolfo was ever able to buy for her. Animando and forte, while she still dares, "Se vuoi"; then no longer so sure, diminuendo, "se vuoi." A deep breath, and bracing her will to help her generous soul, she offers him, broadly and forte, the precious bonnet. Start the third "se vuoi" slowly and piano, and sing broadly and crescendo, with only a quick breath after "serbarla" to the top "ricordo." From the beginning of that phrase the voice should have acquired a spin and a ringing momentum that should make the top B-flat an integral part of it, without any attempt at swelling or banging it, for it must be a note full of love, not a technical feat. It is, of course, acceptable to breathe after "ricordo." It would be beautiful, however, not to have to breathe, to make instead a very light portamento downward from the B-flat to the C of "ricordo," keeping that C in the upper resonances and proceeding to the A-flats of "d'amor" by the continuation of the same spin. To devise the phrase that way, even if it does not turn out to be possible, would prevent the performer from hanging on the B-flat too long, destroying the even level and the continuity of the sound by a rough breath before "d'amor." Everything should be done to give that great phrase the soaring quality its feeling and its writing call for.

The first of the last two "Addio" is on time and very simple. The second is brief, followed by a long breath. The last "senza rancor" is free, with a diminuendo during the fermata on F. Mimi wants Rodolfo to feel that not only does she not resent the failure of their love affair but she also forgives him for revealing to her the critical condition of her health. Is it possible to express, singing beautifully with a beautiful voice, the heartbreak of a lovelorn girl who knows that her death is near? Ideally, that is what this short page demands.

"Vecchia zimarra, senti"   *bass*

Vecchia zimarra, senti,	Old cloak, listen,
io resto al pian,	I stay in the plain,
tu ascendere il sacro monte	you to the sacred mountain
or devi.	now must ascend.
Le mie grazie ricevi.	Receive my thanks.
Mai non curvasti	Never did you bend
il logoro dorso	your threadbare back
ai ricchi ed ai potenti.	before the rich and the powerful.
Passar nelle tue tasche	There passed in your pockets
come in antri tranquilli	as in tranquil dens
filosofi e poeti.	philosophers and poets.
Ora che i giorni lieti fuggir,	Now that the happy days have fled,
ti dico addio, fedele amico mio,	I am saying farewell to you, my faithful friend,
addio.	farewell.

In the final scenes of *La Bohème* the four Bohemians as well as Mimi and Musetta have reached the depth of misery. Mimi will be dead within moments, her friends have neither food nor fire nor money nor any means to shelter her from the cold that invades her body. But their ties of solidarity are so strong that they will find a way to help. Musetta, too late, alas, will sell her earrings to pay for a doctor and some drugs. And Colline, the only one to own a coat—that coat he displayed so happily last Christmas Eve—will go and pawn his coat. After a short, silent meditation he makes his decision and bids the old, precious garment farewell.

There is no introduction to this very short aria. The tempo indicated by Puccini is ♩ = 63, the markings are *allegretto moderato e triste*, not *andante*, not *adagio*. Singing the aria to myself at 63 to the ♩ I found it quite fast at first. At a second try I think I understood Puccini's intention. The dominating drama is that Mimi is dying, is leaving Rodolfo forever, together with all that was her life. If the minor drama of the separation of Colline from his coat were allowed to become a solemn *adagio*, the delicate balance of the scene would be upset, an error that Puccini's infallible instinct would never commit. The problem for the performer is to sing with great emotion, with deep regret, but without tragic pathos or theatrical exteriorization, while reaching the hearts of his listeners through the simple beauty and sincerity of his voice.

You can take advantage of the *allegretto* marking for counting mentally and settling vocally the two eighths of each beat. Leaving the marking *staccatissimo* to the orchestra, sing legatissimo and make the most of the written rallentandos.

During the first phrases Colline is determined not to yield to sentimentality and keeps the tempo steady except for the short ritenuto on "al pian, tu ascen-." For the Italians and the French, the words "sacro monte" hold no mystery, for the Italian pawnshop, like the French, is a city-controlled institution called "monte-di-pietà" or "mont-de-piété," the mountain of mercy. Colline masters his sadness and, half smiling, indulges in a joke: He will stay at a lower level, "pian," while the coat will ascend higher. "Le mie grazie ricevi" is said simply and seriously. There is pride in "Mai non curvasti il logoro dorso" and some scorn in "ai ricchi ed ai potenti." The E-flat on "Passar" must be sung piano and slower, to suggest how unsettled and ephemeral were the possessions—books, for instance—housed in the pockets of the coat. The comparison of those vast pockets with tranquil lairs stresses the melancholy humor of the piece.

To sing the E-flat piano will be no trouble if the voice spins without a break between the middle E in "potenti" and the E-flat immediately following. Even if, as is natural, a short silence separates the two notes, the feeling of spin should be uninterrupted. The idea of a break and a new attack on the E-flat may not result in success.

But even Colline the philosopher cannot always keep his heart in check, and the last lines, starting with "Ora che i giorni lieti fuggir," are genuinely distressed. The few words "ti dico addio, fidele amico mio," sung with more voice, must have Colline on the verge of tears, and a large rallentando will contrast in a pathetic way with the earlier willful steadiness of the piece. Indulge Colline's sorrow, and take a lot of time to sing the first of the final two "addio." The second "addio," however, must be brief, almost suppressed as if to avoid the danger of crying.

Puccini has provided four bars of orchestral conclusion to the aria, four bars of uncommon simplicity. Coupled with the absence of an introduction, they confirm that the aria must move the listeners through its inherent magic and not through any undue theatrical effort on the part of the interpreter. At the end of the aria the audience should not feel like clapping. A furtive tear in many an eye would be ample reward for the performer.

Puccini, *Gianni Schicchi*

"Oh! mio babbino caro" *soprano*

Oh! mio babbino caro,	O my dearest Daddy,
mi piace, è bello, bello;	I like him, he is beautiful;
vo'andare in Porta Rossa	I want to go to Porta Rossa
a comperar l'anello!	to buy the wedding ring!
Sì, sì, ci voglio andare!	Oh yes, I want to go there!
e se l'amassi indarno,	and if I should love him in vain,
andrei sul Ponte Vecchio,	I'd go on the Ponte Vecchio,
ma per buttarmi in Arno!	but to throw myself in the Arno!
Mi struggo e mi tormento!	I am wasting away and agonize!
O Dio, vorrei morir!	O God, I wish I could die!
Babbo, pietà, pietà!	Dad, have mercy!

Lauretta, the daughter of the resourceful, cunning Gianni Schicchi, hopes to be married to Rinuccio, of the Buoso family, on the first of May. But there is an obstacle to the lovers' project: the Buosos consider themselves socially on a higher level than the Schicchis and oppose the marriage. Schicchi, however, is the only one who can help the Buosos get rid of the will of a rich old cousin that would leave all his considerable wealth to the Friars and replace it with a new one favoring the family. Therein lies the hope of the two youngsters. As Schicchi refuses, Lauretta falls on her knees and pleads with him.

This very simple aria is extremely popular, and it deserves to be. The melody is lovely, the feeling warm and true, and the demands on the voice are modest. The danger of this popularity is a drift toward the trivial or even the vulgar, which this aria should not be exposed to and will not be if the singer stays faithful to the music as it is written.

Lauretta's voice is a lyric soprano with a youthful ring, with tenderness and warmth. The tempo, ♪ = 120, is a rather slow *andantino*, at ease but rhythmical. The indication of style, *ingenuo*, is all-important: The singing must be naive, artless, just flowing from the heart, or so it seems. Lauretta is totally sincere in her plea to her father, but she is also clever enough to make it more effective with a strong touch of blackmail. It is a case of artless shrewdness, a normal thing in a young girl in love, and she uses it with great charm.

The dynamic level is piano; the legato helps the pleading quality of the voice. The word "caro" is full of affection, coming after a "babbino" such as a little girl would say, but it is love that increases the intensity of the tone in "mi piace, è bello." What is the proper behavior here? Does the very existence of an A-flat call for a portamento upward and a fermata? No. The bar should stay on time, with at most a tender inflection on the A-flat, but the strong note of the phrase is the E-flat of the second "bello." The music of those first four bars has been heard already as a sonorous interlude between the two verses of Rinuccio's aria earlier in the score and is somehow associated lyrically with the idea of beautiful Florence. A fermata on the A-flat would destroy it.

The next phrase, "vo'andar in Porta Rossa," is firm without becoming forte, as

Lauretta tries to believe that she can still have her way. "Sì, sì, ci voglio andare" is more affirmative. The repeat in bar 11 of the music in bar 3 fills Lauretta's voice with emotion, and a strong crescendo shows her distress at the thought of losing Rinuccio. Here again a fermata on the A-flat would destroy the meaning of the line. It is at this point that the poor, shrewd girl threatens suicide, and with a very precise indication of where and how. How could a father resist that picture? A touch of the pathetic must be heard in the voice, which is at the same time intense and near sobbing. "Mi struggo e mi tormento," the loudest phrase of the aria, is a line of revolt that a slight ritardando can help to strengthen. Now is the time to stress the importance of the two A-flats, the second followed by a diminuendo. The long F on "O Dio" pianissimo must be of a beautiful quality, adding in that way to the irresistible plea.

After the two-bar interlude the pleading voice grows into a strong crescendo, and here a fermata on the A-flat of "pietà" and a portamento downward into the second syllable of "pietà," if done with taste, seem desirable and effective.

The last words are murmured in a prayer of last resort, a comma between the two "pietà" permitting an increasing feeling on the second word.

This is a very simple aria indeed and a deeply touching one, if the soprano avoids the childish satisfaction of making her A-flats loud and long just to show them off—as if an A-flat were a rarity in the soprano voice. Let it be a naive and heartfelt prayer from a girl who knows the power of her simplicity.

Puccini, *Madama Butterfly*

"Un bel dì vedremo"   *soprano*

Un bel dì vedremo	One beautiful day we will see
levarsi un fil di fumo	a thread of smoke rising
sull'estremo confin del mare.	at the extreme limits of the sea.
E poi la nave appare,	And then the ship appears,
poi la nave bianca	then the white ship
entra nel porto,	enters the harbor,
romba il suo saluto.	roars its salute.
Vedi? E venuto!	See? He has come!
Io non gli scendo incontro.	I don't go down to meet him.
Io no.	Not I.
Mi metto là sul ciglio del colle	I place myself here on the brow of the hill,
e aspetto, e aspetto gran tempo	and wait, wait a long while,
e non mi pesa la lunga attesa.	and the long wait does not weigh on me.
E uscito dalla folla cittadina	Out of the city crowd steps
un uomo,	a man,
un picciol punto s'avvia per la collina.	a tiny speck advances toward the hill.

Chi sarà? E come sarà giunto,	Who can it be? And when he arrives,
che dirà, che dirà?	what will he say, what will he say?
Chiamerà "Butterfly" dalla lontana.	He will call "Butterfly" from afar.
Io senza dar risposta	I without answering
me ne starò nascosta,	will remain hidden,
un po' per celia	a bit for teasing,
e un po' per non morire	and a bit not to die
al primo incontro,	at the first encounter,
ed egli alquanto in pena chiamerà:	and he a bit in pain will call:
"Piccina mogliettina,	"My darling little wife,
olezzo di verbena,"	fragrance of verbena,"
i nomi che mi dava al suo venire.	the names he used to give me when he came.
Tutto questo avverrà,	All this will come to pass,
te lo prometto.	I promise you.
Tienti la tua paura,	Restrain your fear,
Io con sicura fede l'aspetto.	I with firm faith wait for him.

This famous, beloved aria is actually an imaginary scene born in the mind of Cio-Cio-San, pleasantly called "Butterfly" by her friends. Three years ago Cio-Cio-San was wed to the American naval lieutenant Pinkerton. For him, it was a "Japanese marriage," convenient for the satisfaction of a passing fancy. For her, it is a lifetime contract, for which she has sacrificed family, ancestral religion, and Japanese honor. Her love is unflinching; she has a little boy to show for it. But Pinkerton has sailed for the United States long ago and, in spite of his promises, has never returned. Butterfly's faithful maid Suzuki still prays for his return but no longer believes in it. Cio-Cio-San, blind and deaf to reality, cannot stand those doubts, and in order to convince Suzuki of her error improvises a precise and passionate description of the return of her husband.

The tempo marking is ♩ = 42, very slow. As the dynamic marking is *pianissimo* and the indication of style *come da lontano* (as if from a distance), the voice must enter very light and attenuated, seemingly coming from nowhere. The first obstacle to achieving this effect lies in the very first syllable, "Un," for two reasons: It is unusual to find an article at the beginning of a phrase on the first downbeat, and the vowel /u/ has a bad reputation with singers and is often distorted in a vain effort to make it easier to sing. The remedy to the first difficulty is to think the whole first bar as a kind of upbeat to "vedremo" and to sing a crescendo from pianissimo on "Un" to mezzo piano on "vedremo." This slight crescendo at the same time stresses Butterfly's absolute faith. The second difficulty is solved if the vowel /u/ is formed by completely extended lips, as for instance in *fool*, that is, very superficially.

The same tenuous, almost misty voice suggests the "thread of smoke" described in the second phrase. The slight decrescendo after "fumo" and the two stresses following it seem to keep the vision well in the distance, as remote as the "confin del mare," the extreme horizon. From that remote world Butterfly's imagination will summon a battleship. Still very light on "E poi" in spite of the range (what an error it would be to sing any chest tones here), the voice comes to life on "la nave appare," said slowly, as if unveiling a stage effect.

There is nothing remote in the accelerando and ritardando of the next phrase, the impatience of the accelerando, the concrete mezzo forte of the slow "entra nel porte."

The following phrase has the same pattern: swift and strong on "romba il suo saluto," broad and triumphant on "Vedi? E venuto!" In one page of music Butterfly has brought the vessel from beyond the horizon to the harbor below the terrace of her garden.

At this point it is advisable for the student to try acting the scene as Butterfly stages it. In contrast with the scope of the preceding description, the restraint of Butterfly, her self-effacing behavior, calls for a very simple way of singing, soft, modest, almost colorless but for one revealing inflection of passion on "e aspetto gran tempo." For her impatience, time passes too slowly. But she is gifted with the self-control of the Japanese and maintains her passive attitude, although the ritardando on "la lunga attesa" is to be stressed as a sign that the long wait becomes a challenge.

Now the spotlight turns on a new character, an animated speck, a man who detaches himself from the crowd down there and climbs the hill toward her house. The first six bars of the new episode are faster, very light in voice, describing a nimble movement. Disbelief will almost seize Butterfly herself as the steep hill slows down the man's progress. "S'avvia per la collina" is much slower and much heavier.

From rehearsal number 14 on, the voice, up to here basically light, becomes much more legato and intense, even when pianissimo, its support deeper. The questions "Chi sarà" and "che dirà" are a complex of anxiety and certainty, the answer coming immediately but said very slowly: "Chiamerà 'Butterfly' dalla lontana." It takes time to report a miracle. As a reaction to it Butterfly creates a marvelous suspense: "me ne starò nascosta" is already quite slow, "un po' per celia" very slow and murmured. Then a long silence, finally but barely broken by a whispered "e un po'." A deep breath should now make "per non morire . . ." an outcry of passion in which is condensed all the fire kept so far under cover.

The next three lines, in which Butterfly puts in the mouth of the imaginary Pinkerton the words she would die for, must be sung as in a state of ecstasy, the low line as in a dream, as far as can be from heavy chest tones.

But even Butterfly's daydreaming has to come to an end. Willing herself to sound totally confident, she returns to reality, at first singing for two bars mezzo forte "Tutto questo avverrà," then in full possession of her strength a great forte, which is a passionate appeal to Suzuki's fortitude, and finally a supreme statement of her faith, fortissimo to *fff* in the last phrase.

"Un bel dì vedremo" covers a very large range of dynamics. From the tenuous thread of voice suggesting the barely visible thread of smoke to the passionate "per non morire" and the vibrant "l'aspetto," there are many steps to be taken and many moods to indicate. The tie holding everything together is Butterfly's personality. Her imagination is so vivid that she can believe and make-believe the nonexistent. Her faith is so strong that it resists three years of betrayal; her self-control seldom fails her. Her passion is a powerful one: love. All those features appear in the aria we are studying. This is something the performer must understand, the consequence being that many different qualities of voice must be found to meet all the psychological demands. There is, therefore, a need for great skill in handling the voice. To find the proper quality of tone, for instance, for the fortissimo "l'aspetto" is not easy after the delicate lines of "Piccina mogliettina" that Butterfly attributes to her imaginary Pinkerton.

Here is a last suggestion: "Tutto questo avverrà, te lo prometto," sung mezzo forte, should be warm and friendly, in a legato voice without an edge, without tense consonants. The same feeling persists on "Tienti la tua paura," although the dynamic is now forte. The G-natural on "tua," the F on "paura," and very soon the G-natural on "sicura" are made of a long true vowel /u/ as in *fool, loose,* which keeps the voice ringing, spinning, and continuous. A ringing vowel /e/ in "fede" prolongs the ring, preparing the groove, at first slim, into which the B-flat on "aspetto" will ring, thus avoiding a sudden explosive, blatant note out of context with the preceding phrases and the true feelings of the music. A sincere emotion can help the voice, but the misuse of the voice may make the rendering of a sincere emotion impossible. Sensitivity and vocal skill are most valuable partners.

Puccini, *Manon Lescaut*

"Donna non vidi mai"   *tenor*

Donna non vidi mai	I have never seen a woman
simile a questa!	such as this one!
A dirle: io t'amo,	Telling her: I love you,
a nuova vita	my soul awakens
l'alma mia si desta.	to a new life.
"Manon Lescaut mi chiamo."	"Manon Lescaut is my name."
Come queste parole profumate	How these fragrant words
mi vagan nello spirto	wander around in my mind
e ascose fibre vanno a carezzare.	and come to caress my innermost fibers.
O susurro gentil,	O gentle murmur,
deh! non cessare!	ah, do not cease!

At the inn in Amiens a group of students are singing and drinking. The young Chevalier Des Grieux has just told them that he does not know "that tragedy or that comedy" called love when the stagecoach stops at the inn and a young girl steps out. Des Grieux no sooner sees her than he is irresistibly attracted to her. He talks to her and finds that her name is Manon Lescaut. Alone again, he cannot detach his mind from that name and that young woman.

This aria, Puccini's first successful one, is written for a spinto voice, vibrant, capable of ringing B-flats, and obviously courting the enthusiastic applause of the listeners. It must be sung in that spirit, intensely contrasting piano and forte, stressing and "milking" the high notes and the vowels, which carry the tonic accent of the phrases and which almost always fall on a strong downbeat. The sweet voice of Manon and her humble name are soon magnified in heroic sounds, and it is the duty of the tenor to provide such amplification.

There is no prelude to the aria, and only one chord precedes the voice. The tempo is indicated in the score, *andante lento*, ♩ = 63. Des Grieux sings softly at first, with great conviction (first four bars of 33) but also with restraint, speaking to himself without knowing it. On "A dirle: io t'amo," however, an upsurge of passion is already felt, which explodes forte on a few notes ("a nuova vita") that must vibrate suddenly, then be restrained on "l'alma mia si desta" by a feeling of sweet surprise. The quotation of Manon's name includes, this first time, an imitation of her harmonious voice, piano, with a tender rallentando on the last two notes of bar 34. The accompaniment is also tender and harmonious, introducing the long phrase "Come queste parole." The phrase unfolds gently, but there is already a strong lyric tone, which should be sustained on "profumate," a crescendo on "nello spirto," and a great forte on "ascose," the B-flat held in a quasifermata, immediately starting a diminuendo. A breath after "fibre" helps to establish the sensuous piano, which fits the words "a carezzare."

The first "O susurro gentil" is said piano on the lips but is well supported. For several bars the sweet piano singing will alternate with intense outbursts of passion, and a constant buildup of the body support is necessary to cope with the rapid changes. Two bars before number 35, "deh! non cessare" and its repeat are a progressive rallentando, with a tenuto on the G on "cessare." On the second bar of number 35, the "deh! non cessare" is accented and forte, sung with passion but not fortissimo; on the one hand, the nuance piano returns immediately, and on the other hand, in spite of the emotions that love at first sight has created in Des Grieux, musical taste protects him from overly noisy utterances.

The second quotation of Manon's words is no longer an imitation but an exuberant enjoyment of their sound, and a cheerful forte is justified. A diminuendo on "chiamo" returns to a tender feeling.

The last line of the aria, faithful to the style of the entire piece, contrasts a soft, slow, touchingly pleading first half, "susurro gentil, deh! non cessar", with a heroic imperious second half. This time a fortissimo is welcome as well as a long fermata on the B-flat, which should be a glorious vocal sound. The last "deh! non cessar" is free in time (*col canto*), with another fermata on the D of "non." Some interpreters have sung these last notes fortissimo, in the same passionate voice as the high B-flat; others have made the last fermata a diminuendo ending pianissimo on the last "cessar." It seems that the marking "staying ecstatic" would speak in favor of the latter choice.

There is a great deal of juvenile ardor in this aria, with perhaps a slight excess of aggressive contrasts. Approached with great enthusiasm, with a feeling of youthfully vibrant strength, but with as yet not an overpowering vocal maturity, this aria can be loved and listened to with love.

"In quelle trine morbide"   *soprano*

In quelle trine morbide . . .   In these delicate laces,
nell'alcova dorata   in the gilded alcove
v'è un silenzio gelido mortal . . .   reigns an icy, deadly silence,
v'è un silenzio, un freddo   a silence, a cold
che m'agghiaccia! . . .   that chills me!
Ed io che m'ero avvezza   And I who had got used

a una carezza voluttuosa	to a voluptuous caress
di labbra ardenti	of burning lips
ed infuocate braccia . . .	and a passionate embrace . . .
or ho . . tutt'altra cosa! . . .	now have . . . a very different thing! . . .
O mia dimora umile,	O my humble dwelling,
tu mi ritorni innanzi . . .	you return before me . . .
gaia, isolata, bianca . . .	gay, isolated, white . . .
come un sogno gentile	like a gentle dream
e di pace e d'amor! . . .	of peace and love! . . .

Thanks to the generosity of old Geronte, Manon lives in elegantly appointed rooms. But, weary of so much luxury without love, she confides her true feelings to her brother Lescaut, the agent of her swift ascent to wealth. These feelings are very different from appearances.

In its two halves this short aria, beautiful in its brevity, contrasts Manon's disillusionment with her present life with the happy memories of bygone, much more humble days. She expresses herself with great simplicity.

There is no introduction. The tempo is *moderato,* not *lento,* and though the voice is poised and even, the syncopations in the orchestra reveal an underlying tension and nervousness. The first four bars, a description of the luxurious room and its gilded alcove, call for a round, rich voice despite Manon's resentment. If possible, add a feeling of scorn to the description. Sing a heart-rending crescendo on the severe accusation "v'è un silenzio gelido mortal." The repeat of the phrase is piano with a strong rallentando, several notes stentato. There seems to be a shudder of loneliness and misery here.

Now the memory of her once ardent love for Des Grieux returns as she recalls the past, starting the phrase "Ed io che m'ero avvezza" piano and dolcissimo. The meaning of the words, however, cause the voice to grow more and more sensuous. A breath after "avvezza" will help inject warmth and sensuousness into "a una carezza voluttuosa." Another breath after "voluttuosa" will render the second part of the phrase intense and telling, with the /r/ in "labbra" and "ardenti" clearly articulated, the sound of the vowel /a/ in "braccia" strong and rich. Although the B-flat on "ho" is the musical climax of the phrase, it must have a different color. It is a rejection and as such must have no tender ring to it but should have power on the vowel /o/. The portamento that carries it into the F must also sound angry, with a fermata on the F forte to the end. After a breath, the "tutt'altra cosa," which refers to Geronte's infatuation, is very abrupt.

Suddenly Manon craves the simplicity of earlier years. Her voice becomes brighter, her expression dreamy, on "O mia dimora umile." She sings with simplicity and charm and with a very young, clear tone, as if describing a vision before her eyes. Although the dynamic marking is *piano,* as she sings above a very lyric phrase of the orchestra, that piano should be ringing and very well supported. The allargando of "gaia, isolata" and the crescendo on the same notes make one curve of the entire phrase from "gaia" to "bianca." The top note, on the syllable "-ta," is mezzo forte, tenuto, after which "bianca" is *a tempo,* exact rhythmically and very light. The delicate dynamic changes are also very gradual, both ways. The last five bars are on time in the graceful movement of the triplets, and the fermata on "e" is light and short. The unexpected silence after that "e" can be explained by saying that Manon almost gasps before being able to say the word "amor." How much she regrets having sacrificed love for wealth!

This very feminine and sincere aria is devoid of frills. It is a melancholy reassessment on the part of Manon of the values that determine the course of her life. The conclusion is sad.

"Sola, perduta, abbandonata" *soprano*

Sola, perduta, abbandonata . . .	Alone, lost, abandoned . . .
in landa desolata . . .	in a desolate moor . . .
Orror!	Horror!
Intorno a me s'oscura il ciel . . .	Around me the sky is darkening . . .
ahimè, son sola!	alas, I am alone!
E nel profondo deserto io cado,	And in the middle of the desert I am falling,
strazio crudel, ah!	cruel torment, ah!
Sola, abbandonata, io la deserta donna!	Alone, abandoned, I the deserted woman!
Ah! non voglio morir, no!	Ah! I don't want to die, no!
non voglio morir!	I don't want to die!
Tutto dunque è finito.	All then is finished.
Terra di pace mi sembrava questa . . .	A land of peace this seemed to me . . .
Ahi! mia beltà funesta	Alas, my fateful beauty
ire novelle accende . . .	ignites new furies . . .
strappar da lui mi si volea;	they wanted to tear me away from him;
or tutto il mio passato orribile	now all my horrible past
risorge	rises again
e vivo innanzi al guardo mio si posa.	and stands alive before my eyes.
Ah! di sangue s'è macchiato!	Ah! it is stained with blood!
Ah! tutto è finito!	Ah! all is finished!
Asil di pace . . .	A refuge of peace . . .
ora la tomba invoco . . .	now I invoke the tomb . . .
No, non voglio morir . . .	No, I don't want to die . . .
amore, aita!	my love, help me!

The passionate story of Manon and Des Grieux is coming to an end. Banished from France, Manon finds herself unwanted even in her new residence in exile. Always escorted by Des Grieux, the most faithful of lovers, she has fled New Orleans but has become lost in the then-deserted plains of Louisiana. Now, overcome by exhaustion, by thirst, by discouragement, she falls to the ground while Des Grieux rushes off to find help somewhere in the immense desert.

This aria did not reach its final form right away, and Puccini worked on it even after the score had been published. In its final form it is a compelling example of the outspoken sincerity of Puccini's inspiration and a challenge to the soprano's power of expression.

Five chords fortissimo, like blows of fate, precede the first vocal phrase. The tempo is very slow, ♪ = 92, but legato, the voice almost dragging from stressed note to stressed note, then interrupting itself, leaving the continuity of the lament in turn to the oboe and the flute. Sixteenths, as in "in landa desolata," must still sound slow and almost delayed in coming. After "orror," Manon, with the coming of night, gives vent to an outburst of fear, going to forte on "ciel" but still keeping the same leaden pace that is the pace of her failing strength. The portamento from the A-flat on "ciel" to "Ahimè" includes the low F and denotes physical and mental exhaustion. A breath can be taken before "Ahimè."

The entire next page, "E nel profondo deserto . . .," is a long legato line, still sung at the same pace, with a touching insistence on the stressed notes in "abbandonata" and on the diminuendo on "io la deserta donna." Then, on rehearsal number 11, the orchestra broadens the tempo, preparing a similar broadening in the great phrase "Ah! non voglio morir," which must be sung fortissimo, in a vibrant, spinning voice, more crescendo with every note till the B-flat. Then, on the third bar after number 11, there is a sudden accelerando, as if Manon were unable to sustain the tension of the preceding great tones and, softly weeping, lets the end of the phrase die piano and pianissimo. The conclusion of that phrase, "Tutto dunque è finito," is sung evenly with a sense of inescapable fate. For the following six bars Manon finds her voice of the happy days again, light, dreamy, but continuously very slow and legato. Note that instead of an accelerando there is a *tratt* (trattenuto), that is, a ritardando written, and another rallentando on "mi sembrava questa." In her enfeebled state Manon has successive, unrelated visions. That last one was a delightful one.

Without any transition, however, she explodes in a violent delirium, berating her beauty and her past. For nine bars she sings forte and very rapidly, with anger at herself. Her violent voice must not become ugly though, and it will not, thanks to a deep support and care in saying the words properly and in an orderly way. On the tenth bar of the *allegro vivo* the tempo slows down considerably. Anger no longer drives Manon, but she feels well-justified horror at the vision of her past. She has caused the death of several men, including her brother Lescaut. The dotted rhythm of the lines "or tutto il mio passato" must be strongly indicated, the voice staying nevertheless legato and sustained, even when singing with full power. Bars 9 to 13 of the *moderato* must rush forward and soar upward with the greatest intensity, bar 14, with an allargando, giving the soprano time to prepare the climactic A. In agreement with the conductor, that A can be held for a very long time, if it has been started with a little less than maximum power, then increased in intensity through a deep support and a mentally repeated vowel /a/ while holding it. After that, "tutto è finito" is a sob of despair, barely sung at all.

But Manon's unhinged mind returns to the illusion of happiness for a few seconds. "Asil di pace" is very slow and dreamy, only to fade immediately and be replaced by the awareness of reality. Sing "ora la tomba invoco" with a dark, hollow voice and in disbelief. Between the two fermatas, the first "non voglio morir" is sung very slowly, with a disembodied voice, but the second is sung with revulsion and, as the score says, "with desperation." This time a breath after the two "no, no" will make the voice rebound to a powerful B-flat before a final collapse on "amore, aita."

Here is a tragic aria which in several ways makes great demands on the singer. Each of the extreme expressions has to be worked out separately before being assembled in stunning contrasts. The constant elements of the voice in this perilous activity are the support of the body and the breath, aimed downward the more the voice soars, and the integrity of the words, always said according to their meaning and their emotional content. There is a continuity even between the most contrasting elements, and in that continuity lies vocal security.

Puccini, *Suor Angelica*

"Senza mamma"   *soprano*

Senza mamma, o bimbo	Without Mama, my little boy
tu sei morto!	you died.
Le tue labbra	Your lips
senza i baci miei	without my kisses
scoloriron fredde,	turned pale and cold,
e chiudesti, o bimbo,	o little boy, and you closed
gli occhi belli!	your beautiful eyes!
Non potendo carezzarmi	Not able to caress me
le manine componesti in croce!	you crossed your little hands.
E tu sei morto	And you died
senza sapere	without knowing
quanto t'amava	how much
questa tua mamma.	your mother here loved you.
Ora che sei un angelo del cielo	Now that you are an angel in heaven,
ora tu puoi vederla, la tua mamma,	now you can see your mamma,
tu puoi scendere giù pel firmamento	you can descend from heaven,
ed aleggiare in torno a me ti sento	and I feel you hovering around me.
Sei qui, mi baci e m'accarezzi.	You are here, you kiss and caress me.
Ah! dimmi, quando in ciel potrò vederti?	Ah! tell me, when can I see you in heaven?
Quando potrò baciarti?	When will I be able to kiss you?
Oh! dolce fine d'ogni mio dolore,	Oh! sweet ending of all my grief,
quando in cielo con te potrò salire?	when can I go to heaven with you?
Dillo alla mamma, creatura bella,	Tell your mamma, beautiful child,
con un leggero scintillar di stella.	with the light sparkling of a star.
Parlami, amore, amor!	Speak to me, love, love!

Angelica, the daughter of noble parents but also the unmarried mother of a little boy, spends her life as a nun in a convent to expiate her unforgivable sin. Seven years have passed in the seclusion and apparent peace of the cloister when Sister Angelica learns that her little son has died. She faints. Then, recovering and alone, she laments her grievous loss.

The aria is written for a lirico-spinto soprano, and from beginning to end it vibrates with several phases of the deepest sorrow. Although the voice must stay extremely flexible and colorful, it often seems to ring at the verge of sobs. No vocal effects should be attempted that are not totally motivated by the despair of Angelica. The poor mother loses herself in visions of the dead child whose presence she almost believes to have resuscitated.

The marking *andante desolato* says it all. The metronomical figure seems a little slow today, and we accept $\flat = 50$ more readily. The imagination of the singer must make her see acutely what she says. Angelica sees her son as he must have looked when dead, and no vision can torture a mother's heart more. While the voice needs absolute control it should identify with each of the almost unspeakable words Angelica forces herself to say. The first phrase, "Senza mamma, o bimbo . . . ," is pianissimo, in a mood of numbed helplessness. Then the mother looks at each of the features of the little body. Observe all the commas in the text, such as the one between "fredde" and its repeat and the tie between the second "fredde" and "e chiudesti," the one before "gli occhi belli." The next line, "non potendo carezzarmi," allows longer phrases; take one breath only, after "carezzarmi." The sight of the child's arms that had nobody to embrace brings the mother to a paroxysm of despair. "E tu sei morto" is a crescendo, "senza sapere" still stronger. Breathe, then sing "quanto t'amava" with tragic intensity, and in a diminuendo that just avoids a collapse sing "questa tua mamma."

Angelica's disturbed mind now suddenly forgets the remains of the child and sees him as an angel in heaven. Her voice becomes lighter and has a kind of serenity. She sings very legato, finding consolation in her illusion. The soprano should feel extremely personal in molding the phrases of number 61, stressing the proximity of the vision with "Sei qui," the warmth of her longing in "quando potrò verderti" and "baciarti." The illusion intensifies its effect: The tempo is more spacious beginning with "Oh! dolce fine," the voice more intense on "quando in cielo con te potrò salire," then broader and mezzo forte on "Quando potrò morir," the A of "morir" being the expression of a happy desire, not a tragic cry. It seems that the word "morir" has awakened in Angelica a thought which, to make it clearer, causes her to repeat "potrò morir" twice, meditatively and more slowly. That is it; she knows it now: To be reunited with her son, she simply has to die. Her serenity turns to ecstasy, and her voice becomes a spiritual crystal. The last lines must be sung pianissimo, on the lips, like the harmonics of a string instrument, only the most external resonances of the face being involved. All the "Parlami, amore" already lie in the high resonances, which will make the high A part of the whole line, just a spin away.

The soprano who would not feel this aria in her fibers does not exist. What is needed here is the courage to be totally involved and the gift to let the voice be so free of technical complications that it seems to ring without a concrete body to hamper its flight.

Puccini, *Tosca*

"Recondita armonia"   *tenor*

Recondita armonia	Hidden harmony
di belleze diverse!	of different kinds of beauty!
E bruna Floria,	Floria is a brunette,
l'ardente amante mia;	my passionare mistress;
e te, beltade ignota,	and you, beautiful unknown woman,
cinta di chiome bionde!	you are crowned with blond hair!

Tu azzuro hai l'occhio,	Your eyes are blue,
Tosca ha l'occhio nero!	Tosca has dark eyes!
L'arte nel suo mistero	Art in its mystery
le diverse bellezze insiem confonde:	combines contrasting beauties:
ma nel ritrar costei	but while painting this woman
il mio solo pensiero	my only thought
ah! il mio sol pensier	ah! my only thought
sei tu, Tosca, sei tu!	is of you, Tosca, of you!

In a church in Rome, Mario Cavaradossi is working on a large religious painting, in particular on the figure of Mary Magdalena whom he has given "large blue eyes and masses of golden hair." "Suddenly he stops painting, takes out of his breast-pocket a medallion containing a miniature, and compares the latter with the picture on the easel," as it says in the Ricordi piano-vocal score (pp. 13, 18). Whatever drama is to happen later in the opera, the opening mood for Cavaradossi is one of radiant love for Tosca, the woman in the medallion, and of happy satisfaction with his blond Magdalena, actually the portrait of a woman who often comes to pray near his scaffolding.

The opening aria requires a fine lyric voice capable of expressing youthful passion and enthusiasm in a happy fashion and with considerable ease. It is a reflective aria unfolding without haste. Prior to the aria the tempo as marked in the score had been ♩ = 48, and there is a *più lento* at the start of the aria. The indication of dynamics is *pianissimo*, but with crescendos and decrescendos in the accompaniment. A good mezzo-piano well sung would be right. The words are beautiful, and the tenor should sing all their vowels with love and tie them smoothly to easy consonants. Tosca's physical character is stressed by the strong consonants /r/ in "bruna" and "ardente," "bruna" stronger, "ardente" going to piano in effusive tenderness. It is quite possible to suggest the Latin glow of Tosca's complexion by a certain shading of the voice and to contrast it with the description of Magdalena, which is given in lyrical, bright tones, no more than mezzo forte in strength, with two grace notes adding elegance to the picture. "Tu azzuro hai l'occhio" paints in clear tones, "Tosca ha l'occhio nero" with a luscious, darker color. All of this is highly pleasurable, a feeling that should appear in the singing.

The smiling bit of philosophy about the compatibility of contrasting beauties, "L'arte nel suo mistero . . ., will be sung with an easy round voice. It is a restful moment, in preparation for the most important lyric phrase about to come. The three quarter notes of "confonde: ma" are broad, well supported, their spin serving as a springboard for "nel ritrar costei," a crescendo-decrescendo with a summit on "co-ste-." "Il mio solo pensiero" is a similar crescendo-decrescendo, and it is from a mezzo-piano strength that the voice spins to an intense A ("ah! il mio sol pensier") and an entire line forte, with a sustained "tu" at the end. The interval between the D and the B-flat of "Tosca" is taken leisurely, the D already felt in the upper resonances that will be needed for the B-flat, the B-flat sung on a vowel /o/ much slimmer than the /ɔ/ of the D. There is bravura in the two grace notes of "Tos-ca," the last notes of the aria all being freely sustained.

What cannot be analyzed is the vibrant quality and the vital energy which throughout the aria must exist in the voice of the tenor, a vibrancy and vitality that come from the mind as well as from the body, better still, from their well-balanced cooperation.

"Vissi d'arte"   *soprano*

Vissi d'arte,	I lived of art,
vissi d'amore,	I lived of love,
non feci mai male	I never harmed
ad anima viva.	a living soul.
Con man furtiva	With a furtive hand,
quante miserie conobbi,	In any misery I knew of,
aiutai . . .	I gave help . .
Sempre con fè sincera	Always, with sincere faith,
la mia preghiera	my prayer rose
ai santi tabernacoli salì.	to the holy tabernacles.
Sempre con fè sincera	Always with sincere faith
diedi fiori agli altar . . .	did I put flowers at the altars . . .
nell'ora del dolore	in the hour of sorrow,
perchè, perchè, Signore	why, why, Lord,
perchè me ne rimuneri così?	why do you reward me thus?
Diedi gioielli	I gave jewels
della Madonna al manto,	for the Madonna's mantle,
e diedi il canto	and gave my song
agli astri, al ciel,	to the stars, to the sky,
che ne ridean più belli . . .	which then smiled more beautifully . . .
nell'ora del dolore,	in the hour of sorrow,
perchè, perchè, Signore	why, why, Lord,
perchè me ne rimuneri così?	why do you reward me thus?

In the scenes preceding this famous aria Floria Tosca, faithful lover of the painter Mario and a celebrated opera singer, has seen her life undergo extreme changes in an incredibly short time. One hour ago she was singing a cantata at the queen's court. Since then, she has seen Mario in chains, tortured, and led off to the gallows; she has barely been able to repulse the physical assault of the odious police chief Scarpia; and now she faces the prospect of having to yield to him in order to save Mario's life. Violent scenes and violent emotions have buffeted the stage and the actors unceasingly for a long while. now there is a sudden silence, for even the relentless Scarpia has to pause, and Tosca, prostrate and bewildered, tries to find her bearings in this new, confused world. Where did she go wrong? Is all this sudden misery the result of some guilt of hers? Why does the Lord punish her in such a horrible way? Those questions are the burden of the aria.

The dynamics is *pianissimo* with the added marking *dolcissimo* (very soft) and *appassionato* (impassioned) and *con grande sentimento* (with great feeling). The tempo is marked at ♩ = 40.

Hence, the beginning of the aria must be sung very piano, very slowly, but with intense feeling. After the preceding turmoil the sound of the soprano voice must create a striking anticlimax and carry with it a different world, one of humanity and goodness. For Tosca, life had consisted of her art, her love, her charity, and her faith. Three of those basic elements are quoted in the first lines. But beneath it all there is Tosca's incapacity to understand why such a life should deserve to be punished.

Sing the first two bars in the mood analyzed above, very legato; mark the comma; sing the next two bars with a little more stress; slowly unfold the triplets of the following bars; allow the voice to surge briefly on "quante miserie"; and let it subside on "aiutai." The next page is devoted entirely to Tosca's faith and describes, still very slowly, her regular prayers at church, her offerings of flowers. It calls for beautiful, melodic singing, still intense within the dynamic limitations and with a majestic crescendo on "diedi fiori agli altar." Now, in an almost confidential tone, Tosca questions the Lord's forsaking her when she needs him so much. The even rhythm in triplets must be very smooth: It seems that Tosca thereby softens her boldness in questioning the Lord.

The score returns to the religious motif as Tosca stresses that she gave the Madonna more than flowers—jewels—and that she gave the starry sky her voice, that sky she had celebrated already in her aria in act 1. The voice is now ready for an immense climax. After containing her sorrow and indignation so far, Tosca, her physical strength recovered, raises her voice to heaven, singing a great forte in a tempo still slower than the slow tempo that has prevailed throughout the aria. The fine point is to build up this climax in a short time and to make the tone as beautiful as it is powerful. The idea that the outcry is directed at the Lord may help the singer conceive a tone as noble as it is strong.

A slight change is accepted that makes the phrase still more singable:

In order to reach the B-flat easily, the preceding D on the syllable "Si-" should be sung very lightly, the impression for the singer being that she spins from the F (end of "perch-è-è") to the B-flat without changing resonances for the D.

If you breathe after the B-flat, you can make a long tenuto on the A-natural of "Ah." Note finally that "perchè me ne rimuneri" has very strong stresses on the first five notes and a fermata on the last one. That fermata must be used and then broken off abruptly, as if by a sob, after which "così" will be sung as written, that is, very short. Holding the E-flat a long time is to be avoided at all cost. Instead of holding a spectacular tone, Tosca has broken down, unable to utter another word.

It is well understood that to do justice to "Vissi d'arte" one must give prime consideration to Tosca's psychological attitude and mold one's voice upon that attitude, which changes from bewilderment to rebellion, from a good length of intense piano singing to a short but outstanding moment of utmost vocal power.

"E lucevan le stelle" — *tenor*

E lucevan le stelle . . .	And the stars were shining . . .
e olezzava la terra,	and sweet smelled the earth,
stridea l'uscio dell'orto . . .	the garden gate squeaked . . .
e un passo sfiorava la rena . . .	and a footstep skimmed over the sand . . .
Entrava ella, fragrante,	She entered, fragrant,
mi cadea fra le braccia . . .	fell into my arms . . .
Oh! dolci baci, o languide carezze,	Oh, sweet kisses, oh, languid caresses,
mentr'io, fremente	while I, trembling,

le belle forme disciogliea	freed the beautiful forms
dai veli!	from their veils!
Svanì per sempre il sogno mio d'amore . .	Vanished forever is my dream of love . . .
l'ora è fuggita . . .	the hour has fled . . .
e muoio disperato . . .	and I die in despair . . .
e non ho amato mai tanto la vita,	and never have I loved life so much,
tanto la vita!	loved life so much!

Contrary to what Scarpia had decided earlier, Mario has not been sent to the gallows but will be executed by a firing squad. In his cell, waiting for the fatal hour, he writes a last message to Tosca. But "after tracing a few lines, engrossed by memories of the past, he ceases writing," to quote from the score.

Nostalgia invades Mario. For our ears it is expressed in a theme that is forever famous. At first, the orchestra sings it repeatedly while Mario only murmurs, remembering his unforgettable nights with Tosca. Following this moving prelude, his nostalgia explodes vehemently, and he sings his heartrending aria based on the same theme.

Although the singer finds himself almost constantly in a rubato situation, let us adopt a basic pace around ♩ = 50–52. While the theme unfolds, Mario's memory recalls visions, perfumes, sounds, all of them faint: distant stars, perfumes from the garden, the creaking of the garden gate, footsteps on the sand, the fragrance of the beloved woman. His eyes, his ears, and his nose assemble their individual offerings to re-create the glorious memory of Tosca as he held her in his arms. It is up to the singer to find the subtle changes of color in his voice that will suggest all this. The voice: very light and clear for "E lucevan le stelle," with a long, deep breath before "e olezzava la terra"; as if listening to a distant, discreet noise on "stridea l'uscio dell'orto"; expressing impatient expectation on "e un passo sfiorava la rena"; full of admiration and already sensuous for "Entrava ella, fragrante"; almost overcome with fulfillment on "mi cadea fra le braccia," said passionately and quite slowly.

In the piano-vocal score there follow two pages that are among the most famous of all opera selections. What has happened (what is still happening?) to them all too often? As they express feelings of the strongest intensity, they have at times been mistaken for very loud pages. Also, since they require a tenor voice of only limited range, they have too often been appropriated by students or amateurs with short voices who have found them convenient for demonstrating the strength of whatever it is they have. On the operatic stage, too, there have been tenors who thought that this aria was their last opportunity of the evening to get a big hand and who tried to wrench it from the audience through the violence of their singing. Yet Mario is a man who, with only one hour to live, has just summoned to his side the presence of the woman he loves and who is now going to savor that supreme illusion.

The marking says *vagamente* (with much feeling), that is, tenderly, gently. The kisses he remembers are "dolci" (soft, sweet), the caresses "languide" (languishing), and he sees himself "despoiling the beautiful body of its light clothing." Can the voice be anything here but a sensuous sigh, warm and flexible? A tenuto is possible on "o languide," and a shudder of emotion can be felt on "fremente." After a breath, the phrase "le belle forme . . ." should be spun with absolute delight, slowly and warmly, from piano to pianissimo and with great flexibility of rhythm: There is greatness in sensuality.

With "svanì per sempre" a sudden hopelessness darkens the voice, which nonetheless stays piano and slow. It is only with "l'ora è fuggita" that sorrow enters into the expression, which will burst out on "e muoio disperato," sung stressing each syllable and without any accelerando. (*Con anima* means "with emotion" and not "more animated.") The second "e muoio disperato" comes after a big diminuendo and is helpless, so that the vital outcry can now explode in its full power, with élan, undiminished by previous unwritten climaxes. The last "tanto la vita" is free and should also be devoid of shouting. On the contrary, it should give its full value to the word "vita," said on its musical pitch with intense yearning. Afterwards, the tenor might burst into tears, as written in the score.

This aria was a personal triumph for Puccini. His librettists had given him several elaborate texts to use at that point in the drama. He rejected them all, one after another, wanting to deal only with the sincere, basic emotions of a young man in love who will die too soon. Nobody should spoil the master's inspiration to serve his own nonartistic purposes.

Puccini, *Turandot*

"Signore, ascolta" *soprano*

Signore, ascolta!	My Lord, listen!
Ah, signore, ascolta!	Ah, my Lord, listen!
Liù non regge più!	Liù cannot bear it anymore!
Si spezza il cor!	My heart is breaking!
Ahimè, quanto cammino	Alas, how far have I walked
col tuo nome nell'anima,	with your name in my soul,
col nome tuo sulle labbra!	with your name on my lips!
Ma se il tuo destino	But if your fate
doman sarà deciso,	is decided tomorrow,
noi morrem sulla strada dell'esilio.	we shall die on the road of exile.
Ei perderà suo figlio . . .	He will lose his son . . .
io l'ombra d'un sorriso!	I, the shadow of a smile!
Liù non regge più!	Liù cannot bear it anymore!
Ah, pietà!	Ah, have mercy!

The action takes place in Peking in legendary times. Liù is a slave girl in the service of Timur, the banished old king of the Tartars. After a long separation Timur and his son Calaf have just been reunited, thanks largely to the devotion of Liù, who has been secretly in love with Calaf since he once smiled at her. Calaf's identity is at present kept secret in fear for his life.

Turandot, daughter of the emperor of China, is a young woman of great beauty and an icy heart who has her royal suitors put to death as they fail, one after the other, to solve the three riddles she asks them. Upon seeing Turandot for the first time, Calaf has fallen passionately in love with her and proposes to pass the murderous test. Desperate, Liù dares attempt to dissuade him.

The arias in *Turandot* (Calaf's two arias, Liù's first aria here, and her second much later in the opera) are short pieces inserted between large ensemble scenes. They are inspired by the theme of absolute finality, death, and their brevity serves to enhance their intensity. The voice of Liù, a strong lyric soprano or lirico-spinto, is heard in ardent supplication, as in this first aria, or in a tragic offering of her life later. It must be a very brilliant voice, with radiant high notes but capable of conveying compelling emotional power in a short span of time.

The marking in the score here calls for an imploring, tearful voice. Liù is a slave who has dared raise her sights to a prince. There is humility in her plea as well as passion and exhaustion. If the soprano tries to feel all these elements in her heart she will find the intense, essentially feminine color of Liù's voice. Singing legato is a must; allowing the voice to soar freely to the high notes is indispensable.

Calaf's old father has failed to make his son renounce his plan. Giving up, he asks for someone's help. That is when Liù raises her voice. "Signore, ascolta" is a desperate attempt to catch Calaf's attention. Tying the "Ah" to "Signore, ascolta" and taking a sharp breath after the "Ah" will create the desired effect of urgency. A similar effect can be achieved by tying "Ahimè" to "Si spezza il cor," making a slight tenuto on the high A-flat. A ritardando on "quanto cammino" will express the weariness of long days of walking; another ritardando, piano, on "col nome tuo" is a humble, loving tribute to Calaf. Liù evokes the memory of her efforts to reach Calaf with tenderness. Looking ahead, her voice becomes tense at the thought of Calaf's fate on "il tuo destino doman sarà deciso," then dramatic, forte and ritardando broadly on "noi morrem," even with a short fermata on the high A-flat. It should be possible to go to the end of the phrase "-la strada dell'esilio" without breathing, but fading a little. The next two bars are said with quiet despair, the second bar slowly, mourning a very great loss. The last four bars, started piano and ending on a ringing and expanding B-flat, will be made easier by the concept of singing the middle A-flats in an upper resonance, which will bring them nearer to the high A-flat, and then to the B-flat, the distance between the well-separated notes being also shortened by a spin upward and by avoiding an attack on the high notes as new sounds unconnected with the middle notes. "Liù non regge più" must sound near exhaustion, but "Ah, pietà" has the intensity of a last effort to win over the immovable Calaf. The soprano must feel deeply involved in that effort. This is not a piece to be sung for the sake of a pleasant vocal achievement only.

"Nessun dorma"   *tenor*

Nessun dorma! Nessun dorma!	Nobody may sleep!
Tu pure, o Principessa,	Even you, oh Princess,
nella tua fredda stanza	in your cold room
guardi le stelle	gaze at the stars
che tremano d'amore e di speranza.	that tremble with love and hope.

Ma il mio mistero è chiuso in me,	But my secret is locked within me,
il nome mio nessun saprà.	my name nobody shall know.
No, no, sulla tua bocca lo dirò,	No, no, on your mouth shall I say it,
quando la luce splenderà.	when daylight will shine.
Ed il mio baccio scioglierà	And my kiss will break
il silenzio che ti fa mia!	the silence which makes you mine!
Dilegua, o notte,	Fade away, oh night,
tramontate, stelle!	go down, stars!
All'alba vincerò!	At dawn I shall win!

Calaf has won the right to possess Turandot but has given the princess a chance to avoid what she considers a humiliating servitude. If before morn she finds out his name, she is free again. Following her orders, the whole city is awake and trying to discover clues to that secret. In this superb aria Calaf, awake himself and sure of his triumph, savors already the rewards the morning reserves for him.

The aria requires a tenor voice of great power, of very easy high range, and capable of vibrant and broad lyricism. Such a voice, handled by an artist, can make the performance of this aria memorable, but no amount of artistry will suffice if the voice of the performer is not a great voice.

The marking reads *andante sostenuto*. The aria is generally sung very slowly, the beginning being as broad as ♩ = 44, with, of course, certain changes farther along, few of them actually in print but felt instinctively both for their emotion and for the glory of the voice.

Repeating the words of the distant chorus, "Nessun dorma," very earnestly, piano but firmly, Calaf creates a mood of spacious silence. But almost immediately waves of the lyricism that flows from him appear in his singing, at first contained by the icy personality of Turandot. The tenor should visualize her consulting the stars from her cold window. His voice, enunciating the words slowly, should find a cold, almost scornful ring in "Principessa," in "nella tua fredda stanza." Use the double *d* and the sixteenth as part of the effect, and slow down still more on "stanza." The voice is raised because of the poetic scope of "guardi le stelle" and warms up somewhat for "che tremono d'amore" before going to piano on "e di speranza," sung slowly and meaningfully.

The next phrase is one of those gems that Puccini found time and again for his tenors and his sopranos. Sing the simple yet irresistible phrase "Ma il mio mistero è chiuso in me" with warmth and amplitude, gaining a little speed for "il nome mio nessun saprà." A breath after "No, no" launches a legatissimo high line of A's, the last one on "lo" the most ringing of the three, before a progressive mellowing makes "la luce' a silky mezzo-forte. After a breath, "splenderà" has a long, delighted fermata diminuendo.

A short orchestral moment introduces the new wave, this one more intimate, more sensuous than the first one, slightly rubato, a little faster on "scioglierà il silenzio," much slower for the enjoyment of "che ti fa mia." Here the choral interludes are almost insufferrably lyric. The voice rises from them to its most glorious, without a breath until after the first "stelle," the A's taking all the time they need to be outstanding. A good ritardando on the second "tramontate, stelle" prepares the words of total confidence, "All'alba vincerò," sung piano with radiant serenity. The last two "vincerò" are really one phrase, started mezzo forte, with a sixteenth note crisp but legato, a tenuto on the G, forte but not fortissimo, no lowering of the resonance for the "vin-" on the D, and a continuous spin to the B fortissimo, vibrant in a vowel /e/ backed by a high dome of resonance in the upper mouth. If good, it can be held for much more than its value, and the final "-rò" can be sustained to the end of its own value.

This aria, one of Puccini's last inspirations, rivals in musical and vocal beauty any of his other creations. Alas, the privilege of performing it is limited to a select few.

"Tu, che di gel sei cinta" *soprano*

Tu, che di gel sei cinta,	You, who wrap yourself in ice,
da tanta fiamma vinta	vanquished by so much fire
l'amerai anche tu!	you, too, will love him!
Prima di questa aurora	Before this dawn,
io chiudo stanca gli occhi,	tired I shall close my eyes,
perchè egli vinca ancora . . .	so that he may win again . . .
per non . . . per non vederlo più!	never . . . never to see him again!

Having passed his dangerous tests victoriously, Calaf in a noble gesture has refused to make Turandot his without giving her another chance. He will renounce his rights to her if she can discover his identity. Turandot has directed the whole city, under the threat of death, to solve the enigma. She has ordered old Timur to be tortured when Liù steps forward and states that she alone knows the name of the mysterious stranger. But even torture fails to make her betray it. Her love is such that she will die to insure Calaf's victory. In a supreme effort she braces herself to speak face to face with Turandot.

The first few phrases of the aria are a challenge to the insensitive princess. The tempo, *andante mosso con un poco d'agitazione*, indicates that many fluctuations will be permitted, many inflections demanded. Liù, showing herself to be the equal of Turandot, sings with vigor and deep earnestness, the voice firm and convincing. Is it possible to make all this appear in "Tu"? It can certainly be done in the description of Turandot as one wrapped in ice—there might even be scorn in that phrase—and defeated. Make "vinta" an aggressive word, "l'amerai anche tu" a challenge, repeated with great emphasis, slowly and forte.

Liù then alludes to her own sacrifice, softly and wearily at first. "Prima di questa aurora" is piano, "io chiudo stanca gli occhi" slow and tired. After a short *a tempo*, however, her determination is expressed, also slowly but in firm tones, "perchè egli vinca ancora." She stops to regain her strength and repeats more strongly "ei vinca ancora." With pathetic simplicity she renounces her hopes, her only joy: to see the inaccessible man she loves. Here her emotions cannot be contained any longer, and she raises her voice in two great lyric phrases, separated by a moment of soft resignation. A great crescendo takes the phrase "Prima di questa aurora" and its amplification to a soaring B-flat, kept vibrant by the fermata. A profoundly weary softness imbues "io chiudo stanca gli occhi" where the longed-for peace of death is detected.

The last six notes are as desperate a cry as has ever been written in opera. Note that all of them are elongated, not accented, by stresses and fermatas and that a soaring spin must take the voice to the B-flat in a superb legato, which will in no way prevent a fortissimo but will give it a scope, a greatness, that no punch can create. It is also very important to be able to sing "veder" with two vowels /e/, vowels which give the very strong vibration of the voice a groove to keep the tone from spreading. It is absolutely possible to sing a vowel /e/ in that range, to give it at the same time a vibrant forward ring and an inner upward resonance for size and richness. Such skills are necessary for doing justice to arias like this one, where one unpleasant tone at a capital moment spoils a most remarkable dramatic effect.

The last word, "più," detached or not from the preceding one by a breath, must not be shouted but must come as a word of simple finality. Within seconds Liù will have stabbed herself to death. I prefer to have her end the final outcry of her despair with the same dignity that has characterized her throughout the opera.

Rossini, *Il Barbiere di Siviglia*

"Largo al factotum"   *baritone*

Largo al factotum della città, largo!	Make room for the factotum of the town, make room!
Presto a bottega, chè l'alba è già, presto!	Quickly to the shop, it's dawn already, quickly!
Ah che bel vivere,	Ah what a beautiful life,
che bel piacere,	what great pleasure,
per un barbiere di qualità!	for a barber of quality!
Ah bravo, Figaro, bravissimo!	Ah bravo, Figaro, bravissimo!
Fortunatissimo per verità, bravo!	Most fortunate indeed, bravo!
Pronto a far tutto	Ready to do everything,
la notte e il giorno,	night and day,
sempre d'intorno,	he is always around,
in giro sta.	always on the move.
Miglior cuccagna per un barbiere	A better opportunity for a barber,
vita più nobile, no, non si dà.	a more noble life can indeed not be had.
Rasori e pettini,	Razors and combs,
lancette e forbici,	lancets and scissors,
al mio comando tutto qui sta.	everything is here at my call.
V'è la risorsa poi del mestiere,	And there are resources besides the job,
colla donnetta,	with the little ladies,
col cavaliere.	with the gentlemen.
Ah che bel vivere,	Ah what a beautiful life,
che bel piacere	what great pleasure
per un barbiere di qualità.	for a barber of quality.
Tutti mi chiedono,	Everybody asks for me,

tutti mi vogliono,	everybody wants me,
donne, ragazze,	ladies, young girls,
vecchi e fanciulle:	old men and little girls:
Qua la parucca,	The wig here,
presto la barba,	quickly, the beard,
qua la sanguina,	there a bleeding,
presto il biglietto,	quickly the note,
Figaro, Figaro, ahimè,	Figaro, Figaro, mercy,
ahimè, che furia!	mercy, what fury!
Ahimè, che folla!	Mercy, what a crowd!
Uno alla volta, per carità!	One at a time, for pity's sake!
Figaro!—Son qua.	Figaro!—Here I am
Ehi, Figaro! Son qua.	Eh Figaro! Here I am.
Figaro su, Figaro giù!	Figaro up, Figaro down!
Figaro qua, Figaro là!	Figaro here, Figaro there!
Pronto, prontissimo,	Fast, faster,
son come il fulmine,	I am like lightning,
sono il factotum della città.	I am the factotum of the town.
Ah bravo, Figaro, bravissimo,	Ah, bravo, Figaro, bravissimo,
a te fortuna non mancherà.	fortune will not be lacking for you.

"To the actor who would play the role of Figaro one cannot recommend enough that he imbue himself thoroughly with the character of the role. If he should see in it more than reason spiced with gaiety and wit, above all, if he should load it with the slightest exaggeration, he would degrade a role which brings honor to [an interpreter] who knows how to master its many nuances and rise to its entire concept" (Beaumarchais, preface to *Le Mariage de Figaro*).

Figaro: "Accustomed to misery I hasten to laugh about everything for fear of being obliged to cry" (*Le Barbier de Séville,* Act I, Scene 2).

It is early morning in Sevilla. Figaro, in high spirits, pauses for a moment on his way to work and makes a survey of the state of his affairs. The state of his affairs is good. With the help of his guitar, forever hanging from his neck, Figaro indulges in a brief celebration of his present success: He has become an important feature in the daily life of the city.

In Rossini's opera Figaro's voice is ideally a ringing lyric baritone, in the same bracket as the coloratura Rosina and the light lyric Almaviva, certainly lighter than Basilio or Don Bartolo. The custom of using a dramatic voice for the role is not new and seems to find great favor with the public. To me it seems that it throws the whole score out of balance for the sake of hearing a big voice singing fast and loud.

In Paris as well as in New York I have had the good fortune to sing Figaro and to make up my mind about this aria, one of the best known and most often quoted of all arias. I have resolved that it is a cheerful aria, an aria of lightheartedness, of self-congratulation, an outburst of such joy that it does not even require a witness, a purely personal, sincere, unpretentious four minutes of happiness. With this resolution I have most certainly not made a great discovery—But I have thereby eliminated the danger of showing off, the desire for boastful pretense, the intemperate interpolations, and the excessive speed. It is difficult to be cheerful when one's mind is centered on dazzling speed. Speed expresses urgency, fretting, haste . . . and speed. It is not easy to be cheerful while thundering through a range extended beyond reason, and for no reason. It is only too easy to transform this aria into a showcase for the singer's unusual powers, and it pays off. But let us take a look at what it is all about:

Allegro vivace, about ♩ = 126–132, a speed that is *vivace* but permits diction, intentions, stresses, all needed for the "many nuances" of the role of Figaro. With his first word the jocular mood of the barber is established: He asks for space in an obviously deserted street. His voice need not be overpowering but it must be happy and must already sing a musical phrase. From "Largo" a crescendo should be made to "città"; it is the E on the second "largo" that is the real forte. The "lala ran la . . ." are like guitar notes made with the voice; the high G is the top note of the forte chord of the guitar, brilliant rather than enormous. The phrase "Presto a bottega" is shaped like the first phrase, going from mezzo forte to forte, full of eagerness, and the "lala ran la . . ." are again like notes from the guitar. During the two bars of interlude Figaro stops his progress to his shop, and for the next ten bars basks in his happiness, singing "Ah che bel vivere . . ." easily, comfortably, adding a touch of conceit in "di qualità," after a touch of elegance added to "piacere," as shown.

By now, Figaro—and the baritone—have firmly established their presence, and the next lines, "Ah bravo, Figaro" and "Fortunatissimo," are sung with full voice, the "lala ran la" staying very light, with the help of the lips. The high A on "bravo" can be used if it adds to the feeling of cheer and ease, not if it causes an impression of strain. The repeats of "Fortunatissimo per verità" should be, for the first, forte, for the second, light, allowing a strong crescendo in the sequence of "lala ran la . . ."

After the interlude, "Pronto a far tutto" is nimble and friendly, "Miglior cuccagna" well rounded in the mouth. The "lala ran la" are proud and forte this time. "Rasori e pettini" should reflect in the clipped words the precise efficiency of the virtuoso barber.

With "V'è la risorsa" the rhythmical element of the music, capitally important so far, eases a little, almost permitting the feeling of a recitative—a meaningful one. Smilingly, Figaro sees himself at work as a messenger between lovers, and the singer should see the scene in his mind, the man and the girl involved, and Figaro's financial reward for his services. There is, moreover, something confidential in the way Figaro speaks of his dealings, but there is great glee when he thinks of his profits. "V'è la risorsa" and "poi del mestiere" are bantering, the two "colla donnetta" graceful and protective, the two "col cavaliere" more manly and full of understanding.

Here an already old custom makes it imperative to add to the original text a number of notes and bars, as follows:

All this must be elegant and brilliant, and must be sung lightly and with amusement. On the sixth bar following the latter addition, a run is added as shown:

Again, these additions make sense only if they are done in a way that adds to the listening pleasure of the audience.

The next section, based on the opening music of the aria, lets the accompaniment sing while the voice, sometimes clipped, sometimes round, sometimes authoritative, impersonates Figaro's many callers. Imagination is in order, but not ugliness or mugging. At the end of the page Figaro summons countless characters in a breathless enumeration of demands and finally calls his own name in the different voices. Here again, taste must work hand in hand with fantasy. Baritones possessing an easy and pleasant falsetto can add a joke at the end of the many calls as shown.

The barber pretends to be overcome by the many demands, pleads for mercy, with a rallentando on the last "Uno alla volta" and, after a life-saving breath, a fermata on "per ca-rità."

The double effect of the several voices calling and Figaro's harried answers is repeated in a different way, "Figaro!—Son qua." Here, no more than in the first series of calls, can triviality, grossness, or even whistles be tolerated. Even when harried the barber is more than able to cope gracefully with all demands.

It is customary to make an accelerando during the four-bar interlude following "della città" and to sing "Ah bravo, Figaro" very rapidly, around ♩ = 160, but very lightly, the tip of the tongue constantly on or very near the upper teeth. The voice becomes more sustained and stronger on "sono il factotum della città," but the pattern of six notes to a bar must be absolutely respected. After singing the high G of "della" the baritone generally stays on the same note for the syllable "ci-" of the last "città" and holds a fermata on it. The whole impression must be one of pride and brilliance, not of heavy, blustering power.

Even if Rossini's music adds a lot of dazzling superficiality to the character of Figaro in this aria, it in no way destroys his "reason spiced with gaiety and wit." Rossini's Figaro is a terminal extrovert, but he must keep his charm and never be degraded by lack of taste. Under that condition a great vocal performance of this aria deserves a triumph.

"Una voce poco fa" *soprano*

Una voce poco fa	A voice, just now,
qui nel cor mi risuonò,	found an echo in my heart,
il mio cor ferito è già,	my heart is wounded already
e Lindor fu che il piagò.	and Lindor is the one who hurt it.
Sì, Lindoro mio sarà,	Yes, Lindoro will be mine,
lo giurai, la vincerò.	I have sworn it, I shall succeed.
Il tutor ricuserò,	I shall refuse my guardian,
io l'ingegno aguzzerò,	my wits I shall sharpen,
alla fin s'accheterà,	in the end he'll be appeased,
e contenta io resterò.	and I will be content.
Sì, Lindoro mio sarà,	Yes, Lindoro will be mine,
lo giurai, la vincerò.	I have sworn it, I shall succeed.
Io sono docile,	I am submissive,
son rispettosa,	I am respectful,
son obbediente,	I am obedient,
dolce, amorosa.	gentle, affectionate.
Mi lascio reggere,	I let myself be governed,
mi fo guidar.	I let myself be guided.
Ma se mi toccano	But if they touch me
dov'è il mio debole	where I have my weak point,

sarò una vipera,	I become a viper,
e cento trappole	and I'll put in play
prima di cedere	a hundred traps
farò giocar.	before giving in.
Io sono docile . . .	I am submissive . . .

"Imagine the prettiest, daintiest girl, sweet, tender, courteous and fresh, whetting the appetite, furtive foot, well-turned waist, plump arms, rosy lips, and what hands, what cheeks, what teeth, what eyes!"—that is the portrait Figaro paints of Rosina in Act II, scene 2 of Beaumarchais's *Le Barbier de Séville*. In Rossini's opera that most charming young lady introduces herself to the audience in the aria "Una voce poco fa." Alone in the room where behind closed blinds she spends many hours, she holds in her hand the letter she will try to send to her inaccessible suitor. She sings, opening her heart confidently, as if nobody could hear and betray her.

What type of voice should Rosina's be? Still imbued with the tradition of Beaumarchais, I would say, "the voice that fits the portrait here above"; the voice my Rosina had when I was Figaro and she was Bidú Sayão or Lily Pons, a young-sounding voice with sparkle and wit. Such voices have usually sung the aria in F. But contraltos and dramatic sopranos have also been tempted by the role and have sung the aria in E. As originally conceived, the aria is in two parts, one in 3/4, the other in 4/4. In the first part Rosina speaks of the love, the trouble, which has invaded her soul recently and of her determination to possess the object of that love. In the second part she reveals a hidden facet of her charming personality, a fierceness she can call upon if need be in order to reach her goals.

The score as printed for voice and piano conveys to perfection the meaning of those two parts, but performer after performer has endeavored to supplement that simple score by adding countless cadenzas to it. Two of the most respected collections of cadenzas devote, respectively, five and two-thirds (Ricci) and even six (Liebling) pages to the cadenzas for this one aria, the length of the cadenzas surpassing the length of the aria in its original form. Little by little the aria and its meaning have disappeared behind flashy vocalises, and Rosina has become a virtuoso vocalist eager to get her big applause in her first scene and postponing until later the building of her character and her participation in the comedy whose central figure she represents. A very well-known anecdote tells us of the aging Rossini listening to the greatest coloratura of his day singing what had originally been "Una voce poco fa" and commenting: "Charming, charming—who is the composer?" According to the usages of classical music in performance, the first part of an aria must be sung straight, the ornamentation reserved for later pages and for repeats. Such a rule would be welcome here. The first sixteen bars of the vocal part would then be sung as printed, and a progressive use of ornamentation would be introduced later. The first change might be that shown here.

The tempo, *andante*, stands at about ♩ = 80, poised and leisurely. Rosina reflects on what has happened to her, well-pleased and slightly puzzled by the new emotion in her heart. She sings piano, warmly but in an intimate mood, actually thinking aloud. The value of the double dotted notes must be sustained to the end, so that the brief thirty-second notes do not create a jumpy rhythm. She sings a sweet legato, interrupted before "qui nel cor" and "mi risuonò" by a sigh of delight. Again, there is a stress of sensitivity on the double dotted notes of "ferito è già." Now the beloved name of Lindor comes for the first time, and, as it will always be, it is said with great love and, this time, with some timidity, as indicated by the portamento downward. But there is a quiet firmness as well as love in the second "Lindor" two bars later, and in the descending line that follows.

The first "lo giurai" has the same quiet firmness, as does the first "la vincerò," quite insinuating with its triplets of sixteenth notes. But the next time (bars 13 and 14) the name of Lindor appears, it is sung forte, and four vigorous accents on the descending scale show a strong determination. The return to piano on "lo giurai" and "la vincerò," bars 15 and 16, show great confidence in a tranquil way.

Here we have the first change of notes indicated earlier, that change showing Rosina's trust in her ability to handle her tutor, a slightly jocular feeling. From here to the end of the section the original music only repeats bars 13 to 16, and a more brilliant variation can be introduced without distorting the character of Rosina. Now is the time to consult Ricci and Liebling and to choose a moderately flashy cadenza, as there is still a long way to go to the end of the aria and we want to keep the best fireworks for the end.

The *moderato* interlude precedes the *moderato* second part, ♩ = 104–108. It would be wise to observe the same policy here as before, singing the original music when it is exposed for the first time, then finding the proper ornamentation for the repeats. By now Rosina has discarded her sentimental mood, her wounded heart, and her worship of the name of Lindor to dedicate herself to the preparation of the project she has sworn to bring to a happy ending. She explains that she has two weapons, her apparent docility and her ability to set merciless traps. The main interest of this second section lies, of course, in the contrast between the two faces of Rosina. The first twelve bars paint her as a sweet little lamb, "io sono docile." All the runs, the alternation of the groups of sixteenths notes and the triplets, create a youthful, vivacious impression. "Sono obbediente," with the accent on "-diente," must be stressed with sweet irony, and any girl will know how to melt a heart with an enchanting "amorosa." With an almost saintly humility Rosina descends to her very low range in "mi fo guidar." By the way it is held, by a clever intonation, this low B can by itself prepare the "surprise." Or, as is generally done, the soprano can ignore the silence and ties the low B to the middle B, stopping abruptly after "Ma." There is certainly nothing wrong with that, or with the tradition of taking a faster tempo starting with "Ma se mi toccano," provided that a threat is felt in Rosina's voice, so far so innocuous.

From this point on to the end of the aria Liebling *(Book of Coloratura Cadenzas)* and Ricci *(Variazoni, Cadenze, Tradizioni per canto)* supersede me, and I surrender happily, only telling dear Rosinas this: Do not attempt what lies beyond the easy limits of your range; while showing, as well you should, your outstanding skill at coloraturas, you must never forget to create admiration and friendly sympathy for Rosina the girl; nor should you forget that good humor is the dominant mood of the piece. No pyrotechnics should cause the listeners to worry, and elegance and beauty of tone have top priority. Quite possibly Rosina will display her most precious artistry in the choice of her inserts, which must be musical, charming, witty, and make her the most lovable of sopranos.

"La calunnia" *bass-baritone*

La calunnia è un venticello,	Calumny is a little breeze,
un'auretta assai gentile,	a very gentle little wind,
che insensibile, sottile,	which insensibly, subtly,
leggermente, dolcemente,	lightly, softly,
incomincia a susurrar.	begins to murmur.
Piano, piano, terra terra,	Softly, softly, crawling along the ground,
sotto voce, sibilando	sotto voce, hissing
va scorrendo, va ronzando;	it glides along, keeps buzzing;
nell'orecchie della gente	in people's ears
s'introduce destramente,	it introduces itself adroitly,
e le teste ed i cervelli	and confuses their heads and brains
fa stordire e fa gonfiar.	and makes them swell.
Dalla bocca fuori uscendo	Out of the mouth and on its way,
lo schiamazzo va crescendo,	the clamor keeps growing,
prende forza a poco a poco,	gains strength little by little,
vola già di loco in loco,	flies already hither and thither,
sembra il tuono, la tempesta	seems a thunder, a storm
che nel sen della foresta	which in the heart of the forest
va fischiando, brontolando	whistles and rumbles
e ti fa d'orror gelar.	and makes you freeze in horror.
Alla fin trabocca e scoppia,	In the end it overflows and breaks out,
si propaga, si raddoppia	it spreads, it redoubles
e produce un'esplosione	and produces an explosion
come un colpo di cannone,	like a cannon shot,
un tremoto, un temporale,	an earthquake, a tempest,
che fa l'aria rimbombar.	that rends the air.
E il meschino calunniato,	And the wretched slandered man,
avvilito, calpestato,	dumbfounded, trampled on,
sotto il pubblico flagello	under the public castigation
per gran sorte va a crepar.	with good luck will croak.

Doctor Bartolo, the guardian of the charming Rosina, plans to marry his ward despite the enormous difference in age between them. He is worried therefore by the presence in town of a young man, probably a student, who has caught Rosina's attention from under her window. Doctor Bartolo would like to eliminate the still-discreet suitor, and he requests the advice of Rosina's music teacher, Don Basilio, a man wise in the ways of the world. Basilio promises to have the young man out of town within four days, through calumny, which he proceeds to explain to Doctor Bartolo.

In the piano and voice score the aria is in D. On the operatic stage it is usually performed in C, the key that fits the bass-baritone voice of Basilio better. The Italian libretto follows the general pattern of the original text by Beaumarchais. Even without the benefit of a musical score, Basilio's imitation of the frightening power of slander is a whirlwind of a speech studded with "pianissimo," "rinforzando," and "crescendo" and ending fortissimo in an explosion of hatred. For a teacher of music that was a natural way of expressing oneself. Rossini used this model to great advantage.

Basilio's concept is that "calunnia" is at first an almost inaudible murmur, that it stays that way during a rather long incubation, meanwhile spreading in all directions and slowly growing in strength until, when ripe and ready, it reaches the size and power of a hurricane and crushes its intended victim to death.

Consequently the performer must sing piano for at least a page and a half in the piano score before his first crescendo, thereby keeping his listeners in a state of expectation for what may seem a long time and enjoying their almost impatient suspense. To achieve the very special effect desired here the singer should suggest that he addresses himself, in a very confidential way, to Bartolo only, his ears checking all the while for any unwelcome eavesdropper.

The prelude of four bars is played sotto voce in an *allegro,* $\downarrow$ = 126, and will be played again twice under the voice, the perfect suggestion of a soft zephyr. The voice matches that softness. It also matches the alternation of legato and nonlegato that describes the vagaries of a very light breeze. "La calunnia" is very legato; "è un venticello" is done as if meant to be legato but with very short interruptions between syllables. The same goes, of course, for "un'auretta" and "assai gentile." The Italian words of the text, both in their meaning and in their sound, blend beautifully well with the music and vice versa. They must constantly keep their descriptive and picturesque value. From the first word of the aria to "susurrar" there is not one word that does not sound like a part of the light breeze that "calunnia" is at first. Justice must be done to "sottile," "leggermente," "dolcemente," "susurrar." The two fermatas following "sottile" and "dolcemente" are short pauses in the movement of the breeze. The notes of "incomincia a susurrar" are staccato and sung without any crescendo. In the following nine bars the voice stays static in the short phrases while the accompaniment starts spreading the gossip all over, the voice joining in that work with "va scorrendo" and "va ronzando," in which the full notes are the first crescendos of the piece.

From there on there will be many waves of sounds. Those waves are made of a great number of eighth notes sung with such an intention of legato that they seem to be attached to each other and each phrase flows and bends like, say, the supple stuff pulled and rounded by the toffee maker. The first wave starts with "s'introduce, s'introduce destramente," swells a little, and falls again to piano. The idea of expectation returns, shortly this time, with "Dalla bocca fuori uscendo." The crescendo starts early, reaches forte at the end of "vola già di loco in loco," and takes possession of the next 21 bars. For the first four of these bars the singer should center his attention on the upper notes of the intervals, increasing the crescendo on the successive D's and E's, doing little for the lower A's. A sense of legato can thus be preserved. The three bars of dotted values must be extremely rhythmical, the silence of the eighth bar used for taking a very deep breath and reinforcing a support that already had to be a very strong one.

The two fortissimos on "cannone" will be most effective if the preceding D's and E-flats have been sung in a full legato and not chopped or barked. When the aria is sung in C, the vowel /o/ in "cannone" will find its color spontaneously. If the aria is sung in D (all the above indications apply to that key), it is advisable to sing the /o/ in exactly the same color as in C, without trying to "cover" its sound. Here it really needs to "explode." For the waves of "un tremoto, un temporale" it will be useful to stay away from chopping and to continue the legato described above. There is no accelerando there; it would only weaken the effect of devastating strength.

The two-bar interlude is usually played a little slower, but the voice comes in *a tempo*, full of scorn for the victim writhing in agony. Note the two accents on "mes*chino*" and "av*vilito.*" A ritardando will be made on "calpestato," especially on the last two quarter notes, expressing extreme gratification at feeling the body of the foe under one's foot. It is customary to add a stringendo to the crescendo in the phrase "sotto il pubblico flagello" and to fill the top note of "crepar" with bitter cruelty. The fermata is followed by a *piano subito*, and the two staccato lines paint, first by the repeat of the same pitch, then by a light wave up and down, the sadistic satisfaction of a successful murder.

For the coda (last eight measures of the aria) it is difficult to resist the temptation of an accelerando and customary to yield to it. The trouble with too much speed would be to fail to satisfy two contrasting needs: one, to stress the double consonants in "sotto, pubblico, flagello," the other to stay legato without a loss of tone.

It is also customary and probably right to sing the last two bars as shown.

"La Calunnia" is a masterpiece of an aria, suggesting so much with such simple means. The longer the subdued singing continues, the more the later explosion will impress. The singer should not fear to tax the patience of his listeners by staying piano and pianissimo for as long as indicated in the score.

As to the meaning of the aria, it conforms so closely to reality and alludes to so many tragedies in real life that, after we have enjoyed its striking originality, we may well shudder at its implications.

Saint-Saëns, *Samson et Dalila*

"Amour, viens aider ma faiblesse"   *mezzo-soprano*

Samson, recherchant ma présence,   Samson, desirous of my presence,
ce soir doit venir en ces lieux.   tonight will come to this place.
Voici l'heure de la vengeance   The hour of vengeance is here,
qui doit satisfaire nos dieux.   which will satisfy our gods.

Amour, viens aider ma faiblesse!	Love, come help my weakness!
Verse le poison dans son sein!	Pour the poison in his heart!
Fais que, vaincu par mon adresse,	See that, defeated by my skill,
Samson soit enchaîné demain!	Samson be in chains tomorrow!
Il voudrait en vain de son âme	He wishes in vain
pouvoir me chasser, me bannir!	to chase and banish me from his soul!
Pourrait-il éteindre la flamme	Could he ever quench the flame
qu'alimente le souvenir?	which memories nourish?
Il est à moi, c'est mon esclave!	He is mine, he is my slave!
Mes frères craignent son courroux;	My brethren fear his wrath;
moi seule, entre tous, je le brave	I alone among all, I defy him
et le retiens à mes genoux.	and hold him down at my knees.
Amour, viens aider . . .	Love, come help . . .
Contre l'amour sa force est vaine;	Against love his strength is vain;
et lui, le fort parmi les forts,	and he, the strongest among the strong,
lui qui d'un peuple rompt la chaîne	he who breaks the chain of a nation
succombera sous mes efforts!	will succumb under my efforts!

The second act of the opera *Samson et Dalila* opens with this aria. At the end of the first act Dalila, a beautiful Philistine, paid the tribute of her love to Samson, chieftain of the Hebrews, who have victoriously revolted against her brethren. Samson has been unable to resist her charms.

At this point, act 2, the stage represents the valley of Soreck where Dalila's house is situated. Night is falling; a thunderstorm rumbles in the distance. Dalila waits for Samson in her garden and, according to the score, "seems to be in a dreamy mood." A few bars of a vigorously rhythmical prelude indicate that she does not dream sweet dreams. When she starts singing, she loses no time revealing what is in her mind. Although she has induced Samson to come back to her arms, her goal is vengeance. She has not betrayed her brethren, and her pretended love is only a ruse. The moment has come when she will need all her strength to defeat Samson, and in order to put all the powers on her side, she will pray to the God of Love for help. That is the burden of the aria, once the first two lines of introduction are sung.

Her first word is "Samson," which is pronounced /sãsõ/. (Incidentally, the name of the composer is pronounced /sẽsãs/.)

At first Dalila sings with strength and animation, with a round voice she has no reason to make dark and heavy. A slight ritardando on "ce soir doit venir en ces lieux" stresses the importance of that particular visit. Let me remark here, in connection with this first low note of the aria, D-flat on "lieux," that a mezzo-soprano is under no obligation to sing very loud and inflated low tones. If her voice is truly a mezzo-soprano and if it is trained toward natural singing, her low notes will have a certain natural size and a feminine resonance. I have heard the love duet of Samson and Dalila many times from the back of the set, after singing my big High Priest scene, and I have wondered at times whether what I was listening to was really heterosexual love, so masculine was Dalila's voice in the lower phrases of her role! Such a phrase is "Voici l'heure de la vengeance." It must grow from an almost hissing piano to a threatening and powerful ending on "nos dieux." Dalila wants revenge not only for herself but for her gods, a goal of much greater scope. The strength of the voice on "nos dieux" will be obtained not by pushing an ugly tone down into the chest but by saying the two words in a ringing, forward tone and with reverence.

From the text of the aria it is easy to understand that Dalila knows and respects the irresistible physical powers of Samson the man and the warrior but also that she is sure of her hold on him through his infatuation with her. What she is asking the God of Love is to maintain and even to increase that hold until love has destroyed strength.

The ten bars of prelude to the aria can be considered an incantation aimed at summoning the God of Love and making him propitious. When Dalila sings, piano over a pianissimo orchestra, it is as a woman of limited strength who needs outside help in order to succeed in her resolute endeavor. The voice is round, harmonious, feminine, especially on "ma faiblesse." It stays legato and even for "verse le poison." That weapon is not brutal, and there is no need to tense the voice and to harden the diction. The same feeling of smooth malevolence pervades "vaincu par mon adresse," but a vigorous articulation and a strong crescendo are needed on "Samson soit enchaîné demain." (Note the sixteenth note on "demain".) The weapon will be suave, the result brutal.

The first seven bars, beginning with letter C, describe the sensual mastery Dalila holds over Samson. It is with a certain scorn that she says, "Il voudrait en vain . . . me chasser, me bannir." The precise rhythm of that phrase must be respected; it gives a meaningful flexibility to the line. "Pourrait-il éteindre la flamme" is almost forte and challenging, then "qu'alimente le souvenir" sensuous like the memory of intense lovemaking. "Il est à moi, c'est mon esclave" does not need to rise above mezzo piano and is sung with smug satisfaction. The crescendo on "craignent son courroux" is not one of fear but one of derision. Starting at letter D there is a very strong accelerando, a sign of pride and boastful confidence. The word "moi" is strongly stressed; the final /s/ in "tous" is pronounced here. There is a great crescendo on "brave" started mezzo forte, reaching forte on the G or the alternate B-flat. Sing the run downward as written, first on sixteenth values, then on thirty-seconds. Be sure to choose the alternate B-flat only if you know it will show your voice to better advantage than the G and if you are able also to handle the two-octave run to your advantage. At any rate, no breath is permissible between "tous" and the low B-flat on the syllable "-ve." It is natural for the voice to ring very differently in the head resonances of the high B-flat and in the mouth resonances of the low B-flat, the high notes seeming to ring vertically through the skull, the low ones out through the front of the mouth. No effort should be made to sing the low B-flat with a black, masculine voice.

After letter E the return of part A is sung forte, more vigorously than the first time, Dalila being surer of her skill, nearer to victory. There is a return of scornful sensuousness in "Contre l'amour sa force est vaine," a sarcasm which makes the vowels swell in "et lui, le fort parmi les forts" and in the word "chaîne."

The last phrase, which, while written in the low range, must have a crushing power, needs much study. Note that the orchestra plays pianissimo. The voice will have its best chance to dominate if you sing vibrantly into forward words. The chest resonance comes naturally for a woman's voice in this range; it should not be induced by pushing and inflating the tone. Besides, the power Dalila suggests is such that she should not labor vocally to make it heard. Even when powerful and merciless, Dalila must still be and sound like a woman.

"Mon coeur s'ouvre à ta voix" *mezzo-soprano*

Mon coeur s'ouvre à ta voix	My heart opens up at [the sound of] your voice
comme s'ouvrent les fleurs	as the flowers open up
aux baisers de l'aurore.	at the kisses of dawn.
Mais, ô mon bien-aimé,	But, o my beloved,
pour mieux sécher mes pleurs,	the better to dry my tears,
que ta voix parle encore.	let your voice speak again.
Dis-moi qu'à Dalila	Tell me that to Dalila
tu reviens pour jamais,	you return forever,
redis à ma tendresse	repeat to my tender love
les serments d'autrefois,	the promises of bygone times,
ces serments que j'aimais.	those promises I loved.
Ah! réponds à ma tendresse,	Ah! surrender to my love,
verse-moi l'ivresse.	fill me with rapture.
Ainsi qu'on voit des blés	Just as you see
les épis onduler	ears of wheat undulate
sous la brise légère,	in a light breeze,
ainsi frémit mon coeur	so my heart sways
prêt à se consoler	ready to be consoled
à ta voix qui m'est chère.	by your voice so dear to me.
La flèche est moins rapide	The arrow is less swift
à porter le trépas	in carrying death
que ne l'est ton amante	than is your lover
à voler dans tes bras.	in rushing into your arms.
Ah! réponds à ma tendresse . . .	Ah! surrender to my love . . .

Samson, torn between his mission to deliver his people from their Philistine captivity and his passion for Dalila, a young Philistine, has decided to see her for the last time tonight. This visit offers Dalila a last chance to discover the secret of Samson's feared superhuman strength. She will make use of all her seductive powers to obtain one more hour of intimacy with Samson. At the same time the Philistines will set a trap to overpower him as soon as Dalila is in possession of his secret. Although totally insincere, Dalila's song of love must overcome all of Samson's resolutions.

The two verses of the song follow the same pattern, an *andantino cantabile* ($\downarrow$ = 66) followed by a most sensuous *un peu plus lent*. In the complete score the second *un peu plus lent* becomes a duet, but taken out of context the aria is always sung with two solo verses. The voice of Dalila must be of a warm color and capable of a perfect legato and long, sustained phrases. The aria is written in the easiest range for a normal mezzo-soprano voice. the low range rings round in the mouth, and no attempt must be made to imitate a male voice by pushing the tone down in the larynx. The high range is limited to G-flat, where all resonances of mouth, face, palate and head can meet gloriously. The pitfall to avoid at all cost is the attempt to blow lower and upper notes up beyond reason, which leaves the middle part of the range (nine-tenths of the aria) small and hollow and gives the impression that the unfortunate Dalila has three voices. What is needed is the skill to let the voice enrich itself freely with the resonances corresponding to the range one sings and to allow the transition between these resonances to be smooth and progressive. Having sung with Dalilas on three continents I regretfully testify that these simple prescriptions were often replaced by monstrous attempts to make a mezzo-soprano voice into something it is not meant to be.

Dalila's first words, "Mon coeur s'ouvre à ta voix," come in reply to Samson's last phrase, "at the risk of my life, Dalila, I love you." For Dalila, victory is near, and she pushes her advantage without delay as a beautiful poetic comparison comes to her talented mind. The first six bars must be sung *dolcissimo e cantabile,* with a radiant voice and with open vowels /œ/ in "coeur" and "fleurs" and a clear vowel /a/ in "voix." But the next bars show that her real goal is yet to be reached. "Mais, ô mon bien-aimé" is the start of a plea: Samson should dry her tears (a crescendo of intensity) with his tender love. "Que ta voix parle encore" is a very sweet prayer, piano. But Dalila wants more; she wants a promise. "Tu reviens pour jamais" is a crescendo, and the recollection of their past liaison makes her sing faster and more intensely ("ces serments que j'aimais"). The long tenuto and ritardando on "j'aimais" is also a long diminuendo, a transition between past joys and the desires for new ones.

This desire is expressed very harmoniously and sensuously in the *un peu plus lent.* The first phrase is generally sung with a break after the G-natural, second note of the third beat of bar 2, and the word "réponds" is repeated.

The first syllable of "réponds" must be pronounced /re/ and not /rø/ because when it is pronounced in the latter way it means "lay another egg" (*pondre* means "to lay eggs," and the prefix *re* means "again").

While the most continuous legato is needed here, the half-tone intervals must stay absolutely clear, crisp, and without slurs, and the ring of the voice must be maintained in the front of the mouth, the more so when going to the low range. Take a breath before the second "verse-moi" in bar 6. In bar 9 a crescendo starts that grows more and more insistent for six bars (9–14) but without any accelerando. Dalila expresses her pretended yearning for Samson's love in a stately way, not in frantic phrases. The successive intervals of sevenths will stay easy if the low note of each of them is started lightly and not with an attempt at heavy darkness. It is, of course, desirable to broaden bar 13 both in time and in power before making a sensuous diminuendo on "verse-moi l'ivresse" (bars 15 and 16). In bar 15 the prevailing custom is to sing the low B-flat as the fifth note of the word "moi" and to sing the syllable "l'i-" of "l'ivresse" on the following F. Throughout that beautiful phrase it is wise to keep the sound of the voice even by lightening the low notes and spinning from them to the high notes, which can then be expanded in resonance. In other words, minimize the length of the intervals instead of stressing it, which would create the impression of a disjointed voice.

While the first verse expresses yearning, the second verse, in the score answering to a new "Je t'aime" from Samson, is a positive, even ardent participation by Dalila in the love scene. The verse could start slightly faster than the first one, become animated on

"La flèche est moins rapide," more animated still on "à voler dans tes bras" before becoming stately again on the second "à voler dans tes bras." The ring of the voice should be much more intense and brilliant than in the first verse, the words more lively, so that when the *un peu plus lent* reappears it comes as a strong contrast with a feeling of almost sensuous fulfillment. The sound of the voice, at first very piano, is ecstatic, becoming exalted in the large phrase "Ah, verse-moi." Here we find a rearrangement of the words similar to that of the first verse: "réponds, réponds à ma tendresse."

Again, in the last "verse-moi l'ivresse" the low B-flat is the fifth note of the syllable "moi," and the syllable "l'i-" of "l'ivresse" comes on the next F.

To this irresistible song of seduction Samson, in the score, brings a solemn conclusion by singing, this time decisively, "Dalila, je t'aime." As an ending is indeed indispensable, it has been agreed that Dalila sing "Samson, je t'aime." It is desirable, however, that she do so on the music as written, that is, with a high B-flat on "je t'aime." Going to a G-flat as is often done creates a depressive feeling not at all in keeping with the winning efforts of Dalila. A mezzo-soprano who has not, either in this aria or anywhere else, pushed her voice down into heavy, inward, dark resonances should be able to perform the suggested ending successfully.

Strauss, *Die Fledermaus*

"Czardas"
soprano

Klänge der Heimat,	Sounds of my homeland,
ihr weckt mir das Sehnen,	you awaken my nostalgia,
rufet die Tränen ins Auge mir.	summon tears to my eyes.
Wenn ich euch höre,	When I hear you,
ihr heimischen Lieder,	you familiar songs,
zieht mich's wieder,	I am drawn again,
mein Ungarland zu dir.	my Hungary, to you.
O Heimat so wunderbar,	O homeland, so wonderful,
wie strahlt dort die Sonne so klar,	how brightly the sun shines there,
wie grün deine Wälder,	how green your forests,
wie lachend die Felder,	how cheerful your fields,
o Land, wo so glücklich ich war.	O country, where I was so happy.
Ja, dein geliebtes Bild	Yes, your beloved image
meine Seele so ganz erfüllt,	fills my soul completely,
dein geliebtes Bild!	your beloved image.
Und bin ich auch von dir weit,	And though I am far from you,
ach, dir bleibt in Ewigkeit doch	to you for eternity
mein Sinn immerdar	my heart always will
ganz allein geweiht.	be devoted.

Feuer, Lebenslust,	Passion, joy of life,
schwellt echte Ungarbrust!	swells a true Hungarian breast!
Hei! zum Tanze schnell,	Hi! quick to the dance,
Czardas tönt so hell!	the czardas sounds brightly!
Braunes Mägdelein,	Brown maiden,
must meine Tänzrin sein,	you shall be my partner,
reich'den Arm geschwind,	give me your arm, quickly,
dunkeläugig Kind!	dark-eyed child!
Zum Fiedelklingen, ho-ha	To the accompaniment of fiddles, ho-ha,
tönt jauchzend Singen, ho-ha-ha!	merry songs resound, ha-ha-ha!
Mit dem Sporn geklirrt,	Rattle the spur,
wenn dann die Maid verwirrt	when the girl then, troubled,
senkt zur Erd' den Blick,	lowers her eyes,
das verkündet Glück!	that forecasts bliss!
Durstge Zecher,	Thirsty revellers,
greift zum Becher,	seize the goblet,
lasst ihn kreisen	pass it round
schnell von Hand zu Hand!	fast, from hand to hand!
Schlürft das Feuer	Sip the fire
im Tokayer,	of the Tokay wine,
bringt ein Hoch aus dem Vaterland!	drink a toast from the fatherland!

At Prince Orlofsky's ball there are guests who are not what they seem to be. Adele, the maid, has been parading successfully in one of her mistress Rosalinde's dresses when, in a stunning, masked Hungarian countess, she recognizes Rosalinde herself. Challenged by Adele to prove her origin, Rosalinde improvises a passionate Hungarian czardas topped by a frenzied *Frischka*. After such a demonstration, who could doubt her authenticity?

The piece is written for a virtuoso soprano or lirico-spinto, by turns forceful, sentimental, nimble, passionate—a great extrovert and an accomplished entertainer. The two parts of the aria are contrasted in every possible way, the czardas stressing nostalgia for the homeland, albeit in unusually fancy ways, the *Frischka* celebrating its people's unrestrained lust for life.

The tempo of the czardas is slow, with many variations, returning basically to approximately ♩ = 60. The sound of the voice is as sensuous as it is nostalgic, truly "gorgeous." In the four bars of the prelude the way the sixteenth notes melt into the following dotted eighth notes and the sudden discretion of the last two bars prepare a favorable ground for a round mezzo forte legatissimo singing. The words "Heimat" and "Sehnen" are very sensitive words. The phrase "rufet die Tränen ins Auge mir" is more piano, the last two words slow to come, as if the interpreter wanted to tone down her expression of sadness. But a fast run in the accompaniment incites her to conjure with force the songs from home. "Wenn ich euch höre" is forte and a little faster, "ihr heimischen Lieder" sentimental, with a *piano subito* on "Lieder," a strong accent on "zieht," a crescendo on "mich's wieder," and, after a breath, a beautiful broad sound for "mein Ungarland" with a large fermata on "Un-" (vowel /u/ please!) and again those melting sixteenth notes slowing down the last words.

The next four bars call for nothing more than gorgeous legato singing, in tones bright as the sun. The accelerando can start as soon as "wie grün deine Wälder" and become stronger, enthusiastically, on the next bar, with a sudden stop before "o Land," whose two notes stand isolated for a short moment until the melting voice concludes slowly, "wo so glücklich ich war." The soprano must respect exactly all the variations of tempo marked for the next bars, but not mechanically. In their capricious changes there is always a true emotion as well as, quite possibly, a desire to catch the attention of the listeners and to intrigue them. "So ganz erfüllt" and "dein geliebtes Bild," legato and piano, must cause a feeling of delight.

With "Und bin ich auch von dir weit" a very different way of expressing nostalgia begins. This time it is expressed with fire and violence. The dotted rhythm is now sharply articulated, the voice is dramatic, the wailing "ach weit, ach" full-voiced, with two fine opportunities to sing beautiful tones on the two fermatas. A sharp, impetuous rhythm reappears for two bars. A breath before "immerdar" helps a new change of mood, sensitive and slow; the majestic high B yields to a progressive diminuendo for the chromatic scale, which then escalates to a surprising short G. Suspense is created before the delightful return of the radiant tribute to the beauty of the homeland and the happy past. The memory of so much beauty suddenly sets the exile's body and soul aflame. The Frischka comes bouncing in, ♩ = 144, with its short periods of two bars, its bold intervals, its sharp word endings, "-lu*st*," "-bru*st*," "schne*ll*," "he*ll*," and so on. The voice here moves swiftly in slim vibrant tones, felt very much forward, between the tip of the tongue, the teeth, and the lips. The sounds seem to bounce off a distant, lively support. The new tempo is established right away, but starting the *Frischka* mezzo piano and making a big crescendo still adds to the effect of striking vitality. After "dunkeläugig Kind," sixteen bars are cut traditionally. The next section is entirely forte with strong stresses on the high first notes of each phrase—"D*urst*-ge," "Schl*ürft*," "*im* To-kayer, b*ringt*"—short silences between the eighth notes, an aggressive treatment of the rhythm of sixteenth notes, as in "*Z*echer," "*B*echer," "*F*euer," "*T*okayer," and in between these chopped measures, two legato lines, "lasst ihn kreisen schnell von Hand zu Hand" and "ein Hoch aus dem Vaterland," sung with a sweeping élan. The long trill on the E of "Ha" is also forte, the beats well stressed. It ties itself to the two-bar run, the first breath coming after the first syncopated A two bars later, the several high A's fortissimo. A boundless energy, a boundless capacity for enjoyment, must appear in these seven bars after "Ha," almost sweeping the listeners to their feet.

But there is more to come in that direction. A moment of relative quiet enhances a still livelier ending. Sing the middle A's slowly and piano, and begin the repeat of part A of the Frischka, "Feuer, Lebenslust," mezzo piano, still in the same fast tempo, not reaching above mezzo forte.

The *più allegro* must be as fast as vocally possible, not forte, in a happy delirium. The trill on the high A is unleashed at the top of the voice, as well as the last five notes on "la la la" to the high A. Much should be done for suspense with the silence preceding the *lento*. Then the high B's and the A of the *lento* must have as fine a quality and intensity as the soprano can provide before spinning into the high D, which, if safe, can be held a little beyond its written value.

It is difficult to imagine a more rousing ending for a rousing aria. Rosalinde must be a highly gifted, well-trained singer, even if other parts of *Die Fledermaus* can be entrusted to good actors without outstanding vocal gifts. The insertion of the "Czardas" in the score was not necessary by any means, but what a sensational piece it is! It brings back to my mind what Maurice Ravel once told me: "The great Strauss, I mean Johann . . ." Wit aside, I am sure he was sincere in a way.

"Mein Herr Marquis"   *soprano*

Mein Herr Marquis,
ein Mann wie Sie
sollt'besser das verstehn,
darum rate ich,
ja genauer sich
die Leute anzusehn!
Die Hand ist doch wohl gar zu fein,
dies Füsschen so zierlich und klein,
die Sprache, die ich führe,
die Taille, die Tournüre,
dergleichen finden Sie
bei einer Zofe nie!
Gestehen müssen Sie fürwahr,
sehr komisch dieser Irrtum war!
Ja sehr komisch, ah ah ah,
ist die Sache, ah ah ah
drum verzeihn Sie, ah ah ah
wenn ich lache, ah ah ah
sehr komisch, Herr Marquis, sind Sie!

Mit dem Profil
im griech'schen Stil
beschenkte mich Natur.
Wenn nicht dies Gesicht
schon genügend spricht,
so sehn Sie die Figur!
Schaun durch die Lorgnette Sie dann
sich diese Toilette nur an, ach
mir scheinet wohl, die Liebe
macht Ihre Augen trübe,
der schönen Zofe Bild
hat ganz Ihr Herz erfüllt.
Nun sehen Sie sie überall,
sehr komisch ist fürwahr der Fall.
Ja sehr komisch, ah ah ah,
ist die Sache, ah ah ah . . .

Dear Marquis,
a man like you
ought to know better,
therefore I advise [you]
to look more closely
at people!
This hand no doubt is much too graceful,
this little foot so delicate and small,
the language I use,
the *taille*, the *tournure*,
you never find the like
with a chambermaid!
You must admit indeed,
this error was very funny!
Yes, very funny, ha ha ha,
is this matter, ha ha ha,
therefore pardon me, ha ha ha,
if I laugh, ha ha ha,
very funny, dear Marquis, are you!

With this profile
in the Greek style
Nature has endowed me.
If this face
does not tell enough already,
then look at the figure!
When you look through your glasses then
at this ball gown, ah,
it seems to me that love
troubles your eyesight,
the image of the pretty chambermaid
has filled your heart completely.
Now you see her everywhere,
the case is very funny indeed.
Yes, very funny, ha ha ha,
is this matter, ha ha ha . . .

At Prince Orlofsky's ball there are guests who are not what they seem to be. Marquis Renard is really Gabriel Eisenstein, a married man who his wife believes has gone to jail that night. And Miss Olga, whom Eisenstein finds charming, looks suspiciously like Adele, his wife's chambermaid, even when dressed most glamorously. But for many reasons neither cares to reveal his or her true identity. To convince Eisenstein that she is a young lady of distinction, Adele takes the limelight and sings this famous song.

Adele's voice is a soubrette's soprano, lively and bright, capable of some modest coloraturas and some good high notes. The chambermaid has theatrical ambitions. In fact, she must show a real talent for comedy in almost every scene of her role, using a wide range of colors in order to impersonate or to fake several different characters. In these "couplets" she tries to prove her rank through her aristocratic features and to dismiss Eisenstein's suspicions by accusing him of being the victim of an amorous obsession.

The tempo, *allegretto*, must have grace and animation without being rushed. The singer must feel at all times that she could dance it instead of singing it and must be completely at ease. The marking, ♩. = 58, seems to permit that feeling. The singer has to deal with a delicate discrimination between Adele's attempts at distinction and her less aristocratic nature, which especially in the comedy situation of Orlofsky's ball induces her to clown a little and to laugh not only at the confusion of her suitor but also at herself playing the part of a lady. For instance, the first eight bars (bars 1 and 2, bars 3 and 4 staccato and light, bars 5 to 8 legato with a very slight ritardando) are, in words and music, dignified and sensible. The same pattern appears in bars 9 to 15. During these fifteen bars Adele sings charmingly, teasingly, being a bit condescending, as a young lady would be. What is not ladylike is the exhibition of her hand, her foot, her silhouette—and the way she praises them all. Her voice can become slightly fussy, with too much stress on the G on "gar" and on the F-sharp on "zierlich," somewhat pedantic on "die Sprache, die ich führe," and too boastful on "die Taille, die Tournüre" with an overly cultivated diction on these adapted French words (fermata and rallentando). Meanwhile, we have had the first two little runs upward on "ah." They are not peals of laughter yet but rather coquettish little guffaws of self-admiration. The peals of laughter will come later. After the fermata the phrases "dergleichen finden Sie" are said with authority from mezzo forte to forte with some strong accents. "Gestehen müssen Sie" teases nicely, but, crescendo and ritardando, "sehr komisch dieser Irrtum war" is much more outspoken.

Now Adele can neither pretend anymore nor contain her hilarity. The staccato notes "ah, ah, ah" are really laughter, not correct and strict pitches and eighth notes. It is essential that they all be sung on a bright vowel /a/, conveying gaiety unrestrained, the kind that cuts your words short, which you try in vain to curtail, and which takes you to a brilliant incursion to high B and a downward cascade of staccato notes. The spell lasts unchanged until the trill on the F-sharp, five bars after the run down from high B. Here the laughter comes in broader waves, a sign that the spell is almost over. The singer must keep the same bright color of voice for the short run to the next high B. The two short "ah" piano, E to A and D to G, with a trill on the E and on the D, are the ebbing of a laughter finally curtailed, and Adele is able now to speak almost normally, with just an involuntary stress on "sehr komisch" and a smiling fermata on "Marquis."

The second verse, musically similar to the first, begins with a further display of Adele's charms. Greek profile, features, figure—Adele details them all. Her voice is bolder now and more provocative, and she challenges the would-be marquis to put on his glasses and examine her still more thoroughly. But the picture of him doing it strikes her as funny, and this time the famous little run upward is clear laughter. The thought that the dress he studies is his wife's makes her laugh again (second little run upward), not too loud yet. But a new idea strikes the resourceful Adele. With a firm legato voice she suggests that Eisenstein is the victim of an amorous obsession concerning a certain chambermaid. The phrase "der schönen Zofe Bild" grows to forte, its repeat strongly accentuated. She has the cheek to confront him with his comical error, crescendo and ritardando, in "sehr komisch ist fürwahr der Fall." Laughter invades her again, as bright and true as in the first verse.

The coda is purely vocal, provided that the color of the voice and the good humor of the singer are maintained throughout. In order to keep alive the élan of the laughing spell it would be advisable to sing the first four bars of the coda without a breath until and including the high D (very brief), and to sing the next four bars again without a breath. The high C, the trill on the F-sharp, and the ending on G would be the third fragment of the coda, attempted boldly, in great spirits, as the sweeping conclusion of a successful prank.

These couplets are generally called "Adele's Laughing Song." It is indeed what they are, if Adele knows how to make her voice laugh on her written music. A correct performance whose laughter does not contaminate the audience is not a successful one. The change in Adele from her initial coquetry to the verge of sarcasm later is worth studying. But infectious laughter should establish itself in the second half of both verses and win the day.

Thomas, *Hamlet*

"O vin, dissipe la tristesse"   *baritone*

O vin, dissipe la tristesse	O wine, undo the sadness
qui pèse sur mon coeur!	which weighs on my heart!
A moi les rêves de l'ivresse	Mine be the dreams of inebriation
et le rire moqueur!	and the mocking laughter!
O liqueur enchanteresse,	O magic beverage,
verse l'ivresse	pour drunkenness
et l'oubli dans mon coeur!	and oblivion in my heart!
Douce liqueur!	Sweet liquor!
La vie est sombre,	Life is gloomy,
les ans sont courts;	the years are short;
de nos beaux jours	of our happy days
Dieu sait le nombre.	God knows the number.
Chacun, hélas, porte ici bas	Every man, alas, carries here on earth
sa lourde chaîne!	his heavy chain!
Cruels devoirs, longs désespoirs	Cruel duties, lasting despairs
de l'âme humaine.	of the human soul.
Loin de nous, noirs présages,	Away with you, dark forebodings,
les plus sages sont les fous!	fools are the wisest of men!
O vin, dissipe la tristesse . . .	Oh wine, undo the sadness . . .

One of the scenes of the Shakespearean tragedy preserved by the librettists of Thomas's opera is the famous scene of the comedians.

Although convinced that his uncle Claudius, presently king of Denmark, has murdered his father, the distraught prince, Hamlet, seeks public proof of the crime. To this effect he instructs a company of traveling comedians to perform in front of the court a play in which the murder of the late king will be faithfully reenacted. It is Hamlet's hope that the sight will unsettle Claudius and reveal his guilt to all present.

There is no drinking song in Shakespeare's tragedy, at this point or anywhere else. In the opera, however, Hamlet welcomes the players with a drink and joins them in drinking. Let me reconstruct for you the aria as I felt it when singing Hamlet. Although different in character from the rest of the role, it still needs to be sung with a beautiful voice.

The preceding scenes have stressed Hamlet's unbalance, his helplessness and irresolution. The players now provide him with a positive opportunity to push his action against the king. Afraid to falter in this endeavor through weakness or timidity, Hamlet expects the wine to give him the strength he will need. I seriously suggest that the baritone think of gulping two fast swallows during the few bars of introduction and several more before "La vie est sombre" as well as before singing part A again after the cadenza and that he try to feel euphoria invading his limbs and his brain. Sometimes the aria is sung as a reflective private solo, sometimes as an almost back-slapping chummy participation in a party, but it should never be sung with a drunken voice.

There should be six bars of introduction before the voice enters. The indicated tempo of $\downarrow$. = 54 has proved absolutely right in performance and should not be altered in favor of high notes or some special effects. Part A is an invocation, a call for help. The first eight bars are contrasted four by four. The first four, sung very legato and like a prayer, show why Hamlet needs the help of wine. The word "vin" almost seems the name of a god, as sadness weighs heavily on his heart. The second four are sung at first fervently—"les rêves de l'ivresse"—then sarcastically—"et le rire moqueur." Note how the same pattern on "dissipe la tristesse" and "les rêves de l'ivresse" can be sung sadly the first time and brilliantly the second. Going to the E-flat the first time denotes sadness; going to the F the second time, exuberance. A serious interpreter must feel these nuances.

The next four bars—"O liqueur enchanteresse"—are sung mezzo forte and warmly, well legato, and diminuendo in the fourth bar, an almost serene moment as if the wine had a momentary soothing effect. "Douce liqueur" starts piano, grows to mezzo forte on the C-sharp and to forte on the fermata. From there to the end of part A the singing is full voice, legato, sustained, with a ringing fermata on the D of the last "dans mon coeur," as if Hamlet were trying to outdo the festive spirit of the players.

If you follow the complete score, there is a six-bar cut at this point, going to four bars before the three sharps. During those four bars Hamlet's mood changes, and he falls back into his dark loneliness. His voice becomes somber (this is done in great part by changing the color of the vowels), and in spite of the long values the singing becomes rather feverish, as suggested by the more animated tempo. The long phrases must be spun unbroken, the first two very evenly and without dynamic changes. "Chacun, hélas" should be more exteriorized and the phrase continued without breathing to after "chaîne." "Cruels devoirs" shows suffering. Stress the sixteenth note to that effect. "Longs désespoirs de l'âme humaine" is a progressive ritardando, weary, depressed, but retaining the breadth and scope that are felt in the whole page.

At this point Hamlet becomes aware that he has drifted away from his guests and violently shakes off his gloom. He drinks and sings "Loin de nous, noirs présages" with full voice, then explodes in an artificial outburst of enthusiasm, the celebrated cadenza that follows "les plus sages sont les fous." The most famous of operatic Hamlets, Tita Ruffo, used the cadenza to display his tremendous high notes, adding an A-natural to the high G with thunderous power. Doing so is certainly permissible, given the effect the cadenza wants to achieve. But in Buenos Aires as well as in Paris and other cities, I sang the cadenza as written, with a modest flourish before the G, a very long fermata fortissimo on the G, a great progressive accelerando on the run down, a breath, a very slow chromatic scale pianissimo upward, with a long trill and an abrupt ending, all of which was accepted wholeheartedly. My goal was to stress once more Hamlet's unbalance: his pretended enthusiasm, the more blatant because faked, his incapacity to sustain the pretense, the return to sorrow, finally a successful attempt at getting hold of himself. The return to part A is given with great vigor at the start, and the dynamic changes are very much like the first time. Both times the singer must pay attention to the expressive value of the few sixteenth notes, refrain from punching the high F's, keep instead an unbroken line in the phrases by shifting the stress from the F's to the following notes, which actually carry the accents of the words:

In the last bar of the aria, when presented as a solo piece, several attempts have been made to find a strong vocal ending to make up for the one provided on stage by the chorus. The addition of a very high note is out of place as no triumph has been achieved. Substituting two F's for the last D and C and holding them in a lengthy fermata provides a solid ending that shows that at best Hamlet has regained some steadiness. He is now ready to prepare his players for their task.

In my opinion the ending as provided in the Schirmer *Operatic Anthology* (compiled by Kurt Adler), which adds a phrase to the original score, is not acceptable.

"A vos jeux, mes amis"   *soprano*

A vos jeux, mes amis
permettez-moi, de grâce,
de prendre part.
Nul n'a suivi ma trace.
J'ai quitté le palais
aux premiers feux du jour . . .
des larmes de la nuit
la terre était mouillée;

In your games, my friends,
allow me, please,
to take part.
Nobody has followed my trace.
I have left the palace
at day's first light . . .
from the tears of the night
the ground was wet;

et l'alouette avant l'aube éveillée	and the lark, awake before dawn,
planait dans l'air.	hovered in the air.
Mais vous, pourquoi vous parler bas?	But you, why speak softly?
Ne me reconnaissez-vous pas?	Do you not recognize me?
Hamlet est mon époux . . .	Hamlet is my husband . . .
et je suis Ophélie.	and I am Ophelia.
Un doux serment nous lie,	A sweet promise unites us,
il m'a donné son coeur	he has given me his heart
en échange du mien . . .	in exchange for mine . . .
Et si quelqu'un vous dit	And if someone tells you
qu'il me fuit et m'oublie	that he avoids me and forgets me,
n'en croyez rien!	do not believe it!
S'il trahissait sa foi,	If he betrayed his promise,
j'en perdrais la raison!	I would lose my reason!
Partagez-vous mes fleurs!	Share my flowers among you!
A toi cette humble branche	For you this humble branch
de romarin sauvage, ah,	of wild rosemary, ah,
à toi cette pervenche . . . ah!	for you this periwinkle . . . ah!
Et maintenant, écoutez ma chanson!	And now, listen to my song!
Pale et blonde	Pale and blond
dort sous l'eau profonde	the Willis with eyes of fire
la Willis au regard de feu!	sleeps under the deep water.
Que Dieu garde	May God protect
celui qui s'attarde	the one who lingers at night
dans la nuit au bord du Lac Bleu!	by the shore of the Blue Lake!
Heureuse l'épouse aux bras de l'époux!	Happy the wife in her husband's arms!
Mon âme est jalouse	My soul is jealous
d'un bonheur si doux.	of such sweet happiness.
Nymphe au regard de feu,	Nymph with eyes of fire,
hélas, tu dors	alas, you are sleeping
sous les eaux du flot bleu.	under the waters of the blue waves.
Ah, cher époux, ah, cher amant!	Ah, dear husband, ah, dear beloved!
Ah, doux aveu, ah, tendre serment!	Ah, sweet avowal, ah, tender promise!
Bonheur suprême!	Utmost happiness!
Ah, cruel, je t'aime!	Ah, cruel man, I love you!
Cruel, tu vois mes pleurs!	Cruel man, you see my tears!
Ah! pour toi je meurs!	Ah! for you I am dying!
Ah, je meurs!	Ah, I am dying!

The gentle Ophelia returned Prince Hamlet's love with simple sincerity. Discouraged by her family early in her love, she has suffered cruel blows since: the increasingly strange behavior of Hamlet, the tragic death of her father killed by the prince. Her tender heart is broken, her innocent mind confused forever. She wanders aimlessly away from the castle, in a world of her own.

In the libretto to the opera by Ambroise Thomas, a group of young villagers, dancing or relaxing in a clearing, are surprised by the arrival of a very pretty young woman. She wears a garland of flowers in her hair and carries flowers in her hands also. She speaks to them sweetly.

Ophélie's voice is a coloratura soprano, light and pure, very secure in singing runs of all kinds but also capable of emotion and of a great variety of colors. When given in concert, the scene can start with a short introduction of six bars before the entrance of the voice. The aria—Or is it a scene?—is divided into several quite disconnected fragments in order to suggest Ophélie's incoherence. Her unpredictable shifting of thoughts and moods is what makes the aria an interesting challenge for the interpreter.

For a while all the lines Ophélie sings are marked *Recit.* That means, of course, that she is free to vary the pace of her speech at will. Nevertheless, the French declamation of her phrases is noted with great accuracy, and the soprano should respect the details of the rhythm as printed in the score. Without introducing herself, Ophélie speaks to the villagers as a friendly child would to other children, in a sweet, humble way, with a youthful, innocent voice, polite and charming (note "mes amis" and "de grâce"). The accompaniment identifies her by playing her theme. Her second phrase, "Nul n'a suivi ma trace" is said mysteriously, as if she asked her new friends to keep her secret. But having said "aux premiers feux du jour" she forgets secrecy. She sees the morning dew; she hears the lark. The andantino "des larmes de la nuit" is sung with a poetic charm, rather slowly, ♪ = 120. The vocalise "planait dans l'air" imitates the singing of the lark, rubato, nimble, light, with crystal-clear notes on the staccato notes high A. The bird seems to be very near during the trill on the A, which grows to forte but moves away on the second trilled A and disappears in the distances with the chromatic run downward. The remaining words "planait dans l'air" forte are no longer an imitation of the bird but a joyful outburst from Ophélie singing with her own voice.

She returns to her modest way of speech, and it is again with innocent charm that she speaks of her delusion. She says with pride, "Hamlet est mon époux," and with humility, "je suis Ophélie." Singing very slowly during the following *andante*, she clings to that vital delusion, alternating delight in "il m'a donné son coeur en échange du mien" with an aggressive denial of what is nearer to the truth, "qu'il me fuit et m'oublie" forte. When she repeats "Hamlet est mon époux," with a short pause after "Hamlet," it should be possible to detect in her voice a doubt that she rejects swiftly. The hesitant "et moi, et moi je suis Ophélie," pianissimo and ritardando, betrays a helplessness still unaccepted. If the phrase "s'il trahissait sa foi" is said with absolute simplicity, it will be pathetic. The music of that page is extremely simple but also perfectly right, and must be sung with great sensitivity.

As the villagers start dancing a waltz, Ophélie distributes her flowers at random. Her voice now is simple and natural, and speaking to one or the other of the young people she sings spontaneously, shorter fragments at first, to be contrasted in dynamics but still light in spirit, then a longer one, quite rustic and gay, before holding a long, happy trill on the note F. Both versions of the last three bars of that section are acceptable. A brilliant coloratura would certainly choose the upper one.

The happy, carefree mood is interrupted suddenly, the dance stops, and Ophélie calls for the attention of the group. "Et maintenant, écoutez ma chanson" is said firmly, as if a sudden inspiration forced Ophélie to sing at that particular instant. The ballad the composer has inserted here in a fortunate move is said to be a Scandinavian folk song. Quiet, sad, and melodious, with a naive text relating to a water nymph, it allows Ophélie to release from her doleful mind the mysterious premonition of her own death. In contrast to the style of the preceding pages and the following ones, the first two phrases are sung in long spans of four bars each, without a breath. (A detail: Pronounce "la *Villiss*." They unfold slowly, with no strong accents, like a long gray ribbon. The next two phrases call for a little more life. Each ends with a wistful fermata; the second one becomes very slow, with a faint gleam of happiness on "D'un bonheur si doux." The last four bars before the end of the song start in the gray color, but a sudden forte on "hélas" seems almost a clear-minded lament, and the song ends in the peace of death.

The cut from *K* to *L* is customary. A strident peal of laughter shatters the mood of the song. From there on, Ophélie's madness explodes in incoherence. A coloratura with an easy high E should sing the upper line on the second bar of *L*, with the final interval from F-sharp to F-sharp going from mezzo forte to piano. From bar 5 to bar 15 the "la la" are meant to be piano with stronger accents stressing the syncopations. The fermata on the C-sharp of bar 16 is forte; then the voice fades with a lazy, dragging feeling on bars 17–20. Bars 21–26 start piano, with a violent crescendo to the high B in bar 23 and a legato diminuendo afterward. The breath comes before the C-sharp fermata in bar 26, and that C sharp is tied to the next bar. By now Ophélie's mind has reached a state of complete disorder, and she cries and laughs alternately in spurts. Bars 1–4 of the 4/4 are piercing notes of grief, bars 5 and 6 uncontrollable laughter. Then in bars 7 to 11 she becomes sentimental while her lines are neither sweet nor loving but for "Bonheur suprême," possibly an unconscious echo of days past.

At this point there is another customary cut, bars 12 to 21 inclusive, ten bars. During bars 22–27 Ophélie recovers enough physical balance to be able to sing full voice with dramatic strength and with despair. The fermata on the silence in bar 27 must be a striking blank, after which "pour toi je meurs" is barely above a whisper. The following run upward begins piano and slowly but very soon accelerates and grows to forte. The notes in bar 30 are interrupted by a panting breath; then the voice soars to the trill on the high A-sharp and, after a sizable silence, to the final "je meurs."

The musical substance of this rather long scene may be neither very original nor very beautiful, but it has a strong impact on the listeners. It also requires great versatility from the singer. To sing with the successive and extreme changes of voice demanded by the text and the music without losing the basic beauty of the sound, to paint Ophélie's agony without forgetting the gentleness of her nature, is not an easy task. But to get away from the pretty singing of so many coloratura parts should be thrilling and refreshing.

Thomas, *Mignon*

"Connais-tu le pays"   *mezzo-soprano*

Connais-tu le pays	Do you know the country
où fleurit l'oranger,	where the orange tree blooms,
le pays des fruits d'or	the country of golden fruits
et des roses vermeilles;	and of crimson roses;
où la brise est plus douce	where the breeze is softer
et l'oiseau plus léger,	and the bird lighter,
où dans toutes saisons	where in all seasons
butinent les abeilles;	the bees are gathering honey;
où rayonne et sourit	where radiates and smiles,
comme un bienfait de Dieu	like a favor from God,
un éternal printemps	an eternal spring
sous un ciel toujours bleu?	under a sky always blue?
Hélas, que ne puis-je te suivre	Alas, why can I not follow you
vers ce pays lointain	to that distant country
dont le sort m'exila?	from which fate exiled me?
C'est là que je voudrais vivre,	That is where I would want to live,
aimer et mourir,	love, and die,
c'est là, oui, c'est là.	yes, it is there.
Connais-tu la maison	Do you know the house
où l'on m'attend là-bas,	where they wait for me,
la salle aux lambris d'or	the gilded hall
où des hommes de marbre	where marble statues
m'appellent dans la nuit	call me in the night
en me tendant les bras;	stretching out their arms to me;
et la cour où l'on danse	and the courtyard where people dance
à l'ombre d'un grand arbre;	in the shade of a big tree;
et le lac transparent	and the clear lake
où glissent sur les eaux	where glide on the waters
mille bateaux légers	a thousand light boats
pareils à des oiseaux?	similar to birds?
Hélas, que ne puis-je te suivre . . .	Alas, why can I not follow you . . .

Given for the first time at the Paris Opéra Comique in 1866, *Mignon* reached its thousandth performance at that theater alone in less than thirty years, and its popularity was universal. Among the arias, which were sung everywhere, "Connais-tu le pays" soon became the most unbearable, for it makes such modest demands on the singer that any girl felt she could sing it. *Mignon* is no longer a pillar of the operatic repertoire, but the easy charm of some selections still recommend them to us.

When first seen in the opera, Mignon appears as part of a gypsy band crossing through Germany. One night, as she refuses to dance in front of an inn, the gypsies threaten to beat her into obedience. But Wilhelm, a young traveler staying at the inn, takes her under his protection. Thinking to buy her freedom from the gypsies, he attempts to find out more about her. The young girl, however, who does not even know her age, remembers little or nothing of her parents and has only vague memories of an earlier home and a country of her own. These memories she tries to assemble in this aria.

The first Mignon, Madame Galli-Marié, who, incidentally, was to be the first Carmen ten years later, was a mezzo-soprano of average vocal power but great charm, whose sensitive rendition of "Connais-tu le pays" started the opera on its road to success from the moment of its premiere. A young voice used with simplicity is the proper one for this aria.

There are two verses: memories of the remote country and memories of the palatial mansion that was hers. The two verses are musically identical and it is the text that provides their different character. The tempo, *allegretto,* is marked by the eighth note, ♪ = 120, at the start and will speed up later. The dynamic is *dolce.* The mezzo-soprano must find the exact amount of voice that will allow her to sing easily, with a warm legato and with glowing admiration in her sound. Hers had been a beautiful country; the pictures, the sounds, the perfumes she remembers are all exalting. Sing the first two bars in one breath, well in rhythm and without shortening the sixteenths. Stay mellow and carry the phrase over to "où fleurit l'oranger." The next four bars must be sung in one breath, with a stronger tone on "d' or," a sweeter one on "roses vermeilles." No breath in the middle of the next four bars, sung pianissimo and very lightly (a breeze, a bird). The sixteenth note on "butinent" in bars 14 and 15 is a nice touch, suggesting the swift, broken flight of the honey-gathering bee.

On bars 17 and 18 Mignon remembers with delight the heavenly climate of her homeland. The voice must shine on "rayonne" (radiate) and "sourit" (smile), make a warm crescendo on "printemps" and end the phrase ("toujours bleu") with a lovely piano that will ring and carry if sung in a precise vowel /ø/, slim and vibrant. With "Hélas," five bars of sadness and regret, sung faster, bring in a new and fleeting mood. And with "C'est là," piano at first, then suddenly forte, the scope of the song changes to an expression of vital longing. The voice soars dramatically to the two F's of "C'est là" and "aimer" and stays vibrant for the next four bars, even in the word "mourir." After the fermata (bar 33) "c'est là" and "oui, c'est là" are sung in an intense piano heavy with longing.

The second verse deals at first with a majestic subject, a mansion with large halls and marble statues. The voice should grow almost stately until "hommes de marbre." Inject a touch of mystery in the music with "m'appellent dans la nuit," a pathetic touch with "en me tendant les bras." Stately trees then replace stately statues, but this time in a happy mood: "et la cour où l'on danse . . ." The memories of the clear lake with its light boats return more charm and lightness to the voice. The words must be said precisely on the lips, and the final sound on "oiseaux" must be as slim and dark as it had been on the "bleu" at the end of the first verse. There is hidden in the humble Mignon the personality of a lady.

The repeat of "Hélas" returns the singer to the same short moment of sadness as with the first verse, and with "C'est là" the dramatic longing takes hold of her soul again. The aria concludes without any new elements.

Very moderate in range, very limited in power except for a few notes, very easy musically (beware of a sloppy rhythm), "Connais-tu le pays" is a perfect training aria. It allows an as yet not very experienced singer to concentrate on finding all the descriptive colors suggested here as well as the succession of emotions they trigger. The last lines of both verses provide a sincere and moving opportunity for emotional involvement. What a reward if the result of the modest study suggested here were a strong and convincing public performance!

Verdi, *Aïda*

"Celeste Aïda"   *tenor*

Se quel guerrier io fossi!	If I were that warrior!
Se il mio sogno si avverasse!	If my dream could come true!
Un esercito di prodi	An army of valiant men
da me guidato . . . e la vittoria . . .	led by me . . . and victory . . .
e il plauso di Menfi tutta!	and the cheers of all Memphis!
E a te, mia dolce Aïda,	And to you, my sweet Aïda,
tornar di lauri cinto . . .	to return covered with laurels . . .
dirti: per te ho pugnato,	to tell you: for you have I fought,
e per te ho vinto!	and for you have I been victorious!
Celeste Aïda, forma divina,	Heavenly Aïda, divine vision,
mistico serto di luce e fior;	mystic wreath of light and flowers;
del mio pensiero tu sei regina,	of my thoughts you are the queen,
tu di mia vita sei lo splendor.	you are the splendor of my life.
Il tuo bel cielo vorrei ridarti,	Your beautiful sky I would give back to you,
le dolce brezze del patrio suol,	the gentle breezes of your homeland,
un regal serto sul crin posarti,	put a royal crown in your hair,
ergerti un trono vicino al sol.	erect a throne for you close to the sun.

At the time of the pharaohs, a war between Egypt and Ethiopia has ended in victory for the Egyptian army. From among the prisoners still held in Memphis, the young Aïda has been chosen to become a slave of Princess Amneris. When the curtain rises on the opera, the High Priest informs Radamès, a brilliant army officer, that Ethiopia has resumed hostilities against the pharaohs. Consequently an army is being assembled and a new commander will be chosen. Left alone in the large hall of the palace, Radamès sings the famous aria "Celeste Aïda" in which he tells of his love for Aïda and his hopes for military glory.

This extremely Italian aria blends the two themes in Radamès' thoughts, glory and love, that is, glory as an offering to love. Both themes will be suggested and then amplified to the limits of musical and vocal powers. The aria requires a tenor voice capable of standing its ground when alternating with some of the sharpest trumpet sounds, yet of matching soon afterward the sweetest-sounding woodwinds and strings, all the while keeping an intense vitality. It must flourish on several heroic B-flats and caress another one with great softness. Few tenors can do this aria justice.

The voice starts *a cappella*, without an indication of tempo. It expresses a wish that is almost a dream, and it could be mezzo forte, swift, with strong accentuations on "*f*ossi" and "avver*a*sse." After the call of the trumpets, the dream almost seems reality, and enthusiasm invades Radamès. Sing "un esercito di prodi" rapidly, "da me guidato" fortissimo and broadly. "E il plauso di Menfi tutta" is a vision of what will later be the triumphal scene. The second theme appears right away, piano, slowly and tenderly, with "E a te, mia dolce Aïda." But the triumphal idea returns immediately, culminating in a resounding "pugnato" and a long, ringing A-flat on "vinto." The trumpets vanish, and barely audible, shimmering violins introduce the song of love.

Here the tempo is marked also for the voice, ♪ = 116, and must be kept, with of course some flexibility for expression. Portamenti will be numerous, some for creating charm ("serto"), some for suggesting passion ("pensiero tu"). The general dynamic is *piano*, with frequent crescendos and diminuendos. This is a song of love, truly of exalting love, and the tenor's goal must be to suggest Aïda's noble beauty through the legato of his singing, the coordination of all his tones, and his respect for all dynamic indications—remember the pianissimo on "di luce e fior." A *piano espressivo* for the winds precedes a matching *dolcissimo* "il tuo bel cielo" where love and sympathy mellow the voice. The constant thought of glory is linked, however, with that of love: "un regal serto" is sung with vitality and a little faster. A deep breath before "ergerti" and a very deep support will make the enthusiastic fortissimo on "trono" physically possible, as well as a long, vibrant B-flat followed by an A still forte. A new intake of breath should allow "vicino al sol" to be sung diminuendo and the following "Ah" to reach pianissimo, during a downward portamento to "Celeste Aïda."

During the repeat of that section pay close attention, as you must have done the first time, to the spin of the voice in the light portamenti between C and F ("Aïda . . . divina") and to the exact color that the vowel /a/ must acquire in order to keep the voice at the same time brilliant and melodious. At the end of the section the declamation on the many F's must be mellow, with very clear vowels. Take a breath after "brezze," keeping the amount of tone as near to piano as possible in the portamento to "un regal." It is only with "sul crin posarti" that the voice regains élan and intensity. During the breath before "ergerti," while checking again on your vitality and deep support, imagine that you can spin the vibration of your voice silently from low B-flat to high B-flat, instead of pulling this high B-flat out of nowhere in an explosive fashion. A very slim vowel /e/, almost /ø/, will help the ringing quality of that most important tone. As before, a breath after "trono" should allow "vicino al sol" to become *ppp*.

The ending of the aria creates a dilemma for the performer. The intention of the composer, marking the last phrase *pianissimo* and *morendo*, must have been to show Radamès' dream ending in sweet ecstasy, of course calling on the vocal ability of the tenor to sing beautiful high tones softly. But—and the same is true in other arias (Don José, Roméo, "Cielo e mar")—not many dramatic tenors can achieve such a feat. Besides, the temptation to deliver a heroic final note is all but irresistible, and the success of the singer may depend on the thirst of the audience for a thundering high note. Although as a performer I have often made the sacrifice of an easy burst of applause for the sake of being faithful to the score, I do not wish to advise Radamès one way or another in this particular case. If a vote were to be taken, my own memory and the testimony of many recordings would forecast that the fortissimos have it.

"Ritorna vincitor" *soprano*

Ritorna vincitor! E dal mio labbro	Return victorious! And from my lips
uscì l'empia parola!	escaped the impious word!
Vincitor del padre mio . . .	Victorious over my father . . .
di lui che impugna l'armi per me . . .	over him who takes up arms for me . . .
per ridonarmi una patria,	to give me back my country,
una reggia,	a palace,
e il nome illustre	and the illustrious name
che qui celar m'è forza!	that here I am forced to conceal!
Vincitor de'miei fratelli . . .	Victorious over my brothers . . .
ond'io lo veggo,	whence I see him,
tinto del sangue amato,	stained with the blood of my loved ones,
trionfar nel plauso	triumph amidst the cheers
del'Egizie coorti!	of the Egyptian troups!
E dietro il carro, un Re . . .	And behind the chariot, a king . . .
mio padre . . . di catene avvinto!	my father . . . bound in chains!
L'insana parola!	These insane words,
O numi, sperdete!	o gods, erase them!
Al seno d'un padre	To her father's embrace
la figlia rendete!	return the daughter!
Struggete, struggete,	Destroy, destroy,
struggete le squadre	destroy the armies
dei nostri oppressor!	of our oppressors!
Ah, sventurata, che dissi?	Ah, wretched woman, what did I say?
E l'amor mio?	And my love?
Dunque scordar poss'io	Can I forget then
questo fervido amore	this fervent love
che, oppressa e schiava	which, oppressed and enslaved so I was,
come raggio di sol	like a ray of sunshine
qui mi beava?	made me happy here?
Imprecherò la morte a Radamès . . .	I should call death upon Radamès . . .
a lui ch'amo pur tanto!	on him whom I love so much!
Ah! non fu in terra mai	Ah! was ever on this earth
da più crudeli angoscie	by more cruel anguish
un core affranto!	a heart broken?
I sacri nomi di padre, d'amante	The sacred names of father, of lover
nè profferir poss'io nè ricordar.	I must neither utter nor remember.
Per l'un, per l'altro	For the one, for the other,
confusa, tremante	confused, trembling,
io piangere vorrei, vorrei pregar.	I would want to weep, want to pray.
Ma la mia prece	But my praying
in bestemmia si muta,	turns into a curse,
delitto è il pianto a me,	a crime is my weeping,
colpa il sospir.	guilt my sighing.
In notte cupa	In deep darkness

la mente è perduta	my mind is lost,
e nell'ansia crudel vorrei morir.	and because of this cruel anxiety I want to die.
Numi, pietà del mio soffrir!	Gods, have mercy on my suffering!
Speme non v'ha pel mio dolor.	There is no hope for my grief,
Amor fatal, tremendo amor,	Fateful love, dreadful love,
spezzami il cor, fammi morir!	break my heart, make me die!
Numi, pietà . . .	Gods, have mercy . . .

The goddess Isis has chosen Radamès to be the new head of the Egyptian army. The priests lead him to the temple for his formal investiture. As the crowd bursts into cheers Aïda joins in the thunderous "Ritorna vincitor" (Return victorious) that sends him on his way. As soon as the words leave her lips Aïda realizes her tragic problem with horror. It is her father's army that Radamès will fight, the army that King Amonasro, her father, has assembled to free her from slavery. Whatever she wishes, whatever she feels, she will commit the crime of betraying either the man she loves or her own father. That is the dramatic burden of this great aria.

"Ritorna vincitor" requires not only a large spinto voice equally at ease in high and low ranges, very flexible and skilled in the use of colors, but also an interpreter capable of extreme intensity and of sincerity in violent contrasts. The aria is composed of several sections, all very well defined, and each of them must be lived and performed to the hilt.

If the aria is given as a solo with piano, it should be preceded by the nine bars of the march concluding the choral scene. The tempo is *allegro agitato*; the metronomical marking in the score gives a good idea of the agitation desired. But, in the first page and several times elsewhere in the aria, a rigorous respect for the markings would be contrary to the spirit of the role, and the soprano must feel herself which parts are relatively strict and which are not. Nevertheless, although the pace may change, the rhythm of the notes as written by Verdi (even quarters, dotted eighths and sixteenths, double dotted notes, and so on) must be preserved. No better declamation than this can be invented.

"Ritorna vincitor" is forte and sung with horror, and it is with disbelief that Aïda hears the words coming from her own lips: "E dal mio labbro uscì . . ." is piano, almost without timbre. After the chords forte by the orchestra, the following phrase, "Vincitor del padre mio," is very rubato, starting moderato as if to give the thoughts time to occur, then growing more intense and horrified. The words "una patria, una reggia" come very fast, but there is more breadth on "il nome illustre . . ." An almost similar pattern will follow the new group of forte chords: Each of the successive short phrases, such as "vincitor de'miei fratelli," is faster and more forte than the one before, reaching a powerful, broad forte on "plauso." The last line of the section, "E dietro il carro . . ." goes accelerando, urged on by the punctuation of the orchestra to a very violent "avvinto." Aïda cannot bear the vision of her enslaved father and rejects it as soon as it appears.

She is moved to pray to the gods to forget her brief madness, to forgive her, and to crush her father's enemies. "L'insana parola" is an ardent but harmonious prayer, still very animated, $\sqcup = 100$. The first two large phrases follow a very clearly indicated crescendo and decrescendo, and the G's on "Struggete" are started with great vigor and slightly diminished (vowel /e/). As soon as the words "nostri oppressor" are said Aïda recoils from her prayer and, torn in her soul, sings a tragic B-flat, which she can hold beyond the written value provided that the tone stays more and more alive and spinning. After a breath, "sventurata, che dissi" are words of utter dejection.

The next section ("E l'amor mio"), changing in a few bars from ecstatic bliss to cruel anguish, is one of the most beautiful melodies ever offered a soprano. It must be performed very freely, with as many fluctuations of tempi as a sincere emotion suggests. The basic tempo could read ♩ = 44–48. The voice is a melodious legato, aiming to blend as perfectly as possible with the accompaniment, soaring to the high notes with élan and fluidity. The intervals, very clean always, must be smoothed out by finding some common resonance between low and high tones. No edge, no asperities, can be tolerated.

Following the invitation of the orchestra to join in the Aïda theme, the voice enters cantabile. A crescendo renders "questo fervido amore" intense. "Schiava" is carried over into "come raggio di sol" in a large, glorious curve, slow and continuous until "sol," followed by "qui mi beava" pianissimo, almost as if it were unutterable. "A lui ch'amo pur tanto," slowly and freely said, is a touching and pure love song. In great contrast the "Ah" on the A-flat is a tragic outcry, forte and tenuto for a long value. After a breath, the descending line "non fu in terra . . ." expresses deep despair which, while absolutely sincere, needs special control of the voice. First, a breath should be taken after "angoscie," for reasons of security as well as for preparing more strength for a crescendo on "un core affranto." Second, the voice, while growing into rounder mouth resonances, must be brought forward and avoid the dark weight of a descent into chest voice. How many Aïdas have I not heard who threatened or destroyed incoming high C's by their practice of a heavy chest voice!

The *allegro giusto* section, ♩ = 100, expresses the feeling of helplessness that makes Aïda want to die. It starts mezzo piano, still legato, with animation, but soon the phrases are broken into anguished fragments. The two phrases "I sacri nomi . . ." and "Per l'un, per l'altro . . ." grow crescendo, with some intensely accented notes, "nè profferir," "io piangere," where we can almost hear sobs. Extreme misery permeates the stronger and more continuous phrases "Ma la mia prece" and "In notte cupa." That section must be sung strictly in time, the emotions being expressed by the way the words are sung and by the color of the voice.

The final, superb section can be read at ♩ = 56–60, without strictness of tempo. The basic dynamic marking is *piano*, the quality of the tone pure, clear, continuous, ready to soar. The meaning, of course, is supplication and prayer. The soaring "tremendo amor" has an allargando on the triplet. After an accelerando on "Numi, pietà" (bars 17 and 18 of that section) and a deep breath, "soffrir" should be carried over into the "Ah" on A-flat (bars 20 and 21) in a large curve culminating in a powerful long note on that "Ah." The bottom of the descending line (bars 24 and 25) is forte, without forcing the voice. Bar 25 is generally sung as shown.

In bars 26–27 the word "numi" is substituted for the first "pietà." The last notes of the aria are a thread of voice fading away, but always clear and pure. Coming as it does after the dramatic moments of the aria, this last part demands exceptional poise from the soprano as well as the talent to convey a deep emotion through the sounds of a pure and melodious voice.

"O Patria mia"   *soprano*

Qui Radamès verrà!	Radamès will come here!
Che vorrà dirmi?	What will he tell me?
Io tremo!	I tremble!
Ah! se tu vieni a recarmi	Ah! if you come to bid me
o crudel, l'ultimo addio,	o cruel man, the last farewell,
del Nilo i cupi vortici	the Nile's dark whirls
mi daran tomba . . .	will offer me a tomb . . .
e pace forse . . .	and peace maybe . . .
e pace forse e oblio . . .	peace and maybe oblivion . . .
O patria mia, mai più ti rivedro.	O my homeland, never again shall I see you.
O cieli azzuri,	O blue skies,
o dolce aure native	o gentle native breezes,
dove sereno	where my early youth
il mio matin brillò . . .	bloomed serene . . .
o verdi colli,	o green hills,
o profumate rive,	o fragrant shores,
o patria mia,	o my homeland,
mai più ti rivedrò.	never again shall I see you.
O fresche valli,	O cool valleys,
o queto asil beato	o quiet, blessed retreat
che un dì promesso	which one day was promised me
dall'amor mi fu . . .	by [my] love . . .
Or che d'amore il sogno	Now that love's dream
è dileguato,	has vanished,
o patria mia,	o my homeland,
mai più ti rivedrò . . .	never shall I see you again.

The moon is full, the night starry. On the bank of the Nile Aïda, bathed in moonlight, secretly expects Radamès, her lover, while in the temple of Isis nearby Amneris prays for the happiness of her own marriage to the young Egyptian hero.

Aïda's life depends on her meeting with Radamès. Should he forsake her, she would throw herself in the river, never again to see her beloved homeland, for which she longs desperately. Anguish, despair, and yearning will find expression in this aria before it turns into a loving hymn to her fatherland, in vocal lines unsurpassed in beauty and sensitivity.

If the aria is sung as a solo, the entire theme of Aïda, ten bars, should be played as a prelude. The aria itself starts with the 6/8 cantabile, but the two pages preceding it are of great importance for setting its mood. The first four bars of the recitative, "Qui Radamès verrà," are quite slow, the words interrupted by two long silences. Aïda sings with a somber voice that conveys a sense of somber premonition. The next four bars are faster and grow in intensity and exteriorization. The voice reaches mezzo forte on "l'ultimo addio." Aïda states her fateful decision forcefully in the next four bars, "del Nilo . . ." The tempo is approximately ♩ = 96, the voice above the suggestive water effect of the basses full and legato. For the next three bars, however, it diminishes and slows down ("e pace forse"), showing the hoped-for peace in death. A pastoral melodic line played by the oboe introduces the thought of the distant homeland. Today it is performed at about ♩ = 56, more slowly than the tempo marked in the piano and voice score. "O patria mia, mai più, mai più ti rivedrò" is sung freely, the first note like a slim sigh, with a slight crescendo on "patria mia," the phrase ending pianissimo and slowly. The remaining words are just a murmur, barely heard. But the moods of the aria have been established—that is, a somber belief in impending death, a yearning without hope for a beloved homeland.

Radiant pictures of Aïda's homeland now rise from the depth of her gloom. The sky at dawn, the verdant hills, the fragrant shores appear with grace, charm, and serenity, and Aïda's voice becomes a silver string vibrating weightlessly, supple, curvacious, respecting the written rhythm but with instinctive changes and inflections impossible to translate into printed notes. Here again today's conductors take a much slower tempo than the printed one, sometimes as slow as ♪ = 66, allowing both singer and orchestra great flexibility. It is well understood, nevertheless, that no sloppiness can be tolerated. The slightly detached notes, the very precise grace sixteenths, the one accented note in the middle of the bar, the *sfumato* (vanishing) C-sharp, a very even color of voice for upper and lower octaves are all part of the ravishing image. In the seventh bar of the verse, the crescendo on "o patria mia" comes in stressed sounds, as if suddenly pouring out from a heavy heart: The beautiful memories have revived Aïda's grief.

Following a wonderfully sensitive contribution by the orchestra in bar 9, Aïda sings the same words again and again, words of despair, made varied and touching by the inspired vocal lines, all full of charm as well as sadness. The soprano voice must stay shining and light. Going to forte, as in bar 17 ("mia"), means growing in intensity and in high resonances, not in loudness. The general dynamic level stays piano, the 3/8 bar (14) is sung more slowly, the downward arpeggio after the high A in bar 17 is sung completely at ease. Bar 17 is a free ritardando with a stress on the "-ve" of "rivedrò". Again the several "mai più" and "no" are almost murmured, as if Aïda could barely grasp their depressing meaning.

Aïda had hoped that Radamès, victorious, would give her country back to her. Now she is filled with dark premonitions that this hope will be betrayed, and in the second verse of the aria she expresses her longing still more strongly. The tempo can be a little faster, the voice slightly more animated but remaining very tender and light—there is another *sfumato* indication on the portamento from "beato" to "che un dì." A breath after the portamento and before the E of "che" will allow the phrase "che un dì promesso" to become more intense and to be contrasted with "Or che d'amore," a phrase of soft sadness. The next "o patria mia" is mezzo forte with a briefly exteriorized despair. Again the orchestra contributes a very sensitive touch, inspiring the voice to great emotion: a crescendo on "o patria mia," a crescendo on "non ti vedrò mai più," tied without a breath to "no, mai più" pianissimo. The voice must be constantly connected with a distant, consistent, but flexible support so that all the inflections just mentioned prepare the ascension to the high C. After a breath just before the C-natural, the vowel /a/ is substituted for /u/, the vibration of the voice is kept intense, and the size of the tone becomes slimmer and slimmer as it goes upward, with a large, high vault of resonance in the back of the upper mouth. If the C is floating and free, it can be held beyond the written value, and the following A-natural and F can be sung freely and very slowly, very tenderly. A breath after that F and another one after "non ti vedrò" give Aïda's statement finality without changing the mood of sweet resignation.

In order to make of the last phrase of the aria the jewel it is meant to be, the soprano must remember that trying to sing heavy chesty tones in the low range (the last "ti rivedrò") constitutes not only an error of characterization but also a danger for the purity and freedom of the two high A's pianissimo. The sounds of the low range must instead be started near the front of the mouth, while well rounded in the mouth, and still keep alive some upper resonances, so that there are no discrepancies between consecutive tones and so that the progressive predominance of the high resonances is achieved by a continuous spin of the tone from wide vowels to taller and slimmer ones. Sopranos who find it difficult to start the first A pianissimo should mentally sing the E of the accompaniment and spin from there into the high A.

This magnificent aria demands a vocal skill so unobtrusive that the listeners might forget the concrete body in back of the tones and believe they soar immaculate from a tender heart and a vibrant soul.

Verdi, *Un Ballo in Maschera*

"Ma dall'arido stelo divulsa" *soprano*

Ecco l'orrido campo	Here is the dreadful place
ove s'accoppia al delitto la morte!	where death is coupled with crime!
Ecco là le colonne . . .	There are the gibbets . . .
La pianta è là,	The plant is there,
verdeggia al piè.	fresh and green, at the foot.
S'inoltri.	Step forward.
Ah, mi si aggela il core!	Ah, my heart turns to ice!
Sino il rumor de'passi miei,	Even the sound of my footsteps,
qui tutto	everything here
m'empie di raccapriccio e di terrore!	fills me with fright and terror!
E si perir dovessi?	And if I should perish?
Perire! Ebben, quando la sorte mia,	Perish! Well then, when such is my fate,
il mio dover tal è, s'adempia	my duty such, may it be fulfilled,
e sia.	may it be so.

Ma dall'arido stelo divulsa	But once from the dry stem
come avrò di mia mano quell'erba,	my hand has plucked that herb,
e che dentro la mente convulsa	so that in my tortured mind
quell'eterea sembianza morrà,	that heavenly image will die,
che ti resta,	what is left for you,
perduto l'amor,	when love is lost,
che ti resta, mio povero cor?	what is left for you [then], my poor heart?
Oh! chi piange,	Oh! who is weeping,
qual forza m'arretra?	what force restrains me?
M'attraversa la squallida via?	What crosses the sordid path?
Su, corragio . . .	Come, be brave . . .
e tu, fatti di pietra,	and you, change to stone,
non tradirmi, dal pianto ristà,	don't betray me, cease your weeping,
o finisci di batter e muor,	or stop beating and die,
t'annienta, mio povero cor!	destroy yourself, poor heart of mine!
Mezzanotte! Ah, che veggio?	Midnight! Ah, what do I see?
Una testa di sotterra si leva,	A head rises from under the ground,
e sospira!	and sighs!
Ha negli occhi il baleno dell'ira	Its eyes flash with anger
e m'affisa e terribile sta! Ah!	and stare at me frighteningly! Ah!
E m'affisa . . .	And stare at me . . .
Deh! Mi reggi, m'aita, Signor,	Ah! give me strength, help me, Lord,
miserere d'un povero cor!	have mercy on a wretched heart!
O Signor, m'aita . . .	O Lord, help me . . .

Amelia has fallen in love with Riccardo, governor of her province, whose close friend and principal assistant is her husband. A woman of honor and honesty, she fights her passion desperately. Ulrica, a fortune-teller, has advised her to gather some magic herbs at midnight, near the gallows, for they will cure her of her illicit love. The stage for this, the second act of the opera shows a lonely field at the foot of a crumbling hill where two gallows are vaguely perceived in the dim moonlight, a sinister landscape. Veiled and wrapped in a large black cape Amelia has entered slowly during the prelude and knelt in prayer. Now she stands up and looks around with fear and distaste.

This aria is a perfect example of Verdi the dramatist and must be sung and acted, even with the voice, for all it is worth. It requires a ringing spinto voice and an interpreter of great intensity and versatility. If it is performed in concert, at least the last nine bars of the prelude should be played as an introduction.

The aria is made up of a recitative and a beautiful cantilena alternating with highly dramatic pages of declamation. The recitative "Ecco l'orrido campo" is an *allegro agitato*, with allowances made, of course, for several variations of tempo according to the fluctuations of Amelia's emotions. The first phrase, $\downarrow = 112$, is nervous and sung with fear and revulsion. The accompaniment in bars 5, 7, 8, and 9 and the vocal phrases in between must accelerate little by little, as if the sight of the gallows, of the magic herbs close by, increased Amelia's nervousness. The fermata in bar 9 is a long silence during which Amelia makes her decision to move forward. "S'inoltri" is sung mezzo forte and as if reluctantly. Her hesitant steps are echoed in the basses. She stops and sings "Ah, mi si aggela il core" legato and much slower. But the orchestra returns to the tempo *agitato*, and the phrase "Sino il rumor . . ." may be thought in cut time, mezzo piano and with a frightened voice, interrupted twice by a start and a shudder, the words "raccapriccio" and "terrore" being articulated very strongly. After the orchestral forte in bars 25 and 26 she sings "E se perir dovessi" more slowly, as if in spite of herself. The following "Perire" can start forte but a diminuendo almost stifles the word while the fortissimo of the orchestra stresses its terrifying meaning. Amelia's willpower, however, overcomes her fears and premonitions, and she sings the last two lines of the recitative more firmly, with very well-sustained tones. A firm tenuto on the A-flat of "s'adempia" shows her renewed strength, and the last "e sia" is short and decisive.

During the incoming *andante* (played nowadays at ♪ = 80–84 rather than the marked 72) Amelia pictures herself being cured of her love for Riccardo but left with an empty heart. Sing the first three phrases very evenly, exactly on time, carefully respecting the exact rhythm of the triplets and the crescendo-decrescendo in the middle of each phrase. In bar 10 there is a strong lyric crescendo and allargando on the words "quell'e-terea," followed by a ritardando and a morendo to "morrà." Bars 12 and 13 return *a tempo*. A deep breath after "l'amor" prepares a tenuto of great emotion on "che ti resta," especially on the high A-flat. Take a short breath after "ti resta," the second time also, and end the phrase slowly, very piano, and with a long, very moving fermata on "povero."

So far the voice, very sensitive, has had a lyric and touching quality. The following page, though in the same tempo, seems much more agitated because of its writing. The broken phrases, sung at least mezzo forte, reveal uncertainty, inner conflicts, and with "Su, coraggio" a transition to a much more dramatic expression. "Non tradirmi," with a tenuto on the first two notes, is already more spinto, and the appeal to the heart to stop crying stays strong despite a diminuendo. An accelerando on "o finisci di battere e muor" precedes an accented A-flat on "t'annienta" and a broad sound on all notes of "t'annienta." The ending of the phrase stays intense. A breath after each "t'annienta" could increase its vigor. It is not necessary to look for a contralto timbre at the bottom of the range. C's and B-naturals will ring very well if sung brightly and frontally with the strong participation of the lips.

The hallucination that fills the next page must be given with utmost strength, a terrified voice, exactly in rhythm, starting quite fast (♪ = 144 seems almost too slow), with the tempo accelerating throughout the page, ending presto in the last four or five bars. In order to avoid any strain, the support of the voice must be kept very low in the lower torso and the search for power kept in the direction of ring and intensity, not of darkness and bulk. Even if the soprano feels the terror of the moment sincerely—and she should—she must control her emotional balance and not try to be expressive through any localized vocal effort. The last words, "e m'affisa" and "terribile sta," should be sung without timbre, as if in complete exhaustion, and preferably with the low A on "sta."

Now the tempo ♪ = 72 for the big, beautiful phrase seems right. The slowness will add to the scope of Amelia's prayer. It starts mezzo piano, already increasing to a good mezzo forte on the A-natural of "aita." "Miserere," a supplication, is almost forte. A breath is advisable after "miserere," another after "povero cor," which is sung forte. The next four notes are sung on the vowel /a/. The G–A–B-flat are forte but not so much so that a crescendo cannot be made by a vibrating spin into the high C. This C deserves a tenuto prior to ending the phrase very slowly and diminuendo.

The word "miserere" will be vibrant and touching if the vowels /i/ and /e/ are sung forward with brilliance. The "miserere" preceding the cadenza can be very slow. It is possible to make the start of the high B-flat easy by tying it mentally, during the silence, to the low C, as if a tone could spin from a low note to a high note even silently. The cadenza is a slow prayer. It is possible to breathe after the D-flat, allowing the soprano to reach the end of the cadenza still supporting the tone well and making it ring forward. The last words are, of course, extremely slow.

This most impressive aria calls for great vocal resources. It will not be dangerous and will bring great rewards if the singer has organized her text and her vocal lines as suggested here, with many justified changes of color, dynamics, and tempi.

"Morrò, ma prima in grazia"   *soprano*

Morrò, ma prima in grazia	I shall die, but first, for mercy's sake,
deh! mi consenti almeno	ah! consent at least
l'unico figlio mio	that my only son
avvincere al mio seno.	I may clasp to my breast.
E se alla moglie nieghi	And if you refuse your wife
quest'ultimo favor	this last favor,
non rifiutarlo ai prieghi	do not deny it to the entreaties
del mio materno cor!	of my motherly heart!
Morrò, ma queste viscere	I shall die, but [allow that] this bosom
consolino i suoi baci;	his kisses may comfort;
or che l'estrema è giunta	now that the end has been reached
dell'ore mie fugaci,	of my fleeting hours,
spenta per man del padre,	when I am put to death by the hand of his father,
la man ei stenderà	his hand he will place
su gl'occhi d'una madre	on the eyes of a mother
che mai più non vedrà!	whom he will never see again!

Amelia, threatened with death by her outraged husband, is kneeling at his feet and pleading for one last favor. She will accept death if she may embrace her son one last time.

This aria is a masterpiece that offers the singer two challenges: first, to sing with a beautiful sound, never rising above mezzo forte until the last cadenza, a sound that is at the same time intensely ringing, feminine, overflowing with sensitivity, convincing, and often on the verge of tears; second, to be able after three pages of this highly communicative but controlled singing to expand it into two very demanding phrases without altering the personality of the voice or the heart-rending sincerity of the plea.

After pages of fury preceding the aria, a cello solo raises its forgiving voice from the orchestra. It will keep pace with Amelia's voice throughout the aria. We hear it for three bars before Amelia, after a breathtaking silence, utters a single word, "Morrò," thus renouncing life in a brief word thrown in as if unimportant, after which the voice takes over legato and in long phrases, replacing the cello, singing long vowels, *"grazia,"* *"meno."* The rhythm ♩ ♪ ♪♩ ♫♩ | ♩ ♩ and its variations in the next bars suggest on the one hand the urgency of the plea and, on the other, by the use of the triplets, great tenderness. Those triplets, to be expressive, can never be legato and flexible enough.

In two different places, bar 12 on "seno" and bar 15 on "favor," the voice slows down and almost seems to falter with emotion. Both times the cello emphasizes this expression, then revives the singing. Bars 16 and 17 include a great crescendo of lyricism to an intense mezzo forte on the /e/ of "prieghi" and a remarkable inflection, as written, on the syllable "-ghi." It seems that a very eloquent prayer is conveyed not only by making a progressive ritardando on the syncopations in bar 18 but also by avoiding a breath between the two "prieghi" in bar 17, breathing instead after the C-flat of the second "prieghi" in bar 18, and making a tenuto on the syllable "-no" of "materno."

The cello now becomes urgent (bar 19) and the voice stronger as Amelia visualizes and feels in her body the cruelty of her farewell to her son. "Viscere" and "baci" are concrete words (much can be done with the sound of the vowel /a/ in "baci.") During bars 24 to 27 she really becomes aware that the end of her life is at hand. A long crescendo starts with "or che l'estrema" and grows to mezzo forte in the run upward on "fugaci," only to die down at the end of that word, stressing the meaning of "fugaci" (fleeting). A breath may be and often is taken before the last note of bar 26 (syllable "fu-" of "fugaci"), allowing a crescendo and ritardando on the upward scale, a fermata on the A-flat (syllable "-ci"), and a morendo to A-natural. The silence at the end of bar 27 may be extended in order to create the feeling of a period, also to suggest Amelia's reluctance to say the painful next phrase, "spenta per man del padre," sung piano and with restraint. There is still a diminuendo on "la man ei stenderà." But now Amelia's sorrow bursts out at the thought that her son will close her eyes, never to see her again. The word "stenderà" should be carried over into "su gl'occhi" with a sudden intensity. The accents on the next notes are akin to sobs, although sobbing itself would be in bad taste here.

The second "su gl'occhi d'una madre" comes like an echo, a brief attempt by Amelia to regain her poise, but in bar 32 "che mai più" grows to forte on "più," then returns to pianissimo on bar 34. She repeats the words as if in disbelief, unable to comprehend such a tragedy. After the short fermata in that bar, the next repeat is made very slowly, with almost detached syllables and a crescendo that the orchestra and the dominant cello pick up emphatically on bar 35. Then the voice enters forte on the F-flat but falls back immediately to pianissimo in bar 36. The effect is repeated in bar 37, the big orchestral crescendo ushering the voice in fortissimo on F-flat, the following notes being sung with force and strong accents until the fermata, then slowly and almost weakly after the fermata. On bar 39 sing the great cadenza rubato, the C-flat with moderate length, the first three descending notes slowly, the next eight faster and slightly unevenly, the two low pairs of sixteenths much more slowly, the last middle G-flat and F still more slowly, and after a breath, the final four notes of the bar adagio with a tenuto on the high G-flat, then giving the final full note its entire value.

The whole last page will be very difficult to perform for a singer who does not trust the vowel /u/. The words "mai più" (by the way, a target for humorists and detractors of opera because sopranos repeat them so regularly) need a true vowel /u/, the one so easy to pronounce in *two* or *I do*, yet so often distorted by singers for no reason whatsoever and with bad results. It is a slim vowel that needs an extension of the lips in order to exist and to stay vibrant and forward to the top of the range. It finds its main location along the face and only resonance, but no bulk, in the space of the upper back of the mouth. Distorted toward /o/ or /œ/, it loses its ring, its quality, and the possibility of handling it easily.

The voice should spin to the high B-flat (bar 38) from the preceding E-flat, still inserted in the same perfect vowel /u/ without any attempt to increase the volume of the voice.

The high C-flat in bar 39 will be easier to sing if, in the preceding bar, you sing the two short phrases "che mai" and "più vedra" very piano, as indicated above, and with a slim voice dying on the lips. During the silence that follows them, the slim vibration of those notes should mentally be spun upward and the sound of the C-flat then started at their size, to be amplified immediately. There should be no "attack" on the C-flat. The descending notes of the cadenza must be brought forward on the way down, the very low ones ringing not on the larynx but very forward in the lower mouth.

It would be a shame for any singer to apply herself to mastering the beautiful vocal lines of this aria as well as its dramatic feeling and then to spoil it all because of a clumsy, labored last page. I hope some attention will be paid to the no doubt tedious but well-tested instructions above, which will help overcome the difficulties of this last page.

"Eri tu che macchiavi"   *baritone*

Alzati! là tuo figlio	Get up! I grant you to see
a te concedo riveder.	your son once more there.
Nell'ombra e nel silenzio,	In darkness and silence
là il tuo rossore	hide your shame there
e l'onta mia nascondi!	and my dishonor!
Non è su lei,	It is not her,
nel suo fragile petto	not her tender breast
che colpir degg'io.	that I must strike.
Altro, ben altro sangue	Another, quite another blood
a terger dessi l'offesa	must cleanse the offense.
Il sangue tuo!	Your blood!
E lo trarrà il pugnale	and my dagger will draw it forth
dallo sleal tuo core:	from your treacherous heart:
delle lacrime mie vendicator!	avenger of my tears!
Eri tu che macchiavi quell'anima	It was you who stained that heart,
la delizia dell'anima mia,	the delight of my heart,
che m'affidi	[you] whom I trusted
e d'un tratto esecrabile	and who in one execrable stroke
l'universo avveleni per me.	poisoned the universe for me.
Traditor!	Traitor!
che compensi in tal guisa	who in such manner

dell'amico tuo primo la fè.	reward the faith of your best friend.
O dolcezze perdute!	O sweet joys lost!
O memorie d'un amplesso	O memories of an embrace
che l'essere india,	that makes man a god,
quando Amelia sì bella, sì candida	when Amelia, so pure, so innocent,
sul mio seno brillava d'amor!	on my heart glowed with love!
È finita.	It is all over.
Non siede che l'odio e la morte	only hatred and death remain
nel vedovo cor.	in this widowed heart.
O dolcezze perdute,	O sweet joys lost,
o speranze d'amor!	o hopes of love!

The role of Renato in *Un Ballo in Maschera,* like that of Don Carlo in *La Forza del Destino* or Posa in *Don Carlo* or Boccanegra in *Simone Boccanegra,* is written for an exceptional baritone voice of great power, long range, and inexhaustible stamina, the kind of voice that came to be known as a "Verdi baritone." There are few such voices in each generation of singers, but without aiming at performing the complete role, it is possible for excellent voices of a little less scope to study and perform excerpts from those great roles that are rewarding for singer and listener alike because of their musical beauty and their dramatic power. Such an aria is "Eri tu . . ."

Renato, friend, secretary, and staunch supporter of Riccardo, count of Warwick, has surprised his wife Amelia in a secret meeting with his master. Much to her own despair Amelia is indeed in love with Riccardo who will not, however, do injury to the honor of his friend. Misinterpreting the situation, Renato enters into a plot to murder Riccardo and decides that Amelia, too, must die in expiation of her crime. In the preceding scene Amelia has pleaded fervently to be spared, attesting her innocence, or at least to be permitted to see her son a last time before dying. Renato yields to her plea, his ferocious initial wrath subsiding while rancor and pity now fight in his heart.

"Alzati" is gruff but not threatening, and the concession "là, tuo figlio . . ." is sung darkly and no more than mezzo forte, rather slowly. On "Nell'ombra e nel silenzio" he sends Amelia away determinedly, masking his hurt and his shame under an air of authority. As he watches her go, while a moving orchestral interlude plays her music, he is left alone with his thoughts, and his better judgment is awakened.

After "Non è su lei" forte and a strong intake of breath, the voice expresses emotion on "suo fragile petto," is resolute on "che colpir degg'io," and acquires a tragic furor on the following line, during which Renato turns toward a portrait of Riccardo on the wall. "Il sangue tuo" is fortissimo, as if spat in the face of the count.

A word of caution: Even the most violent utterances need vocal control, such as a very deep support, a very well-shaped vowel /e/ on "ben," a very well-channeled vowel /u/ on "tuo."

The first two phrases of the *agitato* are like two waves, culminating on "pugnale" and "core." Then the violence spreads over the triplets and vibrates in the /i/ and /e/ of "mie" and on the first "vendicator." The second "vendicator" makes Renato shudder; the third one is said very slowly and wonderingly.

By the end of the four bars of interlude the mood has changed. There is disbelief in "Eri tu" although it is an accusation, growing stronger on "che macchiavi" with its definite crescendo immediately softened, however, by the thought of Amelia, the victim. "Quell'anima" is quite tender, and "la delizia dell'anima mia" is still sung lovingly and piano—a challenge met by all well-trained, big voices. The vowel /i/ in "delizia" must stay bright even when sung piano. Slight portamenti fit the style if they help to express more tenderness.

The accusation grows in intensity and exteriorization. Follow all markings of style, and be sure to sustain to the end of their value all long notes forte, such as "esecrab*ile*," "Trad*itor*," "gu*isa*." The descending line in triplets, "avveleni per me," is rubato, ending much slower. Some Italian baritones avoid the low A at the end of this line and sing instead one octave higher. It would be a much better idea to learn to sing the low A. "Dell'amico tuo primo" is intensely sad. The repeat of "dell" on E-natural is vehement, before the phrase is allowed to turn sentimental and slow, with a very slow turn and a fermata on the B-flat of "primo."

The six bars of interlude with their moving flute duet bring Renato a new dominant mood, the sorrow of a beautiful love lost but still felt in all its sensuous beauty. Singing piano is absolutely compulsory here, piano and very legato, with a velvety voice slightly darkened for intimacy. That applies also to the high notes. Although the rhythm must stay very constant throughout, there are impulses and letups that a musical singer cannot help but feel.

After a very even "O dolcezze perdute," which is soft and nostalgic, "d'un amplesso" is more intense as it prepares the contrast, after a breath, with "che l'essere," which is sung more slowly, with a very lyric slow turn and a slight tenuto on the F (vowel /e/). The next line follows the same pattern: "quando Amelia" is intense, "si bella" slow and tender, with a slight tenuto on the E (vowel /ɑ/). A crescendo on the triplet in "seno" makes the F mezzo forte but without tenseness. "Brillava d'amor" has a ritardando and becomes very slow on "d'amor." Two beats later, on "quando Amelia," the voice extends the orchestral phrase in its same color, then ascends in a lyrical wave to the G on "brillava," rising powerfully and lingering (not too long) on the G (vowel /ɑ/), already receding to mezzo forte on "d'amor," to piano after a breath, and very slow on the concluding "brillava d'amor."

The entrancing memories of happy love abruptly yield to reality. "E finita" is a sigh of despair that turns into an outcry of hatred in "Non siede che l'odio." This cry has a furious echo on the same words, but with "che l'odio e la morte" despair subdues the fury and the words "nel vedovo cor" are sung slowly with a short fermata on the syllable "-vo" of "vedovo" and with great sadness. The repeat of "O dolcezze perdute" blends with the sensitive orchestral line, as does "o speranze d'amor." The vowel /o/ on the high F must be vibrant and spinning, the following turn and the fermata on D very spacious. The repeat of the word "d'amor" should start piano, then reach forte as the orchestra does.

This superbly human and sensitive aria is sometimes considered a test of vocal strength and as such is often presented in auditions—seldom with success. If it is understood as a test of vocal skill put at the service of great sensitivity and a better-than-average voice, then the aria becomes less forbidding. Whether to study and perform it or not is a question of personal wisdom and common sense. How fortunate are those who can truly handle it and truly enjoy singing it!

Verdi, *Don Carlo*

"Ella giammai m'amò"   *bass-baritone*

Ella giammai m'amò!	She never loved me!
No! quel cor chiuso è a me,	No, that heart is closed to me,
amor per me non ha.	She has no love for me.
Io la rivedo ancor	I still see her
contemplar trista in volto	looking with a sad face
il mio crin bianco	at my white hair
il dì che qui di Francia venne.	the day she came here from France.
No, amor per me non ha!	No, she has no love for me!
Ove son?	Where am I?
Quei doppier presso a finir . . .	These candles about to burn down . . .
L'aurora imbianca il mio veron . . .	The dawn whitens my window . . .
già spunta il dì!	already day is breaking!
Passar veggo i miei giorni lenti!	I see my days passing slowly!
Il sonno, o Dio	Sleep, o Lord,
sparì da'miei occhi languenti.	has fled my weary eyes.
Dormirò sol nel manto mio regal,	I shall sleep alone in my royal cloak,
quando la mia giornata è giunta a sera,	when my day will have reached its evening,
dormirò sol sotto la volta nera,	I shall sleep alone under the black vault,
là nell'avello dell'Escurial.	there in the tomb of the Escurial.
Se il serto regal a me desse il poter	If only the royal crown gave me the power
di leggere nei cor	to read in the hearts,
che Dio può sol veder!	what God alone can see!
Se dorme il prence,	If the prince falls asleep,
veglia il traditore,	the traitor watches,
il serto perde il re,	the king loses his crown,
il consorte l'onore!	the husband his honor!

As part of a peace treaty between France and Spain, Elizabeth, daughter of Henri II, king of France, was given in marriage to Felipe II, king of Spain. Originally the young woman was slated to marry Felipe's son, Don Carlos, whom she loved and who loved her. After a sleepless night "Filippo" is meditating deeply, in silence and solitude, as dawn is about to break. To the torments inherent in his great power he must add the grief of a distraught husband, as his marriage has failed.

For concert or audition purposes the long introduction can be shortened to eight bars before the entrance of the voice. The tempo is marked at ♩ = 76, *andante sostenuto*. The aria, one of the greatest ever written for a bass-baritone, begins piano, as if distant, as Filippo lost in thought is singing only half-consciously. The voice, when it enters, should not attack but should blend with the orchestral tremolo from which it seems to have been born. Darkly, the king acknowledges an unalterable fact. Inside the sustained legato the double consonants in "Ella" and "giammai" must be stressed clearly, but none should be invented, as in "ammor" instead of "amor." Note that there is no stress on "amor" the first time it appears. It is a fact, stated sadly but as a fact. The repeat of "per me non ha" simply fades away.

Memory of Elizabeth's arrival comes to Filippo's mind, and some life appears in his voice, "Io la rivedo ancor." But the vision is depressing, and "trista in volto" and "il mio crin bianco" are somber phrases. "Il dì che qui di Francia venne" is written with slightly detached notes, an allusion to Elizabeth's youthful appearance, and somehow creates pathos. After the interlude, the intense "No, amor per me non ha" is a release of inner sorrow, still dark and legato, its repeat pianissimo and rallentando with helpless finality, the voice still distant and dreamy. During the slow arpeggiando that follows, Filippo comes to his senses. The four short sentences, from "Ove son" on, mark his return to clear-mindedness. The first sentence is still a bewildered question; the next three are concerned with the existence of concrete objects and the time. They must be sung with increasing firmness, and with some surprise at the late hour. Filippo has been alone with his thoughts for a long time.

The beautiful next phrase reveals his tragic awareness of his fate. It is anxious and faster; the silence after "Passar" expresses a kind of disbelief, the triplets unfold evenly, and an expressive crescendo grows into "o Dio," which can be held a little beyond its written value—on the vowel /i/. After a deep breath and in spite of a certain tradition, the end of the phrase must be sung wearily, with a long, lasting feeling and without a break. Respect the allargando and the crescendo-decrescendo in "languenti."

The new section, *andante mosso cantabile*, is a majestic and desolate vision of the solitary tomb awaiting Filippo. It is one of the greatest legato phrases ever. The somber voice must flow uninterrupted from syllable to syllable, aware of the scope of its theme but suggesting it without rising above mezzo forte, even for the second "volta." The end of the phrase is almost sinister: The Escorial (or "Escurial") built by Filippo was and is a gloomy monument—palace, convent, and necropolis all in one.

A sudden change of mood occurs. Putting his dark forebodings aside, Filippo reveals the violence of the suspicions and jealousy he usually keeps hidden. In the same majestic tempo but now in a powerful voice he wishes he could read the hearts of Elizabeth and Carlo and others still at the court. His voice flexes in a sweeping vocalise in "che Dio può sol, può sol veder," hurries on in an almost murmured repeat of "Ah, se il serto regal," only to rise and thunder again on the D-flat of "leggere," without doubt a tenuto, to return to an almost mysterious piano on the last "che Dio sol può veder." Then the anxiety of all powerful men seizes him: Is there a conspiracy going on against him, against his marriage? "Se dorme il prence" has the cautious discretion of the plotter's voice. "Il serto perde il re, il consorte l'onore"—these phrases are said with distaste and great reluctance. The middle section of the aria is violently exteriorized, in strong contrast with the meditative quality of the preceding pages. Nevertheless, there must be a sense of greatness in the successive moods, even when the vocal dynamic level is kept very low.

The theme of the eternal sleep returns, the more impressive for coming after the tormented middle section. But even the suffering during his life fails to make the king's solitary rest less sad; it is only more obviously peaceful. A return to the somber legatissimo voice, never louder than mezzo forte, is, of course, indicated, as is the return to an intense voice with the renewed expression of Filippo's intense desire to read the truth in human hearts. This time, "Ah, se il serto regal" begins mezzo forte and reaches fortissimo on the last "nei cor," suggesting the anguished feeling but with a beautiful quality of tone

Observe the long silence before "Ella giammai m'amò." After struggling with or pondering different anxieties, the king's soul suffers most deeply from that particular one, and he cannot chase it away. The singer should feel that obsession and sing slowly and darkly until a powerful upsurge of pain makes him expand the voice in a very broad, intense "amor per me non ha" before ending with a disconsolate repeat of the words, a diminuendo fermata on "me" adding to the pathetic feeling.

A great voice will triumph in this great aria when it is used to stress, suggest, or illustrate the many facets of the king's meditation, with its moments of inner concentration and its moments of ardent exteriorization. When one is penetrated by those emotions one will have no difficulty finding complete sincerity in conveying them.

"O don fatale"   *mezzo-soprano*

Ah! più non vedrò,	Ah! I shall not see again,
ah, più mai non vedrò la Regina!	ah, never see the queen again!
O don fatale,	Oh fateful gift,
o don crudel,	Oh cruel gift,
che in suo furor	that in his wrath
me fece il cielo!	Heaven made me!
Tu che ci fai . . .	You, what are you doing to us . . .
sì vane, altere,	yes, go away, haughty one,
ti maledico, o mia beltà.	I curse you, o my beauty.
Versar sol posso il pianto,	I can but shed tears,
speme non ho,	I have no hope,
soffrir dovrò.	I shall have to suffer.
Il mio delitto è orribil tanto	My crime is so horrible
che cancellar mai nol potrò!	that I shall never be able to erase it!
Ti maledico, o mia beltà.	I curse you, my beauty.
o mia Regina, io t'immolai	O my Queen, I have immolated you
al folle error di questo cor.	to the foolish error of this heart.
Solo in un chiostro	Only in a convent
al mondo ormai	shall I henceforth
dovrò celar il mio dolor!	hide my grief from the world!
Ohimè!	Woe to me!
Oh ciel! E Carlo?	Heavens! And Carlo?
a morte domani . . . gran Dio!	to his death tomorrow . . . great God!
a morte andar vedrò!	I shall see him go to his death!
Ah! . . . un dì mi resta,	Ah! . . . one day is left me,
la speme m'arride,	hope smiles at me,
sia benedetto il ciel,	Heaven be blessed,
lo salverò!	I shall save him!

Princess Eboli is a lady-in-waiting to Queen Elizabeth of Spain. A woman of great beauty, her ambition, her jealousy, and her behavior contribute greatly to the misfortunes of several of the characters in the opera. Mistress of the king but in love with Don Carlo, she is jealous of Elizabeth and has called the king's attention to the couple's unfulfilled romance. However, after witnessing a cruel scene between the king and the queen, her conscience is aroused and she confesses her guilt to Elizabeth, who banishes her from the court and to a convent for life.

The role of Eboli calls for a great voice, a dramatic mezzo-soprano as much at ease in powerful high notes as in the refined elegance of the song of the veil in the second act and capable of expressing a great variety of emotions. There are not many mezzo-sopranos who can master the role. The aria "O don fatale" concludes the grandiose fourth act in a final display of vocal fireworks.

It begins with an explosion of despair fortissimo and allegro, a line divided in two halves by a swift breath before the second "Ah" ("più non vedrò"). The singer must prepare herself beforehand for the apparent disarray of the outcry by a deep and careful buildup of her body and of her supply of air, and by shaping a very precise large vowel /a/ in her mouth, avoiding tension in the throat on the very first note of the aria. She should also avoid a melodramatic descent into chest tones for "vedrò la Regina" for the same reason.

The orchestra attacks the *allegro giusto*, ♩ = 84, with tremendous intensity and biting accents. The singer must understand that she must not do the same: The shortness of her phrases is sufficient indication of the depth of her distress. She should sing very sonorous vowels in well-pronounced words. Her agitation must not disturb the fine sound of her voice. "Il cielo" is forte, without exaggeration, and the vowel on the F is only half open. Three notes, "*Tu che ci fai,*" but no others, are accusingly accented. The triplets on "ti maledico" are smooth and like springboards to the higher notes. The G flat on the second "maledico" is only forte, as the singer still has a long way to go to the climax of that section, and Eboli's mood is so new to her that it has not yet reached full intensity.

The *più mosso* will bring her nearer to the full expression of her curse. Here the mezzo-soprano should sing the first two phrases, "Versar, versar" and "speme non ho" legato and whole, from piano to mezzo forte. Eboli has just begun to realize what her future will be. There is an accusing crescendo on "Il mio delitto," and after a breath before "che cancellar" this fourth phrase is full of despair. The curses are sung in the same *più mosso* tempo. Again, there is no hammering but a smooth unfolding of the triplets, with the sound expanding on the higher notes. The high C-flat is started in a spin, not on a bang, and should be a crescendo while it lasts. After a long fermata on the "o" (F-flat), "mia beltà" should, of course, be fierce, not in a heavy chest voice but in firmly articulate forward tones. Whatever the intensity of her feelings, the singer should have reached this point in the aria without any undue stress.

The *molto meno* section is very feminine in all its fluctuations of mood. It is a page of sorrow, contrition, and penance, very sincere but quite unbalanced. To follow all the markings exactly is the basic requirement; to transform those markings into moving lines is the work to be done.

"O mia Regina, io t'immolai" is legato, mezzo piano, with affection. The silence after "immolai" seems a respiratory spasm, followed by an involuntary attack forte, which turns mezzo forte on the triplet of quarter notes. "Di questo cor" is apologetic and pianissimo, "solo in un chiosto" the accepted, almost welcome penance. There is another involuntary strong note on "dovrò," attenuated in the triplet, almost fading on "il mio dolor." The two "Ohimè" are near tears. There is a little more stability in the next six bars, a good opportunity for an even and warm legato. Then a stringendo and crescendo mark an increase, a wave of violent repentance in Eboli's heart, culminating in an almost hysterical outcry in a broad B-flat forte, tenuto, expanding into the following triplets. A breath comes before "al mondo," the next after "celar." The last notes, "il mio dolor," are sung freely and deeply felt.

All the above indications are nothing but an attempt to put nouns and adjectives where musical markings are. They must be studied and understood and then adapted to the sensitivity of the individual performer. But throughout, whatever is suggested by Eboli's disturbed nerves, the quality of the voice must be maintained, a good quality free of artificial distortions and uncontrolled disorder. Therein lies the art of singing.

At this point a sudden thought hits Eboli and makes her frantic: Carlo is condemned to die the next day. In the *allegro più mosso* she confirms that fact to herself in a broken declamation that is a prelude to a new outburst, this time of crazed hope. The two phrases "Ah! . . un dì mi resta" and "la speme m'arride" are sung freely, broadly, with a ringing voice, the fermata on "m'arride" long and expanded. She blesses heaven for that one day still offered to her efforts to save him. "Sia benedetto il ciel" is sung full voice as well as "lo salverò." When the phrase starts anew with "un dì mi resta," it is both wise and expressive to use a moderate mezzo forte, again for the repeat of the same words, and to begin a crescendo only on "Ah, sia benedetto il ciel." After the word "ciel" the notes F, G, A-flat, and B-flat are usually sung on the vowel /a/, each one with a stress, not a punch, so that the voice spins from note to note without interruption of its vibration. The large silence after the B-flat should allow the singer to regroup and find again a very low support, in order to start the final "lo salverò" in full control of an intense voice, basically slim and vibrant, instead of risking disaster in an attempt to push through a massive tone.

It may seem that, while doing little more than paraphrasing, we have insisted here on saying what not to do. True, some readers of these lines may well have already mastered such passionate writings of Verdi's as this. For those, however, who are not yet masters, caution is compulsory. Intensity should never be confused with violence, and the more dramatic the singing, the more it should rely on coordination and beauty. It should also allow the singer to be in good voice the next morning.

Verdi, *Ernani*

"Ernani, involami" *soprano*

Sorta è la notte, e Silva non ritorna!	Night has fallen, and Silva does not return!
Ah! non tornasse ei più!	Ah! may he never return,
Questo odiato veglio,	this hateful old man,

che quale immondo spettro	who like a filthy ghost
ognor m'insegue.	follows me incessantly.
Col favellar d'amore	With his gibberish of love
più sempre Ernani	he plants Ernani ever more firmly
mi configge in core.	in my heart.
Ernani, Ernani, involami	Ernani, Ernani, take me away
all'abborrito amplesso.	from this abhorred embrace.
Fuggiamo. Se teco vivere	Let's flee. If love grant me
mi sia d'amor concesso,	to live with you,
per antri e lande inospite	to caves and inhospitable moors
ti seguirà il mio piè.	my foot will follow you.
Un Eden di delizia	An Eden of delights
saran quegli antri a me.	those caves will be for me.
Tutto sprezzo che d'Ernani	I disdain what to this heart
non favella a questo core:	does not speak of Ernani:
non v'ha gemma che in amore	there exists no precious stone
possa l'odio tramutar.	that changes hatred to love.
Ah! Vola, o tempo, e presto reca	Ah! Fly, o time, and quickly bring
di mia fuga il lieto istante.	the happy moment of my escape.
Vola, o tempo: a core amante	Fly, o time: for a loving heart
è supplizio l'indugiar!	waiting is torture!

Victor Hugo's drama of *Hernani* was an early and bold product of the romanticism movement. As in that famous drama, Elvira, a young lady of nobility, lives in the castle of Silva, her aging uncle, to whom she is betrothed despite the difference in their ages. That union is repulsive to Elvira, all the more so since she has fallen in love with the outlaw Ernani who leads a group of rebels in revolt against the king of Spain. The young woman sees the rebel secretly in her private apartments when he comes down from his mountain retreat.

Elvira sings this aria in the solitude of her richly appointed bedroom. Silva is absent, and Ernani has not appeared. Her voice is a lirico-spinto, extremely brilliant, nimble, and flexible. The aria consists of a short recitative, a very ornate cavatina, and, after cutting two choral pages, a vivacious cabaletta. Every line of the aria requires vocal security and virtuosity as well as a soaring and romantic flame of love.

The first phrase of the recitative is simply informative, sung mezzo forte, slowly, almost gloomily. The night is dark, the mention of Silva without warmth. The phrase should reveal the melancholy feelings of Elvira, alone and passive. But with "Ah! non tornasse ei più," sung forte and faster, the passionate nature of Elvira reveals itself. "Odiato veglio" and "immondo spettro" are strongly accented words of disgust and hatred, and "ognor m'insegue" is dropped with contempt and little voice. But it is this disgust, this contempt, that makes Ernani even more desirable. While still speaking of Silva, Elvira sings the music of love . "Col favellar d'amore" flourishes on the short run of "amore" (a short fermata is permissible on the second G), and the dear name "Ernani" is sung with rapture, "mi configge in core" with joy. It is possible to sing the final "-ge" of "configge" on the last C of the bar, to breathe, and to sing "in" on the last B-flat, in order to give the end of the phrase, "in core," a fine lyric expansion. The recitative, started in Silva's gloom, has spontaneously turned into Ernani's radiance.

This radiance inspires the whole cavatina. Two bars only are concerned with the hated old man, "l'abborrito amplesso," but through their physical implication they throw Elvira irresistibly into Ernani's arms. The tempo of the *andantino* is basically ♩ = 60, but for both expression and vocal comfort it is subjected to many fluctuations. The voice, ringing, enthusiastic, almost weightless, seems to bounce in almost every phrase from a start in the low range to shining high notes. "Ernani, involami," "Fuggiamo. Se teco vivere," and "mi sia d'amor" are written that way, as is "per antri e lande inospite." A powerful drive animates Elvira's singing, but suddenly she becomes submissive, saying pianissimo, "te seguirà il mio piè," even though she knows that Ernani can offer her only caves and grottos. That irresistible élan finds a more and more outspoken expression with each new musical line, but it also needs an ever more precise and sophisticated vocal treatment. In bars 14–17 ("Un Eden") we find five notes staccato and several strong accents, some on syncopated values, while the dynamic range goes from piano to fortissimo to piano again. The soprano must have trained herself to sing an absolutely free tone, placed in light forward words, bouncing weightlessly on a distant support. That type of singing will now find two contrasted applications in the next lines. "Un Eden" suggests to Elvira a legato, including portamenti (bar 18) and long tenutos (bars 21 and 23–24), or a jubilant pattern of runs ("saran quegli antri per me"). The long values on "Eden" are crescendo-decrescendo, the vowel /e/ vibrant and slim, the face of the singer opened by an enchanted smile. The value of the second long "Eden" can be prolonged at will in the bar with the fermata, provided that the longer tone expresses still greater delight. The coloraturas on "saran quegli antri" are fast but may ease the tempo a little if needed. Their ending is piano and rallentando.

Although various cadenzas have been suggested to end the cavatina, there is nothing wrong with the one printed in the score. The soprano can indulge in a fermata on the high C and make an accelerando on the way down, a ritardando on the last four notes of the run, and a sensitive piano on the G-flat and F of "-den." In order to push the feeling of enthusiasm to its limits, the last few notes can be given as shown.

The cabaletta is an *allegro con brio,* ♩ = 126, marvelously animated, elegant yet still impassioned. In the pages that are cut, the chorus rejoices at the thought of the wedding of Silva and Elvira, whom so many Spanish girls envy. Elvira receives their tribute but, as a challenge aside, rejects all that is not Ernani. The first eight bars of the cabaletta express that rejection. The phrase begins piano, then grows to mezzo forte on Ernani's name (third bar), returns to pianissimo with disdain in "non favella a questo core," and becomes indignant and forte on "possa l'odio tramutar." The silence that cuts the word "tramutar" in two is like a scornful chuckle. Elvira's mood changes suddenly with the trill and the fermata on F, bar 9. That bar is sung very slowly, the trill strong and long, the grace notes and the triplet very soft and prayerlike. With bar 10 comes a vivid *a tempo,* with the same élan as in the cavatina but for four bars with a murmuring voice, in a kind of secret enjoyment. Bars 21 and 22 bring a melting prayer, sung slowly, with soft downward portamenti. The syllable "-re" of "core" is sung on the D of the last triplet of bar 22. Then, after a breath, with the "a-" of "amante" sung on the last note C of that bar, the *allegro con brio* takes hold of the singer and will never relent until the end of the piece. Only one verse of the cabaletta is used, so that after bar 26 there is a cut to the end of the similar run in the second verse, and only the last nine bars of the vocal music are sung, entirely as a vocalise on "Ah," if possible with a slight accelerando, with the full power of the brightest possible voice. The B-flats are no problem if the voice is used weightlessly and with brightness. After the trill fortissimo on the last F, the last B-flat can be held at will. There is tremendous vitality in this ending. Verdi succeeded here in combining vocal virtuosity with passionate intensity. Only a soprano who is capable of both can triumph in this aria. What a worthy challenge to meet!

Verdi, *Falstaff*

"È sogno? o realtà . . ."   *baritone*

È sogno? o realtà . . .	Is this a dream? or reality . . .
Due rami enormi crescon	Two enormous horns are growing
sulla mia testa.	on my head.
È un sogno?	Is it a dream?
Mastro Ford! Dormi?	Master Ford! Are you asleep?
Svegliati! Su . . . ti desta!	Wake up! Come . . . get up!
Tua moglie sgarra	Your wife is straying
e mette in mal'assetto	and debases [puts in bad order]
l'onor tuo, la tua casa	your honor, your house,
ed il tuo letto.	and your bed.
L'ora è fissata,	The time is set,
tramato l'inganno,	the betrayal plotted,
sei gabbato e truffato!	you have been cheated and swindled!
E poi diranno . . .	And yet people will say . . .
che un marito geloso	that a jealous husband
è un insensato.	is a crazy man.
Già dietro a me	Already at my back
nome d'infame conio	they hiss names of infamous meaning
fischian passando;	as I pass;
mormora lo scherno.	sneers are whispered.
O matrimonio: inferno!	Oh matrimony: hell!
Donna: demonio!	Woman: a demon!
Nella lor moglie	In their wives
abbian fede i babbei!	only fools have faith!
Affiderei la mia birra a un Tedesco,	I would entrust my beer to a German,
tutto il mio desco a un Olandese lurco,	all my food to a greedy Dutchman,
la mia bottiglia d'aquavite a un Turco,	my bottle of brandy to a Turk,

non mia moglie a sè stessa.	not my wife to herself.
O laida sorte!	Oh wretched fate!
Quella brutta parola in cor mi torna:	That ugly word turns around in my heart:
"Le corna!" Bue! Capron!	"The horns!" Ox! Old buck!
Le fusa torte!	The twisted horns!
Ah! "Le corna! Le corna!"	Ah! "The horns! The horns!"
Ma . . . non mi sfuggirai!	But . . . you shall not escape from me!
No! Sozzo, reo,	No! Filthy, perverse,
dannato epicureo!	damned epicurean!
Prima li accoppio,	First I shall match them,
e poi li colgo,	and then I shall catch them,
li accoppio, li colgo!	match them, catch them!
Io scoppio!	I am choking!
Vendicherò l'affronto!	I shall avenge this outrage!
Laudata sempre sia	From the bottom of my heart . . .
nel fondo del mio cor . . .	be jealousy
la gelosia.	praised forever.

In the time of this opera there lived in the city of Windsor an enormously fat, conceited, unscrupulous man, a former soldier, a drunkard, Sir John Falstaff. In this chapter of his history he is courting no less than two women, the wives of Windsor's burghers, Alice Ford and Meg Page. The outraged women plot their revenge, and so does Mr. Ford. The latter, however, is not aware of the women's plan. This lack of coordination between the two projects will create a serious misunderstanding. Assuming a false identity, Ford goes to meet Falstaff and becomes convinced that his wife encourages Falstaff's advances, since she has arranged a date with him for that very day. Falstaff's delirious satisfaction is increased by the joy of cuckolding Mr. Ford. Left alone and in deep shock, Ford gives free rein to his jealousy in the aria "È sogno? o realtà."

The aria is written for a lirico-spinto baritone with an excellent high range and great versatility of expressions and colors. A gem filled with opportunities for acting, the aria is also a very telling solo and audition piece.

Before going any further it must be understood that in the tradition of many European countries, a cuckolded husband is marked by horns on his forehead. (In the fourth act of *The Marriage of Figaro*, Figaro, under the delusion of his fiancée's betrayal, tests his forehead while Mozart has the horns playing conspicuously in the orchestra.) In the pages preceding the aria Falstaff has boasted that he will surely make a pair of horns grow on Ford's head. On the music heard in the four bars preceding the aria itself, Falstaff has repeatedly mimicked the growing of the horns. These four bars must be played as a prelude to the aria.

Bewildered, Ford says "sogno" vaguely and slowly, then "o realtà" more concretely. Then, *a tempo,* ♩ = 108, he sings an enormous crescendo form piano "Due rami enormi" to "mia testa" shouted in horror. Trying to reassure himself, he murmurs uncertainly "È un sogno?" That alternation of violence and reflection is one of the striking characteristics of the aria.

As if pinching himself, Ford tries in short, pungent utterances (♩ = 120), "Svegliati, Su . . ti desta," to shake off what he still hopes is only a dream, and again an enormous crescendo reveals his horror fortissimo on "ed il tuo letto." Then he forces himself to check the facts dispassionately. "L'ora è fissata, tramato l'inganno" are somber phrases, and the next one, "sei gabbato," finally admits the inescapable truth. A superb phrase, much broader on time, ♩ = 80, and sung full voice, brings his feelings to a more general scope.

With the return of the tempo ♩ = 120, the motif of the horns returns, and Ford sees himself publicly disgraced and ridiculed. He sings piano as if in hiding, with just a hissing sound on "fischian." Suddenly, rage invades him. The two phrases, "O matrimonio" and "Donna: demonio" are violent curses that end in helplessness with "Nella lor moglie . . ." As the orchestra jumps several times to fortissimo outbursts, he contemplates the paradox of his situation. He would not hesitate to entrust food and drink to gluttons and drinkers, but he cannot entrust his wife to herself. The three phrases "Affiderei . . .," "tutto il mio desco . . .," and "la mi bottiglia . . ." are rather relaxed, with only a slight crescendo from one to the next, but "non mia moglie" is a desperate explosion.

The obsessive motive of the horns is heard again in the orchestra, and Ford loses control of himself. The horns seem to have gained a concrete existence—"Le corna"—and he fights them, shouts at them, sees himself debased to the status of an animal. The fury that has to be expressed in this page is intense, and the singer must not hold back. But it takes great control of the voice to avoid forcing and getting tired. In such circumstances it is best to try for a ring and not for bulk, especially in this aria, for without any transition Ford transfers his intensity to the idea of revenge. The last enraged words "Ah! Le corna! Le corna" must be vocally of a quality that allows them to spin into the "Ma" G-flat, which has to be a tone of beauty and great strength. Now the insults are directed at Falstaff and bring a short relief to Ford's tensions. For "dannato epicureo" the baritone must find round, open vowels /a/ in his mouth resonance in order to avoid letting his expressive words die for lack of sound.

Ford now yields to an irresistible fancy: He will surprise the guilty ones, he will catch them, thinking now in the plural and including his wife in the nightmare. The repetition of the words "colgo" and "accoppio" becomes more and more feverish; he is about to burst. Here is an opportunity for a marvelous work of interpretation, but with constant care to control the expenditure of voice. A crisp, dental, biting type of sound will probably be the safest here. The following orchestral bars give the singer time to regain his complete composure, rebuild his support, check the depth of his breath, and be prepared for the glorious finale that is expected from him.

"Vendicherò l'affronte," although already quite poised, still keeps some of the previous violence. But during the tremolo leading into the much slower tempo ♩ = 80, a sense of greatness must penetrate the singer. The line "Laudate sempre" starts piano with surprising serenity. The voice grows louder on "nel fondo del mio cor," becomes brilliantly lyric on the G ("mio cor"), and must reach its full power at the end of the E-flat ("gelosia"), this last vowel /a/ being repeated and amplified to the end of the value. The climax of this finale is not on the G, as important as that note may be, but in the powerful expansion of the phrase after the G, the word "gelosia" being the keyword of the entire aria.

Let us remember here that an interpreter must have two personalities. While one participates to the hilt in the life of the character impersonated, the other observes from the outside and regulates, guides, and judges the activities of the first. Without the first personality there can be no sincerity, no intensity, no sensitivity. Without the second, there is no security, no style, no proportions. This aria puts their common work to a great test.

Verdi, *La Forza del Destino*

"Pace, pace" *soprano*

Pace,	Peace,
pace, mio Dio!	peace, o Lord!
Cruda sventura m'astringe	Cruel misfortunes forces me,
ahimè, a languir;	alas, to waste away;
come il dì primo da tant'anni	as on the first day of so many years
dura profondo il mio soffrir.	my suffering continues profound.
Pace, pace, mio Dio!	Peace, peace, o Lord!
L'amai, gli è ver,	I loved him, it is true,
ma di beltà e valore cotanta	but with such beauty and valor
Iddio l'ornò,	did God grace him,
che l'amo ancor	so that I love him still
nè togliermi dal core	and could not rip out of my heart
l'immagin sua saprò.	his image.
Fatalità, fatalità . . .	Tragic fate . . .
Un delitto disgiunti n'ha quaggiù.	A crime has separated us here on earth.
Alvaro, io t'amo,	Alvaro, I love you,
e su nel cielo è scritto:	and in heaven above it is written:
non ti vedrò mai più.	I shall never see you again.
O Dio, fa ch'io muoia;	O God, let me die;
che la calma può darmi morte sol.	since death alone can give me repose.
Invan la pace qui sperò quest'alma	In vain did this heart hope for peace,
in preda a tanto duol,	a prey to so much pain,
in mezzo a tanto duol.	in the midst of so much grief.
Misero pane, a prolungarmi vieni	Miserable bread, you come to prolong
la sconsolata vita.	my disconsolate life.
Ma chi giunge?	But who is coming?
Chi profanare ardisce	Who dares profane
il sacro loco?	this sacred place?
Maledizione!	Damnation!

Leonora sings this aria in the concluding scene of a very long opera. It is one of the most desperate arias ever written. Years ago the man Leonora was about to elope with accidentally killed her father. In a vain effort to atone for her sin and in the belief that her lover had died, Leonora became a recluse, living in a grotto near a convent. Her daily bread is placed by her door, and she never sees a human being. At the start of the aria her voice is heard coming from inside the grotto. Then, stepping out and, as always, obsessed with her love and her sin, she calls on the Lord to grant her peace, in life or in death.

Following the insistent motif of fate in the orchestra, the voice enters on a prayer for peace (part A in the voice-piano score), made the more urgent by the extreme weariness of the lonely woman. Her first word is "Pace," a long wail but vocally controlled. A true vowel /a/ is started in a vibrant piano, increased in intensity to forte, and diminished to piano, the length of the value left to the good taste of the soprano, the crescendo and decrescendo absolutely essential. The tempo of the aria then establishes itself at ♩ = 56, stately but nevertheless constantly flexible in order to accommodate the successive tragic changes in Leonora's words. "Pace" is repeated twice, now starting the supplication mezzo forte and letting it fade, as if without hope. "pace, mio Dio" is soft and weary, the triplets sung slowly, the D on the second "Dio" sustained and stressed.

After the four bars of interlude Leonora recalls the cause and length of her misery with extreme sadness. The marking *con dolore* suggests a voice without great power reaching in pain from note to note, dividing the phrases with short breaths after "sventura," after "primo," and after "dura," unfolding the triplets slowly but with an inner tension that precludes any false sobbing or flattening of the end of note values. There is an upsurge of suffering on the F in "Pace," a touching helplessness in the next "pace," but a crescendo in the last "pace, mio Dio," which prepares a startling change of mood.

Part B is given to an ardent affirmation of Leonora's lasting love for Alvaro, a man without peer, a man doomed by fate. Her voice comes suddenly to life, and if the tempo stays the same, the handling of the words and phrases suggests a very different pace. The sixteenth note starting "L'amai" should come abruptly and give the short phrase "L'amai, gli è ver" strength. The voice becomes warmer and rounder on "di beltà e valore," and a breath is taken to prepare a long lyric span, with the next breath coming only after "l'amo ancor." A portamento joins "l'ornò" with "che l'amo ancor" in a sweeping élan of lyricism; "nè togliermi dal core" is firm and in rhythm, "l'immagin sua" slow and tender, the grace notes helping to create a feeling of love.

But fate did not allow that love to be rewarded. "Fatalità" is attacked forte, with the sixteenth note again sharp and abrupt. The repeats of the word are said in defeated sadness, the third one whispered. All Leonora can do is to acknowledge that defeat once more. The descending phrase, "Un delitto disgiunti n'ha quaggiù," is passive, the ending slow and colorless.

Her mood changes again in a second, however, and the name of Alvaro has the ring of worship, "io t'amo" as true a sound as if it were a declaration of young love. With the crescendo on "cielo" and the quotation "non ti vedrò mai più," the next phrase, by stressing the terrible injustice of fate, prepares the desperate outburst that follows. (Note that "non ti vedrò mai più" must be separated from the preceding "scritto.")

Part C is a wild outburst of sorrow, a call for death as the only hope for peace. The fate motif starts it, faster than before, and the words come rapidly and pressing, with a very strong rhythm on "che la calma può darmi morte sol." "Invan la pace" becomes frantic, the long values on "pace" and then on "quest'alma" grow to forte, and "in preda a tanto, tanto duol" goes violently to fortissimo. Here an accepted Italian custom allows breaking the phrase after the E-flat and restarting it on the G-flat, singing a long "Ah" piano, and after a portamento to the middle G-flat singing very piano and slowly "in mezzo a tanto, tanto, duol." If that liberty is taken only as a technical trick, it should not be taken. If it is treated in such a way as to suggest a climax of despair reaching the breaking point, in fact followed by a breakdown, and if the soprano really feels it that way, then it will be acceptable and probably telling for the listener. The high B-flat pianissimo should not be a difficult note if the three preceding middle B-flats have already been sung piano and in very high resonances and the vibration then spun slim and light to the high note. An expression of deep yearning would, of course, help that tone to stay alive and in line with the rest of the music, especially with the incoming high A-flat, which expresses the same overwhelming yearning.

A detail: In the bar after the high B-flat the eighth note on the syllable "-ma" of "alma" can be divided in two sixteenths, the syllable "In-" of "Invan" being sung on the second sixteenth after a breath.

The last two vocal measures of part C are sung freely, more and more slowly, with a fermata on the last "alma" as well as on the last "invan sperò," so as to express an infinite hopelessness and a terminal weariness.

In part D Leonora remakes contact with concrete matters. Sing grimly and without color from "Misero pane" to "vita." The sudden *allegro* paints her violent surprise at hearing human noises reaching her usually deserted retreat. "Ma chi giunge?" is piano. Indignation follows surprise, with a crescendo in the phrase "Chi profanare . . ." The word "Maledizione" is at first sung mezzo forte, but more strongly with each repeat, the last time fortissimo. The long tenuto on the F must be an active moment, the vowel /o/ repeated mentally several times and growing ever more resounding before spinning smoothly into the B-flat without a punch or a muscular drive. It is the perfection of the ring of the voice that will make that last note powerful, not a muscular effort to make it big.

This desperate aria offers an intelligent and sensitive interpreter countless opportunities to be human and feminine, to inspire pity, to move the hearts of the listeners. Even if it has some wild and frantic moments, the sure way to ruin it would be to sing it from forte to fortissimo all the way because it is written for a dramatic soprano. That way would also ruin the singer. In Verdi's music there is always so much sincerity within the dramatic skill that nothing artificial or in questionable taste need be or should be attempted when singing it. Leonora's despair in this aria builds a haunting and powerful tragic scene.

Verdi, *Luisa Miller*

"Quando le sere" *tenor*

Oh! fede negar potessi	Oh! could I refuse to trust
agl'occhi miei! . . .	my eyes! . . .
Se cielo e terra,	If heaven and earth,
se mortali ed angeli	if mortals and angels
attestarmi volesser	wanted to affirm
ch'ella non è rea . . .	that she is not guilty . . .
Mentite! io risponder dovrei,	You are lying! I would have to reply,
tutti mentite!	you are all lying!
Son cifre sue!	This is her writing!
Tanta perfidia!	Such perfidy!
Un'alma si nera!	A soul so black!
si mendace!	so deceitful!
Ben la conobbe il padre!	Well did my father know her!
Ma dunque i giuri,	And yet the promises,
le speranze, la gioia,	the hopes, the joy,
le lagrime, l'affanno . . .	the tears, the sorrow . . .
tutto è menzogna,	all is falsehood,
tradimento, inganno!	betrayal, deceit!
Quando le sere	When on evenings
al placido chiaror	filled with the peaceful glow
d'un ciel stellato	of a starry sky
meco figgea nell'etere	she turned her loving gaze with me
lo sguardo innamorato	to the firmament
e questa mano stringermi	and I felt this hand being pressed
dalla sua man sentia . . .	by her hand . . .
ah! mi tradia!	ah! she deceived me!
Allor, chi'io muto, estatico	While I, mute, in ecstasy,
da'labbri suoi pendea	hang on her words
ed alla in suono angelico	and she in an angelic voice
"amo, amo te sol" dicea,	said "I love you, you alone"
tal che sembrò l'empireo	so that the heavens seemed
aprirsi all'alma mia! . . .	to open themselves for my soul . . .
ah! mi tradia!	ah! she deceived me!

Luisa Miller is the daughter of an old soldier of modest means. She loves the young Carlo, who is passionately in love with her. Carlo passes for a peasant in the village but in truth is Rodolfo, son of Count Walter, the lord of the county. Infuriated by Rodolfo's refusal to renounce Luisa and marry a young woman of his rank, the count takes advantage of other serious conflicts and throws Luisa's father in jail. In the hope of saving his life Luisa agrees to write Rodolfo a letter, telling him that not love but greed for his wealth had attracted her to him. This aria is his desperate reaction to the reading of the letter.

Rodolfo's voice is a lirico-spinto, the same kind of voice for which most of the tenor roles are written in the great Verdi dramas, the voice of his tragic lovers. The enchanting and passionate melody of this aria is framed by a recitative and a coda which require great dramatic power. The case here is that of a dramatic voice required to sing with singular loveliness.

The recitative is immediately fortissimo, the declamation showing a violent indignation as well as cruel suffering. The singer must remember from the start that the power he needs must be well channeled, even in violence. Each phrase, even a short one, must be a continuous vibration aiming at a climactic syllable and avoiding chopping and pounding on the way to its goal. The first phrase aims at the G in "potessi," and after the short silence that stresses growing indignation, the second aims at "miei" with a stress on the B-flat. The same pattern applies in the next phrases to "terra," "angeli," "volesser," and "rea." An incisive vowel /i/ is the principal tone of "mentite." As for "tutti mentite," a real vowel /u/ as in *loose* will make the voice sound its best before returning to the vibrant /i/ as used just before. Constant changes of speed from phrase to phrase and inside a phrase give life and spontaneity to the singing, which here, despite the range, must stay as near as possible to speech. The singer should try several variations of those rubatos and decide on the ones he finds most natural.

"Son cifre sue" carries the expression of despair created by the evidence of the betrayal. Again a true vowel /u/ in "sue" will give the note the right ring. A bitter accusation colors "Un'alma si nera! si mendace" and a rueful, almost sobbing acknowledgment of error the "Ben la conobbe il padre." From "Ma dunque" to "tradimento" the line is a furious crescendo, starting piano in disbelief, getting louder with each noun, exploding on "tutto è menzogna," and still more explosive on "tradimento" before deflating in a helpless "inganno." The beginning of that phrase is the only opportunity in the recitative for singing piano. It should be used to the utmost. The ears of the listeners will receive the full impact of the terrible forte of "tradimento" only if they have had a break from the general forte of the piece, which is almost shocking in its crude sincerity.

The tenor is given only three bars to shift from violence to a still passionate but very harmonious and almost serene cantilena. These bars are, it is true, very slow, but the adjustment nevertheless demands a real mastery of physical control and nervous balance. The tempo of the aria, ♩ = 44, must be absolutely steady. The physical power used to provide for the violence must stay as strong but must be used for sustaining a vibrant mezzo piano tone throughout the two verses of the aria. In fact, the aria is as intense as the recitative, only less outspoken and, of course, in a different mood.

In the tempo indicated everything becomes legato; the sixteenths are no longer short notes but must be sung with the same amount of tone as the longer values. An artist will find the proper color of the voice, as limpid as the evening air, as shining as the stars in the sky, as surrounded with spacious resonances as the spaces trembling with love in such a ritardando as "innamorato," after a passionate crescendo (bar 10 of number 38). It is indeed difficult to describe how to paint in sounds the contact of the lovers' hands. The way must be found through some personal, blessed remembrance. Above all, there should be no accelerando in bars 15 and 16 of number 38. The rhythm as written palpitates with emotion, but the lips of the singer take as much time as they can to say the unforgettable, even more strongly on the last "sentia." The crescendo-decrescendo on the high G and A-flat is full of passion, the fall from it to the last "ah! mi tradia" piano and heartrending, with the long fermata on the C of "tradia."

The intense crescendo comes earlier in the second verse, after a very piano start, and reaches mezzo forte on "angelico" with ecstatic feeling. In bar 10 of number 39 Luisa's words are alive in their briskness, and the ecstatic feeling endures until their repeat (in bar 16 of number 39), which brings grief into the voice, coloring the high G and the A-flat with a sorrow that grows deeper, but still with some restraint, in the resolution of the phrase, bar 19 of number 39.

The restraint will be replaced with open despair in the coda. The high A-flat on "mi tradia," bar 21, is already dramatic; a breath of intensity is taken before the ensuing "mi tradia." The final cadenza starts as if Rodolfo did not have the strength to pass in review the reasons for his grief, as if the words came with difficulty: "in suono angelico." He manages somehow to repeat her words and in five notes fortissimo exhausts what strength is left in him (ringing vowel /i/) before sinking into a deep depression. The last "ah! mi tradia" is sung piano, with a long fermata on the F-flat before the voice dies away.

Such an aria lends itself to exaggeration, but the contrast between the first recitative and the aria must be striking. Rodolfo has received a totally unexpected blow, a deadly one. The sweetness of his memories bears witness to the sincerity of a passion now unrequited. Some accents in the coda almost match the frenzy of the early lines but die in helplessness. When sung with sustained but restrained power, the cantilena is a piece of the greatest beauty.

Verdi, *Macbeth*

"Pietà, rispetto, amore"   *baritone*

Perfidi! All'Anglo contro me v'unite!	Traitors! With the English you unite against me!
Le potenze presaghe han profetato:	The prescient powers have prophesied:
"Esser puoi sanguinario, feroce,	"You can be murderous, ferocious,
nessun nato di donna ti nuoce."	no man born of woman will harm you."
No, non temo di voi,	No, I am not afraid of you,
nè del fanciullo che vi conduce!	or of the child that is leading you!
Raffermar sul trono	This assault will
quest'assalto mi debbe,	steady me on the throne,
o sbalzarmi per sempre.	or unseat me forever.
Eppur la vita sento	Yet I feel life
nelle mie fibre inaridita.	drained out of my entrails.
Pietà, rispetto, amore,	Pity, respect, love,
conforto a'dì cadenti,	the solace of waning days,
ah! non spargeran d'un fiore	ah! not one flower will they strew
la tua canuta età.	on your white-haired age.
Nè sul tuo regio sasso	Nor hope on your royal stone

sperar soavi accenti—	for tender words—
ah! sol la bestemmia, ahi lasso!	ah! only curses, alas!
la nenia tua sarà.	will be your dirge.

Macbeth and Banco, two generals in the army of Duncan, king of Scotland, have been listening to the witches prophesying that Macbeth will become king of Scotland and that Banco's descendants will in turn take Macbeth's place on the throne. Urged on by his own ambition as well as by Lady Macbeth's avidity, Macbeth slays Duncan and indeed becomes king. Later he disposes of Banco in a similar manner. Gathering behind Duncan's young son Malcolm, the noblemen of Scotland, however, revolt against Macbeth. With help from the English they are now holding him at bay in his own castle, and a decisive battle is imminent.

In this aria, although he still feels protected as predicted by the witches, Macbeth nevertheless has a premonition of death approaching. He bemoans having to die without love or respect, a cursed, hated man.

Following the abrupt end of an embattled prelude, Macbeth speaks angrily, with the full power of his voice, which must be richly resonant and dramatic. The recitative preceding the aria is made up of violently contrasting moods. All changes of tempo written for the orchestra also apply to the vocal line, as well as all indications of dynamics. The first word, "Perfidi," must explode with anger, strong consonants *p* and *r* stressing its intensity, and the first phrase confirms the mood. This mood changes during the two orchestra chords, as if they meant "but," the meaning being that the enemy is allied against him in vain. Sing "Le potenze presaghe" forte, with solemnity, with an accent of importance on "pres*a*ghe" and slowing down on the last word, "profetato."

The quotation from the "potenze presaghe" ought to be sung in imitation of the sound Macbeth had heard from them. It was the sound of a distant boy soprano speaking slowly and clearly. It is, of course, not desirable that a strong baritone reproduce a boy-soprano voice, but it can be suggested by attempting to sing the phrase like a light tenor, but with trusting firmness and a crescendo to "feroce," stressing that even Macbeth's crimes were protected by mysterious powers.

In the next bars allegro, the anger is replaced by challenge ("non temo di voi") and scorn ("nè del fanciullo"). The following phrase stresses the importance of the battle for Macbeth, with its alternative effects: "Raffermar sul trono" must be sung with authority and pride before the surprising contrary conclusion, "o sbalzarmi per sempre," which becomes slower and heavy with dark foreboding. The *adagio* prepared in this way is a reluctant acknowledgment of an inner exhaustion and should be sung darkly, note after reluctant note, the D-flat in "inarid*i*ta" pianissimo and tenuto.

The aria is a vocal piece of broad scope that reveals Macbeth's potential greatness. Here he sings like a man who has tested power, who could have used it well, who knows the price he will have to pay for having failed to do so. The words of the text are words of importance, the curb of the musical phrase is ample, the thoughts are far-reaching. Be prepared to sing with a deep support, a round, manly voice, a long legato line, and profoundly felt emotion.

The tempo indicated, $\sqcup$ = 50, meets all these demands. The voice starts with an intensely vibrant piano above a pianissimo orchestra. The C on "rispetto" is a grace note, very brief, so that the vowel /o/ of "rispetto" will be sung on C, grace note, B-flat dotted eighth note, and the vowel /a/ of "amore" will fall on the A-flat sixteenth note. (Some editions read "onore" instead of "amore.") In the second phrase the dots on the triplet of "cadenti" indicate a very light staccato, meaning commiseration. Stress well the syncopation of the C "ah," and make a short crescendo to the D of "non." The two accents on "canuta" indicate weariness. Breathe after "età," sing the following "non spargeran" mezzo forte, its repeat piano and without taking a breath. Breathe after "fiore," then sing the end of the phrase almost like a free cadenza, with a fermata on the D-flat on "tua," a very slow turn, and a tenuto on the "-ta" of "canuta."

The next phrase, "Nè sul tuo regio sasso . . ." is marked *con dolore* and *dolcissimo.* *Con dolore* no doubt requires a slightly darker set of vowels, *dolcissimo* certainly calls for darker vowels /a/ on "sperar" and "soave," and the light staccato again acquires a meaning of pity. Instead of the consolation of respect and affection engraved on his tombstone, for Macbeth in his grave there will only be never-ending curses. The voice must soar with full power for two and a half bars on "ah! sol la bestemmia," then diminish in self-pity before growing more forte, finally fortissimo with despair on the repeats of "sol la bestemmia," and ending the phrase diminuendo and piano.

After the one-bar interlude, the "ahi lasso" is weary and very piano. A new wave of despair creates a new wave of crescendo to the F forte with its fermata five bars before the end of the piece. In that bar a slight change has prevailed.

The words "ahi lasso" four bars before the end are very weary. In the following bar, the first part of the phrase "sol la bestemmia, ahi lasso" is sung vigorously, almost with violence, but the cadenza should be rubato (slow on the way up, faster on the way down, quite slow on the last four notes), piano and legato, with great sensitivity, the last "la nenia tua sarà" broadly sung. There is a considerable fermata on the "sa-" of "sarà" and a slight portamento between "sa-" and "-ra."

This aria is beautiful to sing. It must be done with the most profound earnestness, fitting the meditation of a man about to face a merciless battle who fears the rewards that his crimes deserve. The fact that he is so near death in all likelihood endows his complaint with a noble quality despite his guilt. Verdi has given his singer all he needs for an eloquent rendering of the complex, powerful tragedy taking place in Macbeth's soul.

Verdi, *Otello*

"Credo in un Dio crudel" *baritone*

Vanne; la tua meta già vedo.
Ti spinge il tuo dimone,
e il tuo dimon son io,
e me trascina il mio . . .
nel quale io credo inesorato Iddio.

Credo in un Dio crudel
che m'ha creato simile a sè
e che nell'ira io nomo.
Dalla viltà d'un germe o d'un atomo
vile son nato.
Son scellerato perchè son uomo
e sento il fango originario in me.
Sì! quest'è la mia fè!
Credo con fermo cuor—
siccome crede
la vedovella al tempio—
che il mal ch'io penso
e che da me procede
per mio destino adempio.
Credo che il giusto
è un istrion beffardo
e nel viso e nel cuor,
che tutto è in lui bugiardo,
lagrima, bacio, sguardo, sacrificio ed onor.
E credo l'uom gioco
d'iniqua sorte,
Dal germe della culla
Al verme dell'avel.
Vien, dopo tanta irrision, la Morte.
E poi? e poi? La Morte è il Nulla,
è vecchia fola il Ciel!

Go ahead; I see your fate already.
Your demon urges you on,
and I am your demon,
and mine leads me on . . .
an inexorable God in whom I believe.

I believe in a cruel God
who has created me in his likeness
and whom in anger I name.
From a vile germ or from an atom
vile I was born.
Criminal I am because I am human,
and I feel the original filth in me.
Yes! that is my creed!
I believe with a staunch heart—
as with the faith
of a young widow in church—
that the evil I conceive
and which proceeds from me
I carry out according to my destiny.
I believe that an honest man
is an actor, mocking
by his face as well as in his heart,
that all with him is a lie,
tear, kiss, glance, sacrifice, and honor.
And I believe man to be the toy
of an unjust fate,
from the germ in the cradle
to the worm in the tomb.
Comes, after so much derision, Death.
And then? And then? Death is Nothingness,
and Heaven is an old fable!

Iago, an ensign in the service of Admiral Otello, has been bypassed for promotion in favor of the younger Cassio. His disappointment pushes his evil mind to revenge, and he will satisfy his vengeful fury not only on Cassio but on Otello and his bride Desdemona as well.

"If I were an actor and had to act Iago, I should like to portray rather a spare, tall man, with thin lips, small eyes set close together like a monkey's, a high, receding forehead, and a head well developed at the back. His manner should be vague, nonchalant, indifferent to everything, skeptical, pungent. He should throw off good and evil sentiments lightly, as if he were something quite different from his actual utterances. . . . A man like this should deceive anybody, even his own wife to a certain extent" [Verdi, as quoted in Francis Toye, *Verdi, His Life and Works* (New York: Vintage, 1946), pp. 181–182].

Indeed, that is the way the role was played by Vanni-Marcoux, the great French baritone who spent most of his career in Chicago at the side of Mary Garden and whose place I took on short notice in Paris in 1931—when the Otello happened to be Lauritz Melchior. The monologue written by Boito and known as the "Credo" is not a translation or an adaptation of a Shakespearean monologue, but it assembles and condenses in one page several statements made by Iago in the course of the tragedy and even puts into words the obvious principles that, without being enunciated, guide Iago in his actions. During the short scene with Cassio that precedes the "Credo," Iago still projects the image described by Verdi. As Cassio leaves, he suddenly discards it. Without a witness to betray him, he bluntly reveals his true nature. This is the only time in the opera that Iago finds himself alone on stage and the only time he does not hide behind a disguise. The sudden, violent change comes during the three bars preceding letter *C* and the start of scene 2. The sound of the four figures of three sixteenths and one eighth rises and flutters lightly while a smiling Iago waves good-bye to Cassio—and the four equal figures of three sixteenths and one quarter note hit the ears like clenched fists, the fists of Iago suddenly tense and hardened in scornful hatred. He hates the puppet he has just manipulated and nastily predicts its doom. The first three phrases, to "il tuo dimon son io," must be sung darkly and piano (*cupo*) as if with clenched teeth, exactly on time. "E me trascina il mio" starts piano, with a great crescendo to "Iddio." Iago turns people into puppets, but he himself is the tool of an evil God whose power is now suggested by this crescendo and the following brassy, clamorous chords. During those chords Iago seems to swell with evil pride and sings fortissimo, boisterously, provokingly. (Do not hesitate to breathe after "crudel" in order to have your full power on "a sè." Scotti used to breathe twice during that phrase.) Stay fortissimo on the next phrase. From my own experience I recommend singing as shown here,

e   che nel- l'i -ra   io   no - - mo.

with a crescendo on the B-flat to the E-flat. The next three short phrases are said bitterly but with a touch of strange pride, which will explode on "son scellerato," with something like an excuse on "perchè son uomo," and with violence on "sento il fango originario in me." A tenuto is permissible on "originar*io*." "Sì, quest'è la mia fè" is sung with solemn finality.

A feeling of *scherzando* now replaces the solemnity in the orchestra, and Iago will soon follow it on "siccome crede la vedovella" for a mocking imitation (*ppp*) of a frail woman praying in church. Then he proudly stresses his mission to spread evil, crescendo to forte. Note the double dotted "da *me*" and the staccato dots on "per mio destino."

The next page shows Iago denying in an insulting way the very existence of virtue and justice in a long phrase chopped progressively into shorter bits, slowing down more and more (see the fifth bar of *F*), and culminating in a powerful rallentando on the sixth bar, "sacrifi*cio* ed onor." Holding the last syllable of "sacrifi*cio*" is certainly an intended climactic effect. Start the phrase "E credo l'uom" forte, after a deep breath and a check on your low support, but not fortissimo, for there is still another climax coming on the long

F-sharp on "germe." Be sure to make the accelerando as indicated on the four bars preceding that F-sharp, first, because it reinforces the expression of mad aggression, second, because it gives the voice the impulse needed for making the F-sharp an outstanding one lasting full-strength into the next bar while the words "dela culla" explode with scorn. It has been my experience that throughout these two pages the most efficient way of handling the voice is to settle for a very intense, vibrant sound, very deeply supported, and to avoid the use of a bulky tone, difficult to move and to bring to the feeling of fury implied in text and music.

At letter *G* we find a most impressive suggestion of the tomb that awaits all of us, and Verdi makes us hear, almost feel, the disturbing mastery of the worm. Sing the phrase with a dark, forward tone filling the mouth, and open bitterly the two vowels /ɛ/ in "verme" and "avel." With that phrase you should be able to suggest a shudder.

The clamorous chords return now, but subdued and dulled. Even Iago has to contend with the thought of death—and to wonder about what will happen to him afterward. All bravura is gone now from the voice: Sing meditatively, evenly, and piano. The two fermatas on "E poi" are long and diminuendo to vanishing. The phrase "La Morte è il Nulla" is preceded by (five) *ppppp* and does not carry a sense of tragedy: For a while Iago has been thinking of a punishment for his evil deeds, but if death is nothing, there is nothing to fear, and he can start smiling. Some singers have made the mistake of singing the word "Nulla" without a pitch and forte. I believe they are wrong. "Nulla" should stay *ppppp* and be said with relief. Convinced once more of his impunity, Iago can now give free rein to his satanic joy. He sings with a triumphant full voice, "è vecchia fola il Ciel." In a stage performance, and with the support of the proper acting, it is possible here to burst out in noisy, vocal, well-supported laughter. I found it improper in concert and would advise the performer to end the aria with a brilliant, sustained F, as written.

What type of baritone voice should sing this aria—or the role? As a lirico-spinto voice, mine was accepted in Europe but not in America, where a dramatic baritone was cast in the role. However, Toscanini always chose a lyric voice for Iago, and any solid, flexible, and intelligent baritone has the right to perform this masterly, bitter "Credo."

"Salce" (Willow Song)   *soprano*

Mi parea.	He seemed so to me.
M'ingiunse di coricarmi	He asked me to go to bed
e d'attenderlo.	and to expect him.
Emilia, te ne prego,	Emilia, I beg you,
distendi sul mio letto	spread out on my bed
la mia candida veste nuziale.	my white wedding gown.
Senti. Si pria di te	Listen. If before you
morir dovessi,	I were to die,
mi seppellisci con un di quei veli.	shroud me in one of those veils.
Son mesta tanto, tanto.	I am so sad, so sad.
Mia madre aveva una povera ancella	My mother had a poor maidservant,
innamorata e bella;	in love and beautiful;
era il suo nome: Barbara.	her name was: Barbara.
Amava un uom	She loved a man

che poi l'abbandonò.
Cantava una canzone: "la canzon del salice."
Mi disciogli le chiome.
Io questa sera ho la memoria piena
di quella cantilena:
"Piangea cantando nell'erma landa,
piangea la mesta.
O salce, salce, salce!
Sedea chinando sul sen la testa,
salce, salce, salce.
Cantiamo! Cantiamo!
Il salce funebre sarà la mia ghirlanda."
Affrettati; fra poco giunge Otello.
"Scorreano i rivi
fra le zolle in fior,
gemea quel core affranto;
e dalle ciglia le sgorgava il cor
l'amara onda del pianto.
Salce, salce, salce!
Cantiamo!
Il salce funebre sarà la mia ghirlanda.
Scendean l'augelli
a vol dai rami cupi
verso quel dolce canto.
E gli occhi suoi piangean tanto, tanto
da impietosir le rupi."
Riponi quest'anello.
Povera Barbara!
Solea la storia
con questo semplice suono finir:
"Egli era nato per la sua gloria,
io per amar . . ."
Ascolta! Odo un lamento.
Taci. Chi batte a quella porta?
"Io per amarlo e per morir . . .
Cantiamo, cantiamo!
Salce, salce, salce!"
Emilia, addio.
Come m'ardon le ciglia!
É presagio di pianto.
Buona notte.
Ah! Emilia, addio!

who then abandoned her.
She used to sing a song: the song of the willow.
Unpin my hair.
This evening my memory is full
of this song:
"She wept, singing on the lonely heath,
the sad girl wept.
O willow, willow, willow!
She sat bending her head on her chest,
willow, willow, willow.
Sing! Sing!
the weeping willow will be my garland."
Hurry; shortly Otello will come.
"The brooks were running
through the meadows in bloom,
that broken heart was moaning;
and her heart was flooded
with the bitter flow of tears from her eyes.
Willow, willow, willow!
Sing!
the weeping willow will be my garland.
The birds descended
in a flight of somber doves
to that sweet song.
And her eyes wept so much, enough
to stir the rocks to pity."
Put down this ring.
Poor Barbara!
She used to end the story
with this simple word:
"He was born for his glory,
I to love . . ."
Listen! I hear a moan.
Quiet? Who is knocking at that door?
"I to love him and to die . . .
Sing, sing!
Willow, willow, willow!"
Emilia, farewell.
How my eyes are burning!
It's a foreboding of tears.
Good night.
Ah! Emilia, farewell!

It is night. In Desdemona's bedroom a lamp hung over an image of the Madonna sheds the only light. Emilia, her companion, helps Desdemona undress for bed. Desdemona is sad and depressed. She does not understand why her husband, Otello, whom she loves and respects and who was so devoted to her, has suddenly insulted and mistreated her in public and cursed her. A premonition of death invades her and brings reminiscences of grief to her lips.

Desdemona's voice is a lirico-spinto of clear and warm quality. In the present aria it stays lyric except for one note at the end, and it will be valued for its sensitivity and simplicity. The soprano who sings this aria either on stage or in concert must feel the tragic circumstances in which Desdemona finds herself, unprepared, ignorant of any wrongdoing, and helpless. But the innocence of her soul, her feminine grace, her youth, must ring in her pure voice in spite of all the gloom.

The tempi printed in the score are, of course, right and must be respected.

To Emilia's question, "Era più calmo?"—without which it is indeed difficult to start the aria—Desdemona answers dimly, with a touch of anxiety in "d'attenderlo." When Otello comes, will Death come with him? Desdemona feels she must make her last arrangements. But there is such beauty in her that these arrangements will be made in lovely melodic phrases. The voice comes to life with "Emilia, te ne prego" and soars from piano to mezzo forte on the next phrase, in which words like "candida veste nuziale" must be sung with great purity of sound. A short intake of breath is permissible after "letto." The phrase ends pianissimo. Then, almost without raising her voice but with great intensity of feeling, Desdemona faces the idea of her own death and thinks of her shroud, which she wants to be soft and light. Make a slight crescendo and decrescendo on "veli," the sound on the tip of your lips. Then a stronger complaint breaks Desdemona's composure for a moment. "Son mesta tanto" goes almost to forte, and, after a breath, the second "tanto" is restrained again by willpower, and is all the more touching for it.

Desdemona's mind turns to a memory of her youth, a melancholy one, which fits her mood of the moment; the story of Barbara, her mother's servant, and of her desolate song. While there is here an indication of *recitativo*, the only liberties the soprano should take are in changing a little the pace of each short phrase, not its inner rhythm. Short hesitations before "era il suo nome" and "Barbara" will suggest that the memory comes back to Desdemona as she is singing. A similar short hesitation before "Cantava una canzone" and "la canzone del salice" will avoid the impression that Desdemona recites from a prepared text.

A practical order to Emilia changes the mood for a second, but even this practical voice must have a friendly sound, as it should every time the effect occurs later in the aria. The song is introduced by a lovely phrase, "Io questa sera. . . ." (vowel /e/). Then, respect the rubato—stringendo followed by an allargando—and sing this vowel /e/ again pianissimo on the tip of your lips for "cantilena."

The song is sung with great simplicity and with varied emotions, according to the text of each verse. The voice must stay sustained and vibrant all the time, even though the dynamic level is not above mezzo forte. The purity of the vowels and of the sound remains a must throughout. The quasi-arpeggiando pattern at the beginning of the first three verses must start piano and soar briskly to the F-sharp, brilliantly delivered but without changing the rhythm as written. A fermata on that note is not motivated and therefore not permissible. The first breath comes before "piangea la mesta." All the "salce" should come from a faraway voice whispering to Barbara of the nature of her funeral garland, discreetly and with insistence. The word "salce" is built around a clear vowel /a/, and the *l* that follows must be made by the tip of the tongue against the back of the upper teeth, so that the distant-sounding word stays crisp and understandable.

In the second verse the breath comes before "la testa," and the first "salce" is forte, almost like a threat. "Cantiamo," a soaring, weightless line, is first *dolce*, then still *più piano.* The key phrase, "Il salce funebre . . ." is mezzo forte and intense. It should be sung without a breath. In case of emergency a breath can be taken after "funebre."

The almost spoken phase "fra poco giunge Otello" is loaded with contrary feelings dominated by anxiety. The third verse, longer and more accented, can be sung a little faster and more dramatically. The fourth, soft and fluid, is poetic but ends in desolation. At this point Desdemona, no doubt symbolically divesting herself of her wedding ring, feels that the song must come to an end. It is as if a deep sigh preceded her heartfelt "Povera Barbara," ending pianissimo. She introduces the conclusion of Barbara's song, "Solea la storia . . .," with no more than a murmur. That conclusion is the conclusion of her own life. "Egli era nato per la sua gloria," marcato, seems an exact reference to Otello, as "io per amarlo e per morir," dolcissimo, is an exact reference to herself.

The dramatic interruption of the song has delayed the words "e per morir." They are all the more moving when they are heard, piano and rallentando when the song rings again; and with "Cantiamo," also pianissimo and rallentando, and the remote last "salce" dying away, Desdemona is left to face a barely different reality. The tempo becomes faster, the voice more concrete, the signs of emotion more physical, until at the marking *come prima* the long D-natural in the orchestra suspends all feelings. "Buona notte" is said with absolute simplicity, as though it were any other night. The outburst on the A-sharp must be extremely strong and tenuto; then the words "Emilia, Emilia, addio" tumble down almost in disorder—not quite, of course. During the chords between "Buona notte" and the "Ah! Emilila," without losing her sentimental intensity the soprano can prepare an outstanding high A-sharp by rebuilding her very low support and mentally spinning the vibration of her voice progressively from the F-sharp to the high A-sharp.

That vocal advice should not detract from the understanding that such a page as this does not live by technique and vocal work alone. It reflects the anguish and the dignity of a sensitive soul able to translate into a poetic song the darkest torments. The piece is worthy of the most sympathetic attention of the greatest singers, but it is also an aria that students should practice at length, learning from it that musical cleanliness is the way to human greatness.

"Ave Maria"   *soprano*

Ave Maria piena di grazia,
eletta fra le spose e le vergini sei tu,
sia benedetto il frutto, o benedetta,
di tue materne viscere, Gesù.
Prega per chi adorando a te si prostra,

prega pel peccator, per l'innocente,
e pel debole oppresso;
e pel possente, misero anch'esso,
tua pietà dimostra.
Prega per chi sotto l'oltraggio
piega la fronte,
e sotto la malvagia sorte;
per noi tu prega, prega sempre

Hail Mary full of grace,
chosen are you among the women and virgins,
blessed be the fruit, o blessed one,
of your maternal womb, Jesus.
Pray for the adoring one who prostrates himself
    before you,
pray for the sinner, for the innocent,
and for the weak and oppressed one;
and for the powerful one, who too is miserable,
show your mercy.
Pray for him who under the outrage
bends his head,
and under a malevolent fate;
pray for us, pray always

e nell'ora della morte nostra,
prega per noi, Ave Maria,
Amen.

and in the hour of our death,
pray for us. Hail Mary,
Amen.

After Emilia's exit Desdemona, alone in her room, walks to the image of the Virgin, kneels on the prie-dieu, and says her evening prayer, a very fervent prayer indeed, sung with the same pure voice that has just finished the scene of the "Willow song."

The text of the ritual Ave Maria is psalmodied like a murmur, but exactly on time, in the beautiful sensitive rhythm written by Verdi. On the word "Gesù" all the anxiety in Desdemona's soul seems to overflow, and after holding the name of the Savior for a long time, she lets her personal prayer take the place of the ritual one.

The name of Gesù, started piano with devotion, must become more intense while the vowel /u/ lasts, five to six beats, then melt during the portamento upward into a soft "Prega." A breath can be taken here, a very short one. The phrase "per chi adorando" is humble, the syllables of the words "adorando a te" slightly detached. "Prega pel peccator" is said with simple warmth, while "per l'innocente" with its cresendo-decrescendo may be more personal, although meant in a general way. From there on Desdemona's prayer, couched in general human terms, appears to plead for the healing of Otello's and her personal troubles. The light, detached notes of "pel debole oppresso" actually underline her meaning discreetly. The powerful one in his misery also deserves help, a thought Desdemona stresses with great conviction, going to forte on "misero." The whole phrase, from "e pel debole" to "possente" should be sung in one breath. When this can not be done, it is customary to divide the quarter note on the syllable "-so" of "oppresso" into two eighth notes, singing "-so" on the first one, taking a breath and singing "e" on the second eighth note.

The next phrase, following the markings of *marcato, animando,* and *crescendo,* is dramatic. Desdemona openly prays for herself, passionately, but blames only fate for her ordeal. As above, it is possible to divide the quarter note on the syllable "-te" in "fronte" into two eighth notes, singing "-te" on the first eighth, breathing, and singing "e" on the second eighth.

Hoping that her particular intention has been heard and understood, Desdemona returns to a quieter tempo and addresses herself to the Virgin with confidence and with an intimate voice, again in the words of the ritual prayer, words that call for mercy at the time of our death. There is great serenity in her singing, as if she were already beyond the moment of danger or as if she had accepted the danger and no longer tried to fight it. The intensity of the serene prayer will emerge for an instant in the isolated "prega per noi," especially in the second one. The final "prega," however, on the E-flat rises to heaven free of human ties. At this point it is very important, even in concert, to follow the instructions of the score, which says: "she repeats mentally the prayer of which we hear only the first and last words." These last words, "nell'ora della morte" are replete with a cruel premonition that pride and dignity keep restrained. The last "Ave" takes flight on angels' wings—if the soprano can conceive it as a very slender vibration originating near the lips and kept slim from note to note, the top one heard in the vowel /e/. "Amen" concludes with total simplicity.

Whatever spiritual inspiration the singer feels in this beautiful aria, she has to transmute it into sounds. No soprano should attempt the "Ave Maria" who does not have complete command of the velvety, weightless pianissimo she needs to convey the exalted beauty of this page.

Verdi, *Rigoletto*

"Pari siamo"   *baritone*

Pari siamo! Io la lingua,	We are alike! I have the tongue,
egli ha il pugnale;	he has the dagger;
l'uomo son io che ride,	I am the man who laughs,
ei quel che spegne!	he is the one who kills!
Quel vecchio maledivami!	That old man cursed me!
O uomini, o natura,	O men, o Nature,
vil scellerato mi faceste voi!	a vile scoundrel you have made me!
Oh rabbia! esser difforme!	Oh rage! to be crippled!
Oh rabbia! esser buffone,	Oh rage! to be a jester,
non dover, non poter	not to be allowed, not able
altro che ridere.	to do otherwise than laugh.
Il retaggio d'ogni uom m'è tolto,	Every man's innate right has been taken
il pianto.	from me, the tears.
Questo padrone mio,	That master of mine,
giovin, giocondo, si possente, bello,	young, cheerful, so powerful, handsome,
sonnechiando me dice:	dozing he tells me:
"Fa ch'io rida, buffone."	"Make me laugh, jester."
Forzarmi deggio, e farlo.	I must force myself and do it.
Oh dannazione!	Oh damnation!
Odio a voi, cortigiani schernitori,	I hate you, you spiteful courtiers,
quanta in mordervi ho gioia!	how I enjoy stinging you!
Se iniquo son,	If I am hateful,
per cagion vostra è solo . . .	it is only because of you . . .
Ma in altr'uomo qui mi cangio!	But here I change into another man . . .
Quel vecchio maledivami . . .	That old man cursed me . . .
Tal pensiero, perchè conturba	That thought, why does it keep
ognor la mente mia?	disturbing my mind?
Mi coglierà sventura?	Will it bring me misfortunte?
Ah no, è follia!	Ah no, that's madness!

In the street outside the house where he keeps his daughter sheltered from the world, Rigoletto is accosted by Sparafucile. This assassin-for-hire offers the reluctant jester his services if and when needed. When he is gone Rigoletto reflects on his own fate and condition.

The aria has no introduction, and in concert or audition the accompanist should play the last two bars in F from the preceding number. The aria is a monologue. Rigoletto, thinking aloud, is totally candid and sincere. He has grown bitter, hating his profession, resenting his deformity (he is lame and a hunchback). And a short while ago he was cursed by a father whom he had taunted with the dishonor of his daughter. It is an aria loaded with emotions. The art of the singer will consist in suggesting them all while keeping them in the proportions established by the composer. The voice should aim at a great variety of colors and dynamics, stretching itself to the limits of technical security.

The tempo is *adagio*. Sing very slowly. ♩ = 56 is suggested.

"Pari siamo" is said with a somber voice: Both Rigoletto and Sparafucile are killers. It is not a pleasant fact to admit. They are killers with a difference, however. Sparafucile's weapon is a dagger, Rigoletto's his tongue. Sing "Io la lingua" with a bitter, sarcastic voice and "egli ha il pugnale" with brutality. Keep the same alternation for the next two short phrases, the /i/ in "che ride" acid and with a scornful portamento downward, "che spegne" with an obscure sound and piano, as if with fright. After a few steps suggested in the orchestra, Rigoletto sings the phrase that has been heard repeatedly since the very first bar of the overture, the phrase symbolizing the curse, an essential element of the score. (The original title of the opera was *La maledizione*.) It must be sung with an extreme legato, the voice carried from note to note without a break, starting piano, swelling to mezzo forte while holding the vowel /i/ in "maledivami," and dying away at the end of the phrase. It reveals the instinctive fear that has invaded Rigoletto's mind and nerves, a fear that might easily turn into an obsession.

The *allegro* following must be sung with intensity, anger, and bitterness but without reaching a real forte yet. Be sure to respect the very brief sixteenth notes and to stress the vowels on the downbeats: "*uo*mini," "nat*u*ra," "sceller*a*to," "v*o*i." There is a feeling of rebelling against fate but not yet an explosion. Even the two "rabbia" are more pronounced than exploded. It is too soon to reach a climax.

The next tempo, *adagio,* starts only on "ridere." The phrase "non dover . . ." is still in the *allegro* tempo, with the syncopation on "altro" clearly indicated. "Ridere" is piano and bitter. The whole phrase, "Il retaggio d'ogni uom," is very slow and pathetic, with sincere despair; "il pianto" is on the verge of a sob, started mezzo forte and ending piano.

During the introduction of the *moderato* Rigoletto thinks of his master the duke and, jester that he is, spontaneously impersonates him: tenor voice, carefree rhythm, nonchalance. Sing piano and crisply "Questo padrone mio . . ."; in a head voice very near falsetto, "Fa ch'io rida, buffone"; with a hollow voice "Forzarmi deggio, e farlo"; and, suddenly explosive fortissimo, "Oh dannazione." Now the hatred accumulated in Rigoletto's soul pours out, and the next three lines stay fortissimo. To stay strictly on time is the best way to give the phrases their full authority. The fact that each phrase is written a step higher than the preceding one insures a feeling of crescendo. Note that, if the first two phrases are pure hatred, the last two—still more the last one, "per cagion vostra"— are violent accusations. It is permissible to sing "per cagion" after the chord, to give the greatest possible importance to the voice. The correct rhythm of the phrase is shown.

per ca- gion vos-traè so - lo.

It should be possible to make an ultimate crescendo on "*solo*."

After the three chords fortissimo, on the three bars of *andante*, Rigoletto regains control of himself. He is home now and will return to his role of loving father. Sing a slim, vibrant tone mezzo piano with a very slight accent on each first eighth note in "uomo qui mi cangio." Then, after a long pause, the phrase of the curse is sung again, this time more bitingly, with double dotted quarter notes and sixteenths but with the same crescendo and decrescendo as the first time. Another long pause, during which Rigoletto wonders about the importance he involuntarily gives that curse. And it is with a meditative, somber voice that he says "Tal pensiero, perché . . ." mezzo piano. "Mi coglierà sventura" is a question, clearly enunciated, slightly anguished (stress the /u/ in ven-*tu*ra). But then, discarding his obsession, he says confidently and with a ringing voice "Ah no, è follia."

Tradition, by now irreversible, wants a G instead of the E on the /i/ of "follia." The meaning of his exclamation as a release from anxiety and not as an outcry of anxiety is corroborated by the French text in the original drama by Victor Hugo: "Pourvu qu'il n'aille rien m'arriver! [Haussant les épaules] Suis-je fou?" ("Let us hope that nothing will happen to me! [*With a shrug*] Am I crazy?") The consequence of that concept is that this "è follia" should be as near as possible to a laugh that makes light of the curse and should not be sung with a sad, heavy tone. Besides, it is a pleasure to the ear to hear that brilliant vowel /i/ held for a generous fermata, preparing the entrance of Rigoletto into his house where he hopes to find peace and solace.

Needless to say, a well-studied interpretation of this monologue will do a lot for the understanding of Rigoletto's character, just as the use of many vocal shadings will do a lot for the comfort and beauty of the singing.

"Caro nome"   *soprano*

Gualtier Maldé—
nome di lui si amato,
ti scolpisci nel core innamorato.
Caro nome che il mio cor
festi primo palpitar,
le delizie dell'amor
mi dêi sempre rammentar.
Col pensier il mio desir
a te sempre volerà,
e fin l'ultimo sospir
caro nome, tuo sarà.

Gualtier Maldè—
name of the one so beloved,
you engraved yourself in my heart in love.
Dear name which first
made my heart throb,
love's delights
you will always recall for me.
With every thought my longing
will always fly to you,
and even my last breath,
dear name, will be yours.

Rigoletto, court jester to the duke of Mantua, is a man surrounded by hatred and resentment. His daughter Gilda, whom he has raised in secret, is not aware of her father's true identity or of his occupation. Living in seclusion in the care of a watchful guardian, she has only recently in church noticed a young man who is clearly attracted to her. In the scene preceding the aria "Caro nome," the young man has managed to enter the garden of her secluded house, to declare his love, and to tell Gilda his name. When he is gone, a song of pure adoration rises to the lips of the young girl. The entire aria is dedicated to the young man's name, a name forever tied to the revelation of love in her virgin heart. Whatever the amount of technical skill demanded by the writing of the vocal line, the ecstasy of a first love is what the aria wants to suggest, and runs and coloraturas will only be means to describe and express this ecstasy. Failure to understand that priority must be given to the *emotional* content of the aria turns it into the meaningless showpiece it has become all too often, and turns Gilda into an insensitive puppet. Yet here is a girl who in the end will give her life for her lover!

The tempi must be respected exactly, ♩ = 80 at first, then ♩ = 76 for the E major. The notes must be sung as written, with no high notes or cadenzas added, except possibly in the final cadenza. The demand is for sensitive beauty, not for acrobatics. Gilda is certainly still in her teens, and while, having matured through suffering and misfortune, she may use a more dramatic voice in the third act, here she is, so to speak, still in the bud and must use a crystal-clear voice, mellowed by the sweet joy in her warm heart.

At first Gilda's voice is heard against a background of soaring flutes, and the voice should match their sound with radiance. The vowel /a/ in "Gualtier Maldé" must be bright with pleasure, the words long like a long sigh, the consonants firm but tying the vowels together, not separating them. The same indication applies to the next two lines, except that such figures as ♪· ♪♪· ♪ are made of long dotted notes, with the sixteenths aiming at the next note instead of being brief and dry. A light portamento upward in "ama-to" is permissible, as is a slight rallentando of enjoyment on "innamorato."

"Caro nome" starts piano. The phrase is not staccato but legato, sweetly interrupted by the eighth-note silences. In each bar the dotted half note must be fed by the support. It is as if the pungent little motif of the violins incited it to grow in intensity. This effect will also be obtained if you repeat the vowel mentally on the second and third beat. The portamenti upward on the fourth beats must be clear and light and should never create an impression of dragging. It is easy to breathe on any of the eighth-note rests, but you might feel better organized if you breathe with extreme discretion on the second eighth of the first beat, that is, after "pri-," after "li-," after "sem-," after "-sier."

On the eighteenth bar of the aria the rhythm changes but not the vocal feeling. The trills in the following bars still call for a very light brightness. A short fermata is usually accepted on the G-sharp "e fin l'ultimo," the tone starting mezzo forte and ending piano. Then the phrase concludes in utmost simplicity: Gilda is certain that this name, which she has heard for the first time only minutes before, will remain in her heart until her last breath.

More variety now enters into the singing line. But Gilda's dedication for life translates itself in long phrases: Do not stop the voice or the meaning after "il mio desir" (bar 27), but carry them into bar 28 and to the end of the cadenza, bar 29, which is sung rallentando and greatly diminuendo. This time, on bar 29, a fermata is written on the G-sharp, followed by the marking *dolcissimo*. The tone of the fermata then must be a diminuendo, the *dolcissimo* suggesting the sweet emotion of Gilda thinking of herself repeating the dear name in her last moment. A crescendo of expression fits the A on "caro," bar 31. On bar 32 it is customary to sing the two syllables of "nome" on E and D sharp, to take a breath, to sing a vowel /a/ on A-sharp–B–C-natural–A-natural–F-sharp–D-sharp–C-natural–B and "Caro nome, tuo sara," on the last six notes of the bar.

The incisive violin is heard for the last time on bar 33. The voice becomes still lighter, if possible, in order to easily reach the B on bar 35. Start singing this B as if it were to have a longer value. Once its spin has been established, it can be cut short. The danger here is in making it an insignificant little squeak by trying to start and stop at the same time, without allowing it a short life. There should be no additional high note on bar 37 and no shortening of the downward run. In order to reach the low notes, the tone must be brought as forward as possible on the lips, with a clear sound.

The following line, bars 38 to 40, is sung on the vowel /a/ with a delight that surpasses the meaning of any word. Try the sensation by singing only the upper notes, legato and with emotion. Then sing the line as written, barely touching the lower notes (but neither are they staccato).

There is no reason to make an accelerando on the next bars, as is often done. Bars 41 and 42 will get their life from the crescendo-decescendo written, bars 43 and 44 from the light mellowness of the singing—but all in the same tempo. Bars 45 and 46 are remarkable in the surprising reversal of the vocal line, with its enthusiastic ascent and the sudden emotion of the descent, sung with the same interrupted legato mentioned earlier. Bars 47 to 49 are sung firmly, bar 50 with more accents.

The first part of the last cadenza, going to the high C-natural, is used as printed in the Ricordi edition. The last part is modified most of the time. It seems that the most frequent change is that shown here.

The soprano who chooses to sing this last cadenza as indicated above must not forget to stay in character while getting and giving the satisfaction of her high notes. She must still imbue these high notes with the same radiant beauty present in the whole aria.

While Gilda's exit is not part of the aria, it, too, must stay in character. Standing outside the little garden in the darkness of the street and waiting for my cue, I have witnessed several disasters as some Gildas attempted to sing a totally meaningless high E. I have also had to wait a long time for the applause to stop when a better-advised Gilda exited on a beautiful trill on the middle E, as written by Verdi!

"Parmi veder le lagrime"   *tenor*

Ella mi fu rapita!	She has been stolen from me!
E quando, o ciel . . .	And when, o heavens . . .
ne'brevi istanti	in the short moments
prima che il mio presagio interno	before my premonition
sull'orma corsa ancora mi spingesse!	made my retrace my steps!
Schiuso era l'uscio,	The gate was open,

e la magion deserta! — and the house deserted.
E dove ora sarà — And where could that dear angel
quell'angiol caro? — now be?
colei che prima potè — She, who first was able to
in questo core destar — wake in this heart
la fiamma di costanti affetti? — the flame of constant love?
colei sì pura, — she so pure,
al cui modesto sguardo — by whose chaste glance
quasi spinto a virtù — I feel at times
talor mi credo! . . . — as if driven to decency.
Ella mi fu rapita! — She has been stolen from me!
E chi l'ardiva? — And who dared to?
Ma ne avrò vendetta: — But I shall have vengeance:
lo chiede il pianto — the tears of my beloved
della mia diletta. — demand it.

Parmi veder le lagrime — I seem to see the tears
scorrenti da quel ciglio, — flow from those eyes,
quando fra il dubbio e l'ansia — as in the uncertainty and the fear
del subito periglio — of her sudden danger
dell'amor nostro memore — remembering our love
il suo Gualtier chiamò. — she called her Gualtier.
Ned ei potea soccorrerti — And he could not succor you,
cara fanciulla amata; — dear beloved child;
ei che vorria coll'anima — he who with all his heart
farti quaggiù beata, — wanted to make you happy on earth,
ei che le sfere agli angeli — he who did not
per te non invidiò. — covet for you the angels' heaven.

The duke of Mantua had left Gilda's garden elated to find the young girl responding to his declaration of love. A few hours later he is seen walking in great agitation back and forth in one of the rooms of his palace. Gilda has been mysteriously abducted. Frustrated and mystified, he recalls the moment when, returning to Gilda's house, he found it unlocked and empty.

The piece consists of an extensive recitative and a cantilena aria. The role of the duke is sung by a lyric tenor, sometimes verging on the spinto. In these pages he needs vigor, warmth, flexibility, and a good imagination in order to follow the fast changes of the duke's mood.

The last five bars of the prelude introduce the duke and the recitative. They are very agitated, and the first words "Ella mi fu rapita" are sung rapidly, with a mixture of anger and disbelief, the syllable "-pi-" of "rapita" strongly stressed. "E quando, o ciel" and the following line, which tells how the duke retraced his steps to Gilda's house, reflect his haste in doing so. The words run quickly and freely. The short motif in the accompaniment suggests a sudden, startled stop. That is the expression for "Schiuso era l'uscio"and for "e la magion deserta." But even the duke could not prevent the abduction. He can only wonder about the fate of the "angel" who, he feels was about to lead him back to the path of virtue. The short *adagio* seems to reveal an unsuspected facet of the duke's character: That cynical man still nourishes the illusion that he could be capable of a sincere love. "E dove ora sarà quell'angiol caro" is sung very slowly, sweetly, yet with only moderate concern for Gilda. In contrast, the duke's voice will become more passionate when he thinks of himself in love with her and of the good this love could have done to his own character. The beautiful *andante* calls for great warmth and waves of lyric feeling. Observe the crescendo-decrescendo on "prima potè in questo core" and on "sì pura, al cui modesto" and the light staccato on these words. The last three bars of the *andante,* very light and nimble, may nevertheless color the duke's hopes for a return to virtue with some superficiality. A smile would add the right shading to the tenor's voice.

"Ella mi fu rapita" now suggests growing anger, and wounded pride rings in "E chi l'ardiva." These two lines and "Ma ne avrò vendetta" are fortissimo. A comma after "Ma ne avrò" adds strength to the repeat. But the vision of a despairing Gilda brings in a new *adagio,* in tender sympathy for her. "Lo chiede il pianto" is slow and soft. The cadenza grows from piano to a forte tenuto on the high B-double-flat. The Italian tradition has the tenor breathing after the E-flat in "mia," thus separating the possessive adjective from "diletta." This is done so that he will have plenty of breath for the considerably slower word "diletta." It seems to me that the same result can be reached by breathing before "mia." It is right, of course, to take all the time necessary in order to sing "diletta" with love and elegance.

A touching picture of Gilda in tears appears in the first lines of the aria. The marking is *pianissimo* for the accompaniment, certainly *piano* for the voice, the tone very friendly, slightly moved. The rhythm must be respected perfectly, it is so expressive of a sympathy that is not without some enjoyment. A Gilda in tears may prove to be singularly attractive. The portamento from "da quel ciglio" to "quando" is generally a tie, and a breath is taken after "quando." It would be a better idea, however, to make a portamento upward on "ciglio" and to breathe after the portamento and before "quando." There is nothing wrong in trying to respect both music and syntax, or is there? A good crescendo stresses the seriousness of the "subito periglio," which the duke understands very well. But he cannot think of love without giving himself an important role in it. Sweetly, lightly, he imagines that what happened in that sudden danger is that Gilda called his name, and that idea fills him with pleasure. There is a delight in the words "dell'amor nostro memore," said and repeated, after a breath. The composer has provided a silence in the accompaniment so that "il suo Gualtier chiamò" can be sung very slowly, with more than a little conceit.

There is some sincere regret in "Ned ei potea soccorrerti" and affection in "cara fanciulla amata" but no tragic sorrow of any kind. On the contrary, a certain nonchalance now permeates the duke's attitude toward the whole adventure. (Just as above, the portamento from "amata" to "ei che" can be made on "amata," and a breath can be taken before "ei.") Again the duke's love for Gilda is formulated in such a way that it is his part in it that emerges as the important element. He wanted to make her happy on earth, and that would have been even better for her than paradise. "Farti quaggiù beata" is full and generous; the delights of the angels' sphere ("ei che le sfere agli angeli") are presented in short values the first time, the second time with some more emphasis, providing the opportunity to sing a fine A-flat. But these delights are dismissed with an easy and free "per te non invidiò." There is a beautiful crescendo of range and expression in the next five bars, starting piano on "ei che le sfere," then climbing as if from springboard to springboard (the syncopated accents), with a breath before "per te" on the high A-flat. It is customary and most rewarding to sing the following bar as shown,

te   le   sfe - reagl'an - ge -li   per te

making a long fermata on the E-flat on "per te" before going slowly down the line. The vocalise part of the cadenza is not sung, only the last notes on "non invidiò per te," very slowly, and ending on a long G pianissimo.

It is, of course, possible to sing this aria beautifully with a fine, sonorous, young-sounding voice and without much concern for the psychological implications of the piece. But how much more interesting it is to add important touches to the character of the duke while singing the aria very well vocally. According to the score there is a formal portrait of the duchess on the rear wall of the room. Does it add to or detract from the sincerity of the pretended Gualtier Maldé?

"Cortigiani"   *baritone*

Cortigiani, vil razza dannata	Courtiers, vile accursed race,
per qual prezzo	at what price
vendeste il mio bene?	did you sell my loved one?
A voi nulla per l'oro sconviene,	To you nothing is improper for gold,
ma mia figlia è impagabil tesor.	but my daughter is a priceless treasure.
La rendete,	Give her back,
o se pur disarmata, questa man	or even unarmed this hand
per voi fora cruenta.	boring through you will turn bloody.
Nulla in terra più l'uomo paventa	Nothing on earth frightens a man anymore
se dei figli difende l'onor.	if he defends the honor of his children.
Quella porta, assassini	That door, you murderers,
m'aprite la porta, assassini	open the door for me, murderers,
m'aprite.	open it.
Ah! voi tutti a me contro venite—	Ah! you all go against me—
Ah! Ebben, piango.	Ah! Well, I am crying.
Marullo, signore,	Marullo, my lord,
tu ch'hai l'alma gentil	you whose soul is as kind
come il core,	as your heart,
dimmi tu, dove l'hanno nascosta?	tell me, where have they hidden her?
E là, non è vero?	It is there, isn't it?
Tu taci! Ohimè.	You keep silent! Woe to me.
Miei signori, perdono, pietate,	My lords, forgive me, have mercy,
al vegliardo la figlia ridate,	give his daughter back to the old man,
ridonarla a voi nulla ora costa	it does not cost you anything now,
tutto al mondo tal figlia è per me.	everything in the world this daughter means to me.

The libretto of *Rigoletto* follows exactly the original drama by Victor Hugo, *Le Roi s'a-muse*, to the point of being merely a condensed translation of the French text. In the drama, the scene between Triboulet (Rigoletto) and the courtiers reaches an extraordinary frenzy. The distraught father alternately pulls his hair in despair, hurls torrents of insults at his tormentors in outbursts of incredible violence, and finally sinks to his knees, to plead with his antagonists. The scene is a whirlwind of unleashed emotions, disorderly, fierce, and seemingly with neither plan nor logic.

Of this original, Verdi and his librettist have kept the sequence of moods and episodes and the intense feeling of the whole scene. But they have of necessity organized it according to a certain logic in order to make it suitable for a musical composition. The task of the performer in this formidable scene is to conciliate the respect of the musical structure with the intensity of the emotional contents. Of course, Verdi's music in its classical mold provides all the elements of the dramatic reading.

This scene-aria requires a baritone voice with power, brilliance, range, and a wide spectrum of colors and dynamics. Some of the suggestions made here stem from the experience of a singer who did not have a devastatingly powerful voice but who was able nevertheless to deliver the full impact of the scene.

The subject: Rigoletto's daughter has been abducted from her father's house. After hours of searching for her in vain, the frantic father understands that Gilda is held captive in the duke's bedroom, the prey of his lust. The abductors, he knows, were the courtiers, the usual targets of his sarcasm, now taking their revenge on him. He is at their mercy and faced with their open hostility.

Above the rough waves of the string instruments in the orchestra the voice starts forte, full, all vowels sung broadly, with emphasis on the accented syllables of the short words, "*razza* dan*na*ta . . .," and a strong support. The first twelve bars show a regular pattern: Bars 1 and 2 contain only short words separated by eighth-note silences; bars 3 and 4 contain a larger phrase, with a possible legato; again, there are short figures in bars 5 and 6, a large phrase in bars 7 and 8; and so on. The following bars, 13–16, blossom into a very great phrase, musically and of course vocally. While constantly using a large amount of voice, the singer should vary its color and its intentions according to the above pattern, that is, insulting in bars 1 and 2, not so loud and scornful in bars 3 and 4, indignant in 5 and 6, pathetic in 7 and 8, imperative in 9 and 10, threatening in 11 and 12. Following a great crescendo, the voice reaches a striking climax on bar 16. This would be impossible if the preceding dynamics had been uniformly fortissimo.

It has been accepted once and for all that on this bar the words "difende l'onor" are sung on the notes D–E-flat–G–G–C, with an allargando and a fermata on the first G.

You may think that all the above changes of mood are unnecessarily exaggerated. Two arguments justify them: First, it is unwise and monotonous to sing a uniform fortissimo for any length of time; second, Rigoletto as a jester has the extrovert's gift of expressing himself strongly and colorfully, and here he is also motivated by exceptional emotions.

The next lines are a furious repeat of the same words over and over while Rigoletto fights bodily with the courtiers until they throw him to the ground. There, hurt and defeated, almost in tears, breathless (but always on time), he sings the line "tutti, contro me" on a progressive diminuendo. The D-flat "Ah" and the words "Ebben, piango" are free in rhythm and sung with a seemingly exhausted but, in truth, well-supported voice. On the next bar the change of tempo, from ♩ = 80 to ♩ = 56, introduces two new elements. The orchestral figure suggests a sudden reawakening of Rigoletto's mind, the legato line a concentrated effort at persuasion. The jester has noticed a flicker of sympathy on Marullo's face and tries to take advantage of it by flattering him. With a friendly voice he sings "tu ch'ai l'alma gentil come il core," with insistence "dimmi tu . . ." The following two lines are of the greatest interest to the performer: While the voice becomes more and more piano until it is only a murmur on the last "non è vero," the intensity of the plea grows conversely stronger and stronger. "Tu taci" can be sung on time as written or, if the singer knows how to create a feeling of searing anxiety by his silence, well after the chord. The F is forte, with a sense of horror. The written decrescendo and following "Ohimè" reveal total despair.

The last part of the aria is one of the most beautiful melodic lines offered the baritone voice. While the expression is that of desperate pleading, the singing must be very even, the voice starting each phrase piano, rising to the written crescendos, respecting the decrescendos, sounding fluid while staying strictly on time until the triplets "tutto, tutto al mondo" in the eighth bar of the section. These are free but in agreement with the accompanist when the aria is performed. In the operatic performance the cello solo constantly plays a very difficult line in duet with the voice. This fact precludes any unexpected changes of rhythm on the part of the singer. Starting with bar 10 the voice must find its most moving sound, at first pianissimo, then with a very definite crescendo on bar 12 and a portamento between "pietà" and "ridate." Take a deep breath before "tutto al mondo," bar 13. Then you have two equally acceptable options: (1) Take a breath before the G-flat (last note of bar 13) and carry the voice over from low F to high F on bar 14. In this case the next breath will be before the E-flat, last note of bar 14. Or (2) breathe before the high F on bar 14, after a portamento from the low F, then breathe again after "figlia" in bar 15. In either case there will be a large rallentando on the words "ridate a me la figlia" in bar 14, with a short fermata on the F (second note on the word "me"). This must be done in good understanding with the accompanist or conductor.

me;   ri-da-tea me   la fi -glia;

It will really provide the climax of the aria.

The phrase "ell'è per me" in the low range, still very sad, must be sung with the resonance of the mouth, round enough so that it does not sound puny after the expansion of the preceding phrases. The last phrases are very free, the top F forte, the descending line rubato, the second "pietà, signore" subdued, the final "Ah pietà" very broad, with the roundest tones the singer can muster.

From the fury of the first page to the persuasive middle part to the pathetic ending, justice will be done this aria, obviously written for a great voice, only if a very human artistry is there to complement the vocal beauty.

"La donna è mobile"   *tenor*

La donna è mobile,	Woman is fickle,
qual piuma al vento	like a feather in the wind
muta d'accento e di pensiero.	she changes speech and thoughts.
Sempre un amabile, leggiadro viso,	A lovable, graceful face,
in pianto o in riso è menzognero.	in tears or in laughter is always lying.
E sempre misero	He is always miserable
chi a lei s'affida	who trusts in her,
chi le confida mal cauto il core!	who entrusts his unwary heart to her!
Pur mai non sentesi felice appieno	Yet nobody feels fully happy
chi su quel seno non liba amore.	who on that bosom does not drink love.
La donna è mobil . . .	Woman is fickle . . .

This is one of the most successful arias ever written. It is one that Verdi kept under wraps almost until the very minute the tenor stepped in front of the public the night of the premiere of *Rigoletto* and that everybody was humming as they left the opera house. As part of the fourth act of the opera, the aria becomes a motif representing "the libertine singing of the faithlessness of women at the very moment the woman he has betrayed is about to die for him" (Toye, *Verdi,* p. 304). As an aria sung in concert it seems even more frivolous and has suffered many distortions from tenors who were mainly eager to chalk up a success through loudness and vulgarity. It is, however, quite possible to retain the aria's musical worth while keeping alive its eloquence and its power to seduce an audience.

The orchestra crisply plays part of the tune, then stops abruptly, and the tenor picks up the tune at its beginning. In each of the two verses the phrases must be conceived as groups of four bars, the first breath coming after "vento," the second after "pensiero," and so on. The first group of four bars is brilliant and almost staccato, the second is more subdued and legato. The same is true of the next two groups of four bars. Moreover, there are accents on the first note of the second and fourth bars in the first group, *"mobile"* and *"vento,"* while in the second group there is a grace note on the corresponding beats. It is the same in the following eight bars. As a result, the first groups of four bars must be sung *con brio,* forte and with a mocking bravura, while the second groups are warmer in voice and caressing in feeling, as if the volatile temper of the women in itself made them even more lovable. And so it goes until the sixteenth bar of the voice line. In bars 17 and 18 the voice bounces on "donna" and "mo-" before accentuating "-bil." In bars 19 and 20 it bounces on "piu-ma-al ven-" before accentuating "-to," then sings full and forte "muta d'accento" before turning very light and smiling on "e di pensier." It is customary to make a tenuto on the G-sharp forte of "accento," and this is acceptable provided it is not absurdly long and provided it prepares the diminuendo toward "e di pensier." The repeat of "e di pensier" must be light again and humorous.

The long tenuto on the F-sharp in the following bars starts piano and goes crescendo so that the last "e di pensier" of the stanza is full and vigorous. This long F-sharp must be sung in a definite vowel /e/ as the word is the conjunction *e* meaning *and* and not the verb *è* meaning *is*. While it is sustained, a resonance can be opened and added in the back and above the tone so that there is no narrowness in the sound—but neither is there spreading.

The general effect of the verse is cheerful, carefree, young, and elegant. What an opportunity to show off a voice that has all those qualities!

The second verse seems to allow a little more introspection than the first. It is like the other side of the coin: the fickleness of women as seen and felt by men. There is no sadness, but certainly there is not much bravado, in saying that to trust women is to find misery. It is not out of place to sing those first eight bars in the same style as in the first verse but with a rounder, slightly deeper voice and much less bounce. The next eight bars are a reluctant tribute to the power of women. Who is not given their physical love is never quite happy. While the same alternation of staccato and legato bars is kept, the feeling for the phrases should be more continuous, warmer, and more melodious. In this section the last group of four "chi su quel seno non liba amore" can be sung pianissimo, with a sensuousness that is not lacking in sympathy for the accused. The following bars are similar to the corresponding ones in the first verse, but after the more reflective phrases they should by contrast be still bouncier and brighter.

A kind of coda is provided by another inescapable tradition: The start of the long F-sharp is delayed by two bars, and a cadenza is introduced replacing the last "e di pensier." It is generally done as shown.

The cadenza must be prepared and executed in the same spirit as the aria itself, that is, with carefreeness, elegance, and cheer. Any sign of strain in it would destroy the overall effect. The run should be sung rapidly and lightly but very clearly. A breath should be taken after "di," and the F-sharp preceding the last B should be very light, already in the resonance of the high note, to which the voice should spin without a new attack. The vowel on the B should be the basic /e/, which has the slimness indispensable for a very high tone.

It must be a real joy to have a great success with the audience by singing a brilliant aria with brilliance, without distorting it for egotistic reasons but keeping in the performance the simple dignity of an artist.

Verdi, *Simone Boccanegra*

"Il lacerato spirito"   *bass*

A te l'estremo addio,
palagio altero,
freddo sepolcro dell'angiolo mio!

A last farewell to you,
haughty palace,
cold tomb of my angel!

Nè a proteggerlo valsi!	You were not able to protect her!
Oh maledetto!	O accursed man!
Oh vile seduttore!	O vile seducer!
E tu, Vergin, soffristi	And you, Virgin, suffered
rapita a lei	to be ravished from her
la verginal corona?	her virginal crown?
Ah! che dissi? Deliro!	Ah! what did I say? I am raving!
Ah! mi perdona!	Ah! forgive me!
Il lacerato spirito	The lacerated mind
del mesto genitore	of a distraught father
era serbato a strazio	was held under the torture
d'infamia e di dolore.	of shame and grief.
Il serto a lei de'martiri	The crown of martyrs
pietoso il cielo diè . . .	the merciful Heaven gave her . . .
Resa al folgor degli angeli,	Risen to the splendor of the angels
prega, Maria, per me.	pray, Maria, for me.

In the fifteenth century the head of the government in Genoa was an elected doge. In the prologue to *Simone Boccanegra,* the patrician Fiesco is at the end of his term, and a plebeian, Boccanegra, is about to be elected in his place. Fiesco's daughter Maria had earlier fallen in love with Boccanegra and had had a child by him. Confined in the doge's palace since then, Maria unexpectedly dies on the very day of the election. The distraught Fiesco now leaves forever the palace that has failed to protect the honor or the life of his daughter.

The part of Fiesco is written for a large operatic bass voice. Fiesco is an aristocrat who, although the victim of unjust political condemnation, refuses to betray or to kill in order to regain his rank. His voice should be noble, his declamation earnest and sober. This particular aria presents no problem of range, and the singer can concentrate fully on expressing and creating a sad, dramatic beauty.

The aria is made of two parts. At first Fiesco rebels against all that has tortured him throughout his life, and he goes as far as to become blasphemous. In two lines of transition he pities himself for his misfortunes. A second part is a prayer to his Maria, whom he sees in heaven among the angels.

The first phrase, "a te l'estremo addio," where the beauty of the voice can already be felt, is no more than mezzo forte, solemn and desolate, the sad solemnity still stronger on "palagio altero." The voice will rise from mezzo forte to a tragic forte on "del l'angiolo mio." Fiesco directs a helpless accusation at the palace in "Nè a proteggerlo valsi," But the sorrow turns to violent anger when Fiesco thinks of Boccanegra, whom he calls "accursed," before his voice weakens, as if in shame, on "vile seduttore." The meaning of the next phrase is not always clear to all singers, but the capital *V* in the word "Vergin" should clarify any confusion. In an outburst of resentment Fiesco accuses the Holy Virgin of allowing the virginity of his daughter to be ravished. This is blasphemy. The phrase must be sung bitterly, accusingly. But as soon as the words have rushed out, Fiesco stops, stunned by what he has just said; "Ah! che dissi? Deliro." And he asks for forgiveness in a short phrase, "Ah! mi perdona," which should be slow, sustained, and humble, the voice keeping its round beauty.

Fiesco passively feels that it has always been his fate to suffer. The two half phrases,

"Il lacerato spirito" and "del mesto genitor," are sung very slowly, with a weary pause between them. The sixteenths are not brief but are carried over to the next note, still in rhythm but in extreme legato. From that weariness issues a long, strong phrase of grief, which has a summit on "d'infamia e di" and a diminuendo at its end. But that diminuendo does not happen between "di" and the E-sharp of "dolore"—that note is still mezzo forte—but comes on the half note of "do-*lo*-re."

During the four bars of interlude the father turns his thoughts to the departed Maria who, having suffered dishonor and sorrow, to him seems deserving of the halo of martyrdom. She is now high above, among the angels, and able to intercede for her grieving father. With the change of key the tempo could become a little faster. The voice is at the same time soft, brighter, and full of love. The marking *cantabile* stresses those points. "Resa al folgor degli angeli" is radiant with faith, growing to a rich mezzoforte. "Prega, Maria, per me" is a humble but fervent prayer. The repeat of the phrase one line later is more exalted and reaches forte, the prayer still humble and fervent. The isolated "prega per me" is deeply touching.

The last line starts in the same mood. The descending line on the last "Prega, Maria, per me" is very slow, each note a well-sustained vowel, love and fervor surrounding the name of Maria. No breath is permissible during the length of the descending phrase. The low F-sharp should not be turned into a vocal feat but should show, in a vibrant forward ring capable of a diminuendo, the beautiful and logical ending of a heartfelt piece of music. It would be a good idea for the bass to find the exact color of the vowel, basically /e/, that would make of the C-sharp, of "prega" and the F-sharp of "me" two similar elements of a very simple and moving phrase.

This aria is very often sung in audition by young basses or bass-baritones. Many a one commits the error of using it only for a show of vocal power, sometimes a hollow and muffled power. The aria is a very human piece of music, however, which immediately gives the character of Fiesco a presence and a credibility. It deserves to be well studied and enjoyed as such.

Verdi, *La Traviata*

"Ah, fors'è lui" *soprano*

È strano! È strano!	It's strange! It's strange!
In core scolpiti ho quegli accenti!	Engraved in my heart are those words!
Saria per me sventura un serio amore?	Would a serious love be a misfortune for me?
Che risolvi, o turbata anima mia?	What do you decide, my troubled heart?
Null'uomo ancora t'accendeva . . .	No man has yet inflamed you . . .
o gioja ch'io non conobbi,	oh, joy that I did not know,
esser amata amando . . .	to love and be loved . . .
E sdegnarla poss'io	And I should disdain it

per l'aride follie	in favor of the barren follies
del viver mio? . . .	of my way of living? . . .
Ah, fors'è lui che l'anima,	Ah, maybe he is the one whom my soul,
solinga ne'tumulti,	lonesome in tumultuous crowds,
godea sovente pingere	often enjoyed painting
de suoi colori occulti.	in secret colors.
Lui, che modesto e vigile	He, who modest and watchful
all'egre soglie ascese	came to the door of the sick one,
e nuova febbre accese	and kindled a new fever
destando mi all'amor!	awakening me to love!
Ah quell'amor, quell'amor . . .	Ah, such love, such love . . .
ch'è palpito dell'universo intero,	the heartbeat of the entire universe,
misterioso, altero,	mysterious, proud,
croce e delizia al cor. Ah!	cross and delight for the heart. Ah!
Follie! delirio vano è questo!	Foolishness! it's all a vain illusion!
Povera donna, sola, abbandonata,	Poor woman, alone, forsaken,
in questo popoloso deserto	in this populous desert
che appellano Parigi,	that they call Paris,
che spero or più?	what else can I hope for?
Che far degg'io?	What must I do?
Gioire! di voluttà	Enjoy myself! of voluptuousness
ne'vortici perir!	perish in the whirlwind!
Sempre libera degg'io	Always free I shall frolic
follegiare di gioja in gioja,	from joy to joy,
vo'che scorra il viver mio	I want my life to run
pei sentieri del piacer.	on the paths of pleasure.
Nasca il giorno, o il giorno muoja,	Let the day be born or the day die,
sempre lieta ne'ritrovi, Ah!	let it find me always gay, Ah!
A diletti sempre nuovi	To always new delights
dee volare il mio pensier.	shall my thoughts fly.

Violetta, young, beautiful, intelligent, sensitive, has reached the pinnacle of the Parisian demimonde, thanks to the successive contributions of several benefactors. The dazzling brilliance of her life style, however, hides a physical frailty: Her life is threatened by consumption. On the evening of the opening scene of the opera she was giving a party at her house when she fainted. While she was recovering, a young man, Alfredo, came to her side to offer her, not more wealth and glitter, but true love and companionship. Left alone after the departure of her guests Violetta ponders on this new and unexpected situation.

The part of Violetta is one of the most attractive and most desirable in the entire soprano repertoire. The aria "Ah, fors'è lui" is a highlight of the score. What kind of voice should attempt it? It is made of two parts, the melodic first part obviously written for a lyric soprano of beautiful vocal quality, great sensitivity, and great flexibility; the second part, "Sempre libera," with its many runs and ringing high notes almost invites a coloratura voice. But those features are only stylistic additions to the dramatic core of the music, which expresses deep and stirring emotions calling for a strong, lyric voice. The soprano who sings this aria should be gifted with remarkable vocal ease but also with great skill at coloring and shaping inflections and an intense power of involvement. Not one phrase in the aria is emotionally indifferent.

In the opening recitative the pace of each phrase is free, the goal being to express a variety of emotions as Violetta tries to cope with feelings unknown to her. Inside each phrase it is nevertheless wise to keep the rhythm written by Verdi, which could hardly be improved upon. The first words, "È strano" and their repeat, are spoken more than sung, although there is already a vibrant spin on the vowel /a/. After the silent fermata Violetta reflects, starting piano and ending forte, on the troubling surprise of finding Alfredo's words engraved on her heart. A new concern shows in the phrase "Saria per me sventura . . .," sung piano, with a ritardando on "un serio amore," a thought totally unfamiliar to her. Uncertainty keeps the line "Che risolvi . . . " moderato and without brilliance. Her empty soul seems to suffer when she sings with intensity "Null'uomo ancora t'accendeva" in a strong crescendo. There is tragic envy in "o gioja" sung forte with a long tenuto on the high B-flat, and there is sadness in "ch'io non conobbi," words that come slowly and with nostalgia. A moment of indignation adds almost a touch of violence to "E sdegnar la poss'io," and there is a strong, impulsive rejection in "l'aride follie." This impulse is carried into "del viver mio" although the final short run ends in a morendo, possibly a sign of subconscious shame.

First part of the aria: The first page of "Ah, fors'è lui" is given to the elaboration of a dream, the dream of a quiet, retired, pampered life preceding the awakening of true love, a tremendous uplifting power, even if it brings sorrow as well as rapture. The mood is confidential, the vision pure and bright; the voice must be clear as crystal and, though dreamy, nevertheless very precise in following all the markings of style, especially the grace notes, which must be unhurried and heard clearly. The two bars of "tumulti" and "occulti" are free, as if there were a fermata over the whole bar. A portamento from the C to the high A-flat in these bars is expected, as well as a tenuto on the A-flat pianissimo. But never consider singing a downward portamento from those two A-flats. A true vowel /i/ alone can give the two A-flats their precision and their lightness.

Now the barely conscious, unfulfilled dream becomes concrete in the person of Alfredo. He is seen, at first pianissimo, "modesto e vigile" in his role of the past months, then in his growing influence on Violetta, "e nuova febbre accese," forte and crescendo, waking her to love. Here one bar of singing pianissimo, "destando mi all'amor," prepares with a delicate touch the passionate onrush of love. The fermata on "amor" is long, with a great crescendo of intensity. Some sopranos like to carry the voice over to the next "Ah, quell'amor." My own taste would prefer that the greatest possible intensity be reached on the E-natural "amor," that a breath be taken, that the F on "Ah" be started again full voice, then almost immediately diminished so that the repeat of "quell'amor" will be an ecstatic piano, with a swelling of the tone to meet the scope of "dell'universo intero" and a return to pianissimo, with a light staccato on "misterioso." A new crescendo of pride on "altero" reaches forte on "croce." Violetta is ready to carry the "cross," that is, the torment she guesses to be part of a serious love, as well as to enjoy its delights.

Here starts a cut that ends with the seventh bar before the end of the aria's first part. The words "croce e delizia" are repeated wonderingly. A cadenza sums up the many moods of Violetta that the singer must feel in a most personal way if all the above lines are to serve any purpose. Shown here is one of many possible cadenzas.

It would appear that the ascending line to the C is associated with delights, the descending line with torments, the last short phrases being wistful and uncertain while the resolution is bright and positive.

Second part: After a brief silence the second part of the aria begins with a sudden sharp reversal of Violetta's thoughts. Realistic now, she perceives that her lot can be only a life of dissipation. "Follie," and "delirio vano" are rejections of her dreams. They need not be screamed but on the contrary, must be icy and cutting before Violetta indulges in a few moments of self-pity. From "Povera donna" to "Parigi" her speech is a monotonous psalmody that slows down in helplessness on "che spero or più." It becomes still slower and forte on "Che far degg'io." The cruelty of her fate is summed up in the word "Gioire," intensely vibrant, which unleashes a whirlwind of notes aptly describing the frantic pace of her life. These runs must be sung with virtuosity, a certain amount of rubato, in great contrast with the tragic forte of "di voluttà . . . perir." Note that "Gioir" is pronounced "joe-ear." After the second "Gioir" the high D-flat and the run are sung on the vowel /a/, the rubato becoming an allargando, the ending coming abruptly.

After the first eight bars of the *allegro brilliante* there is usually a three-page cut leading to the repeat of "Sempre libera." In her whole being Violetta feels the fever of dissipation that has been her milieu for years. The printed indication of the tempo, ♩ = 84, is, of course, right. One should not yield to the temptation of greater speed. The marked tempo provides plenty of momentum yet allows for time to sing exactly all the indications of style that dress the rather hard vocal line in lace and silk. "Sempre libera degg'io" already requires a light staccato on the first two notes; an accent on "li-" of "libera"; then after two legato sixteenths another light staccato on the last two notes of the same bar; then a trill on "degg'io" and "follegiare"; staccato eighths for "di gioja," and so on. The impetuosity of the singing is indispensable, but so is the elegance of the details.

A few bars later it is customary to sing both "-tro-" and "-vi" of "ritrovi" on the E-natural and to use the vowel /a/ for the trill on the G and the ringing high C, held freely. A return to a strict *a tempo* must then follow on "a diletti." The accents on the many starts on the word "dee" require taste in order not to be overdone. The long run on "volar" will make no sense unless it is done with a very light voice as the word implies. Besides, each of the starting notes of each section of the run must be piano or at the most mezzo forte, and a crescendo must be made on the descending line of each section. Avoid the temptation to do the contrary. The repeated A-flats that top the next light ascending scale on "volar," as well as the repeated high C's a few bars later, must be only slightly accented, and after a start mezzo fo*r*te each note must be louder than the one before, creating a sense of exaltation and not just a successful production of even but static tones. The difficult runs following these A-flats and these C's require an extremely light voice. A heavy tone can never be nimble. It is customary for the soprano to stay silent instead of singing the last-but-one "il mio pensier" and to come in on the B-flat four bars before the end of the vocal line, singing a vowel /a/ into the high C and the descending pattern and to sing the end as shown.

This aria is a wondrous vehicle for the display of the vocal quality and sensitivity of a soprano. It goes without saying that it should not be attempted as long as the would-be performer has problems of range, of lightness, of vocal nimbleness. For those who have overcome these problems, the psychological unfolding of Violetta's emotions deserves long study, and spontaneous sympathy. One should be able to live the hesitations, the dreamy hope, the hidden sorrow, the surrender to luxury, with sincerity and fervor.

"De'miei bollenti spiriti"   *tenor*

Lunge da lei per me non v'ha diletto!	Away from her there is no pleasure for me!
Volaron già tre lune	Three months have passed already
dacchè la mia Violetta	since my Violetta
agi per me lasciò,	for me gave up comforts,
dovizie, amori,	luxuries, loves,
e le pompose feste,	and the pompous festivities
ov'agli omaggi avvezza,	where, used to homages,
vedea schiavo ciascun	she saw a slave in everybody
di sua bellezza.	of her beauty.
Ed or contenta	And now, content
in questi ameni luoghi	in these pleasant surroundings,
tutto scorda per me.	she forgets everything for me.
Qui presso a lei	Here, near her,
io rinascer mi sento,	I feel myself become reborn,
e dal soffio d'amor rigenerato	and renewed by the breath of love
scordo ne'gaudi suoi	I forget in her enjoyment
tutto il passato.	all the past.
De'miei bollenti spiriti	The youthful ardor
il giovanile ardore	of my excitable impulses
ella temprò col placido sorriso	she tempered with her placid smile
dell'amor.	of love.
Dal dì che disse: vivere	Since the day when she said: I want
io voglio a te fedel,	to live faithful to you,
dell'universo immemore	forgetful of the universe
io vivo quasi in ciel.	I live close to heaven.

Alfredo is a very young man. Introduced into the glittering world of Parisian society, he has fallen in love with a woman his own age, Violetta, a beautiful, gifted, unusual woman but a kept woman, who belongs to whoever can afford her for however long, a woman who in her frenzied dissipation burns up her frail body already sapped by illness. For a year Alfredo has worshiped her from afar. Then, one fateful day, he has offered her his love, and the improbable has happened: Violetta has renounced her life of disorder, and for three months she and Alfredo have been living the blessed life of young lovers in an isolated country house.

When the curtain rises on the second act Alfredo has been hunting but has cut his outing short in order to spend his time with Violetta. The brief prelude *allegro vivace* to the aria describes his speedy return as well as his "bollenti spiriti." Alone, discarding his hunting gear, Alfredo ponders aloud about his present happiness in a clear, young, ringing voice.

The tempo at the beginning of the recitative is brisk, possibly a bit slower than the tempo of the introduction, in order to show ease and relaxation, ♩ = 104–108. The values must be respected, the dotted notes stressed, the short notes kept very light. This is not a marching song but an expression of joy and happiness. An inflection of affection could slow down ever so little "la mia Violetta." The enumeration that follows brings an accelerando: All those things have been discarded by Violetta and matter no more. Is there not a trace of mockery in the pretended solemnity of "e le pompose feste," a good smile on "ov'agli omaggi avvezza," at the memory of Violetta passing like a princess in a crowd? The staccato notes on "vedea schiavo ciascun" show how lightly Violetta used to accept the tributes of her admirers. "Di sua bellezza" brings a ritardando preparing the next tempo and is said with great conviction. The *andante* can be situated around ♩ = 86. It is sung with good humor and cozily, with staccatos that are here a light, detached way of isolating the notes. "Tutto scorda per me" is said with pride and satisfaction. So far, Alfredo has indulged in painting Violetta's happiness, which he believes to be complete and easily achieved. He will now sing of his own bliss, and both tempo and voice will become broader and suggest depth after the superficial lightness of the preceding lines.

The *adagio,* ♩ = 68–72, is very sustained and lyrical, sung with great earnestness and with a manly voice, ringing in beautiful Italian vowels: "*lei,*" "*rinascer,*" "*sento,*" "*rigenerato*" (this last word with great enthusiasm). The ascension to the A-flat starts light and brisk so that the voice can spin easily to the top of the phrase, which is a brilliant vowel /i/ that expands to forte while singing. Even if it sounds excellent, do not dwell on it too long. Take a deep breath before "tutto," and try to sing to the end of the phrase without breathing again. A breath after "tutto" is an unnecessary crutch that robs the final phrase of its fine breadth. The goal of the singer should be to reach the word "passato" with a full supply of air, avoiding a ritardando on "tutto," and then to broaden the several notes of "passato," especially the C on the third beat.

A decision must be made regarding the tempo of the aria. The marking ♩ = 60 is not respected today. Some tenors of preceding generations began the aria in that tempo; some others, then as now, took the aria much faster. A factor in deciding on that tempo must have been the meaning of "De'miei bollenti spiriti" (of my ardent senses, or spirit). Those words incite to speed, as well as the words "giovanile ardore." But what Alfredo tells us is that Violetta's love "temprò," that is, moderated, these ardors with her "placido" (peaceful) smile, and in this way he has been living as if in heaven. Actually, the aria expresses quiet bliss, and the orchestral pattern of an eighth note on the beats followed by three sixteenths, instead of being feverish and pressing, is on the contrary calm and soothing. That does not mean that Alfredo has become dull and indifferent. The repeated ascending phrase "dell'universo immemore" has power and enthusiasm enough to prove this.

Could a tempo based on ♩ - 72 be lively enough and still allow the notion of quiet bliss? It has been said that practicing the shortest values of a piece is a good way to find the limits of speed or slowness. The sixteenths in bars 17 and 18 of the aria appear fast enough in this tempo while being easy to handle and meaningful. To attempt to sing the aria in that moderate tempo seems worthwhile. The voice, throughout, will be bright, young, the face of the singer lifted around the eyes of a warm smile. Sing the first two phrases, bars 2 and 3, bars 4 and 5, with a lilt; the third phrase, bars 6, 7, and 8, in a vibrant legato, without breathing and with a crescendo on "placido sorriso"; the first "dell'amor" staccato, the second pianissimo and tender. The quotation of Violetta's own words, "vivere io voglio," is alive with eagerness—respect the marked accents. A crescendo on "fedel" includes a portamento downward but with a breath before "dell'universo." The great phrase, bars 14, 15, 16, and 17, requires a round, full voice and is at its best when sung exactly on time and without breathing until after "quasi," bar 17. That breath must be very brief so that the second "io vivo quasi in ciel" concludes the phrase practically without a break. Alfredo's happiness is better expressed by the sweeping continuity of the phrase than by any high fermata.

A delighted vitality still bounces lightly on the repeat of the quotation, bars 18–20. (The first of the two "sì" is often replaced by an "Ah.") The great phrase will this time go to a written fortissimo, and this time it would be correct to breathe after "immemore"; then, going from ebullience to contentment, sing from fortissimo to morendo (bars 23 and 24) without any interruption to "quasi in ciel."

The repeat of "io vivo in ciel," bar 26, is dolcissimo, still in full contentment. "Dell'universo immemore" needs a little more tone in order to sustain the long value on /u/ (the same sound as in *loose,* sung with elongated lips). From here to the end of the piece there is a free cadenza. The ascending phrase to "ciel" on A-flat could be rather slow and the forte on the A-flat warm and flexible, so that it allows an immediate diminuendo to dolcissimo on "in cielo," these notes following the A-flat said rather briskly. Start the last G on "quasi" piano, reach a warm mezzo forte, and return to piano. "In ciel" should be pianissimo. Your own taste decides on the length of the fermata. Whatever its length, it must allow you to finish the phrase without breathing. There is no justification in taking a big breath before "in ciel" and in adding a fermata on "in." This type of forced emphasis does not belong in this aria, so simply vital in its contented happiness, a monologue, thought and spoken to oneself alone.

"Di Provenza" *baritone*

Di Provenza il mar, il suol,	The sea, the sun of Provence,
chi dal cor ti cancellò?	who has struck them from your heart?
Al natio fulgente sol,	From your native brilliant sunshine,

qual destino ti furò?	what fate stole you away?
Oh rammenta pur nel duol	Oh, remember in your grief
ch'ivi gioja a te brillò,	that there joy shone for you,
e che pace colà sol	and that there alone peace
su te splendere ancor può.	can still radiate upon you.
Dio mi guidò!	God has guided me!
Ah, il tuo vecchio genitor,	Ah, your old father,
tu non sai quanto soffrì.	you don't know how much he suffered.
Te lontano, di squallor	With you far away,
il suo tetto si coprì.	his house filled with misery.
Ma se al fin ti trovo ancor,	But if at last I find you again,
se in me speme non fallì,	if my hope did not deceive me,
se la voce dell'onor	if the voice of honor
in te appien non ammutì,	is not totally silent in you,
Dio m'esaudì.	[then] God has answered my prayer.

At this point in *La Traviata,* one of the operas most familiar to opera lovers, the older Germont has succeeded in freeing his son from a liaison with a women he considers dangerous. But the young man collapses in an agony of grief. The famous aria "Di Provenza" is the father's attempt to bring a ray of sunshine into the gloom of Alfredo's despair. Germont has come to Paris from his home in Provence, a place whose sun-bathed landscape and seashore fill a childhood and adolescence with radiant memories. By recalling such memories he tries to awaken in Alfredo some hope for the future. The music of the first verse is almost that of a lullaby, the kind one would sing to soothe the pain of an ailing child.

The tempo is marked precisely ♩ = 60, the dynamic indication is *piano* for the brief orchestral introduction and is, of course, valid for the voice also. Besides, for the first four lines of the aria all markings of style stress a great softness and lightness on all the parts of the text referring to Provence (*dolce, pianissimo, dolce,* dots over the eighth notes) while there are two *marcate* on allusions to heart and fate and a strong crescendo on "duol" (pain, sorrow). All these notations help the singer to solve the main problem of this aria: Built in regular, symmetrical sections, it can become monotonous and trite and the expression of the singing indifferent, all the more so if the singer pauses regularly after every seventh note! The first breath should come after "cancellò" (fourteen notes), the second after "il suol" (fourteen notes). The first grace note ("Pro-venza") is soft, the next two (on "cor") are vigorous. The dots on the eighth notes combined with the slur mean that the same vibration of the voice fills the whole phrase but that there is a very discreet suspense between notes. When all the requirements are satisfied, the task of the interpreter is not yet begun. This is an aria sung directly to somebody in order to influence him, to create a reaction in him, to persuade him. Even when singing in concert, the baritone must feel the presence before him of a desperate young man who is his son, whose sorrow he has caused, and whom he wants to rescue. A warm, intense desire to communicate must be the essential guide to the interpretation of "Di Provenza."

Another element of concern is the repetitious character of the aria. I believe that a clever interpreter can turn this potential shortcoming into an asset. In the first stanza, sing "e che pace colà sol" piano and in an insinuating voice the first time, sing very softly on "su te splendere ancor può," then raise your voice to majesty on the second "e che pace," still more so on "splendere." The first "Dio mi guidò" is sung religiously, the second triumphantly (good stentato on "mi"), the third pianissimo and rallentando, with gratitude. If the mind concentrates on the succession of moods, that climactic phrase will be vocally easy.

A similar attitude will make the second stanza even more meaningful. In it Giorgio Germont speaks of his personal feelings in order to touch his son's heart (and I am not sure that this was a good idea on his part). The pattern is the same as in the first stanza. All indications must be respected (breathe after fourteen notes, and so on). I dared to divide the second phrase as follows: "Te lontano/ di squallor il suo tetto si coprì, il suo tetto si coprì di squallore / di squallor," for which I was rudely taken to task by the then reigning critic in Chicago—and I still cannot believe that a man as deeply committed to expression as Verdi would have preferred the monotonous division in 7-7-7-7.

A great sincerity must imbue the phrases "Ma se al fin te trovo ancor" (crescendo of emotion), comma, and "se in me speme non fallì" (more restrained); a large curve covers the following "se la voce dell'onor," and there must be greatness in its repeat forte. Be sure to sustain the B-flat on the word "fallì" so as to connect it with "Dio m'esaudì," which, in contrast to the first stanza, is the end of the phrase. The repeats of "Dio m'esaudì" must carry different meanings (triumph, gratitude). In both stanzas the singer must be sure to calibrate the size of his crescendo so that it is only on the high F–F–G-flat–F notes that the voice reaches its maximum. A premature forte will minimize the climax, tire the voice, and make the return to pianissimo difficult.

The first G-flat of the coda is generally omitted, and the fermata is placed on the second G-flat. Be sure to note that the phrase is written diminuendo and allargando. It seems that a rubato, first fast, then slow, is accepted at this point. A progressive allargando, with a comma after the first "ancor," would better express the emotion of the father, who feels that his plea has a chance of being successful and who lingers a little longer before ending his speech. The last two "Dio m'esaudì" are sung freely, with as warm and rich a voice as possible, a good fermata on the F, a good intake of breath, a very slow ending with a diminuendo and a fermata on the C ("m'esaudì"). If at all possible, the voice should convey that the conclusion of the aria is really wishful thinking. This must be done in such a way, however, that the audience does not get the impression of weakness on the part of the singer.

Verdi, *Il Trovatore*

"Tacea la notte placida" and "Di tale amor"   *soprano*

Tacea la notte placida	The peaceful night lay quiet
e bella in ciel sereno,	and beautiful in a serene sky,
la luna il viso argenteo	the moon showed her silver face
mostrava lieto e pieno,	joyous and full,
quando suonar per l'aere	when ringing in the air,
infino allor si muto,	till then so quiet,
dolci s'udiro e flebili	sweet and moving
gli accordi d'un liuto,	the chords of a lute were heard,
e versi melanconici	and a troubadour
un trovator cantò.	sang melancholy lines,
Versi di prece, ed umile	lines of prayer, humble ones,
qual d'uom che prega Iddio,	as of a man praying to God,
in quella ripeteasi	in which a name kept repeating itself,
un nome—il nome mio!	my name!
Corsi al veron sollecita.	I ran to the balcony in a hurry.
Egli era, egli era desso!	It was he, the same man!
Gioia provai che agli angeli	I felt a joy
solo è provar concesso!	which it is only given to angels to feel!
Al core, al guardo estatico	To my heart, my ecstatic eyes,
la terra un ciel sembrò!	the earth seemed heaven!
Di tale amor, che dirsi	Of such love, what can one
mai può dalla parola,	ever say with words?
d'amor, che intendo io sola,	With a love, that I alone understand,
il cor s'innebriò.	my heart is enraptured.
Il mio destino compiersi	My destiny cannot be fulfilled
non può che a lui d'appresso.	but next to him.
S'io non vivrò per esso,	If I am not going to live for him,
per esso morirò.	for him I shall die!

The action takes place in the fifteenth century. The setting for this scene is a dark night in the gardens of the palace of the prince of Aragon. Leonora, a noble lady of the court, is passionately in love with a knight, the winner of a recent tourney, whom she had crowned herself but whose name and whereabouts are unknown. He may be the man who once came to sing under her balcony at night. With her attendant Inez at her side, Leonora recalls her emotions of that night as she waits anxiously for a new sign of the presence of that mysterious man.

Leonora's voice is the typical lirico-spinto dramatic voice of the great Verdi heroines. The role makes the most extreme demands on the voice, in range, in emotions, in colors, in style. In this section both the cavatina "Tacea la notte placida" and the cabaletta "Di tale amor" will be studied. More contrasted vocal pieces cannot be found, and Leonora is expected to sing them in succession, separated only by a short scene for Inez. In the operatic performance, incidentally, only the second verse of the cabaletta is sung.

The cavatina is introduced in four bars, which create a nocturnal atmosphere and entice the melodic line. The dynamic level for the singing is *mezzavoce,* but a rich *mezzavoce* it must be, and there must be legatissimo singing from the start. The first eight bars describe a beautiful night bathed in moonlight and silence. The voice must be soft, the diction very smooth and light, the triplets of sixteenths in "placida" and "argenteo" very delicately done. But the essential interpretive element is the imagination of the soprano. "Tacea la notte placida" is dominated by the idea of silence. After a breath, "e bella in ciel sereno" has a broader scope and already calls for a rounder voice. The next two phrases are radiant with moonlight and require a brighter tone, but different from one that would describe sunshine—a bright tone attuned to moonlight. These first eight bars may tell an artist from a correct singer. The next four bars, a little fast, are bars of preparation for and expectation of a new, startling element. They are nearer to staccato than to legato, and very piano. The two fermatas on "muto" must make the ears listen intently for what the voice then describes in two successive waves of soaring tone. Here a great voice reveals itself with great expansion and expression. "Flebili" translated here means "touching, moving"; the word "liuto" rings with delight. But the most rousing wave is still to come. It begins pianissimo with "e versi" and culminates in a shining B-flat. Some sopranos are unhappy having to sing the syllables "-nici" of "melanconici" when going to the B-flat and choose instead to sing the sound "Ah" on the E-flat and the high B-flat. A way to free these two notes for an "Ah" is to sing "e versi melanconici, si melanconici, ah." In favor of the change it can be said that this "Ah" when given with full voice and passion can really sound triumphant. A breath is taken after the high B-flat to allow the two fermatas to broaden the end of the phrase in elation. The sound of the lute, that is, the presence of the man, had filled Leonora with an immense joy.

The second verse follows the pattern of the first. Here the reason for the subdued first eight bars lies in the nature of the poem the troubadour had sung, a prayer, a reverent prayer. That religious feeling changes to surprise and emotions: He was praying to her. Without raising her voice, she stresses slightly "un nome," more strongly "il nome mio." "Corsi al veron sollecita" is said faster without distorting the rhythm, nearer to speech than anything before. The first "Egli era" is sometimes sung neglecting the silence preceding it; then "egli era desso" is slower, in disbelief and wonderment. In that case the effect will be that of a rubato, with two faster bars and two slower. Then the two soaring waves rise anew. They are among the most uplifting ever written, the voice seemingly disengaged from the flesh, although it could not rise without a deep support of the body. The climax is reached as the first time, after a breath before the words "la terra," which are replaced by "Ah" on the E-flat and the high B-flat. Another breath after the G on "un ciel" will again allow the end of the phrase to expand broadly. The idea of cutting this second climax, as is sometimes suggested, is simply revolting.

The coda begins again subdued, in an ecstatic piano, whereupon the voice rises once more to a great forte. Here, too, it is customary to replace the words "la terra" (E-flat–B-flat–A-flat–G) with an "Ah" and to hold a fermata on the high B-flat. Many final cadenzas have been written and sung. The one printed in the score is very appropriate. It provides a traditional conclusion to the aria, and nothing else is needed after the splendors of the earlier phrases.

It is acceptable to end here, considering the cavatina a complete aria in itself. It is also possible to tie the cabaletta to it by cutting twenty-eight bars of the score. In this case the eight bars of the *allegretto* introduction should be played, but the singer should start with the second line, after Inez's phrase.

During the introduction the soprano must readjust her voice to prepare for the new task. She chooses mentally a much smaller tone than before, and she thinks it very slim, very forward, very brisk. The piece is pure virtuosity; the singer becomes an acrobat who must discard every possible weight in order to bounce and frisk. She must nevertheless keep a complete sense of legato. If the staccato notes were separated by jerks, the piece would die ungraciously. The staccato notes must instead be the sounds of a legato purposely interrupted for a fraction of a second but ready to ring for the next fraction of that second. Also, the vowels must be extremely precise and very sharp. Here and there it is customary to replace the words with "Ah"; for instance, in bars 7 and 8 the words "il cor" twice, in bars 15 and 16 "per esso" twice. A naive, irresistible joy must pervade the singing. The most should be made of the legato lyricism of "non può che a lui d'appresso." The *poco più mosso* is extremely light in voice. The cadenza is generally ended with the *oppure* printed in the score, with a moderately long fermata on the last F.

No doubt the cavatina is a great singing aria. No doubt even the great voice of Leonora is expected to sing the cabaletta. Such must be the art of the singer.

"Stride la vampa"   *mezzo-soprano/contralto*

Stride la vampa!	The blaze is crackling!
La folla indomita	The unruly crowd
corre a quel foco	runs to that fire
lieta in sembianza!	with a cheerful look.
Urli di gioia	Shouts of joy
intorno eccheggiano;	resound all around;
cinta di sgherri	surrounded by ruffians
donna s'avanza;	a woman advances;
sinistra splende	the mournful flame
sui volti orribili	that rises to the sky
la tetra fiamma	throws a sinister light
che s'alza al ciel!	on their horrible faces.
Stride la vampa!	The blaze is crackling!
Giunge la vittima nero vestita	The victim arrives, dressed in black,
discinta e scalza;	ragged and barefoot;
grido feroce di morte levasi;	a ferocious cry for death is raised;
l'eco il ripete di balza in balza.	the echo repeats it from cliff to cliff.
Sinistra splende sui volti orribili	The mournful flame rising to the sky
la tetra fiamma che s'alza al ciel!	throws a sinister light on their horrible faces!

The curtain rises on part 2 of *Il Trovatore* revealing a gypsy camp. A large fire is burning. Setting aside in their minds the first act they have just heard, the listeners must remember the introduction to the opera and the narration they had heard before the action got underway—the story of the gypsy woman who had been burned at the stake, and of her daughter Azucena who had avenged her death with a horrible crime.

Many years have passed, but the drama has never ceased to obsess Azucena. There, by the large fire burning in the uncertain light of early dawn, she sees once more the unforgettable scene as if it were happening in front of her eyes at this very moment. It is essential to give this aria the character of a hallucination that has taken possession of Azucena's ears and eyes, of her whole being. More than merely describing them, Azucena imitates the various sounds and suggests with her own voice the flickering of the fire on the unruly crowd, the crackling, raging flames, the howling of the people who have come to watch. In the second verse a precise vision of the victim suddenly emerges for a short moment, and then the flames reign again.

The voice of Azucena is a dramatic mezzo-soprano of natural power, very mature, capable of extreme intensity and long range. The part is certainly not to be sung by a young lyric voice.

The tempo, *allegretto*, $\downarrow$. = 60, is absolutely steady, its strictness adding to the feeling of hallucination. Great attention must be paid to the alternation of forte and pianissimo, without ever changing the pace of the singing. The vision, still dim and possibly distant but already disturbing, at first shows the crowd in the flickering light of the crackling fire. Azucena sings piano, with a bitter sound and nervous accents on "Stri-*de*." The trill on the first eighth note and the sharp dotted values in "vampa" suggest instinctively the central element of her obsession, the flames. The descriptive accents, the trill, and the dotted rhythm repeat themselves without a crescendo (bars 7 to 18). Suddenly Azucena's ears remember the shock of the gleeful yells. "Urli di gioia" is a loud forte, with a frightening echo pianissimo, "intorno . . ." Next she sees the escort of the victim, and another shock makes her sing "cinta di sgherri" forte. A strong mezzo-forte then tells of the progress of the victim and again of the uneven light playing on horrible faces. The pattern of accents, trill, and dotted values must be stressed continuously. The flames rise at first in a moderate outburst, "la tetra fiamma," in a crescendo and decrescendo, before they prepare their ascension "s'alza, s'alza al ciel" in the long trill on B, finally exploding upward in the last "che s'alza al ciel." A ritardando on the last two bars would only destroy the violence of the explosion.

The second verse repeats exactly the musical pattern of the first. The fire is still crackling as at first, but Azucena now sees her mother very clearly. "Giunge la vittima" fills her with anxiety and commiseration. "Discinta e scalza" is a horrified piano. "Grido feroce" makes her own voice ferocious, only to dim in terror for "di morte levasi." This time the echo amplifies the sounds and makes them last longer. "Di balza in balza" is the moment when the best contralto sounds of the mezzo-soprano voice should be used. The ending is similar to the first ending. Both times the best effect of the long trill on B will be obtained by starting it almost piano and making a strong crescendo to its end.

The range of this aria presents no difficulty. Throughout the singer can use a very round, mouth-filling sound, and it is that sound which is taken down to pianissimo or brought to fortissimo at the end, which rings easily in the only two low B's written in the aria and vibrates intensely in the only two high G's. As written in many of these pages, the error would be to sing the aria in a kind of furious forte or to obtain the different colors to be suggested by distorting the voice into dark chest tones or shrill upper tones. The imagination of the singer must be in command and must make this cruel aria moving by its sincerity.

"Condotta ell'era in ceppi"   *mezzo-soprano/contralto*

Condotta ell'era in ceppi	She was led in chains
al suo destin tremendo;	to her dreadful fate;
col figlio sulle braccia	with my son in my arms
io la seguia piangendo.	I followed her weeping.
Infino ad essa un varco tentai,	Finally I tried,
ma invano, aprirmi . . .	but in vain, to open a passage for myself,
invan tentò la misera	in vain the unfortunate woman tried
fermarsi e benedirmi!	to pause and bless me!
chè, fra bestemmie oscene	And amongst obscene curses then,
pungendola coi ferri	stinging her with their swords
al rogo la cacciavano	the villainous ruffians
gli scellerati sgherri.	threw her on the pyre.
Allor, con tronco accento	That is when, in a broken voice,
"mi vendica" sclamò.	"avenge me" she cried out.
Qual detto un eco eterno	That word has left an eternal echo
in questo cor lasciò.	in this heart.
Il figlio giunsi a rapir del conte;	I succeeded in stealing the son of the count;
lo trascinai qui meco	I dragged him there with me,
le fiamme ardean già pronto.	the flames were already lively.
Ei distruggeasi in pianto . . .	He wore himself out weeping. . .
io mi sentiva il core	I felt my heart
dilaniato, infranto,	torn to pieces, broken,
quand'ecco agl'egri spirti	when there to my crazed mind
come in un sogno apparve	as in a dream appeared
la vision ferale	the ominous vision
di spaventose larve.	of frightening ghosts.
Gli sgherri! ed il supplizio!	The ruffians! and the execution!
la madre smorta in volto,	my mother's blanched face,
scalza, discinta . . .	barefoot, in rags . . .
il grido—il noto grido ascolto,	the cry—the haunting cry I hear,
"mi vendica."	"Avenge me."
La mano convulsa stendo . . .	I hold out my shaking hand . .
Stringo la vittima . . .	grip the victim tightly . . .
nel foco la traggo . . .	drag him to the fire . . .
la sospingo!	push him in!
Cessa il fatal delirio,	The fateful delirium ceases,
l'orrida scena fugge . . .	the horrible scene vanishes . . .
la fiamma sol divampa	the fire alone rages
e la sua preda strugge!	and destroys its prey!
Pur volgo intorno il guardo	Then I look around me
e innanzi a me vegg'io	and before me I see
dell'empio conte il figlio!	the son of the cruel count!
Il figlio mio, mio figlio	My own son, my son
avea bruciato! Ah!	I had burned! Ah!

Sul capo mio le chiome	On my head I still feel
sento drizzarsi ancor!	my hair standing up!

In the preceding scene Azucena in her hallucination did not address her "Stride la vampa" to anybody in particular, and the gypsies, who had been listening from a distance, disperse when the tale is ended. Manrico now is alone with her. Thinking as always that he is Azucena's son, he begs his mother to tell him what happened after his grandmother had had to suffer that horrible fate. Azucena, shuddering, backs away from the fire and speaks.

In the preceding chapter Azucena's voice has already been described as a dramatic mezzo-soprano or contralto of natural power and long range, in its full maturity.

The narration consists of two parts and a coda. The first part tells of the burning at the stake of Azucena's mother, the second part of the attempted vengeance that failed and turned into a still more horrible tragedy. On stage Manrico interjects a few words, which are dispensed with in the performance of the scene as a solo.

The tempo is *andante* ♪ = 120. The rhythm, very precisely and strongly defined, creates the feeling of a funeral procession during the first sixteen bars of the vocal part. The singer must conform exactly to the many changes of dynamics and accents written in the score. They are elements of the music as essential as the pitches and values. The basic idea for the voice is a lugubrious legato, the voice swelling to the fortes and returning to piano immediately. A different sensitivity appears in "io la seguia piangendo," but the original motif returns and fills the telling of Azucena's attempt to reach her mother with a weary sound. There is more life and a more affectionate feeling in "tentò la misera fermarsi" and, diminuendo, a touching sadness in "e benedirmi." Violence now replaces gloom. Although very accented, "fra bestemmie oscene" is still piano, as if said in shame, but an intense, horrified, revolted forte hammers the words of "al rogo la cacciavano . . ." The mournful voice is used again for the initial motif, "Allor, con tronco accento." The quotation "mi vendica"is not forte, as if, in this moment, Azucena could not bring herself to utter the word which, she says with desperate weariness, resounds forever in her heart.

The second part of the narration begins after one bar of interlude. A fast declamation replaces the precise rhythmic patterns. The abduction of the child and his presence at the fire are told in feverish words. While an ominous pattern appears in the accompaniment, Azucena recalls, in staccato words, the despair of the child and her own broken heart in a soaring "il core" followed by a frantic "dilaniato."

The tempo changes to *allegretto,* ♩. = 60, and the motif of the pyre (see preceding aria, "Stride la vampa") revives in the accompaniment, the theme of Azucena's obsession, above which she mumbles almost without voice the always present words that terrify her, shorten her breath, upset her, until the obsession at its climax finds its way out of her mouth. The singer has to enter wholly into the play and to create a feeling of deep horror, without any vocal outburst, until the A-natural on "mi ve*n*dica," which then must be stunning.

The tempo becomes agitated, ♩ = 92. Azucena, panting with anguish, breathes after every two syllables, even in the middle of a word, until the child is pushed into the fire, "la sospingo." As she did in reality, she regains some poise now and can sing longer spans at a time. At first, still piano, she recalls how she came to her senses. "Cessa il fatal delirio . . ." should be sung without breathing. It seems to be the calm after the storm. But the accompaniment denies it. "La fiamma sol divampa . . . " is not calm but tensely fateful and sung with a voice devoid of expression. Another onrush of the accompaniment prepares the new tragedy. The phrase "Pur volgo intorno il guardo . . .," with its progressive ascending pitches, creates suspense, abruptly resolved with "il figlio" (the high and low E's). The singer must calibrate exactly each moment of the needed crescendo.

Several lines of a desperate fortissimo follow that need no analysis. Heartbreaking always, the many "mio figlio" can be colored in slightly different ways, although this is not the place to be artful. It is wise to delay the most intense "mio figlio" until after singing the B-flat. Verdi has given Azucena one bar of rest before that B-flat. It should be used—by that half of the interpreter that controls the gears while the other half suffers and despairs—to check on the low support, the freedom of the neck, shoulders, and jaws. At the same time it would be a good idea to keep the ring and the spin of the A in "bruciato" present and to tie the two notes mentally and physically, avoiding having to pull the B-flat, a high note even for an excellent mezzo-soprano, out of the blue, possibly with a special effort.

The coda is a moving inspiration of the composer. Azucena has exhausted all her powers of exteriorization. Her horrible and hopeless feeling of loss and guilt can only be expressed, at this point, by a moaning in the lowest range of her voice. The first phrase is still in tempo, but with "senti drizzarsi ancor" there is a progressive allargando which, together with a morendo, will bring the last words to the verge of disappearance. There is here a great temptation for a mezzo-soprano, still greater for a contralto, to display in these last phrases all the strength of her low range. Certainly the quality of emotion and depth of voice must be used to the best of their possibility. But it would be disconcerting to hear Azucena suddenly sing with an almost male baritone, causing surprise instead of creating intense compassion. This tremendous scene deserves a heartrending ending. Verdi's beautiful idea must be treated with a desire for beauty as much as for dramatic pathos.

"Il balen del suo sorriso"   *baritone*

Tutto è deserto;	Everything is deserted,
nè per l'aure ancora	nor does the usual chant
suona l'usato carme . . .	sound in the air . . .
In tempo io giungo.	I arrive in time.
Ardita, e qual furente amore	Bold, such as a passionate love
ed irritato orgoglio	and an irritated pride
chiesero a me.	demanded from me.
Spento il rival,	With the rival dead,
caduto ogni ostacol sembrava	every obstacle to my wishes
a'miei desiri.	seemed to have fallen aside.
Novello e più possente	A new and more powerful one

ella ne appresta,	she sets up,
l'altare . . .	the altar . . .
Ah no! non fia d'altri Leonora!	Ah no! Leonora shall not belong to others!
Leonora è mia!	Leonora is mine!
Il balen del suo sorriso	The radiance of her smile
d'una stella vince il raggio;	wins over the rays of a star;
il fulgor del suo bel viso	the glow of her beautiful face
novo infonde a me coraggio.	inspires me with new courage.
Ah! l'amor ond'ardo	Ah! may the love with which I burn
le favelli in mio favor,	speak to her in my favor,
sperda il sole d'un suo sguardo	may the sunshine of one glance of hers
la tempesta del mio cor!	disperse the tempest in my heart!

Count di Luna is passionately in love with the duchess Leonora, who, indifferent to his pursuit, loves another knight and poet, Manrico. Manrico's origin is clouded in secrecy, but he is a member of a political movement opposed to Luna's. After a battle between the two factions Manrico is assumed dead, and the distraught Leonora decides to take the veil in a nearby convent.

In this scene it is not yet dawn when Luna and his guards, wrapped in cloaks, stealthily enter the cloister of the convent. To his faithful Ferrando, captain of the guards, the count confirms his violent passion for Leonora before singing a fervent, adoring tribute to her beauty.

As often happens in opera, which is, of course, a very conventional art, the whispers of the first lines are soon replaced by sonorous phrases, and nobody is concerned any longer with secrecy. Luna's aria consists of a recitative that grows from piano to fortissimo, and of a cantilena of great beauty, to be sung broadly but also with romantic fondness. The piece calls for a large, round baritone voice, a Verdi baritone, but it would be a regrettable mistake to use that voice loudly. As will be seen, the marking *forte* appears only three times in the score, once at the conclusion of the recitative and twice in the last page of the aria. Not everything is loud in *Trovatore*.

The voice enters after a short prelude made of light pizzicati chords from the strings. The indication of *andante mosso* ♩ = 80 is only a general one, the pace of the recitative being very free and in accordance with the meaning of the words. The cloister is empty of life; no sound rings in the air. "Tutto è deserto" and the first phrase stay in line with the hushed prelude. The word "carme" must carry some amount of tone. "In tempo io giungo" is said with relief. The fact that Ferrando's phrase will not be sung in the concert version has no effect on the music, but it is he who warns Luna that his plan is bold. In his absence, the baritone will do without a justification for the word "Ardita." Luna sings, already mezzo forte and with an inner tension that makes him rush the words "furente amore ed irritato orgoglio" before a short pause after "orgoglio." "Spento il rival" and the phrase until "desiri" must be sung slowly, as they are informative for the audience, and in a hollow voice that reveals the impact on Luna of the loss of his hopes. Anger makes the phrase "Novello e più possente" swell a short moment to mezzo forte, the dotted rhythm sharply stressed. The single word "l'altare" is said with scorn in very brief syllables. A fighting spirit makes Luna sing rapidly and aggressively "non fia d'altri

Leonora." It is in an outburst of pride and passion that "Leonora è mia" concludes the recitative fortissimo. It is customary to insert a high G between the E-natural and the F of "Leonora," giving great lyrical and vocal importance to all the words.

Le - o - no - - ra è mi - a

Three bars of the original pizzicati piano and a long silence allow a new mood to set in, a mood of admiration, devotion, and stirring love. Even if Count di Luna is not the romantic hero of the opera, he must be heard in this aria with the sympathy that a sincere lover deserves, and he must sing like one. The tempo, *largo*, ♩ = 50, allows the display of his deep feelings, as well as the meticulous performance of an elegant and ornate vocal line. Not until the eighteenth bar of the *largo* can the baritone sing *con espansione* and prepare for the powerful ending of the aria. The vocal requirement asks for a naturally large and round voice capable of keeping that character while the singer performs from pianissimo to mezzo-forte in a mellow legato, with constant flexibility and a complete command of soft, high tones.

Luna's enchantment expresses itself as well in the lightness of the staccato notes (not detached, though) as in the legatissimo of all others. The constant arpeggiando in the accompaniment invites flexibility, but only a well-motivated flexibility. In bars 8, 9, and 10, for instance, after a breath, "nove infonde" can be started in a slight rallentando preparing the F dolcissimo. Time is taken for a breath after that F, the repeat of "novo infonde" is a slight accelerando, but "a me coraggio" is a rallentando. "Ah! l'amor" and bars 11 and 12 are on time, even if possible, the turn on the fourth beat of bar 11. In bar 13 the quarter note E-natural on "-li" is usually divided into two eighth notes and "in" sung on the second eighth. The third beat is on time, and a rallentando starts on the fourth beat, which becomes a real ritenuto on the first two beats of bar 15. The *a tempo* will then last a long while except for an allargando on the thirty-second notes in bar 18.

There is nothing pedantic in the above indications, although they seem tedious to read. A study of the ornamentations would seem still more tedious. Each turn, each grace note, must nevertheless be prepared and sung fastidiously. Luna's manly baritone sings of love convincingly, thanks to all these delicate additions to the main vocal line.

While still rich in dynamic changes, the last page of the aria, starting with bar 18, calls for the normal use of a strong baritone voice, full and resounding, especially in the upper range. The rocking rhythm in bars 18 and 19, a wish that his love could persuade Leonora, is followed by a powerful but short expansion with "sperda il sole," the end of the phrase again being a rallentando and a diminuendo, showing the soothing effect of Leonora's glances. The rocking rhythm is then repeated, and the strong expansion returns, but this time there will be an increased accentuation of "sperda il sole" and of "la tempesta," preparing a full-voiced cadenza, customarily sung as shown, and aiming at the forceful release of the expression of an irresistible passion:

sper-da il so - le d'un suo sguar -do, Ah - - la tem-pe - - sta,

la tem - pe - - sta del mio cor.

Two words of advice at this point: It is wise to breathe often during the whole page rather than attempt to sing a high range forte in very long phrases. It is wise to gauge carefully the amount of vocal bulk that can be carried safely into the high phrases. Too often an excess of bulk will mean a loss of ring. A final detail: In bar 24, sing *"favore"* on G and F instead of *"favor"* G, and sing *"sperda"* on the high F, exactly the same as the first time in bar 20. There is a error in some editions.

"D'amor sull'ali rosee"   *soprano*

Timor di me?	Fear for me?
Sicura, presta è la mia difesa!	Sure, quick is my defense!
In quest'oscura notte ravvolta	Wrapped in this dark night
presso a te son io,	I am close to you,
e tu nol sai!	and you don't know it!
Gemente aura, che intorno spiri,	Plantive breeze that sighs around me,
deh, pietosa gli arreca	ah, have pity and bring him
i miei sospiri!	my sighs!
D'amor sull'ali rosee	On love's rosy wings
vanne, sospir dolente,	fly, mournful sigh,
del prigioniero misero	comfort the wretched prisioner's
conforta l'egra mente . . .	ailing mind . . .
com'aura di speranza	Like a breeze of hope
aleggia in quella stanza,	linger in that room,
lo desta alle memorie,	awaken him to the memories,
ai sogni dell'amor!	to the dreams of love!
Ma, deh! non dirgli le pene,	But, ah, do not tell him of the pains,
le pene del mio cor!	the pains of my heart!

Ruiz, a soldier at Manrico's service, has led Leonora to the foot of the tower where Manrico is the prisoner of Count di Luna. Without revealing her own suffering, she pledges her love once more, hoping that her voice will reach and comfort him.

In this aria the voice of the soprano must prove itself highly skillful. It is still a lirico-spinto capable of great dramatic strength, but it is used here with the flexibility, the tenderness, and the refinement of a string instrument of the highest class. The result of the performance must be stunning.

In concert performance it is a good idea to include the recitative in order to place the aria clearly and also for contrast. The tempo is slow, ♩ = 60. Leonora refuses to be afraid and starts singing with force, as if challenging the absent Luna. Saying with deep earnestness, "Sicura, presta è la mia difesa," she looks at a ring she wears on her right hand that contains a deadly poison. She will actually poison herself later in the opera. She has provided for her own fate and can now turn to Manrico. The phrase "In quest'oscura notte . . . e tu nol sai" demands a slow, somber voice wrapped in darkness, as is Leonora herself. "E tu nol sai" is profoundly sad. With great gentleness Leonora then asks the passing breezes to carry her message to the prisoner. In "Gemente aura, che intorno spiri" she attributes to the breezes a mood like her own, then, in "deh, pietosa" and its repeat she asks them for their help with exquisite sweetness. Slowly ascending to the high B-flat, her voice must become a pianissimo thread of crystal-clear vibration, whereupon the end of the phrase is given the same refined tenderness. A grace note E-flat before the final D-flat–C of "sospiri" adds a final touch of elegant gentleness to the end of the recitative.

The aria is an *adagio*, ♩ = 50, and the voice will often ask for even a little more time to express Leonora's many feelings. Constant attention must be paid to the ties between notes—the first two phrases, "D'amor sull'ali rosee' and "vanne, sospir dolente" rock gently, all sounds tied in an almost nonchalant continuity; to the trills, so frequent early in the aria and which are of true value for the expression; to the words, their meaning and their sound, inseparable from the notes in this totally integrated vocal music. Woe to the singer who does not hear the sound her voice should have to do justice to "dolente" with its up-and-down wave, its trill, and its ending pianissimo on the F; who does not feel the need of a crescendo and a firm legato on "del prigioniero misero" and of a sudden pianissimo to start the high A-flat in "conforta." After a breath, "l'egra mente" is a ritardando, the fermata on the B-flat–B-natural long and sensitive. The next four bars are a pure delight to sing, a little louder perhaps, slowly, with a crescendo and decrescendo on each phrase, and always the trill bright as a jewel. "Lo desta alle memorie," dolce and free to find its own pace, is again a beautiful blend of sound and meaning. The phrase concludes with a perfect legato on "ai sogni dell'amor." Take a breath before "dell'amor" in order to sing the sextuplet very slowly, and keep "amor" vibrant to the end of the values. The message of love must be fervent to the end.

With "Ma, deh! non dirgli" a new pattern begins. It expresses Leonora's own torment, not to be revealed to the prisoner. It requires the same beauty of tone, the same refinement as before. There are some practical changes customary in performance: The word "improvvido" is taken out of the text, and the high notes are sung on the sound "Ah." The first two bars of this new section are shown, followed by bars 4 and 5.

They are all sung with the same flexibility and with the constant desire to make the highest note a caress to the ear. But there is now a feeling of sorrow in the voice that contrasts with the loving warmth of the first part of the aria.

The trill on the last-but-one bar is piano. The final cadenza can be kept very similar to the one printed in the score, possibly adding one more opportunity to end the aria in a heavenly pianissimo.

Il Trovatore is replete with beautiful pages for the singers. While the cast for this opera must be endowed with powerful voices, the opportunities are many for this ideal prospect: to sing operatic music with a cultivated voice. But should that not always be so?

Wagner, *Der Fliegende Holländer*

"Die Frist ist um" *baritone*

Die Frist ist um,
und abermals verstrichen
sind sieben Jahr':
voll Überdruss wirft mich
das Meer an's Land.
Ha, stolzer Ocean!
In kurzer Frist

The span of time is over,
and once again
seven years have passed:
with disgust the sea throws me
on land.
Ha, proud Ocean!
In a short while

sollst du mich wieder tragen!	you shall carry me again!
Dein Trotz ist beugsam,	Your insolence is pliable,
doch ewig meine Qual!	but everlasting [is] my torment!
Das Heil, das auf dem Land	The salvation that on land
ich suche,	I search for,
nie werd'ich es finden!	never shall I find it!
Euch, des Weltmeer's Fluten	To you, the ocean's swells
bleib ich getreu,	I remain faithful
bis eure letzte Welle sich bricht,	until your last wave breaks,
und euer letztes Nass versiegt.	and your last drop runs dry.
Wie oft in Meeres tiefsten Schlund	How often in the ocean's deepest abyss
stürzt'ich voll Sehnsucht mich hinab,	did I throw myself longingly,
doch ach! den Tod, ich fand ihn nicht!	but alas! death, I did not find it!
Da, wo der Schiffe furchtbar Grab,	There, where [lies] the ships' frightening grave,
trieb mein Schiff ich	I pushed my ship
zum Klippengrund,	to the cliffs,
doch ach! mein Grab, es schloss sich nicht!	yet alas, my tomb, it did not close.
Verhöhnend droht'ich dem Piraten,	Tauntingly I threatened the pirate,
in wildem Kampf hofft'ich Tod:	in fierce battle I was hoping for death:
Hier, rief ich, zeige deine Taten!	Here, I called, show your feats!
von Schätzen voll ist Schiff und Boot!	full of treasures are ship and boat!
Doch ach, des Meer's barbar'scher Sohn	But alas, the sea's barbarous son
schlägt bang das Kreuz	fearfully makes the sign of the cross
und flieht davon.	and flees.
Wie oft in Meeres tiefsten Schlund	How often in the ocean's deepest abyss
stürzt'ich voll Sehnsucht mich hinab.	did I throw myself longingly.
Da, wo der Schiffe furchtbar Grab,	There, where [lies] the ships' frightening grave,
trieb mein Schiff ich	I pushed my ship
zum Klippengrund.	to the cliffs.
Nirgends ein Grab!	Nowhere a grave!
Niemals der Tod!	Never death!
Dies der Verdamnis Schreckgebot!	This the damnation's terrible precept!
Dich frage ich,	You I ask,
gepries'ner Engel Gottes,	the Lord's exalted angel,
der meines Heil's Bedingung	who won for me the condition
mir gewann,	of my salvation,
war ich Unsel'ger Spielwerk	was I, wretched man, the butt
deines Spottes,	of your derision,
als die Erlösung	when my redemption
du mir zeigtest an?	you indicated to me?
Vergeb'ne Hoffnung!	Futile hope!
Furchtbar eitler Wahn!	Dreadfully vain illusion!
Um ew'ge Treu auf Erden	Eternal faithfulness on earth
ist's getan!	exists no more!
Nur eine Hoffnung soll mir bleiben,	One hope alone shall remain for me,
nur eine unerschüttert steh'n:	one alone stand unshakable:
so lang' der Erde Keim' auch treiben,	as long as the earth's seeds may grow,
so muss sie doch zu Grunde geh'n!	it must perish nonetheless!
Tag des Gerichtes!	Day of Judgment!
Jüngster Tag!	Doomsday!
Wann brichst du an in meine Nacht?	When will you dawn in my night?

Wann dröhnt er,	When will it resound,
der Vernichtungs Schlag,	the clap of annihilation,
mit dem die Welt zusammenkracht?	on which the world collapses?
Wann alle Toten aufersteh'n,	When all the dead shall rise,
dann werde ich in Nichts vergeh'n.	then I shall be lost in nothingness.
Ihr Welten, endet euren Lauf!	Worlds, end your course!
Ew'ge Vernichtung, nimm mich auf!	Eternal perdition, receive me!

The "Holländer," the Dutchman, is a legendary character, a brave and adventurous sea captain whose excessive conceit has brought him to grief. Battling savage seas in his attempt to round the Cape of Good Hope he swore to succeed even if he had to sail for all eternity. The Devil took him at his word and condemned him to keep sailing until Doomsday. Once every seven years he is allowed to land. Should he then find a woman willing to die for him in order to save his soul, the curse would be lifted.

The Dutchman sings his aria as he comes ashore once again after seven years of sailing. The red sails of his silent vessel form the background of the scene, and he stands on top of a rocky cliff surrounded by the ever present sea. Solemn, slow, displaying a frightening calm, he belongs to a distant world, from which he will emerge progressively during the aria. At first overcome by weariness, he later recovers his energy and rises to the highest degree of intensity. Throughout the aria the strong musical presence of the sea serves as a foil for his emotions.

The Dutchman's voice is a dramatic baritone, not necessarily a black, sinister voice. He is a powerful extrovert as much as a brooding introvert. A ringing spinto voice with a fine resonance in the lower range and a broad spectrum of dynamic levels can handle the part. As the first "Dutchman" ever at the Paris Opéra, I was readily accepted in that part even though my voice was not by nature somber and sinister. The tremendous aria we study here should be a challenge for vigorous young singers who are learning the art of giving their all to great music and who have the skill to do so without danger to their voices.

The beginning of the aria is very slow, the voice without any passion, coming from an exhausted man. The phrases are sung practically on time, keeping pace with the short interludes, which suggest the Dutchman's first steps on land. A comma can be inserted after "verstrichen," stressing the weariness of "sind sieben Jahr." "Voll Überdruss" may be given some more voice. Even the challenge "Ha, stolzer Ocean" is cold and not yet forte. Another comma for expression is made after "In kurzer Frist," "doch ewig meine Qual" is very slow and weary, and despair fills "nie werd'ich es finden." The sudden *allegro* starts with an eddy of the surf, and the Dutchman, with some strength but also with cold resignation, spells out the nature of his fate, tied forever to the sea as long as there is a sea. The two phrases "bis eure letzte Welle" and "euer letztes Nass" are said darkly, again slowly, with somber resentment (note the three accents on "letztes Nass"). A forward ring on the last three notes will keep them audible.

The very important *allegro molto agitato* deals with the unsuccessful attempts of the Dutchman to do away with his life, either in the fury of the sea or at the hands of pirates. The sea rages in the furious orchestral writing but softens for the entrance of the voice, which has lost the passivity of the earlier pages. There will be two tempi in the first twenty-two bars of that *allegro:* very agitated in the narration of the struggles, quieter in the account of the failures. The first four bars for the voice, for instance, are a strong and animated crescendo, the next two bars are slowly and sadly piano. The pattern is repeated in the next five bars forte and the following two slower and piano. The *allegro* then prevails for eighteen bars as the episode of the pirates is told with excitement and power. The new failure, "Doch ach, des Meer's barbar'scher Sohn," is slower and bitterly restrained. The repeat of the whole phrase "Wie oft im Meeres tiefsten Schlund," like an obsessed recapitulation, grows from mezzo piano to forte with waves of dynamic changes. The coda of the piece, "Nirgends ein Grab! Niemals ein Tod," is a powerful forte followed by a less ringing but desperately moved conclusion, "Dies der Verdamnis Schreckgebot." But, as Wagner himself stresses in his comments, even a powerful intonation must leave some leeway for more striking volume later. Those lines were only a description of past sufferings. The real explosion of the present despair is still to come.

After a long, dramatic tremolo a new section begins, *maestoso,* ♩ = 66, a difficult page to deal with. Forcing himself to restrain his tension, the Dutchman addresses a direct question to the angel of the Lord who had given him hope for his salvation. He feels a painful bitterness in the suspicion that he was deceived purposely. The singing must be very legato with an insisting continuity, barely above piano, showing an almost sarcastic skepticism, which will explode in anger at the end of the page. This revolt against eternal justice tortures him. The intonation is difficult, the more so because, singing with great continuity on stage, the baritone loses auditive contact with the pianissimo tremolo of the orchestra almost completely. Nevertheless, the phrases should be sung in one breath throughout the piece.

With "Vergeb'ne Hoffnung," still more so with "Furchtbar eitler Wahn" and the next phrase, the Dutchman rebels against the devastating hopelessness of his condition. The whole body of the singer must provide the strength needed by the voice. Crushed by the explosion, the Dutchman stays silent during the interlude *feroce,* whereupon his thoughts turn in a new and startling direction. He now places his last and terrible hope in the end of the world, which would finally allow him, too, to disappear.

The last *allegro (molto appassionato)* in two, ♩ = 84, calls for extreme vocal energy but must not reach its climax until the very end. As the discovery of a surprising possibility, the first phrase "Nur eine Hoffnung" can be sung mezzo piano, and a real forte can wait until "so muss sie doch zugrunde geh'n." "Tag des Gerichtes" and "Jüngster Tag" are full-voiced apostrophes on very convenient E-flats. Several changes of tempi make the page starting with "Wann brichst du an" both passionate and meaningful. "Wann brichst du an" begins piano, grows quickly to forte, the words "meine Nacht" sung with a ritardando. The following short phrases are violent, but "mit dem die Welt zusammenkracht," a frightening wish, slows down toward the end, and a short fermata can be held on "-kracht." A faster tempo, of grim impatience, is used for the whole phrase "Wann alle Toten aufersteh'n." When it ends on a furious upward chromatic pattern in a solemn broadening, the Dutchman stresses the frightening scope of his concept, and the tempo slows down considerably on the last two "in Nichts vergeh'n."

In the last phrase, says Wagner, "the sublimity of the expression must reach its apogee." All possible vocal power should be summoned on "Ihr Welten, endet euren Lauf."

Then, without a diminuendo, an accelerando covers the next four bars. A deep breath is taken before "mich auf," a tenuto on the word "mich," whereafter "auf" may be held for three and three-quarters bars, expanding if still possible. The overwhelming demand of this ending can be met only if the singer has followed precisely all the dynamic markings, tempi, and emotional features of the aria. To sing it with full power most of the time would be an artistic and vocally dangerous error.

"Jo ho hoe" (Senta's Ballad) *soprano*

Jo ho hoe!
Traft ihr das Schiff
im Meere an,
blutrot die Seegel, schwarz der Mast?
Auf hohem Bord der bleiche Mann,
des Schiffes Herr, wacht ohne Rast.
Hui! wie saust der Wind!
Jo ho he! . . .
Hui! wie pfeift's im Tau!
Jo ho he!
Wie ein Pfeil fliegt er hin,
ohne Ziel, ohne Rast, ohne Ruh'.
Doch kann dem bleichen Manne
Erlösung einstens noch werden,
fänd'er ein Weib, das bis in den Tod
getreu ihm auf Erden.
Ach, wann wirst du bleicher Seemann
sie finden?
Betet zum Himmel, dass bald
ein Weib Treue ihm halt'.

Bei bösem Wind und Sturmeswut
umsegeln wollt' er einst ein Cap;
er flucht' und schwur mit tollem Mut:
"in Ewigkeit lass ich nicht ab."
Hui! und Satan hört's,
Jo ho he! . . .
Hui! und nahm ihn beim Wort!
Hui! und verdammt zieht er nun
durch das Meer ohne Rast, ohne Ruh'.
Doch, dass der arme Mann noch
Erlösung fände auf Erden,
zeigt Gottes Engel an
wie sein Heil ihm einst könne werden.
Ach, könntest du, bleicher Seemann,
es finden!
Betet zum Himmel, dass bald
ein Weib Treue ihm halt.

Vor Anker alle sieben Jahr,
ein Weib zu frei'n,
geht er an's Land;

Jo ho hoe!
Did you encounter the ship
on the sea,
blood-red the sails, black the mast?
High on board the pale man,
the ship's master, watches without rest.
Hui! how the wind rushes!
Jo ho he! . . .
Hui! how it whistles in the rigging!
Jo ho he!
Like an arrow he flies along,
aimless, without rest, without peace.
But for the pale man
deliverance one day may still come,
should he find a woman who until death
would be faithful to him on earth.
Ah, when will you, pale mariner,
find her?
Pray to Heaven, that soon
a woman stay faithful to him.

In angry wind and raging storm
he once wanted to sail around a cape;
he cursed and swore with insane courage:
"In all eternity I will not give up."
Hui! and Satan heard it,
Jo ho he! . . .
Hui! and took him at his word!
Hui! and damned he now criss-crosses
the ocean without rest, without peace.
But, so that the poor man
may still find redemption on earth,
the Lord's angel showed
how one day his salvation might come about.
Ah, may you, pale mariner,
find it!
Pray to Heaven, that soon
a woman stay faithful to him.

At anchor every seven years,
to woo a woman
he goes ashore;

er freite alle sieben Jahr,	he married every seven years,
noch nie ein treues Weib er fand.	never yet did he find a faithful wife.
Hui! "Die Segel auf!"	Hui! "Hoist the sails!"
Jo ho he! . . .	Jo ho he! . . .
Hui! "Den Anker los!"	Hui! "Weigh the anchor!"
Jo ho he!. . .	Jo ho he!. . .
Hui! "Falsche Lieb', falsche Treu!	Hui! "False love, false faith!
Auf in See, ohne Rast, ohne Ruh'."	To the sea, without rest, without peace."
Ich sei's die dich durch ihre Treu	I be the one who through her faith
erlöse!	redeem you!
Mög' Gottes Engel mich	May God's angel show me
dir zeigen!	to you!
Durch mich sollst du das Heil erreichen!	Through me you shall obtain salvation!

The scene is set in a large room in the house of Daland, a Norwegian sailor. His daughter Senta, her old nurse, and several of Senta's friends are busy spinning. On one of the walls hangs the portrait of a somber-looking, bearded man. Senta, a robust Nordic girl with a naive and romantic mind, has long been fascinated by the portrait and by the legend of the Flying Dutchman whom the painting purports to represent. After a lovely and gracious choral ensemble, the girls accept Senta's offer to sing for them the ballad of the Dutchman.

Senta's voice is a lirico-spinto soprano. It must be young and brilliant, with a very easy top, but capable of deep feelings, intense sensitivity, and imaginative colors. The whole part is a most desirable one.

In a ten-bar introduction we hear the theme associated with the Dutchman as well as the one associated with the dangerous ocean. After a long, silent fermata, Senta sings, first, the very theme of the mysterious man adapted to a kind of outdoor call, on the syllables, "Jo-ho-hoe." The tempo in 6/8 is *allegro ma non troppo*, ♩. = 63, but the first bars are free. The first call is piano as if it came from a distance, and vibrating a while in a fermata. The second call is stronger and prolonged in the same way. The third call is an echo followed by a vigorous forte, the three notes on "Jo" strongly accented. The ballad itself starts at this point.

The first motif includes two tempi. The first one, marked ♩. = 63, tells the legend of the Dutchman for twelve bars. Then, without a new marking except in the third verse, the music relates to the stormy ocean, and the tempo becomes a *più allegro*, ♩. = 96–100. In the first tempo, although counted in two, we must hear the eighth notes in the voice clearly. In the second, the voice imitates the whistling of the wind and concerns itself with vivid colors and strong accents. In the first tempo the first four bars of the ballad speak of the ship as it seems to be perceived at some distance. There are colors: the red sails, the black mast. The following four bars describe the captain, who is pale and impressive. The singer must convey these important changes and never hesitate to vary the color of her voice. Then the wind must be imitated, the "Hui" with a sharp vowel /i/, the word "pfeift's" also sharp in the same way. The last phrase of the verse, "Wie ein Pfeil," is a crescendo even though the line is descending, and each beat is strongly stressed—"Pfeil," "hin," "Ziel," "Rast," "Ruh"—creating the sensation of harassment. After a long, silent fermata Senta expresses her deep compassion for the

Dutchman in a beautiful legato phrase that is her own theme. The tempo in 6/8, stands now at ♪ = 100, which is very slow. The voice is soft, already moved by the mention of the "bleichen Manne." The phrases are molded by a sensitive feeling for the meaning of the words. A breath after "Manne" allows a discreet stentato on each syllable of "Erlo-̈sung einstens noch werden," even a slight ritardando on "werden." A breath after "Weib" permits a long lyric unfolding of the next phrase until "Erden"; a breath after "wirst du" and one after "zum Himmel" divide the lines into meaningfully articulate elements.

The second verse repeats exactly the pattern of the first. By following all the markings in the accompaniment, by singing the episode of the unfortunate oath with firmness, by showing distaste in such places as "Und Satan hört's" and "nahm ihn beim Wort" and contained horror on "und verdammt zieht er nun durch das Meer," the necessary variety will be achieved. It has to be done in a very personal way.

The *più lento* shows that Senta's compassion for the Dutchman is slowly changing in character. The hope of salvation offered by the angel of the Lord inspires her to pray in earnest, as if the legend were a factual story. In its softness her voice is now more intense. "Ach, könntest du, bleicher Seeman, es finden" is said as to a person who could indeed receive the comfort of her wish. The last words, "dass bald ein Weib Treue ihm halt," carry a very realistic conviction. At the opera this ending is given the support of the chorus as if to magnify its importance.

The pattern is maintained in the third verse. But Senta increasingly shows signs of a deeper obsession, a stronger involvement, and a vivid premonition of some imminent drama. By now, "ein Weib zu frei'n, geht er an's Land" almost suggests that she could be that woman, the "Land" right where she stands. She stops for a fermata, starts singing again more slowly: That man who marries every seven years, could it happen that one day he would come to her? Still more slowly, Senta shares the man's grievous disappointment. Had she been his wife, she would have remained faithful. "Ein treues Weib er fand" is very slow, and the *allegro* becomes more intense. "Die Segel auf," and "den Anker los" are sung bitterly; then the tempo accelerates almost frantically. "Falsche Lieb', falsche Treu" are thrown out like desperate insults. The departure of the ship is hurried, and it is forever.

When singing alone Senta will lose here the support of the anxious chorus devoutly wishing that the faithful woman be found. It is in reply to the softly expressed question of the chorus that she suddenly and vibrantly exclaims that she herself will be the one. But even without the chorus the desired contrast can be obtained by stressing Senta's sorrow strongly in the last words, "Auf in See, ohne Rast, ohne Ruh," letting the accompaniment die pianissimo, making the fermata very long, and then, during the silence, rebuilding body and nerves to a high degree of intensity and beginning the *allegro con fuoco* fortissimo, with ecstatic exaltation. Everything must contribute to the powerful brilliance of the voice. Put a comma after "Ich sei's," spin your tone in a strong vowel /o/ from the F to the A on "Treu," stress the /ø/ in "erlöse," keep your fortissimo as legato as possible for the phrase "Mög' Gottes Engel." Sing very broadly "Durch mich sollst du," take a breath, begin the F in "Heil" forte, and make a crescendo on the long value by repeating in your mind the vowel /a/, bigger and bigger; do the same for "erreichen."

Take a deep breath before the new "das Heil," another deep one before the last "errei-chen," and decide to sing from there to the end without another breath, rubato—a short stress on the high A, a stringendo on the middle notes, a long fermata on the last F—and in a triumphant mood.

Senta's desire to redeem the Dutchman had been smoldering in her for some time and has been rekindled by the singing of the ballad. Now it explodes suddenly like an over-whelming craze, which will eventually take her to her death. One of the most attractive features of the ballad is the contrast between the intensity of Senta's desires, contained for several pages, where the range of the vocal line covers the middle to lower part of the voice, and the boundless exteriorization of that desire in the last page. A true artist will be able to respect that contrast and find, nevertheless, a unifying element between the two equally human facets of Senta's personality.

Wagner, *Lohengrin*

"Einsam in trüben Tagen" (Elsa's Dream)   soprano

Einsam in trüben Tagen	Alone in somber days
hab ich zu Gott gefleht,	I implored the Lord,
des Herzens tiefstes Klagen	my heart's innermost pain
ergoss ich im Gebet:	I poured out in prayer:
da drang aus meinem Stöhnen	then from my moans
ein Laut so klagevoll,	there pressed forth a sound so filled with grief
der zu gewalt'gen Tönen	that it swelled to powerful tones
weit in die Lüfte schwoll:	far through the air:
ich hört' ihn fernhin hallen,	I heard it ring far in the distance
bis kaum mein Ohr er traf;	till it barely reached my ear;
mein Aug ist zugefallen,	my eyes closed,
ich sank in süssen Schlaf.	I sank into sweet sleep.
In lichter Waffen Scheine	Radiant in bright armor
ein Ritter nahte da,	a knight then approached,
so tugendlicher Reine	so chaste and pure
ich keinen noch ersah:	I never saw any yet:
ein golden Horn zur Hüften,	a golden horn on his hip,
gelehnet auf sein Schwert,	leaning on his sword,
so trat er aus den Lüften	so he descended through the air
zu mir, der Recke wert:	to me, the valiant hero;
mit züchtigem Gebahren	with respectful bearing
gab Tröstung er mir ein:	he gave me solace:
des Ritters will ich wahren,	for that knight I shall wait,
er soll mein Streiter sein.	he shall be my champion.
Hört, was dem Gottgesandten	Hear what the envoy of God
ich biete für Gewähr:	I offer as pledge:

in meines Vaters Landen	in my father's countries
die Krone trage er:	he shall wear the crown;
mich glücklich soll ich preisen,	I shall call myself fortunate
nimmt er mein Gut dahin,	if he accepts my possessions,
will er Gemahl mich heissen,	should he make me his wife,
geb'ich ihm, was ich bin.	I give him what I am.

Time: the tenth century. Place: Brabant, a part of today's Belgium, on the River Schelde. The German king Henry I is raising a force to combat the Hungarians who have invaded Germany. But the succession of the late duke of Brabant has left the province in a state of chaos. The legitimate heir, the young Gottfried, has disappeared mysteriously, and his sister Elsa is accused of having murdered him. The accusation is made public before the king and the people of Brabant, and Elsa is summoned to answer it.

The king, his herald, Elsa's accuser Telramund, the men of Brabant, all are rugged, martial people. Trumpets, trombones, horns, and the clatter of swords against shields have created a fitting atmosphere. Then Elsa appears, "luminous and pure," and silent at first, in striking contrast with the crowd surrounding her. She murmurs as if to herself, "mein armer Bruder," then, against a background of flutes and strings, she begins to sing.

The voice of the soprano, a lirico-spinto, must be equally pure and luminous to meet the expectations of the crowd and must basically remain so throughout the aria, with, of course, many variations of dynamics and colors. When sung as a solo, the aria must do without the constant, helpful alternation provided in the score of Elsa's clear voice with the severe, aggressive, powerful voices of the king, Telramund and the chorus. When she sings alone, it is all the more imperative that her voice keep the pure brilliance that is Elsa's distinctive mark. When performed alone, the three fragments of the aria do not need any musical changes to make it a whole. It is enough to cut the text of the chorus and of the king between fragments 1 and 2 and the entire intervening music between fragments 2 and 3, that is, between "mein Streiter sein" and the marking *langsamer*.

The tempo of part 1 is *langsam*, slow. Elsa was alone in the days that followed the disappearance of her brother. Added to her grief at that loss, the accusation of murder became an almost unbearable burden. Her only recourse was prayer. It is that cruel time which she describes at first, very briefly, with great restraint and extreme simplicity. The tempo must not be too slow or it would overemphasize Elsa's statement. $\sJ = 72$ seems right, the voice going easily and softly from vowel to vowel without overly stressing the consonants. The pure quality of the two sounds /a/ in " Einsam" should instantly catch the attention of the ear, and the sustained fervent sound in "Gott" should create sympathy, as should the words "des Herzens tiefstes Klagen" (vowel /ɛ/ in "Herzens").

This is when the first marvel occurred, as she tells it. Her moan became so powerful a lament that it resounded far through the air before fading in the distance. To describe the marvel, the voice starts pianissimo, makes a slight crescendo on "Stöhnen" (long /ø/), a definite crescendo on "klagevoll," after which the voice, like a powerful wave, grows faster and stronger (again a long /ø/ on "Tönen"), expands fully on "weit," and climaxes on "Lüfte" before ending the phrase on a diminuendo. The crescendo on the repeated E-flats must be made not by pressing on the voice but by the expansion of its resonances.

For some sopranos, "Lüfte" poses a problem but not for those who have accepted once and for all the fact that the vowel /y/ is a normal sound that can be sung in any range. It requires a full extension of the lips, the feeling that the vowel is a slim blade along the face, and the decision not to substitute another vowel for it.

Very legato, softly, and progressively slower, Elsa now dims her voice to suggest the coming of peaceful sleep. The long chromatic scale in the orchestra seems to call her back from far away. A theme of the greatest beauty is heard before she enters into the narration of the dream that has dazzled her. Her voice in a radiant pianissimo describes her shining vision. "Scheine" rings very brightly, as well as the vowels /a/ in "nahte da." In the next four bars her rapture makes her sing a bit faster. The rhythm in double dotted notes must be strictly observed but, in order to avoid any edginess, the sixteenths must be carried into the next notes and not cut short and dry: "ich keinen noch ersah: ein golden Horn . . .," the result being a very rhythmical legato.

The vision is now seen in smaller details, and it takes a little more time to single them out. Do not hurry the phrase from "ein golden Horn" to "der Recke wert." A short silence after "so," a short comma after "zu mir," will make Elsa more realistic in her reaction to the vision. Now, raising her voice and singing with animation, she identifies the radiant knight as the champion come to her defense. The phrase "mit züchtigem Gebahren" must flow generously and confidently, reaching its climax on "er soll mein Streiter sein." The repeat of the same words piano expresses a still more exalted adoration, the ritardando still more confidence.

Still in profound exaltation and buoyed by the same marvelous phrase, Elsa reaffirms her faith in her unknown champion. The phrase is a complete piano to forte to piano curve. The orchestra slows down in the bar preceding "Hört" as it prepares a turn in Elsa's mind. She will now state her side of the covenant she offers the knight. Her land and her crown will be his if he deigns to accept them. The first eight bars starting with "Hört" are sung full voice with a sense of glory. Elsa is a princess and the proud ruler of a large domain. On the ninth bar, however, she changes to a more humble mood and lowers her voice slightly as she expresses her fulfillment, should the knight accept her offer.

The accompaniment now dwindles to a tremolo pianissimo. Elsa, also pianissimo at first but very soon with exaltation, offers herself in marriage to him. The soprano should be able to sing the capital line "will er Gemahl mich heissen" in one breath, slower than the preceding phrases, with a great crescendo to "heissen," the vowel /a/ in that word very brilliant, then a decrescendo. (One can brainwash oneself into believing that the /h/ in "heissen" starts very forward in the mouth.) A deep breath precedes "geb' ich ihm . . .," each of the three syllables well stressed, whereupon "was ich bin" is said in total simplicity and very slowly.

In this aria the voice of the soprano, always bright and pure, will suggest solitude and sorrow, marveling, slumber, boundless admiration, adoration, faith and generosity, and finally selfless dedication. When she sings, Elsa does not know who the knight is or what the Grail's music that announces his coming means, but these unknown marvels have put her under a magic spell. It is a beautiful experience both to sing and to hear this aria.

"In fernem Land"

tenor

In fernem Land,
unnahbar euren Schritten,
liegt eine Burg,
die Montsalvat genannt.
Ein lichter Tempel
stehet dort inmitten,
so kostbar ist auf Erden
nichts bekannt.
Drin ein Gefäss
von wundertät'gem Segen
wird dort als höchstes Heiligtum
bewacht:
es ward, dass sein der Menschen reinste
pflegen,
herab vom einer Engelschar gebracht.
Alljährlich naht vom Himmel
eine Taube,
um neu zu stärken seine Wunderkraft.
Es heisst der Gral,
und selig reinster Glaube
erteilt durch ihn sich
seiner Ritterschaft.
Wer nun dem Gral zu dienen
ist erkoren,
den rüstet er
mit überirdischer Macht,
an dem ist jedes Bösen Trug
verloren,
wenn ihn er sieht,
weicht dem des Todes Nacht.
Selbst wer von ihm
in ferne Land entsendet,
zum Streiter für der Tugend Recht
ernannt,
dem wird nicht seine heil'ge Kraft
entwendet,
bleibt als sein Ritter er
dort unerkannt.
So hehrer Art doch
ist des Grales Segen
enthüllt muss er
des Laien Auge fliehn.
Des Ritters drum sollt Zweifel
ihr nicht hegen,
erkennt ihr ihn,
dann muss er von euch ziehn.
Nun hört, wie ich verbotner Frage

In a distant land,
inaccessible to your steps,
there lies a citadel
named Montsalvat.
A shining temple
stands there in its midst,
the value of which
is unequaled on earth.
Therein a vessel
of miraculous blessing
is guarded
as the most sublime relic:
it was, so that the purest of men
may have it in their care,
brought to earth by a heavenly host.
Once a year a dove
approaches from heaven
to renew the strength of its miraculous power.
It is called the Grail,
and the purest, blissful faith
through it is conferred
on its knights.
The one chosen
to serve the Grail,
that one it arms
with supernatural powers,
on him any evil man's deceit
is lost,
when he sees him, [then]
the darkness of death falls away from him.
Even though a man be sent by it
to distant lands,
appointed a champion for virtue's
rights,
its sacred power is not withdrawn
from him,
as long as he remains undetected
there as its knight.
Of such lofty nature, however,
is the Grail's blessing,
that once recognized he must
flee the eyes of the uninitiated.
Therefore do not harbor doubts
about the knight,
if you recognize him,
then he must depart from you.
Now learn how I satisfy

lohne!	the forbidden question!
Vom Gral ward ich zu euch	By the Grail have I
daher gesandt;	been sent to you here;
mein Vater Parzival	my father Parzival
trägt seine Krone,	wears its crown,
sein Ritter ich	I, its knight,
bin Lohengrin genannt.	am called Lohengrin.

Since his magical arrival, the knight who came to be Elsa's champion had kept his identity a secret. Even Elsa, his bride-to-be, was to refrain from questioning him. Despite her promise, however, Elsa eventually infringed upon his order, and now the knight will have to depart. This aria is his farewell to the king, to Elsa, and to the same crowd that had welcomed him when he first appeared, to all of whom he will now reveal his identity.

Basically the metronomic marking can be set at ♩ = 72, but allowance is made for the general flexibility of the phrases and for many inflections. The knight has to explain a subject and reveal facts that are of a nature totally foreign to the minds of his listeners. He will proceed with deep conviction, as well as with patience and precision, to unfold the miraculous tale before them. His origin, his background, his mission are bathed in holiness, in grace, and in blessings, but also in superhuman power and in secrecy. Lohengrin's narration, kept at a serene pace, will actively reflect the many facets of his story. A noble, ample tenor voice, not necessarily a heroic one, is the voice of Lohengrin.

There are four bars of introduction, written with the spiritual and luminous quality inherent in the knight's musical characterization. The narration starts pianissimo, as befits the suggestion of a distant land, and the feeling is one of reverence and mystery. With the word "Burg" the tone becomes more vigorous, and lyric on "Montsalvat." The voice is light and again pianissimo on "ein lichter Tempel" so as to suggest the clear chapel in the midst of a dark fortress. "So kostbar . . . nichts bekannt" shows Lohengrin's pride in and admiration for his temple. All the following phrases are sung with serene beauty. The inflections will come from the understanding of the words. "Segen," "Heiligtum" "Engelschar" will be stressed with devotion, all sounds blending with the serene orchestral line. A slight delay before "Alljährlich" prepares the startling statement, sung slowly and piano, of the yearly coming of the dove. The rejuvenating effect of its visit demands a strong crescendo, and the first time the word "Gral" is heard it must glow with a glorious ring and, above all, without any roughness, sending a serene brilliance over the next phrase.

From there on, it is the writing of the orchestral music that guides the voice. For nine bars the singer's voice entwines with the themes of the Gral and of Lohengrin, the phrases unfolding like silvery waves of a supple fabric, all inflections inspired by the meaning: "überirdischer Macht" cannot sound like "des Todes Nacht." From the tenth bar on, the singer becomes the leader and the orchestra only a background. Lohengrin, in general terms at first, sings now of his own mission. "Selbst wer von ihm in ferne Land" is still piano, in an aura of mystery, but soon more authority and power are used ("seine heil'ge Kraft") alternating with mystery ("sein Ritter er dort unerkannt"). In two long phrases he reveals the law he must obey. Although still imbued with the Gral's holy greatness the singing becomes more earthy, less continuous. A comma after "enthüllt," a silence after "Des Ritters drum," and a general accelerando make the lines different. The crescendo reaches fortissimo on "erkennt ihr ihn." The diminuendo and the fermata piano on "dann muss er von euch ziehn" contrast the inescapability of the law with his personal regrets at leaving. (The markings stress that the fermata is on "euch" and not on "von").

The heart of the whole opera and the key to the entire tale lie in the next lines. Lohengrin reveals his identity and does so with a solemnity and a grandeur that originate not in himself but in his ancestry and his mission. A true artist should feel that his voice, as beautiful, as heroic as he can make it, is meant to convey here a glory that outshines his own brilliance. Sung in that selfless way, the last lines of the narration create a mood of sublime emotion.

After "Nun hört," the phrase "wie ich verbotner Frage" is sung rather quickly and with enthusiasm. A slight broadening of the tempo will allow the capital words "Vom Gral ward ich . . ." to stress their own importance, although no feeling of slowness must be allowed to exist. The fermata after "gesandt" is a silence of suspense. The values in "mein Vater Parzival" must be exact, the eighth note on "Vater" unhurried, in order to maintain a majestic pace. The high A on "Ritter" is a vowel brought as near to a true /i/ as qualms about distorting the short German vowel will allow, and the words "bin Lohengrin" must stand isolated between the two short silences written. Both high A's in "Gral" and "Ritter" can be held a little longer than their written values, but both of them must be soaring sounds totally devoid of muscular tensions or boastful drives.

The range of the "Gral's Erzählung" seems to be accessible to all tenor voices. A light tenor will, of course, have an easy time singing the notes, but he will not be Lohengrin. A dramatic tenor singing with only the idea of power in mind will to his surprise find it difficult to reach the ending of the aria in good vocal condition. This beautiful narration requires a vigorous tenor voice trained to suggest nobility without strain, to stay on a fluid mezzo-forte without losing its presence, and to sing ringing high notes with serenity. Who would not want to be that tenor!

Wagner, *Die Meistersinger von Nürnberg*

"Preislied"   *tenor*

Morgenlich leuchtend im rosigen Schein,
von Blüt' und Duft geschwellt die Luft,
voll aller Wonnen nie ersonnen,
ein Garten lud mich ein,
dort unter einem Wunderbaum,

Radiant in the rosy glow of morning,
the air heavy with blossoms and fragrances,
filled with delights never imagined,
a garden invited me,
there under a wondrous tree

von Früchten reich behangen,	richly hung with fruit
zu schau'n in sel'gem Liebestraum	to see in a blissful dream of love
was höchstem Lustverlangen	what of the highest yearning and desiring
Erfüllung kühn verhiess,	boldly promised fulfillment,
das schönste Weib:	the most beautiful woman:
Eva im Paradies.	Eve in Paradise.
Abendlich dämmernd umschloss mich	At evening's dusk
die Nacht.	night enveloped me.
Auf steilem Pfad war ich genaht	On a steep path I had approached
zu einer Quelle reiner Welle,	a spring of pure water,
die lockend mir gelacht;	that had laughed and tempted me;
dort unter einem Lorbeerbaum,	there under a laurel tree,
von Sternen hell durchschienen,	starlight brightly shining through it,
ich schaut'im wachen Dichtertraum	I saw in a poet's waking dream
von heilig holden Mienen,	of hallowed gentle features,
mich netzend mit dem edlen Nass,	refreshing me with the noble drink,
das hehrste Weib,	the most sublime woman,
die Muse des Parnass.	the Muse of the Parnassus.
Huldreichster Tag,	Most fortunate, gracious day,
dem ich aus Dichters Traum erwacht!	to which from my poet's dream I wakened!
Das ich erträumt, das Paradies	What I had dreamed, Paradise,
in himmlisch neu verklärter Pracht	in heavenly, newly transfigured splendor,
hell vor mir lag.	radiant lay before me.
Dahin lachend nun der Quell	Thereto now the laughing brook
den Pfad mir wies;	showed me the way;
die dort geboren,	the one born there,
mein Herz erkoren,	who has won my heart,
der Erde lieblichstes Bild,	the earth's most lovely image,
als Muse mir geweiht,	destined to be my muse,
so heilig ernst als mild,	hallowed and solemn as much as gentle,
ward kühn von mir gefreit;	boldly was she wooed by me;
am lichten Tag der Sonnen	on a bright sunny day
durch Sanges Sieg gewonnen,	won through the triumph of song,
Parnass und Paradies!	Parnassus and Paradise!

In the mid-sixteenth century the city of Nuremberg is once again holding its midsummer festival of poetry and music. Its high point is a contest of song and poetry in which the Meistersinger are both competitors and judges. In Wagner's lyric poem the prize to be won this year is the hand of Eva, the daughter of Pogner the goldsmith, a Meistersinger himself. A young knight, Walter von Stolzing, is in love with Eva, who also loves him. He finds himself compelled to enter the contest in order to keep alive any hope for their union. With the guidance of Hans Sachs, the cobbler-poet, he is able to overcome the outspoken reluctance of the more conservative among the masters to let him enter the contest, and to compose and perform a Lied, inspired by his love for Eva. He performs it in front of the population of Nuremberg, with its guilds, its corporations, its burghers all devoted to the fine art of music and poetry.

Walter's voice is a lirico-spinto tenor, a lyric tenor of power and brilliance, with a particular beauty in the high medium and the higher part of its range and flexible enough to sing long melodic lines with charm. The Preislied is a perfect example of what is expected from such a voice. The song consists of three verses and grows in lyricism and intensity from verse to verse.

A prelude of five bars precedes the entrance of the voice. The moderate tempo is felt at ♩ = 72 for the first verse. The mood is one of wondrous delight. Words and music unite to describe the vision of the beautiful and desired woman bathed in morning light in the midst of an enchanting garden. The voice begins piano, but with a warm, glowing sound, stressing the beauty of the words, the attenuated brightness of "rosigen Schein," the velvety sounds of "Blüt'," "Duft," "Luft," already starting a crescendo of enthusiasm on the fourth bar, and reaching forte on the radiant word "Wonnen." "Ein Garten lud mich ein" is said in a happy diminuendo; a breath precedes the phrase piano "dort unter einem Wunderbaum" marked "in ecstasy" by the composer. A crescendo will paint the tree loaded with fruit, another one the intensity of the singer's passion. Between these high points the voice softens for a few notes. All those lines mold themselves with flexibility on varied nuances of delight. The last five bars of the verse grow progressively more animated, with a passionate vocal climax on "Weib" and a tender ending on "Paradies."

The second verse follows the same pattern as the first—Evening instead of morning, a mountain instead of a garden, a well instead of a tree, an inspiring vision, the noblest woman instead of the most beautiful, the Muse. She is still Eva, but now presented as the poet's inspiration. All that was pretty is now noble. Walter had sung as a man in love; now he sings as an entranced poet. The tempo of the second verse is usually slightly faster than that of the first, ♩ = 76, and subject only to one variation, a very expressive rallentando in bars 10 to 13. Walter's voice is now firmer and rounder. "Abendlich" and "Nacht" must be suggested, also the "steilem Pfad." The voice brightens and shines on "Quelle" and "Welle." The ritardando prepares in a tantalizing way the vision of the most lovely woman. Again the word "Weib" must be a beautiful sound, but this time the climax of the phrase is in its ending, "die Muse des Parnass," with a true vowel /u/ as in *loose,* and a vowel /a/ expanded as long as the value lasts.

In an ardent outpouring of words and melodies, the third verse assembles not only the two elements of the first two verses, love for Eva and poetic inspiration from her, but also the triumphant feeling of the singer who knows that his talent and his daring have won him the woman and the prize. Phrase follows phrase in rippling waves of crescendos and decrescendos, and it is the first duty of the tenor to obey the ever-changing dynamic markings. The first forte comes almost at the start; high notes as in "Pracht" and "hell" call for an enthusiastic ring. The rhythm seems to accelerate by itself, its speed reaching about ♩ = 88 by "Dahin lachend nun der Quell . . ." A sense of well-knit continuity imposes itself from word to eloquent word. Two shorter phrases, "die dort geboren" and "mein Herz erkoren," are two shorter waves whose crest is "geb*o*ren" and "erk*o*ren." The climactic A of "heilig" is preceded by a kind of very long upbeat of two and a half bars preparing its glory, which then overflows beyond itself. All singing lines are at the same time curvacious and going forward, reaching without a gap the resounding final "Parnass und Paradies." The long value of the A in "Parnass" must be stated forte, but not so forte that it would be impossible to feed the sound to a still more impressive strength at the end of the value. "Und Paradies" sung with a slight ritardando seems the heavenly release of all effort and worry.

Walter's prize song has been in the making throughout the long opera. When it reaches its maturity it is so densely filled with music and thought that there is practically no room left in it for silences. One of the beauties but also a difficulty of the piece is that once the tenor has started it, he is never given an opportunity to relent, the inspiration of poet and musician giving him an increasing flow of material to present in an increasing expansion of musical and vocal enthusiasm. With no note above A to sing, the tenor must nevertheless gauge his physical effort most carefully, so that he can do justice to this great page, and do so to the very end.

Wagner, *Tannhäuser*

"Dich, teure Halle"   *soprano*

Dich, teure Halle, grüss ich wieder,	You, dear hall, I greet again,
froh grüss ich dich, geliebter Raum!	joyfully I greet you, beloved room!
In dir erwachen seine Lieder	In you awaken his songs
und wecken mich aus düstrem Traum.	and rouse me from somber dreams.
Da er aus dir geschieden,	After he left you,
wie öd' erschienst du mir!	how empty you seemed to me!
Aus mir entfloh der Frieden,	Peace fled from me,
die Freude zog aus dir!	joy departed from you!
Wie jetzt mein Busen hoch sich hebet,	As my bosom now swells high,
so scheinst du jetzt mir stolz und hehr;	so you now seem proud and noble to me;
der mich und dich so neu belebet,	the one who gives new life to me and you,
nicht weilt er ferne mehr!	no longer does he stay afar!
Wie jetzt mein Busen hoch sich hebet,	As my bosom now swells high,
so scheinst du jetzt mir stolz und hehr;	so you now seem proud and noble to me;
der mich und dich so neu belebet,	the one who gives new life to me and you,
nicht länger weilt er ferne mehr!	no longer does he stay afar!
Sei mir gegrüsst!	Hail to you!
Du teure Halle, sei mir gegrüsst!	You dear hall, hail to you!

The scene is the Hall of the Minnesingers in the Wartburg, the castle of the landgraves of Thuringia, in the thirteenth century. Lovers of the arts, these landgraves sponsored many contests of music and poetry in the castle. According to Wagner, among the knights who had distinguished themselves in such a contest was Tannhäuser, who had also won the love of Elisabeth, niece of the landgrave. But Tannhäuser had disappeared mysteriously. Now, after a long absence, he has returned to the Wartburg and will again take part in a contest. When the curtain rises, a radiant Elisabeth, her beauty enhanced by a superb costume, steps swiftly into the empty hall and bursts into her aria. A rutilant orchestral prelude sets the mood for her entrance, and her voice soars almost a capella in the great silence that follows it.

Elisabeth is a lirico-spinto soprano of power and brilliance, whose quality of voice must suggest purity, enthusiasm, and devotion. It is an aristocratic voice capable of reaching high intensity without losing its charm and its beauty.

The basic tempo of the aria is a spirited *allegro*, ♩ = 88. Throughout the aria Elisabeth will speak to the hall as if it were a living being, a very present partner. She greets the hall as if it could acknowledge her greeting. This feeling of addressing someone and being listened to does wonders for the vitality of the singing.

The first "Dich" is a personal and hearty word, and the style of singing will proceed from it. Nothing will be done merely technically and coldly, nothing is attacked abruptly—everything flows with a cordial warmth. The first four bars are sung in one breath, in absolute legato, and the long sound on "Halle" overflows into the next words. An accent on "froh" is stressed by an orchestral chord, and "geliebter" is full of affection.

During the six bars of interlude Elisabeth looks around her and for a while memories soften her joyous outburst. The tempo stays exactly the same; it is the mood that changes, as a sweet emotion, expressed by a piano legato sound, invades Elisabeth. A flash by the violins stresses the vivid impact of Tannhäuser's song on her heart, but the voice stays light and poetic. The mood changes again in "Da er aus dir geschieden," the voice saddens, and the long value on "öd' " sounds cold and a little fearful. The long phrase "Aus mir entfloh der Frieden" must start pianissimo and ring like one note from beginning to end, with an increase of intensity on "Frieden." "Die Freude," a lost treasure, is a sad word here, and there is compassion in "zog aus dir," compassion for the hall that had been left empty and silent.

That melancholy past is now canceled by the orchestra, and from here on all is hope, brilliance, and glory. Above the jubilant orchestra the voice of Elisabeth soars, slender, vibrant, resilient, singing each phrase in one breath, without roughness or harshness. The slim vowels /e/ in "hebet" and "hehr" can be of great help. The friendly sharing of her emotions with the hall makes such words as "der mich und dich so neu belebet" sentimental but touching. The two bars containing "nicht weilt er ferne mehr" are slower, to allow time for a triumphant feeling but also to allow the singer to unwind, be it ever so little, before the last two pages. Note the forte that marks these two bars. A wise and artistic singer has certainly noticed it.

The same lines will now be repeated in a more exalted mood, with more vocal power, but still with varied inflections that are humanly true as well as a means of saving the voice. "So scheinst du jetzt" can be only mezzo-forte; "der dich und mich" starts mezzo-forte before a crescendo; the short silence between "nicht" and "länger" allows a deep breath to be taken with poise. There has been no change of tempo yet. The exaltation of the music and the participation of the singer in it must not destroy her physical poise.

With "Sei mir gegrüsst" starts the *più mosso* but not yet the forte. The repeat of the same words one third higher is in itself a crescendo, as is the new step of one third higher for "Du teure Halle." No exertion should be necessary. The syncopation of the two short "Sei mir gegrüsst" adds to the intensity of the music but at the same time seems to create a pent-up energy for the singer, who should then be able to let her voice soar to a ringing B-flat, not so forte that the final "sei mir gegrüsst" cannot be still more powerful.

The meaning, the structure, and the triumphant beauty of the aria are obvious. But too often it has been used as a demonstration of lung power or, on the contrary, has been shied away from as overtaxing, even for dramatic voices. The truth is that, if studied phrase by phrase with the right dynamics, with the right relationship to the orchestra, and delivered with the dominant desire to make it the warm, cordial, youthful explosion of joy of a woman in love, this aria is a very rewarding and very accessible piece of music for the proper voice.

"Blick'ich umher"   *baritone*

Blick'ich umher	As I look around
in diesem edlen Kreise,	in this noble circle,
welch' hoher Anblick	what an exalted sight
macht mein Herz erglühn!	makes my heart glow!
So viel der Helden,	So many knights,
tapfer, deutsch und weise,	valiant, German and wise,
ein stolzer Eichwald,	a proud oak forest,
herrlich, frisch und grün;	magnificent, fresh and green;
und hold und tugendsam	and gracious and virtuous
erblick'ich Frauen,	I see women,
lieblicher Blüten düftereichster Kranz.	of lovely blooms a most fragrant garland.
Es wird der Blick wohl trunken mir	My eyes are drunk
vom Schauen,	from looking,
mein Lied verstummt	my song falls silent
vor solcher Anmut Glanz.	in the luster of so much grace.
Da blick'ich auf	Then I raise my eyes
zu einem nur der Sterne,	to but one of the stars
der an dem Himmel,	which stands in the sky
der mich blendet, steht;	that dazzles me;
es sammelt sich mein Geist	my mind collects its thoughts
aus jeder Ferne,	from afar,
andächtig sinkt die Seele	devoutly my soul sinks
in Gebet.	into prayer.
Und sieh, mir zeiget sich	And lo! a wondrous fountain
ein Wunderbronnen,	shows itself to me,
in den mein Geist	into which my mind
voll hohen Staunens blickt;	gazes filled with amazement;
aus ihm er schöpfet	from it it draws
gnadenreiche Wonnen,	divine delights,
durch die mein Herz	through which it refreshes my heart
er namenlos erquickt.	inexpressibly.
Und nimmer möcht'ich	And never would I want
diesen Bronnen trüben;	to cloud this fountain,
berühren nicht den Quell	or touch that spring
mit frevlem Mut:	with frivolous daring:
in Anbetung möcht'ich mich	worship I would practice,
opfernd üben,	self-effaced,
vergiessen froh	spill gladly
mein letztes Herzensblut.	my heart's last drop of blood.
Ihr Edlen möcht in diesen Worten	Noble men, pray read

lesen,
wie ich erkenn'
der Liebe reinstes Wesen.

in these words,
how I understand
love's purest nature.

"Blick'ich umher": this song represents Wolfram's entry in the singing contest at the Wartburg. Wolfram von Eschenbach, young knight and poet of the German thirteenth century, comes to life again in Wagner's opera, in which he takes an active part. A noble and cordial man, he tries to counsel and protect his adventurous friend Tannhäuser even though both men are rivals in their worship of the pure Elisabeth. A contest of singing may decide their fate, as the winner will be engaged to the noble young woman.

The theme of the contest is the celebration of pure love. Lots are drawn, and Wolfram will be the first to sing. He must get up in front of a large gathering of people, of his suzerain the landgrave, of Elisabeth, and begin without any time for preparing himself. Hence, the aria is an improvisation and must be sung accordingly.

The tempo is moderato, in cut time, but without any strictness. Wolfram accompanies himself on some kind of harp or lute and allows himself a good flexibility while keeping the general feeling of a rhythm in two. As a basis for that rhythm in two, let me suggest ♩ = 56. Almost taken aback by the need to improvise a poem and a song on the spot, Wolfram does not hurry, nor does he lose his poise and dignity. Consequently the aria is structured in two parts. In the first one, until "die Seele im Gebet," Wolfram buys himself time while waiting for inspiration to take shape. In the second part, from "Und sieh" on, he has taken hold of his theme and will sing of his concept of pure love.

One is almost tempted to smile at the candor of Wolfram's opening lines. Anybody who has experienced the sudden need to find a beginning for an improvised speech knows the relief when he has found one. And who, under circumstances similar to Wolfram's, would not do what he does, that is, address first the men, then the women sitting there in their finery and looking very solemn in the Festhalle of the Wartburg, and tell them how honored he feels to be singing for such a distinguished audience?

In the first two lines of his polite praise Wolfram includes the whole assembly. Sing these lines with a mezzo-forte round, even voice, rising on a bright vowel /a/ on "Kreise" and again on "Anblick," and vibrating slimly on the lips on "erglühn." Let me stress right away the need to detach the starting vowel of each word from the preceding consonant: "Blick'/ich/umher," "welch'/hoher/Anblick," and so on, not "Blickich umherin . . .,"as it would be, for instance, in French. At the same time, however, avoid making a glottal attack on this separation, which is never needed.

The next two lines are a compliment to the men in the hall. The voice may reach forte, with a virile sound, a strong expansion on "Eichwald," a strong articulation, especially the *r*'s in "herrlich, frisch und grün." The following two lines are dedicated to the women. They must be sung mezzo-piano, with charm, and a graceful diminuendo on "lieblicher Blüten." Courtly love was in fashion even in those rough and brutal times, and Wolfram practices it.

Again, two lines describe the reaction of a humble and sensitive poet to such surroundings. So much beauty blinds him and leaves him mute. Sing piano, with restraint but always with a ring and a vibration of love in the voice. The vowel /a/ in "A*n*mut" and in "Gl*a*nz" must be well fed and sustained.

Allowing himself time for a short interlude, Wolfram is now able to focus on his subject: Out of so many, there is only one beauty shining in his sky—Elisabeth, of course. In its extreme discretion the phrase "Da blick'ich auf" must express an almost mystic love. Make a crescendo on "der an dem Himmel," then sing piano and as if in parenthesis "der mich blendet" and, as if releasing a sigh, "steht." Another harp interlude introduces a quasi-religious phrase of devotion, "es sammelt sich mein Geist." With that, the period of preparation is over, and Wolfram will sing his song, as warmly, as freely, as vocally as any Italian singer. The tempo is slightly faster than the preceding one, $\downarrow = 60$, but again without strictness.

For sixteen bars the arpeggiando of the harp under the voice leaves the second half of the second beat empty. Consequently it is possible to extend very slightly the value of the dotted halfnotes in the vocal line without creating a disturbance, meanwhile making the vocal line long, full, and effusive. That pattern is discontinued in the following ten bars, from "Und nimmer" on, the new arpeggiando urging the vocal phrase on and placing the main accent of the phrases on the last word "trüben," then "Mut." The first sixteen bars call for piano to mezzo-piano singing, conveying sweet amazement and untold delight, whereas the next ten bars are an intense pledge never to disturb the pure waters of the allegorical spring. They must be sung with great élan, the two top E-flats forte with a soaring quality, the two descending lines fervent but diminuendo, firmly anchored on the last words "trüben" and "Mut." There follow eight bars accompanied by very simple chords to support the words of total dedication in which Wolfram offers his love the last drops of his blood. The voice should be mezzo-forte again with that almost religious ring to it, ending piano but very well sustained and with deep emotion on "mein letztes Herzensblut."

Having done as well as he could under difficult conditions, Wolfram concludes his song by addressing his noble audience brightly. Sing with pride but not boisterously, "Ihr Edlen . . ." Take your time before "wie ich erkenn'," breathe if you wish, and sing a large fermata on "Liebe," the vowel /i/ (as in *sweet*) of radiant brilliance, young and clear without any idea of darkness or cover, of course. The same goes for "reinstes," /a/ as in *Hi*. In these two last phrases there must be a spacious, unhurried, fulfilled feeling.

It might be said that by comparison with the passionate, sensuous entries that Tannhäuser will provide, Wolfram's song is rather tame. But the baritone, free of any preoccupation with range, rhythm, or intonation, devoting himself to the pure expression of love in an innocent heart, can create an emotion very different from unrestrained passion, yet very touching and deep—an emotion that he and his listeners can cherish at the moment of the performance as well as in their memories. I think I always did, and still do.

"O du mein holder Abendstern"   *baritone*

Wie Todesahnung	Like a premonition of death
Dämmrung deckt die Lande,	twilight covers the countryside,
umhüllt das Thal	envelops the valley
mit schwärzlichem Gewande.	in a dark garment.
Der Seele,	The soul
die nach jenen Höh'n verlangt,	which yearns for those heights
vor ihrem Flug	dreads its flight

durch Nacht und Grausen bangt.	through night and terror.
Da scheinest du,	Then you shine,
o lieblichster der Sterne,	oh, most lovely of stars,
dein sanftes Licht	your gentle light
entsendest du der Ferne,	you send out from the distance,
die nächt'ge Dämmrung	the gloomy twilight
theilt dein lieber Strahl,	is broken up by your dear radiance
und freundlich zeigst du	and like a friend you point
den Weg aus dem Thal.	the way out of the valley.
O du mein holder Abendstern,	O you, my lovely Evening Star,
wohl grüsst'ich immer dich so gern.	I have always welcomed you with pleasure.
Vom Herzen, das sie nie verrieth,	From the heart that has never betrayed her,
grüsse sie, wenn sie vorbei dir zieht,	greet her when she passes by you,
wenn sie entschwebt dem Thal der Erden,	when she rises out of this earthly valley
ein sel'ger Engel dort zu werden.	to become a blessed angel there.

Wolfram loves Elisabeth without hope. In the pages preceding this aria, Elisabeth has made him understand that she will end her life and dedicate herself in heaven to the salvation of the sinner she loves. She has left and Wolfram, a lyric poet whose inspiration derives from love, friendship, generosity, self-sacrifice, stays alone in the darkening valley.

Wolfram sings four arias in *Tannhäuser*. They are all constructed according to the same pattern: (*a*) an intellectual or factual or descriptive introduction which must be sung with a certain restraint and extreme clarity and during which the inspiration seems to take form slowly; (*b*) a lyric song, in which the inspiration makes the singer's voice vibrant with one exalting emotion. In the aria discussed here this emotion will be resignation and spirituality.

The first part, until "den Weg aus dem Thal," is in cut time (¢), $\bd = 46$, sung without a strict rhythm. It is an improvisation, but an orderly one, following easily the pattern of the written values. The color of the voice is very dark, suggesting the premonition of death in the twilight of an autumn evening. Dark does not mean throaty or heavy but means a sound ringing in the mouth inside darkened vowels. Sing an extreme legato, the eighth notes long and well connected with the longer values, an accent on "*Lan*de" and on "Ge*wan*de."

The phrase starting with "Der Seele" should be sung with a more lyric voice, with a slim ascending tone on "Seele" to mark the desire of the soul to rise above the gloom. "Vor ihrem Flug" to "bangt" is sung with almost a shiver of fear, very dark.

During the three following bars Wolfram lifts his eyes above the valley and sees the Evening Star. His mood changes and his voice brightens. A star is a poet's friend, and its pure light will bring him companionship now, solace soon. The whole page must be sung with a clear, ringing voice mezzopiano, with the exception of the words "Die nächt'ge Dämmrung," darkened to recall the original mood. (The orchestra is so transparent below the voice that at the old Met, with the star shining through the backdrop, I always sang that page piano, with my back to the audience.) Make a good crescendo on "und freundlich zeigst du" and a decrescendo on "den Weg aus dem Thal." Now the depressing gloom in Wolfram's soul has been replaced by a sensitive resignation, and he will raise his poet's soul to the eternal spheres.

The 6/8 keeps the tempo already established. Be sure to sing the rhythm absolutely even, the value of the eighth notes exactly one-sixth of the value of the whole bar, and sustain these eighths. The song starts piano with a round, vibrant voice. There is a pianissimo subito on "Abendstern," as if the word were almost sacred. Sing the four-bar phrases without interrupting them with a breath, with one exception: Breathe after "grüsse sie" and expand the resonance of "vorbei." The E on "entschwebt" must be slim, vibrant in head resonances, "Thal" round and expanded. Be sure to sing a slim /e/ in "Erden," and sing piano "ein sel'ger Engel dort zu werden." The turn should be done slowly, starting on the second eighth and very light, creating the impression of soaring into the D of "Engel"—a turn with angel's wings.

With the repeat of "wenn sie entschwebt" start a very important ritardando (very often ignored by conductors and singers) that becomes più ritardando two bars later and goes to the end of the song. Without it the song seems suddenly to die in indifference. With the ritardando we sense the awe Wolfram feels at the thought of Elisabeth's soul passing near the star on its way to heaven—and the finality of it all.

A real pianissimo on the word "werden" (light, vibrant vowel /e/, not a muffled, heavy one) with a fermata on the B only will help the song to end in a quiet, pathetic feeling of attenuated sorrow—and will leave the performer with a feeling of deep participation.

If performing the aria in concert and with piano, ask your accompanist to play an abbreviated postlude, playing the four bars following the voice, cutting eight bars, then playing to the end.

Weber, *Der Freischütz*

"Durch die Wälder, durch die Auen"   *tenor*

Nein, länger trag'ich nicht die Qualen,	No, I can no longer bear the torment,
die Angst, die jede Hoffnung raubt!	the fear that plunders all hope!
Für welche Schuld muss ich bezahlen?	For what offense must I pay?
Was weiht dem falschen Glück mein Haupt?	What vows my head to fickle Fortune?
Durch die Wälder, durch die Auen	Through woods and fields
zog ich leichten Sinn's dahin;	I wandered with a carefree mind;
alles, was ich konnt'erschauen,	everything I could behold
war des sichren Rohrs Gewinn.	was the sure barrel's prize.
Abends bracht'ich reiche Beute,	In the evenings I brought home rich booty,
und wie über eignes Glück,	and, as if over her own good fortune
drohend wohl dem Mörder, freute	though threatening the murderer,
sich Agathe's Liebesblick.	Agathe's loving gaze rejoiced.
Hat denn der Himmel mich verlassen?	Has Heaven then forsaken me?
Die Vorsicht ganz ihr Aug' gewandt?	Providence totally turned her eyes away?
Soll das Verderben mich erfassen?	Shall perdition get hold of me?

Verfiel ich in des Zufall's Hand?	Did I fall into the hands of Chance?
Jetzt ist wohl ihr Fenster offen	Now her window must be open
und sie horcht auf meinen Tritt,	and she listens for my steps,
lässt nicht ab vom treuen Hoffen:	does not cease her loyal hoping:
Max bringt gute Zeichen mit.	Max will bring good omen with him.
Wenn sich rauschend Blätter regen,	When the leaves move rustling
wähnt sie wohl, es sei mein Fuss;	she presumes, no doubt, it is my step,
hüpft vor Freuden, winkt entgegen—	jumps for joy, waves—
nur dem Laub den Liebesgruss.	only to the leaves her loving greeting.
Doch mich umgarnen finstre Mächte,	But I am ensnared by dark powers,
mich fasst Verzweiflung, foltert Spott.	despair grabs me, mockery tortures me.
O dringt kein Strahl durch diese Nächte,	Oh, does no ray pierce these nights,
herrscht blind das Schicksal,	does Fate reign blindly,
lebt kein Gott?	is there no God alive?

Before he retires from his post, the head ranger of Prince Ottokar's lands wants to marry his daughter to his loyal assistant Max and make him his successor. Max, usually an excellent shot, seems to have lost his skill just at the time when an old law requires him to pass a shooting test in order to justify his appointment. He feels that unknown dark powers oppose his success, and he is right. Another ranger, Kaspar, who has made a pact with the Devil, has indeed cast a spell upon him. Outdone by a peasant in a local shooting contest, Max has been jeered at and taunted. When alone, he reflects on the painful strangeness of his present condition.

The role of Max is written for a vigorous and manly tenor voice, able to sustain several dramatic climaxes but also to express love, sadness, and the weight of serious aggravations. The aria consists of several sections in which Max alternately tries in vain to shake off the ascendance of the dark powers, recalls at length his love for the gentle Agathe, and finally in a violent outcry revolts against an indifferent God. The line preceding the voice is played fortissimo and violently, at about $\downarrow$ = 132. The voice, also forte and violent, takes a slightly slower tempo in order to be able, as in a declamation, to stress syllables like "Nein," "Qualen," "raubt." The same proportion is maintained for the next two lines, the orchestra a little faster, the voice taking the time to detail the words. In the second phrase, "Schuld" and "bezahlen" must be stressed, as must "Was" and "falschen" in the third phrase. The last two phrases are abrupt questions, urgent but left without an answer. Max is a man under a spell he cannot identify or even trace to some source.

But he seems to be able for a while to turn his thoughts away from it. The orchestra plays a very sentimental transition to the aria, becoming quite intimate slowly and progressively. Max reminisces about his happiness as a hunter and as a lover. The violent, angry singing gives way to a melodious song, still rhythmical and manly but with overtones of joy and tenderness. The tempo *moderato* can be felt at $\downarrow$ = 84. The dotted rhythms must be very precise without being edgy, the voice lyric and round in an easy mezzo-forte. Max was indeed a worthy forester, virile, efficient, and proud, and this must be heard in the first verse of the aria. Love for Agathe dominates the second verse. The first three bars nevertheless still refer to the successful hunter and his booty. A ritardando in the third bar of the second verse, "und wie über eignes Glück" ends the memories of the happy hunter with a sensation of fulfillment. In bar 4 the limelight moves from Max to Agathe as several lines are given to the loving girl's joyful reaction to the visit of her young man. The voice becomes softer and more lyrical, caressing the name of Agathe, celebrating her joy, and at the end of the page, on the last "Agathe's Liebesblick" in a free ritardando, going to a brilliant forte followed by a loving, moved piano. The several dynamic markings must be observed, but they must be justified by a sentimental inspiration; and a good part of the charm of Agathe's name lies in the variations that love can bring to two basically brilliant vowels /a/, which must never be darkened.

A lengthy, sinister tremolo of E-flat notes interrupts the tender reminiscences. Max returns to his unanswered questions, this time at first with a somber, contained voice and rather slowly. At this point, on the operatic stage, the silhouette of the evil spirit is seen passing in the background. Max senses the threatening presence that makes him feel lonely and forsaken. "Die Vorsicht ganz . . ." is sung more broadly and with intensity, and "Soll das Verderben mich erfassen . . ." with a tragic accent, reaching fortissimo on "Verderben," then diminishing and rising again on "in des Zufall's Hand." Here Zamiel, the evil spirit, disappears. After a long, silent fermata Max's mind is free to return to his love, picturing Agathe at her window as she waits to hear his welcome steps. The graceful *andante con moto* reads at ♩ = 76. But what is at first a warm, touching picture of faithful and impatient affection, sung mezzo forte with firmness and charm, will become a sad symbol of disappointment and failure. Already, behind the eagerness of the two short phrases "hüpft vor Freuden, winkt entgegen," the tenor should suggest a nervousness about to become anxiety. And, alas, Agathe's expectations will not be fulfilled: Max is reluctant to visit her. After a short fermata, "nur dem Laub" and its repeat are sung piano, slowly and sadly. The voice revives on "den Liebesgruss," words which refer to Agathe's thoughts, but a pall of gloom covers the last line, with again an expression of deep sadness for the words "nur dem Laub" and this time still more on "den Liebesgruss."

The bittersweet mood abruptly turns into a tortured complaint. The tempo, *allegro con fuoco,* reads about ♩ = 104–108. Zamiel is passing slowly across the stage, causing despair and blasphemy. The voice starts piano but reaches forte on the first "Verzweiflung" and fortissimo on "foltert Spott" seven bars later. The singer must use great vigor, think in terms of long spans of intense singing, and avoid the very real danger of punching, hacking, or barking. Such phrases as "O dringt kein Strahl durch diese Nächte" are superb vocal lines. If found in a different context, such lines could be sung with a full resounding voice and with beauty. The talent of the interpreter will lie in his ability to convey anguish and rebelliousness without ever resorting to edginess or ugliness. He must also find the right proportions. The shorter phrases—"O dringt kein Strahl," "durch diese Nächte," "herrscht blind das Schicksal"—can be said intensely but with less voice than the broad ones. The short orchestral interludes provide the time needed for rebuilding the support, so that the singer will have enjoyed a relative rest before the climactic "lebt kein Gott." The A-natural is obviously meant to be not only fortissimo but also ferocious. Here the error to avoid is that of singing an explosive, guttural consonant /g/ to attack the A-natural. On the contrary, that tone must be the uninterrupted continuation of "lebt kein," tied to these syllables by a spin, slim at first, then amplified by the mental repeat of the vowel /ɔ/ to the end of the value. The same legato power must be maintained throughout the last page of the aria. The diction of the difficult words "mich fasst Verzweiflung" is easier in legato than in staccato, the vigor of the word "Spott" more constant by avoiding an explosive *Sp* at the start of the word. A slight ritardando on the descending line "mich fasst Verzweiflung, foltert Spott" (bars 17 to 11 before the end of the aria) provides a rebound of intensity for the end of the piece.

There is no subtlety in this aria in the changes of mood. They are not the result of a mental process but are thrown upon Max by an outside force. But achieving the resulting contrasts of vocal colors is extremely rewarding, and the emotions, whether spontaneous or provoked, are deeply human.

The first part, until "den Weg aus dem Thal," is in cut time (2/2, $\frac{1}{2}$ = 46, sung without a strict rhythm. It is an improvisation, but an orderly one, following easily the pattern of the written values. The color of the voice is very dark, suggesting the premonition of death in the twilight of an autumn evening. Dark does not mean throaty or heavy but means a sound ringing in the mouth inside darkened vowels. Sing an extreme legato, the eighth notes long and well connected with the longer values, an accent on "*Lan*de" and on "Ge*wan*de."

"Schweig, schweig" *bass*

Schweig, schweig,	Keep silent, keep silent,
damit dich niemand warnt!	that nobody may warn you!
Der Hölle Netz hat dich umgarnt,	Hell's net has ensnared you,
nichts kann vom tiefen Fall dich retten!	nothing can save you from utter ruin!
Umgebt ihn, ihr Geister,	Surround him, you spirits
mit Dunkel beschwingt!	winged with darkness!
Schon trägt er knirschend eure Ketten!	Angrily he already wears your fetters!
Triumph, die Rache gelingt!	Triumph, the revenge is succeeding!

Kaspar, the forest ranger who cast a spell upon Max, is approaching the end of the term of his pact with the Devil. Unless he provides a substitute for himself he will go down to eternal doom. In the scene preceding this aria he has secretly poured a potion into Max's drink, and under its influence Max agrees to join Kaspar in occult practices. In time these should deliver him to the Devil, and Kaspar rejoices at the thought as Max is leaving him late that night.

This difficult aria is not glamorous, but it is powerful and calls for great vocal skill, although not of the bel canto type. If well sung it can bring its performer unexpected recognition. And although it is mostly violent and malevolent, ways must be found to make it vocally interesting or even enjoyable.

After a sinister tremolo pianissimo on D the voice sneaks in on a sibilant *Sch* and a long *w* mezzo-piano on "Schweig," then grows stronger but is otherwise identical on the second "Schweig," held longer than its exact value. The voice then whispers slowly ($\frac{1}{2}$ = 84) in a threatening, dark tone "damit dich niemand warnt." The full note on "Schweige" is again sibilant with a contained crescendo and decrescendo and the repeat of "damit dich" is still dark and hollow, very slow on "niemand warnt."

By now Max is out of earshot, and Kaspar roars with exultation: He has succeeded in transferring the impending doom hanging over him to Max. While the singing is obviously fortissimo and the text deals with Max's delivery to the powers of hell, in this first part of the aria at least Kaspar is elated for whatever evil cause. What is suggested here is that the bass singer avoid distorting his voice into a malignant, hideous scream and that, on the contrary, he keep his voice round and bouncy within the limits of the written notes, the long values sonorous, the strings of eighth notes nimble and relatively light.

The tempo of the *allegro* stands at about ♩ = 92; the rhythm is clear and firm. No monotony must be allowed. After the first two phrases fortissimo, "nichts kann vom tiefen Fall" starts piano and rises with gusto to forte, its repeat rising to fortissimo; "nichts," too, is fortissimo. Now we must count bar: In bar 25 "nichts kann dich retten" is said brightly; in bar 27 "vom tiefen Fall" somber. The long meandering line, bars 29–33, must be a sweep sung with élan and without taking a breath in the middle. Following the same concept, "nichts, nichts," bars 34 and 35, are bright, and the full notes, bars 37–40, are made very dark in the mouth resonance, with a half-contained ring sounding very low.

Still in the same tempo, the second part of the aria is a conjuration, a call for all demons to surround and overpower Max. Now is the time for the voice to become bitter, biting, nasty. But the vocal line lies on top of a very different orchestral fabric, basically piano, with only short thrusts of crescendos. This means that the bass singer, who has enjoyed a healthy, vigorous forte singing in the first part, can now use a character voice that does not exhaust his strength while it awakens a new interest in the ears of the listeners. It also prepares a great contrast with the incoming music. This applies to bars 40–58. It is indispensable to have the meaning of each word present in the mind at all times, as well as its precise diction, which should be very crisp with sharp, forward consonants.

The words "Triumph," fortissimo (and with a real vowel /u/ as in *loose)*, introduce the last part of the aria. In the pages in the key of D we are indeed in the realm of the fortissimo. It seems that Kaspar is completely overcome by his release from doom and goes overboard vocally and even musically. There will be only one short respite for the voice, the return of the conjuration of the demons, and it should not pass unnoticed for either the throat of the singer or the ears of the listeners. The best way to avoid stress singing these loud pages is to stay legato all the time, without punching any note, especially the high notes, and to stay aware of the change of resonances, down and forward in the mouth for the low tones; vibrant and slim in nature, prior to amplification, for the high tones.

In order to ease the vocalization, it is possible to rearrange the words in the long runs up and down.

After the lines shown, note that the D's of "Triumph" are tied to the small grace notes before "die Rache" both times this pattern occurs. The fermatas on "gelingt" are short both times, and the singer goes "breathlessly" ahead with the triplets, as if unable to stop his frenzied pace.

Kaspar's mind is centered on his delivery in the first part of the aria, then becomes centered on his passion for revenge in the last two parts. Max had done him no harm. Kaspar's only motivation for revenge is the fact that he has lived an evil life and wants the righteous ones to pay for his torments. It should be possible to present the aria in such a way that it shows a dramatic progression from a still human elation to a demonic rage, while keeping the voice in a general attitude of balanced and controlled singing.

"Leise, leise, fromme Weise" *soprano*

Wie nahte mir der Schlummer	How sleep used to come
bevor ich ihn gesehn!	before I met him!
Ja, Liebe pflegt mit Kummer	True, love with sorrow
stets Hand in Hand zu gehn.	always goes hand in hand.
Ob Mond auf seinem Pfad wohl lacht?	Could the moon be smiling on his path?
Welch' schöne Nacht!	What a beautiful night!
Leise, leise, fromme Weise,	Softly, softly, pious melody,
schwing'dich auf zum Sternenkreise.	rise up to the firmament.
Lied, erschalle,	Song, ring out,
feiernd walle	let in praise
mein Gebet zur Himmelshalle.	my prayer float to the heavenly vault.
O wie hell die gold'nen Sterne,	Oh, how bright the golden stars,
mit wie reinem Glanz sie glühn!	with what pure brilliance they glow!
Nur dort in der Berge Ferne	Only over there in the distant mountains
scheint ein Wetter aufzuziehn.	a storm seems to be brewing.
Dort am Wald auch schwebt ein Heer	There, too, by the woods a host
dunkler Wolken, dumpf und schwer.	of dark clouds is hanging, sultry and heavy.
Zu dir wende ich die Hände,	To you I raise my hands,
Herr ohn'Anfang und ohn'Ende.	Lord without beginning and without end.
Vor Gefahren uns zu wahren	To protect us from all danger
sende deine Engelscharen.	send your heavenly host.
Alles pflegt schon längst der Ruh';	Everything long since is gone to rest;
trauter Freund, was weilest du?	sweet friend, why do you tarry?
Ob mein Ohr auch eifrig lauscht,	Even though my ear listens eagerly,
nur der Tannen Wipfel rauscht,	only the tops of the pine trees rustle,
nur das Birkenlaub im Hain	only the foliage of the birch trees in the grove
flüstert durch die hehre Stille,	whispers in the solemn silence,
nur die Nachtigall und Grille	only the nightingale and the cricket
scheint der Nachtluft sich zu freun.	seem to enjoy the night air.
Doch wie! Täuscht mich nicht mein Ohr?	But what! Does my ear not deceive me?
Dort klingt's wie Schritte,	There it sounds like steps,
dort aus der Tannen Mitte	there from among the pine trees
kommt was hervor. Er ist's! Er ist's!	something steps forward. It is he!
Die Flagge der Liebe mag wehn!	The flag of love may wave!
Dein Mädchen wacht noch in der Nacht.	Your sweetheart still keeps watch in the night.
Er scheint mich noch nicht zu sehn—	He does not seem to see me yet—
Gott, täuscht das Licht des Monds mich nicht,	God, if the moonlight does not deceive me,
so schmückt ein Blumenstrauss den Hut.	then a nosegay adorns the hat.

Gewiss, er hat den besten Schuss getan!	For sure, he has fired the best shot!
Das kündet Glück für morgen an!	That forecasts luck for tomorrow!
O süsse Hoffnung, neu belebter Mut!	Oh, sweet hope, newly revived courage!
All' meine Pulse schlagen	All my pulses are beating away
und das Herz wallt ungestüm	and my heart flies impatiently,
süss entzückt entgegen ihm.	sweetly enraptured, to meet him.
Konnt'ich das zu hoffen wagen?	Could I dare hope this?
Ja, es wandte sich das Glück	Yes, Fortune has turned around
zu dem teuren Freund zurück.	to my dearly beloved again.
Will sich's morgen treu bewähren?	Will it prove faithful tomorrow?
Ist's nicht Täuschung?	Is it not a delusion?
Ist's nicht Wahn?	Is it not a mistake?
Himmel, nimm des Dankes Zähren	Heaven, accept tears of gratitude
für dies Pfand der Hoffnung an!	for this pledge of hope!
All'meine Pulse schlagen . . .	All my pulses are beating . . .

On the eve of her wedding to Max, Agathe is alone with her cousin Aennchen in her father's house, the head forest ranger's lodge. The two girls, waiting for Max to return from hunting, are of very contrasting moods, Aennchen gay and optimistic, Agathe filled with somber premonitions. When her cousin retires for the night, Agathe steps out on the balcony overlooking the valley, and in the beautiful moonlight pours out her hopes and yearnings and turns to prayer.

The aria requires a lirico-spinto voice of bright texture, capable of singing crystal-clear tones in the first part of the aria, of declaiming vigorously in the middle part, of sustaining the strength of very animated, enthusiastic pages in the last part. It is a voice that can be meditative, introspective, and also suggest the open air, the starry night, the distant valleys. The outdoors plays a large part in the score of *Der Freischütz* and the singing, very often, leaves the walled-in space of rooms and houses to take off and ring in the natural surroundings in nature's infinite space or its sinister glens. It is definitely possible for a skillful singer to find sounds and resonances tuned to the great outdoors.

The one bar of introduction is very slow, soft, veiled. The voice must be light, quiet, and already filled with love. "Bevor ich ihn gesehn" is sung with an intimate and touching warmth. After the same delicate orchestral touch, Agathe sings slowly and earnestly of her premonitions. She needs reassurance and finds it for a while in the splendor of the night. "Ob Mond auf seinem Pfad wohl lacht" is a little louder in voice and slightly hopeful in mood. And "Welch' schöne Nacht," started forte in admiration, spins a long time on the F-sharp and the vowel /ø/ of "schöne," then goes down in a slow, pearly diminuendo, to end in a light, bright vowel /a/ on "Nacht." That short phrase is sufficient for the true artist to describe the whole starry sky.

Over the muted strings Agathe is now inspired to send a very melodic prayer toward the distant firmament. "Leise, leise" unfolds very slowly, ♪ = 69, in perfect legato, in delicate but bright tones, weightless and tender. No darkness should mar the clarity of the vowels, no edge the smoothness of the sound. The appoggiaturas are long and pi-ano. The irresistible attraction of the beautiful night interrupts the prayer before it reaches its main point. Here, in addition to its splendor, the night shows Agathe a symbolic contrast: Above her head, all is bright, and such must be the phrase "O wie hell die goldnen Sterne . . . ," but in the distance, whence Max is to emerge, a storm is brewing. The whole phrase "Nur dort in der Berge Ferne . . ." requires a darker voice and a feeling of concern. Agathe's prayer is more urgent and precise now. Its tempo does not change, but its sound, still legato, pure and bright, becomes a little louder and more intense.

Her prayer concluded, Agathe grows restless. She returns to nature for companionship, but this time to search in its voices for some trace of the delayed Max. The lovely page is an *andante* ($\quarternote$ = 92–96), sung with charm and simplicity in a friendly, well-articulated voice. The sounds of the forest are discreet and well detailed, the last one, the nightingale and the cricket, delightful. Although the expression of longing had been strongly indicated in one phrase only, "trauter Freund, was weilest du," there is a searching anxiety in listening to all those friendly noises. It takes a certain subtlety to convey this complex sensitivity.

Suddenly the horns suggest human steps approaching, and Agathe immediately knows whose steps they are. In the next two pages, alternating free recitatives and measured *agitato* fragments, she releases her varied emotions. At first, listening intently, still in doubt, she murmurs "Doch wie! Täuscht mich nicht mein Ohr," then faster, more positive, and very soon louder, "Dort klingt's wie Schritte." The *agitato* is forte, exactly on time with the chords in the orchestra. With élan Agathe wants Max to know how impatiently he is expected. "Dein Mädchen wacht noch in der Nacht" is an enthusiastic accelerando, and her singing alone should make us see with what eagerness she waves to him.

Her surprised disappointment is expressed in a slow piano phrase: "Er scheint mich noch nicht zu sehn." But it is rapidly, freely and forte again that she fancies she sees the flowers of triumph on his hat. Her joy grows stronger and turns into a measured short hymn, and "Das kündet Glück . . " is round and very legato. The orchestra broadens the tempo before "O süsse Hoffnung," which follows even more broadly, with a real vowel /y/ well sustained on top. "Neu belebter Mut" is cheerful and free. With feverish expectation Agathe breaks into a *vivace con fuoco* ($\halfnote$ = 108), which includes one of the most famous themes of the opera and its overture. When it is introduced here it can be kept at a mezzo-forte level, with a sweet joy still partly contained, for Agathe still has some misgivings, expressed by the repeated question, "Konnt'ich das zu hoffen wagen," which she sings with growing intensity, the third time with an anxious broadening and two fermatas in which there is almost a supplication. After a silent fermata, confidence takes the upper hand. The voice is nimble throughout, and a rallentando on the first "zu dem teuren Freund zurück" brings an affectionate touch to the line. A strong *a tempo* on "Will sichs morgen treu bewähren" and its repeat maintains the enthusiasm. Finally, "Ist's nicht Wahn" is said slowly, with confidence and certainty.

Agathe abandons herself then and there to the morrow's happiness, after thanking heaven in two luminous, broad phrases, "Himmel, nimm des Dankes Zähren" and "für dies Pfand . . . ," sung freely and with great vocal enjoyment. The glorious theme starts the finale of the aria, serene in its exaltation. The voice stays light and nimble on the excited phrases "All'meine Pulse schlagen." The high A on "süss entgegen" is given with the greatest intensity, on a real vowel /y/.

The final thirteen bars for the voice must, for musical reasons as well as for vocal ones, be the crescendo written in the score, starting piano on "entgegen ihm," going slowly to mezzo-forte on "süss entzückt" (bars 7 and 6 from the end), becoming forte only in the fourth bar before the end, and fortissimo only on the high B in the last-but-one bar. A true vowel /e/ on that note will be very helpful for keeping the vibration of the voice slim, intense, and reliable. An enthusiastic but unwise forte used all along may prove too much of a strain and endanger the security of the last bars.

Throughout this most sincere and emotional aria even the most sensitive interpreter must translate her feelings through well-measured and well-balanced vocal effects. Only an impeccable, harmonious form will do justice to the beautiful humanity of this aria.

"Und ob die Wolke"   *soprano*

Und ob die Wolke sie verhülle,	And though the cloud hide it,
die Sonne bleibt am Himmelszelt,	the sun remains on the firmament,
es waltet dort ein heil'ger Wille,	there reigns a hallowed will,
nicht blindem Zufall dient die Welt.	the world does not serve a blind Chance.
Das Auge, ewig rein und klar,	The eye, eternally pure and clear,
nimmt aller Wesen liebend wahr.	protects all beings lovingly.
Für mich wird auch der Vater sorgen,	Of me, too, the Father will take care
dem kindlich Herz und Sinn vertraut,	whom my heart and mind trust candidly,
und wär'dies auch mein letzter Morgen,	though this be my last morning,
rief mich sein Vaterwort als Braut.	though his fatherly word call me, the bride, away.
Sein Auge, ewig rein und klar,	His eye, eternally pure and clear,
nimmt meiner auch mit Liebe wahr.	protects me, too, with love.

Today is the day of the final shooting contest, and Agathe's fate is about to be decided. If Max, her fiancé, is successful, he will become Prince Ottokar's head forester and marry Agathe. Already in her bridal gown, alone in her quaint room, Agathe has been praying before her own altar. She has never lost faith in the final happy outcome of her ordeal, and she rises to offer the Lord the tribute of her confidence.

Agathe's voice is a lirico-spinto soprano, which in this aria uses its qualities of purity and melodious legato more than the dramatic power needed in other parts of the role. But a certain scope and a distinct majesty are no doubt required here. Without one loud phrase in it, the aria must nevertheless unite great charm with an active vitality. The Lord it celebrates is somewhere above in the open spaces. The voice must reach him through its clear, lively, and intense sound, carrying across the large landscapes always associated with *Der Freischütz*.

The aria is written in three sections, parts A, B, and A. The *adagio* tempo can be marked at $\flat$ = 80. The short introduction is highlighted by a cello solo playing the melody that Agathe takes over after a fermata. The voice must soar legatissimo and clear above the attenuated background of dark strings. The first three bars are still a little reserved—the clouds—but "die Sonne bleibt am Himmelszelt" needs a radiant sound, the word "Himmelszelt" said with a caressing feeling. A slightly louder voice, still mezzo piano and legato, stresses the statement of Agathe's belief in a higher power, and "dort" must suggest how far away is that power. The firmness of the statement is maintained to the end of the sustained sound, "Welt." Those first four phrases are all patterned in the same way. The singer must be sure not to make a crescendo on the first three notes or a louder tone on the upper F (the upper E-flat in the last phrase) or a decrescendo ending the line feebly. On the contrary, the dynamic level reached on the high notes must be maintained, the strongest notes being, in each phrase, the last downbeat, *"verhülle,"* "Himmels*zelt*," "W*i*lle," "W*e*lt."

The same remark applies, of course, to the next two phrases, "Das Auge . . ." and "nimmt aller Wesen wahr." The color of those phrases calls for bright vowels /a/ in "Auge," "rein," "klar," and "wahr," for slim vowels /e/ in "ewig" and "Wesen." Also, whenever there are words starting with a vowel, such as "Auge," "ewig," and so on, no glottal attack should be heard, nor should any preceding consonant be carried over. Sometimes a written comma will eliminate the problem, but nothing should interfere with the constant legato of the singing. The meaning and the sound of the word "rein" and "klar" determine the color of the whole verse. An already high resonance on "nimmt" creates an easy approach to the high A-flat. That long note will be satisfactory if started mezzo-piano in a slim tone and then amplified by mentally repeating the vowel /a/ on top of a steady low support. It is desirable to stay on time throughout the word "aller" and to breathe only after "Wesen." The intervals of the last three bars of part A are taken lightly and always legato in spite of the dotted rhythm.

Part B expresses Agathe's supreme trust in the protection of the Lord, a special protection for herself. This part is more personal than part A, where that feeling of protection was more universal. It can be sung with a rounder, warmer voice and in slightly faster tempo than part A. The pattern of the phrases has changed; they are longer, and each must be sung in one breath, without dragging, the quarter note now being the basic unit of time. The feelings expressed are strongly positive. The first two phrases are radiant with an almost childish faith. The last two are a statement of extreme obedience to the Lord. Even if he called Agathe to him on this special day, meant to be the happiest in her life, she would accept his call without hesitation. A robust new firmness makes "und wär'dies auch mein letzter Morgen" a crescendo, soon attenuated by the clear awareness of what she is saying, but a new crescendo stresses "sein Vaterwort" and enhances the words "als Braut." There is no sadness in this stoic acceptance, the voice still serene and generous, flowing with great simplicity.

The return of part A introduces no new elements of interpretation. Coming after the rounder tone used in part B, it should sound even more spiritual than the first time, the voice still more crystal-clear and radiant. Nevertheless it should not sound like a light lyric voice. The colors, the dynamics, the inflections used by a dramatic or lirico-dramatic voice should not alter its basic character but only allow it to impersonate many different human beings—better still, the many facets that a role demands from one particular person, just as real life does.

Index of First Lines